ACT
AMERICAN COLLEGE TESTING PROGRAM

JOAN U. LEVY, Ph.D.
NORMAN LEVY, Ph.D.

Prentice Hall
New York • London • Toronto • Sydney • Tokyo • Singapore

ACT is a registered trademark that is the exclusive property of the American College Testing Program. Arco is a division of Schuster & Schuster, Inc., and is not affiliated with the American College Testing Program. This book has been prepared by Arco and the authors, who bear sole responsibility for its contents.

Fifteenth Edition

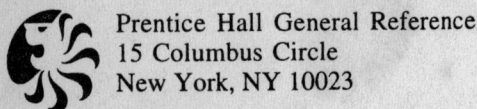
Prentice Hall General Reference
15 Columbus Circle
New York, NY 10023

Copyright © 1994, 1993, 1992, 1991, 1989 by Joan U. Levy and Norman Levy
All rights reserved
including the right of reproduction
in whole or in part in any form

An Arco Book

ARCO and PRENTICE HALL are registered trademarks of Prentice-Hall, Inc.
Colophon is a trademark of Prentice-Hall, Inc.

Library of Congress Cataloging-in-Publication Data

Levy, Joan.
    ACT, American College testting program / Joan U. Levy, Norman Levy.
  —15th ed.
      p. cm.
    "An Arco book"—T.p. verso.
    ISBN 0-671-88822-6
    1. ACT Assessment—Study guides. I. Levy, Norman, 1946–
II. Arco Publishing. III. Title.
LB2353.48.L49   1994
378.1'662—dc20   93-48848
                                   CIP

Manufactured in the United States of America

1 2 3 4 5 6 7 8 9 10

For Joshua Seth and Jessica Dawn
two of our best reasons for writing this book

ACKNOWLEDGEMENTS

A work of this magnitude, scope, and complexity depends not only upon the expertise of its authors, but also relies heavily on the assistance and advice of many other people. We want to thank the following people for their time, input, and their suggestions:

Richard Hresko	for his invaluable assistance on the science and mathematics sections.
The science staff of NJL College Preparation	for their assistance and suggestions on the science sections of this text.

About the Authors

JOAN LEVY, Ph.D.

B.A., City College of New York, M.S. in Guidance and Counseling, Fordham University, Ph.D. in Behavioral Science. Director of NJL College Preparation and Learning Center. Guidance Counselor and Educational Evaluator for the New York City Board of Education with nineteen years of teaching and guidance experience.

NORMAN LEVY, Ph.D.

B.E., City College of New York, M.S. in Operations Research, New York University, Ph.D. in Educational Administration. Executive Director of NJL College Preparation and Learning Center, a private tutoring, test preparation, and college guidance service.

Other ARCO books by Joan Levy and Norman Levy:

MECHANICAL APTITUDE AND SPATIAL RELATIONS TESTS

AP EUROPEAN HISTORY

ESSENTIAL MATH FOR COLLEGE-BOUND STUDENTS

AP UNITED STATES GOVERNMENT AND POLITICS

CONTENTS

Introduction xiii

Part I
Test Busters

Guessing 1

Solving Math Problems 2

Reading Comprehension 8

Part II
ACT Pretest

English Pretest 13

Mathematics Pretest 15

Reading Pretest 17

Science Reasoning Pretest 18

Pretest Answer Key 20

Pretest Explanatory Answers 20

Part III
English Review

English	25
Punctuation	26
The Apostrophe	26
The Colon	27
The Comma	27
The Dash	29
The Exclamation Mark	29
The Hyphen	29
The Period	30
The Question Mark	30
Quotation Marks	30
The Semicolon	31
Capitalization Rules	33
Grammar and Usage	35
Parts of Speech	35
Words Commonly Confused	38
English Practice Exercise One	48
Selected Rules of Grammar	50
English Practice Exercise Two	53
Sentence Structure	55
English Practice Exercise Three	59
Rhetorical Skills	61
Strategy	61
Organization	61
Style	61
Rhetorical Skills Exercise One	62
Rhetorical Skills Exercise Two	62
Rhetorical Skills Exercise Three	63

Rhetorical Skills Exercise Four 64

Part IV
Mathematics Review

Mathematics 69

Operations with Integers and Decimals 70

    Practice Exercise One 71

Operations with Fractions 73

    Fractions and Mixed Numbers 73

    Practice Exercise Two 77

    Verbal Problems Involving Fractions 80

    Practice Exercise Three 81

Variation 85

    Direct Variation 85

    Inverse Variation 86

    Joint Variation 86

    Practice Exercise Four 87

Percent 91

    Practice Exercise Five 95

    Verbal Problems Involving Percent 98

    Practice Exercise Six 100

Statistics and Probability 104

    Statistics 104

    Probability 107

    Practice Exercise Seven 107

Signed Numbers and Equations 115

    Signed Numbers 115

    Practice Exercise Eight 115

    Linear Equations 118

    Practice Exercise Nine 119

Quadratic Equations	123
Practice Exercise Ten	124
Literal Expressions	127
Practice Exercise Eleven	127
Roots, Radical, and Exponents	131
Roots and Radicals	131
Practice Exercise Twelve	133
Factoring and Algebraic Fractions	137
Practice Exercise Thirteen	139
Problem Solving in Algebra	143
Coin Problems	143
Consecutive Integer Problems	143
Age Problems	144
Interest Problems	144
Fraction Problems	144
Mixture Problems	145
Motion Problems	146
Work Problems	148
Practice Exercise Fourteen	149
Geometry	153
Area	153
Perimeter/Circumference	154
Right Triangles	155
Coordinate Geometry	156
Angles	159
Parallel Lines	160
Triangles	161
Polygons	162
Circles	162
Volume	163

Similarity	164
Practice Exercise Fifteen	165
Inequalities	172
Practice Exercise Sixteen	173
Sequences and Logic	177
Practice Exercise Seventeen	179
Trigonometry	182
Practice Exercise Eighteen	185
Discriminant	189
Practice Exercise Nineteen	190
Conic Sections	192
Practice Exercise Twenty	192

Part V
Reading Review

Reading	203
Approaching the ACT Reading Test	203
Practice Reading Passages	205

Part VI
Science Review

The Physical Sciences	221
Earth Science Practice Exercise	223
Biology	226
Biology Practice Exercise	228
Chemistry	231
Chemistry Practice Exercise	233
Physical Science	235
Physical Science Practice Exercise	237

Part VII
Science Reasoning Review

Science Reasoning	241
Data Representation	245
Tables	245
Graphs	248
Diagrams	250
Data Representation Practice Exercise	251
Research Summaries	258
Research Summaries Practice Exercise	261
Conflicting Viewpoints	267
Conflicting Viewpoints Practice Exercise	270

Part VIII
ACT Practice Exams

Practice Exam I	279
SPECIAL SECTION: What You Need to Know About College Financial Aid (excerpted from ARCO's *College Financial Aid*, 5th edition)	color pages
Answer Key for Practice Exam I	321
Explanatory Answers for Practice Exam I	326
Practice Exam II	343
Answer Key for Practice Exam II	383
Explanatory Answers for Practice Exam III	387
Practice Exam III	402
Answer Key for Practice Exam III	443
Explanatory Answers	447
Practice Exam IV	465
Answer Key for Practice Exam IV	503
Explanatory Answers for Practice Exam IV	508

INTRODUCTION

The Enhanced ACT Assessment is a comprehensive evaluation performed in Grades 11 and/or 12. It contains four academic tests designed explicitly to measure student achievement in skills that are developed in high school. The tasks presented in the tests represent a wide range of academic skills. They depend upon the student's skill in applying the content knowledge and reasoning skills acquired in high school.

Purpose of the Test

The Enhanced ACT Assessment has these essential purposes:

1. To help colleges and universities in their college admissions process.
2. To provide educational and vocational planning for high school students.
3. To aid in academic advisement and counseling in post-secondary planning.
4. To aid in recruitment and retention.

Composition of the Test

The Enhanced ACT Assessment consists of four major tests: English, Mathematics, Reading, and Science Reasoning.

Enhanced ACT Assessment Tests

	English	Mathematics	Reading	Science Reasoning
Length of Test (in minutes)	45	60	35	35
Number of Questions	75	60	40	40

English Test

The English Test measures the student's comprehension of standard written English including punctuation, grammar and usage, sentence structure, and rhetorical skills. The test emphasizes analyzing the kinds of prose that students are required to read and write in high school and college, not mere recall of rules of grammar. Three scores are reported:

a total English Test score
a subscore in Usage/Mechanics
a subscore in Rhetorical Skills

Mathematics Test

The Mathematics Test assesses the student's achievement in mathematics. The test emphasizes solving practical problems included in courses taken in Grades 9, 10, and 11 (pre-algebra, algebra, intermediate algebra, plane geometry, coordinate geometry, and trigonometry). The test stresses the application of mathematical skills to quantitative reasoning and problem solving, not rote memorization of formulas, techniques or computational skills. Four scores are reported:

a total Mathematics Test score
a subscore in Pre-Algebra/Elementary Algebra
a subscore in Intermediate Algebra/Coordinate Geometry
a subscore in Plane Geometry/Trigonometry

Reading Test

The Enhanced ACT Assessment Reading Test consists of one 35-minute section which assesses reading comprehension as a result of skill in reasoning and reference. This test requires students to answer questions about several reading passages by referring to what is specifically stated; reasoning to determine implications and inferences; and drawing conclusions, comparisons, and generalizations. The prose passages on the Reading Test are similar to those that appear in high school and college curricula. They include passages in the arts, in literature, in social studies, and in the sciences. Prose fiction and humanities are reported in the Arts/Literature subscore. Social sciences and natural sciences are reported in the Social Studies/Sciences subscore.
Three scores are reported:

A total reading score—based on all 40 items
A subscore in Arts/Literature—based on 20 questions
A subscore in Social Studies/Sciences—based on 20 questions

Science Reasoning Test

The Science Reasoning Test assesses the student's scientific reasoning skills. The test offers several sets of scientific information followed by test items. The scientific information is presented in three different formats:

Data Representation
Research Summaries
Conflicting Viewpoints

Test items require students to understand the basic features of a concept related to the information provided; to examine the relationships between the given information and the conclusions drawn or hypotheses developed; and to generalize from what is presented to gain new information, draw other conclusions or forecast future projections. A single Science Reasoning Test score is reported.

Administration

The Enhanced ACT Assessment tests are given five times a year: in October, December, February, April, and June. New York State does not have a February test date. The Enhanced ACT test is given throughout the United States and Canada. It is also offered three times a year at a variety of overseas test centers.

High school students can obtain a current registration packet from their counselors or a college admissions office. Registration packets may also be obtained by writing to:

ACT
P.O. Box 168
Iowa City, Iowa 52243

Test Scores

The four Enhanced ACT Assessment test scores are reported on a scale ranging from 1–36. A composite score, which is the average of the four test scores, is also reported on a scale of 1–36. The seven subscores are reported on a scale of 1–18.

How to Use This Book

Arco's *ACT* is meant to provide the student with preparation for the four academic tests of the Enhanced ACT Assessment. It begins with a pretest in each of the four content areas to introduce the student to the content and format of each test. Then it provides comprehensive review and practice questions in writing skills, mathematical skills and concepts, reading comprehension, and science reasoning skills. This is followed by three simulated full-length ACT examinations, plus scoring tables. By using this book, the student will be able to review all of the content areas included on the ACT and also become familiar with the format, timing, and types of questions on the test.

Helpful Hints for Test-Takers

1. Go to bed early the night before the test.
2. Follow the directions given to you.
3. Blacken the spaces on your answer sheet carefully.
4. Choose only one answer to each question. If you change an answer, erase the first answer completely and then blacken another space.
5. Read each question and the four or five possible answer choices carefully before answering.
6. Answer every question. You are not penalized for guessing.
7. Use a process of elimination to help you select the best answer to a question.
8. Use any leftover time to look for possible mistakes.
9. Bring the following items to the test:

   - Three No. 2 pencils with erasers
   - Your social security number and picture identification
   - A watch to help pace yourself

Part I

TEST BUSTERS

SHORTCUTS AND STRATEGIES FOR THE ACT

GUESSING

 ### The Fallacy of "First Guess Is Best"

Since your score on the ACT is based on the number of questions you answer correctly, you should answer every question even if you have to guess. But when should you fill in the guess on the answer sheet? It is best to mark in the guess before going on to the next question (which you should do fairly quickly; never get hung up on any one question, since they are all worth the same number of points to you). You should also put a light mark next to the question number on the answer sheet so that at the end of a section, if you have time, you may return to the question with a fresh perspective and perhaps work the problem out and change your answer. If, on the other hand, time runs out on you, then your best guess is already there. You will not have to leave many blanks or guess wildly. (Be sure to erase any light marks you make before you go on to the next section, so that there is no chance of confusing the computer scorer.)

In order to use this flexible strategy of answer-marking effectively, you have to reject a bit of multiple-choice test folklore; the principle that your "first guess is best." This is misleading, to say the least. Research indicates that when people change their answers on tests like the ACT, about two-thirds of the time they go from wrong to right!

SOLVING MATH PROBLEMS

The key to getting answers to math problems you can't solve on the ACT is making effective use of the *extra information* given in these questions: the answer choices, and the diagrams, if any. This material should be considered part of the given information in the problem and can be used to facilitate guessing or to simplify the solving of the problem. It can help you avoid unnecessarily tedious calculations. The ACT is not intended to be a test of donkey arithmetic; the key to success in the math section is to avoid unnecessary math, especially unnecessary calculations. To do this, you must know what the possible answers look like. Thus, the most important point of strategy for the math section of the ACT is to always scan the answer choices before doing any serious calculation. The choices can tell you a great deal about what work you will have to do on a problem. Keep in mind that your basic task on the ACT math section is to select the correct answer, not necessarily to calculate it. Often you can get the answer without extensive calculation. We will examine a number of techniques based on this principle.

Substitution

One common, useful technique is called substitution or "plugging in." Most test-takers find it easier to think through a problem when known quantities, instead of unknowns, are involved. What you do is pick a number to work with when none is specified in the problem, or pick simple, numerical values for variables (x, y, z, etc.) in the question while plugging in the same values in the answer choices. Here are examples of each of these strategies.

example   A square is changed into a rectangle by increasing its length 10% and decreasing its width 10%. Its area

(A) remains the same
(B) increases by 10%
(C) decreases by 10%
(D) increases by 1%
(E) decreases by 1%

solution by substitution   All squares must undergo the same percentage of increase or decrease in area under the circumstances described in the problem. If this is not clear to you, notice that the problem refers to "a square," and that the answers are not qualified or variable. That is, the answers do not say: "Its area decreases if its side measures less than two feet, and increases by 5% if its side measures two feet or more." Your conclusion must be that all squares behave the same in this regard.

Therefore, a square of side 10 behaves the same as any other square does in the situation indicated in the problem. Now increase the length of this square by 10%, so that it becomes 11, and decrease its width by 10%, so that it becomes 9. The area now becomes 11×9, or 99. Since $100 - 99 = 1$, you have a decrease of 1 in area. $\frac{1}{100} = 1\%$. The correct answer, then, is **(E)**.

example   The total number of feet in x yards, y feet, and z inches is

(A) $3x + y + \dfrac{z}{12}$

(B) $12(x + y + z)$

(C) $x + y + z$

(D) $\dfrac{x}{36} + \dfrac{y}{12} + z$

(E) $x + 3y + 36z$

solution by substitution   "Plug in" simple values to arrive at a solution. For instance. let $x = 2$, $y = 2$, and $z = 6$. Since 2 yards = 6 feet and 6 inches = $\frac{1}{2}$ foot, the total is $8\frac{1}{2}$ feet. Which answer choice would equal $8\frac{1}{2}$ feet when the chosen values are plugged in? Answer (B) does not: $12(2 + 2 + 6) = 12(10) = 120$ feet. (C) does not: $2 + 2 + 6 = 10$ feet. (D) does not: $\frac{2}{36} + \frac{2}{12} + 6$ is less than 7. (It is not necessary to take the time to calculate the exact value.) (E) does not: $2 + 3(2) + 36(6)$ is obviously much more than $8\frac{1}{2}$. Only **(A)** works: $3(2) + 2 + \frac{6}{12} = 8\frac{1}{2}$.

You should not have to substitute more than once, except in rare cases. If it should happen that two or more of the answer choices give you the correct number, pick a new set of values and substitute again into those choices.

Working Backwards from the Answer Choices

Another technique you can use when you do not know how to solve a problem using standard methods is working backwards—that is, simply trying each answer and seeing which one works. This approach is useful when you are stuck going forward and is often faster than working in the forward direction.

example   A vendor sold $\frac{1}{2}$ of his hot dogs in the first three innings of a baseball game. At the end of the fourth inning, after selling five more hot dogs, $\frac{3}{8}$ of the original number of hot dogs remained. How many hot dogs did he start with?

(A) 20
(B) 30
(C) 40
(D) 50
(E) 60

solution by working backwards   Working backwards, you see what happens if (A) is right. $\frac{1}{2}$ of 20 is 10, $10 - 5 = 5$, and $\frac{5}{20} \neq \frac{3}{8}$. So (A) is not correct. We try (B). $\frac{1}{2}$ of 30 is 15, $15 - 5 = 10$, and $\frac{10}{30} \neq \frac{3}{8}$. Now (C): $\frac{1}{2}$ of 40 is 20, $20 - 5 = 15$, and $\frac{15}{40} = \frac{3}{8}$, so **(C)** must be correct. Once you find the correct answer you need not examine the remaining choices.

Since ACT math answer choices are arranged in either ascending or descending order (for example, in the preceding question, the answer choices go in ascending order from 20 to 60), it is often most convenient to work backwards starting with the middle choice.

example   A farmer raises chickens and pigs. These animals have a total of 120 heads and 300 feet. How many chickens does the farmer have?

(A) 50
(B) 60
(C) 70
(D) 80
(E) 90

solution by working backwards   Looking for a combination of animals that will have 300 feet, we work backwards starting with choice (C) and see what would happen if there were 70 chickens. In this case, there would be 50 pigs. Thus, there would be 2 × 70 = 140 chicken feet and 4 × 50 = 200 pig feet, for a total of 340 feet. Too many! How do you get fewer feet? We need more chickens and fewer pigs. So we try answer choice (D). This gives you 80 chickens and 40 pigs, that is, 80 × 2 = 160 chicken feet and 40 × 4 = 160 pig feet, giving us a total of 320 feet. Still too many! Now you know (E) is the correct answer, because it is the only one left with more chickens and, therefore, fewer total feet. By working backwards, beginning the process with choice (C), you make sure that you never have to plug in more than two answer choices to identify the correct answer. If our original substitution had resulted in too few feet, we would simply have tried choice (B) with more pigs, and thus, more total feet. Again, we would have known what the right answer was.

Estimation

One important reason for scanning the answer choices before working through the questions is to assess the outlook for estimating. If the answers are spread far apart from each other, estimating is easy. If they are close to each other, you may not be able to estimate effectively. Let's look at a simple case.

example   32% of 1498 = ?

solution by estimation   What you do with a question like this depends on what the answer choices look like. If they are not too similar, a good estimate of the answer will suffice. Here it helps to know some fractional equivalents for percentages. 32% is close to $33\frac{1}{3}$%, which is $\frac{1}{3}$. 1498 is close to 1500. Thus, a good estimate of the answer would be $\frac{1}{3}$ of 1500, which is easily seen to be 500. You should keep track of which way the estimate differs from reality. In this case, $\frac{1}{3}$ is slightly greater than 32%, and 1500 is slightly greater than 1498. Thus, 500 is slightly greater than the true answer. If the answer choices are reasonably spread apart, then you should select the answer choice that is closest to, but smaller than, 500.

Logical Elimination

Sometimes answer choices can be eliminated because you can see without computation that they cannot possibly be right. To eliminate such answers you simply ask yourself, "Is it even *possible* for this answer choice to be correct for this question?"

example Two pipes labelled X and Y are being used to fill an oil tank. Pipe X fills the tank at a rate of 20 gallons per minute, and pipe Y fills it at the rate of 30 gallons per minute. The tank can be filled in 30 hours, 20 hours, or 12 hours depending on whether pipe X alone, pipe Y alone, or both pipes are used. If the tank is filled by using pipe Y all of the time and pipe X half of the time, how many hours will it take to fill the tank?

(A) 7.5
(B) 15
(C) 19.5
(D) 21
(E) 25

solution by logical elimination Here's the way to get the answer to this fairly difficult question by logical elimination. Notice that choices (D) and (E) are impossible because they are longer than the 20 hours it takes when pipe Y works by itself. Choice (A) is impossible because it is less time than it takes when both pipes work together all of the time, 12 hours. Answer (C) is too close to the time it takes pipe Y alone. Surely pipe X working half the time would be worth more than a mere one half of an hour. Therefore, answer **(B)** must be correct.

example Given that EFGH is a square, ETG is an arc of a circle centered at H, ESG is an arc of a circle centered at F, and side EF = 2, what is the area of the shaded region?

(A) $4 - 2\pi$
(B) $\pi - 2$
(C) $2\pi - 4$
(D) $2 + 2\pi$
(E) $4\pi - 4$

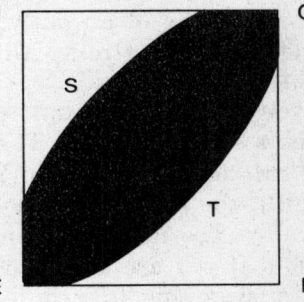

guessing approach Now, suppose that either you were stuck on this question or were too short of time to solve it. You should try to eliminate answers and guess! Choice (A) cannot be correct. 2 times π is more than 6; thus (A) is a negative number, and you will never see negative areas on the ACT! Choice (D) is impossible because it is slightly greater than 8, and the area of the entire square is only 4. If (D) is bad, (E) is even worse, because it is even larger (we don't care by how much). Thus you are down to (B) and (C). Now you can make use of the measurement principle. the leaf-shaped shaded region *looks* as if it is half the area of the square. The area of the square is $2 \times 2 = 4$, so the shaded area should be about 2. Choice (B) is a little more than $3 - 2 = 1$ (remember that π, the Greek letter that represents the ratio of the circumference of a circle to its diameter, is about $3\frac{1}{7}$). Choice (C) is twice as large as (B); it is a little more than $6 - 4 = 2$. Clearly **(C)** is the correct answer.

"Guessperation"

What can you do with a math problem when you have very little time left in the section? Usually not very much, but sometimes there are reasonable guesses that can be made quickly, precisely because the test-writer is trying to make his wrong answers attractive. Try the following "question."

example (?)
- (A) 3.7
- (B) 4.5
- (C) 4.9
- (D) 5.2
- (E) 9.8

guessing approach What is the answer to this question? Oh yes, we are saying here that you do not have time to actually read it. Is there any hope? Not much, but you might look quickly at how the choices compare to each other. Test-writers like to try to hide the correct answer by presenting variations of it as distractors. In other words, when x/y is the correct answer, y/x is a likely distractor. When you see some answers that are variations on a theme, you should suspect that one of them is correct. In this example, you might notice that 9.8 is twice 4.9, so maybe one of these two is the right answer. 9.8 is something of an outlying answer, and so seems less likely, although this principle is not very strong. All in all, 4.9 seems to be the best guess, but is a shaky guess at best.

Suppose, though, you have enough time to skim this question and see that it is a problem about filling a swimming pool. There are two pipes filling the pool while a leak at the bottom empties it, and so on. You notice that the problem asks how long it takes to "half fill" the pool. How does this information affect your guessing confidence? Considerably. The math problems of the ACT are very much tests of reading comprehension. If you are asked to *half* fill a swimming pool, what is a likely distractor? An answer that fills the pool, of course! With this in mind, (C) now becomes a solid guess, because 9.8 is a good distractor if 4.9 is the right answer. Again, let me stress that you should resort to this "psyching out the test-writer" posture only when you cannot otherwise solve the problem.

Making Sure That the Question You Answer Is the Question That Was Asked

Before we leave our discussion of math problems, there is an issue we should talk about that does not concern guessing or shortcuts. It is, however, probably the most common pitfall in every examination, and it is likely that more points are lost from it than any other single cause. This mistake is misreading or forgetting the question. Questions are often long and complicated, and missing the significance of a single word can make the difference between a right and wrong answer. ACT math questions are often difficult not just because of the mathematics involved, but because of how they are formulated. Consider the following example. It is a fairly easy question, but it is also easy to get wrong.

example A delicatessen worker wants to cut a ten-foot long submarine sandwich into smaller pieces. Two pieces are to be 6 inches long, and the rest of the sub is to be cut into pieces that are nine inches long. How many cuts will be necessary?

(A) 12
(B) 13
(C) 14
(D) 15
(E) 16

solution by careful reading A logical approach to this problem is to determine the total number of pieces. The two 6-inch pieces account for one foot of the sub. Nine inches is $\frac{3}{4}$ of a foot. (It is more convenient to work in feet than in inches, since the numbers will be smaller that way.) Thus, the remaining 9 feet will be cut into $\frac{3}{4}$-foot pieces. Thus, the question is: How many $\frac{3}{4}$-foot pieces make up 9 feet? This is found by dividing 9 by $\frac{3}{4}$. Since to divide by a fraction you must invert it and multiply, this would equal 9 times $\frac{4}{3}$, or 12 pieces. Add this to the two 6-inch pieces and you have 14 pieces altogether. This means answer choice (C) is correct, right? Wrong! The question asks for the number of cuts required, not the number of pieces, and there will always be one less cut than pieces. The correct answer is **(B)**. Answer (C) is, of course, a very likely distractor choice. To avoid falling into this trap, take a few seconds after figuring out the answer and before marking it on the answer sheet to ask yourself: "Is this the answer to exactly the question asked?" This small investment of time can save you from unnecessary mistakes.

Overviewing Math Word Problems

One more word about reading technique in the math section of the ACT. Some test-takers like to start writing an equation as soon as they start reading a word problem. This is unwise because you generally cannot tell exactly where you are supposed to be going until you read the entire question and identify carefully what the unknown is and what given information you have to work with. When first approaching a word problem, put down your pencil, read the problem over quickly to get the general idea, identify the desired unknown, and scan quickly over the answer choices. Then, go back and translate the words of the problem into an equation.

READING COMPREHENSION

Solving the Biggest Problem: Motivation

The one thing that will definitely be fatal to your cause in tests that involve reading comprehension items is to lose your concentration while reading the passage. The passages are often quite dry and, for most people, boring. It is very easy for your eyes to move down the page while your mind is occupied elsewhere, perhaps thinking about lunch or the nice weather outside. If you let this happen to you, no amount of reading skill will save you. Conversely, if you are able to maintain the proper attention to the passage, you will do well even if your reading skills are not top-notch.

Make up your mind now that on the day of the exam you will pay sustained attention to the reading material no matter how uninteresting it is to you. Of course, you should not have to rely completely on will power. You can help yourself concentrate by asking yourself specific questions about the material as you read it. (Some useful questions will be provided a little later in our discussion.) In any event, if you find yourself drifting off, you can always focus your efforts by asking yourself the general-purpose question: "What is the author trying to tell me here?"

Focusing Your Reading

Reading for the ACT is not quite the same as reading for a course or for your own information. On the ACT, you are reading specifically to answer multiple-choice questions. For reasons that will be made clear shortly, this means, most fundamentally, getting the answer by elimination. The basic purpose of reading a passage is to obtain enough information to eliminate the distractor choices in the questions. It is not necessary for this purpose, nor is it enough, to memorize the passage or thoroughly understand everything about it. On the other hand, speed reading is not the recommended approach, either. A properly *focused* reading can get you what you need without excessive effort. It will actually end up being faster than speed reading, because you will not have to spend as much time referring to the passage. Let's now talk specifically about *how* to focus your reading effectively.

Suggestions for Reading the Passage

The first suggestion to be made in this section is to preview the question stems before reading the passage. The question stem is the part of the question that asks you something or tells you what to do. It does not include the answer choices. Looking at the answer choices first is bound to be confusing, because by definition, 75 percent of them are wrong! This previewing strategy is only a suggestion; you should try it out in practice and see if you like it. Most, but not all students find it useful if done properly. However, done incorrectly, it could even hurt your score. If you try to use previewing as a substitute for reading—that is, to read the questions, try to memorize them, then go to the passage looking for answers—you are likely to lose track of the main thrust of the passage. You will be too busy keeping the questions in your mind while you look for the answers to really pay attention to what you are reading. You should only spend a few seconds per question previewing to sensitize your mind to recognize what is important in the passage. It gives you just a hint ahead of time about what's important in the passage.

The key words for the reading process itself are included in the famous phrase "active reading." Passive reading is allowing the light rays from the page to enter your eyes with the hope that they will somehow automatically get into your brain. This does not work, partly because in Reading Comprehension you must not only read the lines, but between the lines as well. You must draw inferences about the material, preferably as you read rather than afterwards. If you wait until you have finished the passage before you think about its implications, it will be all too easy to lose track of some of them.

Active reading means thinking as you read, which, in turn, basically means asking yourself and answering questions while you read. Here are some suggested questions to keep in mind that have direct relevance to the goal of eliminating the distractors in the questions.

1. What is the exact subject matter of the discussion?

   This issue can be referred to as the *scope* of the passage. Many of the wrong answers are wrong merely because they are not what the passage is talking about, that is, they are outside the scope of discussion. If you know what that scope is, you will be able to eliminate what is probably the test-writer's favorite form of Reading Comprehension distractor.

2. How forcefully are assertions made about that subject matter?

   This issue may be referred to as the *strength* of the passage. If a passage is highly qualified in its claims and uses cautious phrases, then uncompromising, absolute answers will not be correct. Correct answers must match the passage and the question in scope and strength. To assess strength, be on the lookout for qualifying terms such as "sometimes," "possibly," "under certain circumstances," and the like. In a slightly different vein, be on the lookout for "thought reversing" words and phrases such as "however," "yet," "on the other hand," and the like. They signal transitions in the reasoning of the passage, and the test-writers are very fond of asking questions about such transitions.

3. What is the main idea of the passage?

   This is the single most important element to figure out while reading. If you understand this, everything else in the passage will make sense because the other ideas will be conceptually organized around the point. If you do not get the main idea, then all you will have will be a lot of separate, unorganized details that will be hard to remember. Some test-takers complain that they read a passage and understand it, but cannot remember a thing afterwards! It seems likely that this occurs because the reader "kind of" understood what he or she read, but did not really get the main idea and thus lost track of everything else.

   Incidentally, there are often questions asked about the main idea. It is worthwhile to look at that question first, because if you can figure it out, you will have a description, in the test-writer's own words, of what the main idea is, and that can be of immense help on other questions.

4. How is the passage laid out and what part does each paragraph have in the discussion?

Answering this question will be helpful should you have to go back to the passage to answer a question. You don't want to go back unless it's necessary, but if you need to look back to get the answer, it is best to know just where to look. If you identify, for example, that the first paragraph of a passage introduces an idea, the second produces evidence for it, the third mentions objections to it, and the fourth answers the objections and concludes, when you are asked, "Which of the following is *not* an objection to the author's proposal discussed in the passage?", you will be able to go right to the relevant paragraph without fumbling.

If you can clearly answer the preceding four suggested questions as you read, you will be in great shape to answer the questions that accompany each passage. Now let's talk about that process.

Answering Reading Comprehension Questions

The first thing to remember about answering reading comprehension questions, once again, is the two-word prep course for the ACT, "read carefully." Missing even a single word in a question can lead directly to a wrong answer. The place where speed reading is most dangerous, where you can least afford to try to cut corners to save time, is the reading of the question stem. Poor test-takers try to rush through this step to get the question over with. They end up confused. Good test-takers may even try to reformulate the question as accurately as possible in their own words, to be sure they understand it.

Recent research into verbal test-taking skills has revealed another way in which good test-takers differ from poor ones in this area. Good test-takers hypothesize about what a good answer might look like, before going to the answer choices. This cannot always be done; if a question asks, "Which of the following can be inferred?", there is no point in sitting there making inferences or banging your head against the wall trying to come up with a possible answer to a tough question. But if you can quickly come up with some idea, it will probably help you to navigate through the answer choices even if your idea is wrong. You must remember, of course, that it is only a hypothesis and might not be among the available answers. You will then have to choose the best of those available, because there is no place for write-in answers! Keep in mind also that you cannot pick an answer just because it looks good to you at that moment. You are looking for the so-called "best" answer, and there is a "theory of relativity" that defines "best" as the most appropriate or correct of the five available choices. That is why on any verbal question you should always read all the answer choices, and you should never get too hung up on any one answer until you have seen them all.

Neutralizing the Distractors

Now we get to the bottom line: selecting the right answer from among the four options. Here it is important to understand how the test-writer constructs answers, especially the distractors. On the one hand, at least some of the wrong answers must have some apparent merit, or the correct answer would stand out too much, and the item would be too easy. On the other hand, the correct answer is supposed to be clearly best, and this means that each incorrect answer must have a disqualifying flaw. This is why elimination is the most powerful approach to the reading questions. If you examine the answer choices just looking for merit, you are likely to find two or three answers that have some, and then you must make the tricky judgment of which has the most. But if you also look for the weaknesses and flaws in the answer choices, and can find them in three choices, then you can be more certain that the fourth answer is correct. At the same time, by focusing on flaws you are less likely to get fooled by carefully crafted distractors. This is where the ideas of scope and strength come into play. The test-writers like to construct wrong answers that seem quite plausible standing on their own, which, in fact, are outside the scope of the passage or question or too strong in their statements. The questions to ask yourself as you strive to eliminate distractors is, "Could this answer be wrong?" Which means, fundamentally, "Could this answer be too broad in scope or too strong?" Let's consider the following Reading Comprehension situation:

example   Suppose you have read a passage that is about Darwin's theory of evolution as it relates to literature, and that is all you were able to get from your reading. (This is all that you are going to be told about the passage, but it is a lot, because it defines the subject matter, or scope). You are faced with this question:

Which of the following best describes the meaning of "poet," as the term is used by the author?

 (A) one who writes verse
 (B) deep philosophical thinker
 (C) one who produces works of art
 (D) writer with imagination

"negative reasoning" approach   Take the answers one-by-one and try to object to them: (A) looks like a pure distractor, thrown in for people who don't read the passage or the question. It looks like a definition out of a dictionary, and the question suggests with the words "as the term is used by the author" that we are looking for a special meaning. (B) looks like it has nothing obvious to do with literature, so it is not too attractive an answer. (C) appears to be too broad for the scope of this passage, because it could include sculptors, painters, and composers as well as writers. Still you might not completely throw this answer out. Feel free to hold on to answers with some merit to which you might possibly return after examining the other options. (D) looks very good because it neatly fits the scope of Darwin and literature, and it seems clearly superior to (C) in this regard. It is, in fact, the correct answer.

The approach of "negative reasoning," looking for flaws in scope and strength in the answer choices, is so powerful that you can sometimes zero in on a good guess of the right answer just from reading the question and the answer choices. The choices, in conjunction with the question, sometimes eliminate themselves and each other. Let's try to answer some Reading Comprehension questions without the various passages on which they are based.

example   It is implied by the author that an extreme internationalist is

 (A) opposed to international controls on national government
 (B) opposed to strong governments of any kind
 (C) favorable to only mild forms of regional cooperation
 (D) opposed to national domination of international government

The phrasing of this question goes a long way toward providing the answer, particularly the words "extreme internationalist." Let's try to object to each answer. (A) seems to go against any idea of what an "internationalist" could be. (B) could be wrong and appears to be outside the scope of the question and too strong, as suggested by the phrase, "of any kind." The word "only" is the key to (C); it does not fit with "extreme." How could (D) be wrong, how could an extreme internationalist disagree with this answer? **(D)** is probably correct.

example   In writing about this performance of *Das Rheingold,* the reviewer's reactions could best be described as

   (A) somewhat negative
   (B) genuinely affirmative
   (C) filled with awe
   (D) totally noncommittal

Here you cannot be at all sure about the answer, but (C) seems to be laying it on too thick: reading passages are rarely that emotional. (D) is unlikely because if it were true, why would the author have written a review at all? (A) and (B) are the most likely choices.

Part II
ACT PRETEST
ENGLISH PRETEST

6 Minutes—10 Questions

DIRECTIONS: In the passage below, certain words and phrases are underlined and numbered. In the right-hand column, you will find choices for each underlined part. You are to select the one that best expresses the idea, makes the statement appropriate for standard written English, or is worded most consistently with the style and mood of the passage as a whole. If you think the original version is best, choose "NO CHANGE." You will also find questions about a section of the passage, or about the passage as a whole. These questions are indicated by a number or numbers in a box. For each question in the test, circle the choice you consider best. Read each passage through once before you begin to answer the questions that accompany it. You cannot evaluate most answers without reading several sentences past the phrase in question.

The two-career marriage in which both the
           ———1———
husband and the wife work, is becoming the

accepted norm in American society. Although it

has not radical altered mankind's most basic and
         ———2———
oldest social unit, the family, there have been

some painful adjustments to accommodate

the dual-career concept

when both the husband and the wife are working.
———————————————3———————————————

More than half the nations mothers work outside
                  ———4———

the home. The Traditional American family, still
               ————5————
portrayed in advertising, children's literature, and

popular movies as a working father, a stay-at-

home mother, and one or more children,

represents a scant thirteen percent of the nation's

families. The apparent reason for this dual-career

1. A. NO CHANGE
   B. marriage; in
   C.⃝ marriage, in
   D. marriage: in

2. F. NO CHANGE
   G.⃝ radically
   H. radicalism
   J. radicalness

3. A.⃝ NO CHANGE
   B. when spouses are working.
   C. when two people are working.
   D. OMIT the underlined portion.   ✓D

4. F. NO CHANGE
   G.⃝ nation's
   H. nations'
   J. nation

5. A. NO CHANGE
   B. traditional american
   C.⃝ traditional American
   D. Traditional american

14 / ACT

family is the need for increasing income. The
                                   ———
                                    6
more than nineteen million families that had at

least two wage earners in 1979 made an average

of $509 a week—more than $26,000 a year—

compared with $305 a week for families with

single breadwinners. Does the dual-career family

hurt the child, according to one prominent
         ————————
              7
sociologist, current research indicates that a

working mother does not either hurt or help the

child. "They grow up just like everybody else."

However, more traditionally minded scholars take

a wait-and-see position, noting that it may take

years for the long-term effects of family work
                            ———
                             8
habits to become clear. ⬜9⬜ ⬜10⬜

6. F. NO CHANGE
   G. increases
   H. increase
   J. increased

7. A. NO CHANGE
   B. child: according
   C. child; according
   D. child? According

8. F. NO CHANGE
   G. effect
   H. affect
   J. affects

9. Is the use of the hyphen appropriate in this passage?
   A. No, because hyphens are only used to show division between syllables.
   B. No, because they are not used in formal writing.
   C. Yes, because a hyphen adds excitement to a passage.
   D. Yes, because the hyphen is used between single words to express the idea of a unit.

10. Is the use of quotation marks appropriate in this passage?
    F. No, because the author is telling the reader the results of research.
    G. No, because the passage is not specific enough.
    H. Yes, because quotation marks are used to set off a direct quote.
    J. Yes, because quotation marks indicate a conversation.

MATHEMATICS PRETEST

10 Minutes—10 Questions

DIRECTIONS: Solve each problem. Then circle the correct answer from among the five choices.

Solve as many problems as you can since they all have the same point value. Do not spend too much time on a single problem. Remember: you are not penalized for incorrect answers; only those answered correctly contribute to your final score.

Note: Unless otherwise stated, assume the following:
- All figures lie in a plane.
- Figures are not necessarily drawn to scale.
- All lines are straight.

---

1. What is the slope of the line $x = 2y + 3$?

   A. $\frac{1}{2}$
   B. 1
   C. $\frac{3}{2}$
   D. 2
   E. 3

2. In the figure below $\overline{AC} = \overline{BC}$, if $m\angle B = 50°$, what is the measure of $\angle ECD$?

   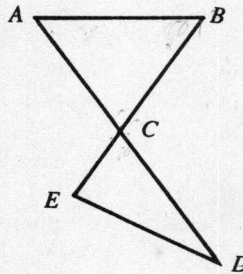

   F. 40°
   G. 50°
   H. 60°
   J. 80°
   K. 100°

3. What is the value of $m^2 n^3$, when $m = -2$ and $n = -1$?

   A. -8
   B. -4
   C. 1
   D. 4
   E. 8

4. On the standard number line below, which integer is the midpoint between points P and Q?

   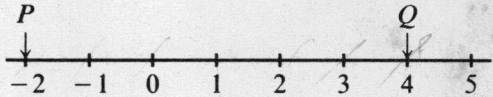

   F. -1
   G. 0
   H. 1
   J. 2
   K. 3

5. In the figure below $\overline{BA} \perp \overline{AD}$ and $\overline{CD} \perp \overline{AD}$. Using the values indicated in the figure, what is the area of polygon $ABCD$?

   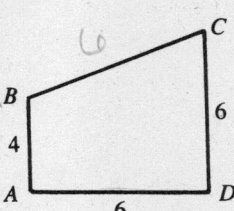

   A. 26
   B. 30
   C. 36
   D. 42
   E. 60

GO ON TO THE NEXT PAGE.

15

6. In the figure below line *m* is parallel to line *n*. If the measure of ∠1 is 30°, what is the measure of ∠2?

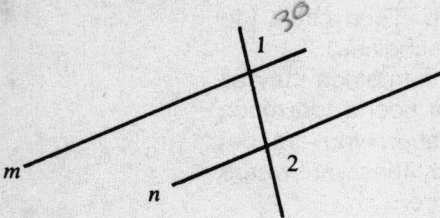

F. 30°
G. 60°
H. 90°
J. 120°
K. 150°

7. Points *N* and *J* have coordinates (−1, −1) and (3, 3) respectively. What is the length of line $\overline{NJ}$?

A. 4
B. √8
C. 6
D. 8
E. 4√2

8. If the area of a circle is π, what is the length of its circumference?

F. 1
G. 2
H. π
J. 2π
K. 3π

9. What is the average of −2, 0 and +5?

A. −3
B. −1
C. $1\frac{1}{2}$
D. 1
E. 3

10. What is the decimal equivalent of the fraction $\frac{3}{5}$?

F. .06
G. .03
H. .3
J. .6
K. 60

READING PRETEST

5 Minutes—5 Questions

DIRECTIONS: There are two passages in this test. Each passage is followed by a number of questions. After reading a passage, circle the most appropriate answer to each question. You may refer to the passages as often as you feel necessary.

Passage I

Movie music is rarely music in any real sense, but has a quality of its own. The men who write it try to fit their notes and phrases to the galloping of hoofs, the lingering kiss, the death, and the lifted mortgage. But above all they struggle with the problem of keeping an orchestra at work on some kind of intelligible sound for a stretch of two hours or more without giving them anything to play that would really catch the hearer's attention. So the score for one picture is about as appetizing and arresting as that for another—it is the cream sauce that does as well for chicken or lamb croquettes or cauliflower or the hanging of wallpaper.

1. The passage suggests that those who prepare music for movies

   A. have a limited knowledge of music.
   B. are hampered by requirements of movie-making.
   C. are not aware of the techniques for making movies.
   D. write music to attract the audience's attention.

2. The passage suggests that movie music

   F. is easy to write.
   G. is more important than what is happening on the screen.
   H. is subordinate to the action on the screen.
   J. is not related to the action on the screen.

3. As used in this passage, the word "score" most nearly means

   A. background music.
   B. sound.
   C. rating.
   D. dialogue.

Passage II

The microscopic vegetables of the sea, of which the diatoms are most important, make the mineral wealth of the water available to the animals. Feeding directly on the diatoms and other groups of minute unicellular algae are the marine protozoa, many crustaceans, the young of crabs, barnacles, sea worms, and fishes. Hordes of the small carnivores, the first link in the chain of flesh eaters, move among these peaceful grazers. There are fierce little dragons half an inch long, the sharp-jawed arrowworms. There are gooseberry-like comb jellies, armed with grasping tentacles, and there are the shrimplike euphausiids that strain food from the water with their bristly appendages. Since they drift where the currents carry them, with no power or will to oppose that of the sea, this strange community of creatures and the marine plants that sustain them are called plankton, a word derived from the Greek, meaning wandering.

4. Which characteristics of diatoms does the passage emphasize?

   F. Size
   G. Feeding habits
   H. Activeness
   J. Numerousness

5. The reader may most safely conclude from this passage that plankton

   A. was given its name by Greek fishermen.
   B. is a valuable source of mineral wealth.
   C. is composed of animal and vegetable life.
   D. is most often found where the currents are strongest.

17

SCIENCE REASONING PRETEST

8 Minutes—10 Questions

DIRECTIONS: Each passage in this test is followed by several questions. After reading a passage, circle the most appropriate answer to each question. You may refer to the passages as often as necessary while answering the questions.

Passage I

An investigation was made of the relation between the flow of electric current through a wire and the power provided. The results are presented in the table below:

Table I

Experiment	Battery (volts)	Current (amps)	Power
1	12	2	24
2	12	4	48
3	12	0.5	6
4	6	2	12
5	6	4	24
6	9	1	9

1. Which of the following would be the correct units for power, based on the data above?

   A. Volts/amps
   B. Amps/volts
   C. Amps + volts
   D. Amps × volts

2. What current would allow a 6-volt battery to deliver 12 units of power?

   F. 6 amps
   G. 12 amps
   H. 2 amps
   J. Cannot be determined.

3. Which experiment would be a control for experiment 3, if one were investigating the relation between power and current?

   A. Experiment 1
   B. Experiment 4
   C. Experiment 5
   D. Experiment 6

4. Which of the following would be the likely result if a 4-volt battery had a current of 2 amps?

   F. 2 units of power
   G. 6 units of power
   H. 8 units of power
   J. 16 units of power

Passage II

To investigate the hypothesis that W, a new drug, is effective as an appetite-suppressant for cats, 3 experiments were performed using cats of similar age, weight, and breed.

Experiment 1
Five cats were given 2 mg of W in their milk in the morning. The average food intake for the cats in this group was 5½ oz. of Meowzer tuna catfood. Each cat also drank 6 oz. of water.

Experiment 2
Five cats were given milk in the morning with no W added. The average food intake for the cats in this group was 8 oz. of Meowzer tuna catfood. Each cat also drank 4 oz. of water.

Experiment 3
Five cats were given 4 mg of W in their milk in the morning. The average food intake for the cats in this group was 3 oz. of Meowzer tuna catfood. Each cat also drank 7 oz. of water.

5. Was it necessary to give the cats in Experiment 2 milk in the morning?

   A. No.
   B. No, because the milk did not have any W in it.
   C. Yes, because otherwise there would be another difference between the cats besides the drug.
   D. Yes, because the cats were hungry.

6. Which of the experiments served as a control to see if drug W affects the food intake of cats?

   F. Experiment 3
   G. Experiment 2
   H. Experiment 1
   J. None

7. Which of the following best summarizes the data found in these three experiments?

   A. The cats were unaffected by W.
   B. The average food intake dropped because one or more cats died in each group.
   C. The average food and water intake decreased with increasing dosage of W.
   D. The average food intake decreased with increasing dosage of W, but water intake increased.

Passage III

Two scientists offer their answers to the question "Can machines think?"

Scientist 1
The idea that only humans, or only a few mammals, have the ability to reason is very short-sighted. The ability to think requires only the ability to take information from the environment, analyze the information into components, and put together new, logically consistent components. It really doesn't matter whether the information enters through eyes and travels through nerves, or comes in through a keyboard and travels through electrical circuits.

Scientist 2
The idea that a machine can think because it can analyze ideas is seriously flawed. All living creatures can perform this task with varying degrees of success. The termite can build complex mounds six feet in height that can last for a century. But not even the greatest termite sympathizer maintains that termites can think. The termite only follows a program. The basis for deciding whether something can think is whether it can independently change its mind based on new information, and this is something that no machine can do.

8. Which of the following, if true, would most successfully refute Scientist 2's arguments?

   F. A computer has been designed that can rewrite its own programs to deal with new situations.
   G. A computer has been designed that can play chess.
   H. A computer has been designed that can pick out spelling errors.
   J. A computer has been designed that can pilot a plane.

9. What assumption does Scientist 2 make about machines?

   A. Sophisticated machines are intelligent.
   B. Machines will never be able to act independently of their programs.
   C. Machines will never have eyes.
   D. Machines could never laugh.

10. According to the definition of thought given by Scientist 1, which of the following could be classified as thinking?

    F. Solving a calculus problem
    G. Building a nest with straw
    H. Neither F nor G
    J. Both F and G

Answer Key for ACT Pretest

1. English Test

1. C		3. D		5. C		7. D		9. D
2. G		4. G		6. J		8. F		10. H

2. Mathematics Test

1. A		3. B		5. B		7. E		9. D
2. J		4. H		6. K		8. J		10. J

3. Reading Test

1. B		3. A		5. C
2. H		4. F		

4. Science Reasoning Test

1. D		3. A		5. C		7. D		9. B
2. H		4. H		6. G		8. F		10. J

Explanatory Answers for ACT Pretest

1. English Test

1. **(C)** Commas are used to set off nonrestrictive clauses or phrases.

2. **(G)** The adverb *radically* correctly modifies the verb *altered*.

3. **(D)** *When both the husband and the wife are working* is redundant. *Dual-career* means *both husband and wife have careers*.

4. **(G)** *Nation's* is the correct possessive. The apostrophe followed by *s* is used to show singular possession.

5. **(C)** Proper nouns and their derivatives are capitalized. *American* must be capitalized, but the adjective *traditional* does not require capitalization.

6. **(J)** The past participle *increased* is the correct verbal form.

7. **(D)** A question mark is used after a direct question.

8. **(F)** The noun *effects* meaning *results* is used correctly. *Affect* means *to influence* and functions as a verb.

9. **(D)** For example, *wait-and-see*.

10. **(H)** The statement, "They grow up just like everybody else" is a direct quote attributed to "one prominent sociologist."

ACT Pretest / 21

2. Mathematics Test

1. **(A)** Change the equation into $y = mx + b$ form.
$x = 2y + 3 \rightarrow 2y = x - 3$
$$y = \frac{x}{2} - \frac{3}{2}$$
$$\text{or } y = \frac{1}{2}x - \frac{3}{2}$$
slope $= \frac{1}{2}$, y-intercept $= \frac{3}{2}$

2. **(J)**

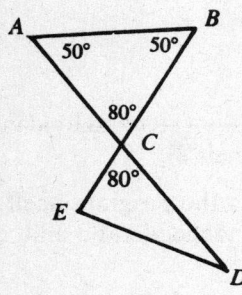

If $\overline{AC} = \overline{BC}$
then $m\angle A = m\angle B = 50°$

In $\triangle ABC$
$m\angle ACB = 180° - (m\angle A + m\angle B)$
$m\angle ACB = 80°$

$m\angle ACB = m\angle ECD$ (vertical angles)
$m\angle ECD = 80°$

3. **(B)** $m^2 n^3 = (-2)^2(-1)^3$
$= 4(-1) = -4$

4. **(H)** midpoint is the average
$$\frac{(-2) + (4)}{2} = \frac{2}{2} = 1$$

5. **(B)**

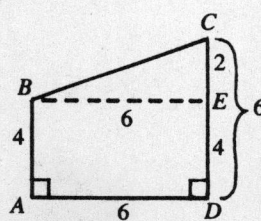

Area of rectangle $ABED$:
$bh = 6(4) = 24$

Area of $\triangle BEC$:
$\frac{1}{2}bh = \frac{1}{2}(6)(2) = 6$

Area of polygon $= 24 + 6 = 30$

6. **(K)**

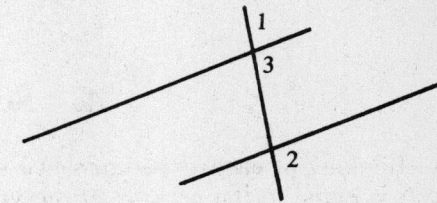

$m\angle 1 = 30°$ (given)

$m\angle 3 = 150°$ (supplementary to $\angle 1$)

$m\angle 2 = m\angle 3 = 150°$ (corresponding angles)

7. **(E)** $N(-1, -1)$
$J(3, 3)$
$d_{\overline{NJ}} = \sqrt{(x_2 - x_1)^2 + (y_2 - y_1)^2}$
$= \sqrt{(3 - (-1))^2 + (3 - (-1))^2}$
$= \sqrt{4^2 + 4^2}$
$= \sqrt{32} = \sqrt{16}\sqrt{2} = 4\sqrt{2}$

8. **(J)** $A = \pi r^2 = \pi$
$\therefore r^2 = 1$
$r = 1$
$C = 2\pi r = 2\pi(1) = 2\pi$

9. **(D)** Average $= \dfrac{\text{Sum of the items}}{\text{Quantity of items}}$
$= \dfrac{-2 + 0 + 5}{3} = \dfrac{3}{3} = 1$

10. **(J)** $\dfrac{3}{5} \rightarrow$ $\begin{array}{r} .6 \\ 5\overline{)3.0} \\ \underline{3\ 0} \\ 0 \end{array}$

3. Reading Test

1. **(B)** The second sentence of the passage states that the music is written to fit in with the action of the movie.

2. **(H)** Since the music must fit in with the action of the movie, it is subordinate to it.

3. **(A)** The word "score" denotes the music for the movie.

4. **(F)** The second sentence of the passage describes diatoms as a part of "... minute unicellular algae ..."

5. **(C)** The last sentence of the passage describes plankton as "... this strange community of creatures and the marine plants that sustain them ..."

4. Science Reasoning Test

1. **(D)** Looking at each experiment we see that power is equal to the product of the volts and the amps. So units will be volts × amps.

2. **(H)** Read across row of Experiment 4.

3. **(A)** In Experiments 1 and 3 the voltage is kept constant, so only current varies and can affect the power.

4. **(H)** 4 × 2 = 8 units.

5. **(C)** Otherwise the food intake of the cats in Experiment 2 might reflect the lack of milk rather than the lack of W.

6. **(G)** These cats are the normal case—no W. The effect of W should be measured against these cats.

7. **(D)** Compare both water and food intakes with control (Experiment 2).

8. **(F)** By rewriting the program itself, the computer can act independently and change its "mind."

9. **(B)** Since Scientist 2 believes that machines will never think, Scientist 2 must assume that machines will never achieve the ability to act independently. Choice D is incorrect because one could program a computer to laugh.

10. **(J)** Scientist 1 requires input of information, analysis, and a resulting action. In G, input is what is seen, analysis is noting the suitability of the straw for nest-building, and the result is the nest. In F, the process is even more apparent.

Part III

ENGLISH REVIEW

ENGLISH

The new ACT English Test is a 45-minute test containing a variety of prose passages and 75 questions that measure your understanding of the conventions of standard written English and of rhetorical skills. Each passage contains words and phrases that are underlined. For each underlined phrase you are presented with four choices. Three options are different from the one that is given. One option is NO CHANGE, meaning that you feel the given choice is best. The questions revolve around topics in grammar, diction, usage, organization, and style. The test focuses on the analysis of the types of prose that you are required to read and write in secondary and college curricula, not on rote memorization of grammar rules. In addition to a total score, two subscores are reported. The chart below indicates the subject areas and subscores for the English Test.

Subject Area	Number of Questions	Subscore
Punctuation	10	
Grammar and Usage	12	Usage/Mechanics
Sentence Structure	18	
Strategy	12	
Organization	11	Rhetorical Skills
Style	12	

This section provides a concise review of the topics on which you will be tested.

PUNCTUATION

The Apostrophe

1. Use an apostrophe to indicate possession. Place the apostrophe according to this rule: "The apostrophe, when used to indicate possession, means *belonging to everything to the left of the apostrophe*."

    Examples: lady's   = belonging to the lady
    ladies'   = belonging to the ladies
    children's = belonging to the children

    NOTE: To test for correct placement of the apostrophe, read *of the*.

    Example: childrens' = of the childrens (obviously incorrect)

    The placement rule applies at all times, even with regard to compound nouns separated by hyphens and with regard to entities made up of two or more names.

    Example: father-in-law's = belonging to a father-in-law

    Example: Lansdale, Jackson, and Roosevelt's law firm = the law firm belonging to Landsale, Jackson, and Roosevelt

    Example: Brown and Son's delivery truck = the delivery truck of Brown and Sons

2. Use an apostrophe in a contraction in place of the omitted letter or letters.

    Examples: haven't   = have not
    we're   = we are
    let's   = let us
    o'clock   = of the clock
    class of '90 = class of 1990

    NOTE: Do NOT begin a paragraph with a contraction.

3. Use an apostrophe to form plurals of numbers, letters, and phrases referred to as words.

    Example: The Japanese child pronounced his *l*'s as *r*'s.

    Example: Solution of the puzzle involves crossing out all the *3*'s and *9*'s.

    Example: His speech was studded with *you know*'s.

The Colon

1. Use a colon after the salutation in a business letter.

   Example: Dear Board Member:

2. Use a colon to separate hours from minutes.

   Example: The eclipse occurred at 10:36 A.M.

3. Use of the colon is optional in the following cases:
   (a) to introduce a list, especially after an expression such as "as follows"
   (b) to introduce a long quotation
   (c) to introduce a question

   Example: My question is this: Are you willing to punch a time clock?

The Comma

1. Use a comma after the salutation of a personal letter.

   Example: Dear Mary,

2. Use a comma after the complimentary close of a letter.

   Example: Cordially yours,

3. Use a comma or pair of commas to set off a noun of address.

   Example: When you finish your homework, Jeff, please take out the garbage.

4. Use a pair of commas to set off parenthetical expressions, words that interrupt the flow of the sentence, such as *however, though, for instance, by the way*.

   Example: We could not, however, get him to agree.

   Example: This book, I believe, is the best of its kind.

   NOTE: Test for placement of commas in a parenthetical expression by reading aloud. If you would pause before and after such an expression, then it should be set off by commas.

6. Use a comma between two or more adjectives which modify a noun equally.

   Example: The jolly, fat, ruddy man stood at the top of the stairs.

   NOTE: If you can add the word *and* between the adjectives without changing the sense of the sentence, then use commas.

7. Use a comma to separate words, phrases, or clauses in a series. The use of a comma before *and* is optional. If the series ends in *etc.*, use a comma before *etc.* Do not use a comma after *etc.* in a series, even if the sentence continues.

   Example: Coats, umbrellas, and boots should be placed in the closet at the end of the hall.

   Example: Pencils, scissors, paper clips, etc. belong in your top desk drawer.

8. Use a comma to separate a short direct quotation from the speaker.

   Example: She said, "I must leave work on time today."

   Example: "Tomorrow I begin my summer job," he told us.

9. Use a comma after an introductory clause or phrase of five or more words.

   Example: Because the prisoner had a history of attempted jailbreaks, he was put under heavy guard.

10. Use a comma after a short introductory phrase whenever the comma would aid clarity.

    Example: As a child she was a tomboy. (comma unnecessary)

    Example: To Dan, Phil was friend as well as brother. (comma clarifies)

    Example: In 1978, 300 people lost their lives in one air disaster. (comma clarifies)

    NOTE: A comma is not generally used before a subordinate clause that ends a sentence, though in long, unwieldy sentences like this one, use of such comma is optional.

11. Use a comma before a coordinating conjunction unless the two clauses are very short.

    Example: The boy wanted to borrow a book from the library, but the librarian would not allow him to take it until he had paid his fines.

    Example: Roy washed the dishes and Helen dried.

12. Use a pair of commas to set off a nonrestrictive adjective phrase or clause. A nonrestrictive phrase or clause is one that can be omitted without essentially changing the meaning of the sentence.

    Example: Our new sailboat, which has bright orange sails, is very seaworthy.

    A restrictive phrase or clause is vital to the meaning of a sentence and cannot be omitted. Do NOT set it off with commas.

    Example: A sailboat without sails is useless.

13. Use a comma if the sentence might be subject to different interpretations without it.

    Example: The banks which closed yesterday are in serious financial difficulty.
    [Some banks closed yesterday and those banks are in trouble.]
    The banks, which closed yesterday, are in serious financial difficulty.
    [All banks closed yesterday and all are in trouble.]

    Example: My brother Bill is getting married.
    [The implication is that I have more than one brother.]
    My brother, Bill, is getting married.
    [Here *Bill* is an appositive. Presumably he is the only brother.]

14. Use a comma if a pause would make the sentence clearer and easier to read.

    Example: Inside the people were dancing. (confusing)
    Inside, the people were dancing. (clearer)

    Example: After all crime must be punished. (confusing)
    After all, crime must be punished. (clearer)

The Dash

1. Use a dash—or parentheses—for emphasis or to set off an explanatory group of words.

   Example: The tools of his trade—probe, mirror, cotton swabs—were neatly arranged on the dentist's tray.

   NOTE: Unless the set-off expression ends a sentence, dashes, like parentheses, must be used in pairs.

2. Use a dash to break up a thought.

   Example: There are five—remember I said five—good reasons to refuse their demands.

3. Use a dash to mark a sudden break in thought that leaves a sentence unfinished.

   Example: He opened the door a crack and saw—

The Exclamation Mark

1. Use an exclamation mark only to express strong feeling or emotion, or to imply urgency.

   Example: Congratulations! You broke the record.

   Example: Rush! Perishable contents.

The Hyphen

1. Use a hyphen to divide a word at the end of a line. Always divide words between syllables.

2. Use a hyphen in numbers from *twenty-one* to *ninety-nine*.

3. Use a hyphen to join two words serving together as a single adjective before a noun.

   Example: We left the highway and proceeded on a well-paved road.

   Example: That baby-faced man is considerably older than he appears to be.

4. Use a hyphen with the prefixes *ex-*, *self-*, *all-*, and the suffix *-elect*.

   Examples: ex-Senator, self-appointed, all-state, Governor-elect

5. Use a hyphen to avoid ambiguity.

   Example: After the custodian recovered the use of his right arm, he re-covered the office chairs.

6. Use a hyphen to avoid an awkward union of letters.

   Examples: semi-independent, shell-like

The Period

1. Use a period at the end of a sentence that makes a statement, gives a command, or makes a "polite request" in the form of a question which does not require an answer.

    Example: I am preparing for my exam.

    Example: Proofread everything you type.

    Example: Would you please hold the script so that I may see if I have memorized my lines.

2. Use a period after the initial in a person's name.

    Example: Gen. Robert E. Lee led the Confederate forces.

3. Use periods after abbreviations.

    Examples: A.M., P.M., Mr., Mrs., Ms., A.D.

    NOTE: Do NOT use a period after postal service state name abbreviations such as AZ (for Arizona) or MI (for Michigan).

The Question Mark

1. Use a question mark after a request for information.

    Example: At what time does the last bus leave?

    NOTE: A question must end with a question mark even if the question does not encompass the entire sentence.

    Example: "Daddy, are we there yet?" the child asked.

Quotation Marks

1. Use quotation marks to enclose all directly quoted material. Words not quoted must remain outside the quotation marks.

    Example: "If it is hot on Sunday," she said, "we will go to the beach."

    NOTE: Do NOT enclose an indirect quote in quotation marks.

    Example: She said that we might go to the beach on Sunday.

2. Use quotation marks around words used in an unusual way.

    Example: A surfer who "hangs ten" is performing a tricky maneuver on a surfboard, not staging a mass execution.

3. Use quotation marks to enclose the title of a short story, essay, short poem, song, article, or chapter titles of books.

    Example: Robert Louis Stevenson wrote a plaintive poem called "Bed in Summer."

NOTE: Titles of books and plays are NOT enclosed in quotation marks. They are printed in italics. In handwritten or typed manuscript, underscore titles of books and plays.

Example: The song, "Tradition," is from *Fiddler on the Roof.*

Placement of Quotation Marks

1. A period ALWAYS goes inside the quotation marks, whether the quotation marks are used to denote quoted material, to set off titles, or to isolate words used in a special sense.

   Example: The principal said, "Cars parked in the fire lane will be ticketed."

   Example: The first chapter of *The Andromeda Strain* is entitled "The Country of Lost Borders."

   Example: Pornography is sold under the euphemism "adult books."

2. A comma ALWAYS goes inside the quotation marks.

   Example: "We really must go home," said the dinner guests.

   Example: If your skills become "rusty," you must study before you take the exam.

   Example: Three stories in Kurt Vonnegut's *Welcome to the Monkey House* are "Harrison Bergeron," "Next Door," and "Epicac."

3. A question mark goes inside the quotation marks if it is part of the quotation. If the whole sentence containing the quotation is a question, the question mark goes outside the quotation marks.

   Example: He asked, "Was the airplane on time?"

   Example: What did you really mean when you said "I do"?

4. An exclamation mark goes inside the quotation marks if the quoted words are an exclamation, outside if the entire sentence including the quoted words is an exclamation.

   Example: The sentry shouted, "Drop your gun!"

   Example: Save us from our "friends"!

5. A colon and a semicolon ALWAYS go outside the quotation marks.

   Example: He said, "War is destructive"; she added, "Peace is constructive."

6. When a multiple-paragraph passage is quoted, each paragraph of the quotation must begin with quotation marks, but ending quotation marks are used only at the end of the last quoted paragraph.

The Semicolon

1. Use a semicolon to separate a series of phrases or clauses each of which contains commas.

   Example: The old gentleman's heirs were Margaret Whitlock, his half-sister; James Bagley, the butler; William Frame, companion to his late cousin, Robert Bone; and his favorite charity, the Salvation Army.

2. Use a semicolon to avoid confusion with numbers.

   Example: Add the following: $1.25; $7.50; and $12.89.

3. You may use a semicolon to join two short, related independent clauses.

   Example: Anne is working at the front desk on Monday; Ernie will take over on Tuesday.

   NOTE: Two main clauses must be separated by a conjunction *or* by a semicolon *or* they must be written as two sentences. A semicolon never precedes a coordinating conjunction. The same two clauses may be written in any one of three ways:

   Autumn had come and the trees were almost bare.
   Autumn had come; the trees were almost bare.
   Autumn had come. The trees were almost bare.

4. You may use a semicolon to separate two independent clauses which are joined by an adverb such as *however, therefore, otherwise,* or *nevertheless*. The adverb must be followed by a comma.

   Example: You may use a semicolon to separate this clause from the next; however, you will not be incorrect if you choose to write two separate sentences.

   NOTE: If you are uncertain about how to use the semicolon to connect independent clauses, write two sentences instead.

CAPITALIZATION RULES

1. Capitalize the first word of a sentence.

    Example: *With* cooperation, a depression can be avoided.

2. Capitalize all proper nouns.

    Example: America, Santa Fe Chief, General Motors, Abraham Lincoln.

3. Capitalize days of the week and months.

    Example: The check was mailed on *Thursday.*

    NOTE: The seasons are not capitalized.

    Example: In Florida, *winter* is mild.

4. Capitalize the word *dear* when it is the first word in the salutation of a letter.

    Examples: *Dear* Mr. Jones:
    My *dear* Mr. Jones:

5. Capitalize the first word of the complimentary close of a letter.

    Examples: *Truly* yours,
    Very *truly* yours,

6. Capitalize the first and all other important words in a title.

    Example: The *Art* of *Salesmanship*

7. Capitalize a word used as part of a proper name.

    Examples: Elm *Street* (but—That *street* is narrow.)
    Morningside *Terrace* (but—we have a *terrace* apartment.)

8. Capitalize titles, when they refer to a particular official or family member.

    Example: The report was read by *Secretary* Marshall. (but—Miss Shaw, our *secretary,* is ill.)

    Example: Let's visit *Uncle* Harry. (but—I have three *uncles.*)

9. Capitalize points of a compass, when they refer to particular regions of the country.

    Example: We're going *South* next week. (but—New York is *south* of Albany.)

    NOTE: Write: the Far West, the Pacific Coast, the Middle East, etc.

10. Capitalize the first word of a direct quotation.

   Example: It was Alexander Pope who wrote, "*A* little learning is a dangerous thing."

   NOTE: When a direct quotation sentence is broken, the *first* word of the *second half* of the sentence is not capitalized.

   Example: "Don't phone," Lily told me, "*because* they're not in yet."

GRAMMAR AND USAGE

Parts of Speech

A **noun** is the name of a person, place, thing, or idea:

    teacher   city   desk   democracy

Pronouns substitute for nouns:

    he   they   ours   those

An **adjective** describes a noun:

    warm   quick   tall   blue

A **verb** expresses action or state of being:

    yell   interpret   feel   are

An **adverb** modifies a verb, an adjective, or another adverb:

    fast   slowly   friendly   well

Conjunctions join words, sentences, and phrases:

    and   but   or

A **preposition** shows position in time or space:

    in   during   after   behind

Nouns

There are different kinds of nouns.

Common nouns are general:

    house   girl   street   city

Proper nouns are specific:

    White House   Jane   Main Street   New York

Collective nouns name groups:

    team   jury   class   Congress

Nouns have *cases:*

Nominative: the subject, noun of address or predicate noun
Objective: the direct object, indirect object or object of the preposition
Possessive: the form that shows possession

Pronouns

A **pronoun** must agree with its antecedent (the noun to which it refers) in gender, person, and number.

Examples: The *girls* handed in *their* assignments.
              The *boy* left *his* jacket at school.

There are several kinds of pronouns. (Pronouns also have cases.)

Demonstrative pronoun: this, that, these, those
Indefinite pronoun: all, any, nobody
Interrogative pronoun: who, which, what
Personal pronoun:

		Nominative Case	Objective	Possessive
SINGULAR	1st person	I	me	my, mine
	2nd person	you	you	your, yours
	3rd person	he, she, it	him, her, it	his, her, hers
PLURAL	1st person	we	us	our, ours
	2nd person	you	you	your, yours
	3rd person	they	them	their, theirs

Adjectives

Adjectives answer the questions "Which one?", "What kind?", and "How many?"

There are three uses of adjectives:

A **noun modifier** is usually placed directly before the noun it describes:

Example: He is a *tall* man.

A **predicate adjective** follows an inactive verb and modifies the subject:

Examples: He is *happy*. I feel *terrible*.

An **article** or **noun marker** are other names for these adjectives: *the, a, an*

Adverbs

Adverbs answer the questions "Why?", "How?", "Where?", "When?", and "To what degree?"

Adverbs are used to modify:

verbs: He walked *quickly*.
adjectives: The water was *extremely* cold.
other adverbs: She whispered *very* softly.

Adverbs should *not* be used to modify nouns.

WORDS COMMONLY CONFUSED

accede—means to agree with.
concede—means to yield, but not necessarily in agreement.
exceed—means to be more than.
   We shall *accede* to your request for more evidence.
   To avoid delay, we shall *concede* that more evidence is necessary.
   Federal expenditures now *exceed* federal income.

access—means availability.
excess—means too much.
   The lawyer was given *access* to the grand jury records.
   The expenditures this month are far in *excess* of income.

accept—means to take when offered.
except—means excluding. (preposition)
except—means to leave out. (verb)
   We *accept* your invitation to the Halloween party.
   The entire class will be there *except* Bill and me.
   The coach refused to *except* any student from the eligibility requirements.

adapt—means to adjust or change.
adopt—means to take as one's own.
adept—means skillful.
   Children can *adapt* to changing conditions very easily.
   The half-starved stray cat was *adopted* by the kindly woman.
   Proper instruction makes children *adept* in various games.
   NOTE: adapt to, adopt by, adept in, or adept at.

adapted to—implies original or natural suitability.
   The gills of the fish are *adapted to* underwater breathing.
adapted for—implies created suitability.
   Atomic energy is constantly being *adapted for* new uses.
adapted from—implies changed to be made suitable.
   Many of Richard Wagner's opera librettos were *adapted from* old Norse sagas.

addition—means the act or process of adding.
edition—means a printing of a publication.
   In *addition* to a dictionary, he always used a thesaurus.
   The first *edition* of Shakespeare's plays appeared in 1623.

advantage—means a superior position.
benefit—means a favor conferred or earned (as a profit).
   He had an *advantage* in experience over his opponent.
   The rules were changed for his *benefit*.
   NOTE: to take advantage of, to have an advantage over.

adverse—(pronounced AD-verse) means unfavorable.
averse—(pronounced a-VERSE) means disliking.
   He took the *adverse* decision poorly.
   Many students are *averse* to criticism by their classmates.

advise—means to give advice. Advise is losing favor as a synonym for notify.
   Acceptable: The teacher will *advise* the student in habits of study.
   Unacceptable: We are advising you of a delivery under separate cover. (SAY: notifying)

affect—means to influence. (verb)
effect—means an influence. (noun)
effect—means to bring about. (verb)
   Your education must *affect* your future.

The *effect* of the last war is still being felt.
A diploma *effected* a tremendous change in his attitude.
NOTE: Affect also has a meaning of pretend.
She had an *affected* manner.

after—is unnecessary with the past participle.
Correct: *After* checking the timetable, I left for the station.
Incorrect: After having checked (omit after) the timetable, I left for the station.

agree—*with* a person
to a plan
in an opinion

ain't—is an unacceptable contraction for am not, are not, or is not.

aisle—is a passageway between seats.
isle—is a small island. (Both words rhyme with pile.)

all ready—means everybody or everything ready.
already—means previously.
They were *all ready* to write when the teacher arrived.
They had *already* begun writing when the teacher arrived.

alright—is unacceptable.
all right—is acceptable.

all-round—means versatile or general.
all around—means all over a given area.
Rafer Johnson, decathlon champion, is an *all-round* athlete.
The police were lined up for miles *all around*.

all together—means everybody or everything together.
altogether—means completely.
The boys and girls sang *all together*.
This was *altogether* strange for a person of his type.

all ways—means in every possible way.
always—means at all times.
He was in *all ways* acceptable to the voters.
His reputation had *always* been spotless.

allude—means to make a reference to.
elude—means to escape from.
Only incidentally does Coleridge *allude* to Shakespeare's puns.

It is almost impossible for one to *elude* tax collectors.

allusion—means a reference.
illusion—means a deception of the eye or mind.
The student made *allusions* to his teacher's habits.
Illusions of the mind, unlike those of the eye, cannot be corrected with glasses.

alongside of—means side by side with.
Bill stood *alongside* of Henry.
alongside—means parallel to the side.
Park the car *alongside* the curb.

alot—is unacceptable. It should always be written as two words: a lot.

among—is used with more than two persons or things.
NOTE: Amongst should be avoided.
between—is used with two persons or things.
The inheritance was equally divided *among* the four children.
The business, however, was divided *between* the oldest and the youngest one.

amount—applies to quantities that cannot be counted one by one.
number—applies to quantities that can be counted one by one.
A large *amount* of grain was delivered to the storehouse.
A large *number* of bags of grain was delivered.

angry—*with* a person
at a thing or an animal
about a situation

annual—means yearly.
biannual—means twice a year. (Semiannual means the same.)
biennial—means once in two years or every two years.

anywheres—is unacceptable.
anywhere—is acceptable.
SAY: We can't find it anywhere.
ALSO SAY: nowhere (NOT nowheres), somewhere (NOT somewheres)

aren't I—is colloquial. Its use is to be discouraged.
SAY: AM I not entitled to an explanation? (preferred to Aren't I . . .)

as—(used as a conjunction) is followed by a verb.
like—(used as a preposition) is NOT followed by a verb.
> Do *as* I do, not *as* I say.
> Try not to behave *like* a child.
> *Unacceptable:* He acts like I do.

as far as—expresses distance.
so far as—indicates a limitation.
> We hiked *as far as* the next guest house.
> *So far as* we know, the barn was adequate for a night's stay.

as good as—should be used for comparisons only.
> This motel is *as good as* the next one.
> NOTE: As good as does NOT mean practically.
> *Unacceptable:* They as good as promised us a place in the hall.
> *Acceptable:* They practically promised us a place in the hall.

as if—is correctly used in the expression, "He talked *as if* his jaw hurt him."
> *Unacceptable:* "he talked like his jaw hurt him."

as . . . so—used for comparison in *positive* statements.
not so . . . as—used for comparison in *negative* statements.
> *Correct:* She was *as* clever *as* her sister.
> *Correct:* He was *not so* deft *as* his father.

ascent—is the act of rising.
assent—means approval.
> The *ascent* to the top of the mountain was perilous.
> Congress gave its *assent* to the President's emergency directive.

assay—means to try or experiment.
essay—means an effort or, the result of an effort.
> We shall *assay* the ascent of the mountain tomorrow.
> The candidate's views were expressed in a well-written *essay*.

attend to—means to take care of.
tend to—means to be inclined to.
> One of the clerks will *attend to* mail in my absence.
> Lazy people *tend to* gain weight.

back—should NOT be used with such words as *refer* and *return* since the prefix *re* means back.
> *Unacceptable:* Refer back to the text, if you have difficulty recalling the facts.

backward
backwards—both are acceptable and may be used interchangeably as an adverb.
> We tried to run *backward* (or *backwards*).
> Backward as an adjective means slow in learning. (DON'T use backwards in this case.)
> A *backward* pupil should be given every encouragement.

badly—an adverb meaning unfavorably.
> It should NOT be used synonymously with *very much*.
> *Correct:* Joshua hurt himself *badly*.
> *Incorrect:* Pearl wanted to go to the play badly. (Use very much instead).

being as
being that—both expressions are nonstandard. *Since* or *because* should be used in their place.
> *Correct:* Since Harold was here first, he got the best seats.
> *Wrong:* Being that Dawn was in his class, the teacher recognized her.

berth—is a resting place.
birth—means the beginning of life.
> The new liner was given a wide *berth* in the harbor.
> He was a fortunate man from *birth*.

beside—means close to.
besides—refers to something that has been added.
> He lived *beside* the stream.
> He found wild flowers and weeds *besides*.

better—means recovering.
well—means completely recovered.
> He is *better* now than he was a week ago.
> In a few more weeks, he will be *well*.

blame—should NOT be used with *on*.
> *Correct:* Don't *blame* her for the accident.
> *Incorrect:* Don't blame the accident on her.

both—means two considered together.
each—means one of two or more.
> *Both* of the applicants qualified for the position.
> *Each* applicant was given a generous reference.
> NOTE: Avoid using expressions such as those on the following page.

Both girls had a new typewriter. (Use *each girl* instead.)
Both girls tried to outdo the other. (Use *each girl* instead.)
They are both alike. (Omit *both*.)

breath—means an intake of air.
breathe—means to draw air in and give it out.
breadth—means width.
Before you dive in, take a very deep *breath*.
It is difficult to *breathe* under water.
In a square, the *breadth* should be equal to the length.

bring—means to carry toward the person who is speaking.
take—means to carry away from the speaker.
Bring the books here.
Take your raincoat with you when you go out.

broke—is the past tense of break.
broke—is unacceptable for without money.
He *broke* his arm.
"Go for broke" is a slang expression widely used in gambling circles.

bunch—refers to things.
group—refers to persons or things.
This looks like a delicious *bunch* of bananas.
What a well-behaved *group* of children!
NOTE: The colloquial use of bunch applied to persons is to be discouraged.
A bunch of boys were whooping it up. (*Number* is preferable.)

calendar—is a system of time.
calender—is a smoothing and glazing machine.
colander—is a kind of sieve.
In this part of the world, most people prefer the twelve-month *calendar*.
In ceramic work, the potting wheel and the *calender* are indispensable.
Garden-picked vegetables should be washed in a *colander* before cooking.

can—means physically able.
may—implies permission.
I *can* lift this chair over my head.
You *may* leave after you finish your work.

cannot help—must be followed by an -ing form.
We *cannot help* feeling (NOT feel) distressed about this.
NOTE: *cannot help but* is unacceptable.

can't hardly
can't scarcely—are double negatives. They are unacceptable.
SAY: The child *can hardly* (or *can scarcely*) walk in those shoes.

capital—is the city.
capitol—is the building.
Paris is the *capital* of France.
The *Capitol* in Washington is occupied by the Congress.
(The Washington Capitol is capitalized.)
NOTE: Capital also means wealth.

cease—means to end.
seize—means to take hold of.
Will you please *cease* making those sounds?
Seize him by the collar as he comes around the corner.

cent—means a coin.
scent—means an odor.
sent—is the past tense of send.
The one-*cent* postal card is a thing of the past.
The *scent* of roses is pleasing.
We were *sent* to the rear of the balcony.

certainly—(and surely) is an adverb.
sure—is an adjective.
He was *certainly* learning fast.
Unacceptable: He sure was learning fast.

cite—means to quote.
sight—means seeing.
site—means a place for a building.
He was fond of *citing* from the Scriptures.
The *sight* of the wreck was appalling.
The Board of Education is seeking a *site* for the new school.

coarse—means vulgar or harsh.
course—means a path or a study.
He was shunned because of his *coarse* behavior.
The ship took its usual *course*.
Which history *course* are you taking?

come to be—should NOT be replaced with the expression *become to be*, since *become* means *come to be*.
True freedom will *come to be* when all tyrants have been overthrown.

comic—means intentionally funny.

comical—means unintentionally funny.
  A clown is a *comic* figure.
  The peculiar hat she wore gave her a *comical* appearance.

compare to—means to liken to something which has a different form.
compare with—means to compare persons or things of the same kind.
contrast with—means to show the difference between two things.
  A minister is sometimes *compared to* a shepherd.
  Shakespeare's plays are often *compared with* those of Marlowe.
  The writer *contrasted* the sensitivity of the dancer with the grossness of the pugilist.

complement—means a completing part.
compliment—is an expression of admiration.
  His wit was a *complement* to her beauty.
  He *complimented* her attractive hairstyle.

conscience—means sense of right.
conscientious—means showing care and precision.
conscious—means aware of one's self.
  Man's *conscience* prevents him from becoming completely selfish.
  He is *conscientious* about getting his work done on time.
  The injured man was completely *conscious*.

concur in—an opinion.
concur with—a person.

consensus of opinion—*of opinion* is redundant.

considerable—is properly used only as an adjective, NOT as a noun.

consul—means a government representative.
council—means an assembly that meets for deliberation.
counsel—means advice.
  Americans abroad should keep in touch with their *consuls*.
  The City *Council* enacts local laws and regulations.
  The defendant heeded the *counsel* of his friends.

convenient to—should be followed by a person.
convenient for—should be followed by a purpose.
  Will these plans be *convenient to* you?
  You must agree that they are *convenient for* the occasion.

copy—is an imitation of an original work. (not necessarily an exact imitation.)
facsimile—is an exact imitation of an original work.
  The counterfeiters made a crude *copy* of the hundred-dollar bill.
  The official government engraver, however, prepared a *facsimile* of the bill.

could of—is unacceptable. (*Should of* is also unacceptable.)
could have—is acceptable. (*Should have* is acceptable.)
  Acceptable: You *could have* done better with more care.
  Unacceptable: I could of won.
  Also avoid: must of, would of.

decent—means suitable.
descent—means going down.
dissent—means disagreement.
  The *decent* thing to do is to admit your fault.
  The *descent* into the cave was treacherous.
  Two of the nine justices filed a *dissenting* opinion.

deduction—means reasoning from the general (laws or principles) to the particular (facts).
induction—means reasoning from the particular (facts) to the general (laws or principles).
  All men are mortal. Since Brad is a man, he is mortal (*deduction*).
  There are 10,000 oranges in this truckload. I have examined 100 from various parts of the load and find them all of the same quality. I conclude that the 10,000 oranges are of this quality (*induction*).

delusion—means a wrong idea that probably will influence action.
illusion—means a wrong idea that probably will not influence action.
  People were under the *delusion* that the earth was flat.
  It is just an *illusion* that the earth is flat.

desert—(pronounced DEZZ-ert) means an arid area.
desert—(pronounced di-ZERT) means to abandon; also a reward or punishment.
dessert—(pronounced di-ZERT) means the final course of a meal.
  The Sahara is the world's most famous *desert*.
  A true friend will not *desert* you in times of trouble.
  Imprisonment was a just *desert* for his crime.
  We had chocolate cake for *dessert*.

differ—with a person.
different—from a thing.
  DO NOT use different than.
  Jessica *differed with* her mother on the importance of homework.
  Norm's interpretation was *different from* that of his colleague.

doubt that— is acceptable.
doubt whether—is unacceptable.
  Acceptable: I *doubt that* you will pass this term.
  Unacceptable: We doubt *whether* you will succeed.

dual—means relating to two.
duel—means a contest between two persons.
  Dr. Jekyll had a *dual* personality.
  Alexander Hamilton was fatally injured in a *duel* with Aaron Burr.

due to—is unacceptable at the beginning of a sentence. Use because of, on account of, or some similar expression instead.
  Unacceptable: Due to the rain, the game was postponed.
  Acceptable: Because of the rain, the game was postponed.
  Acceptable: The postponement was *due to* the rain.

each other—refers to two persons.
one another—refers to more than two persons.
  The two girls have known *each other* for many years.
  Several of the girls have known *one another* for many years.

either . . . or—is used when referring to choices.
neither . . . nor—is the negative form.
  Either you *or* I will win the election.
  Neither Eric *nor* Alex is expected to have a chance.

eliminate—means to get rid of.
illuminate—means to supply with light.
  Let us try to *eliminate* the unnecessary steps.
  Several lamps were needed to *illuminate* the corridor.

emerge—means to rise out of.
immerge—means to sink into. (also immerse)
  The swimmer *emerged* from the pool.
  She *immerged* the dress in the hot, soapy water.

emigrate—means to leave one's country for another.
immigrate—means to enter another country.
  The Norwegians *emigrated* to America in the mid-1860's.
  Many of the Norwegian *immigrants* settled in the Middle West.

endorse on the back of—*on the back of* is redundant.

enthused—unacceptable diction.
  USE: enthusiastic.

equally as—is unnecessary.
  My assignment is *equally* good.

everyone—is written as one word when it is a pronoun.
every one—(two words) is used when each individual is stressed.
  Everyone present voted for the proposal.
  Every one of the voters accepted the proposal.
  NOTE: Everybody is written as one word.

everywheres—is unacceptable.
everywhere—is acceptable.
  We searched *everywhere* for the missing book.
  NOTE: Everyplace (one word) is likewise unacceptable.

feel bad—means to feel ill.
feel badly—means to have a poor sense of touch.
  I feel *bad* about the accident I saw.
  The numbness in his fingers caused him to feel *badly*.

feel good—means to be happy.
feel well—means to be in good health.
  I *feel* very *good* about my recent promotion.
  Spring weather always made him *feel well*.

flout—means to insult.
flaunt—means to make a display of.
  He *flouted* the authority of the principal.
  Hester Prynne *flaunted* her scarlet "A."

formally—means in a formal way.
formerly—means at an earlier time.
  The letter of reference was *formally* written.
  He was *formerly* a delegate to the convention.

former—means the first of two.
latter—means the second of two.

The *former* half of the book was prose.
The *latter* half of the book was poetry.

forth—means forward.
fourth—comes after third.
  They went *forth* like warriors of old.
  The *Fourth* of July is our Independence Day.
  NOTE: spelling of forty (40) and fourteen (14).

get—is a verb that strictly means to obtain.
  Please *get* my bag.
  There are many slang forms of GET that should be avoided.
  Avoid: Do you get me? (SAY: Do you understand me?)
  Avoid: You can't get away with it. (SAY: You won't avoid punishment if you do it.)
  Avoid: Get wise to yourself. (SAY: Use common sense.)
  Avoid: We didn't get to go. (SAY: We didn't manage to go.)

got—means obtained.
  He *got* the tickets yesterday.
  Avoid: You've got to do it. (SAY: You have to do it.)
  Avoid: We have got no sympathy for them. (SAY: We have no sympathy for them.)
  Avoid: They have got a great deal of property. (SAY: They have a great deal of property.)

hanged—is used in reference to a person.
hung—is used in reference to a thing.
  The prisoner was *hanged* at dawn.
  The picture was *hung* above the fireplace.

however—means nevertheless.
how ever—means in what possible way.
  We are certain, *however*, that you will like this class.
  We are certain that, *how ever* you decide to study, you will succeed.

humans—is unacceptable usage.
  Human beings is the noun.
  Human is the adjective.
  Barney treated his antiques as if they were *human beings*.
  The malfunction was traced to *human* error.

if—introduces a condition.
whether—introduces a choice.
  I shall go to Europe *if* I win the prize.
  He asked me *whether* I intended to go to Europe (not if).

in—usually refers to a state of being. (no motion)
into—is used for motion from one place to another.
  The records are *in* that drawer.
  I put the records *into* that drawer.

in regards to—is unacceptable usage.
  USE: in regard to or regarding.
  Regarding your letter, I responded to it immediately.

irregardless—is unacceptable.
regardless—is acceptable.
  Unacceptable: Irregardless of the weather, I am going to the game.
  Acceptable: Regardless of his ability, he is not likely to win.

its—means belonging to it.
it's—means it is.
  The house lost *its* roof.
  It's an exposed house, now.

kind of
sort of—are unacceptable expressions for *rather*.
  SAY: We are *rather* disappointed in you.

last—refers to the final member in a series.
latest—refers to the most recent in time.
latter—refers to the second of two.
  This is the *last* bulletin. There won't be any other bulletins.
  This is the *latest* bulletin. There will be other bulletins.
  Of the two most recent bulletins, the *latter* is more encouraging.

lay—means to place.
lie—means to recline.
Note the forms of each verb:

Tense	Lie (Recline)
Present	The child is *lying* down.
Past	The child *lay* down.
Pres. Perf.	The child *has lain* down.

Tense	Lay (place)
Present	She is *laying* the book on the desk.
Past	She *laid* the book on the desk.
Pres. Perf.	She *has laid* the book on the desk.

Words Commonly Confused / 45

lightening—is the present participle of to lighten.
lightning—means the flashes of light accompanied by thunder.
> Leaving the extra food behind resulted in *lightening* the backpack.
> Summer thunderstorms produce startling *lightning* bolts.

lose out, win out—are unacceptable usage.
> USE: lose or win.
> If you cheat on the examination, you will certainly *lose* in the future.

many—refers to a number.
much—refers to a quantity in bulk.
> How *many* inches of rain fell last night?
> I don't know, but I would say *much* rain fell last night.

may—is used in the present tense.
might—is used in the past tense.
> We are hoping that he *may* come today.
> He *might* have done it if you had encouraged him.

noplace—as a solid word, is unacceptable for no place or nowhere.
> *Acceptable:* You now have *nowhere* to go.

number—is singular when the total is intended.
> The *number* (of pages in the book) is 50.

number—is plural when the individual units are referred to.
> A *number* of pages (in the book) were printed in italic type.

of any—(and of anyone) is unacceptable for all.
> SAY: His was the highest mark of all.
> (NOT of any or of anyone)

off of—is unacceptable.
> SAY: He took the book off the table.

out loud—is unacceptable for aloud.
> SAY: He read aloud to his family every evening.

outdoor—(and out-of-door) is an adjective.
outdoors—is an adverb.
> We spent most of the summer at an *outdoor* music camp.
> Most of the time we played string quartets *outdoors*.
> NOTE: Out-of-doors is acceptable in either case.

people—comprise a united or collective group of individuals.
persons—are individuals that are separate and unrelated.
> The *people* of New York City have enthusiastically accepted "Shakespeare-in-the-Park" productions.
> Only five *persons* remained in the theater after the first act.

persecute—means to make life miserable for someone. (Persecution is illegal.)
prosecute—means to conduct a criminal investigation. (Prosecution is legal.)
> Some racial groups insist upon *persecuting* other groups.
> The District Attorney is *prosecuting* the racketeers.

precede—means to come before.
proceed—means to go ahead. (Procedure is the noun.)
supersede—means to replace.
> What were the circumstances that *preceded* the attack?
> We can *proceed* with our plan for resisting a second attack.
> It is then possible that Plan B will *supersede* Plan A.

principal—means chief or main (as an adjective); a leader (as a noun).
principle—means a fundamental truth or belief.
> His *principal* supporters came from among the peasants.
> The *principal* of the school asked for cooperation from the staff.
> Humility was the guiding *principle* of Buddha's life.
> NOTE: Principal may also mean a sum placed at interest.
> Part of his monthly payment was applied as interest on the *principal*.

reason is because—*is because* is unnecessary.
> USE: reason that.
> The *reason* for Shirley's lateness is *that* the bus broke down.

repeat again—is unnecessary.
> USE: repeat

seldom ever—incorrect usage.
> USE: seldom if ever.

sit—means take a seat (intransitive verb)
set—means place (transitive verb)
Note the forms of each verb:

Tense	Sit (Take a Seat)
Present	He *sits* on a chair.
Past	He *sat* on the chair.
Pres. Perf.	He *has sat* on the chair.

Tense	Set (Place)
Present	He *sets* the lamp on the table.
Past	He *set* the lamp on the table.
Pres. Perf.	He has *set* the lamp on the table.

some time—means a portion of time.
sometime—means at an indefinite time in the future.
sometimes—means occasionally.
 I'll need *some time* to make a decision.
 Let us meet *sometime* after twelve noon.
 Sometimes it is better to hesitate before signing a contract.

somewheres
someplace—are unacceptable.
somewhere—is acceptable.

stationary—means standing still.
stationery—means writing materials.
 In ancient times people thought the earth was *stationary*.
 We bought writing paper at the *stationery* store.

stayed—means remained.
stood—means remained upright or erect.
 The army *stayed* in the trenches for five days.
 The soldiers *stood* at attention for one hour.

sure—for surely is unacceptable.
 SAY: You surely (NOT sure) are not going to write that!

take in—is unacceptable in the sense of deceive or attend.
 SAY: We were deceived (NOT taken in) by his oily manner.
 We should like to attend (NOT take in) a few plays during our vacation.

their—means belonging to them.
there—means in that place.
they're—means they are.
 We took *their* books home with us.
 You will find your books over *there* on the desk.
 They're going to the ballpark with us.

theirselves—is unacceptable for themselves.
 SAY: Most children of school age are able to care for themselves in many ways.

these kind—is unacceptable.
this kind—is acceptable.
 I am fond of *this kind* of apples.
 NOTE: These kinds would be also acceptable.

through—meaning finished or completed is unacceptable.
 SAY: We'll finish (NOT be through with) the work by five o'clock.

try to—is acceptable.
try and—is unacceptable.
 Try to come (NOT try and come).
 NOTE: Plan on going is unacceptable. Plan to go is acceptable.

two—is the numeral 2.
to—means in the direction of.
too—means more than or also.
 There are *two* sides to every story.
 Three *two's* (or 2's) equal six.
 We shall go *to* school.
 We shall go, *too*.
 The weather is *too* hot for school.

wait on—is incorrect usage.
 USE: wait for.
 Sharon could not *wait for* her husband a moment longer.

was
were—If something is contrary to fact (not a fact), use were in every instance.
 I wish I *were* in Bermuda.
 Unacceptable: If he was sensible, he wouldn't act like that.
 (SAY: If he were . . .)

ways—is unacceptable for way.
 SAY: We climbed a little *way* (NOT ways) up the hill.

went and took—(went and stole, etc.) is unacceptable.
 SAY: They *stole* (NOT went and stole) our tools.

when—(and where) should NOT be used to introduce a definition of a noun.
>SAY: A tornado is a twisting, high wind on land. (NOT: is when a twisting, high wind is on land.)
A pool is a place for swimming. (NOT: is where people swim.)

whereabouts—is unacceptable for where.
>SAY: Where (NOT whereabouts) do you live?
>NOTE: Whereabouts as a noun meaning a place is acceptable.
>Do you know his whereabouts?

whether—should NOT be preceded by *of* or *as to*.
>SAY: The president will consider the question *whether* (NOT of whether) it is better to ask for or demand higher taxes now.
>He inquired *whether* (NOT as to whether) we were going or not.

which—is used incorrectly in the following expressions:
>He asked me to stay, which I did. (*Correct:* He asked me to stay and I did.)
>It has been a severe winter, which is unfortunate. (*Correct:* Unfortunately, it has been a severe winter.)
>You did not write; besides which you have not telephoned. (*Correct:* Omit which.)
>*Which* must be preceded by a noun that it modifies.
>SAY: Jessica said that I was always late, a statement *which* is not true.

while—is unacceptable for *and* or *though*.
>SAY: The library is situated on the south side; (OMIT while) the laboratory is on the north side.
>Though (NOT while) I disagree with you, I shall not interfere with your right to express your opinion.
>Though (NOT while) I am in my office every day, you do not attempt to see me.

who
whom—The following is a method (without going into grammar rules) for determining when to use WHO or WHOM.
>"Tell me (who, whom) you think should represent our company?"
>STEP ONE: Change the who-whom part of the sentence to its natural order.
>"You think (who, whom) should represent our company?"
>STEP TWO: Substitute HE for WHO, HIM for WHOM.
>"You think (he, him) should represent our company?" You would say he in this case.
>THEREFORE: "Tell me WHO you think should represent our company?" is correct.

who is
who am—Note these constructions:
>It is I who am the most experienced.
>It is he who is . . .
>It is he or I who am . . .
>It is I or he who is . . .
>It is he and I who are . . .

whose—means of whom.
who's—means who is.
>*Whose* notebook is this?
>*Who's* in the next office?

would of—is incorrect usage.
>USE: would have.
>If I had known the answer, I would have responded.

you all—is unacceptable for you (plural).
>SAY: We welcome you, the delegates from Ethiopia.
>You are all welcome, delegates of Ethiopia.

English Practice Exercise One

DIRECTIONS: Mark each sentence Correct or Incorrect. Correct all incorrect choices.

1. I wish I <u>was</u> a rich man.
   were

2. <u>Try and</u> come over to my apartment tonight.
   to

3. Their <u>principal</u> means of attack was by air.

4. Of the three dresses, she preferred the <u>latter</u>. — only 2
   last

5. My grandparents <u>emigrated</u> to the United States from Poland.
   immigrated

6. We have never been <u>formally</u> introduced.

7. Can you <u>cite</u> any of Shakespeare's soliloquies?

8. We <u>cannot help but</u> feel sorry for her predicament.

9. Please <u>repeat</u> your answer <u>again</u>.

10. I <u>differ from</u> you in many respects.

11. Salt and pepper <u>complement</u> the meal.

12. The <u>reason</u> Josh cannot come is <u>because</u> he is being punished.

13. Jessica is <u>as</u> pretty <u>as</u> Dawn.

14. Did you endorse the check <u>on the back</u>?

15. <u>Neither Daniel or</u> his brother is coming tonight.
    Nor

16. Karen <u>laid</u> down when she was ill.
    lay

17. His <u>principal</u> means of support was his salary.

18. To <u>whom</u> do you wish to speak?

19. The drapes were <u>hung</u> on the rod.

20. Did you heed her excellent <u>advise</u>?

# Explanatory Answers for English Practice
Exercise One

1. **(Incorrect.)** *Were* must be used if something is not a fact.
2. **(Incorrect.)** The correct expression is *try to*.
3. **(Correct.)** *Principal* means main.
4. **(Incorrect.)** *Latter* compares two items only. For three or more items, use *last*.
5. **(Incorrect.)** *Emigrate* means to leave a country. *Immigrate* means to enter a new country.
6. **(Correct.)** *Formally* means in a formal way.
7. **(Correct.)** *Cite* means to quote.
8. **(Incorrect.)** *Cannot help but* is unacceptable. The expression should be *cannot help feeling*.
9. **(Incorrect.)** *Repeat again* is redundant. Use *repeat* and omit *again*.
10. **(Correct.)** One *differs from* another.
11. **(Correct.)** *Complement* means goes together with.
12. **(Incorrect.)** *Reason is because* is incorrect usage. The *reason is that* he is being punished.
13. **(Correct.)** In a positive comparison as . . . as is used.
14. **(Incorrect.)** *Endorse on the back* is redundant. Use *endorse* and omit *on the back*.
15. **(Incorrect.)** *Neither* must be used with *nor*.
16. **(Incorrect.)** The past tense of lie is *lay*.
17. **(Correct.)** *Principal* means main.
18. **(Correct.)** *Whom* is the object of the preposition to.
19. **(Correct.)** Objects are *hung*. People are hanged.
20. **(Incorrect.)** *Advise* is a verb. *Advice* is a noun.

Omit – take out

SELECTED RULES OF GRAMMAR

1. The subject of a verb is in the nominative case even if the verb is understood and not expressed.

   Example: They are as old as *we*. (As we are)

2. The word *who* is in the nominative case. *Whom* is in the objective case.

   Example: The trapeze artist who ran away with the clown broke the lion tamer's heart. (*Who* is the subject of the verb *ran*.)

   Example: The trapeze artist whom he loved ran away with the circus clown. (*Whom* is the object of the verb *loved*.)

3. The word *whoever* is in the nominative case. *Whomever* is in the objective case.

   Example: Whoever comes to the door is welcome to join in the party. (*Whoever* is the subject of the verb *comes*.)

   Example: Invite whomever you wish to accompany you. (*Whomever* is the object of the verb *invite*.)

4. Nouns or pronouns connected by a form of the verb *to be* should always be in the nominative case.

   Example: It is *I*. (Not *me*)

5. The object of a preposition or of a transitive verb should use a pronoun in the objective case.

   Example: It would be impossible for *me* to do that job alone. (*Me* is the object of the preposition *for*.)

   Example: The attendant gave *me* the keys to the locker. (*Me* is the indirect object of the verb *gave*.)

   NOTE: When the first person pronoun (I or me) is used in conjunction with one or more proper names, you may confirm the choice of *I* or *me* by eliminating the proper names and reading the sentence with the pronoun alone.

   Example: John, George, Marylou, and (me or I) went to the movies last night. (By eliminating the names you can readily choose that *I went to the movies* is correct.)

   Example: It would be very difficult for Mae and (I or me) to attend the wedding. (Without *Mae* it is clear that it is *difficult for me* to attend.)

6. *Each, either, neither, anyone, anybody, somebody, someone, every, everyone, one, no one*, and *nobody* are singular pronouns. Each of these words takes a singular verb and a singular pronoun.

   Example: *Neither likes* the pets of the other.
   Everyone must wait *his* turn.
   Each of the patients *carries* insurance.
   Neither of the women *has* completed *her* assignment.

7. When the correlative conjunctions *either/or, neither/nor, both/and, not only/but also* are used, the number of the verb agrees with the number of the last subject.

   Example: Neither John nor *Greg eats* meat.

   Example: Either the cat or the *mice take* charge in the barn.

8. A subject consisting of two or more nouns joined by a coordinating conjunction takes a plural verb.

   Example: Paul *and* Sue *were* the last to arrive.

9. The number of the verb is not affected by the addition to the subject of words introduced by *with, together with, no less than, as well as*, etc.

   Example: The *captain*, together with the rest of the team, *was delighted* by the victory celebration.

10. A verb agrees in number with its subject. A verb should not be made to agree with a noun that is part of a phrase following the subject.

    Example: Mount Snow, one of my favorite ski areas, *is* in Vermont.

    Example: The *mountains* of Colorado, like those of Switzerland, *offer* excellent skiing.

11. A verb should agree in number with the subject, not with the predicate noun or pronoun.

    Example: Poor study *habits are* the leading cause of unsatisfactory achievement in school.

    Example: The leading *cause* of unsatisfactory achievement in school *is* poor study habits.

12. A pronoun agrees with its antecedent in person, number, and gender.

    Example: Since you were absent on Tuesday, you will have to ask Mary or Beth for *her* notes on the lecture. (Use *her*, not their, because two singular antecedents joined by *or* take a singular pronoun.)

13. *Hardly, scarcely, barely, only,* and *but* (when it means *only*) are negative words. Do NOT use another negative in conjunction with any of these words.

    Not: He *didn't have but* one hat. (WRONG)
    But: He had *but* one hat.   OR   He had *only* one hat.

    Not: I *can't hardly* read the small print. (WRONG)
    But: I *can hardly* read the small print.   OR   I *can't* read the small print.

14. *As* is a conjunction introducing a subordinate clause. *Like* is a preposition. The object of a preposition is a noun or phrase.

    Example: The infant was wrinkled and red *as* newborns usually are. (*Newborns* is the subject of the clause; *are* is its verb.)

Example: He behaves *like* a fool.

Example: The gambler accepts only hard currency *like* gold coins.

15. When modifying the words *kind* and *sort*, the words *this* and *that* always remain in the singular.

    Example: This kind of apple makes the best pie.

    Example: That sort of behavior will result in severe punishment.

16. In sentences beginning with *there is* and *there are*, the verb should agree in number with the noun that follows it.

    Example: There *isn't* an unbroken *bone* in her body. (The singular subject *bone* takes the singular verb *is*.)

    Example: There *are* many *choices* to be made. (The plural subject *choices* takes the plural verb *are*.)

17. A noun or pronoun modifying a gerund should be in the possessive case.

    Example: Is there any criticism of *Arthur's* going? (*Going* is a gerund. It must be modified by *Arthur's*, not by *Arthur*.)

18. Do *not* use the possessive case when referring to an inanimate object.

    Not: He had difficulty with the *store's* management. (WRONG)
    But: He had difficulty with the management of the store.

19. When expressing a condition contrary to fact or a wish, use the subjunctive form *were*.

    Example: I wish I *were* a movie star.

20. Statements equally true in the past and in the present are usually expressed in the present tense. The contents of a book are also expressed in the present tense.

    Example: He said that Venus *is* a planet. (Even though he made the statement in the past, the fact remains that Venus *is* a planet.)

    Example: In the book *Peter Pan*, Wendy *says*, "I can fly." (Every time one reads the book, Wendy *says* it again.)

English Practice Exercise Two

DIRECTIONS: For each sentence, choose the word in parentheses that is correct, and circle the word.

1. To (who, *whom*) shall I give the package?

2. Who is it? It is (*me*, I).

3. It is (*my*, me) understanding of the situation that the class was cancelled.

4. Each of the girls (were, was) pleased with the results.

5. Neither Jessica nor Joan (were, *was*) accepted to the college of her choice.

6. Either Josh or his sisters (was, *were*) coming over tonight.

7. Howard together with his friends (*is*, are) on the track team.

8. Washington, D. C. (is, *was*) the capital of the United States.

9. If I (was, *were*) rich, I'd travel extensively.

10. (*Whoever*, Whomever) gets there first should reserve five seats.

Explanatory Answers for English Practice Exercise Two

1. **(Whom.)** Rule 2 states that *whom* is in the objective case (object of the preposition *to*).

2. **(I.)** Rule 4 tells us that the verb *to be* takes nominative pronouns. *Is* is a form of *to be*.

3. **(My.)** Rule 17 states that a gerund, *understanding,* requires the possessive pronoun *my*.

4. **(Was.)** Rule 6 states that *each* is singular and requires the singular verb *was*.

5. **(Was.)** Rule 7 tells us that singular subjects joined by *nor* take a singular verb, *was*.

6. **(Were.)** Rule 7 states that in an *either/or* construction the verb agrees with the nearest subject.

7. **(Is.)** Rule 19 states that the subject of the sentence remains singular and needs the singular verb *is*.

8. **(Is.)** Rule 20 tells us that true statements are expressed in the present.

9. **(Were.)** Rule 19 states that *were* expresses a wish.

10. **(Whoever.)** Rule 3 tells us that *whoever* is in the nominative case.

SENTENCE STRUCTURE

1. Every sentence must contain a verb. A group of words, no matter how long, without a verb is a sentence fragment, not a sentence. A verb may consist of one, two, three, or four words.

   Examples: The boy *studies* hard.
   The boy *will study* hard.
   The boy *has been studying* hard.
   The boy *should have been studying* hard.

   The words that make up a single verb may be separated.

   Examples: It *is* not *snowing*.
   It *will* almost certainly *snow* tomorrow.

2. Every sentence must have a subject. The subject may be a noun, a pronoun, or a word or group of words functioning as a noun.

   Examples: Fish swim. (noun)
   Boats are sailed. (noun)
   She is young. (pronoun)
   Running is good exercise. (gerund)
   To argue is pointless. (infinitive)
   That he was tired was evident. (noun clause)

   In commands, the subject is usually not expressed but is understood to be *you*.

   Example: Mind your own business.

3. A phrase cannot stand by itself as a sentence. A phrase is any group of related words which has no subject or predicate and which is used as a single part of speech. Phrases may be built around prepositions, participles, gerunds, or infinitives.

   Example: The boy *with curly hair* is my brother. (Prepositional phrase used as an adjective modifying *boy*)

   Example: My favorite cousin lives *on a farm*. (Prepositional phrase used as an adverb modifying *lives*)

   Example: Beyond the double white line is out of bounds. (Prepositional phrase used as a noun, the subject of the sentence)

   Example: A thunderstorm *preceding a cold front* is often welcome. (Participial phrase used as an adjective modifying *thunderstorm*)

   Example: We eagerly awaited the pay envelopes *brought by the messenger*. (Participial phrase used as an adjective modifying *envelopes*)

Example: *Running a day camp* is an exhausting job. (Gerund phrase used as a noun, subject of the sentence)

Example: The director is paid well for *running the day camp.* (Gerund phrase used as a noun, the object of the preposition *for*)

Example: *To breathe unpolluted air* should be every person's birthright. (Infinitive phrase used as a noun, the subject of the sentence)

Example: The child began *to unwrap his gift.* (Infinitive phrase used as a noun, the object of the verb *began*)

Example: The boy ran away from home *to become a marine.* (Infinitive phrase used as an adverb modifying *ran away*)

4. A main, independent, or principal clause can stand alone as a complete sentence. A main clause has a subject and a verb. It may stand by itself or be introduced by a coordinating conjunction.

   Example: The sky darkened ominously, and rain began to fall. (Two independent clauses joined by a coordinating conjunction)

   A subordinate or dependent clause must never stand alone. It is not a complete sentence, only a sentence fragment, despite the fact that it has a subject and a verb. A subordinate clause usually is introduced by a subordinating conjunction. Subordinate clauses may act as adverbs, adjectives, or nouns.

   Subordinate adverbial clauses are generally introduced by the subordinating conjunctions *when, while, because, as soon as, if, after, although, as before, since, than, though, until,* and *unless.*

   Examples: *While we were waiting for the local,* the express roared past.
   The woman applied for a new job *because she wanted to earn more money.*
   Although a subordinate clause contains both subject and verb, it cannot stand alone *because it is introduced by a subordinating word.*

   Subordinating adjective clauses may be introduced by the pronouns *who, which,* and *that.*

   Examples: The play *that he liked best* was a mystery.
   I have a neighbor *who served in the Peace Corps.*

   Subordinate noun clauses may be introduced by *who, what,* or *that.*

   Examples: The stationmaster says *that the train will be late.*
   I asked the waiter *what the stew contained.*
   I wish I knew *who backed into my car.*

5. Two independent clauses cannot share one sentence without some form of connective. If they do, they form a run-on sentence. Two independent clauses may be joined by a coordinating conjunction, by a comma followed by a coordinating conjunction, or by a semicolon. Two main clauses may NEVER be joined by a comma without a coordinating conjunction. This error is called a comma splice.

   Example: A college education has never been more important than it is today it has never cost more. (WRONG—run-on sentence)
   A college education has never been more important than it is today, it has never cost more. (WRONG—comma splice)

To correct a run-on sentence:

    a. Divide it into two separate sentences, adding a transitional word if necessary.

        Example: A college education has never been more important than it is today. Also, it has never cost more.

    b. Join the two independent clauses with a comma and a conjunction.

        Example: A college education has never been more important than it is today, and it has never cost more.

    c. Join the independent clauses with a semicolon.

        Example: A college education has never been more important than it is today; it has never cost more.

    d. Make one clause subordinate to the other.

        Example: While a college education has never been more important than it is today, it has also never cost more.

6. Adjectives modify only nouns and pronouns. Adverbs modify verbs, adjectives, and other adverbs.

    Example: One can swim in a lake as *easy* as in a pool. (WRONG)
    One can swim in a lake as *easily* as in a pool. (The adverb *easily* must modify the verb *can swim*.)

    Example: I was *real* happy. (WRONG)
    I was *really* happy. (The adverb *really* must be used to modify the adjective *happy*.)

    Sometimes context determines the use of adjective or adverb.

    Example: The old man looked angry. (*Angry* is an adjective describing the old man. [angry old man])
    The old man looked *angrily* out the window. (*Angrily* is an adverb describing the man's manner of looking out the window.)

7. The antecedent of a pronoun must be a specific word, not an idea expressed in a phrase or clause.

    Not: Although the doctor operated at once, *it* was not a success and the patient died. (There is no specific noun to which *it* can refer.)
    But: Although the doctor performed the operation at once, *it* was not a success and the patient died. (*It* correctly refers to the nearest noun *operation*.)

8. Phrases should be placed near the words they modify.

    Not: We need someone to keep the records *with bookkeeping experience*. (The records cannot have bookkeeping experience.)
    But: We need someone *with bookkeeping experience* to keep the records.

9. Adverbs should be placed near the words they modify.

    Not: The man was *only* willing to contribute one dollar.
    But: The man was willing to contribute *only* one dollar.

10. Relative clauses should be placed immediately after the word they modify.

    Not: The report must be typewritten *which is due tomorrow*.
    But: The report, *which is due tomorrow*, must be typewritten.

11. A modifer must modify something.

  Not: *Running for the bus,* her shoe fell off. (The phrase *running for the bus* has nothing to modify. Obviously a *shoe* cannot *run*.)
  But: *Running for the bus,* she lost her shoe.
  Or: *As she was running for the bus* her shoe fell off. (Either way the addition of the pronoun *she* tells who did the *running*)

12. Express ideas that balance each other in the same grammatical structure.

  Not: *Skiing* and *to skate* are both winter sports.
  But: *Skiing* and *skating* are both winter sports.

  Not: She spends all her time *eating, asleep,* and *on her studies.*
  But: She spends all her time *eating, sleeping,* and *studying.*

  Not: The work is neither *difficult* nor *do I find it interesting.*
  But: The work is neither *difficult* nor *interesting.*

13. Avoid needless shifts in point of view. A change from one tense or mood to another, from one subject or voice to another, or from one person to another destroys parallelism within the sentence.

  Not: After he *rescued* the kitten, he *rushes* down the ladder to find its owner. (Shift from past tense to present tense.)
  But: After he *rescued* the kitten, he *rushed* down the ladder to find its owner.

  Not: *Mary* especially likes math, but *history* is also enjoyed by her. (Shift from active to passive voice)
  But: *Mary* especially likes math, but *she* also enjoys history.

  Not: First *stand* at attention and then *you should* salute the flag. (Shift from imperative to indicative mood)
  But: First *stand* at attention and then *salute* the flag.

  Not: *One* should listen to the weather forecast so that *they* may anticipate a hurricane. (Shift from singular to plural subject)
  But: *One* should listen to the weather forecast so that *one* (or *he*) may anticipate a hurricane.

14. Avoid unnecessary repetition and superfluous words.

  Not: She *began to get started* knitting the sweater.
  But: She *began* knitting the sweater.

  Not: This skirt is *longer in length* than that one.
  But: This skirt is *longer* than that one.

15. Make comparisons logical and complete.

  Not: Wilmington is larger than any city in Delaware. (Not logical since Wilmington is a city in Delaware)
  But: Wilmington is larger than any *other* city in Delaware.

  Not: He is as fat, if not fatter, than his uncle. (Not complete since *as fat* is completed by *as*, not *than*)
  But: He is as fat *as*, if not fatter than, his uncle.

English Practice Exercise Three

DIRECTIONS: Some of the following sentences are correct, but most are incorrect. Rewrite each incorrect sentence.

1. She likes tennis, golf, and to go swimming.

2. He could not deliver the supplies. Because the roads had not yet been plowed.

3. If you want to succeed, one must be willing to work hard.

4. Jeff is taller than any boy in his class.

5. To get to school we nearly walked two miles.

6. The heroine was unbelievable naive.

7. Drive carefully. There may be ice on the roads.

8. Leaning out the window, the garden could be seen below.

9. The hotel room was clean and comfortable that we had reserved.

10. This book is heavier in weight than that one.

Explanatory Answers for English Practice
Test Three

1. She likes tennis, golf, and *swimming*.
   Rule 12 states that parallel ideas should be expressed in the same grammatical structure.

2. He could not deliver the supplies *because* the roads had not yet been plowed.
   Rule 4 states that a subordinate clause cannot stand alone.

3. If you want to succeed, *you* must be willing to work hard.
   Rule 13 cautions against shifts in point of view.

4. Jeff is taller than any *other* boy in his class.
   Rule 15 states that comparisons must be logical. Jeff cannot be compared to himself; therefore, he must be separated from the rest of the boys by the use of the word *other*.

5. To get to school, we walked *nearly two miles*.
   Rule 9 explains that adverbs must be placed near the words they modify. *Nearly* modifies *two miles*, not *walked*.

6. The heroine was *unbelievably* naive.
   Rule 6 indicates that an adverb is needed to modify the adjective *naive*.

7. Correct.
   Rules 1 and 2 verify that each statement is a complete sentence.

8. Leaning out the window, *she could see* the garden below.
   Rule 11 states that every modifier must modify something. Without the addition of *she*, *leaning out the window* has nothing to modify.

9. The hotel room *that we had reserved* was clean and comfortable.
   Rule 8 states that phrases must be placed near the words they modify.

10. This book is *heavier* than that one.
    Rule 14 warns against using unnecessary words. *Heavier in weight* is redundant.

RHETORICAL SKILLS

Rhetorical skills include writing strategies, organization, and style. A range of essay types is used in the ACT to provide a number of rhetorical situations. Questions that measure the comprehension of rhetorical skills may refer to a specific portion of the text or may refer to the passage as a whole.

Strategy

This type of question is new in the ACT. It asks whether a given device in the passage is *useful* or *appropriate* in the context of the essay.

Examples: 1. Is the use of a specific example in this passage appropriate?
2. The author could most effectively strengthen the passage by:

Organization

This type of question deals with the sequence of ideas presented in the passage. It may ask the student to choose the most logical sequence or to decide whether a given idea should be added, deleted or moved to another part of the passage.

Examples: 1. Choose the order of paragraph numbers that is most sensible.
2. What is the best placement for Sentence X?

Style

This type of question deals with the passage as whole—its style and point of view. These questions assess comprehension of the entire passage.

Examples: 1. This passage was written for an audience which:
2. The tone of the passage could best be described as:

The following exercises provide practice in the rhetorical skills included in the ACT. Read each passage and select the best choice for each question.

Rhetorical Skills Exercise One

(1)

People who smoke have a ten times greater chance of getting cancer than people who don't smoke. Overall, smoking causes 30 percent of all cancer deaths. The risk of getting lung cancer from cigarettes increases with the number of cigarettes you smoke, how long you have been smoking, and how deeply you inhale. Smoking also has been linked to cancers of the larynx, esophagus, pancreas, bladder, kidney, and mouth.

(2)

Although stopping is better, switching to low-tar, low-nicotine cigarettes may reduce somewhat your risk of developing lung cancer if you do not inhale more deeply, take more puffs, or smoke more cigarettes than you did before you switched.

(3)

However, switching to low-tar, low-nicotine cigarettes will not reduce your risks of developing other cancers and diseases, such as heart disease. Animal studies also have confirmed that basic byproducts (tar) produced by smoking marijuana can cause cancers.

(4)

Once you quit smoking, your risks begin to decrease at once. The only way to eliminate your cancer risks due to smoking it not to smoke at all.

1. The order that would be most sensible for this passage is

   A. NO CHANGE.
   B. 2, 1, 3, 4.
   C. 2, 1, 4, 3.
   D. 4, 3, 2, 1.

2. The passage could best be strengthened by

   F. providing personal examples.
   G. citing statistics.
   H. quoting a leading authority on cancer.
   J. discussing other diseases.

3. The use of the second person throughout the passage is beneficial because it

   A. is grammatically correct.
   B. conceptualizes what is being discussed.
   C. renders the discussion effective.
   D. personalizes the discussion.

Rhetorical Skills Exercise Two

(1) Residents of Montana laughingly refer to the small, windblown settlement of Ekalaka in the eastern badlands as "Skeleton Flats," but as curious as it may sound, the name is appropriate. (2) So many fossils have been dug up in this otherwise unremarkable town that it has become a paradise for paleontologists, scientists who use fossils to study prehistoric life forms. (3) In fact, dinosaur bones are so plentiful in this area that ranchers have been known to use them as doorstops! (4) Ekalaka's fame began to grow more than 50 years ago when Walter H. Peck, whose hobby was geology, found the bones of a Stegosaurus, a huge, plant-eating dinosaur. (5) The entire population soon took up Peck's pastime, and many people began digging for dinosaur bones. (6) Led by the local science teacher, the people sought new finds and they rarely returned empty-handed. (7) It would seem there is no end to the fossil riches to be found in Ekalaka. (8) Among the most valuable finds are the remains of a Brontosaurus, an 80-foot-long monster that probably weighed 40 tons, and the skeleton of a Triceratops, whose head alone weighed more than 1000 pounds!

4. Is the use of quotation marks in the first sentence appropriate?

   F. No, because it is not a direct quotation.
   G. No, because the quotation marks are irrelevant.
   H. Yes, because names are always put in quotation marks.
   J. Yes, because the quotation marks indicate a nickname.

5. Are the mentions of Brontosaurus and Triceratops in Sentence 8 appropriate?

   A. No, because it is extraneous information.
   B. No, because they detract from the main point.

- C. Yes, because they are necessary to the thesis.
- D. Yes, because they provide examples of the fossils being discussed.

6. This passage was probably excerpted from
   - F. a textbook on earth science.
   - G. an article on fossils.
   - H. a science monograph.
   - J. a guide to Montana.

Rhetorical Skills Exercise Three

(1)

Well, relax, ladies. Nutritionists say that pasta is not as bad as you might think. Two ounces of dry pasta—which is an average dinner portion—contain about 210 calories. Just like a baked potato, it is not the pasta that's fattening, but the stuff one slathers over it that makes the calorie count jump. Pasta holds its own in the nutrition department, too.

(2)

Sophia Loren once confessed to an interviewer that she had always loved pasta and ate it "by the ton." Most women would eat tons, too, if they could end up with a figure like Sophia's, but they don't and won't because they think pasta is fattening.

(3)

Though there is no historical documentation, it's not too hard to imagine how pasta was invented. Somewhere, someone must have carelessly dropped a blob of paste made from flour and water into a pot of boiling water and, after tasting it, decided the accident was worth repeating.

(4)

No one knows who invented pasta, but it is mentioned in Chinese writings from about 5,000 B.C. Marco Polo used to get the credit for introducing pasta to Italy, but that legend was laid to rest when scholars unearthed an Italian cookbook with pasta recipes published about 1290—at least five years before Marco returned from his wanderings through Asia. Now experts believe that Indians, Arabs, or Mongols introduced pasta to Italy as early as the 11th century, though some think the Etruscans were using it in pre-Roman days.

7. Is the use of quotation marks appropriate in the first sentence of Section 2?
   - A. Yes, because it emphasizes the expression in the quotation marks.
   - B. Yes, because colloquial expressions are always in quotation marks.
   - C. No, because it is not a direct quotation.
   - D. No, because the quotation marks are irrelevant.

8. The order that makes the most sense for this passage is
   - F. NO CHANGE.
   - G. 1, 3, 4, 2.
   - H. 2, 1, 3, 4.
   - J. 2, 1, 4, 3.

9. The style of the passage is
   - A. formal.
   - B. narrative.
   - C. informal.
   - D. poetic.

10. Is the use of dates in the passage useful?
    - F. No, because it confuses the reader.
    - G. No, because it is irrelevant.
    - H. Yes, because it adds to the information provided in the passage.
    - J. Yes, because it is necessary to understand the concepts.

11. What function is served by the mentioning of Sophia Loren in the passage?
    - A. None. It is unnecessary.
    - B. None. It obscures the main point of the passage.
    - C. It gives her point of view on pasta.
    - D. It introduces the passage with an interesting anecdote.

Rhetorical Skills Exercise Four

(1) Some people with osteoarthritis don't know they have it even though x-rays show joint damage. (2) For those who do have trouble, the major symptoms are pain in and around joints and noticeable loss of ability to move joints easily. (3) In advanced cases, joints take on an outwardly knobby look. (4) Osteoarthritis, a degenerative joint disease, occurs most often in men and women over 50. (5) It is believed to be related to the wear and tear of the hardest working joints of the body and to other uncertain and unknown factors. (6) The cartilage that protects the ends of the bones in the joints is worn away due to weakness of the supporting structures, such as the tendons, ligaments, and muscles. (7) The bones then grate against each other with accompanying pain and a decrease in mobility. (8) In the beginning only one joint may be affected, but as time goes on, different joints can begin to hurt, usually one at a time.

12. The most logical order for the 8 sentences in this passage is

   F. NO CHANGE.
   G. 4, 5, 6, 7, 8, 1, 2, 3.
   H. 4, 5, 1, 2, 3, 6, 7, 8.
   J. 4, 5, 6, 7, 2, 3, 1, 8.

13. The passage might then go on to discuss

   A. other symptoms of osteoarthritis.
   B. an anecdote related to medicine.
   C. another degenerative joint disease.
   D. a digestive disease.

14. The style of the passage is

   F. informal and anecdotal.
   G. literary.
   H. historical.
   J. didactic and informational.

15. Would the use of a personal example strengthen the passage?

   A. Yes, because it would humanize the passage.
   B. Yes, because it would add a missing element to the selection.
   C. No, because it would detract from the thesis.
   D. No, because it is irrelevant in the context of the presentation.

Answer Key for Rhetorical Skills
Exercises One–Four

1. A	4. J	7. A	10. H	13. C
2. H	5. D	8. J	11. D	14. J
3. D	6. G	9. C	12. G	15. D

Explanatory Answers

1. **(A)** The passage begins with a general statement about smoking and cancer. It gives one alternative and its risks and ends by reiterating the thesis.

2. **(H)** Paragraph 3 could contain a direct or indirect quotation to confirm the assertions.

3. **(D)** By using the second person (you, your), the author directs and personalizes the discussion for the reader.

4. **(J)** The use of quotation marks reinforces the adverb *laughingly*.

5. **(D)** The use of examples provide concrete evidence to support the main point.

6. **(G)** Although the passage is set in Montana, the discussion concerns the fossils to be found there.

7. **(A)** The use of quotation marks emphasizes the expression and points out its informality.

8. **(J)** The anecdote about Sophia Loren serves to introduce the discussion of pasta. The *ladies* addressed in the first sentence of Section 1 refers to the *women* mentioned in Section 2 and so logically follows it. Section 4, which presents a wealth of historical documentation, comes before Section 3, which refers to a lack of historical documentation.

9. **(C)** The language is informal and folksy. *Well, relax, ladies, stuff*, etc. are all informal expressions.

10. **(H)** The dates give a historical perspective on pasta.

11. **(D)** The use of a famous movie star piques the reader's interest.

12. **(G)** This order provides for a logical progression from the definition of osteoarthritis (4) to causes (5, 6, 7) to early stages (8, 1) to early effects (2) to advanced cases (3).

13. **(C)** The passage discusses osteoarthritis. It is likely that it would go on to discuss something related in the next paragraph, namely, another degenerative joint disease.

14. **(J)** The passage discusses osteoarthritis. It instructs and informs the reader.

15. **(D)** The passage is informational. A personal example is unnecessary.

Part IV

MATHEMATICS REVIEW

MATHEMATICS

The mathematics section of the ACT consists of 60 multiple-choice questions. These questions are derived from six major subject areas. A total mathematics score (1 to 36) is reported based solely upon the number of questions answered correctly. In addition to the total score, three subscores (0 to 18) are also reported. The chart below depicts the six major subject areas and their subscore association.

Subject Areas		Number of Questions
Pre-algebra Elementary algebra	Subscore category 1	24
Intermediate algebra Coordinate geometry	Subscore category 2	18
Plane geometry Trigonometry	Subscore category 3	18

You should remember that the test you will take is prepared by persons highly skilled in test construction. The questions on the ACT test your ability to make careful and logical decisions. The choices listed as possible answers for each question are there for a reason. In many cases, the wrong choices offered you are the answers that result from common student errors. Do *not* assume your answer is correct just because it appears among the choices. The key to success is careful reading and accurate computation.

To do well on this section of the test, you should be comfortable with the basic math skills you have been developing in school and be able to apply these skills toward the posed problems. This section will help you review the required skills.

OPERATIONS WITH INTEGERS AND DECIMALS

The four basic arithmetic operations are addition, subtraction, multiplication, and division. The results of these operations are called sum, difference, product, and quotient, respectively. Because these words are often used in problems, you should be thoroughly familiar with them.

When adding integers and/or decimals, remember to keep your columns straight and to write all digits in their proper column according to place value.

Example: Add 43.75, .631, and 5

Solution: 43.75
           .631
           5.
         49.381

When subtracting integers and/or decimals, it is likewise important to put numbers in their proper columns. Be particularly careful in subtracting a longer decimal from a shorter one.

Example: Take .2567 from 3.8

Solution: 3.8000
      − .2567
       3.5433

In order to perform this subtraction, zeros must be added to the top number to extend it to equal length with the bottom number. The zeros in this case are only place fillers and in no way change the value of the number.

When multiplying integers, pay particular attention to zeros.

Example: Find the product of 403 and 30.

Solution: 403
      ×   30
     12090

When multiplying decimals, remember that the number of decimal places in the product must be equal to the sum of the number of decimal places in the numbers being multiplied.

Solution: 4.03
      ×   .3
     1.209

When dividing, it is also important to watch for zeros.

Example: Divide 4935 by 7

Solution: $7)\overline{4935}$ = 705

Since 7 divides evenly into 49, there is no remainder to carry to the next digit. When we divide 7 into 3, it cannot go, so we must put a 0 into the quotient. Carrying the 3, we then divide 7 into 35 evenly.

In dividing decimals, remember that we always wish to divide by an integer. If the divisor is a decimal, we must multiply by a power of ten in order to make it an integer. Multiplying by 10 moves a decimal point one place to the right. Multiplying by 100 moves it two places to the right, and so forth. However, remember to do the same to the number in the division sign. Since division can always be written as a fraction in which the number we are dividing by becomes the denominator, when we remove a decimal point from the divisor, we are really multiplying both parts of the fraction by the same number, which changes its form, but not its value.

Example: Divide 4.935 by .07

Solution: $.07)\overline{4.935}$ → $7)\overline{493.5}$ = 70.5

Practice Exercise One

DIRECTIONS: Work out each problem in the space provided.

Add:

DO YOUR FIGURING HERE.

1. 6 + 37 + 42,083 + 125

2. .007 + 32.4 + 1.234 + 7.3

3. .37 + .037 + .0037 + 37

Subtract:

4. 3701 − 371

5. 1000 − 112

6. 40.37 − 6.983

Multiply:

7. 3147 by 206

8. 2.137 by .11

9. .45 by .06

Divide:

10. 12,894 by 42

11. 34.68 by 3.4

12. .175 by 25

Solutions to Practice Exercise One

1.
```
     6
    37
 42083
   125
 42251
```

2.
```
  .007
 32.4
  1.234
  7.3
 40.941
```

3.
```
   .37
   .037
   .0037
 37.
 37.4107
```

4.
```
  3701
 − 371
  3330
```

5.
```
  1000
 − 112
   888
```

6.
```
  40.370
 − 6.983
  33.387
```

7.
```
   3147
 ×  206
  18882
  62940
 648282
```

8.
```
  2.137
 ×  .11
   2137
   2137
  .23507
```

9.
```
   .45
 × .06
  .0270
```

10.
```
         307
    42)12894
        126
        294
        294
          0
```

11.
```
           10.2
    3.4)34.68
         34
          68
          68
           0
```

12.
```
         .007
    25).175
        175
          0
```

OPERATIONS WITH FRACTIONS

Fractions and Mixed Numbers

A **fraction** is part of a unit. A fraction has a **numerator** and a **denominator**.

Example: In the fraction $\frac{3}{4}$, 3 is the numerator and 4 is the denominator.

In any fraction, the numerator is being divided by the denominator.

Example: The fraction $\frac{2}{7}$ indicates that 2 is being divided by 7.

In a fraction problem, the whole quantity is 1, which may be expressed by a fraction in which the numerator and denominator are the same number.

Example: If the problem involves $\frac{1}{8}$ of a quantity, then the whole quantity is $\frac{8}{8}$ or 1.

A **mixed number** is an integer together with a fraction, such as $2\frac{3}{5}$, $7\frac{5}{8}$, $3\frac{1}{3}$, etc. The integer is the integral part, and the fraction is the fractional part.

A positive **improper fraction** is one in which the numerator is equal to or greater than the denominator, such as $\frac{9}{5}$, $\frac{7}{3}$, $\frac{53}{2}$, $\frac{7}{7}$.

To change a mixed number to an improper fraction:

- Multiply the denominator of the fraction by the integer.
- Add the numerator to this product.
- Place this sum over the denominator of the fraction.

Example: Change $3\frac{4}{7}$ to an improper fraction.

Solution: $7 \times 3 = 21$
$21 + 4 = 25$

$$3\frac{4}{7} = \frac{25}{7}$$

To change an improper fraction to a mixed number:

- Divide the numerator by the denominator. The quotient, disregarding the remainder, is the integral part of the mixed number.
- Place the remainder, if any, over the denominator. This is the fractional part of the mixed number.

Example: Change $\frac{36}{13}$ to a mixed number.

Solution:

$$13\overline{)36}$$

with quotient 2, 26, remainder 10.

$$\frac{36}{13} = 2\frac{10}{13}$$

The numerator and denominator of a fraction may be changed by multiplying both by the same number, without affecting the value of the fraction.

Example: The value of the fraction $\frac{3}{5}$ will not be altered if both the numerator and denominator are multiplied by 2, to yield $\frac{3}{5} \times \frac{2}{2} = \frac{6}{10}$.

The numerator and the denominator of a fraction may be changed by dividing both by the same number, without affecting the value of the fraction. This process is called **reducing the fraction**. A fraction that has been reduced as much as possible is said to be in **lowest terms**.

Example: The value of the fraction $\frac{3}{12}$ will not be altered if both the numerator and denominator are each divided by 3, to yield $\frac{1}{4}$.

Example: If $\frac{6}{30}$ is reduced to lowest terms (by dividing both numerator and denominator by 6), the result is $\frac{1}{5}$.

Addition and Subtraction of Fractions

To add or subtract fractions, you must remember that the numbers must have the same (common) denominator.

Example: Add $\frac{1}{3} + \frac{2}{5} + \frac{3}{4}$

The least number into which 3, 5, and 4 all divide evenly is 60. Therefore, we must use 60 as our common denominator. To add our fractions, we divide each denominator into 60 and multiply the result by the given numerator.

Example: $\frac{20 + 24 + 45}{60} = \frac{89}{60}$, or $1\frac{29}{60}$

Operations With Fractions / 75

To add or subtract two fractions quickly, remember that a sum can be found by adding the two cross products and putting this answer over the denominator product.

$$\frac{a}{b} \divideontimes \frac{c}{d} = \frac{ad + bc}{bd}$$

A similar shortcut applies to subtraction.

$$\frac{a}{b} - \frac{c}{d} = \frac{ad - bc}{bd}$$

Example: $\dfrac{3}{4} - \dfrac{5}{7} = \dfrac{21 - 20}{28} = \dfrac{1}{28}$

All fractions should be left in their lowest terms. That is, there should be no factor common to both numerator and denominator. Often in multiple-choice questions you may find that the answer you have correctly computed is not among the choices but an equivalent fraction is. Be careful!

In reducing fractions involving large numbers, it is helpful to be able to tell whether a factor is common to both numerator and denominator before a lengthy trial division. Certain tests for divisibility help with this.

To test if a number is divisible by:	Check to see:
2	if it is even
3	if the sum of the digits is divisible by 3
4	if the last two digits are divisible by 4
5	if it ends in 5 or 0
6	if it is even *and* the sum of the digits is divisible by 3
8	if the last three digits are divisible by 8
9	if the sum of the digits is divisible by 9
10	if it ends in 0

Example: $\dfrac{3525}{4341}$

This fraction is reducible by 3, since the sum of the digits of the numerator is 15 and the denominator is 12, both divisible by 3.

$$\frac{3525}{4341} = \frac{1175}{1447}$$

The resulting fraction meets no further divisibility tests and therefore has no common factor listed above.

To add or subtract mixed numbers, it is again important to remember common denominators. In borrowing in subtraction, you must borrow in terms of the common denominator.

Addition:

$$43\frac{2}{5} \qquad\qquad 43\frac{6}{15}$$
$$+\ 8\frac{1}{3} \quad\rightarrow\quad +\ 8\frac{5}{15}$$
$$\overline{\qquad\qquad\qquad\qquad 51\frac{11}{15}}$$

76 / ACT

Subtraction:
$$43\frac{2}{5} \quad\rightarrow\quad 43\frac{6}{15} \quad\rightarrow\quad 42\frac{21}{15}$$
$$-\ 6\frac{2}{3} \quad\quad\quad -\ 6\frac{10}{15} \quad\quad\quad -\ 6\frac{10}{15}$$
$$\quad\quad\quad\quad\quad\quad\quad\quad\quad\quad\quad\quad\quad\quad 36\frac{11}{15}$$

Multiplication and Division of Fractions

To multiply fractions, always try to cancel where possible before actually multiplying. In multiplying mixed numbers, always change them to improper fractions first.

Multiply: $\dfrac{2}{\cancel{8}} \cdot \dfrac{\cancel{10}^{\,2}}{\cancel{11}} \cdot \dfrac{\cancel{99}^{\,9}}{\cancel{110}_{\,55}} = \dfrac{18}{55}$

Multiply: $4\dfrac{1}{2} \cdot 1\dfrac{2}{3} \cdot 5\dfrac{1}{5}$

$\dfrac{\cancel{9}^{\,3}}{\cancel{2}} \cdot \dfrac{\cancel{5}}{\cancel{3}} \cdot \dfrac{\cancel{26}^{\,13}}{\cancel{5}} = 39$

To divide fractions or mixed numbers, remember to invert the divisor (the number after the division sign) and multiply.

Divide: $4\dfrac{1}{2} \div \dfrac{3}{4} = \dfrac{\cancel{9}^{\,3}}{\cancel{2}} \cdot \dfrac{\cancel{4}^{\,2}}{\cancel{3}} = 6$

Divide: $62\dfrac{1}{2} \div 5 = \dfrac{\cancel{125}^{\,25}}{2} \cdot \dfrac{1}{\cancel{5}} = 12\dfrac{1}{2}$

To simplify complex fractions (fractions within fractions), multiply every term by the lowest number needed to clear all fractions in the given numerator and denominator.

Example: $\dfrac{\dfrac{1}{2} + \dfrac{1}{3}}{\dfrac{1}{4} + \dfrac{1}{6}}$

The lowest number which can be used to clear all fractions is 12. Multiplying each term by 12, we have

$$\dfrac{6 + 4}{3 + 2} = \dfrac{10}{5} = 2$$

Example: $\dfrac{\dfrac{3}{4} + \dfrac{2}{3}}{1 - \dfrac{1}{2}}$

Again we multiply by 12.

$$\frac{9+8}{12-6} = \frac{17}{6} = 2\frac{5}{6}$$

Practice Exercise Two

DIRECTIONS: Work out each problem in the space provided.

Add:

DO YOUR FIGURING HERE.

1. $12\frac{5}{6} + 2\frac{3}{8} + 21\frac{1}{4}$

2. $\frac{1}{2} + \frac{1}{3} + \frac{1}{4} + \frac{1}{5} + \frac{1}{6}$

Subtract:

3. $5\frac{3}{4}$ from $10\frac{1}{2}$

4. $17\frac{2}{3}$ from 50

5. $25\frac{3}{5}$ from $30\frac{9}{10}$

Multiply:

6. $5\frac{1}{4} \cdot 1\frac{5}{7}$

7. $\frac{3}{4} \cdot \frac{3}{4} \cdot \frac{3}{4}$

8. $12\frac{1}{2} \cdot 16$

Divide:

9. $\frac{1}{5} \div 5$

10. $5 \div \frac{1}{5}$

11. $3\frac{2}{3} \div 1\frac{5}{6}$

78 / ACT

Simplify:

DO YOUR FIGURING HERE.

12. $\dfrac{\dfrac{5}{6} - \dfrac{1}{3}}{2 + \dfrac{1}{5}}$

13. $\dfrac{3 + \dfrac{1}{4}}{5 - \dfrac{1}{2}}$

Solutions to Practice Exercise Two

1. $12\frac{5}{6} = 12\frac{20}{24}$
   $2\frac{3}{8} = 2\frac{9}{24}$
   $+21\frac{1}{4} = 21\frac{6}{24}$
   $\overline{\phantom{+21\frac{1}{4}}} \quad \overline{35\frac{35}{24} = 36\frac{11}{24}}$

2. $\frac{1}{2} = \frac{30}{60}$
   $\frac{1}{3} = \frac{20}{60}$
   $\frac{1}{4} = \frac{15}{60}$
   $\frac{1}{5} = \frac{12}{60}$
   $\frac{1}{6} = \frac{10}{60}$
   $\overline{\frac{87}{60}} = 1\frac{27}{60} = 1\frac{9}{20}$

3. $10\frac{1}{2} = 9\frac{3}{2} = 9\frac{6}{4}$
   $-5\frac{3}{4} = 5\frac{3}{4} = 5\frac{3}{4}$
   $\overline{\phantom{-5\frac{3}{4}}} \quad \overline{\phantom{5\frac{3}{4}}} \quad 4\frac{3}{4}$

4. $50 = 49\frac{3}{3}$
   $-17\frac{2}{3} = 17\frac{2}{3}$
   $\overline{\phantom{-17\frac{2}{3}}} \quad 32\frac{1}{3}$

5. $30\frac{9}{10} = 30\frac{9}{10}$
   $-25\frac{3}{5} = 25\frac{6}{10}$
   $\overline{\phantom{-25\frac{3}{5}}} \quad 5\frac{3}{10}$

6. $\dfrac{\overset{3}{\cancel{21}}}{\cancel{4}} \cdot \dfrac{\overset{3}{\cancel{12}}}{\cancel{7}} = 9$

7. $\frac{3}{4} \cdot \frac{3}{4} \cdot \frac{3}{4} = \frac{27}{64}$

8. $\dfrac{25}{\cancel{2}} \cdot \overset{8}{\cancel{16}} = 200$

9. $\frac{1}{5} \cdot \frac{1}{5} = \frac{1}{25}$

10. $5 \cdot 5 = 25$

11. $\dfrac{\cancel{4}}{\cancel{3}} \cdot \dfrac{\overset{2}{\cancel{6}}}{\cancel{4}} = 2$

12. $\dfrac{25 - 10}{60 + 6} = \dfrac{15}{66} = \dfrac{5}{22}$
    Each term was multiplied by 30.

13. $\dfrac{12 + 1}{20 - 2} = \dfrac{13}{18}$
    Each term was multiplied by 4.

Verbal Problems Involving Fractions

In dealing with fractional problems, we are usually dealing with a part of a whole.

Example: In a class there are 12 boys and 18 girls. What part of the class is boys?

Solution: 12 out of 30 students, or $\frac{12}{30} = \frac{2}{5}$

Be careful to read all the questions carefully. Often a problem may refer to a part of a previously mentioned part.

Example: $\frac{1}{4}$ of this year's seniors have averages above 90. $\frac{1}{2}$ of the remainder have averages between 80 and 90. What part of the senior class has a below 80 average?

Solution: $\frac{1}{4}$ have averages above 90.

$\frac{1}{2}$ of $\frac{3}{4}$ or $\frac{3}{8}$ have averages between 80 and 90.

$\frac{1}{4} + \frac{3}{8}$ or $\frac{5}{8}$ have averages above 80.

Therefore, $\frac{3}{8}$ of the class have averages below 80.

When a problem can easily be translated into an algebraic equation, remember that algebra is a very useful tool.

Example: 14 is $\frac{2}{3}$ of what number?

Solution: $14 = \frac{2}{3}x$

Multiply each side by $\frac{3}{2}$

$21 = x$

If a problem is given with letters in place of numbers, the same reasoning must be used as if numbers were given. If you are not sure how to proceed, replace the letters with numbers to determine the steps that must be taken.

Example: If John has p hours of homework and has worked for r hours, what part of his homework is yet to be done?

Solution: If John had 5 hours of homework and had worked for 3 hours, we would first find he had $5 - 3$ hours, or 2 hours, yet to do. This represents $\frac{2}{5}$ of his work. Using letters, we have $\frac{p - r}{p}$.

Practice Exercise Three

DIRECTIONS: Work out each problem in the space provided. Circle the letter that appears before your answer.

1. A team played 30 games of which it won 24. What part of the games played did it lose?

    A. $\dfrac{4}{5}$

    B. $\dfrac{1}{4}$

    C. $\dfrac{1}{5}$

    D. $\dfrac{3}{4}$

    E. $\dfrac{2}{3}$

DO YOUR FIGURING HERE.

2. If a man's weekly salary is $x and he saves $y, what part of his weekly salary does he spend?

    F. $\dfrac{x}{y}$

    G. $\dfrac{x-y}{x}$

    H. $\dfrac{x-y}{y}$

    J. $\dfrac{y-x}{x}$

    K. $\dfrac{y-x}{y}$

3. What part of an hour elapses between 11:50 a.m. and 12:14 p.m.?

    A. $\dfrac{2}{5}$

    B. $\dfrac{7}{30}$

    C. $\dfrac{17}{30}$

    D. $\dfrac{1}{6}$

    E. $\dfrac{1}{4}$

82 / ACT

4. One half of the employees of Acme Co. earn salaries above $18,000 annually. One third of the remainder earn salaries between $15,000 and $18,000. What part of the staff earns below $15,000?

F. $\dfrac{1}{6}$

G. $\dfrac{2}{3}$

H. $\dfrac{1}{2}$

J. $\dfrac{1}{10}$

K. $\dfrac{1}{3}$

5. David receives his allowance on Sunday. He spends $\dfrac{1}{4}$ of his allowance on Monday and $\dfrac{2}{3}$ of the remainder on Tuesday. What part of his allowance is left for the rest of the week?

A. $\dfrac{1}{3}$

B. $\dfrac{1}{12}$

C. $\dfrac{1}{4}$

D. $\dfrac{1}{2}$

E. $\dfrac{4}{7}$

6. 12 is $\dfrac{3}{4}$ of what number?

F. 16
G. 9
H. 36
J. 20
K. 15

7. A piece of fabric is cut into three sections so that the first is three times as long as the second and the second section is three times as long as the third. What part of the entire piece is the smallest section?

A. $\dfrac{1}{12}$

B. $\dfrac{1}{9}$

DO YOUR FIGURING HERE.

GO ON TO THE NEXT PAGE.

C. $\frac{1}{3}$
D. $\frac{1}{7}$
E. $\frac{1}{13}$

8. What part of a gallon is one quart?

   F. $\frac{1}{2}$
   G. $\frac{1}{4}$
   H. $\frac{2}{3}$
   J. $\frac{1}{3}$
   K. $\frac{1}{5}$

9. A factory employs m men and w women. What part of its employees are women?

   A. $\frac{w}{m}$
   B. $\frac{m+w}{w}$
   C. $\frac{w}{m-w}$
   D. $\frac{w}{m+w}$
   E. w

10. A motion was passed by a vote of 5:3. What part of the votes cast were in favor of the motion?

    F. $\frac{5}{8}$
    G. $\frac{5}{3}$
    H. $\frac{3}{5}$
    J. $\frac{2}{5}$
    K. $\frac{3}{8}$

DO YOUR FIGURING HERE.

Solutions to Practice Exercise Three

1. **(C)** The team lost 6 games out of 30. $\frac{6}{30} = \frac{1}{5}$

2. **(G)** The man spends $x - y$ out of x. $\frac{x-y}{x}$

3. **(A)** 10 minutes elapse till noon, and another 14 after noon, making a total of 24 minutes. There are 60 minutes in an hour. $\frac{24}{60} = \frac{2}{5}$

4. **(K)** One half earn over $18,000. One third of the other $\frac{1}{2}$ or $\frac{1}{6}$ earn between $15,000 and $18,000 inclusive. This accounts for $\frac{1}{2} + \frac{1}{6}$ or $\frac{3}{6} + \frac{1}{6} = \frac{4}{6} = \frac{2}{3}$ of staff, leaving $\frac{1}{3}$ to earn below $15,000.

5. **(C)** David spends $\frac{1}{4}$ on Monday and $\frac{2}{3}$ of the other $\frac{3}{4}$, or $\frac{1}{2}$, on Tuesday, leaving only $\frac{1}{4}$ for the rest of the week.

6. **(F)** $12 = \frac{3}{4}x$. Multiply each side by $\frac{4}{3}$.
$16 = x$

7. **(E)** Let the third or shortest section = x. Then the second section = $3x$. And the first section = $9x$. The entire piece of fabric is then $13x$, and the shortest piece represents $\frac{x}{13x}$, or $\frac{1}{13}$, of the entire piece.

8. **(G)** There are four quarts in one gallon.

9. **(D)** The factory employs $m + w$ people, out of which w are women.

10. **(F)** For every 5 votes in favor, 3 were cast against. 5 out of every 8 votes cast were in favor of the motion.

VARIATION

Variation in mathematics refers to the interrelationship of variables in such a manner that a change of value for one variable produces a corresponding change in another.

This section describes the three basic types of variation: direct, inverse, and joint.

Direct Variation

The expression "x varies directly as y" can be described by any of the following equations:

$$\frac{x}{y} = \text{constant} \qquad \frac{x_1}{y_1} = \frac{x_2}{y_2} \qquad \frac{x_1}{x_2} = \frac{y_1}{y_2}$$

Two quantities are said to vary directly if they change in the same direction. As one increases, the other increases and their ratio (quotient) is equal to a positive constant.

For example, the amount I must pay the milkman varies directly with the number of quarts of milk I buy. The amount of sugar needed in a recipe varies directly with the amount of butter used. The number of inches between two cities on a map varies directly with the number of miles between these cities:

Example: If x varies directly as the square of m and $x = 12$ when $m = 2$, what is the value of x when $m = 3$?

Solution:
$$\frac{x_1}{y_1^2} = \frac{x_2}{y_2^2} \rightarrow \frac{x}{(3)^2} = \frac{12}{(2)^2}$$
$$\frac{x}{9} = \frac{12}{4}$$
$$\frac{x}{9} = 3$$
$$x = 27$$

Inverse Variation

The expression "x varies inversely as y" can be described by any of the following equations:

| $xy = $ constant | $x_1 y_1 = x_2 y_2$ | $\dfrac{x_1}{x_2} = \dfrac{y_2}{y_1}$ |

Two quantities are said to vary inversely if they change in opposite directions. As one increases, the other decreases.

For example, the number of men I hire to paint my house varies inversely with the number of days the job will take. A doctor's stock of flu vaccine varies inversely with the number of patients he injects. The number of days a given supply of cat food lasts varies inversely with the number of cats being fed.

Example: The time t to empty a container varies inversely as the square root of the number of men m working on the job. If it takes 3 hours for 16 men to do the job, how long will it take 4 men working at the same rate to empty the container?

Solution:
$$t_1 \sqrt{m_1} = t_2 \sqrt{m_2}$$
$$3\sqrt{16} = t\sqrt{4}$$
$$3(4) = t(2)$$
$$2t = 12$$
$$t = 6$$

Joint Variation

The expression "x varies jointly as y and z" can be described by any of the following equations:

| $\dfrac{x}{yz} = $ constant | $\dfrac{x_1}{y_1 z_1} = \dfrac{x_2}{y_2 z_2}$ | $\dfrac{x_1}{x_2} = \left(\dfrac{y_1}{y_2}\right)\left(\dfrac{z_1}{z_2}\right)$ |

Example: The area A of a triangle varies jointly as the base b and the height h. If $A = 20$ when $b = 10$ and $h = 4$, find the value of A when $b = 6$ and $h = 7$

$$\dfrac{A_1}{b_1 h_1} = \dfrac{A_2}{b_2 h_2}$$
$$\dfrac{20}{(10)(4)} = \dfrac{A_2}{(6)(7)}$$
$$\dfrac{20}{40} = \dfrac{A_2}{42}$$
$$\dfrac{1}{2} = \dfrac{A_2}{42}$$
$$A_2 = 21$$

Practice Exercise Four

DIRECTIONS: Work out each problem in the space provided. Circle the letter that appears before your answer.

1. If 60 feet of uniform wire weighs 80 pounds, what is the weight of 2 yards of the same wire?

   A. $2\frac{2}{3}$
   B. 6
   C. 2400
   D. 120
   E. 8

2. A gear 50 inches in diameter turns a smaller gear 30 inches in diameter. If the larger gear makes 15 revolutions, how many revolutions does the smaller gear make in that time?

   F. 9
   G. 12
   H. 20
   J. 25
   K. 30

3. If x men can do a job in h days, how long would y men take to do the same job?

   A. $\dfrac{x}{h}$
   B. $\dfrac{xh}{y}$
   C. $\dfrac{hy}{x}$
   D. $\dfrac{xy}{h}$
   E. $\dfrac{x}{y}$

4. If a furnace uses 40 gallons of oil in a week, how many gallons, to the nearest gallon, does it use in 10 days?

   F. 57
   G. 4
   H. 28
   J. 400
   K. 58

DO YOUR FIGURING HERE.

5. A recipe requires 13 oz. of sugar and 18 oz. of flour. If only 10 oz. of sugar are used, how much flour, to the nearest ounce, should be used?

   A. 13
   B. 23
   C. 24
   D. 14
   E. 15

6. If a car can drive 25 miles on two gallons of gasoline, how many gallons will be needed for a trip of 150 miles?

   F. 12
   G. 3
   H. 6
   J. 7
   K. 10

7. A school has enough bread to last 30 children 4 days. If 10 more children are added, how many days will the bread last?

   A. $5\frac{1}{3}$
   B. $1\frac{1}{3}$
   C. $2\frac{2}{3}$
   D. 12
   E. 3

8. At c cents per pound, what is the cost of an ounce of salami?

   F. $\frac{c}{a}$
   G. $\frac{a}{c}$
   H. ac
   J. $\frac{ac}{16}$
   K. $\frac{16c}{a}$

9. If 3 miles are equivalent to 4.83 kilometers, then 11.27 kilometers are equivalent to how many miles?

   A. $7\frac{1}{3}$

DO YOUR FIGURING HERE.

B. $2\frac{1}{3}$
C. 7
D. 5
E. $6\frac{1}{2}$

10. If p pencils cost d dollars, how many pencils can be bought for c cents?

    F. $\dfrac{100pc}{d}$

    G. $\dfrac{pc}{100d}$

    H. $\dfrac{pd}{c}$

    J. $\dfrac{pc}{d}$

    K. $\dfrac{cd}{p}$

11. m varies directly as the square of t. If m is 7 when $t = 1$, what is the value of m when $t = 2$?

    A. 28
    B. 14
    C. 7
    D. $3\frac{1}{2}$
    E. 2

12. m varies jointly as r and l. If m is 8 when r and l are each 1 what is the value of m when r and l are each 2?

    F. 64
    G. 32
    H. 16
    J. 4
    K. 2

DO YOUR FIGURING HERE.

Solutions to Practice Exercise Four

1. **(E)** We are comparing *feet* with pounds. The more feet, the more pounds. This is DIRECT. Remember to change yards to feet:

    $$\frac{\cancel{60}^{3}}{\cancel{80}_{4}} = \frac{6}{x}$$

    $$3x = 24$$
    $$x = 8$$

2. **(J)** The larger a gear, the fewer times it revolves in a given period of time. This is INVERSE.
    $$50 \cdot 15 = 30 \cdot x$$
    $$750 = 30x$$
    $$25 = x$$

3. **(B)** The more men, the fewer days. This is INVERSE.
    $$x \cdot h = y \cdot ?$$
    $$\frac{xh}{y} = ?$$

4. **(F)** The more days, the more oil. This is DIRECT. Remember to change a week to days.
    $$\frac{40}{7} = \frac{x}{10}$$
    $$7x = 400$$
    $$x = 57\frac{1}{7}$$

5. **(D)** The more sugar, the more flour. This is DIRECT.
    $$\frac{13}{18} = \frac{10}{x}$$
    $$13x = 180$$
    $$x = 13\frac{11}{13}$$

6. **(F)** The more miles, the more gasoline. This is DIRECT.
    $$\frac{25}{2} = \frac{150}{x}$$
    $$25x = 300$$
    $$x = 12$$

7. **(E)** The more children, the less days. This is INVERSE.
    $$30 \cdot 4 = 40 \cdot x$$
    $$120 = 40x$$
    $$3 = x$$

8. **(J)** The more salami, the more it will cost. This is DIRECT. Remember to change a pound to 16 ounces.
    $$\frac{c}{16} = \frac{x}{a}$$
    $$x = \frac{ac}{16}$$

9. **(C)** The more miles, the more kilometers. This is DIRECT.
    $$\frac{\text{miles}}{\text{kilometers}} = \frac{\text{miles}}{\text{kilometers}}$$
    $$\frac{3}{4.83} = \frac{x}{11.27}$$
    $$4.83x = 33.81$$
    $$x = 7$$

10. **(G)** The more pencils, the more cost. This is DIRECT. Remember to change dollars to cents.
    $$\frac{\text{pencils}}{\text{cents}} = \frac{\text{pencils}}{\text{cents}}$$
    $$\frac{p}{100d} = \frac{x}{c}$$
    $$x = \frac{pc}{100d}$$

11. **(A)** m varies directly as the square of t can be expressed mathematically as:
    $$\frac{m_1}{t_1^2} = \frac{m_2}{t_2^2}$$
    $$\frac{7}{(1)^2} = \frac{m}{(2)^2}$$
    $$\frac{7}{1} = \frac{m}{4}$$
    $$m = 28$$

12. **(G)** m varies jointly as r and l can be expressed mathematically as:
    $$\frac{m_1}{r_1 l_1} = \frac{m_2}{r_2 l_2}$$
    $$\frac{8}{(1)(1)} = \frac{m}{(2)(2)}$$
    $$\frac{8}{1} = \frac{m}{4}$$
    $$m = 32$$

PERCENT

"Percent" means "out of 100." Understanding this concept, it then becomes very easy to change a % to an equivalent decimal or fraction.

$$5\% = \frac{5}{100} = .05$$

$$2.6\% = \frac{2.6}{100} = .026$$

$$c\% = \frac{c}{100} \text{ or } \frac{1}{100} \cdot c = .01c$$

$$\frac{1}{2}\% = \frac{\frac{1}{2}}{100} = \frac{1}{2} \cdot \frac{1}{100} = .5\left(\frac{1}{100}\right)$$

To change a % to a decimal, we must remove the % sign and divide by 100. This has the effect of moving the decimal point two places to the LEFT.

Example: 37% = .37

To change a decimal to a %, we must put in the % sign and multiply by 100. This has the effect of moving the decimal point two places to the RIGHT.

Example: .043 = 4.3%

To change a % to a fraction, we must remove the % sign and divide by 100. This has the effect of putting the % over 100 and reducing the resulting fraction.

Example: $75\% = \frac{75}{100} = \frac{3}{4}$

To change a fraction to a %, we must put in the % sign and multiply by 100.

Example: $\frac{1}{8} = \frac{1}{8} \cdot 100\% = \frac{100}{8}\% = 12\frac{1}{2}\%$

Certain fractional equivalents of common percents occur frequently enough that they should be memorized. Learning the values in the following table will make your work with percent problems much easier.

Percent-Fraction Equivalent Table

$50\% = \dfrac{1}{2}$ $33\dfrac{1}{3}\% = \dfrac{1}{3}$ $12\dfrac{1}{2}\% = \dfrac{1}{8}$

$25\% = \dfrac{1}{4}$ $66\dfrac{2}{3}\% = \dfrac{2}{3}$ $37\dfrac{1}{2}\% = \dfrac{3}{8}$

$75\% = \dfrac{3}{4}$ $20\% = \dfrac{1}{5}$ $62\dfrac{1}{2}\% = \dfrac{5}{8}$

$10\% = \dfrac{1}{10}$ $40\% = \dfrac{2}{5}$ $87\dfrac{1}{2}\% = \dfrac{7}{8}$

$30\% = \dfrac{3}{10}$ $60\% = \dfrac{3}{5}$ $16\dfrac{2}{3}\% = \dfrac{1}{6}$

$70\% = \dfrac{7}{10}$ $80\% = \dfrac{4}{5}$ $83\dfrac{1}{3}\% = \dfrac{5}{6}$

$90\% = \dfrac{9}{10}$

Most percentage problems can be solved by using the following proportion:

$$\dfrac{\%}{100} = \dfrac{\text{part}}{\text{whole}}$$

Although this method works, it often yields unnecessarily large numbers that are difficult to compute. We will look at the three basic types of percent problems and compare methods for solving them.

1. To Find a Percent of a Number

Example: Find 27% of 92.

PROPORTION METHOD

$\dfrac{27}{100} = \dfrac{x}{92}$

$100x = 2484$

$x = 24.84$

SHORT METHOD

Change the percent to its decimal or fraction equivalent and multiply. Use fractions only when they are among the familiar ones given in the previous chart.

$$\begin{array}{r} 92 \\ \times\ .27 \\ \hline 644 \\ 184 \\ \hline 24.84 \end{array}$$

Example: Find $12\dfrac{1}{2}\%$ of 96.

PROPORTION METHOD

$\dfrac{12\tfrac{1}{2}}{100} = \dfrac{x}{96}$

$100x = 1200$

$x = 12$

DECIMAL METHOD

$$\begin{array}{r} 96 \\ \times\ .125 \\ \hline 480 \\ 192 \\ 96 \\ \hline 12.000 \end{array}$$

FRACTION METHOD

$\dfrac{1}{8} \cdot 96 = 12$

Which method is easiest? It really pays to memorize those fractional equivalents.

2. To Find a Number When a Percent of it is Given

Example: 7 is 5% of what number?

PROPORTION METHOD

$$\frac{5}{100} = \frac{7}{x}$$
$$5x = 700$$
$$x = 140$$

SHORTER METHOD

Translate the problem into an algebraic equation. In doing this, the % must be written as a fraction or decimal.

$$7 = .05x$$
$$700 = 5x$$
$$140 = x$$

Example: 20 is $33\frac{1}{3}$% of what number?

PROPORTION METHOD

$$\frac{33\frac{1}{3}}{100} = \frac{20}{x}$$
$$33\frac{1}{3}x = 2000$$
$$\frac{100}{3}x = 2000$$
$$100x = 6000$$
$$x = 60$$

SHORTER METHOD

$$20 = \frac{1}{3}x$$
$$60 = x$$

Just think of the time you save and the number of extra problems you will get to solve if you know that $33\frac{1}{3}\% = \frac{1}{3}$.

3. To Find What Percent One Number is of Another

Example: 90 is what % of 1500?

PROPORTION METHOD

$$\frac{x}{100} = \frac{90}{1500}$$
$$1500x = 9000$$
$$15x = 90$$
$$x = 6\%$$

SHORTER METHOD

Put the part over the whole. Reduce the fraction and multiply by 100.

$$\frac{90}{1500} = \frac{9}{150} = \frac{3}{50} \cdot 100 = 6\%$$

Example: 7 is what % of 35?

PROPORTION METHOD

$$\frac{x}{100} = \frac{7}{35}$$
$$35x = 700$$
$$x = 20\%$$

SHORTER METHOD

$$\frac{7}{35} = \frac{1}{5} = 20\%$$

Example: 18 is what % of 108?

PROPORTION METHOD

$$\frac{x}{100} = \frac{18}{108}$$

$$108x = 1800$$

Time-consuming long division is necessary to get:

$$x = 16\frac{2}{3}\%$$

SHORTER METHOD

$$\frac{18}{108} = \frac{9}{54} = \frac{1}{6} = 16\frac{2}{3}\%$$

Once again, if you know your fraction equivalents of common percents, computation can be done in a few seconds.

4. When the Percentage Involved is Over 100, the Same Methods Apply

Example: Find 125% of 64

PROPORTION METHOD

$$\frac{125}{100} = \frac{x}{64}$$

$$100x = 8000$$

$$x = 80$$

DECIMAL METHOD

$$\begin{array}{r} 64 \\ \times\ 1.25 \\ \hline 320 \\ 128 \\ 64 \\ \hline 80.00 \end{array}$$

FRACTION METHOD

$$1\frac{1}{4} \cdot 64$$

$$\frac{5}{4} \cdot \overset{16}{64} = 80$$

Example: 36 is 150% of what number?

PROPORTION METHOD

$$\frac{150}{100} = \frac{36}{x}$$

$$150x = 3600$$

$$15x = 360$$

$$x = 24$$

DECIMAL METHOD

$$36 = 1.50x$$

$$360 = 15x$$

$$24 = x$$

FRACTION METHOD

$$36 = 1\frac{1}{2}x$$

$$36 = \frac{3}{2}x$$

$$72 = 3x$$

$$24 = x$$

Example: 60 is what % of 50?

PROPORTION METHOD

$$\frac{x}{100} = \frac{60}{50}$$

$$50x = 6000$$

$$5x = 600$$

$$x = 120\%$$

FRACTION METHOD

$$\frac{60}{50} = \frac{6}{5} = 1\frac{1}{5} = 120\%$$

Practice Exercise Five

DIRECTIONS: Work out each problem in the space provided. Circle the letter that appears before your answer.

1. Write .2% as a decimal.

    A. .2
    B. .02
    C. .002
    D. 2
    E. 20

    DO YOUR FIGURING HERE.

2. Write 3.4% as a fraction.

    F. $\dfrac{34}{1000}$
    G. $\dfrac{34}{10}$
    H. $\dfrac{34}{100}$
    J. $\dfrac{340}{100}$
    K. $\dfrac{34}{10,000}$

3. Write $\dfrac{3}{4}$% as a decimal.

    A. .75
    B. .075
    C. .0075
    D. .00075
    E. 7.5

4. Find 60% of 70.

    F. 420
    G. 4.2
    H. $116\dfrac{2}{3}$
    J. 4200
    K. 42

5. What is 175% of 16?

    A. $9\dfrac{1}{7}$
    B. 28
    C. 24
    D. 12
    E. 22

6. What percent of 40 is 16?

   F. 20
   G. $2\frac{1}{2}$
   H. $33\frac{1}{3}$
   J. 250
   K. 40

7. What percent of 16 is 40?

   A. 20
   B. $2\frac{1}{2}$
   C. 200
   D. 250
   E. 40

8. $4 is 20% of what?

   F. $5
   G. $20
   H. $200
   J. $5
   K. $10

9. 12 is 150% of what number?

   A. 18
   B. 15
   C. 6
   D. 9
   E. 8

10. How many sixteenths are there in $87\frac{1}{2}$%?

    F. 7
    G. 14
    H. 3.5
    J. 13
    K. 15

DO YOUR FIGURING HERE.

Solutions to Practice Exercise Five

1. **(C)** .2% = .002 Decimal point moves to the LEFT two places.

2. **(F)** $3.4\% = \dfrac{3.4}{100} = \dfrac{34}{1000}$

3. **(C)** $\dfrac{3}{4}\% = .75\% = \dfrac{.75}{100} = \dfrac{75}{10,000}$

4. **(K)** $60\% = \dfrac{3}{5}$ $\quad \dfrac{3}{5} \cdot 70 = 42$

5. **(B)** $175\% = 1\dfrac{3}{4}$ $\quad \dfrac{7}{4} \cdot 16 = 28$

6. **(K)** $\dfrac{16}{40} = \dfrac{2}{5} = 40\%$

7. **(D)** $\dfrac{40}{16} = \dfrac{5}{2} = 2\dfrac{1}{2} = 250\%$

8. **(G)** $20\% = \dfrac{1}{5}$, so $4 = \dfrac{1}{5}x \quad 20 = x$

9. **(E)** $150\% = 1\dfrac{1}{2} \quad \dfrac{3}{2}x = 12 \quad 3x = 24$
   $x = 8$

10. **(G)** $87\dfrac{1}{2}\% = \dfrac{7}{8} = \dfrac{14}{16}$

Verbal Problems Involving Percent

Certain types of business situations are excellent applications of percent.

1. Percent of Increase or Decrease

The percent of increase or decrease is found by putting the amount of increase or decrease over the original amount and changing this fraction to a percent as explained in a previous section.

Example: Over a five-year period, the enrollment at South High dropped from 1,000 students to 800. Find the percent of decrease.

Solution: $\frac{200}{1000} = \frac{20}{100} = 20\%$

Example: A company normally employs 100 people. During a slow spell, it fired 20% of its employees. By what % must it now increase its staff to return to full capacity?

Solution: $20\% = \frac{1}{5}$ $\frac{1}{5} \cdot 100 = 20$

The company now has $100 - 20 = 80$ employees. If it then increases by 20, the percent of increase is $\frac{20}{80} = \frac{1}{4}$ or 25%.

2. Discount

A discount is usually expressed as a percent of the marked price, which will be deducted from the marked price to determine the sale price.

Example: Bill's Hardware offers a 20% discount on all appliances during a sale week. How much must Mrs. Russell pay for a washing machine marked at $280?

LONG METHOD	SHORTCUT METHOD
$20\% = \frac{1}{5}$	If there is a 20% discount, Mrs. Russell will pay 80% of the marked price.
$\frac{1}{5} \cdot 280 = \$56$ discount	$80\% = \frac{4}{5}$
$\$280 - \$56 = \$224$ sale price	$\frac{4}{5} \cdot 280 = \$224$ sale price
The danger inherent in this method is that $56 is sure to be among the multiple choice answers.	

Example: A store offers a television set marked at $340 less consecutive discounts of 10% and 5%. Another store offers the same set with a single discount of 15%. How much does the buyer save by buying at the better price?

Solution: In the first store, the initial discount means the buyer pays 90% or $\frac{9}{10}$ of 340, which is $306. The additional 5% discount means the buyer pays 95%

of $306, or $290.70. Note that the second discount must be figured on the first sale price. Taking 5% of $306 is a smaller amount than taking the additional 5% off $340. The second store will therefore have a lower sale price. In the second store, the buyer will pay 85% of $340, or $289, making the price $1.70 less than in the first store.

3. Commission

Many salesmen earn money on a commission basis. In order to inspire sales, they are paid a percentage of the value of goods sold. This amount is called a commission.

Example: Mr. Saunders works at Brown's Department Store, where he is paid $80 per week in salary plus a 4% commission on all his sales. How much does he earn in a week in which he sells $4,032 worth of merchandise?

Solution: Find 4% of $4,032 and add this amount to $80.
$$\begin{array}{r} 4032 \\ \times\ .04 \\ \hline \end{array}$$
$161.28 + $80 = $241.28

Example: Bill Olson delivers newspapers for a dealer and keeps 8% of all money collected. One month he was able to keep $16. How much did he forward to the dealer?

Solution: First we find how much he collected by asking 16 is 8% of what number?
$16 = .08x$
$1600 = 8x$
$200 = x$
If Bill collected $200 and kept $16, he gave the dealer $200 − $16 or $184.

4. Taxes

Taxes are a percent of money spent or money earned.

Example: Nassau County collects a 7% sales tax on automobiles. If the price of a used Ford is $5,832 before taxes, for what amount will Mrs. Behr have to write her check if she purchases this car?

Solution: Find 7% of $5,832 to find tax and then add it to $5,832. This can be done in one step by finding 107% of $5,832.
$$\begin{array}{r} 5832 \\ \times\ 1.07 \\ \hline 408\ 24 \\ 5832\ 0 \\ \hline \$6240.24 \end{array}$$

Example: Mrs. Brady pays income tax at the rate of 10% for the first $10,000 of earned income, 15% for the next $10,000, 20% for the next $10,000 and 25% for all earnings over $30,000. How much income tax must she pay in a year in which she earns $36,500?

Solution:
10% of first $10,000 = $1,000
15% of next $10,000 = $1,500
20% of next $10,000 = $2,000
25% of $6,500 = $1,625
Total tax = $6,125

Practice Exercise Six

DIRECTIONS: Work out each problem in the space provided. Circle the letter that appears before your answer.

1. A suit is sold for $68 while marked at $80. What is the rate of discount?

   A. 15%
   B. 12%
   C. $17\frac{11}{17}$%
   D. 20%
   E. 24%

DO YOUR FIGURING HERE.

2. A man buys a radio for $70 after receiving a discount of 20%. What was the marked price?

   F. $84
   G. $56
   H. $87.50
   J. $92
   K. $90

3. Willie receives r% commission on a sale of s dollars. How many dollars does he receive?

   A. rs
   B. $\dfrac{r}{s}$
   C. $100rs$
   D. $\dfrac{r}{100s}$
   E. $\dfrac{rs}{100}$

4. A refrigerator was sold for $273, yielding a 30% profit on the cost. For how much should it be sold to yield only a 10% profit on the cost?

   F. $210
   G. $231
   H. $221
   J. $235
   K. $240

5. What single discount is equivalent to two successive discounts of 10% and 15%?

   A. 25%
   B. 24%
   C. 24.5%
   D. 23.5%
   E. 22%

GO ON TO THE NEXT PAGE.

6. The net price of a certain article is $306 after successive discounts of 15% and 10% have been allowed on the marked price. What is the marked price?

   F. $234.09
   G. $400
   H. $382.50
   J. $408
   K. none of these

7. If a merchant makes a profit of 20% based on the selling price of an article, what percent does he make on the cost?

   A. 20
   B. 40
   C. 25
   D. 80
   E. None of these

8. A certain radio costs a merchant $72. At what price must he sell it if he is to make a profit of 20% of the selling price?

   F. $86.40
   G. $92
   H. $90
   J. $144
   K. $148

9. A baseball team has won 40 games out of 60 played. It has 32 more games to play. How many of these must the team win to make its record 75% for the season?

   A. 26
   B. 29
   C. 28
   D. 30
   E. 32

10. If prices are reduced 25% and sales increase 20%, what is the net effect on gross receipts?

    F. They increase by 5%.
    G. They decrease by 5%.
    H. They remain the same.
    J. They increase by 10%.
    K. They decrease by 10%.

DO YOUR FIGURING HERE.

11. A saleswoman earns 5% on all sales between $200 and $600, and 8% on all sales over $600. What is her commission in a week in which her sales total $800?

   A. $20
   B. $46
   C. $88
   D. $36
   E. $78

12. If the enrollment at State U. was 3,000 in 1950 and 12,000 in 1975, what was the percent of increase in enrollment?

   F. 125%
   G. 25%
   H. 300%
   J. 400%
   K. 3%

13. 6 students in a class failed algebra. This represents $16\frac{2}{3}$% of the class. How many students passed the course?

   A. 48
   B. 36
   C. 42
   D. 30
   E. 32

14. 95% of the residents of Coral Estates live in private homes. 40% of these live in air-conditioned homes. What percent of the residents of Coral Estates live in air-conditioned homes?

   F. 3%
   G. 30%
   H. 3.8%
   J. 40%
   K. 38%

15. Mr. Carlson receives a salary of $500 a month and a commission of 5% on all sales. What must be the amount of his sales in July so that his total monthly income is $2,400?

   A. $48,000
   B. $38,000
   C. $7,600
   D. $3,800
   E. $25,000

DO YOUR FIGURING HERE.

Solutions to Practice Exercise Six

1. **(A)** The amount of discount is $12. Rate of discount is figured on the original price.
$$\frac{12}{80} = \frac{3}{20} \qquad \frac{3}{20} \cdot 100 = 15\%$$

2. **(H)** $70 represents 80% of the marked price.
$$70 = .80x$$
$$700 = 8x$$
$$\$87.50 = x$$

3. **(E)** $r\% = \frac{r}{100}$
Commission is $\frac{r}{100} \cdot s = \frac{rs}{100}$

4. **(G)** $273 represents 130% of the cost.
$$1.30x = 273$$
$$13x = 2730$$
$$x = \$210 = \text{cost}$$
New price will add 10% of cost, or $21, for profit.
New price = $231

5. **(D)** Work with a simple figure, such as 100.
First sale price is 90% of $100, or $90.
Final sale price is 85% of $90, or $76.50
Total discount was $100 − $76.50 = $23.50
% of discount = $\frac{23.50}{100}$ or 23.5%

6. **(G)** If marked price = m, first sale price = $.85m$ and net price = $.90(.85m) = .765m$
$$.765m = 306$$
$$m = 400$$
In this case, it would be easy to work from the answers.
15% of $400 is $60, making a first sale price of $340.
10% of this price is $34, making the net price $306.
Answers (F), (H), and (J) would not give a final answer in whole dollars.

7. **(C)** Use an easy amount of $100 for the selling price. If profit is 20% of the selling price, or $20, cost is $80. Profit based on cost is $\frac{20}{80} = \frac{1}{4} = 25\%$

8. **(H)** If profit is to be 20% of selling price, cost must be 80% of selling price.
$$72 = .80x$$
$$720 = 8x$$
$$90 = x$$

9. **(B)** The team must win 75%, or $\frac{3}{4}$, of the games played during the entire season. With 60 games played and 32 more to play, the team must win $\frac{3}{4}$ of 92 games in all. $\frac{3}{4} \cdot 92 = 69$. Since 40 games have already been won, the team must win 29 additional games.

10. **(K)** Let original price = p, and original sales = s. Therefore, original gross receipts = ps. Let new price = $.75p$, and new sales = $1.20s$. Therefore, new gross receipts = $.90ps$. Gross receipts are only 90% of what they were.

11. **(D)** 5% of sales between $200 and $600 is $.05(400) = \$20$. 8% of sales over $600 is $.08(200) = \$16$. Total commission = $20 + $16 = $36

12. **(H)** Increase is 9000. Percent of increase is figured on original. $\frac{9000}{3000} = 3 = 300\%$

13. **(D)** $16\frac{2}{3}\% = \frac{1}{6}$
$$6 = \frac{1}{6}x$$
$$36 = x$$
36 students in class. 6 failed. 30 passed.

14. **(K)** $40\% = \frac{2}{5}$
$\frac{2}{5}$ of 95% = 38%

15. **(B)** $500 + .05s = \$2,400$
$$.05s = 1,900$$
$$5s = 190,000$$
$$s = \$38,000$$

STATISTICS AND PROBABILITY

Statistics

The **averages** used in statistics include the **arithmetic mean**, the **median**, and the **mode**.

1. Arithmetic Mean

The most commonly used average of a group of numbers is the **arithmetic mean**. It is found by adding the numbers given and then dividing this sum by the number of items being averaged.

Example: Find the arithmetic mean of 2, 8, 5, 9, 6, and 12.

Solution: There are 6 numbers.

$$\text{Arithmetic mean} = \frac{2 + 8 + 5 + 9 + 6 + 12}{6}$$

$$= \frac{42}{6}$$

$$= 7$$

The arithmetic mean is 7.

If a problem calls for simply the "average" or the "mean," it is referring to the arithmetic mean.

A more frequently encountered type of average problem will give the average and ask you to find a missing term.

Example: The average of three numbers is 43. If two of the numbers are 32 and 50, find the third number.

Solution: Using the definition of average, write the equation

$$\frac{32 + 50 + x}{3} = 43$$

$$32 + 50 + x = 129$$

$$82 + x = 129$$

$$x = 47$$

Another concept to be understood is the **weighted average**.
To obtain the average of quantities that are weighted:

- Set up a table listing the quantities, their respective weights, and their respective values.
- Multiply the value of each quantity by its respective weight.

- Add up these products.
- Add up the weights.
- Divide the sum of the products by the sum of the weights.

Example: Andrea has four grades of 90 and two grades of 80 during the spring semester of calculus. What is her average in the course for this semester?

Solution:

```
  90                    90 · 4 = 360
  90                    80 · 2 = 160
  90                           ─────
  90                           6)520
  80        or                   2
  80                          86─
 ───                            3
6)520
   2
86─
   3
```

Be sure to understand that we cannot simply average 90 and 80, since there are more grades of 90 than 80.

Example: Assume that the weights for the following subjects are: English 3, history 2, mathematics 2, foreign languages 2, and art 1. What would be the average of a student whose marks are: English 80, history 85, algebra 84, Spanish 82, and art 90?

Solution:

Subject	Weight	Mark
English	3	80
History	2	85
Algebra	2	84
Spanish	2	82
Art	1	90

English   3 × 80 = 240
History   2 × 85 = 170
Algebra   2 × 84 = 168
Spanish   2 × 82 = 164
Art   1 × 90 = 90
                   ───
                   832

Sum of the weights: 3 + 2 + 2 + 2 + 1 = 10
832 ÷ 10 = 83.2

$$\text{Average} = \frac{832}{10} = 83.2$$

The final concept of average that should be mastered is that of average rate. The average rate for a trip is the total distance covered, divided by the total time used.

Example: In driving from New York to Boston, Mr. Portney drove for 3 hours at 40 miles per hour and 1 hour at 48 miles per hour. What was his average rate for this portion of the trip?

Solution:

$$\text{Average rate} = \frac{\text{Total distance}}{\text{Total time}}$$

$$\text{Average rate} = \frac{3(40) + 1(48)}{3 + 1}$$

$$\text{Average rate} = \frac{168}{4} = 42 \text{ miles per hour}$$

Since more of the trip was driven at 40 m.p.h. than at 48 m.p.h., the average should be closer to 40 than to 48, which it is. This will help you to check your answer, or to pick out the correct choice in a multiple-choice question.

2. Median

If a group of numbers is arranged in order, the middle number is called the **median**. If there is no single middle number (this occurs when there is an even number of items), the median is found by computing the arithmetic mean of the two middle numbers.

Example: The median of 6, 8, 10, 12, and 14 is 10.

Example: The median of 6, 8, 10, 12, 14, and 16 is the arithmetic mean of 10 and 12.
$$\frac{10 + 12}{2} = \frac{22}{2} = 11.$$

3. Mode

The **mode** of a group of numbers is the number that appears most often.

Example: The mode of 10, 5, 7, 9, 12, 5, 10, 5, and 9 is 5.

Summary Chart

A set of data elements can be viewed in terms of many different data statistics.

Summary Chart of Data Statistics

Data Statistic	Description
average or arithmetic mean	$= \dfrac{\text{the sum of all the data elements}}{\text{quantity of data elements}}$
median	The "middle" data element when the data is arranged in numerical order. In the case of an even number of elements it is the mean of the two "middle" numbers.
mode	The data element that appears most often. A set of data can have more than one mode. If all the elements appear with equal frequency there is NO mode.
range	The difference between the highest valued data element and the lowest.

Probability

The study of probability deals with predicting the outcome of chance events; that is, events in which one has no control over the results.

Examples: Tossing a coin, rolling dice, and drawing concealed objects from a bag are chance events.

The probability of a particular outcome is equal to the number of ways that outcome can occur, divided by the total number of possible outcomes.

Example: In tossing a coin, there are 2 possible outcomes: heads or tails. The probability that the coin will turn up heads is $1 \div 2$ or $\frac{1}{2}$.

Example: If a bag contains 5 balls of which 3 are red, the probability of drawing a red ball is $\frac{3}{5}$. The probability of drawing a non-red ball is $\frac{2}{5}$.

NOTE: If an event is certain, its probability is 1.

Example: If a bag contains only red balls, the probability of drawing a red ball is 1.

NOTE: If an event is impossible, its probability is 0.

Example: If a bag contains only red balls, the probability of drawing a green ball is 0.

Probability may be expressed in fractional, decimal, or percent form.

Example: An event having a probability of $\frac{1}{2}$ is said to be 50% probable.

A probability determined by random sampling of a group of items is assumed to apply to other items in that group and in other similar groups.

Example: A random sampling of 100 items produced in a factory shows that 7 are defective. How many items of the total production of 50,000 can be expected to be defective?

Solution: The probability of an item being defective is $\frac{7}{100}$, or 7%. Of the total production, 7% can be expected to be defective.
$7\% \times 50,000 = .07 \times 50,000 = 3500$

Answer: 3500 items

Practice Exercise Seven

DIRECTIONS: Work out each problem in the space provided. Circle the letter that appears before your answer.

1. The arithmetic mean of 73.8, 92.2, 64.7, 43.8, 56.5, and 46.4 is

   A. 60.6
   B. 61.00
   C. 61.28
   D. 61.48
   E. 62.9

DO YOUR FIGURING HERE.

2. The median of the numbers 8, 5, 7, 5, 9, 9, 1, 8, 10, 5, and 10 is

   F. 5
   G. 7
   H. 8
   J. 9
   K. 10

3. The mode of the numbers 16, 15, 17, 12, 15, 15, 18, 19, and 18 is

   A. 15
   B. 16
   C. 17
   D. 18
   E. 19

4. A clerk filed 73 forms on Monday, 85 forms on Tuesday, 54 on Wednesday, 92 on Thursday, and 66 on Friday. What was the average number of forms filed per day?

   F. 60
   G. 72
   H. 74
   J. 92
   K. 94

5. The grades received on a test by twenty students were: 100, 55, 75, 80, 65, 65, 85, 90, 80, 45, 40, 50, 85, 85, 85, 80, 80, 70, 65, and 60. The average of these grades is

   A. 70
   B. 72
   C. 77
   D. 80
   E. 87

6. A buyer purchased 75 six-inch rulers costing 15¢ each, 100 one-foot rulers costing 30¢ each, and 50 one-yard rulers costing 72¢ each. What was the average price per ruler?

   F. $26\frac{1}{8}$¢
   G. $34\frac{1}{3}$¢
   H. 39¢
   J. 42¢
   K. 49¢

DO YOUR FIGURING HERE.

7. What is the average of a student who received 90 in English, 84 in algebra, 75 in French, and 76 in music, if the subjects have the following weights: English 4, algebra 3, French 3, and music 1?

   A. 81
   B. $81\frac{1}{2}$
   C. 82
   D. 83
   E. 84

Items 8 to 11 refer to the following information.

A census shows that on a certain block the number of children in each family is 3, 4, 4, 0, 1, 2, 0, 2, and 2, respectively.

8. Find the average number of children per family.

   F. 2
   G. $2\frac{1}{2}$
   H. 3
   J. $3\frac{1}{2}$
   K. 4

9. Find the median number of children.

   A. 6
   B. 5
   C. 4
   D. 3
   E. 2

10. Find the mode of the number of children.

    F. 0
    G. 1
    H. 2
    J. 4
    K. 5

11. What is the probability that a family chosen at random on this block will have 4 children?

    A. $\frac{4}{9}$
    B. $\frac{2}{9}$
    C. $\frac{4}{7}$
    D. $\frac{5}{7}$
    E. $\frac{5}{9}$

DO YOUR FIGURING HERE.

12. What is the probability that an even number will come up when a single die is thrown?

    F. $\frac{1}{6}$
    G. $\frac{1}{5}$
    H. $\frac{1}{4}$
    J. $\frac{1}{3}$
    K. $\frac{1}{2}$

13. A bag contains 3 black balls, 2 yellow balls, and 4 red balls. What is the probability of drawing a black ball?

    A. $\frac{1}{2}$
    B. $\frac{1}{3}$
    C. $\frac{2}{3}$
    D. $\frac{4}{9}$
    E. $\frac{4}{5}$

14. In a group of 1000 adults, 682 are women. What is the probability that a person chosen at random from this group will be a man?

    F. .318
    G. .682
    H. .5
    J. 1
    K. 1.5

15. In a balloon factory, a random sampling of 100 balloons showed that 3 had pinholes in them. In a sampling of 2500 balloons, how many may be expected to have pinholes?

    A. 30
    B. 75
    C. 100
    D. 450
    E. 800

DO YOUR FIGURING HERE.

16. Find the average of $\sqrt{.64}$, .85, and $\frac{9}{10}$.

   F. $\frac{21}{25}$
   G. 3.25
   H. 2.55
   J. 85%
   K. $\frac{4}{5}$

17. The average of two numbers is xy. If the first number is y, what is the other number?

   A. $2xy - y$
   B. $xy - 2y$
   C. $2xy - x$
   D. x
   E. $xy - y$

18. 30 students had an average of x, while 20 students had an average of 80. The average for the entire group is

   F. $\frac{x + 80}{50}$
   G. $\frac{x + 80}{2}$
   H. $\frac{50}{x + 80}$
   J. $\frac{3}{5}x + 32$
   K. $\frac{30x + 80}{50}$

19. What is the average of the first 15 positive integers?

   A. 7
   B. 7.5
   C. 8
   D. 8.5
   E. 9

20. A man travels a distance of 20 miles at 60 miles per hour and then returns over the same route at 40 miles per hour. What is his average rate for the round trip in miles per hour?

   F. 50
   G. 48
   H. 47
   J. 46
   K. 45

DO YOUR FIGURING HERE.

21. A number p equals $\frac{3}{2}$ the average of 10, 12, and q. What is q in terms of p?

A. $\frac{2}{3}p - 22$
B. $\frac{4}{3}p - 22$
C. $2p - 22$
D. $\frac{1}{2}p + 11$
E. $\frac{9}{2}p - 22$

22. Darren has an average of 86 in three examinations. What grade must he receive on his next test if he wants to raise his average to 88?

F. 94
G. 90
H. 92
J. 100
K. 96

23. The heights of the five starters on Redwood High's basketball team are 5'11", 6'3", 6', 6'6", and 6'2". The average height of these boys is

A. 6'1"
B. 6'2"
C. 6'3"
D. 6'4"
E. 6'5"

24. Find the average of all numbers from 1 to 100 that end in 2.

F. 46
G. 47
H. 48
J. 50
K. none of these

25. Don had an average of 72 on his first four math tests. After taking the next test, his average dropped to 70. What was Don's most recent test grade?

A. 60
B. 62
C. 64
D. 66
E. 68

DO YOUR FIGURING HERE.

Solutions to Practice Exercise Seven

1. **(E)** Find the sum of the values:
   $73.8 + 92.2 + 64.7 + 43.8 + 56.5 + 46.4 = 377.4$
   There are 6 values.
   Arithmetic mean $= \dfrac{377.4}{6} = 62.9$

2. **(H)** Arrange the numbers in order:
   1, 5, 5, 5, 7, 8, 8, 9, 9, 10, 10
   The middle number, or median, is 8.

3. **(A)** The mode is that number appearing most frequently. The number 15 appears three times.

4. **(H)** Average $= \dfrac{73 + 85 + 54 + 92 + 66}{5}$
   $= \dfrac{370}{5}$
   $= 74$

5. **(B)** Sum of the grades = 1440.
   $\dfrac{1440}{20} = 72$

6. **(G)**
   $75 \times 15¢ = 1125¢$
   $100 \times 30¢ = 3000¢$
   $\underline{50 \times 72¢ = 3600¢}$
   225   7725¢

   $\dfrac{7725¢}{225} = 34\dfrac{1}{3}¢$

7. **(D)**

Subject	Grade	Weight
English	90	4
Algebra	84	3
French	75	3
Music	76	1

   $(90 \times 4) + (84 \times 3) + (75 \times 3) + (76 \times 1)$
   $360 + 252 + 225 + 76 = 913$
   Weight $= 4 + 3 + 3 + 1 = 11$
   $913 \div 11 = 83$ average

8. **(F)**
   Average $= \dfrac{3 + 4 + 4 + 0 + 1 + 2 + 0 + 2 + 2}{9}$
   $= \dfrac{18}{9}$
   $= 2$

9. **(E)** Arrange the numbers in order:
   0, 0, 1, 2, 2, 2, 3, 4, 4
   Of the 9 numbers, the fifth (middle) number is 2.

10. **(H)** The number appearing most often is 2.

11. **(B)** There are 9 families, 2 of which have 4 children. The probability is $\dfrac{2}{9}$.

12. **(K)** Of the 6 possible numbers, three are even (2, 4, and 6). The probability is $\dfrac{3}{6}$, or $\dfrac{1}{2}$.

13. **(B)** There are 9 balls in all. The probability of drawing a black ball is $\dfrac{3}{9}$, or $\dfrac{1}{3}$.

14. **(F)** If 682 people of the 1000 are women, $1000 - 682 = 318$ are men. The probability of choosing a man is $\dfrac{318}{1000} = .318$.

15. **(B)** There is a probability of $\dfrac{3}{100} = 3\%$ that a balloon may have a pinhole.
    $3\% \times 2500 = 75$

16. **(J)** In order to average these three numbers, they should all be expressed as decimals.
    $\sqrt{.64} = .8$
    $.85 = .85$
    $\dfrac{9}{10} = .9$
    $3)\overline{2.55}$
    $.85$ This is equal to 85%.

17. **(A)** Let $b =$ the second number.
    $\dfrac{y + b}{2} = xy$
    $y + b = 2xy$
    $b = 2xy - y$

18. **(J)** $\dfrac{30(x) + 20(80)}{50} =$ Average
    $\dfrac{30x + 1600}{50} = \dfrac{3x + 160}{5} = \dfrac{3}{5}x + 32$

19. **(C)** Positive integers begin with 1.
    Sum $= 1 + 2 + 3 + 4 + 5 + 6 + 7 + 8 + 9 + 10 + 11 + 12 + 13 + 14 + 15 = 120$
    Number of items = 15
    Average $= \dfrac{120}{15} = 8$

    Note: Since these numbers are evenly spaced, the average will be the middle number, 8.

20. (G) Average rate = $\dfrac{\text{Total distance}}{\text{Total time}}$

Total distance = 20 + 20 = 40

Since time = $\dfrac{\text{distance}}{\text{rate}}$, time for first part of trip is $\dfrac{20}{60}$ or $\dfrac{1}{3}$ hour, while time for the second part of trip is $\dfrac{20}{40}$ or $\dfrac{1}{2}$ hour.

Total time = $\dfrac{1}{3} + \dfrac{1}{2}$ or $\dfrac{5}{6}$ hour.

Average rate = $\dfrac{40}{\frac{5}{6}} = 40 \cdot \dfrac{6}{5} = 48$

21. (C) $p = \dfrac{3}{2}\left(\dfrac{10 + 12 + q}{3}\right)$

$p = \dfrac{10 + 12 + q}{2}$

$2p = 22 + q$

$2p - 22 = q$

22. (F) $\dfrac{3(86) + x}{4} = 88$

$258 + x = 352$

$x = 94$

23. (B)
$$\begin{array}{r} 5'11'' \\ 6'\ 3'' \\ 6' \\ 6'\ 6'' \\ 6'\ 2'' \\ \hline 29'22'' \end{array} = 5\overline{)30'10''} \\ 6'\ 2''$$

24. (G) Sum = 2 + 12 + 22 + 32 + 42 + 52 + 62 + 72 + 82 + 92 = 470

Number of items = 10

Average = $\dfrac{470}{10} = 47$

Note: Since these numbers are evenly spaced, the average is the middle number. However, since there is an even number of addends, the average will be halfway between the middle two. Halfway between 42 and 52 is 47.

25. (B) $\dfrac{4(72) + x}{5} = 70$

$288 + x = 350$

$x = 62$

SIGNED NUMBERS AND EQUATIONS

Signed Numbers

Basic to successful work in algebra is the ability to compute accurately with signed numbers.

Addition: To add signed numbers with the same sign, add the magnitudes of the numbers and keep the same sign. To add signed numbers with different signs, subtract the magnitudes of the numbers and use the sign of the number with the greater magnitude.

Subtraction: Change the sign of the bottom number and follow the rules for addition.

Multiplication: If there are an odd number of negative signs, the product is negative. An even number of negative signs gives a positive product.

Division: If the signs are the same, the quotient is positive. If the signs are different, the quotient is negative.

Practice Exercise Eight

DIRECTIONS: Work out each problem in the space provided. Circle the letter that appears before your answer.

1. When $+3$ is added to -5, the sum is

    A. -8
    B. $+8$
    C. -2
    D. $+2$
    E. -15

DO YOUR FIGURING HERE.

2. When -4 and -5 are added, the sum is

    F. -9
    G. $+9$
    H. -1
    J. $+1$
    K. $+20$

115

3. Subtract +3
           −6

   A. −3
   B. +3
   C. +18
   D. −9
   E. +9

4. When −5 is subtracted from +10, the result is

   F. +5
   G. +15
   H. −5
   J. −15
   K. −50

5. (−6)(−3) equals

   A. −18
   B. +18
   C. +2
   D. −9
   E. +9

6. The product of $(-6)\left(+\dfrac{1}{2}\right)(-10)$ is

   F. $-15\dfrac{1}{2}$
   G. $+15\dfrac{1}{2}$
   H. −30
   J. +30
   K. +120

7. When the product of (−4) and (+3) is divided by (−2), the quotient is

   A. $+\dfrac{1}{2}$
   B. $+3\dfrac{1}{2}$
   C. +6
   D. $-\dfrac{1}{2}$
   E. −6

DO YOUR FIGURING HERE.

Solutions to Practice Exercise Eight

1. **(C)** In adding numbers with opposite signs, subtract their magnitudes (5 − 3 = 2) and use the sign of the number with the greater magnitude (negative).

2. **(F)** In adding numbers with the same sign, add their magnitudes (4 + 5 = 9) and keep the same sign.

3. **(E)** Change the sign of the bottom number and follow the rules for addition.
$$\begin{array}{r} +3 \\ +\ominus 6 \\ \hline +9 \end{array}$$

4. **(G)** Change the sign of the bottom number and follow the rules for addition.
$$\begin{array}{r} +10 \\ +\ominus\ 5 \\ \hline +15 \end{array}$$

5. **(B)** The product of two negative numbers is a positive number.

6. **(J)** The product of an even number of negative numbers is positive.
$$(\cancel{6})\left(\frac{1}{\cancel{2}}\right)(10) = 30$$
with 3 above $\cancel{6}$ and 1 above $\cancel{2}$.

7. **(C)** $(-4)(+3) = -12$. Dividing a negative number by a negative number gives a positive quotient.
$$\frac{-12}{-2} = +6$$

Linear Equations

The next step in gaining confidence in algebra is mastering linear equations. Whether an equation involves numbers or only letters, the basic steps are the same.

1. If there are fractions or decimals, remove them by multiplication.
2. Collect all terms containing the unknown for which you are solving on the same side of the equation. Remember that whenever a term crosses the equal sign from one side of the equation to the other, it must pay a toll. That is, it must change its sign.
3. Determine the coefficient of the unknown by combining similar terms or factoring when terms cannot be combined.
4. Divide both sides of the equation by this coefficient.

Example: Solve for x: $5x - 3 = 3x + 5$
Solution: $2x = 8$
$x = 4$

Example: Solve for x: $ax - b = cx + d$
Solution: $ax - cx = b + d$
$x(a - c) = b + d$
$x = \dfrac{b + d}{a - c}$

Example: Solve for x: $\dfrac{3}{4}x + 2 = \dfrac{2}{3}x + 3$
Solution: Multiply by 12: $9x + 24 = 8x + 36$
$x = 12$

Example: Solve for x: $.7x + .04 = 2.49$
Solution: Multiply by 100: $70x + 4 = 249$
$70x = 245$
$x = 3.5$

In solving equations with two unknowns, it is necessary to work with two equations simultaneously. The object is to eliminate one of the two unknowns, and solve the resulting single unknown equation.

Example: Solve for x: $2x - 4y = 2$
$3x + 5y = 14$
Solution: Multiply the first equation by 5:
$10x - 20y = 10$
Multiply the second equation by 4:
$12x + 20y = 56$
Since the y terms now have the same numerical coefficients, but with opposite signs, we can eliminate them by adding the two equations. If they had the same signs, we would eliminate them by subtracting the equations. Adding, we have: $22x = 66$
$x = 3$
Since we were only asked to solve for x, we stop here. If we were asked to solve for both x and y, we would now substitute 3 for x in either equation and solve the resulting equation for y.
$3(3) + 5y = 14$
$9 + 5y = 14$
$5y = 5$
$y = 1$

Example: Solve for x: $ax + by = c$
$$dx + ey = f$$
Solution: Multiply the first equation by e:
$$aex + bey = ce$$
Multiply the second equation by b:
$$bdx + bey = bf$$
Since the y terms now have the same coefficient, with the same sign, we eliminate these terms by subtracting the two equations.
$$aex - bdx = ce - bf$$
Factor to determine the coefficient of x.
$$x(ae - bd) = ce - bf$$
Divide by the coefficient of x.
$$x = \frac{ce - bf}{ae - bd}$$

Practice Exercise Nine

DIRECTIONS: Work out each problem in the space provided. Circle the letter that appears before your answer.

1. If $5x + 6 = 10$, then x equals

   A. $\dfrac{16}{5}$

   B. $\dfrac{5}{16}$

   C. $-\dfrac{5}{4}$

   D. $\dfrac{4}{5}$

   E. $\dfrac{5}{4}$

DO YOUR FIGURING HERE.

2. Solve for x: $ax = bx + c, a \neq b$

   F. $\dfrac{b + c}{a}$

   G. $\dfrac{c}{a - b}$

   H. $\dfrac{c}{b - a}$

   J. $\dfrac{a - b}{c}$

   K. $\dfrac{c}{a + b}$

3. Solve for k: $\dfrac{k}{3} + \dfrac{k}{4} = 1$

   A. $\dfrac{11}{8}$
   B. $\dfrac{8}{11}$
   C. $\dfrac{7}{12}$
   D. $\dfrac{12}{7}$
   E. $\dfrac{1}{7}$

4. If $x + y = 8p$ and $x - y = 6q$, then x is

   F. $7pq$
   G. $4p + 3q$
   H. pq
   J. $4p - 3q$
   K. $8p + 6q$

5. If $7x = 3x + 12$, then $2x + 5 =$

   A. 10
   B. 11
   C. 12
   D. 13
   E. 14

6. In the equation $y = x^2 + rx - 3$, for what value of r will $y = 11$ when $x = 2$?

   F. 6
   G. 5
   H. 4
   J. $3\dfrac{1}{2}$
   K. 0

7. If $1 + \dfrac{1}{t} = \dfrac{t+1}{t}$, what does t equal?

   A. $+1$ only
   B. $+1$ or -1 only
   C. $+1$ or $+2$ only
   D. No values
   E. All values except 0

8. If $.23m = .069$, $m =$

   F. .003
   G. .03
   H. .3
   J. 3
   K. 30

DO YOUR FIGURING HERE.

9. If $35rt + 8 = 42rt$, then $rt =$

   A. $\dfrac{8}{7}$
   B. $\dfrac{8}{87}$
   C. $\dfrac{7}{8}$
   D. $\dfrac{87}{8}$
   E. $-\dfrac{8}{7}$

10. For what values of n is $n + 5$ equal to $n - 5$?

   F. No value
   G. 0
   H. All negative values
   J. All positive values
   K. All values

DO YOUR FIGURING HERE.

Solutions to Practice Exercise Nine

1. **(D)** $5x = 4$
   $x = \dfrac{4}{5}$

2. **(G)** $ax - bx = c$
   $x(a - b) = c$
   $x = \dfrac{c}{a - b}$

3. **(D)** Multiply by 12: $4k + 3k = 12$
   $7k = 12$
   $k = \dfrac{12}{7}$

4. **(G)** Add equations to eliminate y:
   $2x = 8p + 6q$
   Divide by 2:
   $x = 4p + 3q$

5. **(B)** Solve for x: $4x = 12$
   $x = 3$
   $2x + 5 = 2(3) + 5 = 11$

6. **(G)** Substitute given values: $11 = 4 + 2r - 3$
   $10 = 2r$
   $r = 5$

7. **(E)** Multiply by t: $t + 1 = t + 1$
   This is an identity and therefore true for all values. However, since t was a denominator in the given equation, t may not equal 0, as we can never divide by 0.

8. **(H)** Multiply by 100 to make coefficient an integer.
   $23x = 6.9$
   $x = .3$

9. **(A)** Even though this equation has two unknowns, we are asked to solve for rt, which may be treated as a single unknown.
   $8 = 7rt$
   $\dfrac{8}{7} = rt$

10. **(F)** There is no number such that when 5 is added, we get the same result as when 5 is subtracted. Do not confuse choices (F) and (G). Choice (G) would mean that the number 0 satisfies the equation, which it does not.

Quadratic Equations

In solving quadratic equations, remember that there will always be two roots, even though these roots may be equal. A complete quadratic equation is of the form $ax^2 + bx + c = 0$ and frequently can be solved by factoring.

Example: $x^2 + 7x + 12 = 0$

Solution: $(x \quad)(x \quad) = 0$

Since the last term of the equation is positive, both factors must have the same sign, since the last two terms multiply to a positive product.

If the middle term is also positive, both factors must be positive, since they also add to a positive sum.
$(x + 4)(x + 3) = 0$
If the product of two factors is 0, each factor may be set equal to 0, yielding the values for x of -4 or -3.

Example: $x^2 + 7x - 18 = 0$

Solution: $(x \quad)(x \quad) = 0$

We are now looking for two numbers that multiply to -18; therefore, they must have opposite signs. To yield $+7$ as a middle coefficient, the numbers must be $+9$ and -2.
$(x + 9)(x - 2) = 0$
This equation gives the roots -9 and $+2$.

Incomplete quadratic equations are those in which b or c is equal to 0.

Example: $x^2 - 16 = 0$

Solution: $x^2 = 16$
$x = \pm 4$ Remember there must be 2 roots.

Example: $4x^2 - 9 = 0$

Solution: $4x^2 = 9$
$x^2 = \dfrac{9}{4}$
$x = \pm \dfrac{3}{2}$

Example: $x^2 + 4x = 0$

Solution: Never divide through an equation by the unknown, as this would yield an equation of lower degree having fewer roots than the original equation. Always factor this type of equation.
$x(x + 4) = 0$
The roots are 0 and -4.

Example: $4x^2 - 9x = 0$

Solution: $x(4x - 9) = 0$
The roots are 0 and $\dfrac{9}{4}$.

In solving equations containing radicals, always get the radical term alone on one side of the equation, then square both sides to remove the radical, and solve. Remember that all solutions to radical equations *must* be checked by substitution into the original equation.

This is necessary because squaring both sides of the equation during the solution process may sometimes result in extraneous roots.

Example: $\sqrt{x + 5} = 7$

Solution: Square both sides of the equation.
$x + 5 = 49$
$x = 44$
Checking, we have $\sqrt{49} = 7$, which is true.

Example: $\sqrt{x} = -6$

Solution: $x = 36$
Checking, we have $\sqrt{36} = -6$ which is not true, as the radical sign means the positive, or principal, square root only. $\sqrt{36} = 6$, not -6, and therefore this equation has no solution.

Example: $\sqrt{x^2 + 6} - 3 = x$

Solution: $\sqrt{x^2 + 6} = x + 3$
Square both sides of the equation.
$x^2 + 6 = x^2 + 6x + 9$
$6 = 6x + 9$
$-3 = 6x$
$-\frac{1}{2} = x$

Checking, we have $\sqrt{6\frac{1}{4}} - 3 = -\frac{1}{2}$

$\sqrt{\frac{25}{4}} - 3 = -\frac{1}{2}$

$\frac{5}{2} - 3 = -\frac{1}{2}$

$2\frac{1}{2} - 3 = -\frac{1}{2}$

$-\frac{1}{2} = -\frac{1}{2}$

This is a true statement. Therefore, $-\frac{1}{2}$ is a true root.

Practice Exercise Ten

DIRECTIONS: Work out the problem in the space provided. Circle the letter that appears before your answer.

1. Solve for x: $x^2 - 2x - 15 = 0$

   A. $+5$ or -3
   B. -5 or $+3$
   C. -5 or -3
   D. $+5$ or $+3$
   E. None of these

DO YOUR FIGURING HERE.

Signed Numbers and Equations / 125

DO YOUR FIGURING HERE.

2. Solve for x: $x^2 + 12 = 8x$

   F. $+6$ or -2
   G. -6 or $+2$
   H. -6 or -2
   J. $+6$ or $+2$
   K. None of these

3. Solve for x: $4x^2 = 12$

   A. $\sqrt{3}$
   B. 3 or -3
   C. $\sqrt{3}$ or $-\sqrt{3}$
   D. $\sqrt{3}$ or $\sqrt{-3}$
   E. 9 or -9

4. Solve for x: $3x^2 = 4x$

   F. $\dfrac{4}{3}$
   G. $\dfrac{4}{3}$ or 0
   H. $-\dfrac{4}{3}$ or 0
   J. $\dfrac{4}{3}$ or $-\dfrac{4}{3}$
   K. None of these

5. Solve for x: $\sqrt{x^2 + 7} - 2 = x - 1$

   A. No values
   B. $\dfrac{1}{3}$
   C. $-\dfrac{1}{3}$
   D. -3
   E. 3

Solutions to Practice Exercise Ten

1. **(A)** $(x - 5)(x + 3) = 0$
    $x = 5 \text{ or } -3$

2. **(J)** $x^2 - 8x + 12 = 0$
    $(x - 6)(x - 2) = 0$
    $x = 6 \text{ or } 2$

3. **(C)** $x^2 = 3$
    $x = \pm\sqrt{3}$

4. **(G)** $3x^2 - 4x = 0$
    $x(3x - 4) = 0$
    $x = 0 \text{ or } \dfrac{4}{3}$

5. **(E)** $\sqrt{x^2 + 7} = x + 1$
    $(\sqrt{x^2 + 7})^2 = (x + 1)^2$
    $x^2 + 7 = x^2 + 2x + 1$
    $6 = 2x$
    $x = 3$

    check:
    $\sqrt{x^2 + 7} = x + 1$
    $\sqrt{(3)^2 + 7} \stackrel{?}{=} 3 + 1$
    $\sqrt{16} \stackrel{?}{=} 4$
    $4 = 4 \checkmark$

LITERAL EXPRESSIONS

Many students who can compute easily with numbers become confused when they work with letters. The computational processes are exactly the same. Just think of how you would do the problem with numbers and do exactly the same thing with letters.

Example: Find the number of inches in 2 feet 5 inches.

Solution: Since there are 12 inches in a foot, we multiply 2 feet by 12 to change it to 24 inches and then add 5 more inches, giving an answer of 29 inches.

Example: Find the number of inches in f feet and i inches.

Solution: Doing exactly as we did above, we multiply f by 12, giving $12f$ inches, and add i more inches, giving an answer of $12f + i$ inches.

Example: A telephone call from New York to Chicago costs 85 cents for the first three minutes and 21 cents for each additional minute. Find the cost of an eight minute call at this rate.

Solution: The first three minutes cost 85 cents. There are five additional minutes above the first three. These five are billed at 21 cents each, for a cost of $1.05. The total cost is $1.90.

Example: A telephone call costs c cents for the first three minutes and d cents for each additional minute. Find the cost of a call which lasts m minutes if $m > 3$.

Solution: The first three minutes cost c cents. The number of *additional* minutes is $(m - 3)$. These are billed at d cents each, for a cost of $d(m - 3)$ or $dm - 3d$. Thus the total cost is $c + dm - 3d$. Remember that the first three minutes have been paid for in the basic charge, therefore you must subtract 3 from the total number of minutes to find the *additional* minutes.

Practice Exercise Eleven

DIRECTIONS: Work out each problem in the space provided. Circle the letter that appears before your answer.

DO YOUR FIGURING HERE.

1. David had d dollars. After a shopping trip, he returned with c cents. How many cents did he spend?

   A. $d - c$

B. $c - d$
C. $100d - c$
D. $100c - d$
E. $d - 100c$

2. How many ounces are there in p pounds and q ounces?

   F. $\dfrac{p}{16} + q$
   G. pq
   H. $p + 16q$
   J. $p + q$
   K. $16p + q$

3. How many passengers can be seated on a plane with r rows, if each row consists of d double seats and t triple seats?

   A. rdt
   B. $rd + rt$
   C. $2dr + 3tr$
   D. $3dr + 2tr$
   E. $rd + t$

4. How many dimes are there in $4x - 1$ cents?

   F. $40x - 10$
   G. $\dfrac{2}{5}x - \dfrac{1}{10}$
   H. $40x - 1$
   J. $4x - 1$
   K. $20x - 5$

5. If u represents the tens' digit of a certain number and t represents the units' digit, then the number with the digits reversed can be represented by

   A. $10t + u$
   B. $10u + t$
   C. tu
   D. ut
   E. $t + u$

6. Joe spent k cents of his allowance and has r cents left. How many dollars was his allowance?

   F. $k + r$
   G. $k - r$
   H. $100(k + r)$
   J. $\dfrac{k + r}{100}$
   K. $100kr$

Literal Expressions / 129

DO YOUR FIGURING HERE.

7. If p pounds of potatoes cost $\$k$, find the cost (in cents) of one pound of potatoes.

   A. $\dfrac{k}{p}$

   B. $\dfrac{k}{100p}$

   C. $\dfrac{p}{k}$

   D. $\dfrac{100k}{p}$

   E. $\dfrac{100p}{k}$

8. Mr. Unger rents a car for d days. He pays m dollars per day for each of the first 7 days, and half that rate for each additional day. Find the total charge if $d > 7$.

   F. $m + 2m(d - 7)$

   G. $m + \dfrac{m}{2}(d - 7)$

   H. $7m + \dfrac{m}{2}(d - 7)$

   J. $7m + \dfrac{md}{2}$

   K. $7m + 2md$

9. A salesman earns 90 dollars per week plus a 4% commission on all sales over $1000. One week he sells $\$r$ worth of merchandise ($r > 1000$). How much money does he earn that week?

   A. $50 + .04r$
   B. $.04r - 50$
   C. $.04r + 90$
   D. $r + 3.60$
   E. $.04(r - 90)$

10. Elliot's allowance was just raised to k dollars per week. He gets a raise of c dollars per week every 2 years. How much will his allowance be per week y years from now? (Assume y is an even number.)

    F. $k + cy$
    G. $k + 2cy$
    H. $k + \dfrac{1}{2}cy$
    J. $k + 2c$
    K. $ky + 2c$

Solutions to Practice Exercise Eleven

1. **(C)** Since the answer is to be in cents, we change d dollars to cents by multiplying by 100 and subtract the c cents he spent.

2. **(K)** There are 16 ounces in a pound. Therefore, we must multiply p pounds by 16 to change to ounces and then add q more ounces.

3. **(C)** Each double seat holds 2 people, so d double seats hold $2d$ people. Each triple seat holds 3 people, so t triple seats hold $3t$ people. Therefore, each row holds $2d + 3t$ people. If there are r rows, we must multiply the number of people in each row by r.

4. **(G)** To change cents to dimes, we must divide by 10.
$$\frac{4x - 1}{10} = \frac{4}{10}x - \frac{1}{10} = \frac{2}{5}x - \frac{1}{10}$$

5. **(A)** The original number would be $10u + t$. The number with the digits reversed would be $10t + u$.

6. **(J)** Joe's allowance was $k + r$ cents. To change this to dollars, we must divide by 100.

7. **(D)** This can be solved by using a proportion. Remember to change $\$k$ to $100k$ cents.
$$\frac{p}{100k} = \frac{1}{x}$$
$$px = 100k$$
$$x = \frac{100k}{p}$$

8. **(H)** He pays m dollars for each of 7 days, for a total of $7m$ dollars. Then he pays $\frac{1}{2}m$ dollars for $(d - 7)$ days, for a cost of $\frac{m}{2}(d - 7)$. The total charge is $7m + \frac{m}{2}(d - 7)$.

9. **(A)** He gets a commission of 4% of $(r - 1000)$, or $.04(r - 1000)$, which is $.04r - 40$. Adding this to 90, we have $.04r + 50$.

10. **(H)** Since he gets a raise only every 2 years, in y years he will get $\frac{1}{2}y$ raises. Each raise is c dollars, so with $\frac{1}{2}y$ raises his present allowance will be increased by $c\left(\frac{1}{2}y\right)$.

ROOTS, RADICALS, AND EXPONENTS

Roots and Radicals

Rules for addition and subtraction of radicals are much the same as for addition and subtraction of letters. The radicals must be exactly the same if they are to be added or subtracted and merely serve as a label that does not change.

Example: $4\sqrt{2} + 3\sqrt{2} = 7\sqrt{2}$

Example: $\sqrt{2} + 2\sqrt{3}$ cannot be added.

Example: $\sqrt{2} + \sqrt{3}$ cannot be added.

Sometimes, when the radicals are not the same, simplification of one or more radicals will make them the same. Remember that radicals are simplified by removing any perfect square factors.

Example: $\sqrt{27} + \sqrt{75}$

Solution: $\sqrt{9 \cdot 3} + \sqrt{25 \cdot 3}$
$3\sqrt{3} + 5\sqrt{3} = 8\sqrt{3}$

In multiplication and division, the radicals are again treated the same way as letters. They are factors and must be handled as such.

Example: $\sqrt{2} \cdot \sqrt{3} = \sqrt{6}$

Example: $2\sqrt{5} \cdot 3\sqrt{7} = 6\sqrt{35}$

Example: $(2\sqrt{3})^2 = 2\sqrt{3} \cdot 2\sqrt{3} = 4 \cdot 3 = 12$

Example: $\dfrac{\sqrt{75}}{\sqrt{3}} = \sqrt{25} = 5$

Example: $\dfrac{10\sqrt{3}}{5\sqrt{3}} = 2$

In simplifying radicals that contain a sum or difference under the radical sign, we must add or subtract first and then take the square root.

Example: $\sqrt{\dfrac{x^2}{9} + \dfrac{x^2}{16}}$

Solution: $\sqrt{\dfrac{16x^2 + 9x^2}{144}} = \sqrt{\dfrac{25x^2}{144}} = \dfrac{5x}{12}$

Had we taken the square root of each term before combining, we would have $\dfrac{x}{3} + \dfrac{x}{4}$, or $\dfrac{7x}{12}$, which is clearly not the same answer. Remember that $\sqrt{25}$ is 5. However if we write $\sqrt{25}$ as $\sqrt{16 + 9}$ we cannot say it is 4 + 3 or 7. *Always* combine the quantities within a radical sign into a single term before taking the square root.

To find the number of digits in the square root of a number, we must remember that the first step in the procedure for finding a square root is to pair off the numbers in the radical sign in each direction from the decimal point. Every pair of numbers under the radical gives one number in the answer.

Exponents

The general rules are:

$x^a = \underbrace{x \cdot x \cdot x \cdot x \cdot \ldots}_{a \text{ times}}$ Example: $3^4 = 3 \cdot 3 \cdot 3 \cdot 3$	$x^a \cdot x^b = x^{a+b}$ Example: $3^5 \cdot 3^2 = 3^7$	$(xy)^a = x^a y^a$ Example: $(3x)^3 = 3^3 x^3 = 27x^3$	$x^{-a} = \dfrac{1}{x^a}$ Example: $7^{-2} = \dfrac{1}{7^2} = \dfrac{1}{49}$
$x^0 = 1$ Example: $7^0 = 1$ $x^1 = x$ Example: $3^1 = 3$	$\dfrac{x^a}{x^b} = x^{a-b}$ Example: $\dfrac{7^8}{7^2} = 7^6$	$\left(\dfrac{x}{y}\right)^a = \dfrac{x^a}{y^a}$ Example: $\left(\dfrac{2}{3}\right)^2 = \dfrac{4}{9}$	$x^{1/a} = \sqrt[a]{x}$ Example: $16^{1/4} = \sqrt[4]{16} = 2$
$x^{a/b} = \sqrt[b]{x^a} = (\sqrt[b]{x})^a$		Example: $9^{3/2} = \sqrt{9^3} = (\sqrt{9})^3 = 27$	

Roots, Radicals, and Exponents / 133

Practice Exercise Twelve

DIRECTIONS: Work out each problem in the space provided. Circle the letter that appears before your answer.

1. The sum of $\sqrt{12} + \sqrt{27}$ is

    A. $\sqrt{29}$
    B. $3\sqrt{5}$
    C. $13\sqrt{3}$
    D. $5\sqrt{3}$
    E. $7\sqrt{3}$

DO YOUR FIGURING HERE.

2. The difference between $\sqrt{150}$ and $\sqrt{54}$ is

    F. $2\sqrt{6}$
    G. $16\sqrt{6}$
    H. $\sqrt{96}$
    J. $6\sqrt{2}$
    K. $8\sqrt{6}$

3. The product of $\sqrt{18x}$ and $\sqrt{2x}$ is

    A. $6x^2$
    B. $6x$
    C. $36x$
    D. $36x^2$
    E. $6\sqrt{x}$

4. If $\dfrac{1}{x} = \sqrt{.25}$, then x is equal to

    F. 2
    G. .5
    H. .2
    J. 20
    K. 5

5. If $n = 3.14$, then to the nearest hundredth, $n^3 =$

    A. 3.10
    B. 30.96
    C. 309.59
    D. 3095.91
    E. 30959.14

6. The square root of 24336 is exactly

    F. 152
    G. 153
    H. 155
    J. 156
    K. 158

7. The value of $2^0 + 4^{1/2} + \left(\frac{1}{2}\right)^{-1}$ is

   A. $1\frac{1}{2}$
   B. $3\frac{1}{2}$
   C. 4
   D. 5
   E. 8

8. Divide $6\sqrt{45}$ by $3\sqrt{5}$.

   F. 9
   G. 4
   H. 54
   J. 15
   K. 6

9. Find $\sqrt{\frac{y^2}{25} + \frac{y^2}{16}}$

   A. $\frac{2y}{9}$
   B. $\frac{9y}{20}$
   C. $\frac{y}{9}$
   D. $\frac{y\sqrt{41}}{20}$
   E. $\frac{41y}{20}$

10. $\sqrt{a^2 + b^2}$ is equal to

    F. $a + b$
    G. $a - b$
    H. $(a + b)(a - b)$
    J. $\sqrt{a^2} + \sqrt{b^2}$
    K. none of these

11. $4^2 \cdot 4^5 = ?$

    A. 16^7
    B. 8^7
    C. 4^{10}
    D. 4^7
    E. 4^{25}

12. What is the value of $2a^2b^3$ when $a = 2$ and $b = -1$

    F. -16
    G. -8
    H. 8
    J. 16
    K. 18

13. $\dfrac{x^3 y^2}{x^3 y^2} = ?$

   A. 1
   B. 0
   C. xy
   D. $x^3 y^2$
   E. $x^2 y^3$

14. What is the value of $x^2(2x + y)^3$ when $x = 1$ and $y = -1$

   F. -2
   G. -1
   H. 0
   J. 1
   K. 2

15. If $x - y = 10$, what is the value of $x^2 - 2xy + y^2$

   A. 49
   B. 64
   C. 81
   D. 100
   E. 121

16. Simplify $\dfrac{a^{x+1} \cdot a^{2x-1}}{a^{-x+1}}$.

   A. a^{4x-1}
   B. a^{2x+1}
   C. a^{-x+1}
   D. a^{2x-1}
   E. a^{4x+1}

17. Solve for m: $4^{2m} = 2^{m+1}$.

   F. 4
   G. 2
   H. 1
   J. $\dfrac{1}{3}$
   K. $\dfrac{1}{15}$

18. Evaluate $3x^0 + (3x)^0 + x^{-1} + 2x$ when $x = \dfrac{1}{2}$.

   A. -1
   B. $1\dfrac{1}{2}$
   C. $6\dfrac{1}{2}$
   D. 7
   E. 10

Solutions to Practice Exercise Twelve

1. **(D)** $\sqrt{12} = \sqrt{4}\cdot\sqrt{3} = 2\sqrt{3}$
   $\sqrt{27} = \sqrt{9}\cdot\sqrt{3} = 3\sqrt{3}$
   $\phantom{\sqrt{27} = \sqrt{9}\cdot\sqrt{3} = }5\sqrt{3}$

2. **(F)** $\sqrt{150} = \sqrt{25}\cdot\sqrt{6} = 5\sqrt{6}$
   $\sqrt{54} = \sqrt{9}\cdot\sqrt{6} = 3\sqrt{6}$
   $\phantom{\sqrt{54} = \sqrt{9}\cdot\sqrt{6} = }2\sqrt{6}$

3. **(B)** $\sqrt{18x}\cdot\sqrt{2x} = \sqrt{36x^2} = 6x$

4. **(F)** $\sqrt{.25} = .5$
   $\dfrac{1}{x} = .5$
   $1 = .5x$
   $10 = 5x$
   $2 = x$

5. **(B)** $(3)^3$ would be 27, so we want an answer a little larger than 27.

6. **(J)** The only answer that will end in 6 when squared is (J).

7. **(D)** $2^0 + 4^{1/2} + \left(\dfrac{1}{2}\right)^{-1} = 1 + \sqrt{4} + \dfrac{1}{\frac{1}{2}}$
   $= 1 + 2 + 2 = 5$

8. **(K)** $\dfrac{6\sqrt{45}}{3\sqrt{5}} = 2\sqrt{9} = 2\cdot 3 = 6$

9. **(D)** $\sqrt{\dfrac{y^2}{25} + \dfrac{y^2}{16}} = \sqrt{\dfrac{16y^2 + 25y^2}{400}}$
   $= \sqrt{\dfrac{41y^2}{400}} = \dfrac{y\sqrt{41}}{20}$

10. **(K)** Never take the square root of a sum separately. There is no way to simplify $\sqrt{a^2 + b^2}$.

11. **(D)** $x^a \cdot x^b = x^{a+b}$ ∴ $4^2 \cdot 4^5 = 4^{(2+5)} = 4^7$

12. **(G)** $2a^2b^3 = 2(2)^2(-1)^3$
    $= 2(4)(-1)$
    $= -8$

13. **(A)** $\dfrac{x^3y^2}{x^3y^2} = 1$
    The numerator equals the denominator

14. **(J)** $x^2(2x + y)^3 = (1)^2[2(1) + (-1)]^3$
    $= (1)^2(2 - 1)^3$
    $= (1)^2(1)^3$
    $= 1(1) = 1$

15. **(D)**
    $(x - y)^2 = (x - y)(x - y) = x^2 - 2xy + y^2$
    if $x - y = 10$, $(x - y)^2 = x^2 - 2xy + y^2 = (10)^2 = 100$

16. **(A)** $\dfrac{a^{x+1}\cdot a^{2x-1}}{a^{-x+1}} = \dfrac{a^{(x+1)+(2x-1)}}{a^{-x+1}}$
    $= \dfrac{a^{3x}}{a^{-x+1}} = a^{3x-(-x+1)}$
    $= a^{4x-1}$

17. **(J)** $4^{2m} = 2^{m+1}$
    $(2^2)^{2m} = 2^{m+1}$
    $2^{4m} = 2^{m+1}$
    $4m = m + 1$
    $3m = 1$
    $m = \dfrac{1}{3}$

18. **(D)** $3x^0 + (3x)^0 + x^{-1} + 2x$
    Substitute $x = \dfrac{1}{2}$.
    $3\left(\dfrac{1}{2}\right)^0 + \left(3\cdot\dfrac{1}{2}\right)^0 + \left(\dfrac{1}{2}\right)^{-1} + 2\left(\dfrac{1}{2}\right)$
    $3(1) + 1 + \dfrac{1}{\frac{1}{2}} + 1$
    $3 + 1 + 2 + 1 = 7$

FACTORING AND ALGEBRAIC FRACTIONS

In reducing algebraic fractions, we must divide the numerator and denominator by the same factor, just as we do in arithmetic. We can never cancel terms, as this would be adding or subtracting the same number from the numerator and denominator, which changes the value of the fraction. When we reduce $\frac{6}{8}$ to $\frac{3}{4}$, we are really saying that $\frac{6}{8} = \frac{2 \cdot 3}{2 \cdot 4}$ and then dividing numerator and denominator by 2. We do not say $\frac{6}{8} = \frac{3+3}{3+5}$ and then say $\frac{6}{8} = \frac{3}{5}$. This is faulty reasoning in algebra as well. If we have $\frac{6t}{8t}$, we can divide numerator and denominator by $2t$, giving $\frac{3}{4}$ as an answer. However, if we have $\frac{6+t}{8+t}$, we can do no more, as there is no factor that divides into the *entire* numerator as well as the *entire* denominator. Cancelling terms is one of the most frequent student errors. Don't get caught! Be careful!

Example: Reduce $\frac{3x^2 + 6x}{4x^3 + 8x^2}$ to its lowest terms.

Solution: Factoring the numerator and denominator, we have $\frac{3x(x+2)}{4x^2(x+2)}$. The factors common to both numerator and denominator are x and $(x+2)$. Dividing these out, we arrive at a correct answer of $\frac{3}{4x}$.

In adding or subtracting fractions, we must work with a common denominator and the same shortcuts we used in arithmetic.

Example: Find the sum of $\frac{1}{a}$ and $\frac{1}{b}$.

Solution: Remember to add the two cross products and put the sum over the denominator product. $\frac{b+a}{ab}$

Example: Add: $\frac{2n}{3} + \frac{3n}{2}$

Solution: $\frac{4n + 9n}{6} = \frac{13n}{6}$

In multiplying or dividing fractions, we may cancel a factor common to any numerator and any denominator. Always remember to invert the fraction following the division sign. Where exponents are involved, they are added in multiplication and subtracted in division.

Example: Find the product of $\dfrac{a^3}{b^2}$ and $\dfrac{b^3}{a^2}$

Solution: $\dfrac{a^3}{b^2} \cdot \dfrac{b^3}{a^2} = \dfrac{a^3 b^3}{b^2 a^2}$

We divide a^2 into the numerator and denominator:

$$= \dfrac{ab^3}{b^2}$$

Then we divide the numerator and denominator by b^2:

$= ab$.

Example: Divide $\dfrac{6x^2 y}{5}$ by $2x^3$.

Solution: $\dfrac{6x^2 y}{5} \cdot \dfrac{1}{2x^3}$. Divide the first numerator and second denominator by $2x^2$, giving $\dfrac{3y}{5} \cdot \dfrac{1}{x}$. Multiplying the resulting fractions, we have $\dfrac{3y}{5x}$.

Complex algebraic fractions are simplified by the same methods used in arithmetic. Multiply *each term* of the complex fraction by the lowest quantity that will eliminate the fraction within the fraction.

Example: $\dfrac{\dfrac{1}{a} + \dfrac{1}{b}}{ab}$

Solution: We must multiply *each term* by ab, giving $\dfrac{b + a}{a^2 b^2}$. Since no reduction beyond this is possible, $\dfrac{b + a}{a^2 b^2}$ is our final answer. Remember *never* to cancel terms, only common factors.

Certain types of problems may involve factoring the difference of two squares. If an expression consists of two terms that are perfect squares separated by a minus sign, the expression can always be factored into two binomials, with one containing the sum of the square roots and the other the difference of the square roots. This can be expressed by the identity $a^2 - b^2 = (a + b)(a - b)$.

Example: If $x^2 - y^2 = 100$ and $x + y = 2$, find $x - y$.

Solution: Since $x^2 - y^2$ can be written as $(x + y)(x - y)$, these two factors must multiply to 100. If one is 2, the other must be 50.

Example: If $a + b = \dfrac{1}{2}$ and $a - b = \dfrac{1}{4}$, find $a^2 - b^2$.

Solution: $a^2 - b^2$ is the product of $(a + b)$ and $(a - b)$. Therefore, $a^2 - b^2$ must be equal to $\dfrac{1}{8}$.

Practice Exercise Thirteen

DIRECTIONS: Work out the problem in the space provided. Circle the letter that appears before your answer.

1. Find the sum of $\dfrac{n}{6} + \dfrac{2n}{5}$.

    A. $\dfrac{13n}{30}$
    B. $17n$
    C. $\dfrac{3n}{30}$
    D. $\dfrac{17n}{30}$
    E. $\dfrac{3n}{11}$

DO YOUR FIGURING HERE.

2. Combine into a single fraction: $1 - \dfrac{x}{y}$

    F. $\dfrac{1-x}{y}$
    G. $\dfrac{y-x}{y}$
    H. $\dfrac{x-y}{y}$
    J. $\dfrac{1-x}{1-y}$
    K. $\dfrac{y-x}{xy}$

3. Divide $\dfrac{x-y}{x+y}$ by $\dfrac{y-x}{y+x}$.

    A. 1
    B. -1
    C. $\dfrac{(x-y)^2}{(x+y)^2}$
    D. $-\dfrac{(x-y)^2}{(x+y)^2}$
    E. 0

GO ON TO THE NEXT PAGE.

140 / ACT

DO YOUR FIGURING HERE.

4. Simplify: $\dfrac{1 + \dfrac{1}{x}}{\dfrac{y}{x}}$

F. $\dfrac{x+1}{y}$

G. $\dfrac{x+1}{x}$

H. $\dfrac{x+1}{xy}$

J. $\dfrac{x^2+1}{xy}$

K. $\dfrac{y+1}{y}$

5. Find an expression equivalent to $\left(\dfrac{2x^2}{y}\right)^3$.

A. $\dfrac{8x^5}{3y}$

B. $\dfrac{6x^6}{y^3}$

C. $\dfrac{6x^5}{y^3}$

D. $\dfrac{8x^5}{y^3}$

E. $\dfrac{8x^6}{y^3}$

6. Simplify: $\dfrac{\dfrac{1}{x} + \dfrac{1}{y}}{3}$

F. $\dfrac{3x+3y}{xy}$

G. $\dfrac{3xy}{x+y}$

H. $\dfrac{xy}{3}$

J. $\dfrac{x+y}{3xy}$

K. $\dfrac{x+y}{3}$

7. $\frac{1}{a} + \frac{1}{b} = 7$ and $\frac{1}{a} - \frac{1}{b} = 3$. Find $\frac{1}{a^2} - \frac{1}{b^2}$.

   A. 10
   B. 7
   C. 3
   D. 21
   E. 4

8. If $(a - b)^2 = 64$ and $ab = 3$, find $a^2 + b^2$.

   F. 61
   G. 67
   H. 70
   J. 58
   K. 69

9. If $c + d = 12$ and $c^2 - d^2 = 48$, then $c - d =$

   A. 4
   B. 36
   C. 60
   D. 5
   E. 3

10. The trinomial $x^2 + x - 20$ is exactly divisible by

    F. $x - 5$
    G. $x + 4$
    H. $x - 10$
    J. $x - 4$
    K. $x - 2$

DO YOUR FIGURING HERE.

Solutions to Practice Exercise Thirteen

1. **(D)** $\dfrac{n}{6} + \dfrac{2n}{5} = \dfrac{5n + 12n}{30} = \dfrac{17n}{30}$

2. **(G)** $\dfrac{1}{1} - \dfrac{x}{y} = \dfrac{y - x}{y}$

3. **(B)** $\dfrac{x - y}{x + y} \cdot \dfrac{y + x}{y - x}$
   (We inverted the divisor and changed the example to multiplication.) Since addition is commutative, we may cancel $x + y$ with $y + x$, as they are the same quantity. However, subtraction is not commutative, so we may not cancel $x - y$ with $y - x$, as they are *not* the same quantity. We can change the form of $y - x$ by factoring out -1. Thus, $y - x = (-1)(x - y)$. In this form, we can cancel $x - y$, leaving an answer of $\dfrac{1}{-1}$, or -1.

4. **(F)** Multiply every term in the fraction by x, giving $\dfrac{x + 1}{y}$.

5. **(E)** $\dfrac{2x^2}{y} \cdot \dfrac{2x^2}{y} \cdot \dfrac{2x^2}{y} = \dfrac{8x^6}{y^3}$

6. **(J)** Multiply every term of the fraction by xy, giving $\dfrac{y + x}{3xy} \rightarrow \dfrac{x + y}{3xy}$

7. **(D)** $\dfrac{1}{a^2} - \dfrac{1}{b^2}$ is equivalent to $\left(\dfrac{1}{a} + \dfrac{1}{b}\right)\left(\dfrac{1}{a} - \dfrac{1}{b}\right)$.
   We therefore multiply 7 by 3 for an answer of 21.

8. **(H)** $(a - b)^2$ is $(a - b)(a - b)$ or $a^2 - 2ab + b^2$, which is equal to 64.
   $a^2 - 2ab + b^2 = 64$
   $a^2 + b^2 = 64 + 2ab$
   Since $ab = 3$, $2ab = 6$, and $a^2 + b^2 = 64 + 6$, or 70.

9. **(A)** $c^2 - d^2 = (c + d)(c - d)$
   $48 = 12(c - d)$
   $4 = c - d$

10. **(J)** The factors of $x^2 + x - 20$ are $(x + 5)$ and $(x - 4)$.

PROBLEM SOLVING IN ALGEBRA

In solving verbal problems, the most important technique is to read accurately. Be sure you understand clearly what you are asked to find. Once this is done, represent what you are looking for algebraically. Write an equation that translates the words of the problem to the symbols of mathematics. Then solve that equation by the techniques reviewed previously.

We will review some of the frequently encountered types of algebra problems, although not every problem you may get will fall into one of these categories. However, thoroughly familiarizing yourself with the types of problems that follow will help you to translate and solve all kinds of verbal problems.

Coin Problems

In solving coin problems, it is best to change the value of all monies involved to cents before writing an equation. Thus, the number of nickels must be multiplied by 5 to give their value in cents; dimes must be multiplied by 10; quarters by 25; half dollars by 50; and dollars by 100.

Example: Richard has $3.50 consisting of nickels and dimes. If he has 5 more dimes than nickels, how many dimes does he have?

Solution: Let x = the number of nickels
$x + 5$ = the number of dimes
$5x$ = the value of the nickels in cents
$10x + 50$ = the value of the dimes in cents
350 = the value of the money he has in cents
$5x + 10x + 50 = 350$
$15x = 300$
$x = 20$
He has 20 nickels and 25 dimes.

In a problem such as this, you can be sure that 20 would be among the multiple-choice answers. You must be sure to read carefully what you are asked to find and then continue until you have found the quantity sought. The correct answer is 25.

Consecutive Integer Problems

Consecutive integers are one apart and are represented by $x, x + 1, x + 2$, etc. Consecutive even or odd integers are two apart and are represented by $x, x + 2, x + 4$, etc.

Example: Three consecutive odd integers have a sum of 33. Find the average of these integers.

Solution: Represent the integers as x, $x + 2$ and $x + 4$. Write an equation indicating the sum is 33.
$$3x + 6 = 33$$
$$3x = 27$$
$$x = 9$$
The integers are 9, 11, and 13. In the case of evenly spaced numbers such as these, the average is the middle number, 11. Since the sum of the three numbers was given originally, all we really had to do was to divide this sum by 3 to find the average, without ever knowing what the numbers were.

Age Problems

Problems of this type usually involve a comparison of ages at the present time, several years from now, or several years ago. A person's age x years from now is found by adding x to his present age. A person's age x years ago is found by subtracting x from his present age.

Example: Michelle was 12 years old y years ago. Represent her age b years from now.

Solution: Her present age is $12 + y$. In b years, her age will be $12 + y + b$.

Interest Problems

The annual amount of interest paid on an investment is found by multiplying the amount of principal invested by the rate (percent) of interest paid.

Principal × Rate = Interest income

Example: Mr. Strauss invests $4,000, part at 6% and part at 7%. His income from these investments in one year is $250. Find the amount invested at 7%.

Solution: Represent each investment.
Let x = the amount invested at 7%. Always try to let x represent what you are looking for.
$4000 - x$ = the amount invested at 6%
$.07x$ = the income from the 7% investment
$.06(4000 - x)$ = the income from the 6% investment
$$.07x + .06(4000 - x) = 250$$
$$7x + 6(4000 - x) = 25000$$
$$7x + 24000 - 6x = 25000$$
$$x = 1000$$
He invested $1,000 at 7%.

Fraction Problems

A fraction is a ratio between two numbers. If the value of a fraction is $\frac{2}{3}$, it does not mean the numerator must be 2 and the denominator 3. The numerator and denominator could be 4 and 6 respectively, or 1 and 1.5, or 30 and 45, or any of infinitely many other combinations. All we know is that the ratio of numerator to denominator will be 2:3. Therefore, the numerator may be represented by $2x$, the denominator by $3x$ and the fraction by $\frac{2x}{3x}$.

Example: The value of a fraction is $\frac{3}{4}$. If 3 is subtracted from the numerator and added to the denominator, the value of the fraction is $\frac{2}{5}$. Find the original fraction.

Solution: Let the original fraction be represented by $\frac{3x}{4x}$. If 3 is subtracted from the numerator and added to the denominator, the new fraction becomes $\frac{3x-3}{4x+3}$.

The value of the new fraction is $\frac{2}{5}$.

$$\frac{3x-3}{4x+3} = \frac{2}{5}$$

Cross multiply to eliminate fractions.
$15x - 15 = 8x + 6$
$7x = 21$
$x = 3$

Therefore, the original fraction is
$$\frac{3x}{4x} = \frac{9}{12}$$

Mixture Problems

There are two kinds of mixture problems with which you should be familiar. The first is sometimes referred to as dry mixture, in which we mix dry ingredients of different values, such as nuts or coffee. Also solved by the same method are problems such as those dealing with tickets at different prices. In solving this type of problem, it is best to organize the data in a chart of three rows and three columns, labeled as illustrated in the following problem.

Example: A dealer wishes to mix 20 pounds of nuts selling for 45 cents per pound with some more expensive nuts selling for 60 cents per pound, to make a mixture that will sell for 50 cents per pound. How many pounds of the more expensive nuts should he use?

Solution:

	No. of lbs.	×	Price/lb.	=	Total Value
Original	20		.45		.45(20)
Added	x		.60		.60(x)
Mixture	$20 + x$		.50		.50($20 + x$)

The value of the original nuts plus the value of the added nuts must equal

the value of the mixture. Almost all mixture problems require an equation that comes from adding the final column:
.45(20) + .60(x) = .50(20 + x)
Multiply by 100 to remove decimals.
45(20) + 60(x) = 50(20 + x)
900 + 60x = 1000 + 50x
10x = 100
x = 10
He should use 10 lbs. of 60 cent nuts.

In solving the second type, or chemical, mixture problem, we are dealing with percents rather than prices, and amounts instead of value.

Example: How much water must be added to 20 gallons of a solution that is 30% alcohol to dilute it to a solution that is only 25% alcohol?

Solution:

	No. of gals.	×	% alcohol	=	Amt. alcohol
Original	20		.30		.30(20)
Added	x		0		0
New	20 + x		.25		.25(20 + x)

Note that the percent of alcohol in water is 0. Had we added pure alcohol to strengthen the solution, the percent would have been 100. The equation again comes from the last column. The amount of alcohol added (none in this case) plus the amount we had to start with must equal the amount of alcohol in the new solution.
.30(20) = .25(20 + x)
30(20) = 25(20 + x)
600 = 500 + 25x
100 = 25x
x = 4

Motion Problems

The fundamental relationship in all motion problems is that Rate × Time = Distance. The problems at the level of this examination usually derive their equation from a relationship concerning distance. Most problems fall into one of three types.

1. *Motion in opposite directions.* When two objects start at the same time and move in opposite directions, or when two objects start at points at a given distance apart and move toward each other until they meet, then the total distance traveled equals the sum of the distances traveled by each object.

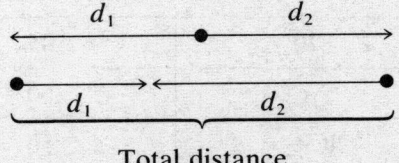

Total distance

In either of the above cases, $d_1 + d_2$ = Total distance.

2. *Motion in the same direction.* This type of problem is sometimes called the "catch-up" problem. Two objects leave the same place at different times and different rates, but one "catches up" to the other. In such a case, the two distances must be equal.
3. *Round trip.* In this type of problem, the rate going is usually different from the rate returning. The times are also different. But if we go somewhere and then return to the starting point, the distances must be the same.

To solve any motion problem, it is helpful to organize the data in a box with columns for rate, time, and distance. A separate line should be used for each moving object. Remember that if the rate is given in *miles per hour*, the time must be in *hours* and the distance in *miles*.

Example: Two cars leave a restaurant at 1 p.m., with one car traveling east at 60 miles per hour and the other west at 40 miles per hour along a straight highway. At what time will they be 350 miles apart?

Solution:

	Rate	×	Time	=	Distance
Eastbound	60		x		$60x$
Westbound	40		x		$40x$

Notice that the time is unknown, since we must discover the number of hours traveled. However, since the cars start at the same time and stop when they are 350 miles apart, their times are the same.

$60x + 40x = 350$
$\quad\quad 100x = 350$
$\quad\quad\quad\quad x = 3\frac{1}{2}$

In $3\frac{1}{2}$ hours, it will be 4:30 p.m.

Example: Gloria leaves home for school, riding her bicycle at a rate of 12 m.p.h. Twenty minutes after she leaves, her mother sees Gloria's English paper on her bed and leaves to bring it to her. If her mother drives at 36 m.p.h., how far must she drive before she reaches Gloria?

Solution:

	Rate	×	Time	=	Distance
Gloria	12		x		$12x$
Mother	36		$x - \frac{1}{3}$		$36\left(x - \frac{1}{3}\right)$

Notice that 20 minutes has been changed to $\frac{1}{3}$ of an hour. In this problem the times are not equal, but the distances are.

$12x = 36\left(x - \frac{1}{3}\right)$
$12x = 36x - 12$
$\ 12 = 24x$
$\ \ x = \frac{1}{2}$

If Gloria rode for $\frac{1}{2}$ hour at 12 m.p.h., the distance covered was 6 miles.

Example: Judy leaves home at 11 a.m. and rides to Mary's house to return her bicycle. She travels at 12 miles per hour and arrives at 11:30 a.m. She turns right around and walks home. How fast does she walk if she returns home at 1 p.m.?

Solution:

	Rate	×	Time	=	Distance
Going	12		$\frac{1}{2}$		6
Return	x		$1\frac{1}{2}$		$\frac{3}{2}x$

The distances are equal.

$6 = \frac{3}{2}x$

$12 = 3x$

$x = 4$

She walked at 4 m.p.h.

Work Problems

In most work problems, a complete job is broken into several parts, each representing a fractional part of the entire job. For each fractional part, which represents the portion completed by one man, one machine, one pipe, etc., the numerator should represent the time actually spent working, while the denominator should represent the total time needed to do the entire job alone. The sum of all the individual fractions should be 1.

Example: John can wax his car in 3 hours. Jim can do the same job in 5 hours. How long will it take them if they work together?

Solution: If multiple-choice answers are given, you should realize that the correct answer must be smaller than the shortest time given, for no matter how slow a helper may be, he does do part of the job and therefore it will be completed in less time.

Let x = the amount of time each spent working together.

$$\frac{\text{Time spent}}{\text{Total time needed to do job alone}} \rightarrow \overset{\text{John}}{\frac{x}{3}} + \overset{\text{Jim}}{\frac{x}{5}} = 1$$

Multiply by 15 to eliminate fractions.

$5x + 3x = 15$

$8x = 15$

$x = 1\frac{7}{8}$ hours

Practice Exercise Fourteen

DIRECTIONS: Work out the problem in the space provided. Circle the letter that appears before your answer.

1. Sue and Nancy wish to buy a gift for a friend. They combine their money and find they have $4.00, consisting of quarters, dimes, and nickels. If they have 35 coins and the number of quarters is half the number of nickels, how many quarters do they have?

   A. 5
   B. 10
   C. 20
   D. 3
   E. 6

2. Three times the first of three consecutive odd integers is 3 more than twice the third. Find the third integer.

   F. 9
   G. 11
   H. 13
   J. 15
   K. 7

3. Robert is 15 years older than his brother Stan. However, y years ago Robert was twice as old as Stan. If Stan is now b years old and $b > y$, find the value of $b - y$.

   A. 13
   B. 14
   C. 15
   D. 16
   E. 17

4. How many ounces of pure acid must be added to 20 ounces of a solution that is 5% acid to strengthen it to a solution that is 24% acid?

   F. $2\frac{1}{2}$
   G. 5
   H. 6
   J. $7\frac{1}{2}$
   K. 10

DO YOUR FIGURING HERE.

GO ON TO THE NEXT PAGE.

5. A dealer mixes *a* lbs. of nuts worth *b* cents per pound with *c* lbs. of nuts worth *d* cents per pound. At what price should he sell a pound of the mixture if he wishes to make a profit of 10 cents per pound?

A. $\dfrac{ab + cd}{a + c} + 10$

B. $\dfrac{ab + cd}{a + c} + .10$

C. $\dfrac{b + d}{a + c} + 10$

D. $\dfrac{b + d}{a + c} + .10$

E. $\dfrac{b + d + 10}{a + c}$

6. Barbara invests $2,400 at 5%. How much additional money must she invest at 8% so that the total annual income will be equal to 6% of her entire investment?

F. $2,400
G. $3,600
H. $1,000
J. $3,000
K. $1,200

7. Frank left Austin to drive to Boxville at 6:15 p.m. and arrived at 11:45 p.m. If he averaged 30 miles per hour and stopped one hour for dinner, how many miles is Boxville from Austin?

A. 120
B. 135
C. 180
D. 165
E. 150

8. A plane traveling 600 miles per hour is 30 miles from Kennedy Airport at 4:58 p.m. At what time will it arrive at the airport?

F. 5:00 p.m.
G. 5:01 p.m.
H. 5:02 p.m.
J. 5:20 p.m.
K. 5:03 p.m.

DO YOUR FIGURING HERE.

9. Mr. Bridges can wash his car in 15 minutes, while his son Dave takes twice as long to do the same job. If they work together, how many minutes will the job take them?

   A. 5
   B. $7\frac{1}{2}$
   C. 10
   D. $22\frac{1}{2}$
   E. 30

10. The value of a fraction is $\frac{2}{5}$. If the numerator is decreased by 2 and the denominator increased by 1, the resulting fraction is equivalent to $\frac{1}{4}$. Find the numerator of the original fraction.

    F. 3
    G. 4
    H. 6
    J. 10
    K. 15

DO YOUR FIGURING HERE.

152 / ACT

Solutions to Practice Exercise Fourteen

1. **(B)** Let x = number of quarters
   $2x$ = number of nickels
   $35 - 3x$ = number of dimes
   Write all money values in cents.
   $25(x) + 5(2x) + 10(35 - 3x) = 400$
   $25x + 10x + 350 - 30x = 400$
   $5x = 50$
   $x = 10$

2. **(J)** Let x = first integer
   $x + 2$ = second integer
   $x + 4$ = third integer
   $3(x) = 3 + 2(x + 4)$
   $3x = 3 + 2x + 8$
   $x = +11$
   The third integer is 15.

3. **(C)** b = Stan's age now
   $b + 15$ = Robert's age now
   $b - y$ = Stan's age y years ago
   $b + 15 - y$ = Robert's age y years ago
   $b + 15 - y = 2(b - y)$
   $b + 15 - y = 2b - 2y$
   $15 = b - y$

4. **(G)**

	No. of oz. ×	% acid =	Amt. acid
Original	20	.05	1
Added	x	1.00	x
Mixture	$20 + x$	.24	$.24(20 + x)$

   $1 + x = .24(20 + x)$ Multiply by 100 to eliminate decimal.
   $100 + 100x = 480 + 24x$
   $76x = 380$
   $x = 5$

5. **(A)** The a lbs. of nuts are worth a total of ab cents. The c lbs. of nuts are worth a total of cd cents. The value of the mixture is $ab + cd$ cents. Since there are $a + c$ pounds, each pound is worth $\dfrac{ab + cd}{a + c}$ cents.

Since the dealer wants to add 10 cents to each pound for profit, and the value of each pound is in cents, we add 10 to the value of each pound.

6. **(K)** If Barbara invests x additional dollars at 8%, her total investment will amount to $2400 + x$ dollars.
   $.05(2400) + .08(x) = .06(2400 + x)$
   $5(2400) + 8(x) = 6(2400 - x)$
   $12000 + 8x = 14400 + 6x$
   $2x = 2400$
   $x = 1200$

7. **(B)** Total time elapsed is $5\frac{1}{2}$ hours. However, one hour was used for dinner. Therefore, Frank drove at 30 m.p.h. for $4\frac{1}{2}$ hours, covering 135 miles.

8. **(G)** Time = $\dfrac{\text{Distance}}{\text{Rate}} = \dfrac{30}{600} = \dfrac{1}{20}$ hour, or 3 minutes. 4 hours 58 minutes + 3 minutes = 5:01.

9. **(C)** Dave takes 30 minutes to wash the car alone.
   $\dfrac{x}{15} + \dfrac{x}{30} = 1$
   $2x + x = 30$
   $3x = 30$
   $x = 10$

10. **(H)** Let $2x$ = original numerator
    $5x$ = original denominator
    $\dfrac{2x - 2}{5x + 1} = \dfrac{1}{4}$ Cross multiply
    $8x - 8 = 5x + 1$
    $3x = 9$
    $x = 3$
    Original numerator is 2(3), or 6.

GEOMETRY

Numerical relationships from geometry should be reviewed thoroughly. A list of the most important formulas with illustrations follows.

Area

1. Rectangle: bh

b = base
h = height

Area = (6)(3) = 18

2. Parallelogram: bh

b = base
h = height

Area = 8 · 4 = 32

3. Rhombus: $\frac{1}{2}d_1d_2$

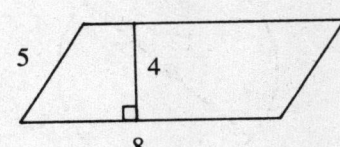

d_1 = diagonal 1
d_2 = diagonal 2

If AC = 10 and BD = 8, then area is $\frac{1}{2}(10)(8)$ = 40

4. Square: s^2 or $\frac{1}{2}d^2$

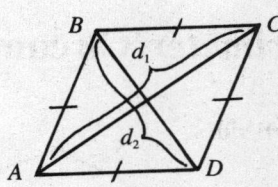

s = side
d = diagonal

Area = 6^2 = 36

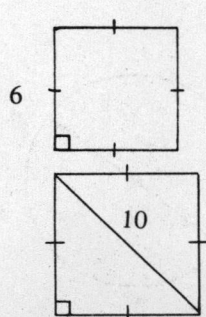

Area = $\frac{1}{2}(10)(10)$ = 50

153

5. **Triangle:** $\frac{1}{2}bh$

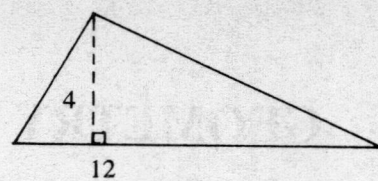

b = base
h = height

Area = $\frac{1}{2}(12)(4) = 24$

6. **Equilateral triangle:** $\frac{s^2}{4}\sqrt{3}$

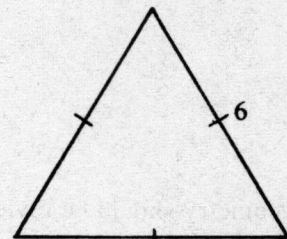

s = side

Area = $\frac{36}{4}\sqrt{3} = 9\sqrt{3}$

7. **Trapezoid:** $\frac{1}{2}h(b_1 + b_2)$

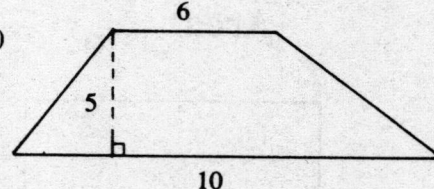

h = height
b_1 = base 1 (top)
b_2 = base 2 (bottom)

Area = $\frac{1}{2}(5)(6 + 10) = \frac{1}{2}(5)(16) = 40$

8. **Circle:** πr^2

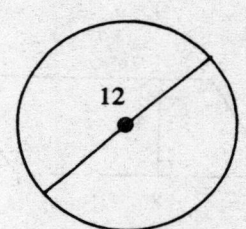

r = radius

Area = $\pi (6)^2 = 36\pi$

Perimeter/Circumference

1. **Any polygon: simply add all sides**

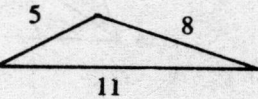

$P = 5 + 8 + 11 = 24$

2. **Circle:** πd or $2\pi r$
   (called circumference)

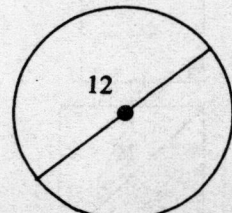

d = diameter
C = circumference
r = radius

$C = \pi (12) = 12\pi$

3. The distance covered by a wheel in one revolution is equal to the circumference of the wheel.

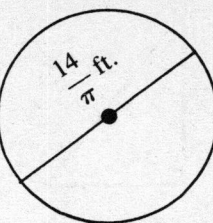

In one revolution, this wheel covers $\pi \cdot \dfrac{14}{\pi}$, or 14 feet.

Right Triangles

1. **Pythagorean Theorem**
   $(\text{leg})^2 + (\text{leg})^2 = (\text{hypotenuse})^2$

   $4^2 + 5^2 = x^2$
   $16 + 25 = x^2$
   $41 = x^2$
   $\sqrt{41} = x$

   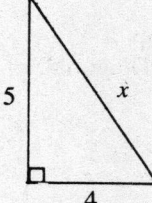

2. **Pythagorean Triples:** These are sets of integers that satisfy the Pythagorean theorem. When a given set of numbers such as 3,4,5 form a Pythagorean triple ($3^2 + 4^2 = 5^2$), any multiples of this set such as 6,8,10 or 15,20,25 also form a Pythagorean triple. The most common Pythagorean triples, which should be memorized, are:

   3,4,5
   5,12,13
   8,15,17
   7,24,25

   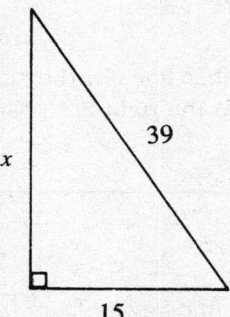

   Squaring these numbers in order to apply the Pythagorean theorem would take too much time. Instead, recognize the hypotenuse as 3(13). Suspect a 5,12,13 triangle. Since the given leg is 3(5), the missing leg must be 3(12), or 36, with no computation and a great saving of time.

3. **The 30°-60°-90° triangle**

   a) The leg opposite the 30° angle is $\dfrac{1}{2}$ hypotenuse.

   b) The leg opposite the 60° angle is $\dfrac{1}{2}$ hypotenuse $\cdot \sqrt{3}$.

   c) An altitude in an equilateral triangle forms a 30°-60°-90° triangle and is therefore equal to $\dfrac{1}{2}$ the side of the equilateral triangle times $\sqrt{3}$. Altitude $= \dfrac{1}{2}s\sqrt{3}$.

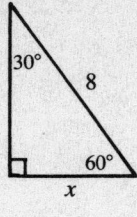 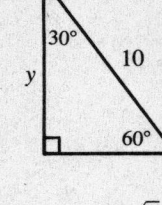 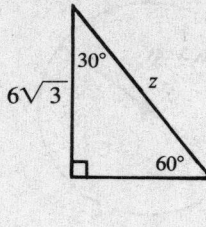 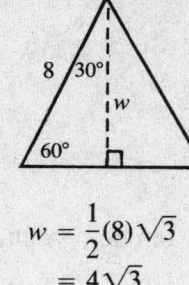

$x = 4$ $\qquad$ $y = 5\sqrt{3}$ $\qquad$ $z = 12$ $\qquad$ $w = \dfrac{1}{2}(8)\sqrt{3}$
$\qquad\qquad\qquad\qquad\qquad\qquad\qquad\qquad\qquad\qquad\qquad\qquad\quad = 4\sqrt{3}$

4. **The 45°-45°-90° triangle (isosceles right triangle)**
   a) Each leg is $\dfrac{1}{2}$ hypotenuse $\cdot \sqrt{2}$.
   b) Hypotenuse is leg $\cdot \sqrt{2}$.
   c) The diagonal in a square forms a 45°-45°-90° triangle and is therefore equal to a side of the square times $\sqrt{2}$. Diagonal $= s\sqrt{2}$.

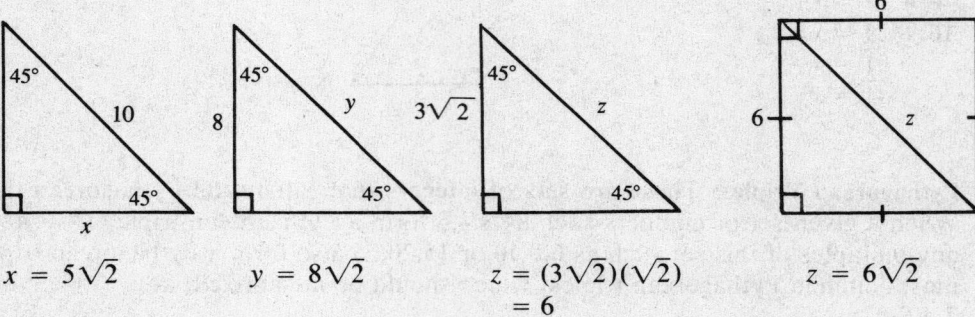

$x = 5\sqrt{2}$ $\qquad$ $y = 8\sqrt{2}$ $\qquad$ $z = (3\sqrt{2})(\sqrt{2})$ $\qquad$ $z = 6\sqrt{2}$
$\qquad\qquad\qquad\qquad\qquad\qquad\qquad\quad = 6$

Coordinate Geometry

Our study of coordinate geometry begins with the number line. In the standard number line, points to the left of zero are negative, while points to the right are positive.

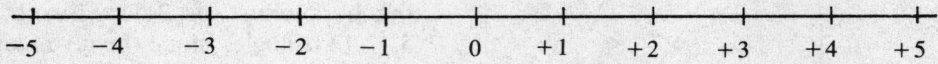

A point is located on the number line as the number of units away from the zero point—the number is positive if the point is to the right of the zero, negative if the point is to the left. Thus a number line gives a physical meaning to signed numbers.

The **distance** between any two points on the number line is the absolute value of the difference between the numbers. Thus, the distance between -2 and $+2$ on the number line is given by $|(+2) - (-2)| = |(+2) + (+2)| = |+4| = +4$. The order of subtraction to represent the distance for -2 to $+2$ can be expressed as $|(+2) - (-2)|$ or $|(-2) - (+2)|$.

The **midpoint** between any two points on the number line is their average. For example, the midpoint between -3 and $+5$ is $\dfrac{(-3) + (+5)}{2} = \dfrac{+2}{2} = +1$ (remember—the average of two numbers is their sum divided by 2).

A coordinate system can be set up by putting two number lines at right angles to each other. Since a point can be located as a positive or negative move from the zero point, and we now have two number lines, we need to give information about two moves, one for each number line (normally called an axis). In order to give this information as concisely as possible, we list the moves inside a set of parentheses, for example, $(-2, 3)$. This point is marked off on the axes drawn below.

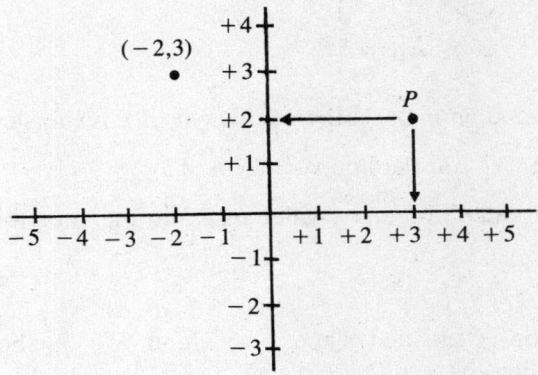

The order is *always* the x axis move (horizontal number line) first, followed by the y axis move.

If a point is drawn on the graph, point P above for example, its coordinates can be found by drawing straight lines to the axes. For point P, the coordinates are (3,2). (Remember that the x coordinate is always written first).

If two points P and Q have coordinates $(x_1 y_1)$ and $(x_2 y_2)$ respectively

- Distance from P to Q is:
$$d = \sqrt{(x_2 - x_1)^2 + (y_2 - y_1)^2}$$
- The coordinates of midpoint between points P and Q are:
$$\text{Midpoint} = \left(\frac{x_1 + x_2}{2}, \frac{y_1 + y_2}{2}\right)$$

Example: The distance from $(-2,3)$ to $(4,-1)$ is
$$\sqrt{[4 - (-2)]^2 + [-1 - (3)]^2}$$
$$\sqrt{(6)^2 + (-4)^2} = \sqrt{36 + 16} = \sqrt{52}$$

Example: The midpoint of the segment joining $(-2,3)$ to $(4,-1)$ is
$$\left(\frac{-2 + 4}{2}, \frac{3 + (-1)}{2}\right) = \left(\frac{2}{2}, \frac{2}{2}\right) = (1,1)$$

We can also plot a straight line on a coordinate graph. The equation of a line is:
$$y = mx + b$$

- m represents the slope (or tilt) of the line
- b represents the y-intercept (the point at which the line crosses the vertical axis)

A point is on a line if its x and y coordinate values, when substituted into the equation for the respective x and y variables, make the equation true.

Example:

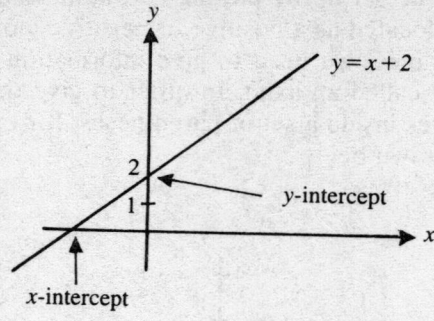

If $y = x + 2$ then $m = 1$ (the coefficient of x is the slope) and $b = 2$

Example: Is the point (3,7) on the line $y = 2x + 1$?

Solution: Insert the x value of 3 and y value of 7 into the equation.
$y = 2x + 1$
$7 = 2(3) + 1$
$7 = 7$
The equation is satisfied when $x = 3$ and $y = 7$, therefore the point is located on the line $y = 2x + 1$.

Equations not in the form $y = mx + b$ can be rearranged as such using standard algebraic techniques.

Example: What is the slope and y-intercept of $2x + 3y = 7$?

Solution: Solve for y
$2x + 3y = 7$
$3y = -2x + 7$
$y = -\frac{2}{3}x + \frac{7}{3}$
slope $= m = -\frac{2}{3}$ $\qquad$ y-intercept $= \frac{7}{3}$

- Two lines are parallel if their slopes are equal.
- Two lines are perpendicular if their slopes are negative reciprocals. (Two slopes are negative reciprocals if they multiply to -1.)

Example: $y = 2x + 3$ and $y = 2x - 7$ are parallel; both have a slope of 2.

Example: $y = 2x + 3$ and $y = -\frac{1}{2}x - 7$ are perpendicular; the slopes are 2 and $-\frac{1}{2}$ respectively.

Example: Are $2y = 4x + 3$ and $3y = 6x - 4$ parallel?

Solution: First rearrange the equations into $y = mx + b$ form.
$2y = 4x + 3$ $\qquad$ $3y = 6x - 4$
$\downarrow$ $\qquad\qquad\qquad$ $\downarrow$
$y = 2x + 3$ $\qquad$ $y = 2x - 4$
The lines are parallel; both have a slope of 2.

Angles

An **angle** is the figure formed by two lines meeting at a point.

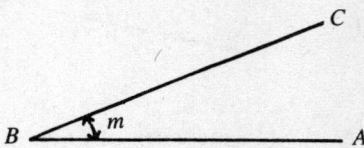

The point *B* is the **vertex** of the angle and the lines $\overline{BA}$ and $\overline{BC}$ are the **sides** of the angle. There are three common ways of naming an angle:

1. By a small letter or figure written within the angle, as ∠*m*.
2. By the capital letter at its vertex, as ∠*B*.
3. By three capital letters, the middle letter being the vertex letter, as ∠*ABC*.

When two straight lines intersect (cut each other), four angles are formed. If these four angles are equal, each angle is a **right angle** and contains 90°. The symbol ∟ is used to indicate a right angle.

Example:

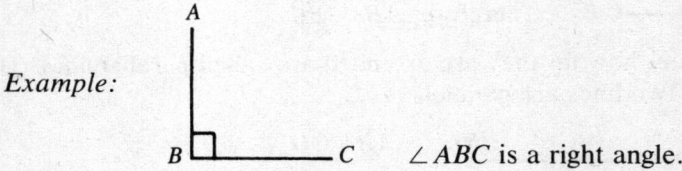

∠*ABC* is a right angle.

An angle less than a right angle is an **acute angle**.

If the two sides of an angle extend in opposite directions forming a straight line, the angle is a **straight angle** and contains 180°.

An angle greater than a right angle (90°) and less than a straight angle (180°) is an **obtuse angle**.

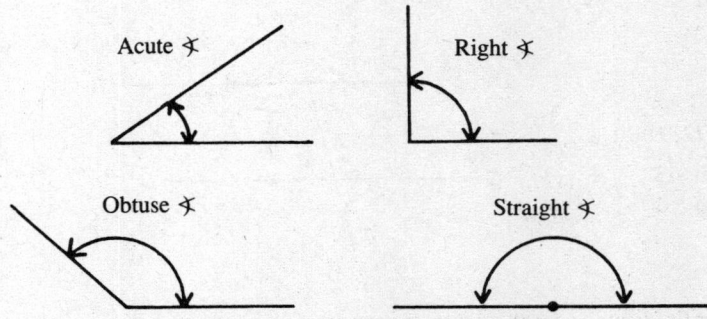

Two angles are **complementary** if their sum is 90°. To find the complement of an angle, subtract the given number of degrees from 90°.

Example: The complement of 60° = 90° − 60° = 30°.

Two angles are **supplementary** if their sum is 180°. To find the supplement of an angle, subtract the given number of degrees from 180°.

Example: The supplement of 60° = 180° − 60° = 120°.

When two straight lines intersect, any pair of opposite angles are called **vertical angles** and are equal.

∠a and ∠b are vertical angles
m∠a = m∠b
∠c and ∠d are vertical angles
m∠c = m∠d

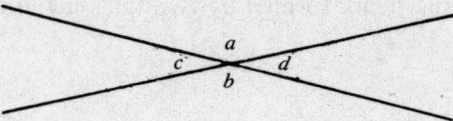

NOTE: The symbol m∠a is read "the measure of angle a." It represents the number of degrees in the angle.

Two lines are **perpendicular** to each other if they meet to form a right angle. The symbol ⊥ is used to indicate that the lines are perpendicular.

Example:

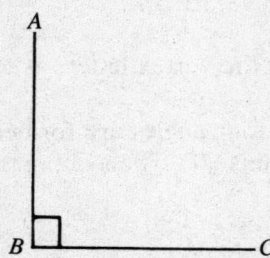

∠ABC is a right angle.
Therefore, $\overline{AB} \perp \overline{BC}$.

Lines that do not meet no matter how far they are extended are called **parallel lines**. The symbol ∥ is used to indicate that two lines are parallel.

Example: A ———————————— B. $\overline{AB} \parallel \overline{CD}$

C ———————————— D

Parallel Lines

1. If two parallel lines are cut by a transversal, the alternate interior angles are congruent.

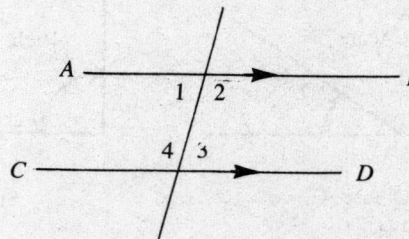

If $\overline{AB} \parallel \overline{CD}$, then
m∠1 ≅ m∠3
m∠2 ≅ m∠4

2. If two parallel lines are cut by a transversal, the corresponding angles are congruent.

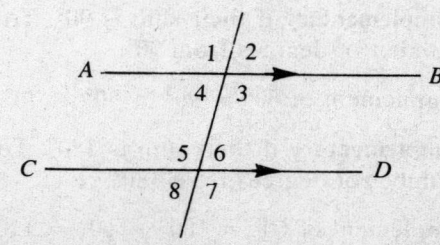

If $\overline{AB} \parallel \overline{CD}$, then
m∠1 ≅ m∠5
m∠2 ≅ m∠6
m∠3 ≅ m∠7
m∠4 ≅ m∠8

3. If two parallel lines are cut by a transversal, interior angles on the same side of the transversal are supplementary.

If $\overline{AB} \parallel \overline{CD}$, then

$m\angle 1 + m\angle 4 = 180°$
$m\angle 2 + m\angle 3 = 180°$

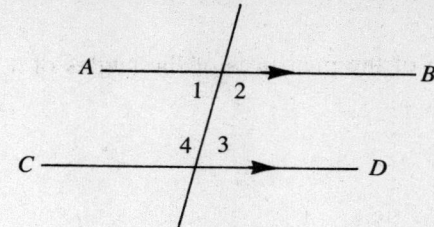

Triangles

1. If two sides of a triangle are equal, the angles opposite these sides are equal.

If $\overline{AB} = \overline{AC}$, then
$m\angle B = m\angle C$.

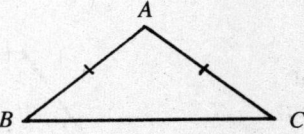

2. If two angles of a triangle are equal, the sides opposite these angles are equal.

If $m\angle C = m\angle B$, then
$\overline{AB} = \overline{AC}$.

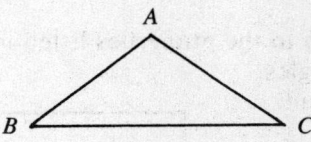

3. The sum of the measures of the angles of a triangle is 180°.

$m\angle A + m\angle B + m\angle C = 180°$

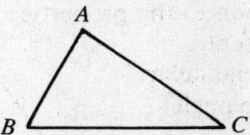

4. The measure of an exterior angle of a triangle is equal to the sum of the measures of the two remote interior angles.

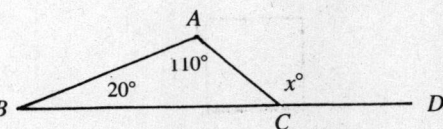

$x = 20 + 110 = 130$

5. If two angles of one triangle are equal to two angles of a second triangle, the third angles are equal.

$m\angle D = m\angle A$

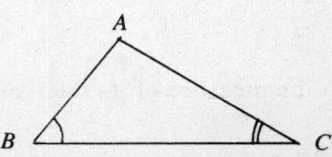 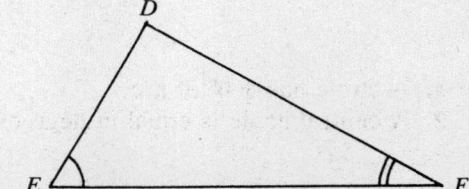

162 / ACT

Polygons

1. The sum of the measures of the angles of a polygon of *n* sides is $(n - 2)180°$.

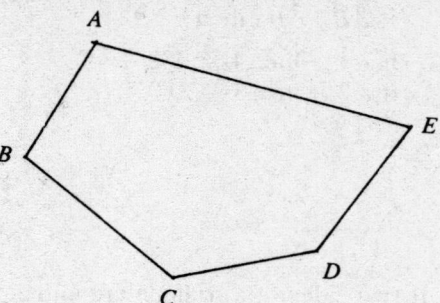

Since *ABCDE* has 5 sides, then

$m\angle A + m\angle B + m\angle C + m\angle D + m\angle E$
$= (5 - 2)180° = 3(180°) = 540°$

2. In a parallelogram:
   a) Opposite sides are parallel.
   b) Opposite sides are congruent.
   c) Opposite angles are congruent.
   d) Consecutive angles are supplementary.
   e) Diagonals bisect each other.
   f) Each diagonal bisects the parallelogram into two congruent triangles.

3. In a rectangle, in addition to the properties listed in (2) above:
   a) All angles are right angles.
   b) Diagonals are congruent.

4. In a rhombus, in addition to the properties listed in (2) above:
   a) All sides are congruent.
   b) Diagonals are perpendicular.
   c) Diagonals bisect the angles.

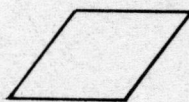

5. A square has *all* of the properties listed in (2), (3), and (4) above.

Circles

1. A circle has 360° of arc.
2. A central angle is equal in degrees to the measure of its intercepted arc.

If the measure of arc $AB = 80°$,
then $m\angle AOB = 80°$

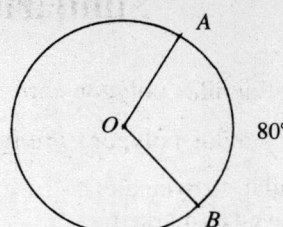

3. An inscribed angle is equal in degrees to one-half the measure of its intercepted arc.

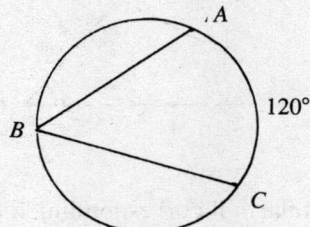

If the measure of arc $AC = 120°$,
then $m\angle ABC = 60°$

Volume

1. The volume of a rectangular solid is equal to the product of its length, width, and height.

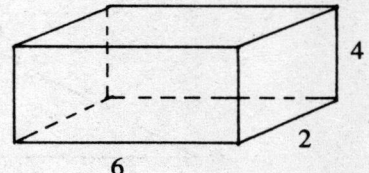

$V = lwh$
$V = (6)(2)(4) = 48$

2. The volume of a cube is equal to the cube of an edge.

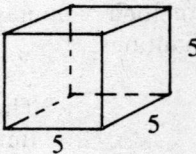

$V = e^3$
$V = (5)^3 = 125$

3. The volume of a cylinder is equal to π times the square of the radius of the base times the height.

$V = \pi r^2 h$
$V = \pi(3)^2(10) = 90\pi$

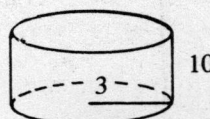

Similarity

1. Corresponding angles of similar polygons are equal.

2. Corresponding sides of similar polygons are in proportion.

   If triangle *ABC* is similar to triangle *DEF*, and the sides are given as marked, then $\overline{EF}$ must be equal to 6, as the ratio between corresponding sides is 4:8, or 1:2.

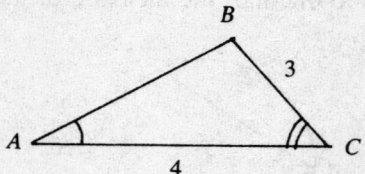
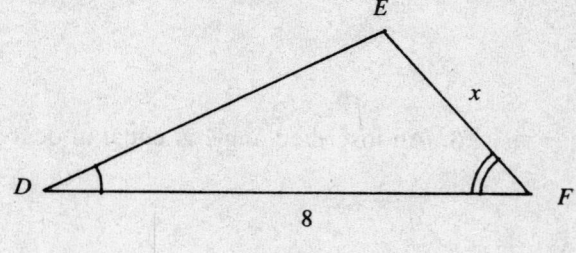

3. When figures are similar, all corresponding linear ratios are equal. The ratio of one side to its corresponding side is the same as perimeter to perimeter, apothem to apothem, altitude to altitude, etc.

4. When figures are similar, the ratio of their areas is equal to the square of the ratio between two corresponding linear quantities.

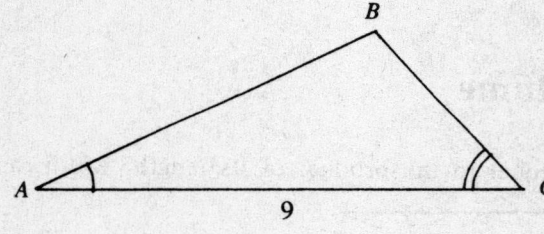

If triangle *ABC* is similar to triangle *DEF*, the area of triangle *ABC* will be 9 times as great as that of triangle *DEF*. The ratio of sides is 9:3 or 3:1. The ratio of areas will be the square of 3:1, giving 9:1.

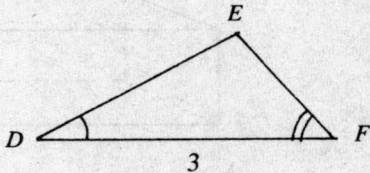

5. When figures are similar, the ratio of their volumes is equal to the cube of the ratio between two corresponding linear quantities.

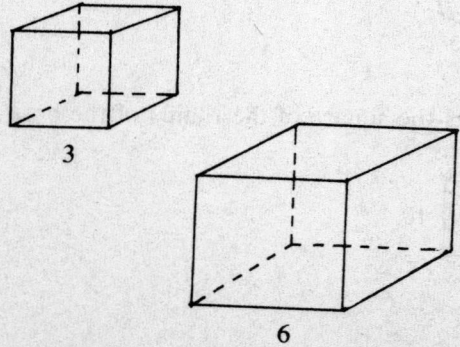

The volume of the larger cube is 8 times as large as the volume of the smaller cube. If the ratio of sides is 3:6, or 1:2, the ratio of volumes becomes the cube of this, or 1:8.

Practice Exercise Fifteen

DIRECTIONS: Work out the problem in the space provided. Circle the letter that appears before your answer.

1. If the angles of a triangle are in the ratio 2:3:7, the triangle is

   A. acute.
   B. isosceles.
   C. obtuse.
   D. right.
   E. equilateral.

2. If the area of a square of side x is 5, what is the area of a square of side $3x$?

   F. 15
   G. 45
   H. 95
   J. 75
   K. 225

3. If the radius of a circle is decreased by 10%, by what percent is its area decreased?

   A. 10
   B. 19
   C. 21
   D. 79
   E. 81

4. A spotlight is 5 feet from one wall of a room and 10 feet from the wall at right angles to it. How many feet is it from the intersection of the two walls?

   F. 15
   G. $5\sqrt{2}$
   H. $5\sqrt{5}$
   J. $10\sqrt{2}$
   K. $10\sqrt{5}$

5. A dam has the dimensions indicated in the figure. Find the area of this isosceles trapezoid.

   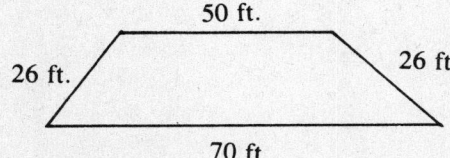

   A. 1300
   B. 1560
   C. 1400
   D. 1440
   E. Cannot be determined from information given

DO YOUR FIGURING HERE.

6. In parallelogram PQRS, angle P is four times angle Q. What is the measure in degrees of angle P?

   F. 36
   G. 72
   H. 125
   J. 144
   K. 150

7. If $\overline{PQ} = \overline{QS}$, $\overline{QR} = \overline{RS}$ and m∠PRS = 100°, what is the measure, in degrees, of angle QPS?

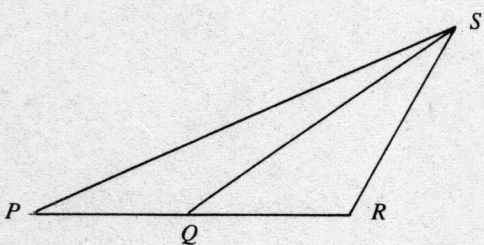

   A. 10
   B. 15
   C. 20
   D. 25
   E. 30

8. A line segment is drawn from the point (3,5) to the point (9,13). What are the coordinates of the midpoint of this line segment?

   F. (3,4)
   G. (12,18)
   H. (6,8)
   J. (9,6)
   K. (6,9)

9. A rectangular box with a square base contains 6 cubic feet. If the height of the box is 18 inches, how many feet are there in each side of the base?

   A. 1
   B. 2
   C. $\sqrt{3}$
   D. $\dfrac{\sqrt{3}}{3}$
   E. 4

10. The surface area of a cube is 150 square feet. How many cubic feet are there in the volume of the cube?

   F. 30
   G. 50
   H. 100
   J. 125
   K. 150

11. Peter lives 12 miles west of school and Bill lives north of the school. Peter finds that the direct distance from his house to Bill's is 6 miles shorter than the distance by way of school. How many miles north of the school does Bill live?

   A. 6
   B. 9
   C. 10
   D. $6\sqrt{2}$
   E. None of these

12. A square is inscribed in a circle of area 18π. Find a side of the square.

   F. 3
   G. 6
   H. $3\sqrt{2}$
   J. $6\sqrt{2}$
   K. cannot be determined from the information given

13. A carpet is y yards long and f feet wide. How many dollars will it cost if the carpet sells for x cents per square foot?

   A. xyf
   B. $3xyf$
   C. $\dfrac{xyf}{3}$
   D. $\dfrac{.03yf}{x}$
   E. $.03xyf$

14. If a triangle of base 6 has the same area as a circle of radius 6, what is the altitude of the triangle?

   F. 6π
   G. 8π
   H. 10π
   J. 12π
   K. 14π

DO YOUR FIGURING HERE.

168 / ACT

15. The vertex angle of an isosceles triangle is p degrees. How many degrees are there in one of the base angles?

   A. $180 - p$
   B. $90 - p$
   C. $180 - 2p$
   D. $180 - \dfrac{p}{2}$
   E. $90 - \dfrac{p}{2}$

16. In a circle with center O, arc $RS = 132$ degrees. How many degrees are there in $\angle RSO$?

   F. $66°$
   G. $20°$
   H. $22°$
   J. $24°$
   K. $48°$

17. The ice compartment of a refrigerator is 8 inches long, 4 inches wide, and 5 inches high. How many ice cubes will it hold if each cube is 2 inches on an edge?

   A. 8
   B. 10
   C. 12
   D. 16
   E. 20

18. In the figure, $\overline{PSQ}$ is a straight line and $\overline{RS}$ is perpendicular to $\overline{ST}$. If angle m$\angle RSQ = 48°$, how many degrees are there in angle PST?

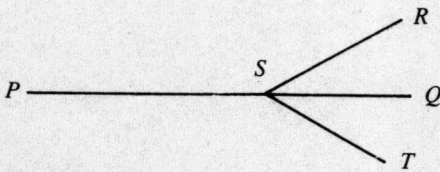

   F. $48°$
   G. $132°$
   H. $90°$
   J. $136°$
   K. $138°$

DO YOUR FIGURING HERE.

19. A cylindrical pail has a radius of 7 inches and a height of 9 inches. If there are 231 cubic inches to a gallon, approximately how many gallons will this pail hold?

   A. 6
   B. $\dfrac{12}{7}$
   C. 7.5
   D. 8.2
   E. 9

20. In triangle PQR, $\overline{QS}$ and $\overline{SR}$ are angle bisectors and m$\angle P = 80°$. How many degrees are there in angle QSR?

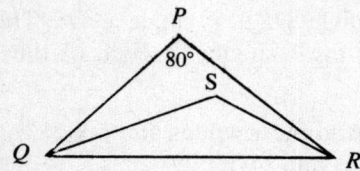

   F. 115°
   G. 120°
   H. 125°
   J. 130°
   K. 135°

DO YOUR FIGURING HERE.

Solutions to Practice Exercise Fifteen

1. **(C)** Represent the angles as $2x$, $3x$, and $7x$.
   $$2x + 3x + 7x = 180$$
   $$12x = 180$$
   $$x = 15$$
   The angles are 30°, 45°, and 105°. Since one angle is between 90° and 180°, the triangle is called an obtuse triangle.

2. **(G)** If the sides have a ratio 1:3, the areas have a ratio 1:9. Therefore, the area of the large square is 9(5), or 45.

3. **(B)** If the radii have a ratio of 10:9, the areas have a ratio of 100:81. Therefore, the decrease is 19 out of 100, or 19%.

4. **(H)**

   $$5^2 + 10^2 = x^2$$
   $$25 + 100 = x^2$$
   $$x^2 = 125$$
   $$x = \sqrt{125} = \sqrt{25}\sqrt{5} = 5\sqrt{5}$$

5. **(D)**

   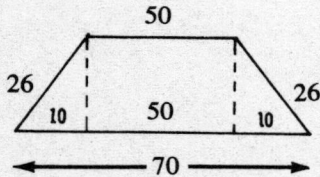

   When altitudes are drawn from both ends of the upper base in an isosceles trapezoid, the figure is divided into a rectangle and two congruent right triangles. The center section of the lower base is equal to the upper base, and the remainder of the lower base is divided equally between both ends. The altitude can then be found using the Pythagorean theorem. In this case, we have a 5,12,13 triangle with all measures doubled, so the altitude is 24.

   The area is $\frac{1}{2}(24)(120)$, or 1440.

6. **(J)** The consecutive angles of a parallelogram are supplementary, so $x + 4x = 180$
   $$5x = 180$$
   $$x = 36$$
   Angle P is 4(36), or 144°.

7. **(C)**

   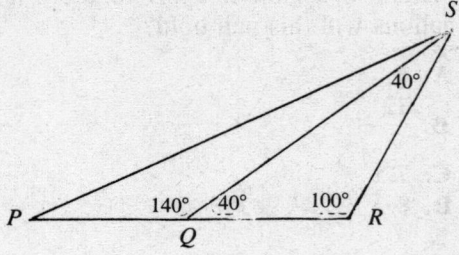

   Since $\overline{QR} = \overline{RS}$, angle RQS = angle RSQ. There are 80° left in the triangle, so each of these angles is 40°. Angle SQP is supplementary to angle SQR, making it 140°. Since $\overline{QP} = \overline{QS}$, angle QPS = angle QSP. There are 40° left in the triangle, so each of these angles is 20°.

8. **(K)** Add the x values and divide by 2. Add the y values and divide by 2.

9. **(B)** Change 18 inches to 1.5 feet. Letting each side of the base be x, the volume is $1.5x^2$.
   $$1.5x^2 = 6$$
   $$15x^2 = 60$$
   $$x^2 = 4$$
   $$x = 2$$

10. **(J)** The surface area of a cube is made up of 6 equal squares. If each edge of the cube is x, then,
    $$6x^2 = 150$$
    $$x^2 = 25$$
    $$x = 5$$
    Volume = (edge)^3 = 5^3 = 125

11. **(B)**

    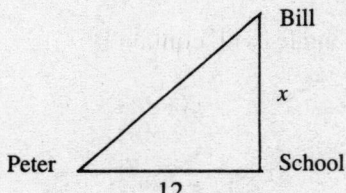

    The direct distance from Peter's house to Bill's can be represented by means of the Pythagorean theorem as $\sqrt{144 + x^2}$. Then
    $$\sqrt{144 + x^2} = (12 + x) - 6$$
    $$\sqrt{144 + x^2} = x + 6$$
    Square both sides.
    $$144 + x^2 = x^2 + 12x + 36$$
    $$144 = 12x + 36$$
    $$108 = 12x$$
    $$9 = x$$

12. (G)

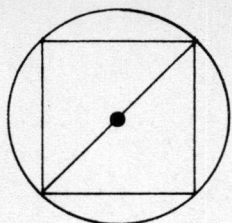

The diagonal of the square will be a diameter of the circle.
$\pi r^2 = 18\pi$
$r^2 = 18$
$r = \sqrt{18} = \sqrt{9}\sqrt{2} = 3\sqrt{2}$
Then the diameter is $6\sqrt{2}$ and, since the triangles are $45° - 45° - 90°$, a side of the square is 6.

13. (E) We want the area in square feet, so change y yards to $3y$ feet. The area is then $(3y)(f)$, or $3yf$ square feet. If each square foot costs x cents, we change this to dollars by dividing x by 100. Thus, each square foot costs $\dfrac{x}{100}$ dollars. The cost of $3yf$ square feet will be $(3yf)\left(\dfrac{x}{100}\right)$, or $\dfrac{3xyf}{100}$.

Since $\dfrac{3}{100} = .03$, the correct answer is (E).

14. (J) The area of the circle is $\pi(6)^2$, or 36π.
In the triangle $\dfrac{1}{2}(6)(h) = 36\pi$
$3h = 36\pi$
$h = 12\pi$

15. (E) There are $(180 - p)$ degrees left, which must be divided between 2 congruent angles. Each angle will contain $\dfrac{180 - p}{2}$ or $90 - \dfrac{p}{2}$ degrees.

16. (J)

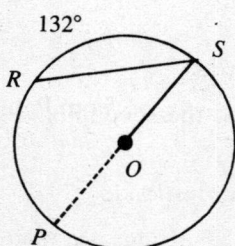

By extending $\overline{SO}$ until it hits the circle at P, arc PRS is a semicircle. Therefore, arc $PR = 48°$, and the measure of inscribed angle $RSO = 24°$.

17. (D)

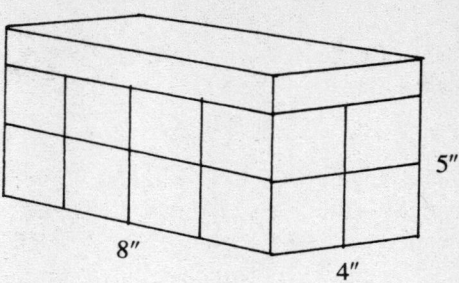

To fill the bottom layer, we can fit two rows of 4 cubes each. We can fit another layer above this, leaving a height of 1 inch on top empty. Therefore, the compartment can hold 16 cubes.

18. (K)

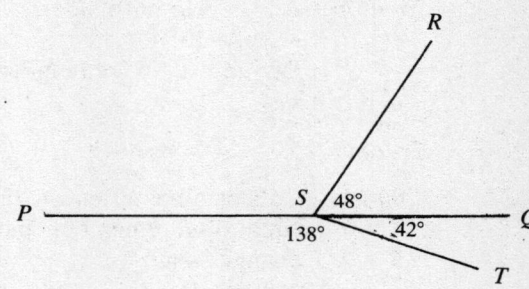

Since $\angle RST$ is a right angle, $42°$ are left for $\angle QST$. Since PSQ is a straight angle of $180°$, $\angle PST$ contains $138°$.

19. (A) The volume of the pail is found using the formula $V = \pi r^2 h$. Since our answers are not in terms of π, it is best to use $\dfrac{22}{7}$ as a value for π, since the 7 will cancel with r^2, $V = \dfrac{22}{7} \cdot 49 \cdot 9$. Rather than multiply this out, which will take unnecessary time, we divide by 231 and cancel wherever possible.
$$\dfrac{\overset{2}{\cancel{22}} \cdot \cancel{7} \cdot \overset{3}{\cancel{9}}}{\underset{\underset{3}{\cancel{33}}}{\cancel{231}}} = 6$$

20. (J) If $\angle P = 80°$, there are $100°$ left between angles PQR and PRQ. If they are both bisected, there will be $50°$ between angles SQR and SRQ, leaving $130°$ in triangle SRQ for angle QSR.

INEQUALITIES

In solving algebraic inequality statements, we solve them as we would an equation. However, we must remember that whenever we multiply or divide by a negative number, the order of the inequality, that is, the inequality symbol, must be reversed.

Example: Solve for x: $3 - 5x > 18$

Solution: Add -3 to both sides:
$-5x > 15$
Divide by -5, remembering to reverse the inequality:
$x < -3$

Example: $5x - 4 > 6x - 6$

Solution: Collect all x terms on the left and numerical terms on the right. As with equations, remember that if a term crosses the inequality symbol, the term changes sign.
$-x > -2$
Divide (or multiply) by -1:
$x < 2$

In working with geometric inequalities, certain postulates and theorems should be reviewed. The list follows.

1. If unequal quantities are added to unequal quantities of the same order, the result is unequal quantities in the same order.

2. If equal quantities are added to, or subtracted from, unequal quantities, the results are unequal in the same order.

3. If unequal quantities are subtracted from equal quantities, the results are unequal in the opposite order.

4. Doubles, or halves, of unequals are unequal in the same order.

5. If the first of three quantities is greater than the second, and the second is greater than the third, then the first is greater than the third.

6. The sum of two sides of a triangle must be greater than the third side.

7. If two sides of a triangle are unequal, the angles opposite these sides are unequal, with the larger angle opposite the larger side.

8. If two angles of a triangle are unequal, the sides opposite these angles are unequal, with the larger side opposite the larger angle.

9. An exterior angle of a triangle is greater than either remote interior angle.

Inequalities / 173

Example:

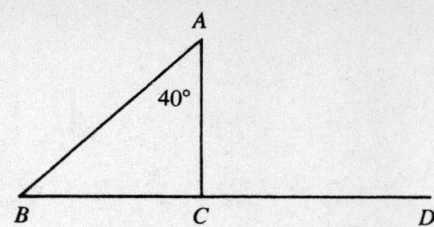

If $\overline{BCD}$ is a straight line and $\angle A = 40°$, then angle ACD contains
(A) 40°
(B) 140°
(C) less than 40°
(D) more than 40°
(E) 100°

Solution: The correct answer is (D), since an exterior angle of a triangle is always greater than either of the remote interior angles.

Example:

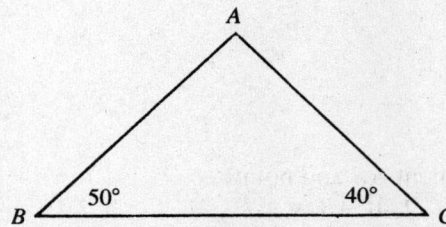

Which of the following statements is true regarding the above triangle?
(A) $\overline{AB} > \overline{AC}$
(B) $\overline{AC} > \overline{BC}$
(C) $\overline{AB} > \overline{BC}$
(D) $\overline{AC} > \overline{AB}$
(E) $\overline{BC} > \overline{AB} + \overline{AC}$

Solution: The correct answer is (D), since a comparison between two sides of a triangle depends upon the angles opposite these sides. The larger side is always opposite the larger angle. Since angle A contains 90°, the largest side of this triangle is BC, followed by AC and then AB.

Practice Exercise Sixteen

DIRECTIONS: Work out the problem in the space provided. Circle the letter that appears before your answer.

1. If $x < y$, $2x = A$, and $2y = B$, then

   A. $A = B$
   B. $A < B$
   C. $A > B$
   D. $A < x$
   E. $B < y$

DO YOUR FIGURING HERE.

2. If $a > b$ and $c > d$, then

   F. $a = c$
   G. $a < d$
   H. $a + d = b + c$
   J. $a + c < b + d$
   K. $a + c > b + d$

3. If $ab > 0$ and $a < 0$, which of the following is negative?

   A. b
   B. $-b$
   C. $-a$
   D. $(a - b)^2$
   E. $-(a + b)$

4. If $4 - x > 5$, then

   F. $x > 1$
   G. $x > -1$
   H. $x < 1$
   J. $x < -1$
   K. $x = -1$

5. Point X is located on line segment $\overline{AB}$ and point Y is located on line segment $\overline{CD}$. If $\overline{AB} = \overline{CD}$ and $\overline{AX} > \overline{CY}$, then

   A. $\overline{XB} > \overline{YD}$
   B. $\overline{XB} < \overline{YD}$
   C. $\overline{AX} > \overline{XB}$
   D. $\overline{AX} < \overline{XB}$
   E. $\overline{AX} > \overline{AB}$

6. In triangle ABC, $\overline{AB} = \overline{BC}$. D is any point on side $\overline{AB}$. Which of the following statements is always true?

   F. $\overline{AD} < \overline{DC}$
   G. $\overline{AD} = \overline{DC}$
   H. $\overline{AD} > \overline{DC}$
   J. $\overline{AD} \leq \overline{DC}$
   K. $\overline{AD} \geq \overline{DC}$

DO YOUR FIGURING HERE.

7. In the diagram at the right,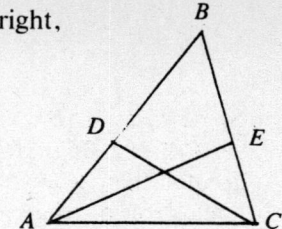
   $\overline{BD} = \overline{BE}$ and $\overline{DA} > \overline{EC}$. Then

   A. $\overline{AE} > \overline{DC}$
   B. $\angle BCA > \angle BAC$
   C. $\angle DCA > \angle EAC$
   D. $\overline{AB} < \overline{BC}$
   E. $\overline{AD} < \overline{BD}$

8. In the diagram at the right, which of the following is always true?
   I. $a > b$
   II. $c > a$
   III. $d > a$

   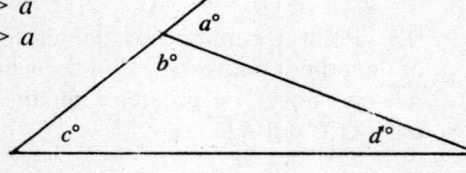

   F. I only
   G. II and III only
   H. I, II, and III
   J. II only
   K. None of these

9. If point X is on line segment $\overline{AB}$, all of the following may be true except

   A. $\overline{AX} = \overline{XB}$
   B. $\overline{AX} > \overline{XB}$
   C. $\overline{AX} < \overline{XB}$
   D. $\overline{AB} > \overline{XB}$
   E. $\overline{AX} + \overline{XB} < \overline{AB}$

10. If $x > 0$, $y > 0$, and $x - y < 0$, then

    F. $x > y$
    G. $x < y$
    H. $x + y < 0$
    J. $y - x < 0$
    K. $x = -y$

Solutions to Practice Exercise Sixteen

1. **(B)** Doubles of unequals are unequal in the same order.

2. **(K)** If unequal quantities are added to unequal quantities of the same order, the results are unequal in the same order.

3. **(A)** If the product of two numbers is > 0 (positive), then either both numbers are positive or both are negative. Since $a < 0$ (negative), b must also be negative.

4. **(J)** $4 - x > 5$
   $-x > 1$
   Divide by -1. Change inequality sign.
   $x < -1$

5. **(B)**

   If unequal quantities are subtracted from equal quantities, the results are unequal in the opposite order.

6. **(F)** Since $\overline{AB} = \overline{BC}$, $\angle BAC = \angle BCA$. Since $\angle BCA > \angle DCA$, it follows that $\angle BAC$ is also greater than $\angle DCA$. Then $\overline{DC} > \overline{DA}$. If two angles of a triangle are unequal, the sides opposite these angles are unequal, with the larger side opposite the larger angle.

7. **(B)** $\overline{BA} > \overline{BC}$. If equal quantities are added to unequal quantities, the sums are unequal in the same order. It follows in triangle ABC, that the angle opposite $\overline{BA}$ will be greater than the angle opposite $\overline{BC}$.

8. **(K)** An exterior angle of a triangle must be greater than either remote interior angle. There is no fixed relationship between an exterior angle and its adjacent interior angle.

9. **(E)** Point X could be so located to make each of the other choices true, but the whole segment $\overline{AB}$ can never be greater than the sum of its parts $\overline{AX}$ and $\overline{XB}$.

10. **(G)** If x and y are both positive, but $x - y$ is negative, then y must be a larger number than x.

SEQUENCES AND LOGIC

Sequences

A **sequence** is a list of numbers based on a certain pattern. There are three main types of sequences.

If each term in a sequence is being increased or diminished by the same number to form the next term, then it is an **arithmetic sequence**. The number being added or subtracted is called the **common difference**.

Examples: 2, 4, 6, 8, 10 . . . is an arithmetic sequence in which the common difference is 2.

14, 11, 8, 5, 2 . . . is an arithmetic sequence in which the common difference is -3.

If each term of a sequence is being multiplied by the same number to form the next term, then it is a **geometric sequence**. The number multiplying each term is called the **common ratio**.

Examples: 2, 6, 18, 54 . . . is a geometric sequence in which the common ratio is 3.

64, 16, 4, 1 . . . is a geometric sequence in which the common ratio is $\frac{1}{4}$.

If the sequence is neither arithmetic nor geometric, it is a **miscellaneous sequence**. Such a sequence may have each term a square or a cube, or the difference may be squares or cubes; or there may be a varied pattern in the sequence that must be determined.

A sequence may be ascending, that is, the numbers increase; or descending, that is, the numbers decrease.

To determine whether the sequence is arithmetic:

Subtract the first term from the second, and the second term from the third, etc. If the difference is the same in each case, the sequence is arithmetic.

To determine whether a sequence is geometric:

Divide the second term by the first, and the third term by the second, etc.. If the ratio is the same in each case, the sequence is geometric.

To find a missing term in an arithmetic sequence:

1. Subtract any term from the one following it to find the common difference.
2. Add the common difference to the term preceding the missing term.
3. If the missing term is the first term, it may be found by subtracting the common difference from the second term.

Example: What number follows $16\frac{1}{3}$ in this sequence:

$$3, \quad 6\frac{1}{3}, \quad 9\frac{2}{3}, \quad 13, \quad 16\frac{1}{3} \ldots$$

Solution: $6\frac{1}{3} - 3 = 3\frac{1}{3}, \; 9\frac{2}{3} - 6\frac{1}{3} = 3\frac{1}{3}$

The sequence is arithmetic; the common difference is $3\frac{1}{3}$.

$$16\frac{1}{3} + 3\frac{1}{3} = 19\frac{2}{3}$$

Answer: The missing term, which is the term following $16\frac{1}{3}$, is $19\frac{2}{3}$.

Example: Find the first term in the sequence:

$$\underline{\quad}, \; 16, \; 13\frac{1}{2}, \; 11, \; 8\frac{1}{2}, \; 6 \ldots$$

Solution: $13\frac{1}{2} - 16 = -2\frac{1}{2}, \quad 11 - 13\frac{1}{2} = -2\frac{1}{2}$

The sequence is arithmetic; the common difference is $-2\frac{1}{2}$.

$$16 - \left(-2\frac{1}{2}\right) = 16 + 2\frac{1}{2} = 18\frac{1}{2}$$

Answer: The term preceding 16 is $18\frac{1}{2}$.

To find a missing term in a geometric sequence:

1. Divide any term by the one preceding it to find the common ratio.
2. Multiply the term preceding the missing term by the common ratio.
3. If the missing term is the first term, it may be found by dividing the second term by the common ratio.

Example: Find the missing term in the sequence:
2, 6, 18, 54, ___

Solution: $6 \div 2 = 3, \; 18 \div 6 = 3$
The sequence is geometric; the common ratio is 3.
$54 \times 3 = 162$

Answer: The missing term is 162.

Example: Find the missing term in the sequence:
___, 32, 16, 8, 4, 2

Solution: $16 \div 32 = \frac{1}{2}$ (common ratio)

$$32 \div \frac{1}{2} = 32 \times \frac{2}{1}$$
$$= 64$$

Answer: The first term is 64.

If, after trial, a sequence is neither arithmetic nor geometric, it must be one of a miscellaneous type. Test to see whether it is a sequence of squares or cubes or whether the difference is the square or the cube of the same number; or the same number may be first squared, then cubed, etc.

Logic

This section briefly discusses the relationship of a statement to its inverse, converse, and contrapositive.

Given a statement such as: "If it is blue, then it is heavy," we can define the following:

Name	Illustration
Converse (reverse, backwards)	Statement $p \rightarrow q$: If it is blue, then it is heavy. Converse $q \rightarrow p$: If it is heavy, then it is blue.
Inverse*	Statement $p \rightarrow q$: If it is blue, then it is heavy. Inverse $\sim p \rightarrow \sim q$: If it is **not** blue, then it is **not** heavy.
Contrapositive (Inverse of the converse) or (converse of the inverse)	Statement $p \rightarrow q$: If it is blue, then it is heavy. Contrapositive $\sim q \rightarrow \sim p$: If it is not heavy, then it is not blue.

*The inverse is obtained by negating the hypothesis and negating the conclusion.

A statement and its contrapositive always have the same truth value. The inverse and converse of a statement always have the same truth value as each other (they are contrapositives) but not necessarily the same truth value as the original statement. Two sentences that always have the same truth value are called **logically equivalent.**

Example: What is the inverse of: "If it rains, then the sun doesn't shine."

Solution: "If it does not rain, then the sun shines."

Practice Exercise Seventeen

DIRECTIONS: Find the missing term in each of the following sequences:

1. ___, 7, 10, 13

2. 5, 10, 20, ___, 80

3. 49, 45, 41, ___, 33, 29

4. 1.002, 1.004, 1.006, ___

5. 1, 4, 9, 16, ___

DO YOUR FIGURING HERE.

6. 10, $7\frac{7}{8}$, $5\frac{3}{4}$, $3\frac{5}{8}$, ___

7. ___, 3, $4\frac{1}{2}$, $6\frac{3}{4}$

8. 55, 40, 28, 19, 13, ___

9. 9, 3, 1, $\frac{1}{3}$, $\frac{1}{9}$, ___

10. 1, 3, 7, 15, 31, ___

11. Which of the following is the converse of the statement: "If it is red, then it is not blue"?

    A. If it is not blue, then it is not red.
    B. If it is not red, then it is blue.
    C. If it is not blue, then it is red.
    D. If it is not red, then it is not blue.
    E. If it is blue, then it is not red.

12. Which is logically equivalent to the statement: "If I live, then I love"?

    F. If I don't live, then I don't love.
    G. If I love, then I live.
    H. If I don't love, then I don't live.
    J. If I don't love, then I live.
    K. If I don't live, then I love.

DO YOUR FIGURING HERE.

Solutions to Practice Exercise Seventeen

1. This is an ascending arithmetic sequence in which the common difference is $10 - 7$, or 3. The first term is $7 - 3 = 4$.

2. This is a geometric sequence in which the common ratio is $10 \div 5$, or 2. The missing term is $20 \times 2 = 40$.

3. This is a descending arithmetic sequence in which the common difference is $45 - 49$, or -4. The missing term is $41 - 4 = 37$.

4. This is an ascending arithmetic sequence in which the common difference is $1.004 - 1.002$, or .002. The missing term is $1.006 + .002 = 1.008$.

5. This sequence is neither arithmetic nor geometric. However, if the numbers are rewritten as 1^2, 2^2, 3^2, and 4^2, it is clear that the next number must be 5^2, or 25.

6. This is a descending arithmetic sequence in which the common difference is $7\frac{7}{8} - 10 = -2\frac{1}{8}$. The missing term is $3\frac{5}{8} - 2\frac{1}{8} = 1\frac{4}{8}$, or $1\frac{1}{2}$.

7. This is a geometric sequence in which the common ratio is:
$$4\frac{1}{2} \div 3 = \frac{9}{2} \times \frac{1}{3}$$
$$= \frac{3}{2}$$
The first term is $3 \div \frac{3}{2} = 3 \times \frac{2}{3}$
$$= 2$$
Therefore, the missing term is 2.

8. There is no common difference and no common ratio in this sequence. However, note the differences between terms:

$$55 \underset{\substack{15 \\ 5 \times 3}}{\frown} 40 \underset{\substack{12 \\ 4 \times 3}}{\frown} 28 \underset{\substack{9 \\ 3 \times 3}}{\frown} 19 \underset{\substack{6 \\ 2 \times 3}}{\frown} 13$$

The differences are multiples of 3. Following the same pattern, the difference between 13 and the next term must be 1×3, or 3. The missing term is then $13 - 3 = 10$.

9. This is a geometric sequence in which the common ratio is $3 \div 9 = \frac{1}{3}$. The missing term is $\frac{1}{9} \times \frac{1}{3} = \frac{1}{27}$.

10. This sequence is neither arithmetic nor geometric. However, note the difference between terms:

$$1 \underset{\substack{2 \\ 2^1}}{\frown} 3 \underset{\substack{4 \\ 2^2}}{\frown} 7 \underset{\substack{8 \\ 2^3}}{\frown} 15 \underset{\substack{16 \\ 2^4}}{\frown} 31$$

The difference between 31 and the next term must be 2^5, or 32. The missing term is $31 + 32 = 63$.

11. (C) The converse of a statement reverses the hypothesis and conclusion.
Statement: If it is red, then it is not blue.
Converse: If it is not blue, then it is red.

12. (H) The contrapositive of a statement is always logically equivalent to the statement.
Statement: If I live, then I love.
Contrapositive: If I don't love, then I don't live.

TRIGONOMETRY

The three basic trigonometric functions—**sine**, **cosine**, and **tangent**—can be viewed in relationship to a right triangle.

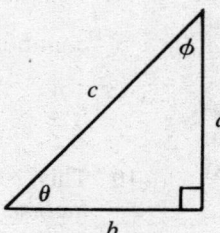

NOTE: The side **opposite** is the side **opposite** the referenced angle.
The side **adjacent** is the side **next to** the referenced angle, but not the hypotenuse.
The **hypotenuse** is the side opposite the right angle.

Trigonometric Function	Abbreviation and Definition (see triangle above)
sine	$\sin \theta = \dfrac{\text{side opposite angle } \theta}{\text{hypotenuse}} = \dfrac{a}{c}$
cosine	$\cos \theta = \dfrac{\text{side adjacent to angle } \theta}{\text{hypotenuse}} = \dfrac{b}{c}$
tangent	$\tan \theta = \dfrac{\text{side opposite angle } \theta}{\text{side adjacent to angle } \theta} = \dfrac{a}{b}$

Example: Using the right triangle below, express the value of sin A, cos A, tan A, sin B, cos B, tan B

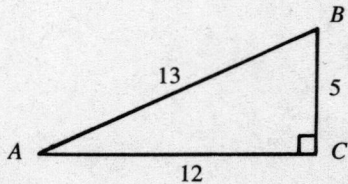

Solution: $\sin A = \dfrac{\text{side opposite angle } A}{\text{hypotenuse}} = \dfrac{5}{13}$

$\cos A = \dfrac{\text{side adjacent to angle } A}{\text{hypotenuse}} = \dfrac{12}{13}$

$\tan A = \dfrac{\text{side opposite angle } A}{\text{side adjacent to angle } A} = \dfrac{5}{12}$

$\sin B = \dfrac{\text{side opposite angle } B}{\text{hypotenuse}} = \dfrac{12}{13}$

$\cos B = \dfrac{\text{side adjacent to angle } B}{\text{hypotenuse}} = \dfrac{5}{13}$

$\tan B = \dfrac{\text{side opposite angle } B}{\text{side adjacent to angle } B} = \dfrac{12}{5}$

Some useful trigonometric relationships are:

$\tan x = \dfrac{\sin x}{\cos x}$	$\dfrac{\cos x}{\sin x} = \dfrac{1}{\tan x}$	$\sin^2 x + \cos^2 x = 1$
$\sin^2 x = 1 - \cos^2 x$		$\cos^2 x = 1 - \sin^2 x$

Example: If $\sin x = \dfrac{5}{13}$ and $\cos x = \dfrac{12}{13}$, what is the value of $\tan x$?

Solution: $\tan x = \dfrac{\sin x}{\cos x} = \dfrac{\frac{5}{13}}{\frac{12}{13}} = \dfrac{5}{12}$

Example: If $\sin 30° = \dfrac{1}{2}$, what is the value of $\tan 30°$?

Solution: First construct a right triangle whose $\sin 30° = \dfrac{1}{2}$.

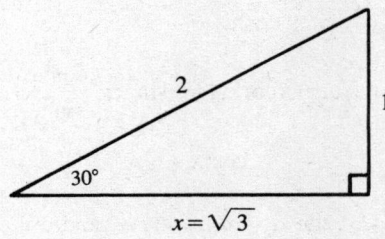

Find the value of the third side of the triangle using the Pythagorean theorem.

$x^2 + 1^2 = 2^2$
$x^2 + 1 = 4$
$x^2 = 3$
$x = \sqrt{3}$

$\tan 30° = \dfrac{\text{side opposite 30° angle}}{\text{side adjacent to 30° angle}} = \dfrac{1}{\sqrt{3}}$ or $\dfrac{\sqrt{3}}{3}$

Example: What is the value of $\sin^2 4x + \cos^2 4x$?

Solution: $\sin^2 x + \cos^2 x = 1$ indicates that for the same angle x, the value of $\sin^2 x$ added to the value of $\cos^2 x$ equals 1.

$\sin^2 4x + \cos^2 4x$ is exactly the correct form. It represents the square of the sine of the angle (in this case, $4x$) added to the square of the cosine of the angle.

$\therefore \sin^2 4x + \cos^2 4x = 1$

Cotangent, Secant, and Cosecant

Trigonometric Function	Abbreviation and Definition
cotangent	$\cot \theta = \dfrac{1}{\tan \theta} = \dfrac{\text{side adjacent to angle } \theta}{\text{side opposite angle } \theta}$
secant	$\sec \theta = \dfrac{1}{\cos \theta} = \dfrac{\text{hypotenuse}}{\text{side adjacent to angle } \theta}$
cosecant	$\csc \theta = \dfrac{1}{\sin \theta} = \dfrac{\text{hypotenuse}}{\text{side opposite angle } \theta}$

The three new trigonometric functions—cot, sec, and csc—are the reciprocals of tan, cos, and sin, respectively.

Some additional trigonometric relationships are:

$(\sin \theta)(\csc \theta) = 1$	$(\cos \theta)(\sec \theta) = 1$	$(\tan \theta)(\cot \theta) = 1$

$$\cot \theta = \frac{\cos \theta}{\sin \theta}$$

Example: Simplify $(\sin^2 x)(\cot^2 x) + (\sec^2 x)(\cot^2 x)$

Solution: $\cot^2 x = \dfrac{\cos^2 x}{\sin^2 x}$, $\sec^2 x = \dfrac{1}{\cos^2 x}$

$\therefore \quad (\sin^2 x)(\cot^2 x) + (\sec^2 x)(\cot^2 x) = (\sin^2 x)\left(\dfrac{\cos^2 x}{\sin^2 x}\right) + \left(\dfrac{1}{\cos^2 x}\right)\left(\dfrac{\cos^2 x}{\sin^2 x}\right)$

$= \cos^2 x + \csc^2 x$

Example: Find $\sin \alpha$, $\cos \alpha$, $\tan \alpha$, $\cot \alpha$, $\sec \alpha$, and $\csc \alpha$.

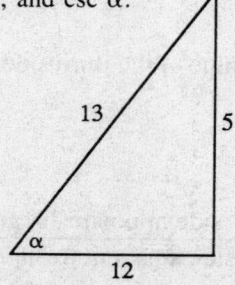

Trigonometry / 185

Solution: $\sin \alpha = \dfrac{opp}{hyp} = \dfrac{5}{13}$ $\csc \alpha = \dfrac{1}{\sin \alpha} = \dfrac{13}{5}$

$\cos \alpha = \dfrac{adj}{hyp} = \dfrac{12}{13}$ $\sec \alpha = \dfrac{1}{\cos \alpha} = \dfrac{13}{12}$

$\tan \alpha = \dfrac{opp}{adj} = \dfrac{5}{12}$ $\cot \alpha = \dfrac{1}{\tan \alpha} = \dfrac{12}{5}$

Practice Exercise Eighteen

DIRECTIONS: Work out the problems in the space provided. Circle the letter that appears before your answer.

1. In the figure below, what is the value of $\sin B$?

    A. $\dfrac{24}{7}$

    B. $\dfrac{7}{24}$

    (C.) $\dfrac{7}{25}$

    D. $\dfrac{24}{25}$

    E. $\dfrac{25}{24}$

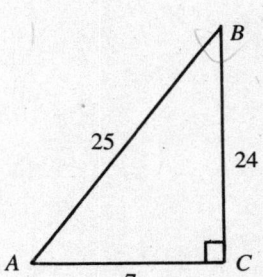

DO YOUR FIGURING HERE.

sin = opp / hyp.

2. In the figure below $\triangle LMN$ has its right angle at M. If $\tan L = \dfrac{4}{3}$, what is the value of $\sin N$?

    (F.) $\dfrac{3}{5}$

    G. $\dfrac{4}{5}$

    H. $\dfrac{3}{4}$

    J. $\dfrac{4}{3}$

    K. $\dfrac{5}{3}$

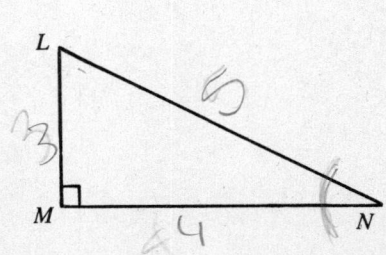

186 / ACT

3. If $\sin x = \frac{5}{7}$, which of the following could be the value of $\cot x$?

   A. $\frac{\sqrt{6}}{7}$
   B. $\frac{2\sqrt{6}}{7}$
   C. $\frac{5}{7}$
   D. $\frac{5\sqrt{6}}{12}$
   E. $\frac{2\sqrt{6}}{5}$

4. If $\sin 60° = \frac{\sqrt{3}}{2}$, what is the value of $\sin^2 30 + \cos^2 30$?

   F. $\frac{\sqrt{3} + 1}{2}$
   G. $\sqrt{5}$
   H. $\frac{\sqrt{5}}{2}$
   J. $\frac{3}{4}$
   K. 1

5. What is the value of $2\sin^2 3x + 2\cos^2 3x$?

   A. 1
   B. 2
   C. 3
   D. 4
   E. 9

6. In triangle NJL, angle J is the right angle. If $\sin N = \frac{2}{3}$, what is the value of $\cos N$?

   F. $\frac{1}{3}$
   G. $\frac{8}{9}$
   H. $\frac{3\sqrt{5}}{5}$
   J. $\frac{\sqrt{5}}{2}$
   K. $\frac{\sqrt{5}}{3}$

DO YOUR FIGURING HERE.

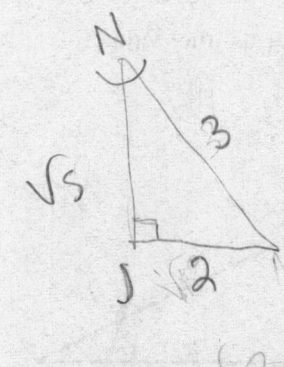

7. In the figure below, sin x is $\frac{3}{5}$. What is the length of $\overline{BC}$?

   A. 3
   B. 6
   C. 8
   D. 9
   E. $\frac{4}{5}$

   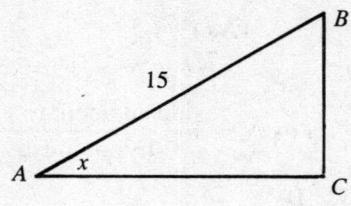

8. Simplify $(1 - \sin x)(1 + \sin x)$

   F. sin x
   G. $\cos^2 x$
   H. tan x
   J. 1
   K. $\sin^2 x$

9. In right triangle RST, S is the right angle. If $\sin R = \frac{1}{4}$, what is the value of tan T?

   A. 4
   B. $\sqrt{15}$
   C. 1
   D. $\frac{4\sqrt{15}}{15}$
   E. $\frac{\sqrt{15}}{16}$

10. $\frac{\cos x \tan x}{\sin x} = ?$

    F. sin x
    G. cos x
    H. tan x
    J. sin x cos x
    K. 1

Solutions to Practice Exercise Eighteen

1. **(C)** $\sin B = \dfrac{\text{side opposite } \angle B}{\text{hypotenuse}} = \dfrac{7}{25}$

2. **(F)** $\tan L = \dfrac{\text{side opposite } \angle L}{\text{side adjacent to } \angle L} = \dfrac{4}{3}$

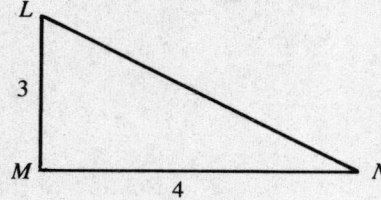

$(\overline{LN})^2 = 3^2 + 4^2$
$\overline{LN} = 5$
$\sin N = \dfrac{\text{side opposite } \angle N}{\text{hypotenuse}} = \dfrac{3}{5}$

3. **(E)** Construct a right triangle whose $\sin x = \dfrac{5}{7}$.

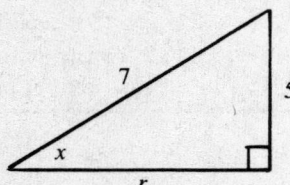

Calculate the third side of the triangle using the Pythagorean theorem.
$r^2 + 5^2 = 7^2$
$r^2 + 25 = 49$
$r^2 = 24$
$r = \sqrt{24} = \sqrt{4}\sqrt{6} = 2\sqrt{6}$

$\cot x = \dfrac{1}{\tan x} = \dfrac{1}{\frac{5}{2\sqrt{6}}} = \dfrac{2\sqrt{6}}{5}$

4. **(K)** $\sin^2 x + \cos^2 x = 1$ regardless of the value of $\angle x$.

5. **(B)** $2\sin^2 3x + 2\cos^2 3x = 2[\sin^2 3x + \cos^2 3x]$
$= 2(1)$
$= 2$

6. **(K)**

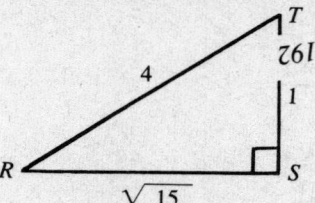

$(\overline{NJ})^2 + 2^2 = 3^2$
$(\overline{NJ})^2 + 4 = 9$
$(\overline{NJ})^2 = 5$
$\overline{NJ} = \sqrt{5}$

$\cos N = \dfrac{\text{side adjacent to } \angle N}{\text{hypotenuse}} = \dfrac{\sqrt{5}}{3}$

7. **(D)**

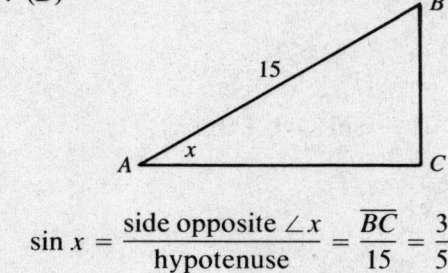

$\sin x = \dfrac{\text{side opposite } \angle x}{\text{hypotenuse}} = \dfrac{\overline{BC}}{15} = \dfrac{3}{5}$
$5(\overline{BC}) = 45$
$\overline{BC} = 9$

8. **(G)**
$(1 - \sin x)(1 + \sin x) =$
$1 + \sin x - \sin x - \sin^2 x = 1 - \sin^2 x$

Rearranging the identity:
$\sin^2 x + \cos^2 x = 1$
$\cos^2 x = 1 - \sin^2 x$

9. **(B)** Construct right triangle RST with $\sin R = \dfrac{1}{4}$.

Calculate the length of the third side of the triangle using the Pythagorean Theorem.
$t^2 + 1^2 = 4^2$
$t^2 + 1 = 16$
$t^2 = 15$
$t = \sqrt{15}$

$\tan T = \dfrac{\text{side opposite } \angle T}{\text{side adjacent to } \angle T} = \dfrac{\sqrt{15}}{1} = \sqrt{15}$

10. **(K)** substitute:

$\dfrac{\cos x \tan x}{\sin x} = \dfrac{(\cos x)\left(\dfrac{\sin x}{\cos x}\right)}{\sin x} = \dfrac{\sin x}{\sin x} = 1$

DISCRIMINANT

If a quadratic equation is written in the form $ax^2 + bx + c = 0$, the nature of the roots and a description of the graph can be determined from the **discriminant**.

$$\text{discriminant} = b^2 - 4ac$$

Nature of the Roots

	\multicolumn{4}{c}{Value of the discriminant}
	negative "−"	**zero** "0"	**positive, perfect square** i.e., 1, 4, 9, 16, 25 ...	**positive, not a perfect square** i.e., 2, 3, 5, 11, 17, 18 ...
NATURE of the Roots	imaginary	real equal rational	real unequal rational	real unequal irrational
Graph	Either totally above or below the x-axis	Tangent to the x-axis	Intersects the x-axis in 2 distinct pts.	Intersects the x-axis in 2 distinct pts.

Example: Describe the nature of the roots for the equation $2x^2 + 3x - 4 = 0$.

Solution: discriminant $= b^2 - 4ac = (3)^2 - 4(2)(-4) = 9 + 32 = 41$.
Since 41 is positive and not a perfect square, the roots are:
real
unequal
irrational

Practice Exercise Nineteen

1. Which of the following best describes the graph of $2x^2 + 3x + 2 = 0$?

   A. Intersects the x-axis in more than 2 points
   B. Intersects the x-axis at exactly 2 places
   C. Is tangent to the x-axis
   D. Is either totally above or below the x-axis
   E. Is a straight line

2. Which best describes the nature of the roots of the equation $x^2 - 3x + 4 = 0$?

   F. real and equal
   G. real and unequal
   H. imaginary
   J. real and irrational
   K. rational and equal

3. Which best describes the nature of the roots of the equation $x^2 + 4x - 3 = 0$?

   A. real and equal
   B. real and unequal
   C. imaginary
   D. real and rational
   E. equal and irrational

4. If the graph of a quadratic equation is tangent to the x-axis, which of the following best describes the nature of the roots?

   F. imaginary
   G. zero
   H. equal
   J. unequal
   K. irrational

DO YOUR FIGURING HERE.

Solutions to Practice Exercise Nineteen

1. **(D)** discriminant $= b^2 - 4ac = (3)^2 - 4(2)(2) = 9 - 16 = -7$. Since the discriminant is negative, the graph is either totally above or below the x-axis.

2. **(H)** discriminant $= b^2 - 4ac = (-3)^2 - 4(1)(4) = 9 - 16 = -7$. Since the discriminant is negative, the roots are imaginary.

3. **(B)** discriminant $= b^2 - 4ac = (4)^2 - 4(1)(-3) = 16 + 12 = 28$. Since the discriminant is positive and not a perfect square, the roots are real, unequal, and irrational.

4. **(H)** If the graph is tangent to the x-axis, the discriminant $= 0$; therefore the roots are: real, equal, and rational.

CONIC SECTIONS

This section describes the four basic types of conic sections: **parabola, circle, ellipse,** and **hyperbola.**

Parabola

The graph and equation of a typical parabola are represented below.

$$y = ax^2 + bx + c$$

The roots are the *x*-values where the curve intersects the *x*-axis. They are the values of *x* that make the quadratic equation equal to zero.

The axis of symmetry is the line that symmetrically divides the curve in half. The equation of the axis of symmetry is:

$$x = \frac{-b}{2a}$$

The sum of the two roots is: **Sum** $= \dfrac{-b}{a}$

The product of the two roots is: **Product** $= \dfrac{c}{a}$

If the roots cannot be determined by factoring, the roots can always be found using the quadratic formula.

$$\text{roots} = \frac{-b \pm \sqrt{b^2 - 4ac}}{2a}$$

Example: Given the quadratic equation $y = 3x^2 - x - 4$
 a. Find the equation of the axis of symmetry.
 b. Find the sum of the roots.
 c. Find the product of the roots.
 d. Find the values of the roots by factoring and by the quadratic formula.

Solution: For the given equation $a = 3,\quad b = -1,\quad c = -4$

a. $x = \dfrac{-b}{2a} = \dfrac{-(-1)}{2(3)} = \dfrac{1}{6} \quad \rightarrow \quad x = \dfrac{1}{6}$

b. $\text{Sum} = \dfrac{-b}{a} = \dfrac{-(-1)}{3} = \dfrac{1}{3}$

c. $\text{Product} = \dfrac{c}{a} = \dfrac{-4}{3}$

d. by factoring: $3x^2 - x - 4 = 0$
$(3x - 4)(x + 1) = 0$
$3x - 4 = 0 \quad | \quad x + 1 = 0$
$x = \dfrac{4}{3} \quad | \quad x = -1$

by quadratic formula: $x = \dfrac{-b \pm \sqrt{b^2 - 4ac}}{2a}$

$= \dfrac{-(-1) \pm \sqrt{(-1)^2 - 4(3)(-4)}}{2(3)} = \dfrac{1 \pm \sqrt{1 + 48}}{6} = \dfrac{1 \pm \sqrt{49}}{6} = \dfrac{1 \pm 7}{6}$

$x = \dfrac{1 + 7}{6} = \dfrac{8}{6} = \dfrac{4}{3} \qquad x = \dfrac{1 - 7}{6} = \dfrac{-6}{6} = -1$

Circle

The graph and equation of a circle with its center at the origin and with radius r are represented below.

$$x^2 + y^2 = r^2$$

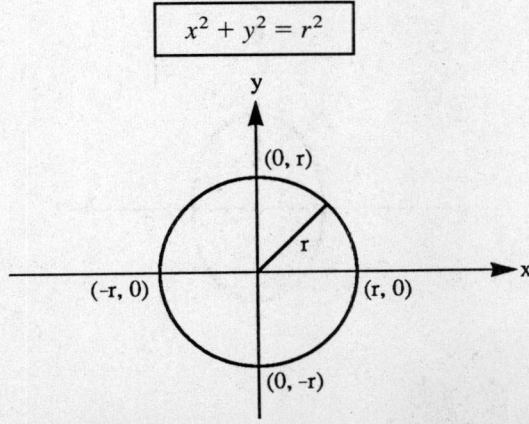

Example: What is the area of the circle with the equation $\frac{x^2}{9} + \frac{y^2}{9} = 1$?

Solution: First rearrange the equation into standard form:

$$x^2 + y^2 = 9$$

This represents a circle with center at (0,0) and radius = 3.

$$A = \pi r^2 = \pi(3)^2 = 9\pi$$

Ellipse

The ellipse is "oval" in shape and has one of two forms depending on whether the major (longer) axis is parallel to the *x*-axis or to the *y*-axis.

The graphs and equations of a typical ellipse with center at the origin and major axis on the *x*-axis or *y*-axis are represented below.

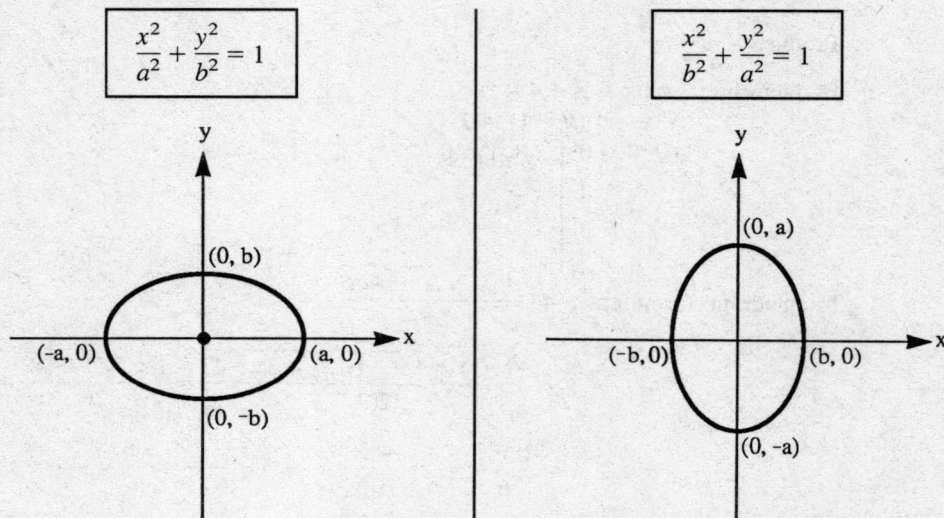

In the figures above, *a* is the distance from the center (origin) to the vertex on the major (longer) axis and *b* is the distance from the center to the vertex on the minor (shorter) axis. If *a* = *b*, the ellipse becomes a circle.

Example: In the figure below, what is the equation of the graphed ellipse?

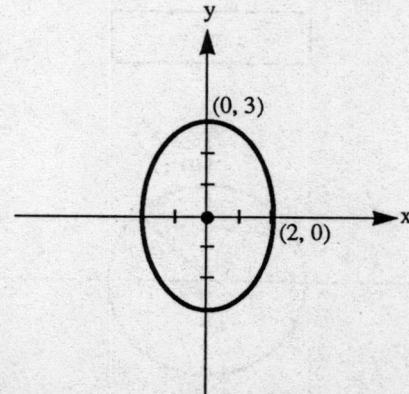

Solution: A vertical ellipse has an equation of the form $\dfrac{x^2}{b^2} + \dfrac{y^2}{a^2} = 1$

a = distance from center to major axis vertex = 3
b = distance from center to minor axis vertex = 2

$$\frac{x^2}{2^2} + \frac{y^2}{3^2} = 1 \quad \rightarrow \quad \frac{x^2}{4} + \frac{y^2}{9} = 1$$

Hyperbola

The equations and graphs below represent the more common forms of a hyperbola centered at the origin.

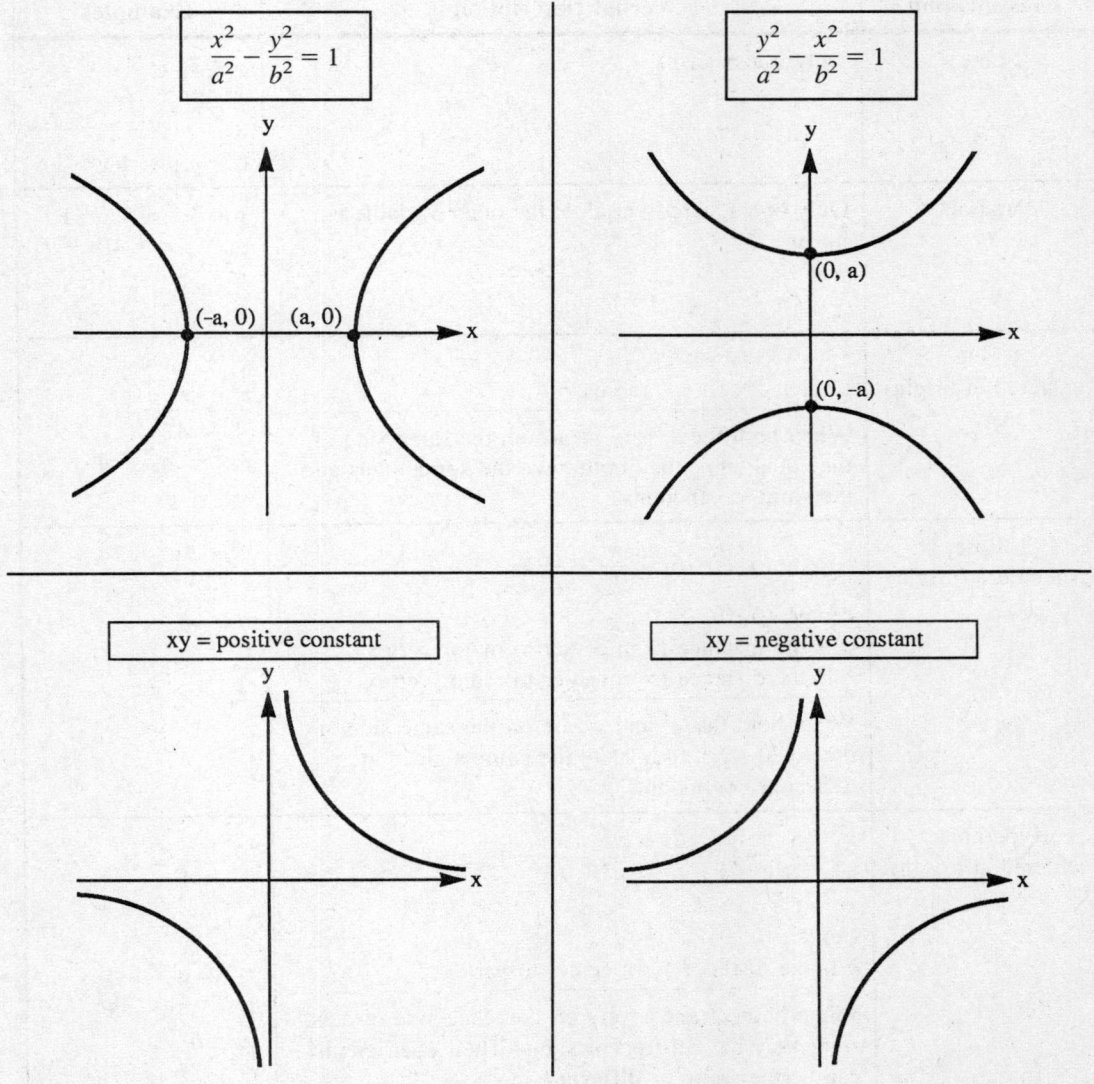

In the figures above, a is the distance from the center to the vertex of either branch of the hyperbola. The value a^2 is always the denominator of the positive term. The positive term, either x^2 or y^2, is determined by the axis intersected by the hyperbola.

Example: Through which quadrants does the graph of $xy = 7$ pass?

Solution: $xy = 7$ is an example of a hyperbola, i.e.: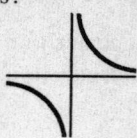

It passes through the first and third quadrants only.

Summary

Classification	Verbal Description	Examples
Line	Only linear terms	$y = 2x + 3$ $\frac{x}{3} + \frac{y}{2} = 1$ $(y - 3) = 4(x - 1)$
Parabola	Only one squared variable; the other variable is linear	$y = 3x^2 + 4x - 1$ $(y - 3)^2 = 4(x - 7)$ $\frac{x^2}{2} + \frac{y}{3} = 7$
Circle (centered at origin)	$x^2 + y^2 = r^2$ Center: (0, 0) radius = r When both the x^2 and y^2 are on the same side of the equal sign, they both have the **same** signs and the **same** coefficients.	$x^2 + y^2 = 9$ $\frac{x^2}{4} + \frac{y^2}{4} = 1$ $3x^2 + 3y^2 = 6$
Ellipse (centered at origin)	$\frac{x^2}{a^2} + \frac{y^2}{b^2} = 1$ or $\frac{x^2}{b^2} + \frac{y^2}{a^2} = 1$ center: (0, 0) a is the distance from center to major vertex b is the distance from center to minor vertex When both the x^2 and y^2 are on the same side of the equal sign, they have the **same** signs and **different** coefficients.	$x^2 + 3y^2 = 7$ $\frac{x^2}{9} + \frac{y^2}{4} = 1$ $\frac{x^2}{3} + y^2 = 4$
Hyperbola (centered at origin)	$\frac{x^2}{a^2} - \frac{y^2}{b^2} = 1$ or $\frac{y^2}{a^2} - \frac{x^2}{b^2} = 1$ $xy = c$ Center: (0, 0) a is the distance from center to vertex When both x^2 and y^2 are on the same side of equal sign, they have **different** signs. Their coefficients can be the **same** or **different**.	$\frac{x^2}{3} - \frac{y^2}{4} = 1$ $\frac{x^2}{3} - \frac{y^2}{3} = 1$ $3x^2 - 4y^2 = 1$ $4x^2 - 4y^2 = 1$ $xy = 6$ $xy = {}^-6$

Practice Exercise Twenty

1. Which of the following is not the equation of a circle?

   A. $x^2 + y^2 = 10$
   B. $x^2 = 15 - y^2$
   C. $y^2 = 15 - x^2$
   D. $y^2 = 15 + x^2$
   E. $\dfrac{x^2}{7} + \dfrac{y^2}{7} = 3$

2. What is the equation of the hyperbola graphed below?

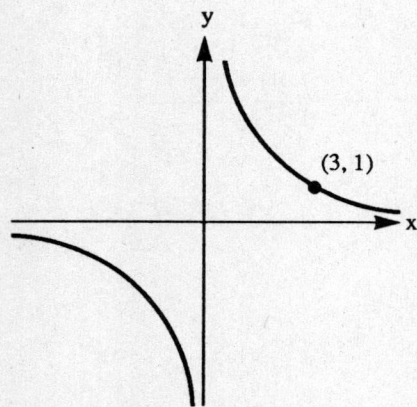

   F. $\dfrac{x^2}{3} + \dfrac{y^2}{1} = 1$
   G. $\dfrac{x^2}{9} + \dfrac{y^2}{1} = 1$
   H. $xy = 3$
   J. $xy = -3$
   K. $3x^2 + y^2 = 1$

3. What is the equation of a circle with center (0, 0) that passes through the point (3, 4)?

   A. $3x^2 + 4y^2 = 1$
   B. $\dfrac{x^2}{9} + \dfrac{y^2}{16} = 1$
   C. $xy = 12$
   D. $x^2 + y^2 = 25$
   E. $x^2 + y^2 = 5$

4. What is the equation of the ellipse graphed below?

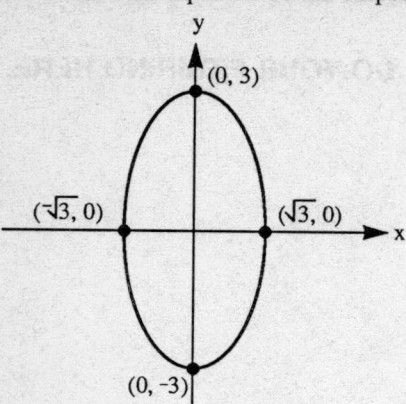

F. $9x^2 + 3y^2 = 1$
G. $3x^2 + 9y^2 = 1$
H. $\dfrac{x^2}{9} + \dfrac{y^2}{3} = 1$
J. $\dfrac{x^2}{3} + \dfrac{y^2}{9} = 1$
K. $27x^2 + 27y^2 = 1$

5. If the roots of a quadratic equation are 6 and -3, what is the equation of its axis of symmetry?

A. $x = 2$
B. $x = -2$
C. $x = \dfrac{1}{2}$
D. $x = 1$
E. $x = \dfrac{3}{2}$

6. What is the equation of the parabola graphed below?

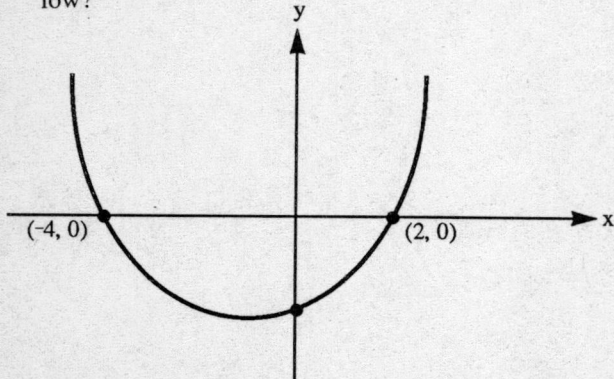

F. $y = x^2 - 4x + 2$
G. $y = x^2 + 2x - 8$
H. $y = x^2 - 2x + 8$
J. $y = x^2 + 2x - 4$
K. $y = x^2 + 3x - 5$

Solutions to Practice Exercise Twenty

1. **(D)** When both the x^2 and y^2 are on the same side of the equal sign, it is a circle if they have the same signs and the same coefficients. Choice **(D)** becomes:
   $y^2 - x^2 = 15$.

2. **(H)** The hyperbola is of the form $xy = $ constant. If we substitute $x = 3$ and $y = 1$ from the point $(3, 1)$, we obtain
   $$xy = c$$
   $$3(1) = c$$
   $$c = 3$$
   $$\therefore xy = 3$$

3. **(D)** The radius is the distance from $(0, 0)$ to $(3, 4)$.
   $d = \sqrt{(3-0)^2 + (4-0)^2} = \sqrt{25} = 5$
   $x^2 + y^2 = r^2$
   $x^2 + y^2 = (5)^2 = 25$

4. **(J)** The ellipse is of the form $\dfrac{x^2}{b^2} + \dfrac{y^2}{a^2} = 1$.
   $a = 3$, $b = \sqrt{3}$
   $\dfrac{x^2}{(\sqrt{3})^2} + \dfrac{y^2}{3^2} = 1 \quad \rightarrow \quad \dfrac{x^2}{3} + \dfrac{y^2}{9} = 1$

5. **(E)** Roots are: 6 and -3
   Factors are: $(x - 6)(x + 3)$
   Equation is: $y = x^2 - 3x - 18$
   Axis of symmetry is: $x = \dfrac{-b}{2a} = \dfrac{-(-3)}{2(1)} = \dfrac{3}{2}$

6. **(G)** Roots are: -4 and 2
   Factors are: $(x + 4)(x - 2)$
   Equation is: $y = x^2 + 2x - 8$

Part V

READING REVIEW

READING

The ACT contains one 35-minute section that measures reading comprehension. The test includes four passages with ten questions based on each passage. The questions deal with information *stated* or *implied* in the passage, not on the student's general knowledge. The types of passages in the Reading Test encompass literary, historical, artistic, musical, architectural, theatrical, fictional, sociological, psychological, anthropological, and scientific topics. They are categorized as social sciences, natural sciences, prose fiction, and humanities.

You should answer every question presented. If you allow 2 to 3 minutes to read each passage and about 35 seconds for each question, you will complete the test with a minute or two left to recheck your work.

Three scores are reported for the ACT Reading Test: a total score based on all 40 items and two subscores as indicated in the chart below.

Text Type	Number of Questions	Subscore
Prose Fiction	10	Arts/Literature
Humanities	10	
Social Sciences	10	Social Studies/ Sciences
Natural Sciences	10	

Approaching the ACT Reading Test

STEP 1   First read the questions.

- Get an idea of what is being asked about the passage.
- *Underline* significant words or phrases in the question.
- *Do not* read the answer choices at this point; it is not necessary.

STEP 2   Read the passage once.

- Bear in mind the questions you have read.
- *Underline* significant words or phrases in the passage.

204 / ACT

STEP 3 Answer the questions.

- *Look back* to the passage to justify your answer.
- Use a *process of elimination*. Cross off the wrong answers. This will ensure that you read each choice.

STEP 4 Answer every question.

- Since wrong answers and omitted answers are counted equally, it is to your advantage to answer everything.

Practice Reading Passages

DIRECTIONS: There are eleven practice passages given. Each passage is followed by a number of questions. After reading a passage, select the most appropriate answer to each question. You may refer to the passages as you work as often as you feel necessary. Use the 4-Step Approach to maximize your correct answers!

Passage 1

There is evidence that the usual variety of high blood pressure is, in part, a familial disease. Since families have similar genes as well as similar environments, familial diseases could be due to shared genetic influences, to shared environmental factors, or to both. For some years, the role of one environmental factor commonly shared by families, namely dietary salt (i.e., sodium chloride), has been studied at Brookhaven National Laboratory. These studies suggest that chronic excess salt ingestion can lead to high blood pressure in man and animals. Some individuals, however, and some rats consume large amounts of salt without developing high blood pressure. No matter how strictly all environmental factors were controlled in these experiments, some salt-fed animals never developed hypertension whereas a few rapidly developed very severe hypertension followed by early death. These marked variations were interpreted to result from differences in genetic constitution.

By mating in successive generations only those animals that failed to develop hypertension from salt ingestion, a resistant strain (the "R" strain) has been evolved in which consumption of large quantities of salt fails to influence the blood pressure significantly. In contrast, by mating only animals that quickly develop hypertension from salt, a sensitive strain ("S" strain) has also been developed.

The availability of these two strains permits investigations not heretofore possible. They provide a plausible laboratory model on which to investigate some clinical aspects of the human prototypes of hypertension. More important, there might be the possibility of developing methods by which genetic susceptibility of human beings to high blood pressure can be defined without waiting for its appearance. Radioactive sodium 22 was an important "tool" in working out the characteristics of the sodium chloride metabolism.

1. Which of the statements best relates the main idea of this article?

   A. When salt is added to their diets, rats and human beings react in much the same way.
   B. The near future will see a cure for high blood pressure.
   C. The medical field is desperately in need of research.
   D. A tendency toward high blood pressure may be a hereditary factor.

2. The study of the effects of salt on high blood pressure was carried out

   F. because members of the same family tend to use similar amounts of salt.
   G. to explore the long-term use of a sodium-based substance.
   H. because it was proven that salt caused high blood pressure.
   J. because of the availability of chemically pure salt and its derivatives.

3. It can be implied that the main difference between "S" and "R" rats is their

   A. need for sodium 22.
   B. rate of mating.
   C. reaction to salt.
   D. type of blood.

4. The reader can infer from the article that sodium 22 can be used to

F. cure high blood pressure caused by salt.
G. tell the "S" rats from the "R" rats.
H. determine what a sodium chloride metabolism is like.
J. control high blood pressure.

5. Among the results of the research discussed in this article, the most beneficial might be

A. the early identification of potential high blood pressure victims.
B. development of diets free of salt.
C. an early cure for high blood pressure.
D. control of genetic agents that cause high blood pressure.

Passage 2

Inertial guidance is the name given to those types of systems which guide and keep track of the location of vehicles that are free to move in three dimensions. Vehicles which move only on a plane surface, such as ships or automobiles, require only an accurate compass, sextant, and clock to keep track of their present position. When a vehicle can travel up or down as well as north or east, it is much more difficult to fix its position. An inertial platform is used in inertial guidance to measure vehicle altitude and acceleration which are then integrated to provide position and velocity. The inertial platform consists of three gyroscopes and three accelerometers mounted in the inner gimbal of the four-gimbal platform. The purpose of the inertial platform is to allow the vehicle to move in any direction about the inner gimbal containing the gyros and accelerometers, without disturbing or turning them from their original orientation. Thus the gyros and accelerometers do not turn when the vehicle turns so they sense altitude and acceleration with respect to their original inertial reference frame. If the acceleration is always known with respect to this original inertial reference frame, it can be integrated to provide velocity and then integrated again to provide distance. Thus the distance and velocity of the vehicle with respect to its starting point are known.

Inertial guidance systems are used today in airplanes, submarines, and spacecraft. They display for the pilot his pitch, roll and yaw angles, his heading, his speed, and his latitude and longitude. These are very important items to have readily available, whether one is in a high-speed vehicle with very low visibility due to poor weather, or in a spacecraft travelling in lunar orbit. The main features of inertial systems are that they are automatic and do not require any external information. Thus, the pilot does not have to feed in any information except the original position and altitude. Inertial systems serve a need on fast-moving vehicles moving in a three-dimensional plane, where position information is required by the pilot almost constantly.

6. It can be inferred from the article that an inertial guidance system is similar to

F. a gyroscope.
G. a high-speed vehicle.
H. a navigator.
J. an accelerometer.

7. According to the selection, the basic concern of the inertial guidance system is

A. space in three dimensions.
B. poor visibility and meteorological conditions.
C. the altitude and position of a vehicle.
D. spacecraft productivity.

8. The inertial platform is mainly used to

F. prevent the ship or plane from moving off course.
G. send information from the ground control unit.
H. relay information from the pilot.
J. prevent a change in the system's orientation.

9. This article would probably appeal to

A. the general public.
B. readers interested in space navigation.
C. psychologists of the behaviorist school.
D. chemists and biologists.

Passage 3

When school was out, I hurried to find my sister and get out of the schoolyard before seeing anybody in my class. But Barbara and her friends had beaten us to the playground entrance and they seemed to be waiting for us. Barbara said, "So now you're in the A class." She sounded impressed.

"What's the A class?" I asked.

Everybody made superior yet faintly envious giggling sounds. "Well, why did you think the teacher moved you to the front of the room, dopey? Didn't you know you were in the C class before, way in the back of the room?"

Of course I hadn't known. The Wenatchee fifth grade was bigger than my whole school had been in North Dakota, and the idea of subdivisions within a grade had never occurred to me. The subdividing for the first marking period had been done before I came to the school, and I had never, in the six weeks I'd been there, talked to anyone long enough to find out about the A, B, and C classes.

I still could not understand why that had made such a difference to Barbara and her friends. I didn't yet know that it was disgraceful and dirty to be a transient laborer and ridiculous to be from North Dakota. I thought living in a tent was more fun than living in a house. I didn't know that we were gypsies, really (how that thought would have thrilled me then!), and that we were regarded with the suspicion felt by those who plant toward those who do not plant. It didn't occur to me that we were all looked upon as one more of the untrustworthy natural phenomena, drifting here and there like mists or winds, that farmers of certain crops are resentfully forced to rely on. I didn't know that I was the only child who had camped on the Baumann's land ever to get out of the C class. I did not know that school administrators and civic leaders held conferences to talk about the problem of transient laborers.

I only knew that for two happy days I walked to school with Barbara and her friends, played hopscotch and jump rope with them at recess, and was even invited into the house for some ginger ale—an exotic drink I had never tasted before.

10. The tone of this passage as a whole is

   F. reflective.
   G. disparaging.
   H. impersonal.
   J. defensive.

11. This passage as a whole is presented from the point of view of

   A. an understanding teacher.
   B. a younger sister.
   C. a mature adult.
   D. a helpful parent.

12. The narrator had most probably been placed in the C class because

   F. she was a poor reader.
   G. she had come from a small school.
   H. the marking system confused her.
   J. all migrant children were placed in the C class.

13. The basic reason the people in the community distrusted the transient workers was that the transient workers

   A. tended to be lawbreakers.
   B. had little schooling.
   C. were afraid of strangers.
   D. were temporary residents.

14. After the narrator was moved to the A class, what was the attitude of Barbara and Barbara's friends towards her?

   F. Dislike
   G. Acceptance
   H. Apology
   J. Jealousy

15. In the fifth paragraph, the underlying theme is that of

   A. intolerance.
   B. patriotism.
   C. greed.
   D. envy.

16. In the fifth paragraph, the author tries to achieve a desired effect through the use of

   F. rhetorical questions.
   G. repetition.
   H. literary allusions.
   J. quotations.

17. The phrase "untrustworthy natural phenomena" in lines 30–31 is used to describe the

   I. gypsies' tents.
   II. farmers' crops.
   III. transient workers.

   A. I only
   B. I and II
   C. III only
   D. I, II, and III

18. In line 41, the word "exotic" most nearly means

   F. strange.
   G. strong.
   H. delicious.
   J. sparkling.

Passage 4

The others, who have avoided all of these deaths, get up in the morning and go downtown to meet "the man." They work in the white man's world all day and come home in the evening to this fetid block. They struggle to instill in their children some private sense of honor or dignity that will help the children to survive. This means, of course, that they must struggle, stolidly, incessantly, to keep this sense alive in themselves, in spite of the insults, the indifference, and the cruelty they are certain to encounter in their working day. They patiently browbeat the landlord into fixing the heat, the plaster, the plumbing; this demands prodigious patience; nor is patience usually enough. In trying to make their hovels habitable, they are perpetually throwing good money after bad. Such frustration, so long endured, is driving many strong admirable men and women, whose only crime is color, to the very gates of paranoia.

19. Which phrase best expresses the main ideas of this passage?

    A. The working day
    B. The nonwhite environment
    C. The white employers
    D. The hope of the world

20. Which one word best describes the ideas of this passage?

    F. Hope
    G. Work
    H. Survival
    J. Prayer

21. In maintaining his house, a nonwhite encounters

    A. resistance by the city council.
    B. careless neighbors.
    C. impatient relatives.
    D. indifferent landlords.

22. According to the passage, an important problem for the nonwhite is to

    F. maintain his identity.
    G. provide for his burial.
    H. send his children to school.
    J. change the white man's conception of him.

23. In this passage the nonwhite is shown to be

    A. patriotic.
    B. persistent.
    C. indifferent.
    D. uncommitted.

24. In the last sentence, which word is used in an *ironic* sense?

    F. Frustration
    G. Paranoia
    H. Admirable
    J. Crime

25. The paragraph preceding this one most probably dealt with

    A. white employers.
    B. Puerto Ricans versus blacks.
    C. the urban nonwhite.
    D. police and fire protection.

Passage 5

Next to his towering masterpiece, *Moby Dick*, *Billy Budd* is Melville's greatest work. It has the tone of a last testament, and the manuscript was neatly tied up by his wife, Elizabeth, and kept in a trunk for some thirty years. It was not until 1924 that it was first published. Slowly it has become recognized as the remarkable work it is. *Billy Budd* has been dramatized for Broadway, done on T.V., made into an opera, and reached a highly satisfying form in Ustinov's movie.

Scholars disagree, somewhat violently, about what Melville was trying to say. He did make it pretty clear that he was recounting a duel between Good and Evil.

Several times he remarked that Billy Budd is as innocent and ignorant as Adam before the fall. His enemy is like Satan in Milton's *Paradise Lost*.

When Billy Budd destroys the letter, and is sentenced to be hanged according to the letter of the law, controversy exists as to whether the Captain is simply a mortal man preserving order, or a Jehovah-like figure, dispensing cruel justice.

Melville, it is claimed, cleverly took pains to hide his heretical feelings. *Billy Budd* is written as if told by a pious, God-loving man.

Ironically, Melville's iconoclasm has largely misfired, for the story today is accepted as either one of simple suspense or a reverent parable of God,

Satan, and Adam. Meanwhile the scholars are still arguing, and *Billy Budd* remains like a porcupine, thorny, with interesting ambiguities.

26. The phrase that best expresses the ideas of this passage is

    F. a controversial work.
    G. the dramatization of *Billy Budd*.
    H. life's ambiguities.
    J. the Captain's revenge.

27. Regarding *Billy Budd*, critics seem to disagree about the book's

    A. plot.
    B. theme.
    C. mood.
    D. setting.

28. As used in this passage, the word "recounting" (paragraph 2) most nearly means

    F. adding up.
    G. adding again.
    H. figuring.
    J. telling.

29. The passage suggests that the character Billy Budd was

    A. Satanic.
    B. ambiguous.
    C. naive.
    D. brutal.

30. The author's purpose in writing this passage seems to be to

    F. point out aspects of *Billy Budd*.
    G. show that *Billy Budd* is well written.
    H. defend Melville against his critics.
    J. defend Melville's iconoclasm.

31. The passage indicates that the Captain

    A. disobeyed the law.
    B. was responsible for discipline.
    C. treated his crew very badly.
    D. disliked Billy intensely.

32. Certain lines in this passage suggest that Melville was

    F. Jehovah-like.
    G. childishly naive.
    H. very scholarly.
    J. rather shrewd.

Passage 6

We still have, in short, all the weapons in the arsenal of satire: the rapier of wit, the broadsword of invective, the stiletto of parody, the Damoclean swords of sarcasm and irony. Their cutting edges are bright and sharp; they glisten with barbs guaranteed to stick and stay stuck in the thickest hide, or stab the most inflated Polonius in the arras. Yet though they hang well-oiled and ready to our hands, we tend to use them separately and gingerly. We are afraid of hurting someone's feelings or of being hurt in a return bout. We tremble at the prospect of treading on someone's corns. We are too full of the milquetoast of human kindness. We always see the Other Side of the Case, always remember that our Victim may have a Mom who loves him, always fear that we may be setting him back a few hundred hours in his psychiatric progress toward the Terrestrial City of Perfect Readjustment. Oh, yes. We poke and pry a bit. We pin an errant butterfly to a board or two. But for real lessons in the ungentlest of the arts we must turn back to the older masters.

33. What title best expresses the main idea of the passage?

    A. Idle Weapons
    B. The Well-Adjusted Person
    C. Writing and Psychiatry
    D. Lessons and Past Masters

34. According to the passage, we avoid using satire because we

    F. are afraid of it.
    G. do not understand it.
    H. feel inferior to the older masters.
    J. are not inquisitive.

35. As used in the passage, the word "gingerly" most nearly means

    A. insincerely.
    B. effectively.
    C. clumsily.
    D. carefully.

36. Which device does the author *not* use in the passage?

   F. Literary allusions
   G. Metaphor
   H. Anecdotes
   J. Sarcasm

37. The passage suggests that modern man chiefly aspires to

   A. a sense of security.
   B. a feeling of aggressiveness.
   C. material wealth.
   D. freedom from hunger.

38. The tone of the latter part of the passage is one of

   F. outraged dignity.
   G. quiet irony.
   H. grudging distrust.
   J. calm resignation.

39. The passage suggests that Polonius was

   A. sensitive.
   B. religious.
   C. tough.
   D. egotistical.

40. The passage suggests that "invective" is

   F. thin.
   G. obvious.
   H. gentle.
   J. careless.

41. In this passage the author seems concerned that we

   A. do not have certain weapons available to us.
   B. pin butterflies to boards.
   C. are too considerate of our fellow man.
   D. do not appreciate art.

42. The "ungentlest of arts" is

   F. satire.
   G. sarcasm.
   H. wit.
   J. parody.

Passage 7

It would be difficult today to name as many as a dozen practicing essayists in this country; a half dozen would be nearer to the mark. We have article writers, novelists, poets by the thousands, but only a handful of professional
5 writers devoted to one of the oldest of literary forms, and still, potentially at least, one of the most delightful and rewarding to read. From the time of Montaigne, who fathered it, the essay has had its roots in personality; the day may not be too far distant when articles can be pro-
10 duced by supermachines, and, indeed, many of them already have that flavor, for the article need be little more than a marshalling of facts, fortified perhaps by the forging of an argument for or against what the facts present. But the essay is the product of a ruminative mind, and its
15 value depends not upon the weight of the facts assembled (it may not assemble any), but upon the character and quality of that mind—its perceptiveness, its attitudes, its sharpness, its imagination. It can take off from the most trivial incident or observation and end in the empyrean.
20 Why has the essay fallen into disrepute? Most magazine editors think that the essay is an outmoded form, that it has no place in our world. Of facts we have a surfeit, and we have not yet digested those of which we are already in possession. Our need is not so much for the acquisition of
25 more, as for reflection upon those we have; not so much for arguments based upon as for meditations on what they suggest and what they mean. For modern man, the acquisition of facts is like a habit-forming drug; the more he takes, the more he craves. Like the drug, they eventually
30 bog him down. There are few periodicals left in which an essay can find publication, though there is an abundant market for factual pieces and for critical analyses, which command higher prices. Yet neither is comparable to a first-rate essay. Still, writers, like butchers, must pay
35 their bills.

43. The title below that best expresses the main ideas of this passage is

   F. "The Faults of the Essay."
   G. "The Status of the Essay."
   H. "More Fact than Fiction."
   J. "Characteristics of the Essay."

44. The tone of the passage suggests that the author has a feeling of

   A. optimism.
   B. regret.
   C. anger.
   D. pride.

45. The essay is declining, the author believes, because

    I. man is becoming less of a thinker.
    II. man is becoming too idea-conscious.
    III. society is becoming too impersonal.

    F. I only
    G. I and II
    H. I, II, and III
    J. II only

46. The passage suggests that modern man has a passion to

    A. write.
    B. dream.
    C. succeed.
    D. consume.

47. The author regards many contemporary articles as being

    F. logical.
    G. tasteless.
    H. artful.
    J. literary.

48. As used in line 14, the word "ruminative" most nearly means

    A. acquistive.
    B. fact-conscious.
    C. scientific.
    D. thoughtful.

Passage 8

. . . It was the voyageur who captured my imagination—he who carried the tremendous loads, paddled from dawn to dark fighting waves and storms, existing on a diet of pea soup and a daily spoonful of fat. His muscle and brawn supplied the power for all the exploration and trade, but in spite of the harshness of his life—the privation, suffering, and constant threat of death by exposure, drowning, and Indian attack—he developed a nonchalance and joy in the wilderness that has never been equaled in man's conquest and exploitation of a new land. These exuberant French-Canadian canoe men, with red sashes and caps and songs in the face of monotony and disaster, were the ones who stood out.

Their barely adequate contracts with the various fur companies proved that profit had little to do with their choice of work, that it must have been something else—perhaps the lure of far places, the romance and adventure of a way of life they had never known before. Whatever the reason, they practically deserted the villages along the St. Lawrence for the *pays d'en haute* . . . But in spite of long absences from family and friends, grueling work on lakes and portages, they fought for the chance to go and were proud when chosen for the brigades. No worse fate could befall a young man than to be forced to remain at home.

. . . What I learned in the land of the voyageurs taught me what to look for everywhere, convinced me that history means the warmth of human associations, that while great events may find their place in books and museums, it is the people themselves who really counted. No longer did a country provide only opportunities for fishing, hunting, and camping. When one followed the trails of the past, no matter who the legendary figures were—voyageurs, conquistadors, or gold-seekers—their feelings came through; and when they did, the land glowed with warmth and light.

49. The phrase below that best expresses the main ideas of this passage is

    F. "the last of the voyageurs."
    G. "the new land."
    H. "the value of history."
    J. "the appeal of the voyageur."

50. The author indicates that the voyageurs

    A. were a select group.
    B. were largely men who were single.
    C. received considerable military training.
    D. disliked military life.

51. The *pays d'en haute* (paragraph two) is most probably

    F. a frontier town.
    G. a military camp.
    H. the wilderness.
    J. a fur company.

52. According to the passage the voyageurs were

   A. harsh in their treatment of Indians.
   B. overcome by monotony.
   C. suspicious of foreigners.
   D. optimistic as a whole.

53. The reader can most safely conclude that an outstanding quality of the voyageurs was their

   F. imaginativeness.
   G. courage.
   H. sense of humor.
   J. inventiveness.

54. In the passage the author indicates that history can best be understood by

   A. reading the statements of voyageurs.
   B. becoming aware of the sentiments of a people.
   C. reading about military men.
   D. trusting the word of a people.

55. In this passage, the word "brigades" (paragraph two) most nearly means

   F. military forces.
   G. gold-seekers.
   H. canoe parties.
   J. village militia.

56. In this passage, the third paragraph serves to

   I. illustrate the ideas of the other two paragraphs.
   II. contradict the ideas of the other two paragraphs.
   III. generalize from the ideas of the other two paragraphs.

   A. I only
   B. I and II
   C. III only
   D. I, II, and III

57. One of the author's purposes in writing this passage seems to be to

   F. defend the voyageurs from unfair criticism.
   G. be obviously critical of the voyageurs's motives.
   H. point out the disadvantages of village life.
   J. describe the lifestyle of the voyageurs.

Passage 9

You know how infuriating it is to listen to a child sitting at a piano and hitting notes for fun, without any connection, without a trace of sequence or development. Suppose you were tone-deaf; you
5 would probably feel the same irritation whenever you heard real music. A short march or a hymn would be a mild annoyance. A symphony in four movements would be an absolute torment, because you would be totally unable to grasp any links
10 between all these meaningless noises which the conductor was extruding from the orchestra and sending through the air in a perfectly arbitrary pattern.

In the same way, a poem-deaf man, who thinks
15 that all words should be used only to express logical constructions between ideas and facts, will be profoundly irritated if he is forced to read a poem in which there is a structure that is not logical, not explicable in words, and perhaps perceptible only
20 when it stirs deep and powerful emotions which he prefers to leave unstirred, far beneath the surface. Shelley's friend and biographer Hogg illustrates this by a story about a famous Cambridge mathematician who had never read *Paradise Lost*. A friend told
25 him it was a great poem which everyone ought to read. So he went away and read it, and came back saying it was a waste of time.

"I have read your famous poem! I read it attentively: but what does it prove? There is more
30 instruction in half a page of Euclid! A man might read Milton's poem a hundred, aye, a thousand times, and he would never learn that the angles at the base of an isosceles triangle are equal!"

58. The phrase that best expresses the main ideas of the passage is

   A. "a parallel between response to music and to poetry."
   B. "a basic appeal of poetry."
   C. "the difference between music and poetry."
   D. "the reason mathematicians dislike poetry."

59. In this passage, the author suggests that music

   F. sounds like meaningless noise.
   G. requires a special kind of hearing ability.
   H. does not appeal to people without a sense of humor.
   J. becomes boring after a while.

60. The author indicates that some people dislike poetry because they

    A. feel that poetry is for the intelligent only.
    B. ignore the value of ideas and facts.
    C. feel too superior to understand poetry.
    D. cannot accept the structure of poetry.

61. The author uses the story about the mathematician to

    F. contradict his main idea.
    G. introduce his main point.
    H. support his main point.
    J. lead into the next main idea.

62. The main idea of the passage is indicated in lines

    A. 1–4
    B. 4–6
    C. 7–13
    D. 14–21

Passage 10

Having been seen at the window, having been waved to, made Anna step back instinctively. She knew how foolish a person looking out of a window appears from the outside of a house—as though waiting for something that does not happen, as though wanting something from the outside world. A face at the window for no reason is a face that should have a thumb in its mouth: There is something only-childish about it. Or, if the face is not foolish it is threatening—blotted white by the darkness inside the room it suggests a malignant indoor power. Would Portia and Thomas think she had been spying on them?

Also, she had been seen holding a letter—not a letter that she had got today. It was to escape from thoughts out of the letter that she had gone to the window to look out. Now she went back to her escritoire which, in a shadowed corner of this large light room, was not suitable to write more than notes at. In the pigeonholes she kept her engagement pad, her account books; the drawers under the flap were useful because they locked. At present, a drawer stood open, showing packets of letters; and more letters, creased from folding, exhaling an old smell, lay about among slipped-off rubberbands. Hearing Thomas's latchkey, the hall door opening, Portia's confident voice, Anna swept the letters into the drawer quickly, then knelt down to lock everything up. But this sad little triumph of being ready in time came to nothing, for the two Quaynes went straight into the study; they did not come upstairs.

63. Anna disliked being seen at the window because she

    F. had been hiding out from these people.
    G. did not want to appear expectant.
    H. wanted to see these people before they saw her.
    J. had told these people she was busy.

64. Anna went to the window in order to

    A. gain light to read by.
    B. observe Portia and Thomas.
    C. distract herself from her musings.
    D. put an end to her loneliness and boredom.

65. Anna's treatment of her possessions suggests that she

    F. is disorganized.
    G. cherishes accuracy.
    H. values her privacy.
    J. dislikes everyone.

66. From the passage we can most safely conclude that

    A. Anna's room is not on the first floor of the house.
    B. Anna has somehow offended Portia and Thomas.
    C. Anna is jealous of Portia.
    D. an evil power inhabits the house.

67. In this passage, what is the author's chief purpose?

    F. To describe the room clearly
    G. To determine Anna's likes and dislikes
    H. To create sympathy for the Quaynes
    J. To indicate Anna's concerns

68. Which most probably happened prior to the events in this passage?

    A. The Quaynes had been away from the house.
    B. The Quaynes mailed a letter to Anna.
    C. The Quaynes delivered Anna's mail to her.
    D. Anna saw a face at the window.

69. Which is the best example of the author's point of view in this passage?

   F. "There is something only-childish about it"
   G. "Or, if the face is not foolish it is threatening"
   H. "Would Portia and Thomas think she had been spying on them?"
   J. "This sad little triumph"

70. The point of view in this passage gives the reader

   I. only what Anna knows and experiences.
   II. Anna's thoughts.
   III. the author's understanding of Anna's thoughts.
   IV. an objective picture of the entire household.

   A. I only
   B. II and III
   C. I, II, and III
   D. I, II, III, and IV

Passage 11

Justice in society must include both a fair trial to the accused and the selection of an appropriate punishment for those proven guilty. Because justice is regarded as one form of equality, we find in its earlier expressions the idea of a punishment equal to the crime. Recorded in the Old Testament is the expression "an eye for an eye, and a tooth for a tooth." That is, the individual who has done wrong has committed an offense against society. To atone for this offense, society must get even. This can be done only by inflicting an equal injury upon him. This conception of retributive justice is reflected in many parts of the legal codes and procedures of modern times. It is illustrated when we demand the death penalty for a person who has committed murder. This philosophy of punishment was supported by the German idealist Hegel. He believed that society owed it to the criminal to administer a punishment equal to the crime he had committed. The criminal had by his own actions denied his true self and it is necessary to do something that will counteract this denial and restore the self that has been denied. To the murderer nothing less than giving up his own life will pay his debt. The exaction of the death penalty is a right the state owes the criminal and it should not deny him his due.

Modern jurists have tried to replace retributive justice with the notion of corrective justice. The aim of the latter is not to abandon the concept of equality but to find a more adequate way to express it. It tries to preserve the idea of equal opportunity for each individual to realize the best that is in him. The criminal is regarded as being socially ill and in need of treatment that will enable him to become a normal member of society. Before a treatment can be administered, the cause of his antisocial behavior must be found. If the cause can be removed, provisions must be made to have this done. Only those criminals who are incurable should be permanently separated from the rest of society. This does not mean that criminals will escape punishment or be quickly returned to take up careers of crime. It means that justice is to heal the individual, not simply to get even with him. If severe punishment is the only adequate means for accomplishing this, it should be administered. However, the individual should be given every opportunity to assume a normal place in society. His conviction of crime must not deprive him of the opportunity to make his way in the society of which he is a part.

71. The style of the passage could best be considered

   F. argumentative.
   G. fictional.
   H. even-handed.
   J. relaxed.

72. The best title for this selection is

   A. "Fitting Punishment to the Crime."
   B. "Approaches to Just Punishment."
   C. "Improvement in Legal Justice."
   D. "Attaining Justice in the Courts."

73. Hegel would view the death sentence for murder as

   F. inadequate justice.
   G. an admission of not being able to cure a disease.
   H. the best way for society to get revenge.
   J. an inalienable birthright of the murderer.

74. The passage implies that the basic difference between retributive justice and corrective justice is the

   A. type of crime that was proven.
   B. severity of the punishment.
   C. reason for the sentence.
   D. outcome of the trial.

75. The punishment that would be most inconsistent with the views of corrective justice would be

   F. forced brain surgery.
   G. flogging.
   H. solitary confinement.
   J. the electric chair.

76. The Biblical expression "an eye for an eye, and a tooth for a tooth" was presented in order to

   A. prove that equality demands just punishment.
   B. justify the need for punishment as a part of law.
   C. give moral backing to retributive justice.
   D. show that man has long been interested in justice.

Answer Key for Practice Reading Passages

1.	D	20.	H	39.	D	58.	A
2.	F	21.	D	40.	G	59.	G
3.	C	22.	F	41.	C	60.	D
4.	H	23.	B	42.	F	61.	H
5.	A	24.	J	43.	G	62.	D
6.	H	25.	C	44.	B	63.	G
7.	C	26.	F	45.	F	64.	C
8.	J	27.	B	46.	D	65.	H
9.	B	28.	J	47.	G	66.	A
10.	F	29.	C	48.	D	67.	J
11.	C	30.	F	49.	J	68.	A
12.	J	31.	B	50.	A	69.	J
13.	D	32.	J	51.	H	70.	B
14.	G	33.	A	52.	D	71.	F
15.	A	34.	F	53.	G	72.	B
16.	G	35.	D	54.	B	73.	J
17.	C	36.	H	55.	H	74.	C
18.	F	37.	A	56.	C	75.	J
19.	B	38.	G	57.	J	76.	D

Explanatory Answers

1. **(D)** Choice D is the best expression of the main idea of the article and is also the hypothesis of the study.

2. **(F)** The basis of the Brookhaven study was to determine the extent of familial diseases and, in particular, high blood pressure. Choice (F), then, is the best answer.

3. **(C)** Both the "R" and "S" strains of rats were fed salt. It was each group's varying reaction to the salt that provided the main difference between the two groups.

4. **(H)** Choice (H) is directly stated in the last sentence of the passage.

5. **(A)** Because the study was concerned with high blood pressure strains within families, this can lead to an early identification of the problem in family members, and preventive measures can be taken. This is most beneficial and is best explained in answer (A).

6. **(H)** Since an inertial guidance system keeps track of a vehicle's location, it is most like a navigator.

7. **(C)** Answer (A) cannot be considered correct, as the inertial guidance system is used to measure the three dimensional space of moving vehicles only. Answers (B) and (D) are wrong because the system does not track these conditions. Choice (C) is the correct answer. The system tracks altitude and position.

8. **(J)** Choice (D) is supported in the middle of paragraph 1. The inertial platform does not do any of the things suggested in answers (F), (G), or (C).

9. **(B)** The first sentence of paragraph 2 states: "Inertial guidance systems are used today in airplanes, submarines, and spacecraft." Thus readers interested in space navigation would find this article of value.

10. **(F)** The passage describes a childhood incident in the life of the author as she looks back upon it.

11. **(C)** The passage is written in the past. The point of view is that of an adult contemplating her childhood experiences.

12. **(J)** The passage states: "... I was the only child who had camped on the Baumanns' land ever to get out of the C class."

13. **(D)** The passage states: "... we were regarded with the suspicion felt by those who plant toward those who do not plant."

14. **(G)** Barbara and her friends walked to school with the narrator, played with her, and invited her to the house.

15. **(A)** The adjectives used in the fifth paragraph, "disgraceful," "dirty," "untrustworthy," all denote intolerance.

16. **(G)** The author repeats the same theme with different examples throughout the paragraph.

17. **(C)** The paragraph is describing the lack of trust with which the community treated the migrant workers.

18. **(F)** The author had never tasted ginger ale before; therefore, it was strange to her.

19. **(B)** The passage discusses the working and home environment of the nonwhite.

20. **(H)** The passage describes how "... they must struggle, stolidly, incessantly, to keep this sense alive in themselves ..."

21. **(D)** Problems include heat, plaster, and plumbing.

22. **(F)** The author states: "They struggle to instill in their children some private sense of honor or dignity that will help the children to survive."

23. **(B)** The passage uses such words as "patience," and "strong, admirable," to describe the nonwhite.

24. **(J)** The author is expressing the view that color is the only factor making the lives of the nonwhites so difficult. It is no crime.

25. **(C)** The paragraph begins with "The others, who have avoided all of these deaths ..." Thus the preceding paragraph must have described the "deaths" endured by other urban nonwhites.

26. **(F)** The passage describes how scholars disagree about *Billy Budd*.

27. **(B)** Paragraph two states: "Scholars disagree ... about what Melville was trying to say."

28. **(J)** Recounting means explaining or telling.

29. **(C)** The third paragraph describes Billy Budd "... as innocent and ignorant as Adam before the fall."

30. **(F)** The author discusses some elements of Melville's work.

31. **(B)** The fourth paragraph describes the role of the Captain in disciplining Billy Budd.

32. **(J)** Paragraph five states: "Melville ... cleverly took pains to hide his heretical feelings."

33. **(A)** The weapons of satire are idle because the author feels that we are afraid to use them.

34. **(F)** The passage states: "We are afraid of hurting someone's feelings or of being hurt in a return bout."

35. **(D)** We use the weapons carefully because we are afraid of them.

36. **(H)** There are no anecdotes, or humorous examples, in the passage.

37. **(A)** Modern man does not wish to be hurt; he craves security.

38. **(G)** The author presents modern man's excuses for not using the weapons of satire in an ironic tone.

39. **(D)** The author describes "... the most inflated Polonius ..."

40. **(G)** The "... broadsword of invective ..." means that the invective was quite obvious.

41. **(C)** The author states: "We are too full of the milquetoast of human kindness."

42. **(F)** The "ungentlest of the arts" mentioned in the last sentence refers to the first sentence and main idea of the passage, namely, the "weapons in the arsenal of satire ..."

43. **(G)** The passage discusses the status of the essay in current society.

44. **(B)** The second paragraph describes the author's regrets at the downfall of the essay.

45. **(F)** The author states: "... the essay is the product of a ruminative mind ...," one which exists less and less in modern society.

46. **(D)** Modern man's concern with the acquisition of more and more facts is a form of consumption.

47. **(G)** The author describes the mere marshalling of facts to bog man down.

48. **(D)** The essay depends upon "... the character and quality of that mind ...," namely, a thoughtful one.

49. **(J)** The passage begins with: "It was the voyageur who captured my imagination..."

50. **(A)** The second paragraph states: "...they fought for the chance to go and were proud when chosen..."

51. **(H)** Since they deserted the villages, *pays d'en haute* must be something quite different from civilization.

52. **(D)** The voyageurs were described in the first paragraph as "...exuberant...with red sashes and caps and songs in the face of monotony and disaster..."

53. **(G)** The voyageurs "...developed a nonchalance and joy in the wilderness that has never been equaled in man's conquest and exploitation of a new land."

54. **(B)** The last paragraph states that "...history means the warmth of human associations..."

55. **(H)** The brigades refer back to the first sentence of the passage, which describes the voyageur who paddled all day.

56. **(C)** The third paragraph takes the example of the voyageurs described in the first two paragraphs and extrapolates from it the generalizations about all of history.

57. **(J)** The author describes how the voyageurs lived, the dangers they faced, and the courage that they showed.

58. **(A)** The passage begins with an example using music and then draws the analogy to poetry.

59. **(G)** The example of the tone-deaf person shows that appreciating music requires the ability to hear tones and link patterns.

60. **(D)** The second paragraph describes how poetry may have an emotional rather than a logical structure.

61. **(H)** The mathematician could only relate to fact and logic; he was "poem-deaf."

62. **(D)** The main idea is in the beginning of the second paragraph. The author believes that one must be open to the emotional structure of poetry in order to appreciate it.

63. **(G)** The second sentence of the passage describes how she feels "...as though waiting for something that does not happen..."

64. **(C)** The second sentence of the second paragraph describes Anna's looking out of the window "...to escape from thoughts out of the letter."

65. **(H)** Anna used drawers that locked; therefore, she values privacy.

66. **(A)** The last sentence of the passage tells that the Quaynes did not come upstairs, ostensibly to Anna's room.

67. **(J)** The entire passage describes what Anna is thinking and doing.

68. **(A)** Anna is seeing the Quaynes for the first time in a while.

69. **(J)** The quote expresses the author's view of Anna as a person to be pitied.

70. **(B)** The passage gives us Anna's thoughts throughout. The passage also tells us the author's point of view in his use of adjectives.

71. **(F)** The article argues a definite point of view; therefore, it is considered an argumentative essay.

72. **(B)** The article discusses two approaches to punishment—retributive and corrective.

73. **(J)** The last sentence of paragraph one clearly illustrates that the death penalty is a right of the murderer. The author's discussion of Hegel's views further substantiates this argument.

74. **(C)** The philosophy of equal injury in retributive justice differs from the philosophy, in corrective justice, of treating the criminal in order to return him to society. The reason for each type of justice, therefore, is quite different.

75. **(J)** The philosophy behind corrective justice is one of treatment and rehabilitation, not death. The electric chair results in death and is therefore inconsistent with the philosophy of corrective justice.

76. **(D)** The Biblical reference shows how long man has been concerned with justice.

Part VI

SCIENCE REVIEW

THE PHYSICAL SCIENCES

The field of earth science has given the other sciences many questions to work on. Chemistry has been given the question of discovering the composition of the many types of rock that make up the earth. Physics has been given the problem of gravity. The fossil record has given biology much to study and think about. It is not an exaggeration to say that earth science is a meeting place for most of the other sciences.

We are going to concentrate on three areas in earth science: astronomy, geology, and meteorology. In astronomy we are going to look only at the motion of the earth in space, and at how the motion of the earth affects the amount of solar energy any region gets. In meteorology we will examine the water cycle. In geology we will discuss the different types of rocks and rock erosion.

For many centuries it was believed that the geocentric theory of Ptolemy, which held that all the stars, the moon, the sun, and the planets moved in circles (or moved on circles that rested on circles) around the earth. The theory of Copernicus removed the earth from the center of the universe and made it a planet moving around the sun. The earth moves around the sun in a slightly lopsided circle called an ellipse. It takes a year for the earth to complete a full circuit around the sun.

In addition to its motion around the sun, the earth spins like a top at a constant speed of 15 degrees per hour, so that a point on the surface of the globe has travelled a complete circle in one day. The line, or axis, that the earth spins around is not perpendicular to the orbit of the earth around the sun, but is off by 23.5 degrees. This angle never changes, and the axis always points in the same direction. Because of this tilt and the fact that the earth doesn't wobble, the northern and southern hemispheres (halves of the earth) have different seasons. Consider the diagram below, which looks down at the sun and on top of the northern hemisphere of the earth.

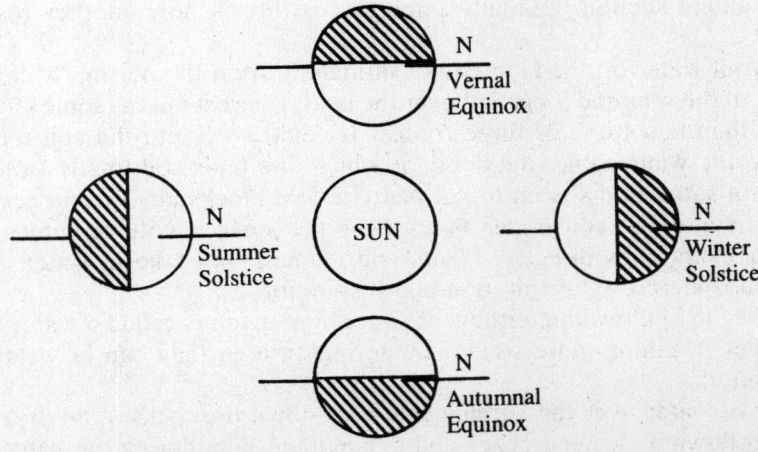

The line sticking through the earth is the axis of rotation. Notice that the axis always points in the same direction. Summer in the north occurs when the northern part of the axis points towards the sun, which allows the north to get more of the direct, or vertical, rays of sunlight. The south, because its part of the axis points away from the sun, has winter. The situation is reversed on the right hand side of the diagram. The time of year when the axis of rotation is pointing directly towards the sun (from either the southern or northern side) is called a solstice. On the solstice one hemisphere will receive light for the longest time of the year (because its half of the axis is pointing as directly as possible at the sun) while the other half will have its shortest day of the year.

At the top and the bottom of the diagram are the spring (vernal) and autumnal equinoxes, when the north and the south get equal amounts of light because neither the northern nor southern portions of the axis is pointing towards the sun. Both halves will have equal amounts of daylight. At equinox, day and night are the same length.

The warming of a hemisphere in summer and the amount of direct sunlight that the hemisphere receives are interrelated because both heat and light are forms of energy. Light is made of two waves, one an electric field, the other a magnetic field, as is shown below:

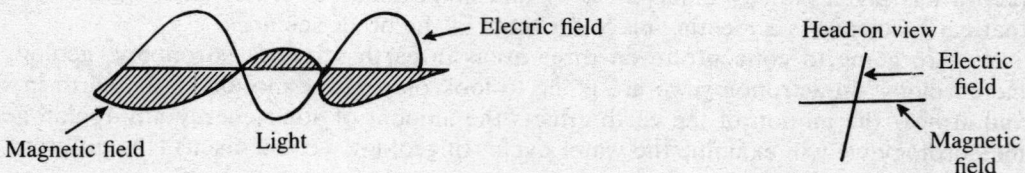

Heat is also a form of energy. This energy can cause atoms and molecules to move around more quickly. This energy of movement is called kinetic energy (see the section on physical science). Temperature is the average kinetic energy of the atoms and molecules. Heat and light can be transformed from one into the other. For example, a light bulb gives off light only because the small tungsten wire gets hot when electricity is passing through it. And if you leave ice cream sitting underneath that light bulb while it's on, you'll find that ice cream can melt pretty quickly!

The warmth of summer is therefore caused by the sunlight being converted into heat. The more sunlight there is, the warmer it can get. This is why if the sunlight comes in perpendicularly to the surface (direct rays), the surface can get warmer than if the light comes in at an angle (slanted rays). The amount of solar energy coming in for a given area is called insolation.

Solar energy is important not only because of the heat energy it gives to us. Plants take the light energy and convert it into chemical energy by a process called photosynthesis. (See the biology section.) Equally important to life is how another resource—water—is distributed.

Virtually all water on the land comes ultimately from the ocean. Water evaporates from the surface of the seas and is carried over the land, where it falls as some kind of precipitation. The water then takes one of three routes. It could seep into the soil through the zone of aeration, to the water table, the depth at which one finds soil totally saturated with water. (This zone of saturation sits on top of bedrock that blocks any further seepage.) Water that doesn't seep into the soil either flows over the surface until it enters a body of water (runoff), or evaporates directly. Plants and animals that take in water also release water into the atmosphere by transpiration and respiration.

A record of the inflow and outflow of water in a region is called a water budget. A surplus in the budget, meaning more water is entering an area than can be evaporated or stored, becomes runoff.

The flow of water over the surface can wear down the rocks in an area. These rocks are also broken down as water freezes and expands in them during the winter. A third way of breaking down rocks is by the wind blowing fine particles over them, scrubbing them like a brush. All of these processes are referred to as weathering or erosion.

If only erosion took place, the land would eventually be worn flat and overcome by the sea. But there are processes that produce new rocks. Igneous rocks are formed by the cooling of hot molten rock coming up from the earth's interior. Sedimentary rocks are formed by the gradual binding together of small grains of other rocks or minerals, sometimes with plants or animals trapped inside to become fossils. Metamorphic rocks are formed by changes in igneous or sedimentary rocks brought about by heat, pressure, or chemical reactions.

In addition to the formation of individual rocks, whole mountain ranges can be created or destroyed by the movement of whole pieces of the earth's crust over the surface. As these pieces, called plates, collide they can buckle the ground like a car hood in a crash. Or, if they move, they can bring about earthquakes and cause land to slip under the surface. Wegener, the first to propose this theory of how the surface of the earth changes, called his theory plate tectonics.

Earth Science Practice Exercise

1. A number of objects are grouped on the basis of common properties. What is this process called?

   A. Observation
   B. Inference
   C. Classification
   D. Measurement

2. Which event would be the most predictable one year in advance?

   F. A hurricane in Florida
   G. An earthquake in California
   H. A volcanic eruption in Japan
   J. An eclipse of the sun

3. In which phase (state) do most earth materials have their greatest density?

   A. Solid
   B. Liquid
   C. Gas
   D. Molten

4. What is the exact shape of the earth's orbit around the sun?

   F. The orbit is a slightly eccentric ellipse.
   G. The orbit is a very eccentric ellipse.
   H. The orbit is an oblate spheroid.
   J. The orbit is a perfect circle.

5. During which month does the minimum duration of insolation occur in the northeast United States?

   A. February
   B. July
   C. September
   D. December

6. What is the density of a rock that has a mass of 35 grams and a volume of 7 cubic centimeters?

   F. 5.0 g/cm^3
   G. 0.2 g/cm^3
   H. 28 g/cm^3
   J. 42 g/cm^3

7. Which is the best indication that the moon's distance from the earth varies?

   A. The apparent change in the shape of the moon
   B. The apparent change in the diameter of the moon
   C. The apparent change in the altitude of the moon
   D. The apparent change in the color of the moon

8. The circumference of the earth is about 4.0×10^4 km. This value is equal to

   F. 400 km
   G. 4,000 km
   H. 40,000 km
   J. 400,000 km

9. The environment is in dynamic equilibrium when it is gaining

    A. less energy than it is losing.
    B. more energy than it is losing.
    C. the same amount of energy it is losing.
    D. no energy.

10. Which process is most likely to remove pollutants from the air?

    F. Precipitation
    G. Evaporation
    H. Transpiration
    J. Runoff

Answer Key for Earth Science Practice Exercise

1. C
2. J
3. A
4. F
5. D
6. F
7. B
8. H
9. C
10. F

Explanatory Answers for Earth Science Practice Exercise

1. **(C)** Classification is the grouping together of events or objects. Inference is a conclusion that something will happen a certain way because similar cases have acted that way before. Observation and measurement are ways of collecting data.

2. **(J)** The movements of heavenly bodies are very predictable.

3. **(A)** The molecules or ions of a substance are normally most tightly packed in the solid phase. A major exception is water, where the liquid is more dense (ice floats).

4. **(F)** The difference between maximum and minimum distance between the earth and the sun is slight.

5. **(D)** Minimum insolation occurs when light strikes the surface at its sharpest angle—which occurs at the winter solstice.

6. **(F)** Density is mass/volume. Also, units in answer should give a clue.

7. **(B)** The closer an object is, the larger it will appear.

8. **(H)** The positive exponent of the ten means "move the decimal point four places to the right."

9. **(C)** Equilibrium means balance, so losses and gains must cancel out.

10. **(F)** Precipitation is the only process mentioned that takes something *out* of the air.

BIOLOGY

Biology is concerned with the study of life in all its stages and forms. What life actually is, is a difficult point to pin down. Scientists, however, have settled on a number of activities that are performed by every creature that can be considered to be alive. These activities are:

Nutrition—the taking in (ingestion) of food.
Transport—the movement of nutrients, water, and other materials from one portion of the organism to another.
Catabolism—the breaking down of complex molecules into smaller ones in order to release energy and create simple building blocks for new molecules (respiration, the oxidation of food, is a special case of catabolism).
Anabolism—the building up of new complex molecules from simpler ones.
Excretion—the elimination of waste products.
Reproduction—the creating of new individuals.

Anabolism and catabolism are two opposing processes, one building and the other tearing down molecules. The two together are referred to as the metabolism of the organism. The metabolism tends to adjust itself to achieve a constant internal environment. This tendency towards balance is called homeostasis.

Two fundamental theories of biology are 1) all living things are made of units called cells, and 2) all cells now in existence are descended from other, similar cells. The theory that all life descends from life came about as a result of experiments that disproved the theory of spontaneous generation. The theory of spontaneous generation states that certain environmental conditions can cause dead matter to give rise to complex life. For example, rotting meat was believed to create maggots, and dirty straw was supposed to breed mice. Experiments showed that the maggots really came from eggs laid on the meat by flies, and the mice from other mice that took up residence in the straw. The simplest way of stating the modern view that replaced spontaneous generation is that life comes from life.

The question of how life brings new life into being is studied in the fields of genetics and embryology. The goal of reproduction is to give the new organism the blueprints necessary so that it "knows" that it is a paramecium, a frog, or a human being. These blueprints are written in a code on the spiral staircase molecules of DNA found in the cell's nucleus. This genetic code consists of three letter words (codons), where each letter is one of the four chemicals (called nucleotide bases) that make up the rungs of the DNA ladder. Each word is a command for hooking up a specific amino acid into a chain. This chain of sometimes hundreds of amino acids is called a protein, and proteins are the workhorse molecules of living things—they are the building blocks for the structure of the cell, the molecules used to transport nutrients, the enzymes that speed up the thousands of chemical reactions that are essential for life. In a very real way, it is the collection of proteins that makes the cell a paramecium, or a cheek cell, or whatever. A long string of bases that makes one protein is called a gene. Genes are strung together in strands of DNA called chromosomes. So for a cell to give rise to a new cell it must give it a copy of its protein plans. For simple cells this process of making a copy of the chromosomes and passing it to a new cell is called mitosis.

The problem with mitosis is that it is too perfect. The two cells that come from the mitotic division of the parent are carbon copies of each other. There is no variety except by an accident in recording the chromosomes—a mutation. Variety is desirable because it allows for a greater chance of some individuals surviving. If every member of a species is perfectly adapted to its surroundings and all are exactly alike, a slight change in the environment or a new disease could wipe them all out. For example, if the fur of all animals of a species were the same color in order to blend into the surroundings, and the surroundings changed by, say, getting sootier, then all of the animals would be at risk. But, if some were light and others dark, at least some would be able to blend into the new environment. Shuffling the "genetic deck" also makes it possible to experiment with new combinations of qualities, to try to build a better version of the organism. The mechanism that does this is called sex.

All organisms that reproduce sexually have two copies of each chromosome—one from the mother, and one from the father. This means that the sex cell (gamete) from each parent (the egg and the sperm) each had only one copy of the chromosome. The process that produces gametes with half the number of chromosomes of a normal (somatic) cell is called meiosis.

Since each copy of a given chromosome comes from a different parent, the corresponding genes can be different. If they are, one can dominate the other and have things done its way. The dominant gene will determine the phenotype, how the organism will appear. This is the case with brown versus blue eyes. If a person receives one gene for brown eyes and one gene for blue eyes, the person will be brown-eyed. The gene for blue eyes is referred to as recessive.

One special pair of chromosomes determine the gender of the offspring. Both sex chromosomes of a female resemble the letter "X." Males, however, have one "X" and one with a missing branch that looks like a "Y." Because of that missing branch, if there is a defect on the male's X chromosome (which is inherited from the mother), the male will suffer the results of the defect. Such sex-linked defects include color-blindness and hemophilia.

Embryology is the branch of biology that follows the development of the new organism from fertilized egg to birth. As the embryo develops two changes occur. There is an increase in size as the embryo grows. There is also specialization of the new cells, some becoming skin cells, others nerves, and so on.

The theory of evolution states that all life comes from simpler life. Charles Darwin, in "Origin of Species" (1859), believed that the change from one species to another was gradual, and the result of the survival and reproduction of the fittest. Modern evolutionary theory adds the idea that mistakes in the transmission of the genetic code (mutations) provide the variety of experiments from which the natural selection process can pick the fittest.

Evidence for evolution comes from two fields: earth science and biochemistry. Earth science has added information about the relative ages of different layers of rock (strata) containing imprints of plants, animals, and even tracks left by the animals. Normally, the oldest stratum is the deepest one as well. Biochemistry, by comparing key proteins (generally ones found in blood such as cytochrome C), can find out how closely two species are related by how few amino acids are different in the same protein.

Another major concern of biology is the use of energy. Plants store solar energy in a form that is useful for them in a process called photosynthesis. In photosynthesis, carbon dioxide and water are combined with light energy to give oxygen, glucose (a simple sugar), and water. This combination is done by a protein, chlorophyll, that organizes the molecules and speeds up reaction. Proteins that speed up reactions are called enzymes. Plants can obtain the minerals and other building blocks for their proteins from the soil through their roots.

Especially helpful is decayed organic matter, since much of the material is already "collected" in small molecules like amino acids.

Animals utilize the solar energy stored in the glucose by either eating the plant or eating another animal that has eaten the plant. The animal releases the energy in the glucose by chemically breaking it back down into carbon dioxide and water. The energy is then stored in a molecule called ATP until needed. So plants and animals must both be present for there to be a balanced environment.

Living things adjust to their surroundings in order to take the greatest advantage of what nourishment is available. They also try to minimize the harmful elements in their environment. This is why plants grow towards the light, and mice scurry to corners when they hear sounds. Such movement toward or away from a stimulus is called a tropism.

Animals and plants both need signals to help them decide how and in what ways to grow. These signals are given by a group of molecules called hormones. Giving a living thing extra hormones may cause a change in the rate or amount of development. There have been cases, for example, of athletes who have taken steroids (a type of hormone) in order to be able to grow larger muscles. As of this writing, "help" of this sort is still illegal and dangerous in athletic competition.

The final area of biology that we will consider is the structure of the cell.

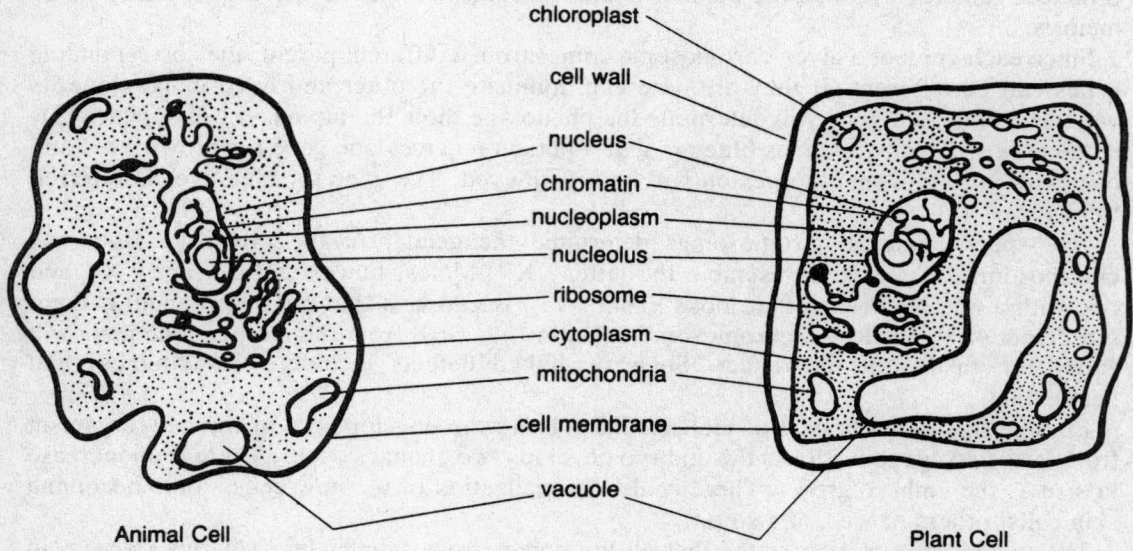

The cell is surrounded by a membrane that allows only limited amounts and types of materials to pass through it into and out of the cell's fluid, the protoplasm. If it is a plant cell it has a wall on the outside of this plasma membrane. Within all cells there are mitochondria, which are the powerhouses of the cell, and ribosomes for the synthesis of proteins. Many cells have their DNA in a nucleus. Animal cells have centrioles, which are active during mitosis. Plant cells have chloroplasts, where the chlorophyll for photosynthesis is stored.

Biology Practice Exercise

1. Which is characteristic of an enzyme?

   A. It is an inorganic catalyst.
   B. It is destroyed after each chemical reaction.
   C. It provides energy for any chemical reaction.
   D. It speeds up the rate of a chemical reaction.

2. Which organisms add more oxygen to the atmosphere than they remove?

   F. Grasshoppers
   G. Bread molds
   H. Corn plants
   J. Mushrooms

3. Which equation best represents the change in chromosome number in the process of normal fertilization in animals?

   A. n + 2n → 3n
   B. n + n → 2n
   C. n → n
   D. 2n + 2n → 5n

4. A chromosome consists of smaller units known as

   F. lipids.
   G. amino acids.
   H. genes.
   J. polysaccharides.

5. It is thought that all citrus fruit trees evolved from a common ancestor because of their common ability to synthesize citric acid. This kind of evidence of evolution is known as

   A. comparative embryology.
   B. comparative biochemistry.
   C. geographical distribution.
   D. anatomical similarity.

6. In an organism, the regulation of internal bodily functions in the face of a constantly changing external environment is done to maintain

   F. catabolism.
   G. homeostasis.
   H. synthesis.
   J. respiration.

7. In a species of corn, the diploid number of chromosomes is 20. What is the number of chromosomes found in each of the normal egg cells produced by this species?

   A. 5
   B. 10
   C. 20
   D. 40

8. Which concept is NOT included in Darwin's theory of evolution?

   F. Genetic variations are produced by mutations and sexual recombinations.
   G. Organisms that survive are best adapted to their environment.
   H. Population sizes remain constant due to a struggle for survival.
   J. Favorable traits are passed from one generation to another.

9. Digestive enzymes and hormones are found to be similar in many mammals. These findings are examples of

   A. similar anatomical structures.
   B. similar homologous structures.
   C. embryological similarities.
   D. biochemical similarities.

10. Normally, a complete set of chromosomes (2n) is passed on to each daughter cell as a result of

    F. reduction division.
    G. mitotic cell division.
    H. meiotic cell division.
    J. nondisjunction.

Answer Key for Biology Practice Exercise

1. D	3. B	5. B	7. B	9. D
2. H	4. H	6. G	8. F	10. G

Explanatory Answers for Biology Practice Exercise

1. **(D)** Enzymes are proteins that act as catalysts. Proteins are organic, so A is wrong. B and C are never true for a catalyst.

2. **(H)** Corn plants are the only ones listed that use photosynthesis, a process that produces oxygen.

3. **(B)** Meiosis reduces the number of chromosomes in sex cells to half the normal number, so that when sperm and egg combine, the offspring has the correct number of chromosomes.

4. **(H)** Chromosomes are long strands of DNA that contain all the cell's information *in the order of nucleotide bases*. The chromosomes are subdivided into genes that control individual traits.

5. **(B)** Production of a particular molecule is a matter of biochemistry.

6. **(G)** Homeostasis is the internal balance of a living thing.

7. **(B)** All sex cells contain half the normal number of chromosomes.

8. **(F)** Genetics as a science was unknown to Darwin.

9. **(D)** Hormones and enzymes are biomolecules, so the similarity is biochemical.

10. **(G)** If a complete set is passed, mitosis took place. Meiosis is only for sex cells.

CHEMISTRY

Chemistry is the study of how material is put together and reacts at the molecular level. Organic chemistry deals with the structure, reactivity, and construction (synthesis) of compounds containing carbon. Inorganic chemistry is concerned with compounds made of anything except carbon. Physical chemistry studies how the nature of a compound influences its physical properties, such as its ability to dissolve in water. Biochemistry is the study of the thousands of chemical reactions in living organisms.

All matter is composed of atoms. These atoms have a small core, called a nucleus, that contains positively charged particles called protons, and neutrons, which have no electrical charge. The number of protons in the nucleus, the atomic number, determines the identity of the atom. If the atom has seven protons, then it is a nitrogen atom, if seventy-nine, then it is gold. Since protons and neutrons have almost equal masses, the sum of the protons and neutrons tells us how "heavy" the atom is. So carbon, with six protons and six neutrons, has an atomic mass of twelve. Since the identity of an atom depends only on the atomic number, the number of neutrons in the nucleus can be different for atoms of the same type. Thus it is possible for different atoms of the same element to have different masses. For example, carbon may have eight neutrons instead of the six mentioned above, which would give it a mass of fourteen. Atoms of the same element with different masses are called isotopes.

Moving around outside the nucleus of the atom are small, negatively charged bodies called electrons. Since it would take 1840 electrons to equal the mass of one proton, and since no atom has more than about a hundred electrons, the true mass of an atom is, for all practical purposes, the atomic mass mentioned above.

If the number of electrons outside the nucleus is equal to the number of protons inside the nucleus, then the atom has no net charge, because all the charges cancel out. If the atom has a positive charge it is called a cation, and has fewer electrons than protons. An anion, an atom with a negative charge, has more electrons than protons.

The electrons in the atom can be thought of as being on different levels or shells surrounding the nucleus. Each shell can hold only a limited number of electrons. The innermost shell has the electrons with the least energy. The outermost shell, the valence shell, has the electrons with the most energy. Most chemical reactions involve the electrons in the valence shell.

Atoms always try to have a completely filled valence shell. Since all neutral atoms, except for helium, neon, xenon, and krypton do not have full valence shells, the atoms must react in some way to get a full shell. There are three possible ways to get a full shell: grab enough electrons to fill up the shell, drop the electrons you have in the valence shell so that the next shell, which is full, is the new outermost shell, or share electrons with a neighbor.

The first two ways are practical only if you are short or over a full valence shell by three electrons or fewer. Reactions involving the transfer of electrons from one atom to another are called redox reactions. The result of these reactions is the making of cations and anions that can "stick" together because of the attraction of positive and negative charges. The force that holds the ions together is called an ionic bond.

When two atoms share electrons, they are held together by a covalent bond. Collections of atoms held together by covalent bonds are called molecules. The molecular weight is just the sum of the atomic masses of all the atoms in the molecule, so molecular weight gives some indication of the size of the molecule.

Because atoms are so small (It takes about 3 million billion billion or 3×10^{24} protons to equal the mass of one nickel!), the chemist talks about taking a large number of them at a time. The way a grocer might talk about eggs by the dozen, the chemist will talk about molecules by the mole. The chemist's "dozen" contains not twelve, but 6.02×10^{23} number of molecules (this number is called Avogadro's number). This number was chosen because if the molecular mass is, say, 44 protons and neutrons, the weight of one mole will be 44 grams.

Chemical compounds react by coming into contact with each other. Since each compound can have a different weight it is not possible to say that one gram of A will react exactly with one gram of B. (Would it make any sense to say that one hundred pounds of girl can date one hundred pounds of boy?) Since we have to deal with numbers of molecules instead of weights, we can use our "large dozens," the moles, to write out the results of a reaction. Consider the following reaction:

$$3A + B \rightarrow 2C + 4D$$

This reaction says that three moles of A combine with one mole of B (no number in front means one mole) to yield two moles of C and four of D. In a chemical reaction, the number of atoms of one type on one side of the arrow must be the same as the number of atoms of the same type on the other side of the arrow. When a reaction is written so that this is true for all the atoms in the reaction it is called a balanced equation.

Sometimes it is easier to handle and react chemicals if they are dissolved in some liquid. In order to determine how much of the chemical is dissolved in the liquid, divide the number of moles put into solution by the volume of solvent used. This quantity, the molarity, has units of moles/liter.

One type of reaction that is of great importance is acid-base chemistry. Acids are compounds that lose an H^+ ion, while bases pick up H^+. In a way, acid-base reactions are like a chemical game of catch, with the acid being the pitcher, the base being the catcher, and the H^+ playing the role of the ball.

Because the ball is so important, chemists have developed a simple way of saying what concentration of H^+ you have in solution, the pH. The pH of a water solution is a number from 0 to 14. A solution with a pH less than 7 is acidic, while a solution with a pH greater than 7 is basic. A solution with a pH of exactly 7 is neither acidic nor basic. This happens when the amount of acid exactly balances the amount of base. In titrations a chemist adds acid or base to a solution until neutral pH is achieved. The point at which balance is achieved between acid and base is called the equivalence point.

Sometimes a chemist is interested in not only what a chemical reaction will produce, but also how the reaction occurs step by step. The branch of chemistry that studies the mechanism of how a reaction occurs and how fast the reaction happens is called kinetics.

Kinetics studies are done by observing the change in the rate of reaction when the concentration of one of the starting materials is changed. In this way the chemist can see the effect of the starting material on rate. An equation that describes the rate is: rate = constant $\times$ [A] $\times$ [B], where [A] is the concentration of starting material A, and [B] is the concentration of starting material B.

If the rate does not change if you change the concentration of starting material, the material has no effect, and would not appear in an equation to calculate the rate. If the rate doubles when the concentration doubles, then the rate equation would have the concentration included. If the rate increases four times when the concentration doubles, then the concentration in the rate equation would be squared (because the effect on the rate is equal to the square of what was done to the concentration of the starting material).

Sometimes a reaction will not use up all its starting materials. It is as though the reaction just "ran out of steam." This kind of situation is known as equilibrium. It is possible to force a reaction to continue by applying a "stress." Consider this simple reaction:

A + B → C + D

If the reaction stops before all of A and B reacts (assuming we have the right proportions so that we have neither A nor B left over), we could force the reaction to make more C and D by adding more A or B to the reaction, or by pulling some C or D out of the flask. We could force the reaction to go backwards by adding C or D, or pulling out some A or B. The ability to manipulate reaction mixtures this way is referred to as LeChatelier's Principle.

Chemistry Practice Exercise

1. In the reaction $Zn + Cu^{+2} \rightarrow Zn^{+2} + Cu$, the Cu ions

    A. gain electrons.
    B. lose electrons.
    C. gain protons.
    D. lose protons.

2. Isotopes of the same element must have the same

    F. number of protons.
    G. atomic weight.
    H. number of electrons.
    J. number of neutrons.

3. Which particle has a mass approximately 1/1836 of the mass of a proton?

    A. A gamma ray
    B. A neutron
    C. An alpha particle
    D. An electron

4. The formula H_2 represents one

    F. gram.
    G. liter.
    H. atom.
    J. molecule.

5. How many moles of electrons would be required to completely reduce 1.5 moles of Al^{+3} to Al?

    A. 0.5
    B. 1.5
    C. 3.0
    D. 4.5

6. What is the percent by mass of hydrogen in NH_3 (mass N = 14, mass H = 1)?

    F. 5.9%
    G. 17.6%
    H. 21.4%
    J. 82.4%

7. What is the total number of molecules in 1.0 moles of Cl (atomic weight = 35)?

    A. 35
    B. 70
    C. 6.02×10^{23}
    D. 12×10^{23}

8. The atomic number of an atom is always equal to the total number of

    F. neutrons in the nucleus.
    G. protons in the nucleus.
    H. neutrons plus protons in the atom.
    J. protons plus electrons in the atom.

9. All atoms of argon have the same

    A. mass number.
    B. atomic number.
    C. number of neutrons.
    D. number of nucleons.

10. Which particle has a negative charge?

    F. Positron
    G. Electron
    H. Proton
    J. Neutron

Answer Key for
Chemistry Practice Exercise

1. A
2. F
3. D
4. J
5. D
6. G
7. C
8. G
9. B
10. G

Explanatory Answers for
Chemistry Practice Exercise

1. **(A)** Going from +2 to zero charge, the Cu must have picked up two negative charges. (Protons do not leave an atom unless there is a nuclear reaction.)

2. **(F)** Each element is identified by the number of protons in the nucleus. If it is the same element, the number of protons must be the same.

3. **(D)** Electrons are the small, negatively charged particles that orbit around the nucleus.

4. **(J)** The formula shows that two atoms of hydrogen form one molecule.

5. **(D)** You need three electrons to cancel the positive-three charge on each ion. If you have 1.5 moles of ions, you need 3 × 1.5 moles = 4.5 moles.

6. **(G)** Total mass = 14 + 1 + 1 + 1 = 17. H makes up (3/17) × 100 = 17.6% of the mass.

7. **(C)** A mole of anything is 6.02×10^{23} molecules (Avogadro's number).

8. **(G)** Each element is identified by the number of protons it has in its nucleus.

9. **(B)** All atoms of argon have the same atomic number. The number of protons in its nucleus is 18. Isotopes of argon have different numbers of neutrons and therefore differ in atomic mass.

10. **(G)** Electrons are the small, negatively charged particles that orbit the nucleus.

PHYSICAL SCIENCE

Physics is concerned with the movement and interaction of bodies and energy. The two fundamental questions we can ask about movement are how much and which way. A scalar is an answer to the first question. For example, ten pounds is a scalar. So is fifty-five miles per hour. A vector answers both questions. Fifty-five miles per hour going north on Route 80 is a vector.

Some students have trouble with vectors and scalars when they are asked questions about speed and velocity. Speed is just how quickly something is moving. It is always a positive number, because you can't move any slower than not moving at all. Velocity is a vector because it has a direction (like north) and an amount (55 mph). You can go backwards (yes, backwards is a direction) and have a negative velocity, or forwards and have a positive velocity. If you don't move you have a zero velocity as well as a zero speed.

Another trouble spot is the difference between velocity and acceleration. Acceleration is how fast the velocity is *changing*. So an object can move one hundred miles a minute and have *zero* acceleration if the velocity hasn't changed. No acceleration means that neither the speed nor the direction of the object has changed. The object moves in a *straight* line with a *constant* speed.

A force is a push or a pull on a body. Because a push or pull must come from some direction, force is a vector quantity. A force causes a change in the velocity of an object. (Just remember the last time you were shoved!) Therefore, a force causes an acceleration. If there are a number of forces acting on a body they are added together if they push or pull in the same direction, or are subtracted if they are going in opposite directions. If there is a net force after all the forces are added and subtracted, there is a change in the velocity of the object. In other words: *If there is a net force, there is an acceleration.*

If a force is applied over a distance then we say that work has been done on the object. To do that work energy must have been used (how often have you said that you are out of energy and can't work any more?) Power is just how much work can be done in a given amount of time.

Energy, the ability to do work, can be present in two forms: energy of motion (kinetic energy), and energy of position (potential energy). The total energy is the sum of the two forms. In ideal pendulums, springs, and falling bodies the energy of the object can go from being all potential at the top of the swing or cliff to all kinetic at the bottom. But since you can't create or destroy energy (a law called conservation of mass and energy) the potential energy at the top must equal the kinetic energy at the bottom.

One area of interest to physicists is wave motion. Sound and light are waves, as well as the more familiar water waves and wiggling ropes. Waves can be described by how high or low they get (amplitude) and by their wavelength, which is the distance they travel before they start repeating themselves. Since a wave can travel only so fast, the higher the frequency, the shorter the wavelength. The frequency of the wave tells how many waves can pass a given point in a second. The higher the frequency, the higher the energy. Higher energy sound waves are higher in pitch than lower energy sound waves. Blue light, which has a higher frequency than red, is higher in energy. That is why iron in a fire first glows red, but gives off bluish light when heated until it melts.

All matter is made up of atoms, and all atoms are made up of protons, neutrons, and electrons (except hydrogen, which lacks a neutron). Protons have an electrical charge of $+1$, and electrons have a charge of -1. The signs plus and minus mean that the charges are different, not that electrons are missing something or protons have something extra. We could just as easily use north and south like a magnet. And, just like a magnet, opposites attract. All atoms start out with equal numbers of protons and electrons, so that they have no net charge—they are neutral.

Because electrons are small, fast, and in the outer regions of the atom, they can become detached and move away. If they do, the atom now has more protons than electrons and therefore has a net positive charge. Such an atom is called a cation.

It takes energy to separate positive and negative charges since electrons and protons are attracted to each other. A device that has this energy is called a battery. When the two ends of a battery are connected by a wire, the wire provides an "escape route" that allows the charges to get back together. This is pictured as the positive charges moving around the wire to get to the negative side of the battery. This movement of positive charges is called the current, and the wire and the battery form a closed loop called a circuit. A wire with current flowing through it will throw off a magnetic compass put near it. The compass needle will point at the wire instead of the North Pole. This is because a moving charge (current) makes a magnetic field at right angles to the direction the charges move. This also works the other way around: If you move a magnetic field at right angles to a wire you will make current flow through the wire. This is how generators work.

The following list of equations summarizes the material covered. A key is provided at the end of the list.

$$d = vt + \frac{1}{2}at^2 \qquad W = Fd \qquad P.E. = mgh$$

$$a = \frac{\Delta v}{\Delta t} \qquad W = \Delta E \qquad P = \frac{W}{t}$$

$$F = ma \qquad E = K.E. + P.E. \qquad f = \frac{v}{l}$$

$$w = mg \qquad K.E. = \frac{1}{2}mv^2 \qquad V = ir$$

Key

a—acceleration
d—distance
E—energy
F—force
f—frequency
g—acceleration of gravity (on Earth)
h—height above the surface
i—current
$K.E.$—kinetic energy
l—wave length
m—mass

P—power
r—resistance
t—time
$P.E.$—potential energy
V—voltage
v—velocity
W—work
w—weight
Δ (delta)—change in
Δv—change in velocity
Δt—change in time

Physical Science Practice Exercise

1. Acceleration is a vector quantity that represents the time-rate change in
    A. charge.
    B. velocity.
    C. distance.
    D. energy.

2. Which is constant for a freely falling body?
    F. Displacement
    G. Speed
    H. Velocity
    J. Acceleration

3. Energy is measured in the same units as
    A. force.
    B. momentum.
    C. work.
    D. power.

4. A force of 3 newtons and a force of 5 newtons act concurrently to produce a resulting force of 8 newtons. The angle between the forces must be
    F. 0°
    G. 60°
    H. 90°
    J. 180°

5. Which is a vector quantity?
    A. Velocity
    B. Energy
    C. Speed
    D. Power

6. If a woman runs 100 meters north and then 70 meters south, her total displacement will be
    F. 30 meters north
    G. 30 meters south
    H. 170 meters north
    J. 70 meters south

7. If the velocity of an automobile doubles, its kinetic energy
    A. decreases to one-half.
    B. doubles.
    C. decreases to one-fourth.
    D. quadruples.

8. A change in the average kinetic energy of the molecules of an object may best be detected by measuring a change in the object's
    F. mass.
    G. speed.
    H. weight.
    J. temperature.

9. Which particle has no charge?
    A. Electron
    B. Neutron
    C. Proton
    D. Positron

10. A magnetic field will be produced by
    F. moving electrons.
    G. moving neutrons.
    H. stationary protons.
    J. stationary neutrons.

Answer Key for Physical Science Practice Exercise

1. **B**
2. **J**
3. **C**
4. **F**
5. **A**
6. **F**
7. **D**
8. **J**
9. **B**
10. **F**

Explanatory Answers for Physical Science Practice Exercise

1. **(B)** Acceleration is the change in velocity over time.

2. **(J)** A freely falling body is under a constant force, gravity, so it feels a constant acceleration.

3. **(C)** Work is the change in energy, so the two must have the same units.

4. **(F)** The two forces must be working together. If they are pulling together the angle between them must be zero.

5. **(A)** Velocity has both amount and direction.

6. **(F)** Since she moves in opposite directions you subtract the distances.

7. **(D)** Kinetic energy is $\frac{1}{2}mv^2$. If v doubles, kinetic energy becomes $\frac{1}{2}m(2v)^2 = \frac{1}{2}m(4v^2) = 2mv^2$. The kinetic energy increases by a factor of four.

8. **(J)** Temperature is a measure of the average kinetic energy of the particles in a sample.

9. **(B)** Protons and positrons are positively charged; electrons are negatively charged.

10. **(F)** Moving charges produce magnetic fields. Neutrons have no charge.

Part VII

SCIENCE REASONING REVIEW

SCIENCE REASONING

The science reasoning test of the ACT consists of 40 questions asked about several different passages. These passages are descriptions of two or more opposing hypotheses, descriptions of experiments, and data presented in tables, graphs, or charts. You will be asked to perform three different types of tasks. You are going to be asked to retrieve information from graphs and tables. You will also be required to draw conclusions and predict results based on summaries of experiments described to you. Finally, you will be tested on your ability to compare two opposing views, and to draw conclusions about those ideas.

You do not need to remember every detail of every chapter of every science course in order to do well on the science reasoning section. (You will need to know some of the basic ideas from earth science, biology, chemistry, and physical science that are reviewed in this book.) In order to do well in this section you will have to be comfortable with using given information and thinking about experiments the way a scientist does. That is why this part of the exam is called science reasoning instead of science knowledge. Before we develop strategies for dealing with specific types of questions, let us look at how scientific research is done.

Scientific reasoning is a process that involves several steps. These steps are hypothesis, experimental design, collecting and organizing data, and drawing conclusions. Let us look at each part in turn.

Step One: Form a Hypothesis

A scientist conducts an experiment in order to try to prove or disprove an idea. This idea is an attempt to explain how something works and is called a hypothesis. The hypothesis is what helps the scientist to decide what experiments to do and what things to measure. For example, a scientist might formulate the hypothesis that drivers are more likely to break the traffic laws when they are not being watched. Her next step would be to design experiments to prove whether or not her hypothesis is reasonable.

Step Two: Design an Experiment

The scientist might decide, in this case, to test how likely it is for drivers to break one particular rule, like running a red light, and to see whether a driver is more likely to break the rule at night or during the day. In doing this the scientist realizes that she is assuming there is a correlation between the time of day and a driver's perception of being watched. In limiting herself to very specific things to test, our scientist has shown an understanding of good experimental design.

Good experimental design has two requirements. First, you look for the effect of only one variable at a time. Our scientist would not want to compare how often people run red lights at night in a blizzard to how often they run them on a spring afternoon. If she did, how would she know how much of the red light running was due to the dark, and how much was because of the weather? She may record the results for all kinds of weather, but she will keep in mind that she can only compare directly those experiments that are different in just one variable. When she designs the experiment, she will try to make the only difference between the day and night drivers the fact that one set drove during the day, and the other at night. So she will probably make all her observations at one intersection, on the same day of the week (could it make a difference if she compared Monday afternoon to Saturday night?), under the same weather conditions.

The second requirement for good experimental design is that there must be a control group. A control group tells you if there is any real change in results when you change the factor. If our scientist told you that two percent of the night drivers run red lights you might be tempted to think that drivers pretty much always obey the law no matter what. But when she tells you that only one tenth of one percent of the daytime drivers break that law, you realize that a driver is twenty times more likely to run the light at night. A control group gives you a context in which to judge your results.

Step Three: Observe and Record Information

Once the experiment has been designed, the scientist has to collect the information. But just getting the facts together isn't enough. The facts have to be organized so that others can make sense out of what has been done. One way to do this is to describe how the experiment was done, what a given observation would mean, and what the result of the experiment actually was. This is called a research summary. Research summaries are often prepared for experiments that test for color changes or some other data that is not easy to put into numbers.

In some experiments just having numbers is not good enough. For example, if our scientist reported that ten cars ran a red light on a warm, clear night, that information would not mean much to you. Even if she added that only five cars ran that same light during the day, you still have not learned much. The information means very little because it does not answer the original question of how likely a driver is to break the law. To answer this question you also need to know how many cars went through the intersection during the day and during the night. If fifty cars went through the intersection during the day and one hundred during the night, the fact that twice as many cars ran red lights at night does not prove the hypothesis. However, if fifty cars went through the intersection during the day, and only twenty went through at night, the facts about running red lights take on a very different look. In this study the scientist would obviously have to calculate percentages before beginning to analyze the data and she would have to arrange the data in such a way that trends are easy to spot. There are three common ways to organize data: tables, graphs, and charts. All three help a scientist to relate a change in one factor to a change in another.

Tables are almost always the first step in organizing data. (In fact, most scientists set up the empty tables to fill in while they are doing the experiments.) Tables are arranged into columns and rows. Every column and every row describes the results for one condition. For example, consider the table on the facing page our scientist might have prepared.

Each row describes the weather conditions and temperature at the time the data for that row was taken. The columns indicate the conditions to be compared. This method of organizing makes it easy to compare data by looking in straight lines either across or up and down. But be careful if you choose to look straight down a column. The weather, dry or wet, would be a third variable in addition to those of temperature and time of day (day or night). And remember that you can *not* compare three variables at once. This is why all the "dry" readings are clumped together at the top of the table and all the "wet" ones are clumped at the bottom. It is very important to watch for columns that are divided by having

Table I—Percent Running Red Lights

Weather	Temperature (F°)	Day (%)	Night (%)
dry	0–19	1	1
dry	20–39	2	1
dry	40–59	3	4
dry	60–79	5	6
dry	80–up	7	10
wet	0–19	1	2
wet	20–39	0	2
wet	40–59	1	2
wet	60–79	3	5
wet	80–up	6	8

an extra variable, like dry and wet in this example. But even with this warning to keep in mind, it is easy to look for trends in a table—you will always be looking in a straight line.

Another common way to organize data is to use graphs. Once again, we will be comparing only one factor in relation to another. The value of one factor becomes the abscissa (the x coordinate or independent variable) and the value of the other becomes the ordinate (the y coordinate or dependent variable). The two together make a point on the graph. We can use tables to read off the points for our graph. We would use the value for a row for one axis, and the value in the column for that row for the other axis.

Let's look at a graph for the effect temperature in dry weather has on the likelihood a daytime driver will run a red light. (Notice that we won't mix the "wet" and "dry" values. Why?)

Because we claim that temperature influences the driving, we make temperature the x axis or independent variable. One point on this graph will have an x value of 20–39. To know what the y value is, we look to the correct column and read the number in the row marked 20–39. A y value of 2 is present at the intersection of the row marked "20–39" and the column labeled "day." Doing that for all the points in the "dry" half, we get a graph that looks like this:

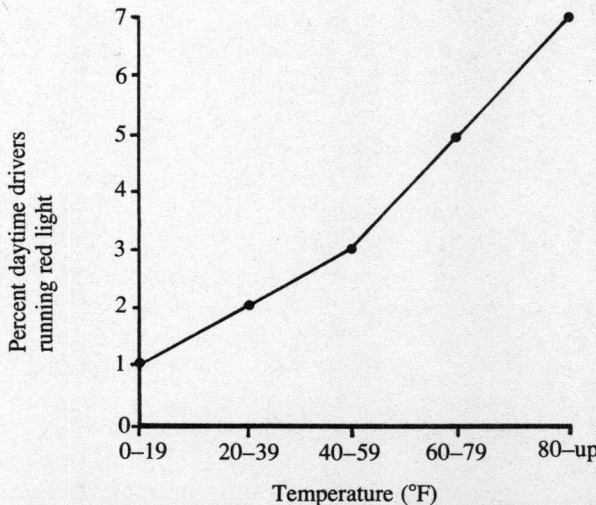

Notice that the *x* and *y* axes are clearly marked with what they measure. The above graph can be described as "the percentage of daytime drivers who run red lights as it changes with (or depends on) temperature." Graphs can give a lot of information at a glance about the relation of one variable to another. If the line connecting the points slants upwards (positive slope) that implies that the variable on the *y* axis increases as the variable on the *x* axis increases. The graph above does that. If there is no relation we won't get a line at all—just a random scattering of points on the graph. We will look at examples of different kinds of graphs in the data representation portion of this section. Another way to show relationships between variables is to make a map, chart, or diagram. You have probably seen maps showing air pressure or temperature curves in earth science and diagrams of the ear or the digestive system in biology. These are other ways of organizing information to show relationships.

Step Four: Draw a Conclusion

From the collected and organized information, the scientist will draw a conclusion as to whether her hypothesis is correct. Based on that conclusion, other experiments will be designed to test how general the rule is, or to make the relationship even clearer. Our scientist, for example, might conclude that there is indeed a relation between driving habits and whether it is day or night. If she thinks this is because drivers are more likely to break the law when it is dark (her original hypothesis), she might compare driving during a full moon to driving during a new moon. Or she might try to see if law-breaking trends are the same for speeding as well as red light running. You can probably think of several other experiments that could help answer questions about the hypothesis. As you think of those experiments, you will be getting involved in experimental design. And you will be starting to reason like a scientist. With that in mind, let's go on to look at the type of questions you'll be asked on the ACT:

- Data Representation
- Research Summaries
- Conflicting Viewpoints

DATA REPRESENTATION

Tables

There are three types of questions that can be asked about tables of data: nature of data, recognizing trends, and drawing conclusions. In order to answer any of them you have to understand what is being presented to you. Start by reading the headings on the columns. These will be the variables of the experiments. Then check the rows to see what variables were changed in each trial. Next, read through a column noting the trend as the row variable changes (as you go down a column, you go through the intersection of the column and the first row, then the column and the second row, and so on.) Finally, using the headings and any explanations provided above or below the table, try to picture how the experiment was done.

Try working on this problem:

A scientist investigated the variables that affect the age at which a female of the animal species *taedi periculum* first gives birth. Some of the results of this study are summarized in the table below.

Table I

Experiment	Temperature (°C)	Average food intake (g)	Age when first gave birth (mo.)
1	25	15	7
2	25	30	6
3	25	45	4
4	35	15	5
5	35	30	3
6	35	45	3

One of the first things you should notice is that you are looking at the effect of two variables, temperature and food, on the sexual maturity of the animal. If you are interested in the effect of food, look down the age column and compare experiments 1, 2, and 3, or compare experiments 4, 5, and 6. In each of those groupings temperature remains constant so that a change in age can only be related (as far as we know) to a change in the amount of food. If you want to look at the effect of temperature, you have to compare rows where the only factor that changes is the temperature. Can you pick out rows that will allow you to look for the effect of temperature? We'll return to that shortly with the correct answer.

If you haven't already done so, figure out what the trends are for the effects of increasing food and increasing temperature on the age of sexual maturity. When you have done that, take a moment to picture in your mind how the experiments might have been performed. Once you have completed all the steps outlined, you are ready to handle typical ACT questions about the table.

Sample Questions—Nature of Data

1. Which of the following would be a good animal to use for the experiment?

    A. Adult females
    B. Newborn females
    C. Newborn males
    D. Adult males

You should be able to eliminate choices C and D right away. You cannot use a male at any age to determine the age at which a female gives birth. You can rule out A with a little thought. If you start the experiment with adults, then you have no way of knowing how big a role the current control of their environment has on them compared to their past. The correct answer is B.

2. Which of the pairs of experiments listed below would be useful for studying the effect of temperature on age of first birth?

    F. 1 and 2
    G. 1 and 5
    H. 1 and 4
    J. 2 and 6

As referenced earlier, we will now get back to the temperature trend question. The correct answer is the one in which the only factor that varies is the one you are interested in. Only choice H includes two experiments in which food intake is the same (15g) and temperature varies.

Questions 1 and 2 illustrate one type of data interpretation question. They ask something about the nature of the experiment, about how it should be set up or studied. Questions 3 through 5 represent another type of data interpretation question. These questions ask you to predict what will happen if you change a variable in the experiment or to compare the results of two or more trials. Answering these questions requires a knowledge of the trends.

3. If all other variables are kept constant, which of the following will result in an increase in the age at which the animals give birth?

    A. Increase in temperature from 25°C to 35°C
    B. Increase in food from 15g to 45g
    C. Decrease in food from 30g to 15g
    D. Increase in temperature from 25°C to 30°C

Both an increase in food and an increase in temperature will cause a decrease in the age at first birth. You are asked for the factor that will cause an *increase* in the age! A decrease in temperature or food will cause a rise in the birth age. The correct answer is C.

The above question is a reminder that you must answer the question that was actually asked, not the one you assumed was asked. If you are not careful, you can lose points on questions that you really can answer.

4. Which experiment was the control for temperature for experiment 5?

   F. Experiment 1
   G. Experiment 2
   H. Experiment 3
   J. Experiment 6

This question is really asking for the same information as question 2. Once again you must look for two experiments that can be compared, which means two experiments that have only one variable that differs. The answer therefore has to be either G if you are looking for the effect of temperature (food is kept constant—food is the control), or J if you are looking for the effect of food with temperature controlled. If you read the question carefully, you will see that the correct answer is J.

5. If an experiment was set up with the temperature set at 30°C and the food intake at 30g, which of the following would be a reasonable prediction of the age in months of the animals when they first gave birth?

   A. 7.5
   B. 6.0
   C. 4.5
   D. 2.5

To solve this problem you have to compare this experiment to experiments 2 and 5. (Remember, you can only estimate the effect of the change in temperature if you hold the food variable constant.) The table shows that an increase in temperature from 25°C to 35°C results in a decrease in age from 6 months to 3 months. It is, therefore, not unreasonable to conclude that the age at first birth at 30°C will be between three and six months. Therefore the answer is C.

Question 6 illustrates the third type of data interpretation question. It requires you to draw conclusions based on the data presented. The major difficulty with this type of question is drawing conclusions that are not valid because you are making assumptions that are not justified by the data.

6. Which of the following conclusions is consistent with the data presented in Table I?

   F. The weight of the firstborn is proportional to the food intake.
   G. The weight of the firstborn is related to the temperature.
   H. The age of the mother at time of first offspring's birth increases with decreasing food intake.
   J. The age of the mother at time of first offspring's birth decreases with decreasing food intake.

In answering this question, keep in mind that all you know about is the effect of temperature and food on the mother. You know nothing about the offspring at all. So even though it might not be unreasonable to suppose that some of the extra food goes to the infant, you have no information to back up that idea. Therefore, neither F nor G can be correct. To decide between H and J look at the table and note the trend. The age of the mother decreases with increasing food intake, so food and age go in opposite directions—as one goes up, the other goes down. Choice J has both age and food going down simultaneously. Choice H has one going up while the other goes down. The correct answer is choice H.

Graphs

Graphs show the relationship between two variables, one giving the x coordinate and the other giving the y coordinate. The shape of the curve that you get from plotting the data points tells you about the relationship between the variables. The two most important kinds of curves are the straight (called "curves" even if they are straight) curve and the parabolic curve.

A straight line means that there is a simple (linear) relationship between the variables that can be described by that familiar equation, $y = mx + b$. Just multiplying the x value by some number (which is the slope) and adding a constant gives you the value for the other variable. To make life even simpler, in many cases b, the y intercept, equals zero, so we not only start at the origin of the coordinate system, but can focus our attention on the slope. The slope can be positive, negative, or zero. If the slope is positive, then the value of the y variable increases as the value of the x variable increases. An example of that is case A below:

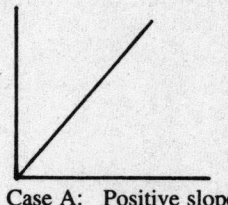

Case A: Positive slope

A special case of a positive slope is when the x variable and the y variable being plotted are the same. For example, if you plot force on the x axis, and mass times acceleration on the y axis, the x and y values for any point will be the same (because $F = ma$). The straight line that results will be at a 45° angle.

A second possibility is that the y variable decreases as the x variable increases. The result is a curve as in case B, with a negative slope.

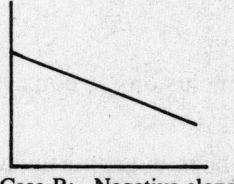

Case B: Negative slope

The final possibility is one in which the y variable does not depend on the x variable at all (that is, the y variable does not change no matter what x value you give it). This results in a zero slope, which gives a flat (horizontal) line, as in case C.

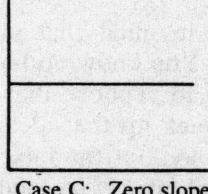

Case C: Zero slope

The other type of curve you'll have to be able to understand is a parabolic curve, shown below. This curve means that the y value is obtained by first squaring the x value and then multiplying by some number, for example, when plotting kinetic energy versus velocity.

Kinetic energy is given by the equation $K.E. = \left(\frac{1}{2}\right)mv^2$. If the x axis represents the velocity v, then the y axis represents the square of the x value multiplied by $\frac{1}{2}m$.

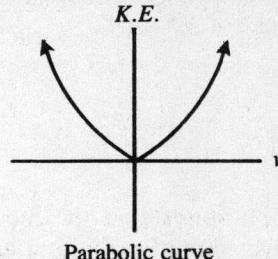

Parabolic curve

When answering questions on graphs you should carefully look over the graph to see what is being measured on each axis and the units of measure used (if given).

The next three questions are based on the following information and graph:

The kinetic energy of an object with mass m (measured in grams) after a fall from a height h (measured in cm) was recorded for different heights. A graph was made representing the kinetic energy versus height.

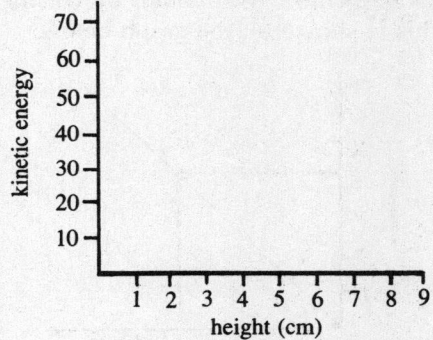

7. If the kinetic energy is given in units of g cm²/s², what units must the slope have?

A. g cm/s
B. g cm/s²
C. s cm/g
D. s²/(g cm)

We know that the units of the slope multiplied by the units of the x value must give us the units of the y value ($y = mx + b$). Choice B multiplied by the cm of the x axis gives us the correct units. The answer is choice B.

8. It is discovered that if we redo the experiment with an object with twice the mass the kinetic energy obtained for every height is doubled. The slope of the new set of experiments can be obtained by doing what to the old slope?

F. Multiplying by 2
G. Dividing by 2
H. Squaring
J. Taking the square root

The slope is the change in the y variable divided by the change in the x variable. If the heights used are the same as in the previous experiment, but the kinetic energy has doubled, then the denominator of the slope hasn't changed while the numerator of the slope is multiplied by two. So the new slope is the old slope multiplied by two. The answer is choice F.

9. What would be the kinetic energy in g cm²/s² of an object of mass *m* if it was dropped from a height of 4.5 cm?

    A. 45
    B. 4.5
    C. 90
    D. 9.0

The information above the graph states that the measurements are for an object with mass *m*, so you can read the answer directly from the graph (if the question asked about a mass of 2*m* you would have to double the amount on the *y* axis). Locate 4.5 on the *x* axis; then run a pencil straight up to the line. From the point where the pencil mark hits the line, draw a straight line to the *y* axis and read the correct *y* value for the *x* value, 45. The answer is choice A.

This question shows that given a graph and a value for one variable, you can find the value of the other variable by running a straight line from the value you know to the line, and then from the line straight to the other axis. Thus, if you knew that the kinetic energy of an object of mass *m* was 45g cm²/s² you could, by tracing those same lines, determine the height of the object. This is shown on the graph below:

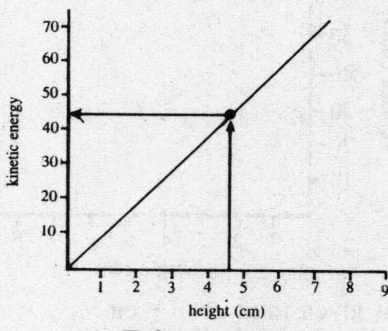

Diagrams

Diagrams and maps are most often used to show information related to how variables change or are connected in space. It is important to pay close attention to what is being measured or related in space, including noticing what units are being used. The next two questions are based on the following information and contour map:

Isotherm (°C) contour map of a table top containing an ice cube and a caged mouse. (Isotherms are closed curves that surround regions of constant temperature.)

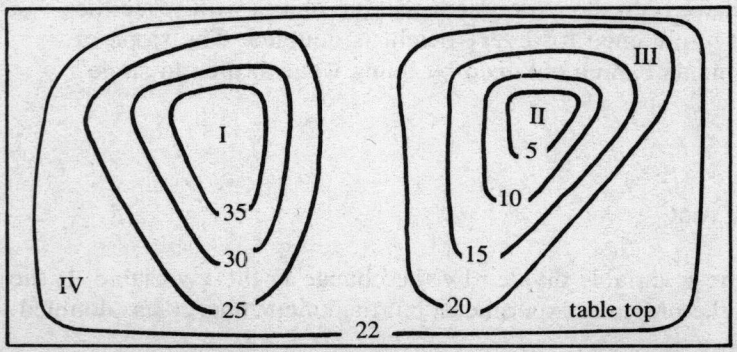
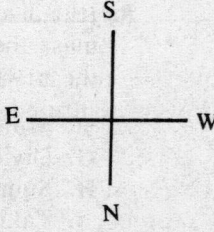

10. Near which number is the caged mouse?

    F. I
    G. II
    H. III
    J. IV

The mouse, being the warmest item on the table, will be at the isotherm with the highest temperature. The correct choice is F.

11. There was a slight breeze over the table top. From which direction did the breeze come?

    A. North
    B. South
    C. East
    D. West

The isotherm curves bulge downward on the diagram. That is due to the breeze coming from the top side of the diagram. Looking at the key, you can see that the top is the south side of the table. The correct choice is B.

This question was set up as a warning not to assume anything about the diagram. There is no law requiring the north to always be on the top. *Always read the data carefully!*

Data Representation Practice Exercise

Passage I

Table I shows the percentages of certain materials in the blood entering the kidney and the percentages of the same materials in the urine leaving the body.

Table I

Substance	Percent in blood	Percent in urine
Protein	7.0	0.0
Water	91.5	96.0
Glucose	0.1	0.0
Sodium	0.33	0.29
Potassium	0.02	0.24
Urea	0.03	2.70

1. According to Table I, which substance is more highly concentrated in the urine than the blood?

    A. Water
    B. Sodium
    C. Protein
    D. Glucose

2. According to Table I, which substance is more highly concentrated in the blood than the urine?

    F. Protein
    G. Water
    H. Potassium
    J. Urea

3. What is the likeliest explanation for the increase of water going from blood to urine?

    A. The kidney manufactures water.
    B. Blood is naturally dehydrated.
    C. The percentage of water increased because other substances were removed.
    D. The water becomes hydrogen bonded to the potassium and sodium salts.

4. Which of the following is NOT a valid conclusion based on the data?

    F. The composition of urine is different from that of blood.
    G. The volume of water leaving the body is greater than the volume of water entering the kidney.
    H. The protein in the blood is not passed into the urine.
    J. The glucose in the blood is not passed into the urine.

5. A scientist wishes to investigate the effect of age on urine content. Which of the following sets of experiments might give him the clearest answer?

   A. Analyze urine samples of people at the age of 65.
   B. Analyze urine samples of people with varying disease states.
   C. Analyze urine samples of people who differ only in age.
   D. Analyze people who do not differ in age.

6. What hypothesis is supported by the above data?

   F. All bodily fluids should have equal concentrations of substances in order to maintain homeostasis.
   G. All salts are harmful to the body.
   H. The body manufactures glucose.
   J. The healthy body will not excrete useful materials.

7. A similar study was done on another individual of the same species. The results were not identical. A reasonable hypothesis explaining this is

   A. that there will be some variation among individuals in a species.
   B. the second experiment was run improperly.
   C. the first experiment did not measure the concentration of glycerol.
   D. the second experiment must have been performed on a female instead of a male.

8. In order to investigate the effect of time of day on the blood and urine chemistry, a scientist might reasonably

   F. test five individuals once a day at the same time.
   G. test one individual five different times during a day.
   H. alternate between male and female subjects for each blood test.
   J. test subjects who have different work schedules.

Passage II

Q is a substance believed to inhibit molting in grasshoppers. A scientist investigated the relation between consumption of Q and age in days at time of first molting. The data is presented below.

Table II

Experiment	Amount of Q per feeding (mg)	Age at first molt (days)
1	0	4
2	1	3
3	2	5
4	4	6
5	6	10
6	8	Does not molt

9. What is the effect of Q on molting?

   A. A small amount triggers early molting; larger amounts slow first molting.
   B. First molting occurs later if Q is fed to grasshoppers.
   C. All moltings occur later in grasshoppers fed Q.
   D. Only the first molting is affected by the presence of Q in the diet.

10. What effect does Q have on crickets?

    F. The same because crickets belong to the same genus as grasshoppers
    G. The same because crickets have the same life cycle
    H. Different because crickets are a different species than grasshoppers
    J. Not enough data

11. Which experiment was the control?

    A. Experiment 1
    B. Experiment 2
    C. Experiment 3
    D. There was no control.

12. When would a grasshopper eating 5 mg of Q be likely to molt for the first time?

    F. 5 days
    G. 8 hours
    H. 8 days
    J. never

13. If a scientist were interested in how long the second molting were delayed he would do best to

    A. continue observing the current experiments.
    B. repeat the experiment with older grasshoppers.
    C. increase the dosage of Q.
    D. decrease the dosage of Q.

14. Which of the following factors would not influence the outcome of the experiment?

    F. Species of grasshopper
    G. Temperature
    H. Type of clock
    J. How dose of Q was given

Passage III

A scientist investigated the number of fossils per cubic foot through several feet in a quarry. The results are presented below.

Table III

Layer	Fish	Shells	Plants	Land Reptile
1 (TOP)	0	0	3	1
2	0	1	8	2
3	1	10	4	0
4	5	18	1	0
5	7	20	0	0

15. When was the site most likely above water?

    A. During the formation of Layers 1 and 2
    B. During the formation of Layers 2 and 3
    C. During the formation of Layers 1 and 4
    D. During the formation of Layer 3

16. Was the site most recently above or below water?

    F. Above
    G. Below
    H. Borderline
    J. Not enough data

17. What assumption is made to relate the fossil record to the environment?

    A. No assumption
    B. That fossils don't affect the environment
    C. That the fossils are mostly from plants and animals that lived in the region
    D. That only animal fossils are important

18. No trilobite fossils were found. This proves

    F. that no trilobites were in the region.
    G. that the layers were formed before trilobites existed.
    H. that the layers were formed after the trilobites died out.
    J. nothing about the presence of the trilobite in the region.

19. A nautilus shell was found in Layer 3. This proves

    A. that Layer 3 formed while the nautilus still existed.
    B. that Layer 3 is newer than Layer 2.
    C. that Layer 3 is older than Layer 2.
    D. that the nautilus once lived on land.

20. Where will the newest layer form?

    F. Under Layer 4
    G. Over Layer 1
    H. Across all the Layers
    J. Layers no longer form

Passage IV

Graph I shows the relationship between the relative rates of activity of enzymes A and B and temperature. Graph II shows the relationship between the relative rates of activity of enzymes A and B and pH.

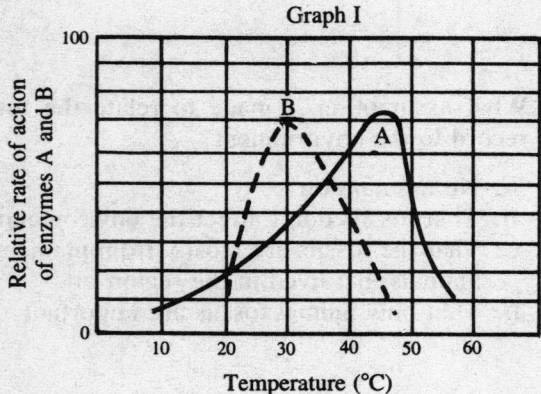

Graph I

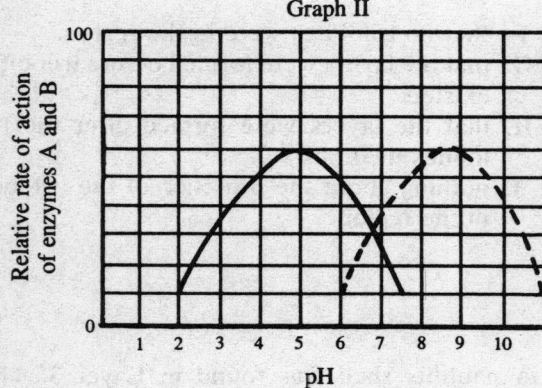

Graph II

21. Under which conditions is enzyme A most effective?

   A. 40°C and a pH of 5
   B. 45°C and a pH of 5
   C. 45°C and a pH of 9
   D. 50°C and a pH of 9

22. The optimum environment for enzyme B is

   F. acidic.
   G. basic.
   H. either acidic or basic.
   J. neutral.

23. At which of the following temperatures do A and B exhibit the same relative rate of action?

   A. 6.9°C
   B. 10°C
   C. 37°C
   D. 47°C

24. At which pH do A and B exhibit the same relative rate of action?

   F. 6.9
   G. 10
   H. 37
   J. 47

25. At what temperature does A have half the activity of B?

   A. 20°C
   B. 30°C
   C. 42°C
   D. 53°C

26. At what temperature does B have half the activity of A?

   F. 20°C
   G. 30°C
   H. 42°C
   J. 53°C

27. Over what range of pH will both A and B be active?

   A. 1 to 3
   B. 3 to 6
   C. 6 to 8
   D. 8 to 10

28. At what pH will A and B both be at their maximum activity?

   F. 2
   G. 5
   H. 8.5
   J. No such pH

Passage V

A seismographic station can detect how far away an earthquake occurred, but not the direction. Any given station can therefore report that the epicenter of an earthquake occurred somewhere on the circumference of a circle. The map below shows the data recorded for an earthquake at three different seismic stations A, B, and C.

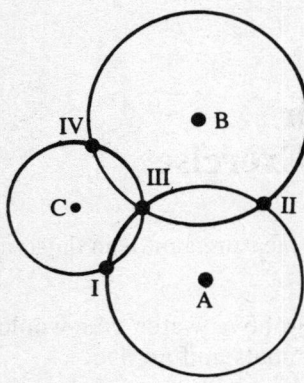

29. Which station was closest to the epicenter?

   A. A
   B. B
   C. C
   D. Can't be determined from data

30. Given the information from stations A and B only, which site(s) is (are) possible for the epicenter?

   F. I only
   G. III only
   H. II and III
   J. I and III

31. Given the information from stations A and C only, which site(s) is (are) possible for the epicenter?

   A. I only
   B. III only
   C. II and III
   D. I and III

32. Given the information from all three stations, which site(s) is (are) possible for the epicenter?

   F. I only
   G. III only
   H. I and III
   J. II and III

33. If a fourth seismic station gave a report, at what point must its curve meet A's curve?

   A. I
   B. II
   C. III
   D. IV

34. If a fourth seismic station gave a report, at what point must its curve meet C's curve?

   F. I
   G. II
   H. III
   J. IV

35. What is the minimum number of points where two circumferences from two seismic stations, both measuring the same earthquake, can meet?

   A. 1
   B. 2
   C. 3
   D. Infinite

Answer Key for Data Representation Practice Exercise

1.	A	6.	J	11.	A	16.	F	21.	B	26.	H	31.	D
2.	F	7.	A	12.	H	17.	C	22.	G	27.	C	32.	G
3.	C	8.	G	13.	A	18.	J	23.	C	28.	J	33.	C
4.	G	9.	A	14.	H	19.	A	24.	F	29.	C	34.	H
5.	C	10.	J	15.	A	20.	G	25.	B	30.	H	35.	A

Explanatory Answers for Data Representation Practice Exercise

1. **(A)** Water has a higher percentage in the urine column than in the blood column.

2. **(F)** Protein has a higher percentage in the blood column than in the urine column.

3. **(C)** As materials are removed, the *percentage* of what remains increases because the sum of all the percents must be 100.

4. **(G)** Percentages give *no* information on absolute amounts!

5. **(C)** This set will provide only one new variable, age.

6. **(J)** Protein and glucose, useful materials, were not passed into urine.

7. **(A)** Not every individual is identical. Consider height and hair color, for example.

8. **(G)** This way the only variable is time, which is what is being tested.

9. **(A)** Compare Experiments 1, 2, and 3.

10. **(J)** The experiments provide no information about the effect of Q on crickets. Choice H assumes a difference without data to back up the assumption.

11. **(A)** Q is not normally in the grasshopper's diet, so the normal condition to which everything else is compared is Experiment 1.

12. **(H)** Expect a value between Experiments 4 and 5. Note the units.

13. **(A)** In the current experiments all the proper variables are controlled.

14. **(H)** Since measurement is in days, clocks really don't matter.

15. **(A)** When above water you would expect to see land animals and no fish.

16. **(F)** The uppermost layer is the most recent layer.

17. **(C)** If it is not assumed that the plants and animals lived at the site where found, there is no information to be gained from their presence there.

18. **(J)** It is possible that no trilobite in the region was fossilized.

19. **(A)** The nautilus must have been present while Layer 3 formed for its shell to end up in the layer.

20. **(G)** See 16.

21. **(B)** Look for where the A curve is at a maximum in both graphs.

22. **(G)** Look at curve B in Graph II. The maximum is at a high pH, which is basic.

23. **(C)** Look for a point where A and B touch in Graph I.

24. **(F)** Look for a point where A and B meet in Graph II.

25. **(B)** Look for a point on Graph I where the value of the A curve is one-half the value of the B curve on a vertical line (same temperature).

26. **(H)** Look for the temperature (on Graph I)

where the height of the A curve is twice the height of the B curve.

27. **(C)** Look for the region in Graph II (pH graph) where there is an overlap of A and B curves.

28. **(J)** In Graph II we see that A and B have maximums at different pH's.

29. **(C)** C has the smallest radius.

30. **(H)** A and B touch only at points II and III.

31. **(D)** A and C touch only at points I and III.

32. **(G)** All three meet only at one point, III.

33. **(C)** It must touch the epicenter.

34. **(H)** See 33.

35. **(A)**

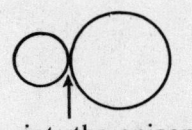

one point; the epicenter

RESEARCH SUMMARIES

Research summaries are used when the data that are collected are not suitable for a table or graph. This can be because the data involve changes that cannot easily be put into numbers, like a change in color or a change in pitch of a sound, or because the experiment is done on a model. Models are used to get a simplified picture of what processes are occurring in real life. So, while the actual measurements are meaningless, the general trends (if the model is valid) are useful. For example, a model of an eardrum can be made by stretching a thin rubber sheet across a round metal hoop. A set of experiments could be run on this model to see how changing the frequency or loudness of a sound affects how the sheet vibrates. Even though a measure of the response of the sheet tells us little in and of itself, the pattern of responses might suggest why we seem to hear shriller noises better than lower pitched ones, and why we can't hear dog whistles.

Research summaries of experiments are just descriptions of how particular experiments were carried out, and the results of those experiments. If any special information is needed, such as the meaning of a chemical test result, it will be spelled out in the description of the experiment. Research summaries may also explain the hypothesis that the experiments were designed to test before discussing the experiments.

Three basic types of questions can be asked about research summaries. The first category consists of questions about the design of the experiments. These can be questions asking you to identify what a given part of the experiment represents. Going back to the ear model for a moment, you might be asked what the metal hoop represents (the supporting bone for the eardrum). Another question might focus on the controlled variables in the experiment (the rubber sheet and the metal hoop).

The second category of questions involves predicting results, taking into account the trends you observed in the experiments. These questions are very similar to the questions on tables discussed earlier, only the answers are not in numerical form. Because of this, it is important to be sure that not only the experiment itself, but also any special results (like the meaning of a certain color or the forming of a solid), are well understood.

The final category of questions involves relating experiments to hypotheses. You may be asked how the experiments can be altered to test a new hypothesis, or which of a group of hypotheses a particular experiment supports. In redesigning the experiments to test a new hypothesis the first step is to determine what the new factor to be varied will be. Then decide what variables will now have to be fixed. The correct answer will have the correct variable as the only factor that can change.

To pick the hypothesis that is supported by an experiment, a good rule of thumb is to choose the *most specific* hypothesis that is in line with the data. Going back to the ear model again, a hypothesis that stated something about flexible membranes on round frames would be better than one that made claims about flexible membranes on frames in general. The reason for this is that the first hypothesis does not generalize to cases (we have no information about non-round frames) while the second hypothesis does.

Let's work on the following passage:

To investigate the hypothesis that the quality of the detail of a fossil depends on the size of the particles that make up the rock surrounding the fossil, three experiments were performed using a particular type of leaf with many fine veins.

Experiment 1

A leaf was placed on a flat bed made of a paste of extra-fine plaster. The leaf was then completely covered with more of the same plaster paste. A glass cover with a five-pound weight was placed on top of the paste for one hour, until the plaster set. The plaster was then baked for 30 minutes at 250°C. When the cast was opened, the imprint of the leaf showed all of the veins, including the finest ones.

Experiment 2

A leaf was placed on a flat bed made of a paste of fine grade plaster. The leaf was then completely covered with more of the same plaster paste. A glass cover with a five-pound weight was placed on top of the plaster for one hour. The plaster was then baked for 30 minutes at 250°C. When the cast was opened, all the main veins were visible, but only isolated traces of the finer veins were found.

Experiment 3

A leaf was placed on a flat bed made of a paste of coarse grain plaster. The leaf was then completely covered with more of the same plaster paste. A glass cover with a five-pound weight was placed on top of the plaster for one hour. The plaster was then baked for 30 minutes at 250°C. When the cast was opened, only the thickest veins were visible, and some of the edge of the leaf was difficult to discern.

1. Should the investigator have used a different type of leaf in each experiment?

    A. Yes, because different types of structure could be studied.
    B. Yes, because in real life many different types of fossils are found.
    C. No, because the fossil served as a controlled variable.
    D. No, because the nature of the fossil is not important.

In this question you are asked to think about how the experiment was set up. You know from the hypothesis that the only factor you want to change is the coarseness of the plaster. In order to compare the casts you should be looking at the same imprints so that you can easily see the differences. So the answer is "no." But which "no," C or D? The answer is "no" precisely because the leaf is a controlled variable. So the correct choice is C.

2. When a fossil is formed, the sediment that surrounds it is normally compressed by the tons of earth deposited over it. What part of the model simulates this sediment?

    F. The five-pound weight
    G. The glass
    H. The upper layer of paste
    J. The baking oven

In order to answer this question you must ask yourself what the sediment does to the fossil. From the question itself it is obvious that the sediment applies pressure to the fossil. Which part of the experiment supplies only pressure? Clearly not J. The upper layer of paste makes the upper half of the imprint. So the choice is between F and G. While the glass supplies some pressure to the plaster, it basically serves to spread the weight of the five-pound weight evenly over the plaster. So the weight is what simulates the pressure, making choice F the correct answer.

Questions 1 and 2 tested your ability to understand the model being used. Question 3 tests your ability to predict results based on experiments.

3. A fourth experiment was set up the same way as the previous three, except that the paste was made by mixing equal amounts of very coarse sand with the extra-fine plaster. The investigator is likely to discover

   A. no change from Experiment 1 because only the plaster counts.
   B. no change because the same kind of leaf is used.
   C. the imprint is better than Experiment 1 because the sand provides air pockets.
   D. the imprint is worse than Experiment 1 because the average particle size is bigger.

The three experiments show that the larger the particles in the plaster, the fewer details are visible in the imprint. You could then conclude that mixing the plaster with a coarser grain would make the image worse. The correct choice is D.

It often helps to work out the answer to the question before looking at the choices because, occasionally, some of the reasons given are so bizarre that you might be led to wonder about whether you had forgotten to take something into account.

Questions 4 and 5 relate the experiments to hypotheses.

4. Which of the following hypotheses are supported by the results of Experiment 1 alone?

   F. The finer the sediment the greater the detail of the resulting fossil.
   G. Hardened sediment can preserve the imprint of a specimen.
   H. All fossils must have been baked at high temperatures.
   J. Only organic material can leave imprints in sediment.

Choices H and J can be ruled out because they claim knowledge that is not provided by Experiment 1. No experiment was done that attempted to make the imprint without baking, so we don't know that baking is a requirement. Also, there was no attempt to make an imprint of anything besides the leaf, so there is no support for the claim that only organic material can leave imprints. Experiment 1 shows that a very fine plaster produces imprints with detail. There is no way of knowing that it produced an imprint superior to coarser grades of plaster until you examine the results of Experiments 2 and 3. So choice F cannot be supported by "Experiment 1 alone." Remember to read the question carefully! The correct choice is G.

5. Which of the following changes in the experiments would have permitted a test of the hypothesis that the quality of a fossil imprint depends on the pressure applied?

   A. Repeat the experiments except for using a ten-pound weight in Experiment 2, and a twenty-pound weight in Experiment 3.
   B. Choose one of the plasters, and run experiments using the same plaster in all trials while varying the weights.
   C. Rerun all the experiments without the glass.
   D. Vary the depth of the leaf in each new trial, because in nature increased pressure means the fossil is at a greater depth.

Choice A is bad because it provides two factors that vary—pressure and plaster. Choice C doesn't deal with the problem at all. Choice D is closer—there will be a slight difference in pressure due to the difference in the weight of plaster pressing down on the leaf. But unless the difference in depth is very large, it will be difficult to distinguish among the samples. Choice B has only one variable that changes, the one that you are interested in. The correct choice is B.

Research Summaries Practice Exercise

Passage I

To study the response of a spider to being repeatedly "tricked," 3 experiments were performed.

Experiment 1

A small blade of grass was used to vibrate a magnum spider's web at fifteen-minute intervals. On the first two trials the spider responded within 35 seconds. On the third trial, the spider responded in 41 seconds. On the fourth trial, in 50 seconds. The spider did not respond to any further trials.

Experiment 2

One small, live fly was placed in the web of a magnum spider every quarter hour. The struggles of the fly caused the web to vibrate. On every trial the spider moved to the fly in 30 to 35 seconds.

Experiment 3

A small blade of grass was used to vibrate a magnum spider's web at fifteen-minute intervals. On the first two trials the spider responded within 35 seconds. On the third trial the spider responded in 42 seconds. On the fourth trial a live fly was used to vibrate the web instead of the blade of grass. The response time was 49 seconds. On the fifth and sixth trials a blade of grass was used and the spider responded within 35 seconds.

1. Which experiment served as a control?

   A. Experiment 1
   B. Experiment 2
   C. Experiment 3
   D. There was no control.

2. What conclusion can be drawn from Experiment 2 alone?

   F. Spiders can distinguish between a fly and a blade of grass by the vibration.
   G. Spiders can smell their prey.
   H. Spiders respond to vibrations in their webs.
   J. Spiders can tell the size of their prey from the amount of vibration in the web.

3. What conclusion can be drawn from Experiment 1?

   A. Spiders will not continue to respond unless rewarded.
   B. Spiders will increase response time and eventually stop responding if there is no reward.
   C. Spiders will decrease response time and eventually stop responding if there is no reward.
   D. Spiders lose their ability to respond to vibrations as they age.

4. What conclusion can be drawn from Experiments 1 and 3?

   F. Spiders will not continue to respond unless rewarded.
   G. Spiders will increase response time and eventually stop responding.
   H. Spiders will decrease response time and eventually stop responding.
   J. Spiders lose their ability to respond to vibrations as they age.

5. What conclusion can be drawn from all three experiments?

   A. The response time will increase if the spider is not rewarded, but will return to normal if the spider is given a reward.
   B. The response time will decrease if the spider is not rewarded, but will return to normal if the spider is given a reward.
   C. The response time will increase until the spider no longer responds at all, unless it is rewarded with a fly. If rewarded, it will react with normal response times on future trials.
   D. The response of the spider is unpredictable.

6. Which of the following is necessarily a controlled variable in the experiments?

   F. The flies
   G. The blade of grass
   H. The response of the spider
   J. The species of spider

7. What would be the likely result if the spider in Experiment 2 were tricked once on the sixth trial?

   A. Response time on the seventh trial will increase compared to the sixth trial.
   B. Response time on the seventh trial will decrease compared to the sixth trial.
   C. Response time on the seventh trial will be identical to the sixth trial.
   D. Cannot be predicted.

Passage II

A scientist wished to investigate factors affecting inheritance of eye color of the Australian kiwi flea. All Australian kiwi fleas have either red or blue eyes. For the experiments the scientist used fleas from lines of pure red- and pure blue-eyed fleas. The results of the investigator's breeding experiments are given below.

Experiment 1

A tank was set up with conditions conducive to the growth of the Australian kiwi flea. One hundred red-eyed fleas and one hundred blue-eyed fleas were placed in the tank. Three out of four fleas in the first generation were red-eyed, the rest blue-eyed. This proportion did not change, even after twelve generations.

Experiment 2

A tank was set up with conditions conducive to the growth of the Australian kiwi flea. Red-eyed males and blue-eyed females were placed in the tank. The first generation of fleas were all red-eyed. After ten generations about one quarter of the fleas were blue-eyed. A single white-eyed flea was observed in the seventh generation.

Experiment 3

A tank was set up with conditions conducive to the growth of the Australian kiwi flea. Only red-eyed fleas were placed in this tank. After ten generations of fleas only red-eyed fleas were observed.

8. Which experiment served as a control for purity of strain of flea?

   F. Experiment 1
   G. Experiment 2
   H. Experiment 3
   J. There was no control.

9. What is the likeliest explanation for the appearance of the white-eyed flea in Experiment 2?

   A. A red-eyed male and a blue-eyed female give rise to white-eyed offspring.
   B. A blue-eyed male and a red-eyed female give rise to white-eyed offspring.
   C. The white-eyed flea was blinded.
   D. The white-eyed flea was a mutation.

10. Which of the following is a reasonable control for purity of strain?

    F. Experiment 2
    G. Experiment 1
    H. A tank with only blue-eyed fleas
    J. A tank with only red-eyed male fleas

11. Which of the following conclusions can be supported by Experiment 3 alone?

    A. Red-eyed fleas are infertile.
    B. Red-eyed fleas give rise to large numbers of mutants.
    C. Red-eyes are a dominant trait.
    D. Red-eyed fleas in this batch give rise to red-eyed fleas.

12. Why should there have been a difference in the outcomes of Experiments 1 and 2?

    F. There was no difference. By the tenth generation the results were the same.
    G. The fleas were different in each experiment.
    H. In one experiment a red-eyed flea had to mate with a blue-eyed flea.
    J. There must have been extra ultraviolet light in the tank with the mutated flea.

13. Which of the following is a valid conclusion based on the experiments?

    A. Red eyes is a dominant trait among Australian kiwi fleas.
    B. All red-eyed Australian kiwi fleas are female.
    C. Blue eyes is a dominant trait among Australian kiwi fleas.
    D. All blue-eyed Australian kiwi fleas are heterozygous.

14. If a fourth experiment used red-eyed males and blue-eyed females, how would the results differ from Experiment 2?

    F. The proportions of red and blue eyes would be reversed.
    G. There will be fewer mutations.
    H. There will be more mutations.
    J. No difference.

Passage III

An investigation was done to determine the relationship between the color of light to which a Diffnia plant is exposed and the number of flowers it develops. A summary of the investigation is presented below.

Experiment 1
Ten Diffnia were grown under green lights at constant temperature with controlled amounts of moisture and food. The plants had, on average, two flowers each.

Experiment 2
Ten Diffnia were grown under normal sunlight at constant temperature with controlled amounts of moisture and food. The plants produced, on average, four flowers each.

Experiment 3
Ten Diffnia were grown under blue lights at constant temperature with controlled amounts of moisture and food. The plants produced, on average, six flowers each.

Experiment 4
Ten Diffnia were grown under red lights at constant temperature with controlled amounts of moisture and food. The plants did not produce flowers.

15. Which experiment served as a control?

    A. Experiment 1
    B. Experiment 2
    C. Experiment 3
    D. Experiment 4

16. Which is a valid conclusion based on Experiment 3 alone?

    F. Blue lights make Diffnia produce more flowers than normal.
    G. Blue lights make Diffnia produce fewer flowers than normal.
    H. The Diffnia produces flowers if exposed to blue light.
    J. The Diffnia produces flowers only if exposed to blue light.

17. Which of the following is a method for checking whether red light stops the growth of flowers?

    A. That was checked in Experiment 4.
    B. Grow ten Diffnia under both red and blue lights shown simultaneously.
    C. Mix green and blue light to produce red light, and grow ten Diffnia under this light.
    D. Cannot be done.

18. If the investigator wished to study the effect of light intensity on flower production, which of the following would be most helpful?

    F. Since intensity depends on color, the investigator should repeat the experiments with more colors.
    G. All the experiments should be repeated with a different wattage bulb for each color.
    H. One of the first three experiments should be repeated several times, with a different wattage bulb each time.
    J. The fourth experiment should be repeated several times, using a different wattage bulb each time.

19. Which of the following was a variable in this series of experiments?

    A. Temperature
    B. Color
    C. Food
    D. Species studied

20. Which of the following is a valid conclusion based on Experiments 2 and 4?

    F. Light slows flower production.
    G. A decrease in light causes a decrease in the number of flowers produced.
    H. An increase in light causes a decrease in the number of flowers produced.
    J. A change in the color of light affects the number of flowers produced by Diffnia.

Passage IV

An investigation was conducted to determine the relationship between electric currents and magnetism. The results are presented below.

Experiment 1

A compass pointing north was placed over a copper wire pointing north. The needle continued to point north.

Experiment 2

A compass pointing north was placed over a copper wire pointing north. As soon as a current of 2 amps was passed south to north through the wire, the compass needle pointed west.

Experiment 3

A compass pointing north was placed under a copper wire pointing north. As soon as a current of 2 amps was passed south to north through the wire, the compass needle pointed east.

21. Which of the following is the best reason for performing Experiment 1?

    A. To make sure that the compass was working
    B. To act as a control for gravitational fluctuations
    C. To act as a control for the influence of the wire on the compass
    D. To see whether the magnetic field of the compass would induce a current in the wire

22. Which of the following conclusions is valid based on Experiment 2 alone?

    F. There is a magnetic field, above the wire, directed west.
    G. There is a magnetic field, above the wire, directed east.
    H. There is a magnetic field, above the wire, directed south.
    J. Compasses are unreliable indicators of magnetic field direction.

23. Which of the following conclusions is valid based on all three experiments?

    A. A wire carrying a south-to-north current creates magnetic fields of opposite directions above and below the wire.
    B. The needle of a compass is deflected to the west by a wire carrying current.
    C. The needle of a compass is deflected to the east by a wire carrying current.
    D. Compasses are unreliable indicators of magnetic field direction..

24. Which of the following will most likely cause a compass, above a wire pointed north and carrying a current, to point east?

    F. Pass a current north to south.
    G. Pass a current south to north.
    H. Pass a current east to west.
    J. Pass a current west to east.

25. Which of the following is the most likely result of bringing a compass pointing north above a wire pointing east, with no current?

    A. The needle of the compass must be deflected, so it will point south.
    B. The needle of the compass will be deflected to the west.
    C. The needle of the compass will be deflected east.
    D. The needle of the compass will continue to point north.

26. Which of the following is the best method for testing the relationship between current and the effect on the compass?

    F. Repeat Experiment 2 or 3 using different wires measured against the amount of deflection.
    G. Repeat Experiment 2 or 3 measuring the distance between the wire and the compass against the amount of deflection.
    H. Repeat Experiment 2 or 3 with different currents measured against the amount of deflection.
    J. Repeat Experiment 2 or 3 measuring the amount of deflection based on varying the current and the compass-to-wire distance.

Answer Key for Research Summaries Practice Exercise

1. B	5. C	9. D	13. A	17. B	21. C	25. D
2. H	6. J	10. H	14. J	18. H	22. F	26. J
3. B	7. C	11. D	15. B	19. B	23. A	
4. F	8. H	12. H	16. H	20. J	24. F	

Explanatory Answers for Research Summaries Practice Exercise

1. **(B)** This is the normal situation from which changes will be noted.

2. **(H)** Remember to answer on the basis of Experiment 2 *only*. Do not draw upon information provided by Experiments 1 and 3.

3. **(B)** This answer is more specific than choice A.

4. **(F)** Experiment 1 shows that the spider will stop responding, while Experiment 3 shows that a reward will keep the spider coming on more trials.

5. **(C)** Choice C is more specific than A (it mentions that the spider will stop responding under certain conditions).

6. **(J)** There may be a major difference in the results if the species were to differ.

7. **(C)** Use results of Experiments 1 or 3. Only repeated trickery causes increase in response time.

8. **(H)** Only "reds" were used to see whether reds could produce blues.

9. **(D)** If the genetic code normally allows only red or blue, another color must be a mutation.

10. **(H)** If a check for purity is desired, mixing different types introduces a new variable.

11. **(D)** Choice C is invalid because in considering only Experiment 3 we have no counter-gene for red to be dominant over.

12. **(H)** In the other experiment all combinations were possible: blue-blue, red-blue, and red-red, because there were males and females of both strains present.

13. **(A)** More red-eyes appear.

14. **(J)** There would still be only red-blue matings possible in the first generation. Dominance is a trait of the gene, not the carrier of the gene.

15. **(B)** This is the experiment that is set up under natural conditions.

16. **(H)** Since *only* Experiment 3 is to be considered, no comparisons are possible; thus choices F and G are invalid. There is no information provided in Experiment 3 about the effect of any other light on the production of flowers.

17. **(B)** If red stops flower production, then fewer flowers will be produced under a combination of red and blue light than would be produced under all blue light.

18. **(H)** This way the intensity will be the only variable.

19. **(B)** This variable was changed in each experiment.

20. **(J)** We can make a comparison between normal conditions and one color only.

21. **(C)** Experiment 1 is a control.

22. **(F)** The compass will deflect in the direction of the magnetic field.

23. **(A)** When there is a current in the wire, there is a magnetic field that circles around the wire and deflects the compass. A south-to-north current causes the compass to deflect west above the wire and east below the wire.

24. **(F)** Based on Experiments 2 and 3, a south-to-north current causes a compass deflection to

the west above the wire and to the east below. A reversal of the current (north to south) causes a reversal of the effect.

25. **(D)** There is no magnetic field if there is no current in the wire. The compass will not be deflected and will continue to point north.

26. **(J)** The amount of deflection depends on both the distance from the wire and the amount of current. Both should be tested independently.

CONFLICTING VIEWPOINTS

The third and final type of passage that you will be given to analyze is called conflicting viewpoints. These passages begin with a question like, "Why is the sky blue?" and are followed by remarks by Scientist 1 and Scientist 2. Scientist 1 will give an answer to the question presented that will include both facts and his interpretation of the facts. Scientist 2 will then argue against Scientist 1's view by giving alternative explanations for the same facts and/or other facts that do not appear to be consistent with Scientist 1's hypothesis.

Three types of questions can be asked about a conflicting viewpoints passage. You can be asked to predict results based on Scientist 1's or Scientist 2's point of view. This kind of question is no different from the questions in data representation or research summaries that required you to use a trend to predict a result. In fact, because the hypothesis is argued from trends discovered in data already collected, part of your job has already been done for you.

The second type of question asks you to spot the assumptions made about the data used in building the hypothesis. These assumptions may or may not be justified; the key thing is that they are not proven to be true. You can sometimes spot an assumption because of the use of "weak" phrases such as "may be," or "it is likely that," or "this could indicate."

The third type of question asks you to pick the best argument for or against the hypothesis. To do this, you should concentrate on the assumptions made about the data, as well as on the central point of the hypothesis. The reason for concentrating on the assumption is that the assumption is the weakest part of the hypothesis, and therefore an argument attacking or supporting it will have the most telling effect on the hypothesis.

Let's examine a sample passage:

What was the earth's early atmosphere like? Two different views are presented below.

Scientist 1

The atmosphere of the earth was at one time almost totally lacking in oxygen. One piece of evidence supporting this assertion is the very fact that life got started at all. The first chemical reactions that are necessary for the origin of life, the formation of amino acids, require ultraviolet light. Most of the ultraviolet light coming from the sun is now absorbed by oxygen in the atmosphere. If there were as much oxygen in the atmosphere then as now there would have been too little ultraviolet light available to enable life to begin. Also, the oldest bacteria, the ones which have the shortest DNA, are almost all anaerobes—they either do not need or die if exposed to oxygen. Most of the oxygen that exists now entered the atmosphere later from volcanic fumes.

Scientist 2
The prevailing opinion is that the atmosphere, though thicker now than it was in the past, is not essentially different in composition. The argument that the earth must originally have been deficient in oxygen is flawed. First of all, the presence of iron and other oxides in the rocks from this time indicates that there was oxygen available. Secondly, the requirement for a great deal of ultraviolet light holds only if there is a low concentration of the starting materials in the water. If the water in some prehistoric lake began to freeze, the starting materials would be concentrated in a small volume of unfrozen water. The high concentration of the starting materials would offset the so-called deficiency of ultraviolet light, and life could begin.

1. According to the hypothesis of Scientist 1, which of the following would have been among the last living things to evolve?

    A. Anaerobes
    B. Plants
    C. Insects
    D. Viruses

Scientist 1 maintains that the earth had very little oxygen in its early atmosphere, so creatures that require oxygen must be relative latecomers. The only creatures among the answer choices that require oxygen are the insects, choice C.

2. According to the information presented by Scientist 1, if his theory of the origin of oxygen in the atmosphere is correct, the total amount of oxygen in the air over the next million years, on the average, should

    F. decrease, then increase.
    G. increase, then decrease.
    H. increase.
    J. decrease.

If Scientist 1 is right, and volcanoes provide extra oxygen to the atmosphere, then the total amount of oxygen will increase, choice H. Since he gives no mechanism to tie up oxygen, no answer that involves a decrease in oxygen is in keeping with his hypothesis.

The first two questions asked about trends. The next two questions deal with assumptions.

3. Underlying the argument of Scientist 2 is the assumption that the oxygen in the oxides in the rocks was

    A. always tied up in the rocks.
    B. involved in biological reactions.
    C. all gaseous during the early days of the atmosphere.
    D. proportional to the oxygen in the atmosphere at the time.

The correct choice is D. Scientist 2 must assume that there is a connection between the oxygen in the rock and the oxygen in the air, otherwise there is no point in bringing up the oxides at all. This rules out A. His argument is based on the idea that there was some oxygen in the atmosphere at the time, but does not necessarily require that all the oxygen in the rock had to have been free, so C is too strong an assumption. Choice B is totally irrelevant to the argument.

4. Underlying Scientist 1's suggestion that the evolutionary record supports the idea of an oxygen deficiency on the early earth is the assumption that

   F. the oldest living things have the shortest DNA.
   G. the oldest living things have the most fragmented DNA.
   H. the oldest living things have changed radically.
   J. the oldest life forms must have died out.

Scientist 1 holds that the behavior of the anaerobic bacteria is based on the environment in which it developed—one lacking in oxygen. For this to matter in a discussion of the early earth the anaerobes would have to be among the oldest living things. Scientist 1 assumed that because the anaerobes have short DNA they indeed must be among the oldest. The correct choice is F.

The final two questions ask you to pick arguments that either support or contradict one of the hypotheses.

5. Which of the following is the strongest argument Scientist 1 could use to counter Scientist 2's suggested mechanism for the origin of life?

   A. There wasn't enough ultraviolet light available.
   B. Chemical reactions occurred differently then.
   C. The temperature at the surface of the earth at that time was always above 35°C because of geothermal heat release.
   D. Most lakes would not have covered large enough areas to guarantee that all the essential building blocks were present.

Choice A just goes back to the original argument. Trying to prove something by using the assumption itself as an argument is two things—circular reasoning and wrong. Choice B is an argument with no foundation. Choice C is a winning argument because, if true, there could be no freezing lake at all. Choice D is a weak argument, as most arguments based on probability are. Furthermore, Scientist 2 only needs to counter with "it only had to happen once," to defuse the argument. The best choice is C.

6. To refute Scientist 1's hypothesis, Scientist 2 might best

   F. show that the amount of oxide in rocks has changed little over the past four billion years.
   G. show that there are ways of making the biologically important molecules without ultraviolet light.
   H. show that there are complex anaerobic bacteria.
   J. show that the atmospheric pressure hasn't changed over the earth's history.

The key point of Scientist 1's argument is that only if ultraviolet light could filter through the atmosphere could life begin. Choice G, if true, destroys his argument completely. Choice F can be used as an argument for either side—Scientist 1 could claim that the fact that the amount of oxide doesn't change just shows that it isn't relevant to what is going on in the atmosphere, while Scientist 2 claims that the fact indicates that the atmosphere has also held a constant amount of oxygen. Choice H is, at best, a weak comeback against Scientist 1's second point. Scientist 1 could easily respond by saying that the complex anaerobe evolved later under special circumstances. Choice J says nothing at all about composition, and so is totally useless. (It is possible for the pressure to stay the same while the relative amounts of the gases change.) Choice G is the best answer.

Conflicting Viewpoints Practice Exercise

Passage I

How did life originate on the planet Earth? Two opposing views are presented.

Scientist 1

The idea that earth could have given rise to life independently is mistaken. Life on this planet must have come from elsewhere for several reasons. First of all, complex life appears very suddenly in the geological record. Secondly, all life on earth has a very similar biochemistry. If life originated on earth, one would expect regional variations in biochemistry, similar to the variations in species spread over large areas. Finally, the time when life first appeared in the geological record was also a time when large numbers of meteorites struck the earth. The meteorites must have caused life to appear on the earth. The simplest hypothesis is that the meteorites brought life with them.

Scientist 2

Life need not have been imported from outer space. The chemicals required for life existed on the surface of the earth at the time life first appeared. The fact that all life has a similar biochemistry can be explained by considering that any group of chemicals that won the race to life would probably have used the almost-living as food. Since we can offer explanations for what happened without relying on a meteorite of unknown composition that might have fallen to earth, we should stick to hypotheses that have fewer unknowns.

1. Which of the following is an assumption of Scientist 1?

   A. Complex life forms can develop quickly.
   B. Meteorites burn up as soon as they hit the earth's atmosphere.
   C. There is a cause-and-effect relationship between meteors falling and the origin of life.
   D. The changes on the earth's surface due to the presence of life attracted meteor showers.

2. Which of the following, if true, strengthens Scientist 2's argument the most?

   F. Only 5% more meteors than normal fell on the earth during the time life began.
   G. Only 5% of the meteorites studied contained organic molecules.
   H. A simulation of early earth chemistry showed the spontaneous formation of complex biomolecules.
   J. Meteorites containing amoebas have been found.

3. Which of the following, if true, strengthens Scientist 1's argument the most?

   A. Only 5% more meteors than normal fell on the earth during the time life began.
   B. Only 5% of the meteorites studied contained organic molecules.
   C. A simulation of early earth chemistry showed the spontaneous formation of complex biomolecules.
   D. Meteorites containing amoebas have been found.

4. Which explanation of the similar biochemistry of all life on earth would Scientist 1 most likely agree with?

   F. A single chemical pathway to life exists.
   G. Life arose from a single source.
   H. Life is not varied.
   J. Meteors are simple.

5. Which explanation of the similar biochemistry of all life on earth would Scientist 2 most likely agree with?

   A. A single chemical pathway to life exists.
   B. Life arose from a single source.
   C. Life is not varied.
   D. Meteors are simple.

6. Which scientist would be likely to disagree with the idea that life on different planets could have different biochemistries?

   F. Scientist 1
   G. Scientist 2
   H. Both
   J. Neither

7. Which of the following questions would be the most difficult for Scientist 1 to defend his theory against?

   A. Why was there more meteorite activity earlier in earth's history?
   B. Why haven't other meteors brought other life based on a different biochemistry?

C. Why did complex life emerge suddenly?
D. Why should meteor activity have any connection to the origin of life?

8. Could Scientist 2 believe that life exists on other planets without affecting his hypothesis?

   F. Yes, as long as he believes that life elsewhere has a different biochemistry.
   G. Yes, because wherever the chemicals required for life exist, life can begin.
   H. No, because then he has to admit that meteorites brought life from these planets.
   J. No, because then he has to admit that meteorites that came from pieces of similar planets brought life to the earth.

Passage II

What will the end of the universe be like? Two opposing views are presented.

Scientist 1

The universe will die out with a whimper because the energy of the big bang that created the universe will spread itself out over larger and larger regions of space. Since there is only so much energy in the universe, every cubic foot must hold, on the average, less energy as time goes on. In the end everything will get so cold that all motion will stop. That will be the true end of time.

Scientist 2

The idea that the universe will spread itself too thin and freeze is seriously flawed. Such theories do not take into account the gravitational attractions of the bits of matter in the universe for each other. Gravity can act as a cosmic glue to keep the universe from dissolving in nothingness.

9. Which of the following is a major assumption of Scientist 1?

   A. All matter consists of atoms.
   B. There is a limited amount of energy in the universe.
   C. Gravity doesn't exist in interstellar space.
   D. The universe is contracting.

10. Which of the following facts, if true, does not help Scientist 2's hypothesis?

    F. It is shown that the galaxies are moving away from each other with a constant speed.
    G. It is shown that the galaxies are moving towards each other with a constant speed.
    H. It is shown that the galaxies are moving towards each other with a constant acceleration.
    J. It is shown that the galaxies are not moving at all relative to each other.

11. It has been calculated that if the universe has a mass greater than or equal to m, then the universe will eventually collapse on itself. Scientist 1 would be most likely to say that the mass of the universe

    A. is equal to m.
    B. is less than or equal to m.
    C. is greater than m.
    D. is less than m.

12. If Scientist 2 claims that the universe is contracting, what would he expect the average temperature of the universe to be ten billion years from now?

    F. Higher than now
    G. Lower than now
    H. Same as now
    J. No comparison possible

13. What must be true about the energy content of the universe if Scientist 1 is correct?

    A. It is increasing.
    B. It is decreasing.
    C. It is a constant.
    D. It increases at the moment of the big bang, and decreases afterwards.

14. What assumption does Scientist 1 make about the energy of the universe?

    F. It is increasing.
    G. It is decreasing.
    H. It is a constant.
    J. It increases at the moment of the big bang, and decreases afterwards.

15. What would happen if the forces moving the galaxies farther out were exactly balanced by forces pulling them together?

    A. The galaxies would stop moving.
    B. The galaxies would move in a straight line with constant speed.
    C. The galaxies would move in a straight line with constant acceleration.
    D. The galaxies would move back and forth in a straight line.

Passage III

How old is the earth? Two opposing views are presented.

Scientist 1

The earth is approximately five billion years old. We know this to be true because of radioactive dating. Some chemical elements are unstable and will fall apart into smaller pieces over time. This disintegration occurs over a period of time that is very regular for the particular element. In general, we talk about the half-life of the element, which is the time necessary for one half of the material to disintegrate. This time is constant whether we have an ounce or a ton of the material. So, by measuring the relative amounts of the material left and the disintegration products, we can form an accurate idea of how old the earth is by determining how many half-lifes have occurred.

Scientist 2

The argument that supports the hypothesis that the earth is only five billion years old is seriously flawed. What the argument fails to take into account is that the earth is the constant recipient of a shower of cosmic debris in the form of meteorites. These meteorites replenish the stock of radioactive material on the surface of the earth, making it seem as though the earth has gone through fewer half-lives than it really has. Therefore, all estimates of the age of the earth based on radioactive dating are too low.

16. Which of the following is a major assumption of Scientist 1?

    F. The earth has life that recycles carbon-14.
    G. The earth is five billion years old.
    H. The radioactive material was formed at the same time as the earth.
    J. There is no longer any radioactivity on the earth.

17. Which of the following is a major assumption of Scientist 2?

    A. The meteorites that land on the earth are radioactive.
    B. Few meteorites have landed on the earth.
    C. The earth is greater than five billion years old.
    D. The earth is highly radioactive.

18. Which of the following, if true, would best refute Scientist 2's argument?

    F. Recent meteorites have been found to be radioactive.
    G. The earth has a greater amount of radioactive material on the surface than in the mantle.
    H. The earth's orbit intersects the orbits of a number of meteorites.
    J. Few meteorites have been found to contain radioactive material.

19. Which of the following would be most likely if Scientist 2's hypothesis were correct?

    A. The amount of radioactive material and its disintegration products on the earth has decreased over time.
    B. The amount of radioactive material and its disintegration products has increased over time.
    C. The amount of radioactive material and its disintegration products has stayed essentially the same over time.
    D. The earth will reach a critical mass and explode.

20. Which of the following would be most likely if Scientist 1's hypothesis were correct?

    F. The amount of radioactive material and its disintegration products has decreased over time.
    G. The amount of radioactive material and its disintegration products has increased over time.
    H. The amount of radioactive material and its disintegration products has stayed essentially the same over time.
    J. The earth will reach a critical mass and explode.

21. Which of the following conditions, if true, would prevent an estimation of the earth's age by Scientist 1's method?

    A. No radioactive disintegration has occurred.
    B. Only some of the radioactive material has disintegrated.
    C. Eighty percent of the radioactive material has disintegrated.
    D. All of the radioactive material has disintegrated.

Answer Key for Conflicting Viewpoints Practice Exercise

1. C	4. G	7. B	10. F	13. C	16. H	19. B
2. H	5. B	8. G	11. D	14. H	17. A	20. H
3. D	6. J	9. B	12. F	15. B	18. J	21. D

Explanatory Answers for Conflicting Viewpoints Practice Exercise

1. **(C)** Scientist 1 assumes that because both events occurred at the same time that one must cause the other.

2. **(H)** His assumption that the earth could produce life would be best supported by this experiment.

3. **(D)** This would be proof that living creatures could come from meteorites, which is the main point of his hypothesis.

4. **(G)** He would further claim that that source came from a meteorite.

5. **(B)** He would further claim that that source came from the earth.

6. **(J)** Neither scientist requires that life be the same at all places in the universe.

7. **(B)** He would either have to say it was coincidence or claim that all life is identical throughout the universe—a claim for which he has no proof.

8. **(G)** F is too strong—as long as the life didn't come here its biochemistry is irrelevant.

9. **(B)** If there is unlimited energy, then there will be more energy to replace what spreads out.

10. **(F)** If the galaxies are moving away from each other at constant speed there is no force pulling them back.

11. **(D)** Scientist 1 argues that the universe will spread out forever, so he will claim that it will not have sufficient mass to collapse. B is wrong because if the mass is equal to m the universe will collapse.

12. **(F)** Because the energy will be more concentrated.

13. **(C)** See 9.

14. **(H)** See 9.

15. **(B)** The net force is zero, which means no acceleration. An object in motion moves in a straight line with a constant speed under the conditions of zero acceleration. See Physical Science Review.

16. **(H)** Otherwise there is no connection between the radioactive "clock" and the age of the earth.

17. **(A)** For the landing of the meteorites to upset the "clock" they would have to contain either radioactive material or its disintegration products. Since Scientist 2 claims the estimate of the earth's age is too low, the meteorites must contain radioactive material.

18. **(J)** See 17.

19. **(B)** Because the meteorites would bring more material, while the earth has no way of getting rid of it.

20. **(H)** Since meteorites are not important for Scientist 1, there is no new source of material, and none is lost (radioactive material decomposes into its disintegration products, but the products don't disappear), the answer is H.

21. **(D)** There would be no way of telling how much time has passed since the "clock" ran out and all the material would be gone.

Part VIII

ACT PRACTICE EXAMS

Answer Sheet for Practice Exam I

1. English Test

1 Ⓐ Ⓑ Ⓒ Ⓓ	11 Ⓐ Ⓑ Ⓒ Ⓓ	21 Ⓐ Ⓑ Ⓒ Ⓓ	31 Ⓐ Ⓑ Ⓒ Ⓓ	41 Ⓐ Ⓑ Ⓒ Ⓓ	51 Ⓐ Ⓑ Ⓒ Ⓓ	61 Ⓐ Ⓑ Ⓒ Ⓓ	71 Ⓐ Ⓑ Ⓒ Ⓓ
2 Ⓕ Ⓖ Ⓗ Ⓙ	12 Ⓕ Ⓖ Ⓗ Ⓙ	22 Ⓕ Ⓖ Ⓗ Ⓙ	32 Ⓕ Ⓖ Ⓗ Ⓙ	42 Ⓕ Ⓖ Ⓗ Ⓙ	52 Ⓕ Ⓖ Ⓗ Ⓙ	62 Ⓕ Ⓖ Ⓗ Ⓙ	72 Ⓕ Ⓖ Ⓗ Ⓙ
3 Ⓐ Ⓑ Ⓒ Ⓓ	13 Ⓐ Ⓑ Ⓒ Ⓓ	23 Ⓐ Ⓑ Ⓒ Ⓓ	33 Ⓐ Ⓑ Ⓒ Ⓓ	43 Ⓐ Ⓑ Ⓒ Ⓓ	53 Ⓐ Ⓑ Ⓒ Ⓓ	63 Ⓐ Ⓑ Ⓒ Ⓓ	73 Ⓐ Ⓑ Ⓒ Ⓓ
4 Ⓕ Ⓖ Ⓗ Ⓙ	14 Ⓕ Ⓖ Ⓗ Ⓙ	24 Ⓕ Ⓖ Ⓗ Ⓙ	34 Ⓕ Ⓖ Ⓗ Ⓙ	44 Ⓕ Ⓖ Ⓗ Ⓙ	54 Ⓕ Ⓖ Ⓗ Ⓙ	64 Ⓕ Ⓖ Ⓗ Ⓙ	74 Ⓕ Ⓖ Ⓗ Ⓙ
5 Ⓐ Ⓑ Ⓒ Ⓓ	15 Ⓐ Ⓑ Ⓒ Ⓓ	25 Ⓐ Ⓑ Ⓒ Ⓓ	35 Ⓐ Ⓑ Ⓒ Ⓓ	45 Ⓐ Ⓑ Ⓒ Ⓓ	55 Ⓐ Ⓑ Ⓒ Ⓓ	65 Ⓐ Ⓑ Ⓒ Ⓓ	75 Ⓐ Ⓑ Ⓒ Ⓓ
6 Ⓕ Ⓖ Ⓗ Ⓙ	16 Ⓕ Ⓖ Ⓗ Ⓙ	26 Ⓕ Ⓖ Ⓗ Ⓙ	36 Ⓕ Ⓖ Ⓗ Ⓙ	46 Ⓕ Ⓖ Ⓗ Ⓙ	56 Ⓕ Ⓖ Ⓗ Ⓙ	66 Ⓕ Ⓖ Ⓗ Ⓙ	
7 Ⓐ Ⓑ Ⓒ Ⓓ	17 Ⓐ Ⓑ Ⓒ Ⓓ	27 Ⓐ Ⓑ Ⓒ Ⓓ	37 Ⓐ Ⓑ Ⓒ Ⓓ	47 Ⓐ Ⓑ Ⓒ Ⓓ	57 Ⓐ Ⓑ Ⓒ Ⓓ	67 Ⓐ Ⓑ Ⓒ Ⓓ	
8 Ⓕ Ⓖ Ⓗ Ⓙ	18 Ⓕ Ⓖ Ⓗ Ⓙ	28 Ⓕ Ⓖ Ⓗ Ⓙ	38 Ⓕ Ⓖ Ⓗ Ⓙ	48 Ⓕ Ⓖ Ⓗ Ⓙ	58 Ⓕ Ⓖ Ⓗ Ⓙ	68 Ⓕ Ⓖ Ⓗ Ⓙ	
9 Ⓐ Ⓑ Ⓒ Ⓓ	19 Ⓐ Ⓑ Ⓒ Ⓓ	29 Ⓐ Ⓑ Ⓒ Ⓓ	39 Ⓐ Ⓑ Ⓒ Ⓓ	49 Ⓐ Ⓑ Ⓒ Ⓓ	59 Ⓐ Ⓑ Ⓒ Ⓓ	69 Ⓐ Ⓑ Ⓒ Ⓓ	
10 Ⓕ Ⓖ Ⓗ Ⓙ	20 Ⓕ Ⓖ Ⓗ Ⓙ	30 Ⓕ Ⓖ Ⓗ Ⓙ	40 Ⓕ Ⓖ Ⓗ Ⓙ	50 Ⓕ Ⓖ Ⓗ Ⓙ	60 Ⓕ Ⓖ Ⓗ Ⓙ	70 Ⓕ Ⓖ Ⓗ Ⓙ	

2. Mathematics Test

1 Ⓐ Ⓑ Ⓒ Ⓓ Ⓔ	9 Ⓐ Ⓑ Ⓒ Ⓓ Ⓔ	17 Ⓐ Ⓑ Ⓒ Ⓓ Ⓔ	25 Ⓐ Ⓑ Ⓒ Ⓓ Ⓔ	33 Ⓐ Ⓑ Ⓒ Ⓓ Ⓔ	41 Ⓐ Ⓑ Ⓒ Ⓓ Ⓔ	49 Ⓐ Ⓑ Ⓒ Ⓓ Ⓔ	57 Ⓐ Ⓑ Ⓒ Ⓓ Ⓔ
2 Ⓕ Ⓖ Ⓗ Ⓙ Ⓚ	10 Ⓕ Ⓖ Ⓗ Ⓙ Ⓚ	18 Ⓕ Ⓖ Ⓗ Ⓙ Ⓚ	26 Ⓕ Ⓖ Ⓗ Ⓙ Ⓚ	34 Ⓕ Ⓖ Ⓗ Ⓙ Ⓚ	42 Ⓕ Ⓖ Ⓗ Ⓙ Ⓚ	50 Ⓕ Ⓖ Ⓗ Ⓙ Ⓚ	58 Ⓕ Ⓖ Ⓗ Ⓙ Ⓚ
3 Ⓐ Ⓑ Ⓒ Ⓓ Ⓔ	11 Ⓐ Ⓑ Ⓒ Ⓓ Ⓔ	19 Ⓐ Ⓑ Ⓒ Ⓓ Ⓔ	27 Ⓐ Ⓑ Ⓒ Ⓓ Ⓔ	35 Ⓐ Ⓑ Ⓒ Ⓓ Ⓔ	43 Ⓐ Ⓑ Ⓒ Ⓓ Ⓔ	51 Ⓐ Ⓑ Ⓒ Ⓓ Ⓔ	59 Ⓐ Ⓑ Ⓒ Ⓓ Ⓔ
4 Ⓕ Ⓖ Ⓗ Ⓙ Ⓚ	12 Ⓕ Ⓖ Ⓗ Ⓙ Ⓚ	20 Ⓕ Ⓖ Ⓗ Ⓙ Ⓚ	28 Ⓕ Ⓖ Ⓗ Ⓙ Ⓚ	36 Ⓕ Ⓖ Ⓗ Ⓙ Ⓚ	44 Ⓕ Ⓖ Ⓗ Ⓙ Ⓚ	52 Ⓕ Ⓖ Ⓗ Ⓙ Ⓚ	60 Ⓕ Ⓖ Ⓗ Ⓙ Ⓚ
5 Ⓐ Ⓑ Ⓒ Ⓓ Ⓔ	13 Ⓐ Ⓑ Ⓒ Ⓓ Ⓔ	21 Ⓐ Ⓑ Ⓒ Ⓓ Ⓔ	29 Ⓐ Ⓑ Ⓒ Ⓓ Ⓔ	37 Ⓐ Ⓑ Ⓒ Ⓓ Ⓔ	45 Ⓐ Ⓑ Ⓒ Ⓓ Ⓔ	53 Ⓐ Ⓑ Ⓒ Ⓓ Ⓔ	
6 Ⓕ Ⓖ Ⓗ Ⓙ Ⓚ	14 Ⓕ Ⓖ Ⓗ Ⓙ Ⓚ	22 Ⓕ Ⓖ Ⓗ Ⓙ Ⓚ	30 Ⓕ Ⓖ Ⓗ Ⓙ Ⓚ	38 Ⓕ Ⓖ Ⓗ Ⓙ Ⓚ	46 Ⓕ Ⓖ Ⓗ Ⓙ Ⓚ	54 Ⓕ Ⓖ Ⓗ Ⓙ Ⓚ	
7 Ⓐ Ⓑ Ⓒ Ⓓ Ⓔ	15 Ⓐ Ⓑ Ⓒ Ⓓ Ⓔ	23 Ⓐ Ⓑ Ⓒ Ⓓ Ⓔ	31 Ⓐ Ⓑ Ⓒ Ⓓ Ⓔ	39 Ⓐ Ⓑ Ⓒ Ⓓ Ⓔ	47 Ⓐ Ⓑ Ⓒ Ⓓ Ⓔ	55 Ⓐ Ⓑ Ⓒ Ⓓ Ⓔ	
8 Ⓕ Ⓖ Ⓗ Ⓙ Ⓚ	16 Ⓕ Ⓖ Ⓗ Ⓙ Ⓚ	24 Ⓕ Ⓖ Ⓗ Ⓙ Ⓚ	32 Ⓕ Ⓖ Ⓗ Ⓙ Ⓚ	40 Ⓕ Ⓖ Ⓗ Ⓙ Ⓚ	48 Ⓕ Ⓖ Ⓗ Ⓙ Ⓚ	56 Ⓕ Ⓖ Ⓗ Ⓙ Ⓚ	

3. Reading Test

1 Ⓐ Ⓑ Ⓒ Ⓓ	6 Ⓕ Ⓖ Ⓗ Ⓙ	11 Ⓐ Ⓑ Ⓒ Ⓓ	16 Ⓕ Ⓖ Ⓗ Ⓙ	21 Ⓐ Ⓑ Ⓒ Ⓓ	26 Ⓕ Ⓖ Ⓗ Ⓙ	31 Ⓐ Ⓑ Ⓒ Ⓓ	36 Ⓕ Ⓖ Ⓗ Ⓙ
2 Ⓕ Ⓖ Ⓗ Ⓙ	7 Ⓐ Ⓑ Ⓒ Ⓓ	12 Ⓕ Ⓖ Ⓗ Ⓙ	17 Ⓐ Ⓑ Ⓒ Ⓓ	22 Ⓕ Ⓖ Ⓗ Ⓙ	27 Ⓐ Ⓑ Ⓒ Ⓓ	32 Ⓕ Ⓖ Ⓗ Ⓙ	37 Ⓐ Ⓑ Ⓒ Ⓓ
3 Ⓐ Ⓑ Ⓒ Ⓓ	8 Ⓕ Ⓖ Ⓗ Ⓙ	13 Ⓐ Ⓑ Ⓒ Ⓓ	18 Ⓕ Ⓖ Ⓗ Ⓙ	23 Ⓐ Ⓑ Ⓒ Ⓓ	28 Ⓕ Ⓖ Ⓗ Ⓙ	33 Ⓐ Ⓑ Ⓒ Ⓓ	38 Ⓕ Ⓖ Ⓗ Ⓙ
4 Ⓕ Ⓖ Ⓗ Ⓙ	9 Ⓐ Ⓑ Ⓒ Ⓓ	14 Ⓕ Ⓖ Ⓗ Ⓙ	19 Ⓐ Ⓑ Ⓒ Ⓓ	24 Ⓕ Ⓖ Ⓗ Ⓙ	29 Ⓐ Ⓑ Ⓒ Ⓓ	34 Ⓕ Ⓖ Ⓗ Ⓙ	39 Ⓐ Ⓑ Ⓒ Ⓓ
5 Ⓐ Ⓑ Ⓒ Ⓓ	10 Ⓕ Ⓖ Ⓗ Ⓙ	15 Ⓐ Ⓑ Ⓒ Ⓓ	20 Ⓕ Ⓖ Ⓗ Ⓙ	25 Ⓐ Ⓑ Ⓒ Ⓓ	30 Ⓕ Ⓖ Ⓗ Ⓙ	35 Ⓐ Ⓑ Ⓒ Ⓓ	40 Ⓕ Ⓖ Ⓗ Ⓙ

4. Science Reasoning Test

1 Ⓐ Ⓑ Ⓒ Ⓓ	6 Ⓕ Ⓖ Ⓗ Ⓙ	11 Ⓐ Ⓑ Ⓒ Ⓓ	16 Ⓕ Ⓖ Ⓗ Ⓙ	21 Ⓐ Ⓑ Ⓒ Ⓓ	26 Ⓕ Ⓖ Ⓗ Ⓙ	31 Ⓐ Ⓑ Ⓒ Ⓓ	36 Ⓕ Ⓖ Ⓗ Ⓙ
2 Ⓕ Ⓖ Ⓗ Ⓙ	7 Ⓐ Ⓑ Ⓒ Ⓓ	12 Ⓕ Ⓖ Ⓗ Ⓙ	17 Ⓐ Ⓑ Ⓒ Ⓓ	22 Ⓕ Ⓖ Ⓗ Ⓙ	27 Ⓐ Ⓑ Ⓒ Ⓓ	32 Ⓕ Ⓖ Ⓗ Ⓙ	37 Ⓐ Ⓑ Ⓒ Ⓓ
3 Ⓐ Ⓑ Ⓒ Ⓓ	8 Ⓕ Ⓖ Ⓗ Ⓙ	13 Ⓐ Ⓑ Ⓒ Ⓓ	18 Ⓕ Ⓖ Ⓗ Ⓙ	23 Ⓐ Ⓑ Ⓒ Ⓓ	28 Ⓕ Ⓖ Ⓗ Ⓙ	33 Ⓐ Ⓑ Ⓒ Ⓓ	38 Ⓕ Ⓖ Ⓗ Ⓙ
4 Ⓕ Ⓖ Ⓗ Ⓙ	9 Ⓐ Ⓑ Ⓒ Ⓓ	14 Ⓕ Ⓖ Ⓗ Ⓙ	19 Ⓐ Ⓑ Ⓒ Ⓓ	24 Ⓕ Ⓖ Ⓗ Ⓙ	29 Ⓐ Ⓑ Ⓒ Ⓓ	34 Ⓕ Ⓖ Ⓗ Ⓙ	39 Ⓐ Ⓑ Ⓒ Ⓓ
5 Ⓐ Ⓑ Ⓒ Ⓓ	10 Ⓕ Ⓖ Ⓗ Ⓙ	15 Ⓐ Ⓑ Ⓒ Ⓓ	20 Ⓕ Ⓖ Ⓗ Ⓙ	25 Ⓐ Ⓑ Ⓒ Ⓓ	30 Ⓕ Ⓖ Ⓗ Ⓙ	35 Ⓐ Ⓑ Ⓒ Ⓓ	40 Ⓕ Ⓖ Ⓗ Ⓙ

1. ENGLISH TEST

45 Minutes—75 Questions

DIRECTIONS: In the passage(s) below, certain words and phrases are underlined and numbered. In the right-hand column, you will find choices for each underlined part. You are to select the one that best expresses the idea, makes the statement appropriate for standard written English, or is worded most consistently with the style and mood of the passage as a whole. If you think the original version is best, choose "NO CHANGE." You will also find questions about a section of the passage, or about the passage as a whole. These questions are indicated by a number or numbers in a box. For each question in the test, choose the choice you consider best and blacken the corresponding space on your answer sheet. Read each passage through once before you begin to answer the questions that accompany it. You cannot determine most answers without reading several sentences beyond the phrase in question.

Passage I

As befits a nation made up of immigrants from all over the Christian world, Americans have no distinctive Christmas symbols, but we have taken the symbols of all the nations and made them our own. The Christmas tree, the holly and the ivy, the mistletoe, the exchange of gifts, the myth of Santa Claus, the carols of all nations, the plum pudding and the wassail bowl are all elements in the American Christmas of the late twentieth century as we know it today. Though we have no Christmas symbols of our own, the American Christmas still has a distinctive aura by the virtue of two character elements.

The first of these is when, as might be expected in a nation as dedicated to the carrying on of business as the American nation, the dominant

1. **A.** NO CHANGE
   B. symbols but
   C. symbols; but
   D. symbols: but

2. **F.** NO CHANGE
   G. as it is known today
   H. known as it is today
   J. OMIT the underlined portion.

3. **A.** NO CHANGE
   B. characters
   C. characterized
   D. characteristic

4. **F.** NO CHANGE
   G. is that
   H. is which
   J. is where

279

role of the Christmas festivities has become to
                                       ─────────
                                          5
serve as a stimulus to retail business. The themes of Christmas advertising begin to appear as early as September, and the open season on Christmas shopping begins in November. 50 years ago,
                                        ───────────
                                             6

Thanksgiving Day was regarded like it was the
                                ──────────────
                                      7
opening day of the season for Christmas shopping; today, the season opens immediately after Halloween. Thus virtually a whole month has been added to the Christmas season—for
                                              ──────────
                                                  8
shopping purposes.

   Second, the Christmas season of festivities has insensibly combined with the New Years
                              ─────────
                                  9
celebration into one lengthened period of Saturnalia. This starts with the office parties a few days before Christmas continues on Christmas
                ──────────────────────
                          10
Eve, now the occasion in America of one of two large-scale revels that mark the season—save that the Christmas Eve revels are often punctuated by a visit to one of the larger churches for midnight Mass, which has increasingly tended to become blended into a part of the entertainment aspect of the season—and continues in spirited euphoria until New Year's Eve, the second of the large-scale revels. New Year's Day is spent resting,

5. A. NO CHANGE
   B. have become
   C. having become
   D. becomes

6. F. NO CHANGE
   G. 50 year ago
   H. Fifty years ago
   J. One time ago

7. A. NO CHANGE
   B. like as
   C. as
   D. like

8. F. NO CHANGE
   G. season. For
   H. season, for
   J. season: for

9. A. NO CHANGE
   B. New Year's
   C. New Years'
   D. New Year

10. F. NO CHANGE
    G. Christmas, continues
    H. as Christmas continues
    J. Christmas as continues

possibly regretting somebody's excesses,
                            11

watching a football "bowl" game. [12]

11. A. NO CHANGE
    B. everyone's
    C. someone's
    D. one's

12. Is the use of quotation marks appropriate in the passage?

    F. No, because the passage has no dialogue.
    G. No, because commas would be more appropriate.
    H. Yes, because quotation marks are used to set off words used out of context.
    J. Yes, because quotation marks are used around titles of books, plays, and poems.

Passage II

> The following paragraphs may or may not be in the most logical order. Each paragraph is numbered in parentheses, and item 24 will ask you to choose the sequence of paragraph numbers that is most logical.

(1)

Can you spot a criminal by his physical characteristics? When the science of criminology was founded in the nineteenth century, an imaginative Italian observer decided that criminals are born that way and are distinctly by certain physical
                                    13
marks. They are, he claimed, "a special species, a subspecies having distinct physical and mental characteristics. In general, all criminals have long, large, protruding ears, abundant hair, a thin beard, prominent front sinuses, a protruding chin, large cheekbones." Rapists, he argued, have "brilliant eyes, delicate faces" and murderers may be distinguished by "cold, glassy eyes, nose always large and frequently aquiline;

13. A. NO CHANGE
    B. distinguish
    C. distinguished
    D. distinguishing

jaws strong; cheekbones large, hair curly, dark and abundant." ⬚14 ⬚15

(2)

But the myth doesn't die *easily*. During
                              ──────
                                16
the 1930s, a German criminologist, Gustav Aschaffenburg, declared that stout, squat people with large abdomens are more liable to be
                                    ──────────
                                        17
occasional offenders, while slender builds and slight muscular development are common among habitual offenders. In the 1940s, according to writer Jessica Mitford, a group of Harvard sociologists who study sociology, decided that
               ──────────────────
                       18
criminals are most likely to be "mesomorphs," muscular types with large trunks who walk assertively, talk noisily, and behave aggressively. Watch out for those kind.
                 ──────────
                      19

14. Is the use of a question appropriate to begin Paragraph 1?

   F. No, because questions are not used in formal writing.
   G. No, because the question is not answered.
   H. Yes, because it varies sentence structure and interests the reader.
   J. Yes, because an essay should always begin with a question.

15. Is the use of quotation marks in this paragraph appropriate?

   A. No, because this paragraph contains no dialogue.
   B. No, because too much physical detail is confusing.
   C. Yes, because the paragraph discusses a theory of criminology.
   D. Yes, because quotation marks are used around direct quotations.

16. F. NO CHANGE
    G. easy
    H. easiest
    J. easier

17. A. NO CHANGE
    B. likely
    C. likely apt
    D. possible

18. F. NO CHANGE
    G. whom study sociological changes
    H. who studied sociology
    J. OMIT the underlined portion.

19. A. NO CHANGE
    B. those sort
    C. them kind
    D. those

(3)

Around about the turn of the century, a British
physician made a detailed study of the faces of
three thousand convicts and compared them with
a like number of English college students,
measuring the noses ears eyebrows and chins of
both groups. He could find no correlation among
physical types and criminal behavior. [23] [24]

20. F. NO CHANGE
    G. At about
    H. Around
    J. OMIT the underlined portion.

21. A. NO CHANGE
    B. compare
    C. compares
    D. comparing

22. F. NO CHANGE
    G. noses ears and eyebrows and chins
    H. noses; ears; eyebrows and chins
    J. noses, ears, eyebrows, and chins

23. This passage was probably excerpted from
    A. a general sociology textbook
    B. a technical monograph on criminology
    C. a news magazine
    D. a biography of Gustav Aschaffenburg

24. Choose the order of paragraph numbers that will make the essay's structure most logical.
    F. NO CHANGE
    G. 3, 2, 1
    H. 1, 3, 2
    J. 2, 3, 1

Passage III

> The following paragraphs may or may not be in the most logical order. Each paragraph is numbered in parentheses, and item 37 will ask you to select the order of paragraph numbers that is most logical.

(1)

The history of modern pollution problems show
that most have resulted from negligence and
ignorance. We have an appalling tendency to
interfere with nature before all of the possible
consequences of our actions have been studied
into completeness. We produce and distribute
radioactive substances, synthetic chemicals, and

25. A. NO CHANGE
    B. shown
    C. shows
    D. showed

26. F. NO CHANGE
    G. a lot
    H. for completeness
    J. in depth

many other potent compounds before fully comprehending their effects on living organisms.
                                    ——27——

Synthetic means manmade. Many of today's
————————————————28————————————————
fashions are made with synthetic fibers. Our
————————————————————————————————
education is dangerously incomplete.

(2)

It will be argued that the purpose of science is to move into unknown territory; to explore, and
                                ———29———
to discover. It can be said that similar risks have been taken before, and that these risks are necessary to technological progress. [30]

(3)

These arguments overlook an important
                          ————31————
element. In the past, risks taken in the name of scientific progress were restricted to a small place and brief period of time. The effects of the processes we now strive to master are not either
                                      ——32——
localized nor brief. Air pollution covers vast urban areas. Ocean pollutants have been discovered in nearly every part of the world. Synthetic chemicals spread over huge stretches of forest and farmland may remain in the soil

27. **A.** NO CHANGE
    B. effectiveness
    C. affect
    D. affects

28. **F.** NO CHANGE
    G. Synthetic fibers are manmade.
    H. Many of today's fashions are made with synthetic fibers.
    J. OMIT the underlined portion.

29. **A.** NO CHANGE
    B. territory:
    C. territory,
    D. territory

30. The writer could most effectively bolster the passage at this point by adding which of the following?

    F. An example of one of these risks argued by some to be necessary for technological progress.
    G. The sentence "The risks are necessary." to gain rhetorical emphasis.
    H. A brief description of an unknown territory.
    J. A definition of the word "science."

31. **A.** NO CHANGE
    B. a important
    C. importance
    D. important

32. **F.** NO CHANGE
    G. either
    H. not neither
    J. neither

for decades and years to come. Radioactive
pollutants will be found in the biosphere for
generations. The size and persistent of these
problems have grown with the expanding power
of modern science.

(4)

One might also argue that the hazards of
modern pollutants are small comparison for the
dangers associated with other human activity. No
estimate of the actual harm done by smog, fallout,
or chemical residues can obscure the reality that
the risks are being taken before being fully
understood.

(5)

The importance of these issues lies in the
failure of science to predict and control. Human
intervention into natural processes. The true
measure of the danger is represented by the
hazards we will encounter if we enter the new
age of technology without first evaluating our
responsibility to environment. [37] [38]

33. A. NO CHANGE
    B. for decades.
    C. for years to come in decades.
    D. for decades and years.

34. F. NO CHANGE
    G. persistence
    H. persevering
    J. persisting

35. A. NO CHANGE
    B. consideration for
    C. comparing with
    D. compared to

36. F. NO CHANGE
    G. control human
    H. control; human
    J. control and human

37. Choose the order of paragraph numbers that will make the essay's structure most logical.

    A. NO CHANGE
    B. 2, 4, 3, 1, 5
    C. 1, 3, 2, 4, 5
    D. 5, 1, 2, 3, 4

38. This passage was probably intended for readers who

    F. lack an understanding of the history of technology
    G. are authorities on pollution and its causes
    H. are interested in becoming more aware of our environmental problems and the possible solutions to these problems
    J. have worked with radioactive substances

Passage IV

> The following paragraphs may or may not be in the most logical order. Each paragraph is numbered in parentheses, and item 49 will ask you to choose the sequence of paragraph numbers that is most logical.

(1)

Many men can be of greatest service to a company by staying around in the laboratory. A
<u>39</u>
single outstanding discovery may of had a far
<u>40</u>
greater impact on the company's profit picture five years hence than the activities of even the most able administrator. It is simply good sense—
<u>41</u>
and good economics—to allow qualified researchers to continue their work. Granting these men maximum freedom to explore their scientific ideas is also eminently good sense.

(2)

In recent years however this theory has fallen
<u>42</u>
into wide disrepair. Companies find that many
<u>43</u>
researchers continue to be highly productive throughout their careers. There is every reason to allow these men to continue their pioneering work.

(3)

Some years ago, the theory was rampant that after the age of about 40, the average researcher

39. A. NO CHANGE
    B. remaining
    C. remaining around
    D. staying up

40. F. NO CHANGE
    G. maybe
    H. might of had
    J. may have

41. A. NO CHANGE
    B. most ablest
    C. more ablest
    D. most abled

42. F. NO CHANGE
    G. years, however
    H. years, however,
    J. years however,

43. A. NO CHANGE
    B. argument
    C. ill repute
    D. disrepute

began losing their creative spark. The chance of
his making a major discovery was believed to
drop off sharply. Hence, there really wasn't much
point to encouraging a man of 45 or 50 to do
research. 45

(4)

Companies are also convinced that the traditional guideposts in establishing salaries are not completely valid. In former years of long ago, the size of a man's paycheck was determined primarily by the size of his annual budget. On this basis, the researcher—however brilliant—who had perhaps one assistant and never spent much money made an extremely poor showing. Companies now realize that the two very important criteria that must also be considerable are a man's actual contributions to the company and his creative potential.

(5)

In today's era of scientific manpower shortages, companies have more reason than ever to encourage scientists to do the work for which they are most qualified. They also have greater reason than ever to provide within the laboratory the environ-

44. F. NO CHANGE
    G. its
    H. his
    J. theirs

45. Suppose that at this point in the passage the writer wanted to increase the information about creative contributions from researchers. Which of the following additions would be most relevant to the passage as a whole?

    A. A bibliography of books about retirement
    B. A description of a few of the contributions older researchers have made to science
    C. A list of today's most prominent researchers
    D. A brief description of a model retirement benefits plan

46. F. NO CHANGE
    G. a long time ago
    H. long ago
    J. OMIT the underlined portion.

47. A. NO CHANGE
    B. considered
    C. most considerable
    D. considerable of

288 / ACT

ment in which the creative processes of research
can be carried out most effectively.

48. F. NO CHANGE
G. about which
H. of which
J. into which

49. Choose the sequence of paragraph numbers that will make the essay's structure most sensible.

A. NO CHANGE
B. 1, 2, 4, 3, 5
C. 1, 2, 3, 5, 4
D. 3, 2, 1, 4, 5

50. Is the author's use of the dash appropriate in the passage?

F. No, because a dash is never used in formal writing.
G. No, because commas would have been as effective for emphasis.
H. Yes, because the dash gives emphasis to the sudden break in thought or interruption in the sentence in which it was used.
J. Yes, because using a dash adds excitement to the passage.

Passage V

The following paragraphs may or may not be in the most logical order. Each paragraph is numbered in parentheses, and item 63 will ask you to select the order of paragraph numbers that is most logical.

(1)

What are those of us whom have chosen careers in science and engineering able to do about meeting our current problems?

(2)

Second, we can identify the many areas in which science and technology, more considerately used, can be of greatest service in the future than in the past to improve the quality of life. While we can make many speeches, and pass many laws, the quality of our environment will be

51. A. NO CHANGE
B. who
C. whose
D. what

52. F. NO CHANGE
G. problems.
H. problems!
J. problems.?

53. A. NO CHANGE
B. great
C. more great
D. greater

improved only threw better knowledge and better
                    ——
                    54
application of that knowledge.

(3)

Third, we can recognize that much of the dissatisfaction we suffer today results from our very successes of former years in the past. We
                                          ————————
                                                55
have been so eminently successful in attaining material goals that we are deeply dissatisfied of the fact that we cannot attain other goals more
————————
      56
rapidly. We have achieved a better life for most people, but we are unhappy that we have not spread it to all people. We have illuminated many sources of environmental deterioration, because of
                                          ——————
                                              57
we are unhappy that we have not conquered all of them. It is our raising expectations rather than
                ——————
                   58
our failures which now cause our distress.

(4)

First, we can help destroy the false impression that science and engineering have caused the current world troubles. Quite the contrary, science
                                ——————————————
                                       59
and engineering have made vast contributions to better living for more people. ☐60

(5)

Granted that many of our current problems must be cured more by social, political, and economic instruments than by science and technology, yet science and technology must still

54. F. NO CHANGE
    G. through
    H. though
    J. from

55. A. NO CHANGE
    B. of the past
    C. being in the past
    D. OMIT the underlined portion.

56. F. NO CHANGE
    G. in the fact that
    H. about
    J. that

57. A. NO CHANGE
    B. despite
    C. but
    D. also

58. F. NO CHANGE
    G. arising
    H. rising
    J. raised

59. A. NO CHANGE
    B. Contrary to,
    C. Contrasted with,
    D. OMIT the underlined portion.

60. Suppose at this point the writer wanted to add more information about the benefits of science and engineering. Which of the following additions would be most relevant?

    F. A list of the colleges with the best science and engineering degree programs
    G. Specific examples of contributions from the areas of science and engineering that have improved the standard of living
    H. a brief explanation of the current world troubles
    J. the names of several famous scientists and engineers

be the tools to make further advances in such
things as clean air, clean water, better transportation, better housing, better medical care, more adequate welfare programs, purer food, conservation of resources, and many other areas. [62] [63]

61. A. NO CHANGE
    B. advances, in
    C. advances. In
    D. advances—in

62. This passage was probably written for readers who
    F. are college graduates
    G. are interested in an environmental services career
    H. are in a career or contemplating a career in science or engineering
    J. are frustrated with the current world problems.

63. Choose the sequence of paragraph numbers that will make the essay's structure most logical.
    A. NO CHANGE
    B. 1, 4, 2, 3, 5
    C. 5, 4, 2, 3, 1
    D. 4, 2, 3, 1, 5

Passage VI

With increasing prosperity, West European youth am having a fling that is creating distinctive consumer and cultural patterns.

The result has been the increasing emergence in Europe of that phenomenon well known in America as the "youth market." This here is a market in which enterprising businesses cater to the demands of teenagers and older youths in all their rock mania and pop-art forms.

The evolving European youth market has both

64. F. NO CHANGE
    G. youths is
    H. youth be
    J. youth is

65. A. NO CHANGE
    B. here idea
    C. here thing
    D. OMIT the underlined portion.

similarities and differences from the American
youth market.

The markets basis is essentially the same—
more spending power and freedom to use it in the hands of teenagers and older youths. Young consumers also make up an increasing high proportion of the population.

Youthful tastes in the United States and Europe extend over a similar range of products—records and record players, tapes and CDs, transistor radios, leather jackets and "wayout" clothing, cosmetics, and soft drinks, generally it now is difficult to tell in which direction transatlantic teenage influences are flowing.

As in the United States, where "teen" and "teenager" have become merchandising terms, Europeans also have adapted similar terminology. In Flemish and Dutch it is "tiener" for teenagers. The French have simply adopted the English word "teenager." In West Germany the key word in advertising addressed to teenagers is "freizeit," meaning holidays or time off.

The most obvious difference among the youth market in Europe and that in the United States is in size. In terms of volume and variety of sales, the market in Europe is only a shadow of its

66. F. NO CHANGE
    G. similarity
    H. similarities to
    J. similar

67. A. NO CHANGE
    B. markets'
    C. market's
    D. market

68. F. NO CHANGE
    G. increasingly high
    H. increasing higher
    J. high increasing

69. A. NO CHANGE
    B. drinks. Generally
    C. drinks, in general
    D. drinks generally

70. F. NO CHANGE
    G. Trans-Atlantic
    H. trans-Atlantic
    J. Trans-atlantic

71. A. NO CHANGE
    B. picked up
    C. added
    D. adopted

72. F. NO CHANGE
    G. betwixt
    H. amongst
    J. between

American counterpart, but it's a growing
shadow.   75

73. Is the author's use of quotation marks appropriate in this passage?

   A. No, because quotation marks are used to set off a direct quote.
   B. No, because the passage has no dialogue.
   C. Yes, because quotation marks are used to set off words used in a special sense.
   D. Yes, because quotation marks indicate a conversation.

74. This passage was probably written for readers who

   F. are interested in new trends in the consumer patterns of the world's youth
   G. are parents of teenagers
   H. are teenagers
   J. are interested in the different cultural patterns of West Germany

75. Is the use of the dash appropriate in this passage?

   A. Yes, because the dash is used to set off interruptions, additions, and illustrations.
   B. No, because the dash is never used in formal writing.
   C. Yes, because the dash adds flair to the passage.
   D. Yes, because the dash is more effective than brackets or parentheses.

STOP!

This is the end of the English Test.
Do not proceed to the next section until the allotted
time expires.

2. MATHEMATICS TEST

60 Minutes—60 Questions

DIRECTIONS: Solve each problem. Then select the correct answer from among the five choices and darken the corresponding space on the answer sheet.

Solve as many problems as you can since they all have the same point value. Do not spend too much time on a single problem. Remember: You are not penalized for incorrect answers; only those answered correctly contribute to your final score.

NOTE: Unless otherwise stated, assume the following:

- All figures lie in a plane.
- Figures are not necessarily drawn to scale.
- All lines are straight.

---

1. What is the additive inverse of $-\frac{2}{3}$?

   A. $\frac{2}{3}$
   B. $\frac{3}{2}$
   C. $-\frac{3}{2}$
   D. 1
   E. 0

2. Which of the following is an element of the solution set of the equation $x^2 + 6x + 8 = 0$?

   F. -8
   G. -2
   H. 8
   J. 6
   K. 4

3. In the figure below, if $\angle AOC$ is a central angle and the measure of $\angle AOC = 70°$, what is the measure of $\angle ABC$?

   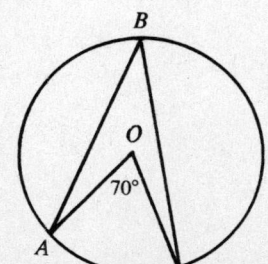

   A. 22°
   B. 35°
   C. 50°
   D. 70°
   E. 140°

DO YOUR FIGURING HERE.

GO ON TO THE NEXT PAGE.

4. In the figure below $l_1 \parallel l_2$. If the measure of $\angle x = 70°$ and the measure of $\angle y = 105°$, what is the measure of $\angle r$?

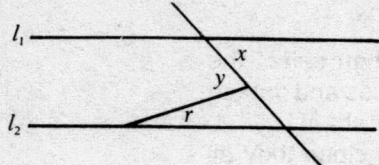

- F. 35°
- G. 45°
- H. 85°
- J. 145°
- K. 175°

5. $A = \dfrac{2gr}{g + r}$. What is the value of g, when $r = 1$ and $A = 4$?

- A. -2
- B. 2
- C. 4
- D. $\dfrac{4}{7}$
- E. $\dfrac{8}{5}$

6. The figure below represents which of the following equations?

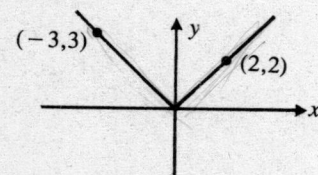

- F. $y = x$
- G. $y = -x$
- H. $y = |x|$
- J. $|y| = x$
- K. $y = x^2$

7. Which of the following is an illustration of the distributive property?

- A. $(12 \times 25)(4) = 12(25 \times 4)$
- B. $7n + 2 - 3n = 7n - 3n + 2$
- C. $(17)(b^2)(5) = (17)(5)(b^2)$
- D. $ab + ac = ba + ca$
- E. $x(x + 2) = x^2 + 2x$

GO ON TO THE NEXT PAGE.

8. Joshua buys a television set for $600. If the sales tax is 7%, what is the total cost of the purchase?

   F. $4.20
   G. $42.00
   H. $420.00
   J. $604.20
   K. $642.00

9. What is the value of $-x^2 - 2x^3$ when $x = -1$?

   A. -3
   B. -1
   C. 0
   D. 1
   E. 3

10. What is the average (arithmetic mean) of the numbers represented by $n + 3$, $2n - 1$, and $3n + 4$?

    F. $\dfrac{5n + 6}{3}$
    G. $2n + 2$
    H. $3n + 3$
    J. $\dfrac{6n + 7}{3}$
    K. $6n + 6$

11. What is the value of $x^0 + x^{1/2} + x^{-2}$ when $x = 9$?

    A. $3\dfrac{1}{81}$
    B. $4\dfrac{1}{81}$
    C. $5\dfrac{7}{18}$
    D. $76\dfrac{1}{2}$
    E. $77\dfrac{1}{2}$

12. $4\sqrt{3} + 3\sqrt{27} = ?$

    F. $7\sqrt{30}$
    G. $10\sqrt{3}$
    H. $13\sqrt{3}$
    J. 63
    K. 108

13. Jessica Dawn received marks of 87, 93, and 86 on three successive tests. What grade must she receive on a fourth test in order to have an average of 90?

    A. 90
    B. 91
    C. 92
    D. 93
    E. 94

DO YOUR FIGURING HERE.

GO ON TO THE NEXT PAGE.

14. In terms of x, what is the total number of cents in $4x$ dimes?

   F. $.04x$
   G. $.4x$
   H. $4x$
   J. $40x$
   K. $400x$

15. Which of the following is shown by the graph below?

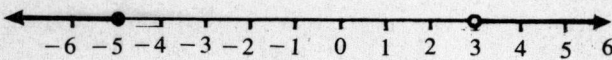

   A. $-5 \leq x < 3$
   B. $-5 < x$ or $x < 3$
   C. $-5 \leq x$ or $x > 3$
   D. $-5 \leq x \leq 3$
   E. $-5 \geq x$ or $x > 3$

16. $2\frac{2}{5} - 1\frac{7}{8} = ?$

   F. $\frac{7}{13}$
   G. $\frac{21}{40}$
   H. $\frac{11}{40}$
   J. $\frac{19}{40}$
   K. $1\frac{5}{40}$

17. In a circle with radius 6, what is the measure (in degrees) of an arc whose length is 2π?

   A. $20°$
   B. $30°$
   C. $60°$
   D. $90°$
   E. $120°$

18. If $\frac{2x}{3\sqrt{2}} = \frac{3\sqrt{2}}{x}$, what is the positive value of x?

   F. 3
   G. 9
   H. $2\sqrt{3}$
   J. $\sqrt{6}$
   K. $\sqrt{3}$

19. If $f(x) = 2x - x^2$ and $g(x) = x - 4$, what is the value of $g(f(2))$?

   A. -8
   B. -4
   C. -2
   D. 0
   E. 3

20. What is the solution set of the equation $|5 - 2x| = 7$?

   F. $\{6, -1\}$
   G. $\{6\}$
   H. $\{-1\}$
   J. $\{1\}$
   K. $\{\ \}$

21. Which of the following is equivalent to $\dfrac{3 - \dfrac{3}{x}}{x - 1}$?

   A. $\dfrac{1}{x-1}$
   B. $\dfrac{1}{3}$
   C. $x + 1$
   D. 3
   E. $\dfrac{3}{x}$

22. What is the slope of the line that passes through the points $(-3, 5)$ and $(4, 7)$?

   F. $\sqrt{53}$
   G. 2
   H. $\dfrac{1}{2}$
   J. $\dfrac{2}{7}$
   K. $\dfrac{7}{2}$

23. In the figure below, diameter $\overline{AB}$ is perpendicular to chord $\overline{CD}$ at E. If $\overline{CD} = 8$ and $\overline{OE} = 3$, what is the length of the radius of the circle?

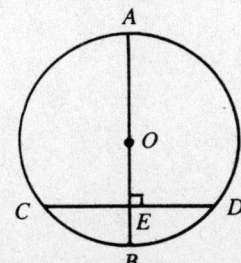

   A. $\sqrt{3}$
   B. $\sqrt{5}$
   C. $\sqrt{7}$
   D. $\sqrt{15}$
   E. 5

GO ON TO THE NEXT PAGE.

24. The diagonals of parallelogram ABCD intersect at point E. If $\overline{DB} = 4x + 2$ and $\overline{DE} = x + 4$, what is the value of x?

    F. 3
    G. 2
    H. 1
    J. 0
    K. $\frac{2}{3}$

25. If the measure of the central angle of a sector of a circle is 120°, what is the area of the sector, if the radius is 6?

    A. 4π
    B. 6π
    C. 8π
    D. 10π
    E. 12π

26. If the statement "If two triangles are red, then they are equal in area" is true, then which of the following must be true?

    F. If the two triangles are not equal in area, then they are not red.
    G. If the two triangles are equal in area, then they are red.
    H. If the two triangles are equal in area, then they are not red.
    J. If the two triangles are not red, then they are not equal in area.
    K. If the two triangles are not red, then they are equal in area.

27. If $\frac{a}{b} = \frac{r}{t}$, then which of the following is not necessarily true?

    A. $\frac{a}{r} = \frac{b}{t}$
    B. $\frac{a}{t} = \frac{b}{r}$
    C. $\frac{a+b}{b} = \frac{r+t}{t}$
    D. $\frac{b}{a} = \frac{t}{r}$
    E. $at = rb$

28. If $-2x + 5 = 2 - (5 - 2x)$, then $x = ?$

    F. 6
    G. 5
    H. 4
    J. 3
    K. 2

GO ON TO THE NEXT PAGE.

29. $\dfrac{(1 + \sin x)(1 - \sin x)}{(1 + \cos x)(1 - \cos x)}$ is the equivalent to which of the following?

A. $\cos x$
B. $\tan x$
C. $\tan^2 x$
D. $\cos^2 x$
E. $\cot^2 x$

30. In the figure below, $\triangle ACB$ is a right triangle. $\overline{CE}$ is the median to hypotenuse $\overline{AB}$, and $\overline{AB} = 14$. What is the length of $\overline{CE}$?

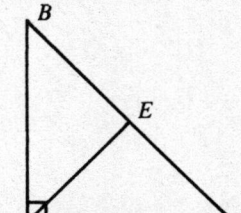

F. 5
G. 6
H. 7
J. 8
K. Cannot be determined from the given information

31. If y varies directly as x, and $y = 10$ when $x = \dfrac{1}{5}$, what is the value of y when $x = \dfrac{1}{2}$?

A. 1
B. 4
C. 7
D. 16
E. 25

32. $\dfrac{(-1)(2)(-3)(4)(-5)}{(5)(-4)(3)(-2)(1)} = ?$

F. 1
G. -1
H. 2
J. -2
K. 3

33. In the diagram below, chords $\overline{AB}$ and $\overline{CD}$ of circle O intersect at E. If $\overline{AE} = 6$, $\overline{EB} = 4$, $\overline{CE} = x$, and $\overline{ED} = 6x$, then $x = ?$

A. 1
B. $1\dfrac{3}{7}$
C. 2
D. 4
E. 6

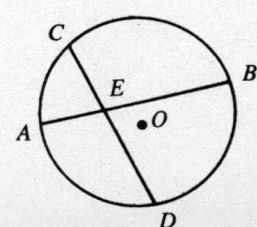

GO ON TO THE NEXT PAGE.

34. The measure of the vertex angle of an isosceles triangle is 50 degrees. What is the measure, in degrees, of each base angle?

    F. 40°
    G. 50°
    H. 65°
    J. 75°
    K. 130°

35. Using the table below, what is the median of the following data?

Score	Frequency
20	4
30	4
50	7

    A. 20
    B. 30
    C. 40
    D. 50
    E. 60

36. Which of the following is the graph of the solution set of $x^2 - 2x - 3 > 0$?

    F.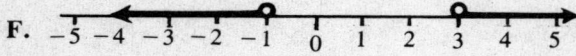
    G.
    H.
    J.
    K.

37. The expression $\sin x + \dfrac{\cos^2 x}{\sin x}$ is equal to which of the following?

    A. 1
    B. $\sin x$
    C. $\cos x$
    D. $\dfrac{1}{\sin x}$
    E. $\dfrac{1}{\cos x}$

38. The value of $(2.5 \times 10^5)^2$ is equal to which of the following?

   F. 6.25×10^7
   G. 6.25×10^{10}
   H. 2.5×10^7
   J. 2.5×10^{10}
   K. 5×10^7

39. If $A * B$ is defined as $\dfrac{AB - B}{-B}$, what is the value of $-2 * 2$?

   A. -3
   B. -1
   C. 0
   D. 1
   E. 3

40. If one of the roots of the equation $x^2 + kx - 12 = 0$ is 4, what is the value of k?

   F. -1
   G. 0
   H. 1
   J. 3
   K. 7

41. In the figure below, D is a point on $\overline{AB}$ and E is a point on $\overline{BC}$ such that $\overline{DE} \parallel \overline{AC}$. If $\overline{DB} = 4$, $\overline{AB} = 10$, and $\overline{BC} = 20$, what is the length of $\overline{EC}$?

   A. 4
   B. 6
   C. 8
   D. 10
   E. 12

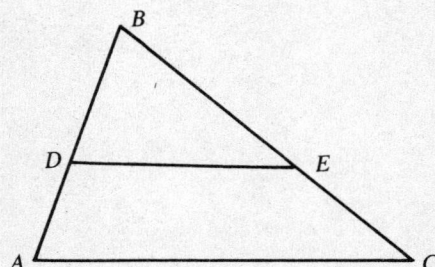

42. $(x + 2)(x - 4) - (x + 4)(x - 2) =$

   F. 0
   G. $2x^2 + 4x - 16$
   H. $-4x$
   J. $4x$
   K. $-4x - 16$

GO ON TO THE NEXT PAGE.

43. If the sum of the measures of the interior angles of a polygon equals the sum of the measures of the exterior angles, how many sides does the polygon have?

    A. 3
    B. 4
    C. 5
    D. 6
    E. 7

44. If the perimeter of an equilateral triangle is 12, what is its area?

    F. $2\sqrt{3}$
    G. $4\sqrt{3}$
    H. 8
    J. $6\sqrt{3}$
    K. $36\sqrt{3}$

45. Two complementary angles are in the ratio of 8:1. What is the number of degrees in the measure of the smaller angle?

    A. 10
    B. 20
    C. 30
    D. 40
    E. 80

46. GIVEN: a square, a rectangle, a trapezoid, and a circle. If one of the figures is selected at random, what is the probability that the figure has four right angles?

    F. 1
    G. $\frac{3}{4}$
    H. $\frac{1}{2}$
    J. $\frac{1}{4}$
    K. 0

47. A man travels 320 miles in 8 hours. If he continues at the same rate, how many miles will he travel in the next 2 hours?

    A. 6
    B. 40
    C. 80
    D. 120
    E. 240

DO YOUR FIGURING HERE.

GO ON TO THE NEXT PAGE.

48. $\dfrac{\sin x}{\cos x} + \dfrac{\cos x}{\sin x} = $?

  F. 1

  G. $\sin x$

  H. $\dfrac{1}{\sin x \cos x}$

  J. $\tan x$

  K. $\dfrac{\sin x + \cos x}{\sin x \cos x}$

49. The average temperatures for five days were 82°, 86°, 91°, 79°, and 91°. What is the mode for these temperatures?

  A. 79
  B. 82
  C. 85.8
  D. 86
  E. 91

50. A booklet contains 30 pages. If 9 pages in the booklet have drawings, what percent of the pages in the booklet have drawings?

  F. 30%
  G. 9%
  H. 3%
  J. 1%
  K. $\dfrac{3}{10}$%

51. Which of the following represents $-7t + 6t^2 - 3$ when it is completely factored?

  A. $(3t - 1)(2t + 3)$
  B. $(3t + 1)(2t - 3)$
  C. $(6t - 1)(t + 3)$
  D. $(6t + 1)(t - 3)$
  E. $(2t - 1)(3t + 3)$

52. What is the solution set of $2^{x^2+2x} = 2^{-1}$?

  F. $\{1\}$
  G. $\{-1\}$
  H. $\{1, -1\}$
  J. $\{2\}$
  K. $\{\ \}$

GO ON TO THE NEXT PAGE.

53. Jessica is 3 years younger than Joshua. If x represents Joshua's age now, what was Jessica's age four years ago in terms of x?

A. $x - 1$
B. $x - 3$
C. $x - 4$
D. $x - 6$
E. $x - 7$

54. In a drama club, x students contributed y dollars each to buy an $18 gift for their advisor. If three more students had contributed, each student could have contributed one dollar less to buy the same gift. Which of the following sets of equations expresses this relationship?

F. $xy = 18$
   $(x + 3)(y - 1) = 18$

G. $xy = 18$
   $(x - 3)(y + 1) = 18$

H. $xy = 18$
   $(x + 3)(y + 1) = 18$

J. $xy = 18$
   $(x - 3)(y - 1) = 18$

K. $xy = 18$
   $(x + 1)(y - 3) = 18$

55. $\frac{1}{2}\sqrt{112} - \sqrt{28} + 2\sqrt{63} =$

A. $6\sqrt{7}$
B. $7\sqrt{7}$
C. $8\sqrt{7}$
D. $9\sqrt{7}$
E. $10\sqrt{7}$

56. What is the value of x for the following set of simultaneous equations?

$$\frac{1}{x} + \frac{1}{y} = \frac{1}{4}$$
$$\frac{1}{x} - \frac{1}{y} = \frac{3}{4}$$

F. 4
G. 2
H. $\frac{1}{2}$
J. $\frac{1}{4}$
K. -4

57. Which set could represent the lengths of the sides of a triangle?

   A. {1, 3, 6}
   B. {2, 4, 7}
   C. {2, 10, 12}
   D. {4, 6, 8}
   E. {4, 4, 10}

58. What is the solution set, in terms of a and b, for the following system of equations?

   $ax + y = b$
   $2ax + y = 2b$

   F. $\left\{-\dfrac{b}{a}, 1\right\}$
   G. $\{-a, b\}$
   H. $\left\{\dfrac{b}{a}, 0\right\}$
   J. $\left\{\dfrac{b}{a}, \dfrac{a}{b}\right\}$
   K. $\left\{\dfrac{2a}{b}, \dfrac{2b}{a}\right\}$

59. In the figure below, $\sin \theta = \dfrac{r}{4}$. What is the value of $\cos \theta$?

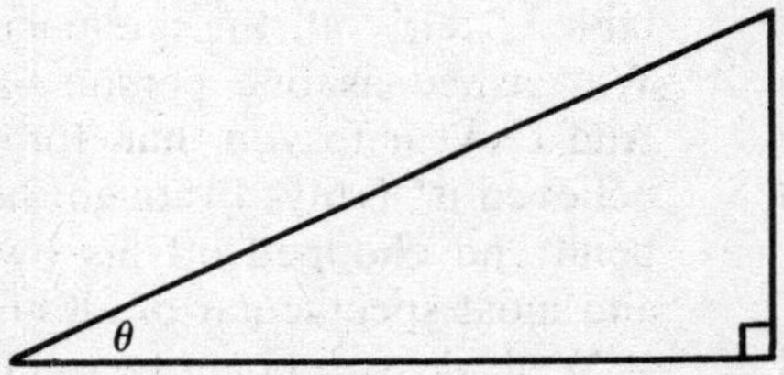

   A. $\dfrac{\sqrt{16 - r^2}}{4}$
   B. $\dfrac{4 - r}{4}$
   C. $\dfrac{\sqrt{16 - r^2}}{2}$
   D. $\dfrac{4 - r}{2}$
   E. $\dfrac{\sqrt{16 - r^2}}{r}$

60. If 3 copier machines can copy 300 sheets in 3 hours, assuming the same rate, how long (in hours) will it take 6 such copiers to copy 600 sheets?

   F. 2
   G. 3
   H. 4
   J. 6
   K. 9

DO YOUR FIGURING HERE.

STOP!
This is the end of the Mathematics Test.
Do not proceed to the next section until the allotted time expires.

3. READING TEST

35 Minutes—40 Questions

DIRECTIONS: There are four passages in this test. Each passage is followed by ten questions. After reading a passage, select the most appropriate answer to each question and blacken the corresponding space on your answer sheet. You may refer to the passages as often as you feel necessary.

Passage I

Richard Burton and Laurence Olivier are great actors. They obviously respect each other.

Burton tells this story of Laurence Olivier's acting genius: Larry, as Richard Burton called him, was starring in a Shakespearean play. There is a famous scene during which the King is compelled to chop off his own left hand with a hatchet. Burton speaks telling how realistically Olivier played the scene.

"The King says a fond and rueful farewell to his hand; that's what it amounts to. As you know, the speech takes place *before* the removal of the hand, and there was Larry—crooning and mooning and kissing his dear hand as though it were a lost, pathetic child. It was brilliant! I had never seen him so truthful, so real. There was a freshness, a newness, an illusion of the first time, a spontaneity unlike anything I've ever seen from Larry. It brought me bolt upright in my seat, my eyes and ears wide open.

"Up to this moment, he had been the same old Larry—expert and crisp—but now he began to moon and whimper and kiss the hand he was about to lose. He brought each finger to his lips, he pressed the palm to his cheek, he turned it this way and that and held the wrist with his right hand as though to memorize the thumb, the wrinkles in the knuckles, each tiny blue vein, each fingernail. He murmured to it longingly, like some passionate Casanova. The effect of the scene was overwhelming. It was so *intimate*, like something played out behind closed doors. At one point, he all but turned his back on the audience for several lines, several kisses, as though he too was aware that this was all too private. I was absolutely hypnotized by the way he moved his mouth about the hand while his other hand caressed it, stopping here to pinch—and there to touch—it was as though the whole business had been choreographed! A beautiful dance of the hands! Such an artistic pattern; such a moving design . . .

"Well, indeed it was a design—as we soon found out. For when he finally came to the end of the speech, he stopped his crooning and caressing; he straightened his shoulders and placed his beloved hand flat against a table top; then he accepted the hatchet from a soldier, swung it a great roundhouse whack through the air, brought it down into that butcher's block as though he were chopping firewood, let out one of his hair-raising shrieks, and bounded across the stage—leaving his own hand, dismembered, sitting all alone on that mad little table. I tell you, the audience was thunderstruck. We gasped as one person—a few ladies fainted! And I swear to you that, for one awful moment, I believed it! Truly, I thought he had gone round the bend and chopped off his own left hand: the last and most spectacular of all his effects!

"Well, do you begin to smell out the sordid facts of all this business? Method? Sincere feeling? Psychological drama? Nothing of the kind. He had to do the speech in just that way. He needed all the pauses to give himself time to undo the artificial hand which was attached to his arm and his costume. The bent shoulders, the passionate-looking hunch came from having to withdraw his own true hand carefully up his sleeve. The kissing and caressing and back-turning and touching with the other hand were all necessary to conceal the nuts and bolts and ratchets, the springs and screws he was putting carefully into place. He didn't choose to play the scene that way—it was thrust upon him. It was inevitable! Method indeed—it was a magic act! And beautiful, too. He's the Harry Houdini of the stage—the greatest trickster of them all."

1. In the passage, what clue most clearly indicates that Burton and Olivier know each other well?

   A. Burton praises Olivier.
   B. Burton calls Olivier by his nickname.
   C. Both have acted in plays by Shakespeare.
   D. Burton went to the theater to watch Olivier act.

2. Burton compares Olivier's emotional attitude toward his hand to that which occurs in a

   F. murder mystery.
   G. musical comedy.
   H. love drama.
   J. medieval tragedy.

3. The speech most impressed Burton because it was

   A. the first time he had ever heard it.
   B. the first time Olivier had said it.
   C. as though Olivier had just made it up.
   D. as though Olivier were reading it.

4. As used in the passage, the word "choreographed" refers to

   F. drawing.
   G. engineering.
   H. transportation.
   J. dancing.

5. Burton gives the listener the impression that Olivier's acting usually is

   A. skillful and concise.
   B. deceptive and smooth.
   C. emotional and flashy.
   D. acrobatic and dynamic.

6. At what point in the scene did Olivier act out the chopping off of his hand?

   F. Just before he ended his speech
   G. Immediately at the end of his speech
   H. In the middle of his speech
   J. Before he began his speech

7. After Olivier chopped off his hand, a loud shriek came from

   A. Olivier.
   B. a few ladies.
   C. Burton.
   D. the audience.

8. For a moment Burton thought that Olivier had

   F. dropped the hatchet.
   G. chopped off both his hands.
   H. insanely chopped off his hand.
   J. accidentally chopped off his hand.

9. Burton says that Olivier played the scene the way he did in order to

   I. make the audience pity him.
   II. follow an acting method.
   III. add psychological excitement.
   IV. have time to take off his artificial hand.

   A. I and II
   B. III and IV
   C. I, II, and III
   D. IV only

10. What tone of voice would Richard Burton most probably use in telling this story?

    F. Amazed
    G. Sarcastic
    H. Humorous
    J. Angry

Passage II

During the night the lightning fluttered perpetually, making the whole sky white. He must have waked again. The world hung livid round him for moments, fields a level sheen of gray-green in dark bulk, and
5 the range of clouds black across a white sky. Then the darkness fell like a shutter, and the night was whole. A faint flutter of a half-revealed world, that could not quite leap out of the darkness! Then there again stood a sweep of pallor for the land, dark
10 shapes looming, a range of clouds hanging overhead. The world was a ghostly shadow, thrown for a moment upon the pure darkness, which returned ever whole and complete. And the mere delirium of sickness and fever went on inside him—his brain
15 opening and shutting like the night—then sometimes convulsions of terror from something with great eyes that stared round a tree—then the long agony of the march, and the sun decomposing his blood— then the pang of hate for the Captain, followed by
20 a pang of tenderness and ease. But everything was distorted, born of an ache and resolving into an ache.

In the morning he came definitely awake. Then his brain flamed with the sole horror of thirstiness! The
25 sun was on his face, the dew was steaming from

his wet clothes. Like one possessed, he got up. There straight in front of him, blue and cool and tender, the mountains ranged across the pale edge of the morning sky. He wanted them—he wanted
30 them alone—he wanted to leave himself and be identified with them. They did not move, they were still and soft, with white, gentle markings of snow. He stood still, mad with suffering, his hands crisping and clutching. Then he was twisting in a paroxysm
35 on the grass.

11. In line 3, the use of the expression, "The world hung livid round him for moments," gives the reader

    A. an opportunity to get to know the soldier
    B. an idea of how the plot will develop
    C. a feeling of the world at a standstill
    D. a brief pause in the story

12. In line 6, the word "shutter" allows the reader to

    F. "hear" the darkness fall
    G. sense the danger
    H. hear the thunder
    J. identify with the soldier

13. In the phrase, "the range of clouds black across a white sky," (line 5), the words *black* and *white* are used to

    A. frighten the soldier
    B. suggest thunder and lightning
    C. describe the fall of darkness
    D. emphasize contrast

14. As used in line 7, the repetition of "flutter" from line 1 has the effect of

    F. renewing the flashing of the lightning
    G. renewing the darkness
    H. enabling the reader to see the action
    J. lighting up the fields and the trees

15. As used in lines 9–10, the effect of "dark shapes looming" is to

    A. reemphasize the "level sheen of gray-green light"
    B. reinforce the phrase "dark bulk"
    C. introduce the "delirium of sickness"
    D. dramatize the "pang of tenderness"

16. The word "pang" is used in line 19 and repeated in line 20 in order to emphasize the main character's

    F. emotional needs
    G. extreme sadness
    H. mental confusion
    J. spiritual feelings

17. The events described in the passage probably take place

    A. after a battle
    B. before a battle
    C. in the character's imagination
    D. during basic training

18. As used in lines 27–28, the description of the mountains as "blue and cool and tender" suggests a

    F. happy ending
    G. new conflict
    H. feeling of calmness
    J. love of nature

19. The tone of the passage is conveyed through the use of a succession of

    A. thoughts
    B. conflicts
    C. fears
    D. word pictures

20. The mood of the passage as a whole is one of

    F. indecision
    G. suffering
    H. grief
    J. protest

Passage III

There was a stumbling rush for the cover of fortification proper; and there the last possible line of defense was established instinctively and in a moment. Officers and men dropped on their knees behind the low bank of earth and continued an irregular deliberate fire, each discharging his piece as fast as he could load and aim. The garrison was not sufficient to form a continuous rank along even this single front, and on such portions of the works as were protected by the ditch, the soldiers were scattered almost as sparsely as sentinels. Nothing saved the place from being carried by an assault except the fact that the assailants were unprovided with scaling ladders. The adventurous fellows who had flanked the palisade rushed to the gate, and gave entrance to a torrent of tall, lank men in butternut or dirty gray clothing, their bronzed faces flushed with the excitement of supposed victory, and their yells of exultation drowning for a minute the sharp outcries of the wounded, and the rattle of the musketry. But the human billow was met by such a fatal discharge that it could not come over the rampart. The foremost dead fell across it, and the mass reeled backward. Unfortunately for the attack, the exterior slope was full of small knolls and gullies, besides being cumbered with rude shanties, of four or five feet in height made of bits of board, and shelter tents, which had served as the quarters of the garrison. Behind these covers, scores if not hundreds sought refuge and could not be induced to leave them for a second charge.

21. Which statement is true of the final defense line?

   A. It was arranged without command.
   B. It was organized by the officers.
   C. It was abandoned by the cowardly.
   D. It was discharged by the officers.

22. Which was a handicap of the defenders?

   F. Improper communications
   G. The ditch
   H. No protection whatsoever
   J. Too few men

23. The reader can infer from this passage that

   I. there are many guards in the garrison.
   II. sentinels are placed widely apart.
   III. sentinels are usually officers.

   A. I only
   B. II only
   C. I and II
   D. II and III

24. The men who were attacking the garrison lacked

   F. sufficient food.
   G. adequate medical supplies.
   H. a battle plan.
   J. special equipment.

25. Which statement is most probably true of the men who flanked the palisade?

   A. They were warmly dressed.
   B. They followed up an initial advantage.
   C. They were supported by the sentinels.
   D. They were scattered widely in the attack.

26. The attackers were most hindered in their attack by

   F. the terrain.
   G. their wounded.
   H. lack of ammunition.
   J. their presupposed victory.

27. Many of the attackers

   A. surrendered to the garrison.
   B. were hampered by inferior training.
   C. refused to make another assault.
   D. were overwhelmed by superior numbers.

28. The expression "the human billow" means the

   F. wounded.
   G. guards.
   H. attacking force.
   J. brave defenders.

29. This passage probably takes place during

   A. The Civil War.
   B. The Korean War.
   C. World War II.
   D. The Vietnam War.

30. The tone of the passage is

   F. analytical.
   G. dispassionate.
   H. dramatic.
   J. cantankerous.

Passage IV

Some years ago a young man applied to a large United States optical firm for a job as a lens designer. He apologized for lack of training, but on announcing that he owned two copies of the classic Conrady *Applied Optics and Optical Design*, one for his office and a second for his bedside table, he was

GO ON TO THE NEXT PAGE.

hired on the spot. Perhaps the story will be repeated some day with Buchdahl's *Introduction to Hamiltonian Optics* as a similar credential.

Hamiltonian theory describes with powerful generality the overall properties of optical systems considered as "black boxes," although it does not describe the detailed structure needed to construct the systems and achieve these properties. Buchdahl's book is therefore on the subject of geometrical optics, but it is not about how to design lenses. It is, however, a compact, comprehensive account of the fundamentals of the theory written with the lens designer's needs very much in mind. Every lens designer worth his salt has at some time in his career attempted to apply the broad concepts of Hamiltonian optics to the solution of practical problems. Success has been sufficiently rare that the theory, as such, has made little direct contribution to techniques for optical instrument design. The failures have been frustrating because of the obvious fundamental power of the theory and because of its conceptual elegance. The indirect effects have been large, however, both in contributing to an understanding of fundamental principles that govern the overall behavior of optical systems and in pointing the way to other, more practical, theoretical approaches.

Buchdahl approaches the subject not only as a capable mathematical physicist, but as one who with a knowledge of practical optics has made a significant contribution to geometrical optical theory. Buchdahl's approach to higher-order aberration theory has, over the last decade, had a major impact on modern lens design with computers. Thus he brings to this exposition of Hamiltonian optics a familiarity with practical optics not usually found in authors on this subject.

The author claims his book to be nonmathematical, and indeed it might be so viewed by a professional mathematician. From the point of view of many physicists and engineers, it will appear to be quite mathematical. Moreover, this is a tightly written book. The subject matter is developed with precision, and the author expects the reader, at every point, to be master of the preceding exposition.

31. Hamiltonian theory allows the lens crafter to

   A. obtain specific information necessary to design lenses.
   B. understand the details of geometrical optics.
   C. get an overview of optical properties.
   D. utilize an easy method of lens crafting techniques.

32. The fact that lens designers have high failure rates shows that

   F. Hamiltonian theory does not provide practical know-how.
   G. there are little or no direct benefits to Hamiltonian theory.
   H. Hamiltonian theory is not supported by what is known about geometrical optics.
   J. Hamiltonian theory was too oversimplified to cover the intricacies of lens design.

33. Hamiltonian theory met with failure as a result of

   A. newer findings related to the wave particle nature of light.
   B. very intricate concepts too difficult to understand by most lens designers.
   C. too much mathematical detail in the theory.
   D. not enough practical information offered by the theory to allow for use by lens crafters.

34. The author of this passage implies that *Introduction to Hamiltonian Optics* is

   F. valuable only to those beginning to study optics.
   G. necessary to those interested in developing new optical systems.
   H. useless to those interested in practical optics.
   J. valuable to any student of optics.

35. The story of the young man's applying for a job was told to show the

   A. value of a personal library.
   B. author's high opinion of this new book.
   C. need for practical and easily understood books.
   D. author's high opinion of classical books.

36. The author's implication regarding Mr. Buchdahl's ability to write about Hamiltonian optics is

   F. aided by the practical applications he attaches to the theory.
   G. hampered by the frustrations of his work with the theory.
   H. helped by his practical experience with optics.
   J. hindered by his shortcomings in mathematics.

37. The article points out that the greatest benefits of Hamiltonian optics have been found in

    A. indirect ways.
    B. a fundamental power within the theory.
    C. the conceptual elegance of the theory.
    D. the practical applications of the theory in finding new approaches to old problems.

38. It is implied that Buchdahl's book could best be approached

    F. as a source for practical solutions to optical problems.
    G. by browsing to discover the general theory.
    H. in connection with *Applied Optics and Optical Design*.
    J. by studying it systematically from start to finish.

39. This passage is probably excerpted from

    A. a review of *Introduction to Hamiltonian Optics*.
    B. a chemistry textbook.
    C. an optician's manual.
    D. a general science text.

40. *Introduction to Hamiltonian Optics* would be considered mathematical by

    I. mathematicians.
    II. physicists.
    III. engineers.

    F. I only
    G. I and II
    H. II and III
    J. I, II, and III

STOP!

This is the end of the Reading Test.
Do not proceed to the next section until the allotted
time expires.

4. SCIENCE REASONING TEST

35 Minutes—40 Questions

DIRECTIONS: Each passage in this test is followed by several questions. After reading a passage, select the most appropriate answer to each question and blacken the corresponding space on your answer sheet. You may refer to the passages as often as necessary while answering the questions.

Passage I

Part of our understanding of the Earth comes from a consideration of its physical properties. A table of selected properties is presented below:

Property	Value
Mass	6×10^{24} kg
Diameter	6×10^{6} m
Orbital Radius	1.5×10^{11} m
Period of Revolution	365.3 days
Period of Rotation	24 hours

Below is a table comparing the other planets of the solar system to the Earth:

	Earth	Jupiter	Mars	Mercury	Neptune	Pluto	Saturn	Uranus	Venus
Diameter	1	10	0.55	0.38	4.3	?	9.4	4.1	0.98
Mass	1	320	0.10	0.58	17	?	95	14	0.83
Surface Gravity	1	2.7	0.40	0.40	1.2	?	1.2	1.1	0.90
Volume	1	1320	0.15	0.58	42	.729	760	50	0.90
Avg. Distance to Sun	1	5.3	1.5	0.40	30	40	10	19	0.70
Period of Revolution	1	12	2	0.25	165	248	30	84	0.60
Period of Rotation	1	0.40	1	60	0.50	0	0.40	0.50	240

The following are a few basic equations:

1) density = $\dfrac{\text{mass}}{\text{volume}}$
2) distance = rate × time
3) volume of a sphere = $\dfrac{4}{3}\pi r^3$

where r is the radius of the sphere

1. Based on the tables above, what is the approximate ratio of the period of revolution in days to the period of rotation in days for Mercury?

   A. 240
   B. $\frac{2}{3}$
   C. $\frac{1}{240}$
   D. $\frac{3}{2}$

2. Which planet is as dense as the planet Earth?

   F. Mercury
   G. Venus
   H. Mars
   J. None

3. Which planet orbits the sun at the slowest rate?

   A. Mercury
   B. Jupiter
   C. Neptune
   D. Pluto

4. Analysis of the tables above shows that surface gravity most likely depends on

   F. mass alone.
   G. volume and mass.
   H. density alone.
   J. density of the planet and proximity to the sun.

5. Assuming that both the Earth and Pluto are spherical, what is the diameter of Pluto?

   A. 0.729 × radius of Earth
   B. 0.9 × radius of Earth
   C. 1.8 × radius of Earth
   D. 2.7 × radius of Earth

6. How many millions of miles separate the most separated planetary neighbors?

   F. 40 × Earth's orbital radius
   G. 11 × Earth's orbital radius
   H. 9 × Earth's orbital radius
   J. 10 × Earth's orbital radius

Passage II

A scientist wished to observe the effects of overcrowding. To study this, he decided to study the changes over time in body weight and in the concentration of a hormone X, which is known to trigger aggressive behavior in mice. Below is a description of various experiments:

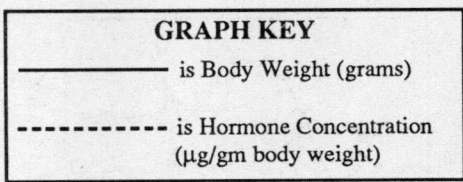

Experiment 1

Five mice were kept in a cage with dimensions 50 cm × 50 cm × 50 cm. The cage was kept at a constant 75°F. Eight grams of standard laboratory rat food were provided per mouse per day. Water was provided by a water bottle that was kept filled at all times. Sixteen hours of daylight were provided by natural spectrum light bulbs. Every day for eleven days the mice were weighed every six hours, and a blood sample was taken. The blood was analyzed for hormone X, and the concentration was reported in micrograms per gram of body weight. Averages of the readings were used in preparing the graph presented below:

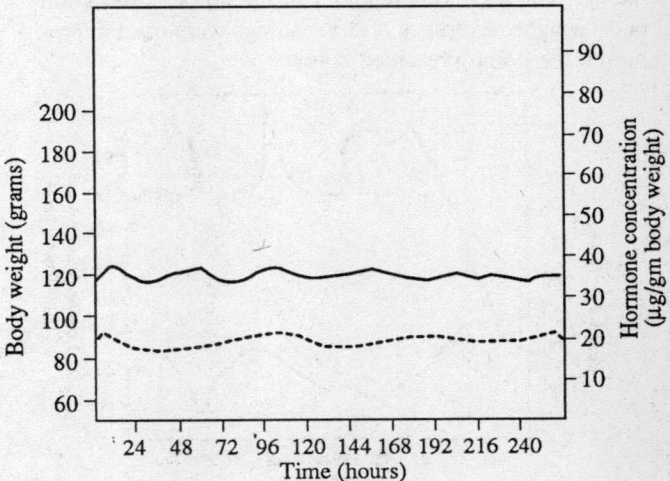

Experiment 2

Ten mice were kept in a cage with dimensions equal to 50 cm × 50 cm × 50 cm. The cage was kept at a constant 75°F. Eight grams of standard laboratory rat food were provided per mouse per day. Water was provided by a water bottle that was kept filled at all times. Sixteen hours of daylight were provided by means of natural spectrum light bulbs. Each day for eleven days the mice were weighed every six hours, and a blood sample was taken. The blood was analyzed for hormone X, and the concentration was reported in micrograms per gram of body weight. Averages of the readings were used in preparing the graph presented below:

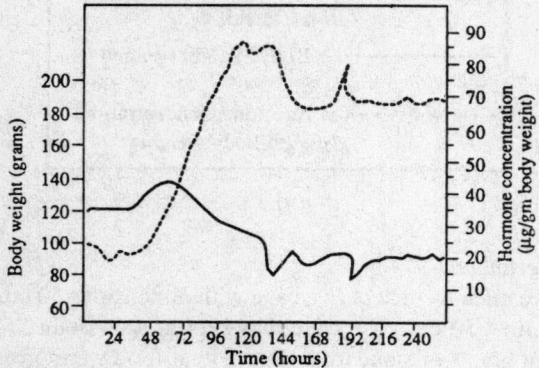

Experiment 3

Twenty mice were kept in a cage with dimensions 50 cm × 50 cm × 50 cm. The cage was kept at a constant 75°F. Eight grams of standard laboratory rat food were provided per mouse per day. Water was provided by a water bottle that was kept filled at all times. Sixteen hours of daylight were provided by means of natural spectrum light bulbs. Each day for eleven days the mice were weighed every six hours. Also, blood samples were taken every day. The blood was analyzed for hormone X, and the concentration was reported in micrograms per gram body weight. Averages of the readings were used in preparing the graph presented below:

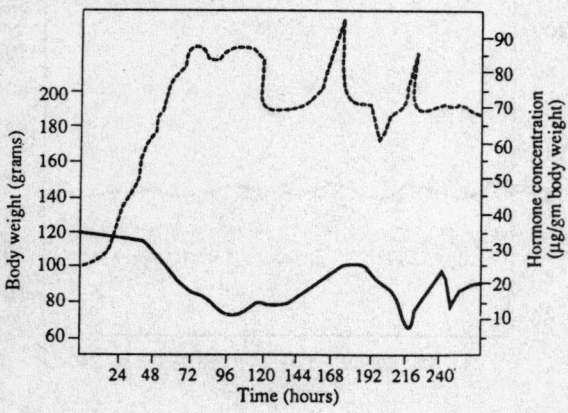

7. In Experiment 3, during which time period did the greatest percentage drop in weight occur?

   A. From 0 to 24 hours
   B. From 24 to 48 hours
   C. From 192 to 216 hours
   D. From 216 to 240 hours

8. Which of the following, if true, would most weaken the ability to compare the experiments legitimately?

   F. More mice died in experiment 3.
   G. Hormone X concentrations were determined by different methods in the three experiments.
   H. Different average initial weights
   J. Different average final weights

9. What was the average total weight of hormone X present in a mouse in Experiment 2 at the 132-hour mark?

   A. 6800 μg   B. 85 μg   C. 80 μg   D. 5.3 μg

10. Which of the following most accurately describes the relation between hormone X and body weight?

    F. An increase in hormone X causes a drop in body weight approximately a day later.
    G. An increase in body weight is caused by a drop in hormone X concentration in the previous 24 hours.
    H. An increase in hormone X is followed by a drop in weight approximately one day later.
    J. The relationship is directly proportional with a proportionality constant of 2.5.

11. What is the normal concentration of hormone X for the mice used in these experiments?

    A. 100   B. 70   C. 25   D. 20

Passage III

The solubility of materials in liquids depends not only on the nature of the solute and the solvent, but also on temperature. A graph showing the solubilities of several substances in water is presented on page 315.

12. Which of the following has a solubility most sensitive to temperature throughout the range shown?

    F. $NaNO_3$
    G. KNO_3
    H. $NaCl$
    J. NH_3

13. The solubility of sodium salts is

    A. high because sodium is an alkali metal.
    B. low because sodium combines with anions to make salts.
    C. dependent on what salt it forms.
    D. always greater than 20 grams per 100 grams of water.

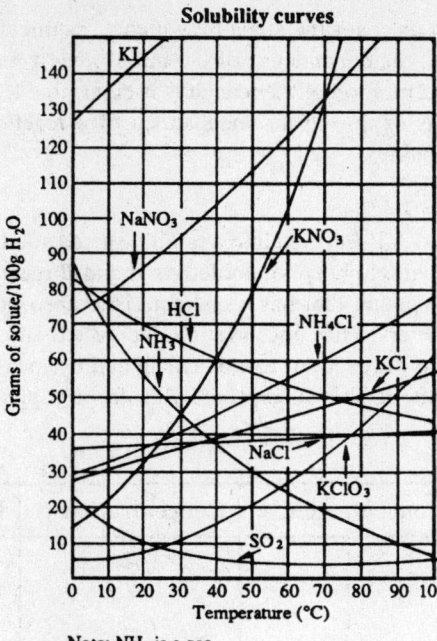

Solubility curves

Note: NH₃ is a gas

14. A 250 ml alcoholic solution of KNO₃ at 50°C contains how many grams KNO₃ at saturation?

   F. 80
   G. 200
   H. 30
   J. Insufficient data is provided.

15. A solution containing equal amounts of NaNO₃ and KNO₃ is allowed to cool until a white powder begins to appear at the bottom of the flask. That powder is

   A. KNO₃
   B. NaNO₃
   C. A mixture of both
   D. Insufficient data is provided.

16. The solubility curve of NH₃ suggests an explanation of why

   F. divers get the bends (nitrogen bubbles in the blood) if they rise too quickly.
   G. soda goes flat.
   H. warm lemonade is sweeter than cold lemonade.
   J. hot air balloons rise.

Passage IV

The chart shows the time periods when several species of organisms lived on the Earth and the type of environment, either ocean or land, in which each species lived.

The diagram shows the fossils of these organisms that are found in the rock layers (A through H) of two separate outcrops that are 25 kilometers apart. Each rock layer contains a complete fossil record of the organisms that existed in the depositional environment during the time of deposition. If a fossil symbol is not shown in a rock layer, the species either lived in the other environment or did not exist at the time that the rock formed.

CHART

DIAGRAM

FOSSIL RECORD IN THE ROCK LAYERS

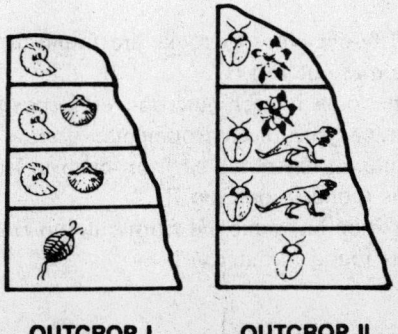

OUTCROP I   OUTCROP II

17. According to the chart, when did dinosaurs live on the Earth?

   A. Between 225 and 65 million years ago
   B. Between 225 and 136 million years ago
   C. Between 570 and 435 million years ago
   D. Between 395 and 280 million years ago

18. Which rock layer in outcrop I could be the same age as layer F in outcrop II?

   F. A
   G. B
   H. C
   J. D

19. According to the chart, when did flowering plants become extinct?

   A. During the Jurassic period
   B. During the Tertiary period
   C. At the same time the insects became extinct
   D. The chart does not give information on the extinction of flowering plants.

20. The extinction of the spirifers occurred at most nearly the same time as the

   F. extinction of the insects.
   G. beginning of the trilobites.
   H. beginning of flowering plants.
   J. extinction of the dinosaurs.

21. Based on fossil evidence, during which time period was rock layer E most likely deposited?

   A. Tertiary
   B. Triassic
   C. Permian
   D. Ordovician

22. Which statement best explains the differences between the types of fossils found in outcrop I and outcrop II?

   F. Different types of rocks are found at outcrop I than at outcrop II.
   G. The rocks in each outcrop were deposited in different types of environments.
   H. Faulting has removed from outcrop I those fossils found in outcrop II.
   J. Erosion has removed from outcrop II those fossils found in outcrop I.

Passage V

In order to discover the steps by which a chemical reaction occurs, the dependence of the initial rate of reaction on the concentration of the reactants is determined. Three experiments exploring the mechanism of a reaction are presented below:

Experiment 1

Compound A is injected into a rapidly stirred solution of B in hexamethyl phosphoramide. As A and B react, they form a compound that has a characteristic absorption at 520 nanometers. The concentration of product, and therefore the rate of reaction, can be calculated by measuring the strength of the absorption. Results are presented below:

Trial	Concentration A	Concentration B	Rate
1	4	4	60
2	2	2	30
3	4	2	30
4	4	8	120

Experiment 2

Compound A is injected into a rapidly mixed solution of B in carbon tetrachloride. The product of the reaction is identical to the product in the previous experiment. The course of the reaction is followed by spectrophotometric methods as in Experiment 1.

Trial	Concentration A	Concentration B	Rate
1	3	3	27
2	6	6	108
3	6	3	54
4	12	6	216

Experiment 3

Compound A is injected in a swirling solution of B in a 1:1-by-volume mixture of carbon tetrachloride and hexamethyl phosphoramide. The formation of product, as before, is followed by spectrophotometry.

Trial	Concentration A	Concentration B	Rate
1	9	9	54
2	9	4.5	27
3	4	4.5	18
4	4	9	36

23. Which of the following best describes the effect of concentration A on the rate of reaction in Experiment 1?

   A. Rate increases with increasing A.
   B. Rate increases by the square of the concentration of A.
   C. Rate increases by the square root of the concentration of A.
   D. Rate is independent of the concentration of A.

24. Which of the following best describes the effect of concentration of A on the rate of reaction in Experiment 2?

   F. Rate increases with increasing A.
   G. Rate increases by the square of the concentration of A.
   H. Rate increases by the square root of the concentration of A.
   J. Rate is independent of the concentration of A.

25. Which of the following best describes the effect on rate of the concentration of A in Experiment 3?

   A. Rate increases with increasing A.
   B. Rate increases by the square of the concentration of A.
   C. Rate increases by the square root of the concentration of A.
   D. Rate is independent of the concentration of A.

26. What is the likeliest explanation for the results obtained in Experiment 3?

   F. A mechanism intermediate between the ones found in Experiments 1 and 2
   G. Some of the molecules react by Experiment 1's mechanism, others by Experiment 2's mechanism.
   H. An entirely different mechanism is responsible.
   J. There is an averaging of the mechanisms.

27. What is the best conclusion that can be drawn from this set of experiments?

   A. Rate is increased by changing solvents.
   B. Reactions may depend on solvent effects as well as on the nature of the reactants.
   C. Mechanisms can always be changed by use of an appropriate solvent.
   D. Reactions depend on solvent effects as well as on the nature of the reactants.

Passage VI

Acceleration is defined as the change in the velocity of an object divided by the length of time during which that change took place. Contrary to popular belief, Galileo did not base his conclusion on the acceleration of gravity on experiments done with cannonballs dropped from the Leaning Tower of Pisa. Instead, he used the motion of objects moving down an inclined plane to develop his theory. In the following sets of experiments, a student studies the motion of bodies on an inclined plane.

(NOTE: For all of the following experiments, time is measured in seconds, distance in meters, and velocity in meters per second. The distance (d) an object travels at a constant acceleration (a) in time (t) assuming it starts from rest, is given by the equation: $d = \frac{1}{2} at^2$

Experiment 1

A student set up a smooth wooden board at an angle of 30° from horizontal. The board had a length of 10 meters. Using a stroboscope, the student was able to determine the position of a 100-gram steel ball that was rolled down the incline. Velocity was determined by means of a radar gun. The results are presented below:

Time	Distance	Velocity
0	0	0
0.5	0.44	1.75
1.0	1.75	3.5
1.5	3.94	5.25
2.0	7.00	7.00

Experiment 2

The same 10-meter wooden board was used in the second experiment. The angle used was once again 30°. The object used this time was a 100-gram sled made of the same material as the ball in Experiment 1. The stroboscope and the radar gun were used to determine its position and velocity as it slid down the inclined plane. The results are presented below:

Time	Distance	Velocity
0	0	0
0.5	1.13	2.45
1.0	2.45	4.90
1.5	5.51	7.35
2.0	9.80	9.80

Experiment 3

The same board at the same angle was used in the third experiment as in the previous two. In this experiment a 100-gram box made of the same material as the ball and the sled was used. The same recording devices were used, and the results presented below:

Time	Distance	Velocity
0	0	0
1.0	0.33	0.66
2.0	1.31	1.32
3.0	2.97	1.98
4.0	5.28	2.64
5.0	8.25	3.30

Experiment 4

The board in the previous experiments was carefully oiled. Once again the board was placed at an angle of 30° from horizontal. Each of the objects was then allowed to move down the inclined plane, and the time required to reach the bottom of the plane is recorded below:

Object	Time
sled	2.02
ball	2.39
box	4.08

28. Which object in the first three experiments has the greatest acceleration?

    F. Ball
    G. Sled
    H. Box
    J. Ball and sled are equal.

29. The acceleration of the ball relative to that of the sled is due to the ball's

    A. rolling.
    B. friction.
    C. rolling and friction.
    D. being the same mass as the sled, and therefore having the same acceleration.

30. The acceleration of the ball relative to that of the box is due to

    F. the ball's rolling only.
    G. the ball's friction only.
    H. the ball's rolling and friction.
    J. the ball's having the same mass as the box, and therefore having the same acceleration.

31. Based on these four experiments, the ratio of the acceleration of the ball to the acceleration of the sled is

    A. 1
    B. $\frac{5}{7}$
    C. dependent on amount of friction.
    D. time dependent

32. Based on these four experiments, the ratio of the acceleration of the ball to the acceleration of the box is

    F. 1.
    G. $\frac{5}{7}$.
    H. dependent on amount of friction.
    J. dependent on time.

Passage VII

What was the fate of Neanderthal man? Two differing views are presented below.

Scientist 1

Neanderthals were very similar to modern humans in appearance. It is true that Neanderthals were somewhat more muscular than modern humans, and that the way the muscles seem to have been arranged on the skeleton was, in a few minor ways, different. This we are able to deduce from the places on the surviving bones that mark where the ligaments were once attached. For example, the neck and wrists of Neanderthals were far thicker than is natural to modern humans. Some of the facial structure was also different, especially the protusion of the brow. But differences between the appearance of Neanderthal and modern humans have been exaggerated, being based on the skeleton of one individual who was later discovered to have been suffering from severe arthritis. It is not unlikely that because of the low population density, and the nomadic lifestyle that spread the few individuals over ever larger areas that Neanderthal and early modern humans interbred and eventually merged into one species. The notion that some sort of "war" broke out between these different species (or, more likely, subspecies) of humans is an attempt to look out of early human eyes with a modern perspective.

Scientist 2

Whenever two species compete for the same niche there is a conflict. In this conflict the loser either moves to a different niche or dies out. It is unusual for two species to interbreed. The difference between early modern humans and Neanderthals physically may not appear great to an anatomist, but to the average man on the street, or prehistoric man in the forest, the differences are not subtle. And it was these individuals, not the anatomists, that had to decide whether or not to mate. And even if early modern humans and Neanderthals did mate the result—us—would look more like a mix of the two rather than like modern humans. Early modern humans and Neanderthals, because they were so close to each other physically, must have been deadly enemies. The population was thinly dispersed at that time because the resources available would not support a greater population density. There literally was not room enough on the planet for the two species. They could not combine because they were so different in appearance, so only one answer remained. We survived because we killed our cousin.

33. Underlying the hypothesis of Scientist 1 is the assumption that

    A. Early modern humans and Neanderthals did not compete for the same kinds of food.
    B. Early modern humans and Neanderthals were genetically close.
    C. Early modern humans and Neanderthals did not necessarily live in the same area.
    D. Early modern humans and Neanderthals often fought.

34. Underlying the hypotheses of both scientists is the assumption that

    F. Early modern humans and Neanderthals understood the consequences of their actions.
    G. Early modern humans and Neanderthals both lived in exactly the same type of environment.
    H. Early modern humans and Neanderthals both lived in the same geographical regions.
    J. Early modern humans were more intelligent than Neanderthals.

35. If an isolated community of Neanderthals were discovered, whose hypothesis would be more damaged?

    A. Scientist 1's because his theory does not allow for such a community to survive.
    B. Scientist 2's because all the Earth is inhabited by early modern human's descendants and therefore there should be no community of Neanderthals.
    C. Both hypotheses are disproved.
    D. Neither is affected.

36. Which of the following, if true, would most support the hypothesis of Scientist 2?

    F. The camps of early modern humans are often close to the camps of Neanderthals.
    G. The camps of early modern humans are never close to Neanderthal camps.
    H. Bones of Neanderthal and early modern humans are often found near each other.
    J. Chipped Neanderthal bones are found with early modern human weapons.

37. The fact that lions and tigers fight when brought together even though they can be interbred supports which hypothesis to the greater extent?

    A. Scientist 1 because it proves two species can interbreed.
    B. Scientist 1 because two species still exist that share the same niche.
    C. Scientist 2 because it suggests that two species that can interbreed may not do so under natural conditions.
    D. Scientist 2 because lions and tigers fight when brought together.

38. According to the hypothesis of Scientist 2, what should be the result of interbreeding lions and tigers?

    F. The offspring should be infertile.
    G. The offspring will resemble one parent only.
    H. The offspring will possess a mixture of traits.
    J. Scientist 2's hypothesis makes no conjectures on the point because lions and tigers would not interbreed.

39. What other assumption do both Scientist 1 and Scientist 2 make about Neanderthals and early modern humans?

    A. That early modern humans were directly involved in the disappearance of Neanderthals.
    B. That early modern humans were the more intelligent of the two.
    C. That Neanderthals differed little from early modern humans.
    D. That early modern humans only inhabited regions that were hospitable for Neanderthals.

40. If a burial site containing over one hundred early modern human and Neanderthal remains were discovered, and if two Neanderthal skeletons were found with early modern human spearpoints in them, which hypothesis would be the most strengthened?

    F. Scientist 1 because the spearpoints need not have been what killed the two Neanderthals.
    G. Scientist 2 because two Neanderthals were killed by early modern humans and no early modern humans were killed by Neanderthals.
    H. Scientist 2 because the spearpoints prove that the early modern humans had more developed weapons.
    J. Scientist 1 because only a couple of the individuals buried together died violently.

STOP!

This is the end of the Science Reasoning Test.
When the allotted time for this section expires, the entire test is completed.

WHAT YOU NEED TO KNOW ABOUT COLLEGE FINANCIAL AID

John Schwartz, Staff Reporter, *Washington Post*

Adapted from

ARCO's *College Financial Aid*, 5th Edition

- **Anyone Can Pay for College**
- **The World of Available Aid—Public Channels**
- **The World of Available Aid—Private Channels**
- **Putting Together Your Financial Aid Package**
- **Glossary of Financial Aid Terms**
- **At-a-Glance Financial Aid Calendar**

Anyone Can Pay for College

The Short Course: What This Section Will Tell You

This section is filled with fundamental information about financial aid for people in a hurry. You'll find capsule descriptions of the basic kinds of financial aid, some tips here and there, and a few warnings to make sure you don't lose out. The section also includes a long-term and short-term view of trends in paying for college that could help you plan for the near and distant future.

There Are Right and Wrong Ways to Pay for College

In *Citizen Kane*, Charles Foster Kane tells an associate, "It ought to be easy to make money—if that's all you want to do." When he made that statement, Kane—like the man he was modeled on, publishing magnate William Randolph Hearst—was a millionaire many times over. You, the reader, are probably not a millionaire many times over. Even if Kane was right, college is not the time to make moneymaking your sole goal. When you're going to college, the last thing you want to do is to spend so much time trying to pay the bills that you can't enjoy the experience—or worse, can't keep up with your studies.

There are plenty of bad ways to pay your way through college. The most common is simple overwork: taking on two or more jobs to make ends meet. One friend was working his way through law school with no less than three part-time jobs. He ended up spending a semester recuperating from hepatitis, and almost had to put off graduating. (Today he's a successful attorney—still overworked, but getting paid handsomely for it.) Other diseases, such as mononucleosis, commonly spring from exhaustion. Why ruin four great years of your life by keeping your nose so close to the grindstone that you can't even enjoy your studies, much less develop a social life? If you decide to work through your college days, choose your employment wisely.

Another way to pay college expenses that gets students into trouble is taking on an oversized debt burden. Education funding experts have warned that taking on too heavy a burden of debts may cause students to look toward safer, higher-paying careers than they might otherwise be attracted to. The same experts also fear that the prospect of being in debt could be enough to scare many lower-income students away from college, or from majors they might find personally fulfilling (say, teaching) but which they feel will never allow them to repay the loans. We lose a lot of good teachers to the ranks of lawyers and engineers that way. While student loans are an increasingly important part of financial aid packages, most schools still have some discretion as to how much of your aid package should be made up of loans and how much should be made up of outside grants.

Some ideas aren't just bad: they're illegal. Shady moneymaking schemes attract a number of students for the same reason that they attract criminals: quick money, and lots of it. However, the risk often outweighs the reward, and few students show the street smarts to escape the long arm of the law.

It is essential to know how to spend your time wisely and get the maximum amount of financial aid funds from the most lucrative sources. That way, you'll be less likely to run yourself into the ground trying to make up for aid money you might otherwise have gotten.

Figuring Out What College Will Really Cost

The student is more than just a seeker of knowledge—he or she is also a consumer in the academic marketplace. And all good shoppers know the value of comparison shopping. Comparing colleges, while a complex task, pays off. The main areas of comparison are these: tuition and fees, books and supplies, room and board, transportation, and personal expenses. Most colleges publish a "consumer brochure"—a handy resource that sets out expenses. That brochure is a helpful starting point for any student or family.

Tuition and fees vary widely, but the most basic dividing line between institutions is public versus private. Private schools simply tend to be pricier. However, public schools are far from cheap—and out-of-state tuition at many of the most respected public universities rivals that of many private schools.

Books and supplies don't vary as much from school to school as do tuition and fees, but they can add hundreds of dollars each semester to the bill and must be counted in. These costs vary depending on the field of study, so it is important to find out typical figures from the academic department or from students within the major.

Room and board can be measured simply if the student is living in a dormitory: it's part of the total bill. But don't think living at home will simply clear that cost from the college budget. For one thing, you won't save as much money as you think on wholesome, home-cooked meals. Irregular class hours will force the student to buy at least one meal a day on or near campus. And if the student is going to live off campus, living expenses could run even higher, with variations from school to school. The differences between paying for an apartment in Athens, Georgia, and Cambridge, Massachusetts, are enough to skew comparisons of schools that might otherwise appear to be similarly priced.

Personal and travel expenses may add up to more than parents expect. Although students have historically lived on the cheap, the Benetton generation is more prone to fancy accessories than its grubbier parents, for whom a year-old pair of (non-designer) blue jeans could be considered formal wear. Even the 1993 Seattle/Grunge fad could be expensive if you went to fancy department stores for those fashionably worn-out lumberjack shirts. Again, geographic variation wreaks havoc on expense estimates. Travel expenses might include air fare for out-of-state students or simply gas and car repair for commuters. In any case, this easily overlooked category can add thousands to the college bundle of costs. Finally, don't forget to add in known medical costs, such as treatment and pharmaceuticals for an existing medical condition.

When you start to see the real cost of college, you might give serious consideration to getting a degree from one of those institutions that advertises on matchbook covers, or to exploring a career in auto repair. DON'T PANIC! Expensive institutions know that they cost more than most people can pay, and they often have the resources to help you.

Once you know what different schools might cost, it's time to work out what you and your family can afford to pay. Taking the difference between what the college costs and what you can afford to pay gives you the amount of your need. This deceptively simple term, "need," doesn't necessarily mean what you think it ought to mean, or what you would like for it to mean. It's a specific, technical term for the amount you cannot pay on your own, and is the amount left after your expected Family Contribution (FC) is subtracted from your cost of education. Your family's contribution to college costs will be determined through a formula developed by the College Scholarship Service (CSS), an arm of the College Board, based on information you provide by filling out the Financial Aid Form (FAF). Family Contribution is the product of a formula, too: it is derived from the family's income after basic expenses are subtracted, along with a portion of the family's assets outside of those needed for retirement or business.

Financial Aid: What It Is

Financial assistance comes in three basic flavors: grants, loans, and work-study. Grants do not need to be repaid, while loans must be repaid some day. Work-study lets students work in order to gain the money to pay for school. You and the financial aid administrator at the college of your choice will negotiate a financial assistance package that will probably contain some combination of these three varieties of aid.

Your aid will come from a number of sources, from the most massive federal programs down to institutional funds unique to your school. Aid might come from the state, private foundations, the school, or even your employer. If the aid comes from a federal government program or a state agency, it is known as public aid; sources such as employers, donors, or foundations are known as private aid.

Federal Aid

Since the federal government is the largest source of student aid, it pays to know something about the major federal programs. The federal government, through the Department of Education, offers the best-known college financial aid programs. These are:

Pell Grants

5.5 billion in Pell grants went to about 4.3 million students in the 1992-93 school year. This program was once known as the Basic Educational Opportunity Grant program, and you might see it referred to as such in older materials. These grants are distributed based on family need and education costs at your school. The maximum available in the 1993-94 school year is $2,300 per year, though the maximum amount changes from year to year depending on how Congress funds the program. Eligibility is determined by a standard formula which was passed into law by Congress; this formula places you along a Student Aid Index which is used by the schools to determine how much money you will receive. The amount of the grant you may receive is not standardized. Different schools, with their varying tuitions, disburse different amounts. Pell Grants are available until you get your undergraduate degree. While Pell Grants once went only to students who attend school at least half-time (another term with a strict definition—see the glossary for more details), part-time students are now eligible so long as their expected family contribution is in line with federal requirements. By the way—even if you think you will not qualify for a Pell Grant, you need to apply. Many schools won't consider you for aid until they see your Pell results.

OTHER AID

■ Federal Supplemental Educational Opportunity Grants (FSEOG): These are grants, as the name indicates, and need not be repaid. As the word "Supplemental" indicates, SEOG's are often used to supplement grants already in place, such as those to Pell Grant recipients. The amount can total as much as $4,000 each year depending on need, the availability of FSEOG funds at the school, and the size of your own aid package. Unlike Pell Grants, which the government promises to pay to all eligible students, SEOG funds come to schools in a set amount. Once that fund dries up, there's no more until next year.

■ Federal Work-Study (FWS): This is basically a part-time job, funded by the federal government and administered by your school. Most undergraduates are paid by the hour, and often at the minimum wage. Graduate students may be paid by the hour or may receive a salary. The jobs are awarded on the basis of need, the size of FWS funds at your school, and the size of your aid package.

■ Federal Perkins Loans (formerly National Direct Student Loans): These are loans made by the school with federal money, and have to be repaid. These loans offer low interest—five percent—and can total as much as $15,000 for undergraduate study. ($3,000 per year for each year of undergraduate study.) Repayment usually begins nine months after you leave school, and you have up to ten years to repay the loan. Interestingly, payment on your loan can be temporarily deferred or cancelled if you enter such programs as Head Start, VISTA, or the Peace Corps, or work as a full-time teacher, nurse or employee of a child or family service agency; the armed services will also repay part of Perkins Loans. The federal government has targeted schools with high default rates on Perkins Loans and is giving less money to schools with a high proportion of deadbeats. You may be able to borrow more than the amounts given if you're attending a school that has a default rate no higher than 7.5%. So when comparing schools, it's worth asking at the financial aid office about the default rate—it could determine whether or not you will get any of that wonderfully cheap five-percent-interest money.

■ Stafford Student Loans (SSL): These used to be called Guaranteed Student Loans. Like all loans, they must be repaid. They are generally reserved for low-income students who pass a needs test. These loans are made through a lender such as a bank, credit union, or savings and loan—and they can charge you an insurance fee that varies from lender to lender, so it's worth shopping around. The "guarantee" in the program's former title comes from the fact that a guarantee agency in your state insures the loans, which are reinsured by the federal government. Like the Pell, the Stafford is an "entitlement" program: if you qualify, you get the money. Freshmen in 1993 will pay no higher than nine percent for repayment. In your first year of school you can borrow up to $2,625, $3,500 in your second year; upper class students can borrow $5,500 annually, up to a total of $23,000 for undergraduates and $65,500 for graduate or professional study (including any Stafford Loans received). These figures include a five percent loan origination fee for subsidized loans (and a 6.5% origination and insurance fee for unsubsidized loans) that goes back to Uncle Sam to help defray the costs of running the program, so you don't get quite as much money as it seems. Unsubsidized repayment begins six months after graduation or leaving school, and must amount to monthly payments of at least $50.

Like SSL's, PLUS Loans and Supplemental Loans for Students (SLS) provide additional funds for educational expenses after high school—but you can get PLUS and SLS loans without requiring a needs test. You do, however, have to have already applied for a Pell Grant and a Stafford Student Loan before you can apply for PLUS or SLS. PLUS loans go to parents, while SLS loans go to students. Interest rates for SLS and PLUS loans are set anew each June; during the 1992-93 school year the rate was 7.36 percent (actually almost two percentage points lower than in 1991-92, so recessions are good for something). The new PLUS loan laws allow parents to borrow the cost of education minus any estimated financial aid the child receives for each dependent child enrolled at least half-time. Under SLS, independent undergraduates are allowed to borrow $4,000 a year for the first and second years of school, $5,000 a year for the third and fourth years (total undergraduate $23,000) and $10,000 a year for graduate studies (with a total not exceeding $73,000 for undergraduate and graduate combined). Debtors usually must begin repaying interest on these loans within sixty (60) days after first getting the money, though other arrangements can be negotiated.

The best sources of information on local standards set for Stafford Student Loans, PLUS Loans, SLS Loans, and other forms of state student aid are your state educational agencies.

Three of the federal programs are "campus-based": FSEOG, FWS, and Perkins Loans. "Campus-based" simply means that the programs are administered by financial aid officers at each school. As we mentioned above, these are not entitlement programs like the Pell Grant or the Stafford Loans. The government gives each school a set amount of cash; when it's gone, it is really gone—no more campus-based aid can be had until the next year's allotment comes through. The schools set their own deadlines for these programs, so ask at your school's financial aid office and apply as early as possible to catch some of the money before it runs out.

The federal government has several other ways of helping students get through school. The government provides a tuition-free education for thousands of students. The only catch is that the schools are owned by Uncle Sam: They are the military academies. If you don't mind the haircut and want to serve your country through the military, the service academies are an excellent way to do so while getting your degree. If you don't get into these highly competitive academies, the service branches maintain ROTC units on many campuses. The ROTC is another rich lode of scholarships. The ROTC also has a number of scholarships geared toward helping minority students, and to boost the number of students entering important-but-strained career fields such as the health professions.

State Aid

In 1992-93, states expected to award more than $2.57 billion in total grant aid to more than 1,700,000 postsecondary students. About 75 percent will be in need-based aid to undergraduates—states collectively award nearly $2 billion in need-based grants to undergraduates, according to the authoritative National Association of State Scholarship and Grant Programs. That group expected to see an 8.1 percent increase in the 1992-93 school year, bringing the total to $1.94 billion. It's part of a continuing trend among the states to increase their support for higher education. However, each state is different, and some states spend far more than others. About 80 percent of the aid is awarded by the 14 states that spend the most—more than $50 million apiece; five sparsely-populated states expected to spend less than $1 million in the 1992-93 school year.

Also, states go through cycles of generosity and stinginess that are virtually impossible to predict. But look for programs that state legislatures have instituted in order to attract more students to certain career fields, such as teaching, and so-called "non-need-based" programs (usually academic scholarships), which are booming.

College Funds

This money includes everything from athletic to academic, or merit, scholarships. The last few years have also been building years for college and university endowments, with hundreds of millions of dollars flowing into schools as diverse as Harvard University and Arizona State. Some, but certainly not all, of this endowment money has gone into scholarship funds. Other college funds might find their way to students in the form of tuition discounts for prepayment, aid in receiving loans, and other innovative programs. Most schools also keep funds on hand for short-term emergency loans for students.

Employers

Many employers help put students through college through the burgeoning field of cooperative education, in which students alternate semesters of school with semesters of work. Not only does this provide professional skills and a leg up in the employment game, it also puts money in the student's pocket. It is best developed at technical and engineering schools like Georgia Tech, which places hundreds of students into positions in a five-year degree program, but all kinds of institutions offer cooperative education programs—almost 1,000 schools boast such programs.

Many employers also pay their employees to go to school. Millions of employees have the right to go back to school on their company tab, though relatively few choose to take the time. Other programs pay for the dependents of employees to attend school.

Private Scholarships

This is a relatively small part of the financial aid picture, and many carry daunting eligibility requirements—the old "red-haired Methodist from Georgia" problem. There's a lot more money to be drawn from federal and state programs, but hundreds of millions of dollars are nonetheless available in private scholarships—not an amount to turn your nose up at. There really are scholarships for left-handed students; Juniata College in Huntington, Pennsylvania, has had one since 1978. Just remember to go after the big money first and early, and then look around for whatever private scholarships you might be able to pick up.

The Long-Term Trends in Paying for College

The long-term trends in paying for college have repercussions for every student and every family. Three main trends have shown up lately: Families are paying a larger share of college costs these days and will continue to do so; financial aid funding is shifting away from grants and toward loans; and the number of college-age students is decreasing. Let's look at each individually.

Students and parents are indeed paying an increasing share of college costs, because federal aid to education hasn't kept up with student need. During the Reagan years, the emphasis in federal aid shifted to the needs of the poorer students as funds dwindled. Between 1980 and 1988, the number of students overall who received federal aid plummeted, and Pell Grants went from being a program for middle- and low-income students to being almost exclusively a low-income program. In 1980, 31.5 percent of all freshmen received Pell Grants; in 1988 the percentage had dropped to just 15.6 percent—the lowest level in the history of the program, according to the Cooperative Institutional Research Program. Other federal aid programs showed similar declines. The percentage of freshmen receiving Supplemental Educational Opportunity Grants dropped from eight percent in 1980 to less than four percent in 1988. And fewer students than ever are entering the federally funded Federal Work-Study program, which, during the same time dropped to less than seven percent from 14.5 percent.

The dropoff in federal assistance has sent students to other sources to make up their college funds. "These trends suggest that the burden of paying for college is increasingly falling on students, their families, and the nation's colleges," said Alexander W. Astin, professor of higher education at UCLA's Graduate School, who directs the annual survey of freshmen that provides the information cited above for the American Council on Education. Family contribution, savings, loans, and institutional grants are on the rise. A 1985 study by the National Institute of Independent Colleges and Universities points out that between 1979-80 and 1983-84, the average family contribution toward paying the price of attending an independent college or university grew from $3,313 to $5,705 for recipients of federal aid—a jump from 53 to 62 percent. The rate of increase was largest for low-income families, soaring 97 percent from $329 to $648 for families with annual incomes of less than $20,000. Nearly 80 percent of freshmen depended on their families for meeting college costs in 1988—a record high, up from about 70 percent in 1980. The percentage of freshmen relying on college grants and scholarships jumped from about 13 percent in 1980 to 20 percent in 1988.

At the same time that families have been required to shoulder more of the burden of college costs, the nature of the remaining aid has changed radically. The past few years have seen a marked shift in aid away from grants, which do not need to be repaid, and toward loans, which must eventually be repaid. Today loans make up about half of the aid that goes to college students, which means that recent graduates go into the world with a debt burden that is nothing short of massive—especially for graduates of professional and medical schools.

One trend that shows an eventual silver lining is the sweep of demographics. The post-World War II baby boom is coming to an end. Demographic predictions indicated higher education enrollments would have already started to drop off in the 1980s as the baby boomers waned. The dropoff has not happened yet—largely because of a 15 percent growth in the enrollment of 22- to 34-year-olds between 1980 and 1988. Still, the 18-year-old population will continue to ebb into the 1990s, until a baby "boomlet" that is expected to push enrollments back to mid-70s levels by the year 2000. All this means a coming drop in the pool of college-age students. While the best-known and most prestigious public and private schools will continue to attract a steady stream of applicants, the nation's smaller private schools will suffer. In the last decade nearly 150 small liberal arts colleges shut down, as more students in a shrinking overall pool of college-age students opted for less expensive public education.

The reason that this news is good news for students is that it means many colleges are working harder to attract students. As a corollary to that trend of a diminishing pool of college-aged students, we can expect to see continued strong demand for students with high scholastic achievement. Such scholarships are not based on need, and will remain popular since bringing these students into a school helps the reputation and academic climate of a campus—and because such programs are the easiest student aid to sell to alumni and other sources of contributions.

Of course, the shrinking population of college-age students could also be bad news. The danger is that fewer students will mean less tuition for the schools. That could start a vicious cycle in which schools, pressed for money, will have to raise their tuition to bring in more bucks; that will in turn drive away more students, so the remaining students will have to pay even more, and so on. It makes sense, then, to think about the nature of a school's endowment in making your choice of a college. Schools that are largely dependent on tuition for their income will be more likely to raise tuition in this environment than those that have cushy endowments. Most schools publish a breakdown of the sources of their money; read it and choose wisely.

One final note on demographics: While minority enrollment has been growing over the past few years, it has not kept pace with the minority groups' greater representation within the larger population. At the same time, the portion of the school-age population that is made up of minority students is growing; minority students could make up almost a third of Americans between the ages of 18 and 24. The effects of such changes can only be guessed at so far, but there is a distinct possibility of a greater percentage of aid money being committed to providing educational opportunities for black and Hispanic students in coming years.

The World of Available Aid — Public Channels

In this section we will go into greater detail about the publicly funded sources of financial aid. We will cover federal programs and state programs. The federal programs make up the bulk of all funding for financial aid. On the state side, we will compare state appropriations to show which states are the big spenders and which are the skinflints. We will also describe the range of programs available from the states.

Federal Government Programs

Pell Grants

Before we even describe Pell Grants and how tough it is to get money out of this need-based federal program, here's a point about them that we can't stress enough: EVEN IF YOU THINK YOU COULDN'T POSSIBLY BE ELIGIBLE FOR A PELL GRANT, YOU SHOULD APPLY. Many other aid programs require that you first apply for a Pell. If you bypass the Pell, you pass up a great deal of possible aid, including the Stafford Loan program. So if you're serious about applying for financial aid, APPLY FOR A PELL GRANT EVERY YEAR THAT YOU ARE IN COLLEGE.

What It Is: Pell Grants are, as the name implies, grants—they need not be repaid. These undergraduate grants go to students who are enrolled at least half-time. (As you can imagine, "half-time" is a term with a very specific definition. The Department of Education defines that this way: "At schools measuring progress by credit hours and academic terms (semesters, trimesters, or quarters), 'half-time' means at least six semester hours or quarter hours per term. At schools measuring progress by credit hours but not using academic terms, 'half-time' means at least twelve semester hours or eighteen quarter hours per year. At schools measuring progress by clock hours, 'half-time' means at least twelve hours per week." If that isn't confusing enough, individual schools can set higher minimum requirements—which means you should check with your school to find out its definition.) Though the funding for Pell Grants comes from the federal government, your school gives you the money—or, in some cases, merely credits your tuition account. Your school will tell you which forms you must fill out to apply for a Pell Grant; different schools require different forms.

Prior to 1980, Pell Grants were called Basic Educational Opportunity Grants; older materials might refer to them as such. If you see terms like BEOG or Guaranteed Student Loan (until recently, the name for the Stafford Loan Program), you shouldn't use those outdated materials. Times change, and the old stuff can steer you wrong.

The budget for Pell Grants is not limited: there is no cap on the number of Pell Grants that will be handed out in a given year. Washington budgets according to its expectations and hopes for the best. However, if program budgets get tight, the maximum award can be shaved somewhat by the Secretary of Education. The important thing to remember with Pell Grants is that if you qualify and apply on time—no later than May 1—you will get your money. The early bird doesn't get a better worm when it comes to Pells, but missing your deadline means getting no money at all.

Pell Grants can be used for five years of undergraduate study, or six if the student is pursuing a course of study that requires more than four years. Factors that exempt students from the five- and six-year limits include death of a relative, personal illness or injury to the student, or the need to take remedial courses. Your school might have other rules for extending Pell support.

How to qualify: Students must be U.S. citizens and must be attending school at least half-time.

Whether or not you will get a Pell Grant depends on a formula, passed into law by Congress, that is applied to the information you provide in your financial aid application. The formula produces a Student Aid Index number. The lower the Student Aid Index number, the more money you can get in your grant. The maximum available in 1992-93 was $2,400. These grants are distributed based on family need and education costs at your school.

Supplemental Educational Opportunity Grants (SEOG)

What it is: SEOG is another grant for undergraduates. As grants, SEOG's do not need to be repaid. This is a campus-based program, which means it is administered by the schools. It provides up to $4,000 a year, depending on your need. Unlike Pell Grants, SEOG funds are "campus-based," which means they come to schools in a set amount. Once that fund is depleted, there's no more until next year. The lesson: apply early (your school sets its own deadline for these grants).

How to qualify: They are earmarked by Congress for students with exceptional financial need, and first priority goes to Pell Grant recipients. Schools decide whether to give SEOG's to students who do not attend more than half-time.

College Work-Study

What it is: CWS lets you earn while you learn in jobs either on- or off-campus, administered through the financial aid office. The amount you earn will depend on the kind of work that the school finds for you. The total amount you earn will be determined by the school; working more hours than those assigned will not get you more money.

The range of work-study jobs is limited only by the imagination of your school aid office, and many aid officers have surprisingly broad imaginations. Thus your school might have arranged myriad jobs on campus in each academic department, from cleaning out the baboon cages to helping run the projectors for college movies. Off-campus jobs abound, too, and often involve working for a private or public nonprofit organization or a local, state, or federal agency. And many schools have linked up with private employers near the campus to give you valuable real-world job experience. Some colleges even have large employment offices to help students sort out all their options. (College Work-Study is not the same as cooperative education, in which the school helps students divide their time between school and a career-oriented job.)

How to qualify: Both undergraduates and graduate students are eligible for this campus-based program. Financial aid administrators dole out work study jobs based on your need. Part-time students may be eligible, depending on the school. Again, since work-study is campus based, the money is allocated to the school in a lump. Once it's gone, it's gone. Pay attention to the school's application deadlines.

Perkins Loans (formerly National Direct Student Loans)

What it is: This is a broad program of federal loans—and loans have to be paid back, with interest. However, Perkins Loans offer extremely low interest—five percent—which is far better than you can get at a commercial lending institution. The school will either pay you directly or credit your tuition account.

Depending on how much money you need and how much money the school can give out, Perkins Loans can give you quite a bit of money. You can borrow up to $9,000 for your four years of college—$4,500 in the first two years of school alone.

How to qualify: Perkins Loans are available to full-time students who demonstrate need, and some schools also give them to part-time and half-time students. These loans are made through your school's financial aid office. This is another campus-based program, which means that the amount of funds are limited by how much money your school got from Washington. So find out the application deadlines at your school and get the applications in early.

When to pay it back: If you are a "new borrower"— that is, if you enroll after July 1, 1987, and you have no other outstanding Perkins Loans or National Direct Student Loans or have paid off your own loans—then you have a grace period of nine months after you graduate, leave school, or drop below half-time attendance. Your school might have different rules concerning payback for students who drop below half-time, so check with your school's financial aid office before dropping too many classes. If you are not a new borrower, your grace period is six months. In either case, you will have as much as ten years to repay your loan.

You can stop the clock on your Perkins Loan so long as you continue your studies at least half-time. You can also hold off repayment for up to three years by working in the Peace Corps or ACTION Programs, or comparable full-time volunteer work for a tax-exempt organization; active duty in the Armed Forces or in the commissioned corps of the U.S. Public Health Service; or serving in the National Oceanic and Atmospheric Administration Corps. Uncle Sam also now allows deferments if you work as a teacher in a federally-defined "teacher shortage area;" your school's education department should have information on which programs qualify you for that deferment. You can also hold off payments for as much as three years if you become temporarily totally disabled, or can't work because you're caring for a spouse or other dependent who becomes temporarily totally disabled. Certain internships can get you a two-year deferment, and mothers of preschool aged children who are working at a salary that pays no more than a dollar above minimum wage get a one-year deferment. There's even a parental leave deferment of up to six months for pregnant borrowers, or borrowers who are caring for newborn or newly adopted children. If you become unemployed, your school may have programs to defer the principal of your loan during your period of unemployment. Being on your way to employment can also get you a deferment: under certain conditions, an internship or residency program that is required to begin professional practice or service. But none of these deferments is automatic; you have to apply for a deferment through your school, and you have to continue paying off your loans until the deferment goes through. Otherwise, you could be found in default. You can even get all or part of your loan forgiven altogether. Part of your loan will be wiped off the books if you become a teacher of handicapped children, or teach in a designated elementary or secondary school that serves low-income kids. In either case, your entire loan will be cancelled in the fifth straight year of full-time teaching. Your college can provide you with a list of designated schools that will help you do well for yourself by doing good. Working in certain Head Start programs will also cancel a portion of your loan; by your seventh Head Start year, the slate will be wiped clean for your entire loan. And as much as 70 percent of your loan can be cancelled if you volunteer for the Peace Corps or VISTA. Finally, the military often repays a portion of your loan as an incentive to sign up.

Stafford Loans

What it is: Stafford Loans, like Perkins Loans or any loans, have to be repaid with interest. These low-interest loans are made by a lender such as a bank, a credit union, or a savings and loan—your financial aid officer or state guarantee agency can help you connect with a lender. Sometimes the school itself is the lender. The federal government reinsures the loans that the lender has made, making them more amenable to the idea of lending to students. While the rate of interest isn't as low as with Perkins Loans, Stafford Loans are easier to obtain—and the rate is awfully good.

How good are they? The interest rate charged on Stafford Loans has fluctuated over time, but has consistently remained below market value for loans—and in fact, is a better deal than can be found anywhere this side of the five percent Perkins Loan. The present interest rate is eight percent for the first four years of repayment; it jumps to 10 percent after that. Depending on your need, Stafford Loans can add up to $2,625 a year for first- or second-year undergraduates and $4,000 a year if you have moved on to third-year status, up to a total of $17,250 for undergradate debt.

These loans cost some money up front: an "origination fee" of five percent, which is deducted from the loan in installments. The state guarantee agency might also take its cut—up to three percent—also to be taken out proportionately from each loan disbursement as an insurance premium.

How to qualify: Students must be attending school at least half-time. Both undergraduate and graduate students are eligible. Students must demonstrate need. But like the Pell Grant program, there is no cap on the number of students who can receive these loans.

When to pay it back: You have to dig into your pocket six months after you graduate, leave school, or drop below half-time status. You usually have five years to repay the debt, though some allow as much as 10 years. As with Perkins Loans, Uncle Sam has made provision for deferments: up to three years for serving in the military, the Public Health Service, Peace Corps, VISTA, ACTION, or the National Oceanic and Atmospheric Adminstration; up to three years of full-time volunteer work for a tax-exempt organization that does work similar to that performed by VISTA or Peace Corps, or for teaching in a teacher shortage area; up to three years for temporary total disability, or while caring for a spouse with a temporary total disability; up to three years for volunteer work in certain tax-exempt organizations; up to two years for internships that are required for professional practice; up to twenty-four months while actively seeking but unable to find full-time employment; up to twelve months for mothers with preschool age children, just entering or returning to the work force for wages not more than one dollar more than minimum wage; or six months for parental leave. The debt is cancelled in the case of death, permanent total disability, or bankruptcy.

As with Perkins Loans, you can even get all or part of your loan forgiven altogether. If you become totally and permanently disabled, or if you die, the loan will be forgiven. That's cold comfort. Also, Uncle Sam wants you so badly that if you enlist in the active military service, he will pay up to 33 percent of the loan for each year you serve.

PLUS Loans and Supplemental Loans for Students (SLS)

What they are: Like Stafford Loans, PLUS Loans and Supplemental Loans for Students (SLS) provide additional funds for educational expenses—but these are not need-based. SLS is for independent undergraduate students. PLUS loans go to parents. As with Stafford Loans, these low-interest loans are made by a lender such as a bank, a credit union, or a savings and loan—your financial aid officer or state guarantee agency can help you connect with a lender. Sometimes the school itself is the lender. Freshmen and their families will have variable interest rates on their SLS and PLUS loans. During the 1992-93 award year the rate was set at 6.64 percent, down from over 7 percent the year before. Parents can borrow $4,000 a year up to a total of $20,000 in PLUS loans for each dependent child enrolled at least half-time. Independent undergraduates are allowed to borrow the same amount on top of Stafford Loan limits.

How to qualify: PLUS loans are open to parents who have a child who is enrolled at least half-time and is a dependent student. SLS loans are open to independent undergraduate students and graduate students.

When to pay it back: Debtors usually must begin repaying interest on these loans within sixty days after first getting the money, though other arrangements can be negotiated. Deferments are the same as for the Stafford Loan. In the case of PLUS Loans, parents can get deferments if they are in school, unemployed, temporarily totally disabled, or unable to work while caring for a temporarily totally disabled dependent. Parents repaying PLUS loans are not eligible for the other Stafford Loan deferments, though the cancellation conditions do apply.

A Note on Repayment

Loan consolidation: Until 1983, students could lump together all of their education loans into one loan with a low, federally subsidized interest rate under a program known as OPTIONS. Consolidation disappeared for a while while Congress tried to figure out how to make the program, which was convenient for students and their families, less costly for the government.

The government brought back consolidation with the Higher Education Amendments of 1986. Today's consolidation is more tightly controlled and costs the borrower more. Here are the details:

Consolidation loans can replace any combination of $5,000 worth of four federal student loans, which includes Stafford Loan, Supplemental Loans for Students (SLS), Perkins Loans, and Health Professions Student Loans (HPSL). Once you begin paying your loans, you can consolidate them—so long as you haven't fallen behind more than ninety days on any of them. The new lender pays off the old lender, and you only have one check to fill out each month. Consolidation rates are no bargain. The rate of interest is the weighted average of the rates of the original loans, but not less than nine percent. If you were able to qualify for dirt-cheap student loans, some of which have been available for as low as three percent, consolidation will cost plenty.

Besides paying a flat rate over the life of the loan, repayment can take three optional forms: an extended payment program that stretches your loans out over more than ten years; a graduated repayment program that makes you repay smaller amounts in early years and larger amounts later, as you get started in your career; or income-sensitive repayment, which is pegged to a percentage of your income.

A warning about consolidation: the payment options, such as extended payment and graduated and income-sensitive repayment, do indeed make it easier to pay off your loans. They also make repayment more expensive—any time you are paying interest over a longer period of time, your costs rise.

The amount of time you have varies depending on how much you have to pay:

Total Loans	Years to Repay
$5,000 to 7,499	10
$7,500 to 9,999	12
$10,000 to 19,999	15
$20,000 to 44,999	20
$45,000 and up	25

Signing up for consolidation also limits the number of deferments available to you. For federal loans, those options include military service, parental leave, Peace Corps service, and more. Borrowers of consolidated loans have precious few deferments: full-time study (or half-time if the student borrows additional Stafford Loan or SLS money), temporary and total disability, and unemployment. And during deferment, interest still needs to be paid—the deferment applies only to repayment of the principal.

The 1986 amendments opened up the field of potential lenders, too. While before consolidation was handled through the Student Loan Marketing Association (Sallie Mae), now many more commercial lenders are eligible, along with the state guarantee agencies and state secondary markets. That means more choice, and it means more trouble: loan plans differ substantially from lender to lender. But Uncle Sam has hooked you again: you are obligated to take a loan from any of the lenders who gave you your original student loans if one of those lenders offer, however attractive other lenders' offers might be.

In short, the new consolidation plans are convenient, but expensive—and many borrowers will find it worth their while to simply send out a few more checks each month and save money.

Other Avenues to Federal Funds

The Military

The U.S. victory in the Persian Gulf brought a lot of attention to the armed forces. For many students, the Gulf victory made the military a more glamorous and attractive option. Others found the harsh reality of reservists being called up for active duty a little too real for their tastes; having signed up for military training as a way to get through college, they had never expected to be sent overseas to fight a war. So how you feel about the military in general will determine whether you skip the next few paragraphs or not. The simple point is this: unless you have conscientious objections to serving in the Armed Forces, the military could be a way to help finance your college education. The military offers a number of ways to help students pay for college, though none of today's programs match the largesse of the GI Bill that educated the post-World War II generation. In return for the years of military service, you receive everything from a cheaper education to one that costs you no money at all. Service academies such as West Point offer a tuition-free college education. Each branch of the service has its own academy with its own character and traditions. These academically rigorous institutions are excellent, especially for the technical fields, and you can't beat the price.

If you'd rather not attend a service academy—or can't get in—chances are that your school will have a Reserve Officer Training Corps—and that organization, too, can help you pay for college. Standing scholarships are available that put $100 each month into your pocket for as much as five years, and ad hoc scholarships are announced all the time to attract students into areas the military feels a need to beef up—usually in the technical fields. Even without ROTC scholarships, students in the ROTC earn $100 each month in their junior and senior years (though they receive nothing as freshmen and sophomores). Once on active duty, students stand a good chance of being sent back to school and having all or part of their tuition picked up by Uncle Sam. The New GI Bill matches the soldier's contribution to a college fund; after emerging from the Armed Services, a student-to-be can amass a war chest of more than $10,000. There are also state programs to help members of the military, as well as funds from public and private sources for families of former military. Healthy benefits are also available to those who enlist in the National Guard.

Whether or not you care for the military, be sure that you have registered for the draft if you are male. Uncle Sam is now tying aid to draft registration: if you don't sign up, you can't sign up for aid.

Programs Offered Through the Department of Health and Human Services

Other federal programs that do not come from the Education Department have millions of dollars to spread around. Many of them are directed toward influencing career choices—say, producing more medical professionals. Here are a few of the most prominent ones:

■ Several campus-based programs get their funding from the Department of Health and Human Services. As campus-based programs, they are administered by the school and funded in a lump sum from the federal government. Campus-based programs can run out of money, and so it is important to check your school's deadline and apply early in order to be sure to get all the money you can get.

■ Nursing Student Loan Program applies to nursing students attending certain nursing schools. Both full-time and half-time students are eligible, depending on the school. Students must demonstrate financial need. The student can then receive up to $2,500 each year (and $4,000 annually in the last two years of your program) for a maximum of $13,000. Repayment of the five percent loans begins nine months after the borrower leaves school and can stretch over ten years, with deferments for active duty in the armed forces, Coast Guard, National Oceanic and Atmospheric Administration, or the U.S. Public Health Service or as a Peace Corps volunteer.

■ Financial Assistance for Disadvantaged Health Professions Students provides up to $10,000 per year to full-time students in medicine, osteopathic medicine and dentistry. Not only must students prove exceptional financial need, but they must also come from a disadvantaged background.

■ Undergraduates pursuing degrees in Pharmacy can also qualify for two programs that are otherwise restricted to graduate students. These are the Health Profession Student Loan (HPSL) and the Health Education Student Loan (HEAL). Your departmental financial aid advisor should be able to help you with information on these programs.

For More Information on Federal Programs

Write or call one of the regional offices of the U.S. Department of Education:

REGION I

Connecticut, Maine, Massachusetts, New Hampshire, Rhode Island, Vermont
U.S. Department of Education
Office of Student Financial Assistance
J.W. McCormack Post Office and Courthouse Building
Room 502
Boston, MA 02109
(617) 223-9338

REGION II

New Jersey, New York, Puerto Rico, Virgin Islands, Panama Canal Zone
U.S. Department of Education
Office of Student Financial Assistance Programs
26 Federal Plaza, Room 3954
New York, NY 10278
(212) 264-4427

REGION III

Delaware, District of Columbia, Maryland, Pennsylvania, Virginia, West Virginia
U.S. Department of Education
Office of Student Financial Assistance
3535 Market Street, Room 16200
Philadelphia, PA 19104
(215) 596-0247

REGION IV

Alabama, Florida, Georgia, Kentucky, Mississippi, North Carolina, South Carolina, Tennessee
U.S. Department of Education
Office of Student Financial Assistance
101 Marietta Tower, Suite 2203
Atlanta, GA 30323
(404) 331-0556

REGION V

Illinois, Indiana, Michigan, Minnesota, Ohio, Wisconsin

U.S. Department of Education
Office of Student Financial Assistance
401 South State Street, Room 700D
Chicago, IL 60605
(312) 353-8103

REGION VI

Arkansas, Louisiana, New Mexico, Oklahoma, Texas

U.S. Department of Education
Office of Student Financial Assistance
1200 Main Tower, Room 2150
Dallas, TX 75202
(214) 767-3811

REGION VII

Iowa, Kansas, Missouri, Nebraska

U.S. Department of Education
Office of Student Financial Assistance
10220 North Executive Hills Boulevard, 9th Floor
Kansas City, MO 64153
(816) 891-8055

REGION VIII

Colorado, Montana, North Dakota, South Dakota, Utah, Wyoming

U.S. Department of Education
Office of Student Financial Assistance
1244 Speer Boulevard, Suite 310
Denver, CO 80204-3582
(303) 844-3676

REGION IX

Arizona, California, Hawaii, Nevada, American Samoa, Guam, Federated States of Micronesia, Marshall Islands, Republic of Palau, Wake Island

U.S. Department of Education
Office of Student Financial Assistance
50 United Nations Plaza
San Francisco, CA 94102
(415) 556-5689

REGION X

Alaska, Idaho, Oregon, Washington

U.S. Department of Education
Office of Student Financial Assistance Programs
915 Second Avenue, Room 3388
Seattle, WA 98174-1099
(206) 220-7820

Endnotes on Federal Aid

If reading about federal sources of aid makes your brain hurt and you still need answers, there is a Federal Student Aid Information Center. Its toll-free number is 1-800-433-3243. The people on the other end of the line can tell you if the school you're applying to participates in federal aid programs, help you file an application, explain student eligibility requirements, and more. They accept calls between the hours of 9:00 a.m. and 5:30 p.m. Eastern Standard Time, Monday through Friday. Usually, they are even pleasant—no small trick these days.

State Programs

The fifty states vary widely in the amount of aid that each gives to education, according to the authoritative National Association of State Scholarship and Grant Programs. In 1992-93, states expected to award more than $2.57 billion in total grant aid to more than 1.7 million college-aid students—about eight percent more than the previous year's spending. $1.5 billion of that money goes to undergraduates for need-based aid. The National Association of State Scholarship and Grant Programs predicts another eight percent growth over the previous year.

Some states are haves, others are have-nots. Whether the states like it or not, some do spend more than others. A lot more. Fourteen states awarded more than $40 million apiece in the 1992-93 school year—and those states make up some three-fourths of the grant dollars awarded by all states. The biggest of the big spenders on grant aid for the 1992-93 school year were, in descending order:

New York	$577 million
California	$237 million
Illinois	$225 million
Pennsylvania	$173 million
Texas	$131 million
New Jersey	$129 million
Ohio	$94 million
Michigan	$84 million
Minnesota	$83 million
Florida	$76 million
North Carolina	$70 million
Iowa	$64 million

Massachusetts	$59 million
Indiana	$56 million

Eleven states pony up less than $2 million each year for aid. You know who you are.

Don't pack the car and head for New York yet. While there are plenty of ways to look at how much money states spend on their college students, it's hard to come by numbers that make sense. Less populous states argue that just citing raw dollar amounts spent overall is misleading, because they end up spending more per capita on their small number of students. Some also complain that the full extent of their aid doesn't show up in standard measures: for instance, several states argue that their schools are so inexpensive that students don't need much financial aid—so that the states are penalized in the rankings for having a strong economic climate and helping students out with low tuition.

Not all of the arguments can be addressed, but the NAASP has tried to address some of them. Rather than be accused of unfairness, the NAASP tries to look at other measures of spending, such as how much the states spend per student. One listing the organization provides ranks states by how much each spends on its undergraduates, both full- and half-time—an imperfect measure, but within the ballpark. The estimated top ten spenders of grant aid per full-time undergraduate for 1992-93 were:

New York	$997
New Jersey	$867
Illinois	$696
Minnesota	$590
Iowa	$587
Pennsylvania	$498
Vermont	$483
Oklahoma	$427
California	$366
New Mexico	$360

Source: National Association of State Scholarship & Grant Programs 21st Annual Survey Report.

Types of State-Administered Programs

The range of state aid is dizzyingly broad, and shows the political process at work. Along with the standard varieties of need-based aid, states are now moving heavily into non-need-based aid programs that reward, say, outstanding academic achievement. The state legislatures also try to influence future careers by offering money to students who pursue certain areas of study or professions, just as the federal government rewards students entering the health professions. Many states push math and science studies for students who intend to go into teaching, while others boost a kaleidoscopic array of professions ranging from bilingual education to teaching. Here's an example: the national nursing shortage, which has been covered extensively and frighteningly in the news media, is already having an effect on financial aid. Six states have announced new or upcoming program initiatives to attract students to nursing: Colorado, Connecticut, Iowa, Maryland, North Carolina, and Rhode Island. Iowa's plan, if implemented, would repay nursing students' Stafford and PLUS loans.

Other state programs try to reward people less for what they do than who they are. Minority group programs, and programs to aid the dependents of prisoners of war or police officers killed in active duty all fall under this broad heading. Many also offer low-interest loan programs that are similar to federal loan aid. And to make the state's private colleges more attractive, several states now offer "equalization" money to help the private colleges' tuition match that of the public institutions.

The best benefit a state offers is the protection it gives its own citizens in the form of in-state tuition at its public institutions. Resident status is also a requirement for eligibility for certain aid programs. If you plan to attend a public school out of state, some students find it worthwhile to take the time beforehand to establish residency in the state of choice—often by moving there early and getting a job. But since establishing residency takes two years in some states, many students feel they just don't have the time.

Attracted to an academic program offered in another state but don't want to give up possible aid from your own state? Many states have established agreements to allow you to take advantage of your home state's aid while studying elsewhere.

The No-Need Aid Trend

Remember that trend toward non-need-based aid? In all, twenty-nine states now have non-need based programs and gave $202 million to more than 200,000 undergraduates during the 1989-90 school year. The five-year growth rate has been 71 percent, almost double the 39 percent growth rate in need-based grants during the same period. Of the non-need pool, the biggest chunk of cash went into academic scholarships. So study up! It pays.

Non-need-based aid is usually broken down into three categories:
(1) Tuition equalization programs, which help reduce the difference in tuition costs between public and private schools;
(2) Scholarship programs or merit awards, which reward academic achievement and are largely aimed at charming academic talent into staying in state;
(3) Categorical aid programs, which encourage students to go into particular fields of study such as math and science, or which help special constituencies like veterans and policemen.

As with all state programs, some give a lot more money than others. The top nine state programs will hand out as much as $50 million in no-need merit scholarships this year—that's 97 percent of the total. Most of the other states will give less than half a million dollars. Those nine best states to be smart in are, in order: New York, Colorado, Florida, Ohio, New Jersey, Illinois, Maryland, Missouri, and Massachusetts.

As you've probably figured out from the list of states above, having a new program doesn't automatically mean that money will shower upon you. The spurt in no-need monies is still puny compared to the massive $1.5 billion that go to undergraduates based on need annually. Starting new programs makes legislators feel good; actually giving those programs enough money to make a difference makes state legislators feel decidedly less good. Thus when you exclude behemoth programs like New York's Part-Time Student Grant Program and Ohio's Student Choice Program, the average allotment for these programs drops off dramatically. That's why the 19th annual report from the National Association of State Scholarship and Grant Programs said that "adding new programs has contributed little to the growth of state grant aid." Of course, a million dollars is not pocket change; most of us would be very happy with just a fraction of that. Simply keep this advice in mind: don't get so hung up on cashing in on the new that you ignore the larger sums that are available from more traditional programs.

State-Administered Programs With Federal Funding

Several federally funded aid programs are administered by individual states. This gives a little more consistency to the crazy quilt of state aid programs, giving you some program names to look out for when going over state aid information.

- State Student Incentive Grants: While the states administer the program and decide individually whether the grants apply to full- or half-time students, the program is partially funded by the federal government. Annual maximum: $2,500.

- Robert C. Byrd Honors Scholarship Program: this program recognizes ten students from each congressional district for outstanding academic achievement, providing $1,500 for the first year of higher education study.

- Paul Douglas Teacher Scholarship Program: a merit-based, state-administered program intended to encourage students who graduate in the top 10 percent of their graduating classes to enter the field of teaching. The states may give each student up to $5,000 a year for up to four years; the student is then obligated to teach for two years.

The World of Available Aid — Private Channels

In this section we discuss the many sources of financial aid outside of the government. The world of private aid is more complex than that of public aid—and the public aid, as we have already seen, is pretty complex. But the sources of public aid are limited to the federal government and the fifty states. Private sources of aid are not only more numerous, but are also tougher to track down—they range from the colleges themselves to private foundations, companies, and other programs such as the National Merit Scholarship Corporation. Trying to keep track of all of these sources on your own borders on the impossible.

Since the field of private financial aid is so dauntingly broad, we recommend that you not try to master it on your own. Find out who knows about sources of aid and pick their brains. Your search should take you to those people who know about the financial aid sources for your school and for your career area. High school counselors can provide the information you need on locally available scholarships. For special programs available through your college, consult the school's financial aid office—America's colleges have about $5 billion in their own funds to help students. For corporate programs, ask your boss (or your parents' bosses) or the company officer in charge of employee benefit programs. This may mean a lot of telephone calls, personal visits, and letters. But this will be time well spent.

A note about organization: This section covers all aid from colleges' own funds. Some of those colleges may be state-run, "public" institutions, but even so, we will include them here with the private schools, if for no other reason than to simplify matters.

A Warning About the True Value of Scholarships

There's a caveat that we should deal with before getting to the goods: getting a scholarship may not help you pay for college. That's because the school will probably either count the award into what it was already going to give you, or add it to your ability to pay. Either way, you are left digging into your pocket for the same amount of money as before. The school is then able to divert the money that would have gone to you to another student who has not been as enterprising as yourself. Sound like a ripoff? Maybe. But it's one way schools have found to stretch their much-needed aid dollars. And remember: getting the scholarship gives you plenty of what you might call "prestige points." These honors look good on your resume, which could help you in your later application to graduate school or job hunt. That warning behind us, let's look at the sources of funds:

College Funds

In days gone by, many schools held out a "need-blind" admissions policy. The phrase means that if a student is accepted at a college, that student will be able to attend; money will be found somewhere. However, few schools have been able to preserve "need-blind" as anything more than a concept in these cash-tight days.

In fact, "need-blind" puts schools in an uncomfortable cycle: by guaranteeing to subsidize the costs for so many of their students, they often find themselves needing to raise tuition—creating even more need for the school to have to fill somehow. The result can be chilling: Smith College, facing 20 percent annual increases in its financial aid budget over the last five years, decided that enough is enough. Starting in 1991, the school decided it would rank students who have been accepted for admission and hand out the money from the top down. Students highest on the list will see all of their financial aid needs met; below the fateful line, students will be on their own unless Smith can find the money elsewhere.

So again, a little investigative work is in order on your part. You should check in with the college financial aid office to see if the school maintains a "need-blind" policy. You might be surprised—it's not just the Ivies. Smaller schools like Franklin and Marshall College in Pennsylvania have managed to hold on to need-blind values. Still, if a school tells you it has need-blind admissions, try to find out what that actually means in practice. Don't be afraid to ask tough questions; for the kind of money you'll be spending, you deserve answers.

Today we look to the colleges for supplements to our education funding that include endowed scholarships, scholarships for athletic or academic prowess, work-study, and even loans from the school's own funds. Some private schools even offer "tuition remission"—that is, a discount on the official cost of tuition.

All of these college gambits cost money. As a practical matter, this means that it behooves you as an academic consumer to keep in mind the school's bottom line while you are trying to make your college choice. It may seem an obvious point, but a school with a bountiful endowment like billionaire Harvard is going to be in a better position to offer you financial aid than a less wealthy institution. And a school that is truly strapped financially could burden you with tuition increases once you enter—or even fold. It happens.

With that chilling thought behind us, let's look at each broad category of student aid from the colleges:

Grants and Scholarships

Academic scholarships: Just as the states have been providing increasing amounts of money for programs to attract academic stars, the individual schools have been hustling to gain the prestige of enrolling academically talented students. If you earn a certain grade point average, or score higher than a certain level on the SAT or ACT, most schools will offer enticements to attend. Some schools also provide special lures for valedictorians or students who have achieved other academic honors. Not every school promotes academic scholarships; the nation's most prestigious institutions attract a consistently high level of scholar, so many don't refer to academic scholarships as such. Academic scholarships are most important to schools on the make: those institutions that are trying to build an academically strong student body but don't have academic traditions of the Ivy League schools as a draw.

Money comes to scholars in a number of ways. The school may offer the awards according to a formula or set of conditions, such as a set SAT score. In addition to the funds available under the standard formula, the school might hold money in reserve to offer to especially promising students in order to sweeten the pot. Instead of actually spending money on bright students, many private schools simply offer tuition remission.

Need is a factor in most academic scholarships. Most of them offer a no-need minimum of a small amount —often less than $300. Beyond that, demonstrated need can up the annual award into the thousands. It's worth asking your school whether there are special no-need scholarships above the need-based variety, and whether you can qualify.

Athletic scholarships: Don't laugh. Even if you're not going to win the Heisman Trophy, there could be athletic scholarships for you out there. (If you are going to win the Heisman Trophy, you're not going to be reading this book, anyway.) Sure, the super-jocks have got football, basketball, baseball, and the like sewn up. But most colleges also have money to help students who show promise. The best jocks will be wooed by the biggest schools. But one of the smaller schools you are considering may have an ambitious sports program in a sport you might be pretty good at. Though your skills might not have gotten you far at Big State U, the other school might be happy to have you—and willing to supply a little money to entice you. And not just in football, basketball, or baseball. Many schools offer scholarships in sports you might never have thought of, including: archery, badminton, bowling, crew, fencing, gymnastics, lacrosse, sailing, skiing, synchronized swimming, and volleyball. Come on—if they're going to make curling an Olympic sport, can varsity tiddly-winks be far behind?

At the beginning of this section, we talked about contacting the people who know where the money is. In this case you need to talk not just with your high school guidance counselor but also with your coach. Together you can figure out which schools' athletic programs might want you. Numerous college guides break down athletic scholarships by sport, to make your search easier. Contact the college coaches at the most likely schools with a letter detailing your athletic achievement and pointing out that you would need financial aid. Be ready to provide the coaches who respond to your letter with more information and letters of recommendation.

The college as bank: Many colleges now offer long-term or short-term emergency loans out of their own funds. Ask at your financial aid office to see if your school has such a program. Many of them help students who do not otherwise qualify for need-based aid, and offer lower interest than commercial banks. Fairleigh Dickinson University of New Jersey uses its foundation money to subsidize interest on parent loans to keep the interest rates low. Other schools such as Lafayette College in Pennsylvania pay the interest on student loans while the student is in college, taking the pressure off students and their families during the college years. The school must be paid back within twelve years of graduation.

Looking for more funding power, thirty of the most prestigious colleges in New England banded together to form a group known as The Consortium on Financing a Higher Education; together with private enterprises such as the New England Loan Marketing Corporation (NELLIE MAE) and the Educational Resources Institute, they have created a loan program that they dubbed SHARE. Parents can borrow up to $20,000 annually at a reasonable interest rate.

Other Private Sources of Funds

Student organizations: You can make your social life pay off. Many student organizations sponsor scholarships for deserving students. Many fraternities, sororities, honor societies, and campus professional groups, among others, have programs, which are almost always limited to their members. If you're a joiner, you might open up some financial aid opportunities. Your school's financial aid office should have the breakdown of programs by organization, as will the organizations themselves.

National Merit Scholarships

Just about everybody who intends to go on to college ends up taking the PSAT/NMSQT test in their junior year of high school. It's preparation for the SAT—and more important, it puts you into competition for financial awards that can put a good deal of money in your pocket. But the competition is stiff: a mere 13,500 of the million students who take the PSAT/NMSQT each year are eligible to compete for these awards. Some schools, like Texas A&M University, work extra hard to recruit National Merit finalists and scholars because of the prestige that winning the award brings to the institution. So even though the actual amount of money received by finalists is usually not that great, it can get you offers of more attractive financial aid packages as schools vie for you. The three types of awards are:

■ $2,000 National Merit Scholarship. There are about 1,800 of these awarded each year; they are one-time-only awards. Need is not considered in these awards.

■ College-sponsored scholarships. Schools offer finalists scholarships out of their own pockets. Fewer than 250 colleges offer about 2,100 scholarships to National Merit finalists each year, including institutions ranging from the University of Chicago to Texas A&M University. The scholarships range from an annual $250 non-need grant to a maximum of $2,000 annually. Beyond that $250 minimum, the award must make up half of the student's calculated need.

■ Corporate-sponsored scholarships. Like the school-sponsored awards, the roughly 1,700 corporate-sponsored awards are renewable and can be received for all four years of college. And like the school-sponsored awards, they range from a minimum of $250 to $2,000 per year, though some go higher. While some of these programs apply to students with no direct tie to the corporation—say, those who live in the vicinity of one of the sponsoring company's plants—very, very few of these awards go to students whose parents do not work for the sponsoring corporation. For the most up-to-date information available on the National Merit Scholarships program, call the organization directly at (708) 866-5100.

Selected Schools that Sponsor National Merit Scholarships

American University
Arizona State University
Auburn University
Baylor University
Boston University
Bowling Green State University
Carleton College
Case Western Reserve
College of the Holy Cross
College of William and Mary
DePauw University
Emory University
Florida State University
Furman University
George Washington University
Georgia Institute of Technology
Grinnell College
Harvey Mudd College
Iowa State University
Johns Hopkins University
Louisiana State University
Macalester College
Miami University
Michigan State University
Mississippi State University
New York University
Northwestern University
Oberlin College
Ohio State University (all campuses)
Rensselaer Polytechnic Institute
Rice University
Rose-Hulman Institute of Technology
Rutgers, The State University of New Jersey (all campuses)
Southern Methodist University
Texas A&M University (all campuses)
Trinity University
Tulane University
University of Alabama
University of Arizona
University of California at Davis
University of California at Los Angeles
University of California at San Diego
University of Chicago
University of Delaware
University of Florida
University of Georgia Foundation
University of Houston
University of Maryland (all campuses)
University of Miami
University of New Orleans
University of Missouri–Columbia
University of Nebraska–Lincoln
University of Oklahoma
University of Rochester
University of South Carolina (all campuses)
University of Southern California
University of Texas at Austin
University of Washington
Vanderbilt University
Virginia Polytechnic Institute and State University
Washington University
Wheaton College (Illinois)

Selected Corporations that Provide National Merit Scholarships

These are some of the corporations listed in the fall 1992 Student Bulletin of the National Merit Scholarship Corporation. Since the American corporate landscape is changing rapidly due to mergers, acquisitions, and general belt-tightening, this list tends to shift a great deal from year to year. Check with your employer even if it is not mentioned on this list, and make sure your company still supports the program if it is on the list.

Abbott Laboratories
ADT Security Systems
Allied-Signal
American Cyanamid
American Home Products Corporation
Amoco
ARCO
Armstrong World Industries
Arthur Andersen
Avon Products
B & W Nuclear Technologies
BASF Corporation
Bechtel
Bell & Howell
BellSouth
BFGoodrich
BFI Corporation
Black & Decker
Blount
Boeing
Boston Edison
BP America
Bridgestone/Firestone
Bristol-Myers
Brown & Williamson Tobacco
Burroughs Wellcome
California Medical Education and Research
Capital Cities/ABC
CIBA-GEIGY
CIGNA Corporation
Collins & Aikman Corporation
ConAgra
CONSOL
Consolidated Papers
Continental Corporation
Cooper Industries
Crum and Forster
CSX Corporation
Data General
Deluxe Corporation
Digital Equipment Corporation
Dow Chemical Company
Dow Corning
Dow Jones
Dresser Industries
Dun & Bradstreet
Duracell
Eastman Kodak
Eaton Corporation
Equitable Life Assurance Society of the U. S.
Ethyl Corporation
Fisher-Price
Fleming Companies
FMC Corporation
GATX Corporation
General Mills
Georgia-Pacific Corporation
Gillette
Goodyear Tire & Rubber
Greyhound Lines
GTE Corporation
Harsco Corporation
Hoechst Celanese Corporation
Honeywell
ICI Americas
Ingersoll-Rand
Inland Steel-Ryerson
Interlake
International Paper
ITT Hartford Fire Insurance
K mart
Thomas J. Lipton
Litton Industries
Lockheed
Loews
LTV Corporation
Lucky Stores
MAXUS Energy Corporation
May Department Stores
Maytag
McDermott
McDonald's Corporation
McGraw-Hill
McKesson Corporation
Meredith Corporation
Metropolitan Life
Miles
Minnesota Mining and Manufacturing (3M)
Mobil
Monsanto
Motorola
National Distillers Distributors
National Medical Enterprises
Navistar
New Jersey Bell Telephone
New York Times Company
Norfolk Southern
Occidental Petroleum
Olin Corporation
Owens-Corning Fiberglas
Paramount Communications

Parker Hannifin Corporation
Penn Mutual
Pennsylvania Power & Light
PepsiCo
Pet
Pfizer
Phelps Dodge
Philadelphia Electric
Polaroid
PPG Industries
Prudential
Public Service Enterprise
Quaker Oats
Quantum Chemical
Raytheon
Rexham Corporation
RJR Nabisco
Rockwell International
Rohm and Haas
Santa Fe Pacific Corporation
Sara Lee
Schering-Plough Corporation
Shell Oil
Siemens
Sony Corporation of America
State Farm Companies
Sterling Winthrop
Stone & Webster
Sun Company
Tenneco
Textron
Times Mirror Company
Transamerica Corporation
Transco Energy Company
TRINOVA Corporation
Unilever United States
Union Electric
Union Pacific Corporation
United Airlines
United Services Automobile Association
United States Fidelity & Guaranty
United States Shoe Corporation
Upjohn
UPS
USG Corporation
Warner-Lambert
Weyerhaeuser Company
Robert W. Woodruff Foundation
Xerox

A number of other programs are looking for ways to give a hand to academically gifted students. The National Honor Society provides about 250 scholarships worth $1,000 each year. (You apply through the chapter at your high school.) The famous Westinghouse Science Scholarships distributes about $140,000 among forty winners. (Write Science Service, 1719 N Street, NW, Washington, DC 20036.) The federal government has weighed in with programs like the Robert C. Byrd Honors Scholarship Program, a state-administered gold mine that recognizes outstanding academic achievement by giving ten students from each congressional district a one-time, $1,500 scholarship for their first year of college study. Another program, the Presidential Scholars, rewards about 120 high scorers on standardized entrance exams with a free trip to Washington; the Dodge Foundation then gives each recipient $1,000. You don't apply for this one, though—the program chooses you. And, of course, more and more states are trying to help bright students. Some of these programs are based on financial need, but a growing number are not.

Employers

Employer tuition plans: This is the great unclaimed area of financial aid, with billions of dollars available to millions of employees. Unfortunately, there's a Catch-22 involved: many companies won't hire you for a good position until you have your college degree. But if you are willing to attend college part-time, and to start in a lowly position, you will find many companies that will pay for your higher education. Though guides to employers with such programs are commercially available, they also tend to be expensive; you can also find them in the public library or through your school library or guidance counselor.

The company wants to make sure it will get its money's worth, so plans generally come with a hitch or two. The most important hitch: you have to make the grade. In "reimbursement" plans, in which you have to put up the tuition money at first, you get the money back only when you have successfully completed the course—in some programs, that means with a grade of "B" or better. In other programs the company pays up front—but you will still have to repay the company if you drop out or flunk. Also, you might have to prove that the courses you are taking are somehow related to your work. Still, an understanding boss can help you to frame your educational needs in such a way that they fit in nicely with the company objectives.

The cooperative way: In co-op education, you combine your time in the classroom with practical experience on the job. It's something for everyone: you the student get a job and the employer gets a highly motivated work force. Co-op programs not only put money in your pocket—roughly $1 billion a year in co-op wages nationwide—they also provide you with job contacts for the future. You get to try out your chosen profession—kick the tires, drive it around the block—to see if it's really what you would like to do. If it is, you have another advantage: often the firm you worked for is the one that hires you after graduation. Fully 40 percent continue working for their co-op employer after graduation. Another 40 percent find work in fields directly related to their co-op assignments, while about 15 percent enroll in law or other professional schools. Add up those percentages, and its pretty easy to see that co-oping it leads to jobs.

Roughly 1,000 colleges have cooperative programs of some kind or another—including some schools where virtually all of the students are in cooperative education programs, such as Antioch College in Yellow Springs, Ohio, Drexel University in Philadelphia, and Northeastern University in Boston. Some 50,000 employers hire on the co-op plan—including the largest provider of co-op jobs, the federal government, which hires nearly 12,000 students each year.

Co-oping takes time. Whether you alternate semesters of work and study or work part-time while attending school, the programs usually require five years. Still, 200,000 students each year seem to feel the time is worth spending. You can get more data on all schools with co-op programs by writing:

National Commission for Cooperative Education
360 Huntington Avenue
Boston, MA 02115

Getting help from your future colleagues: If you have made your career choice, you might be eligible for aid from the professional association, or associations, that serve the field. Of course, if you really want to get financial aid in your chosen career field and want to get a head start besides, you should consider attending a college that has a cooperative education program. But if your school doesn't provide such programs, then you might be able to get help from the professional association. There is an industry group for every trade and profession, from dental hygienists to hotel management to wine experts. Of course, most of this money gravitates toward schools that have well-regarded programs in the field, such as journalism at Northwestern University or meat science at Sul Ross State University. For suggestions on the strongest schools in your career area, you should consult guides such as *Rugg's Recommendations on the Colleges*. Still, many professional groups offer "portable" scholarships that are not tied to a particular school.

There are thousands of professional associations, so it is worth your while to find out about any other opportunities offered by your professional group. Trade groups are easy enough to find: reference works like *Gale's Encyclopedia of Associations*, available at the library, can give you the addresses and telephone numbers. Once you have the addresses, write to request their scholarship information, including a stamped, self-addressed envelope.

The Junior Fellowship Program

The Junior Fellowship program resembles cooperative education, but with some important differences: for one thing, your boss is the federal government. Also, you join the Junior Fellowship program in high school—though you don't begin working until college—and apply through your high school guidance counselor. Unlike cooperative education, which is only offered through certain schools, Junior Fellows can attend any school—you work during breaks in the college term. You also have to have very good grades and prove financial need. And here's the good part: though the program is limited to 5,000 participants at a time, it has historically had thousands of vacancies. If your high school guidance counselor doesn't have information on this program, you can write for it yourself:
Director, Office of Personnel Management
1900 E Street, NW
Washington, DC 20415

Other Private Aid Sources

Many organizations provide scholarships, though the amount is usually small. If you have already gotten all you are going to get from the big-ticket sources of financial aid, like federal and state programs and your college resources, you may be able to get a little extra from sources you might not have considered. Here's a list to start you on your way:

Your local government: Your city, county, or even your school district might have scholarship money or other special programs. Though many of these only amount to a few hundred dollars, some offer funds in the thousands. Finding them involves investigative work on your part, since relatively few of these make their way into the big scholarship databases. But you can find them: your high school or college financial aid officer should have some information about these programs. The Chamber of Commerce and public library might have leads, too. Keep an eye out for scholarships in the local news section of your newspaper.

Unions: Despite the tough times that America's unions are going through, many still offer funds for the education of their members' children. For information you should contact the secretary of your union local. Union programs are offered both by the national organization and by the local chapters. You can get some information from your local; to get the fullest amount of information, write for the comprehensive AFL-CIO guide, which is free to members: *AFL-CIO Guide to Union Sponsored Scholarships, Awards and Student Financial Aid*.

Department of Education, AFL-CIO
815 16th Street, NW
Washington, DC 20006

Foundations: Many private foundations and educational trusts provide funds for students. Organizations like the Hattie M. Strong Foundation provide Strong Foundation Loans from $1,000 to $2,500 per year, on average, to students who are a year away from college graduation. Some have rather odd restrictions: the Ernestine Matthews Trust Scholarships, for example, offers around $750 per year—but recipients must sign a statement that they will neither smoke nor use alcoholic beverages while receiving the scholarship.

Community organizations in general: Don't forget to check into scholarship programs available as a multitude of awards, including a $2,000 scholarship at the national level for children of veterans called The American Legion Auxiliary National President's Scholarship. There's also a National High School Oratorical Contest with a grand prize of $16,000 and many $1,000 scholarships. More important, each state organization and its auxiliary offer scholarships. The Legion is most valuable to students who are the children of veterans, but not exclusively to them. For the most up-to-date listing of the Legion's programs and contests, you should send two dollars to get a copy of *Need a Lift?* Write to:

The American Legion
National Emblem Sales
P.O. Box 1055
Indianapolis, IN 46206

Religious organizations: Churches and religious organizations also have money to give. Groups like the Aid Association for Lutherans host contests and offer scholarships and loans. Find these groups through your church, your campus Bible Chair, or in *Gale's Encyclopedia of Associations*. You might run into a number of restrictions, including a requirement of religious study or of attending a church-sponsored school.

Ethnic societies: Sure, you're proud to be an Armenian. But did you know that your Armenian ancestry could qualify you for scholarships? The Armenian Relief Society (80 Bigelow Ave, Watertown, MA 02172) has many available. So does the Armenian General Benevolent Union, which offers both scholarships and loans (585 Saddle River Road, Saddle Brook, NJ 07662). Are you a woman of Greek descent? Perhaps you have a relative in the Daughters of Penelope. If so, you might qualify for one of that organization's awards, such as Helen Karagianis Memorial Award or the Pota Sarastis Memorial Award. (Scholarship Committee, Daughters of Penelope, Supreme Headquarters, 1422 K Street, NW, Washington, DC 20005).

We've only scratched the surface of ethnic funds available. Many national groups in the U.S. sponsor programs to help each new generation better itself through higher education. If you or your parents aren't members of such organizations, you can find their names and addresses in *Gale's Encyclopedia of Associations*, available in your library. Send them a request for information on college aid along with a stamped, self-addressed envelope.

Youth clubs and jobs: Think back to your childhood—or to more recent high school experience. You can find scholarships for former Boy Scouts, newspaper carriers, and even golf caddies. Really. The Western Golf Association maintains an Evans Scholars House, where lucky former caddies live for free, at fourteen universities—Colorado, Illinois, Indiana, Marquette, Miami (Ohio), Michigan State, U of Michigan, Minnesota, Missouri, Northern Illinois State U at DeKalb, Northwestern, Ohio State, Purdue, and Wisconsin. The sponsoring organization also covers tuition. Students at state universities that do not have an Evans House can get their tuition and a housing allowance paid by the sponsoring organization. Caddies who served for more than two years and show financial need may apply to the Western Golf Association, Golf, IL 60029.

As for your participation in high school activities, you might have made yourself eligible for scholarships if you were a member of 4-H, Future Homemakers of America, or distributive education programs. You might also want to check with your high school counselor for other awards that get overlooked.

The contest route: Many of the organizations alluded to above sponsor contests in essay writing and oratory. That's just the tip of the iceberg for competitions ranging from science competitions to beauty pageants. Many of them sponsor scholarships for prizes. Each summer, the National Association of Secondary School Principals puts its stamp of approval on a long roster of these programs in its Advisory List of National Contests and Activities. For a copy of this list, send a request for publication #210-9293 $5.00 plus $3.00 for shipping and handling to:

National Association of Secondary School Principals
1904 Association Drive
Reston, VA 22090

Warning: entering a lot of contests can be time-consuming—and you're going to need a lot of time to apply for the traditional channels of financial aid. Don't get lost on a rabbit trail—go after the big game first by applying for financial aid through your school's financial aid office. Once you've done that, and if you have a little extra time, you might give some of the contests listed by the principals a try—your odds of winning are no worse than those on getting many of the private foundation scholarships.

If there's any lesson here, it is simply this: get to know your college financial aid officer. This is the person who can help you ferret out money, and who has some power, however limited, to ease your financial aid burden. The position of student aid administration is fast becoming a hardship post. Aid officers report that angry students have hit them and threatened their lives. And one tragic case ended in death. A student threw coffee on Willie Pappas, director of financial aid at Delgado Community College in Louisiana. When Pappas followed the student out into a parking lot, the student shot him.

Obviously, this is no way to get your financial aid package improved. Financial aid officers don't take the job to abuse students and pinch pennies; they are in the business of helping students. Unfortunately, they are also working within the school's budgetary limits—and the school is juggling the financial needs of students with its own priorities for research, faculty pay, physical improvements, and shiny new leather chairs for the trustees to sit on at their meetings. And so they are tough.

But not necessarily heartless. They will listen to reason, and respond to real problems. With solid negotiation, you might be able to get your financial aid officer to adjust the formula for computing your need: the officer can adjust your family contribution down or the cost of education up to reduce your aid burden. The key is to deal with financial aid officers politely and responsibly. Don't try to con them—students sharper than you have tried, and failed. Have all your ducks in a row: keep track of your financial records and be ready to back up your case with documentation.

Putting Together Your Financial Aid Package

The Three Commandments of Applying for Financial Aid

Before getting down to the nuts and bolts of applying for financial aid, it's worth keeping three "commandments" in mind. Without them, a hundred pages of instruction are useless. The three commandments are:

1: Be Prompt!

Meet each deadline. Since many programs work from a fund of limited size, wasting time can waste money. Start applying for financial aid right after January 1—as soon after you receive your W-2 forms as possible. That's when you can begin filling out your IRS forms, too. That will make filling out the financial aid forms easier. Besides, if you have a refund coming you'll get it faster.

2: Be Accurate!

Fill in all of the blanks on every form, and fill them out accurately and legibly. Read the instructions fully. Any blank spaces or mistakes can cause the overworked aid agencies to send your form back to you to be filled in again. You'll not only have to do more work, but you'll delay the processing of your financial aid application—and that delay could keep you from receiving as much aid as you could have gotten.

3: Be Organized!

If there was ever a reason to get organized, this is it. You have to keep track of all of your applications to different colleges and the financial aid applications to those colleges. Make copies of every piece of correspondence you send out, keeping all of it in a fanfold organizer or file box, organized by school. Many financial aid guides go so far as to recommend sending all aid correspondence via certified mail so that you will have a record of having sent items and of their being received. The College Board, on the other hand, says registered mail is a bother and slows the application process. We say: If you are applying well in advance, spend the money for a little security.

Another reason for all this organization: By getting organized from the start, you will find it easier to fill out your forms again next year—and remember, you have to apply for aid every year.

Your Financial Aid Timetable

Junior Year of High School

October: Take the PSAT exam. This important test will not only give you a taste of what's in store on the SAT; it will also qualify you for the National Merit Scholarship.

If you have not already begun to consider your college choices, you should be sending off for college brochures and financial aid information. Talk to friends from high school who have attended the colleges, and to alumni. It's a good time to begin touring the campuses that seem the most promising to you. While on campus, be sure to check out the financial aid office. Does it appear to be efficiently run? Does it look like the sort of place where you will get personalized service? If possible, schedule an interview with a financial aid adviser at the school to determine the school's resources and how much of your college costs your family will be expected to provide.

Senior Year of High School/Year Before Going to College

Fall: Begin narrowing down your college choices to the ones that interest you the most. Ask those schools for admissions applications and financial aid forms. Send in your applications for admission to your favorites well before the deadlines that each school lists. Be sure to take your time writing any essays the school requires; you want to stand out as a lucid thinker and a clear writer, not as someone who doesn't care enough to do a good job on an application.

January 1: You can't apply for financial aid before January 1 of the year you intend to go to college. But you should apply as soon as the ball drops in Times Square. People who file at the time of the deadline risk losing out on the college's own aid and those funds from campus-based federal financial aid programs. When you hear Auld Lang Syne, think about your financial aid forms.

April 15: If you haven't done your financial aid forms yet because your IRS forms weren't done, you've probably just lost that excuse. Time's a-wastin'. A lot of students and their families have already turned in financial aid forms—and their tax forms besides. And they've probably already gotten their IRS refunds back, too.

May 1: Your aid application must be received by the processing agency listed on the form by the first of May. It's really very late by now—and the processing agency is still going to take four to six weeks to run your forms through, so it's later than you think. Still, better late than never. Before you buy the hot dogs for your Memorial Day picnic, make sure you've got the forms into the mail.

June 30: Your school's financial aid office must receive your application and your student aid report—the forms you get back from the processing agency—by this deadline. If you are already in college, your deadline is the last day of enrollment for that year. Again, this is the absolute deadline. It's much better to get this in far ahead of time, and beginning January 1.

Freshman Year, Sophomore Year, etc.

January 1: Apply for financial aid all over again. You need to do this every year.

Applying for Financial Aid: The Nuts and Bolts

Applying for financial aid begins with your applications at the federal level; other aid providers look to the information you provide to the federal government. Your school will tell you which forms to fill out, but the basics of applying for federal aid are the same for whatever form you use.

Are You Eligible?

There are eligibility requirements for financial aid. You must be enrolled at least half-time to receive aid from the Pell Grant, GSL, PLUS, and SLS programs. Half-time enrollment is not required for the campus-based student aid programs such as Supplemental Educational Opportunity Grants (SEOG), College Work-Study, and Perkins Loans. Individual schools have various qualifications for the campus-based programs. You must be what the government calls a "regular student," which means you are enrolled in an institution to get a degree or certificate, or are completing course work that enables you to qualify for admission.

Eligibility also depends on citizenship: You must be a citizen, or an eligible noncitizen. If you are not a citizen, you must be a U.S. national or a U.S. permanent resident with an Alien Registration Receipt Card—or you must fall into one of several other arcane categories (for example, those whom the Immigration and Naturalization Service has designated "Cuban-Haitian entrant, status pending" are eligible for aid, while students on an F-1 or F-2 student visa are not).

You can be knocked out of eligibility if you are already in default on federal loans, including a Perkins Loan, a Guaranteed Student Loan, a PLUS Loan, or SLS.

And to clinch your eligibility, you will have to sign several pieces of paper: You must sign a "statement of educational purpose" that promises you will use your federal student aid funds for school-related expenses only. You must also sign a "statement of registration status" that states you have registered for the draft, if you are required to do so. If you don't register, you can't get aid. (If you say you registered but you really didn't, there could be repercussions: The Education Department has begun to turn the list of liars over to the Justice Department.) After you have applied for aid and received your Student Aid Report, you will have to add a "statement of updated information" to your aid request that certifies that the items listed in your Student Aid Report are still correct.

Dependent or Independent?

Few financial aid questions are as important as whether you will be considered a dependent or independent student. If you are considered a dependent student, your parents must report their income and assets along with yours (and with your spouse's, if you are married). If you are classified as an independent student, you report only your own income and assets (along with your spouse's, if you are married). Unless you are a rock star, you probably make less money than your parents, and you will be eligible for more aid if you can be certified as an independent student. You should answer these questions to see if you can make the independent classification:

Are you 24 years old or older? You will be automatically considered an independent student if you are 24 years old by December 31 of the year you receive the financial aid award.

Are you a vet? A veteran of the U.S. Armed Forces is also automatically considered an independent student. This doesn't apply to former National Guardsmen, Reservists, or to former members of the Armed Forces who received a dishonorable discharge.

Are both of your parents dead, or are you a ward of the court? Wards of the court are also independent, as are students whose parents are dead and who don't have an adoptive parent or legal guardian.

Do you have legal dependents other than a spouse? That includes your child, so long as the child gets at least half its support from you, or any other legal dependents who get more than half their support from you and who will continue to get that support through the award year.

Do your parents claim you as a tax exemption? If you are a SINGLE undergraduate student with no dependents and if your parents or guardian didn't claim you as a dependent on the previous two tax returns, you might qualify as an independent student. You must also prove that you had annual total resources other than what the folks have kicked in, of more than $4,000 in those years. This includes wages, salaries, tips, student financial aid, personal loans for educational purposes, interest income, dividend income and other income or benefits such as fellowships.

If you are MARRIED and can say that your parents or guardian won't claim you as a dependent on their next tax return, you will also be considered independent.

Living with your parents, by the way, does not automatically make you a dependent. But the school aid administrator can nonetheless take a hard look at the situation and can factor in the cost of room and board at home— among other support—to determine whether to increase the amount of parental contribution, the student contribution, or otherwise to fiddle with your financial aid package.

Your school's aid administrator can change your status from dependent to independent if he or she thinks circumstances warrant the switch. Though the financial aid officer has every reason to want to look to your parents to shoulder the burden of your financial aid, the switch to independent status occurs from time to time. See the passage below on dealing with financial aid officers.

Special Circumstances

If you don't qualify as an independent student by the basic rules outlined above but feel that special circumstances dictate that you should be considered as an independent student anyway, you will be happy to know that the school aid administrator has the power to reclassify you as he or she sees fit. The aid administrator has the power to adjust your family contribution, or some element of your cost of education, such as tuition at private schools. However, you shouldn't assume that just because that person has the power that you will get your status changed—far from it. So it would be especially foolish for you to fill out your aid application as an independent if you don't automatically qualify unless you have gotten specific instructions from your aid administrator. The procedure for making the change will depend on the aid applications used and the individual school's rules, so you definitely need to follow the lead of the aid administrator.

A radical change in your life will change the way the aid administrator sees you and your plea for aid. If one of your parents dies, you should list only the income of the surviving parent. If the parent dies after you have filed, you should contact the school's financial aid office, since the loss in family income certainly needs to be reflected in your aid package. If one of your parents becomes unemployed, that can also change your status. Losing benefits such as child support or Social Security can sway an administrator. Anything that makes you substantially poorer affects your chances to receive aid.

Other family issues that come up when filling out the forms include the following:

■ If you are a single student with dependent children and you provide more than half the support for the children, independent status is automatic. But if you and your dependent children live with your parents and they provide more than half the support, you probably won't be classified as independent.

■ If you are separated or divorced, give the aid administrator information that applies directly to you— report only your own share of the joint asssets and liabilities.

■ If your parents are divorced, the aid administrator wants the information from the parent you have lived with for the most time over the year before you file. That parent should fill out the form as a single head of household, and only list his or her income and his or her portion of the joint assets and debts. If you didn't live with either parent, or you lived with each an equal amount of time, you should list the parent who gave you the most financial support in the year before you file. If you got no support from either parent or if you got equal support from each in that time, list the parent who gave the most in a previous, uneven year.

■ If you have a stepparent who has married the parent who supports you, you should provide that person's financial information along with that of your natural parent's.

The Application Process

The forms you need to fill out in order to apply for aid vary from state to state and from institution to institution, depending on the "need analysis service" used by the state or institution. Your school will let you know which forms you must complete and will provide them to you. The most common forms are:

■ The U.S. Department of Education's Free Application for Federal Student Aid (FAFSA), which is the main application for the Pell Grant

■ The College Scholarship Service's Financial Aid Form (FAF)

■ The American College Testing Program's Family Financial Statement (FFS)

■ The Pennsylvania Higher Education Assistance Agency's Application for Pennsylvania State Grant and Federal Student Aid (PHEAA)

■ The Student Aid Application for California (SAAC)

■ The Illinois State Scholarship Commission's Application for Federal and State Student Aid (AFSSA)

The forms, while not easy, are not impossible to fill out on your own.

The state forms tend to be shorter and easier to complete than the nationally distributed forms. You don't have to fill out the FAFSA if you are filling out one of the other forms; those forms let you apply for Pell Grants and other federal aid at the same time. Checking a box on the forms tells the state to send your financial information along to a federal processing center.

Your school's application instructions will give you the information you need about applying for other forms of aid—several states, for instance, require that you fill out still more forms to apply for their own aid programs. The school's own application, and the state applications, might have separate deadlines that you will have to pay heed to.

Once you have applied, the processing agency will take between four and six weeks to turn your application around. You may be asked to confirm information or to correct the forms and then return them to be processed again. (You didn't listen to the second commandment!) The reprocessing will add another two or three weeks to your wait.

After processing your data, you will begin to receive a lot of paper. Your application for federal aid through the FAFSA or the other forms will be used to generate a Student Aid Report, or SAR. The SAR puts your data into a financial aid Cuisinart and figures out whether you qualify for federal student aid. It generates a Student Aid Index number, which lets you know whether you qualify for a Pell Grant, and a Family Contribution number, which will be used to see whether you qualify for campus-based programs such as SEOG, College Work-Study, Perkins Loans, and the Guaranteed Student Loan programs.

If you qualify for a Pell Grant, your SAR will arrive in three parts. The Information Summary, Part 1, will tell you how to check the SAR for errors. You use Part 2, the Information Review Form, to correct any errors in the SAR. Your school will use Part 3, Pell Grant Payment Document, to decide how much money you will receive. Immediately make copies of Part 1 and send one to the financial aid office of each school you are applying to. You'll submit all three parts of the SAR to the school you ultimately decide to attend.

Didn't get the Pell? Don't worry—very few applicants do. But now you have something very important: your family contribution number. Send that information to your financial aid administrator, who will use it to figure out whether you qualify for other federal student aid.

If you are very unlucky, the Department of Education or your school might decide that you need to submit to "verification." This is like an IRS audit. You may have to verify everything from income to household size to federal taxes paid. You may have a long one-on-one with your aid administrator, and have to produce documents or fill out a verification worksheet. If you don't comply, kiss your aid goodbye. Some schools require verification from every financial aid applicant.

How Need Analysis Works

How was it determined that you would or would not receive a Pell Grant?

By strict exercise of the Pell Grant Methodology. If you want to look it up, the Education Department publishes it each year in the Federal Register. But if you do look it up, you might be disappointed; it does not even purport to be an accurate look at your family's financial ability. It's just the numerical filter that the Education Department uses to ration the amount of Pell Grant money it has decided that it needs. As far as the Pell Grant Methodology goes, your school is only interested in whether your Student Aid Index qualifies you for a Pell, and pays little attention to what it purports to say about your financial status.

To figure out the family's financial strength, most schools now rely on what is known as the Uniform Methodology—or, in its latest form, the Congressional Methodology. Congress has mandated through the Higher Education Amendments of 1986 that schools will use the Congressional Methodology to determine the expected family contribution for campus-based and GSL programs. Thus far, 33 schools use the CM exclusively, and others are making the switch. So even though the next few paragraphs promise to be slow going, it's worth slogging through to understand how your school will judge your ability to pay.

For DEPENDENT STUDENTS, the expected family contribution (EFC) is broken down into four parts:

- contribution from parental income
- contribution from parental assets
- contribution from student income
- contribution from student assets

For INDEPENDENT STUDENTS, EFC boils down to:

- contribution from student (and spouse, if any) income
- contribution from student (and spouse, if any) assets

When families earn $15,000 or less, the need analysis excludes any consideration of assets. While the Pell Grant and Congressional methods both take into account required expenses such as taxes and unusual medical expenses, and while both let the family set aside a certain amount for retirement or emergencies, the two methodologies part ways when figuring out how that income and those assets can be sheltered, and how much. Also, both methodologies make allowances for the expected family contribution whenever another member of the family heads off to college.

Getting the Award Letter

Once the school has all the information it needs, it can put together an aid package that will probably include a combination of grants (precious few), loans (too many), and work-study employment. You will get your notification of what your aid package contains in an award letter. This document gives you an idea of your probable cost of attendance, how your need was determined, what your need turned out to be, and the composition of that aid package. If you are satisfied with the aid package, you sign the documents that come with the form and send them back to the school.

Even if you haven't decided which school to attend, you should move quickly to accept the aid package from each school that offers one. That's the only way to keep your options open. Schools set response deadlines: If you don't respond to your aid letter within that time, you could miss out on the funds that have been offered to you. Accepting the aid package does not obligate you to attend the school. This isn't to say you should keep a number of colleges on a string—choose your college as quickly as possible so that the schools you don't choose can distribute the money to other students.

But before you leap to accept that award letter, evaluate your offers with a cold eye. Don't be fooled by big numbers; pay special attention to how much of the offer is made up of grants and how much is made up of loans. Which schools are tossing in special awards for academic or athletic merit? If scholarships are offered, are they renewable or are they one-shot wonders that will leave you high and dry next year? Break out your calculator and compare the loan interest rates offered by different institutions, and check out whether the payback requirements for those loans are especially onerous. And as for work-study offers, keep in mind the study load before you and ask yourself whether you will be able to juggle work and school right off the bat. You may accept part of the award and reserve the right to appeal any objectionable parts.

Getting More: Appealing to the Financial Aid Officer

Say you want to attend a certain school, but the award letter was a major disappointment. Is there anything you can do to change the school's mind? As we have already seen, the aid officers have a degree of latitude within which to change their estimate of a student's need, especially in cases of hardship. If you are dissatisfied with your award, you might want to put together your case for more aid and present it to the school's financial aid officer. The sooner the better: As matriculation day approaches, the aid officer's discretionary power dries up with his or her funds.

Try for a face-to-face meeting, so long as (1) the travel expenses aren't prohibitive or (2) the school is not too big to provide that kind of personal service. If you get your foot in the door, politely present youself in the best possible light to the financial aid officer—make the school want you. Push your abilities and accomplishments and the reasons that you and the school make a good match.

You'll do best if you remember the old adage: it's nice to be nice. Financial aid officers suffer a lot of abuse. You do not want to add to the stress in your financial aid officer's life. Read your Dale Carnegie to polish those people skills, and take a look at a remarkably handy guide: "Financial Aid Officers—What They Do To You and For You." Written by a financial aid officer, the $3.00 booklet outlines a winning strategy for helping a harried financial aid officer see your side of things. (Octameron Associates, P.O. Box 3437, Alexandria, VA 22302.)

Glossary of Financial Aid Terms

Ability to Benefit: Applies to most students who are admitted to a postsecondary institution but who do not have a high school diploma or a GED high school diploma equivalency. To receive federal student aid, a student admitted on the basis of ability to benefit must fulfill one of the following conditions:

(1) Pass a standardized admissions test that measures the student's aptitude successfully to complete the course of study. If the student fails the test, he or she must complete step #2 to qualify for aid.

(2) Enroll in and successfully complete a remedial program that is required by the school and that does not exceed one academic year. If the student fails the admissions test mentioned in step #1, or if the student is admitted on the basis of counseling given by the school, he or she would be required to enroll in the remedial program.

(3) Receive a GED before graduating from the course of study or by the end of the first year of the course of study—whichever comes first.

Local financial aid administrators will have more information as to the specifics at your school.

Assets: Savings and checking accounts, home or business value, stocks, bonds, money market funds, mutual funds, real estate, trust funds, etc. Cars are not considered assets, nor are possessions such as stamp collections or musical instruments.

Campus-Based Programs: Supplemental Educational Opportunity Grants (SEOG's), College Work-Study (CWS), and Perkins Loans. These federal programs are called campus-based because they're administered by the financial aid administrator at the school. Your financial aid package may contain aid from one or more of these programs.

Citizen/Eligible Noncitizen: You must be one of the following to receive federal student aid:
1. U.S. citizen
2. U.S. national
3. U.S. permanent resident who has an I–151 or I–551 (Alien Registration Receipt Card)

If you're not in one of these categories, you must have a Departure Record (I–94) from the U.S. Immigration and Naturalization Service (INS) showing one of the following designations:
1. "Refugee"
2. "Asylum Granted"
3. "Indefinite Parole" and/or "Humanitarian Parole"
4. "Cuban–Haitian Entrant, Status Pending"
5. "Conditional Entrant" (valid only if issued before April 1, 1980)
6. Other eligible noncitizen with a Temporary Resident Card (I–688)

Also, you're eligible for federal student aid if you have a suspension of deportation case pending before Congress.

If you're in the U.S. on an F1 or F2 student visa only, or on a J1 or J2 exchange visitor visa only, you cannot get federal student aid. NOTE: Only citizens and noncitizen nationals can receive a GSL, PLUS, or SLS for study at a foreign institution.

Residents of Palau are eligible for all the student aid programs mentioned in this section. Some residents of the Federated States of Micronesia and the Marshall Islands may be eligible for Pell Grants, Supplemental Educational Opportunity Grants (SEOG's), or College Work-Study only. These residents should check with their financial aid administrators.

Cost of Education (or Cost of Attendance): The total amount it will cost a student to go to school. It is usually expressed as a yearly figure. The cost of education covers tuition and fees; on-campus room and board (or a housing and food allowance for off-campus students); and allowances for books, supplies, transportation, child care, costs related to a handicap and miscellaneous expenses. Talk to the financial aid administrator at the school you're planning to attend if you have any unusual expenses that may affect your cost of education or your ability to pay that cost.

Default: Failure to repay a student loan according to the terms agreed to when you signed a promissory note. If you default on a student loan, your school, lender, state government, and the federal government all can take action to recover the money. Default may affect your future credit rating, and you won't be able to receive additional federal aid or a deferment of your loan repayments, if you decide to return to school. Also, you may be liable for expenses incurred in collecting the loan. Finally, the Internal Revenue Service may withhold your income tax refund so that your loan will be repaid.

Dislocated Worker: A person so classified by the appropriate state agency (such as the state employment service or job service). Generally, a dislocated worker is unemployed because 1. He or she has been terminated or laid off; 2. The plant or other facility where he or she worked has closed; 3. He or she was self-employed, but is not now because of poor economic conditions in the community or because a natural disaster has occurred.

If one of these conditions applies to you, to your spouse, or to your parents, your (and/or their) financial circumstances will be specially considered in determining the ability to pay for your education.

To find out if you, your spouse, or one of your parents qualifies as a dislocated worker, contact your local state employment service or local Job Training Partnership Act (JTPA) service (listed under state agencies in the telephone book). Or contact your city or county employment and training program (listed under city or county agencies). If you have any trouble finding these offices, your financial aid administrator should have a list of Employment and Training offices you can contact.

Displaced Homemaker: Someone who—

1. Has not worked in the labor force for a substantial number of years (for example, approximately five years or more), but during those years has worked in the home providing unpaid services for family members;
2. Has depended on public assistance or on the income of another family member, but is no longer receiving that income, or who has been receiving public assistance because of dependent children in the home;
3. Is unemployed or underemployed and is having trouble obtaining or upgrading employment. "Underemployed" means not working this week but being available for work and having made specific efforts to get a job sometime during the last four weeks. "Underemployed" means working part-time (even though full-time employment is desired), because work is slack or because only part-time work is available.

If all of these conditions apply to you, to your spouse, or to your parents, your (and/or their) financial circumstances will be specially considered in determining the ability to pay for your education.

Eligible Program: A course of study that leads to a degree or certificate at a school that takes part in one or more of the student aid programs described in this booklet. To get a Pell Grant, SEOG, Perkins Loan, or a College Work-Study job, you must be enrolled in an eligible program. The same is true for a GSL or SLS, with a single exception: if your school has told you that you must take certain course work to qualify for admission into one of its eligible programs, you can get a GSL or SLS for up to 12 months while you're completing that course work, as long as you're attending at least half-time. You must also meet the usual student aid eligibility requirements.

Exit Interview: A counseling session you must attend before you leave your school, if you have any of the loans described in this section. At this session, your school will give you information on the average amount borrowers owe, the amount of your monthly repayment, and about deferment, refinancing, and loan consolidation options.

Family Contribution (FC): This figure is determined by a formula and indicates how much of your family's financial resources should be available to help pay for school. This amount is used to determine your eligibility for aid from the campus-based GSL, PLUS, and SLS programs. This number is important because your financial aid administrator will subtract it from your cost of education to find out how much you can't pay. To determine your contribution, the information you fill in on an aid application is evaluated. Factors such as your (and your family's) taxable and nontaxable income, as well as assets such as savings or the net worth of a home, are considered in determining your family's financial strength. Certain allowances are subtracted from both income and assets to protect part of them for future needs. A portion of the remaining amount is considered available to help pay for postsecondary educational costs.

If you have any unusual expenses that may affect your family contribution, make sure that you notify your financial aid administrator.

Family Financial Statement (FFS): An American College Testing Program form to assess the student's need for monetary aid. If requested by the student, the need assessment will be sent to a college's financial aid office.

Financial Aid Form (FAF): Form provided by the College Board College Scholarship Service for assessing and informing specified colleges of a student's family's financial situtation. It is generally available from high school guidance offices as well as from the colleges that prefer the results of this form.

Financial Aid Package: The total amount of financial aid a student receives. Federal and nonfederal aid such as loans, grants, or work-study are combined in a "package" to help meet the student's need. Using available resources to give each student the best possible package of aid is one of the major responsibilities of a school's financial aid administrator.

Financial Aid Transcript: A record of the Department of Education student aid you've received. If you've received federal student aid and you transfer, you must request that your old school(s) send your financial aid transcript to the school you'll be attending. If your new school doesn't receive a financial aid transcript from the old one(s), you won't receive aid from Department of Education programs.

Part 1 of the 1993-94 Student Aid Report contains a statement of registration status. You must sign either that one or a similar one prepared by your school. (Some schools require all students to sign a statement, indicating either that the student has registered or is not required to do so.)

NOTE: If you already have a statement on file with your school, you do not have to sign another one unless your registration status has changed.

Guarantee Agency: The organization that administers the GSL, PLUS, and SLS programs in your state. The federal government sets loan limits and interest rates, but each state is free to set its own additional limitations, within federal guidelines. This agency is the best source of information on GSL's, PLUS loans, and SLS loans in your state.

Half-time: You must be attending school at least half-time to be eligible to receive a Pell Grant, a GSL, a PLUS, or an SLS. Half-time enrollment is not a requirement to receive aid from the campus-based programs.

At schools measuring progress by credit hours and academic terms (semesters, trimesters, or quarters), "half-time" means at least six semester hours or quarter hours per term. At schools measuring progress by credit hours but not using academic terms, "half-time" means at least 12 semester hours or 18 quarter hours per year. At schools measuring progress by clock hours, "half-time" means at least 12 hours per week. Note that schools may choose to set higher minimums than these. Also, GSL, PLUS, and SLS requirements may be slightly different.

Internship Deferment: A period during which loan payments can be deferred if a borrower is participating in a program of supervised practical training required to begin professional practice or service. For a new borrower, an internship also means a degree or certificate program offered by a postsecondary school, hospital, or health care facility with postgraduate training. If you're enrolled in an internship program, you may defer repayment of your Guaranteed Student Loan (GSL), SLS, or Perkins Loan for up to two years.

New Borrower: For Perkins Loans, you're a new borrower if your period of enrollment begins on or after July 1, 1987, and you have no outstanding Perkins Loans (or NDSL's)—either because you've never had any or because you've paid off any you've had. Once you qualify as a new borrower, those loan conditions automatically apply to any future Perkins Loans.

For GSL, PLUS, or SLS, you're a new borrower if your period of enrollment begins on or after July 1, 1987, and you have no outstanding GSL, PLUS, SLS, or consolidated loans—either because you've never had any or because you've paid off any you've had. Once you qualify as a new borrower, those loan conditions automatically apply to any future GSL, PLUS, or SLS loans.

The new borrower definition affects only the loan program you're applying to, and doesn't affect other student loans you may have. You could be a new borrower for the Perkins Loan Program and an old borrower for the GSL Program at the same time. For example, if you've paid off a previous Perkins Loan and apply for a new one after July 1, 1987, but still have an outstanding GSL, you're a new borrower for your Perkins Loan.

Parental Leave Deferment: A period of up to six months during which loan payments can be postponed if a borrower is pregnant, or if he or she is taking care of a newborn or newly adopted child. The borrower must be unemployed and not attending school. To get this deferment, you must apply within six months after you leave school or drop below half-time status.

Promissory Note: The legal document you sign when you get a student loan. It lists the conditions under which you're borrowing and the terms under which you agree to pay back the loan.

Regular Student: One who is enrolled in an institution to obtain a degree or certificate. (There is an exception for GSL, PLUS, and SLS borrowers.)

Satisfactory Progress: To be eligible to receive Federal student aid, you must maintain satisfactory academic progress. If you're enrolled in a program that is no longer than two years, the following definition of satisfactory progress applies to you: you must be maintaining a "C" average by the end of your second academic year of study or have an academic standing consistent with your institution's graduation requirements. You must continue to maintain satisfactory progress for the rest of your course of study.

If you're enrolled in a program that is shorter than two years, you must meet your school's written standard of satisfactory progress. Check with your school to find out what that standard is.

Statement of Educational Purpose: You must sign this statement in order to receive federal student aid. By signing it, you agree to use your student aid only for education-related expenses. Part 1 of the 1993-94 Student Aid Report (SAR) contains such a statement. You must sign either this one or a similar one prepared by your school.

Statement of Registration Status: If you are required to register with the Selective Service, you must sign a statement indicating you have done so before you can receive any federal student aid. This requirement applies to males who were born on or after January 1, 1960, are at least 18, are citizens or eligible noncitizens, and are not currently on active duty in the Armed Forces. (Permanent residents of the Federated States of Micronesia, the Marshall Islands, or Palau are exempt from registering.)

Statement of Updated Information: You must sign a statement certifying that the following Student Aid Report (SAR) items are still correct at the time you submit your SAR to your school: your status as a dependent/independent student, the number of your family members, and the number of those members enrolled in postsecondary education at least half-time. If information for any items changes after you submit your application, you must update the information so that it is correct as of the date you sign your SAR. Otherwise, you will not be able to receive Federal student aid. The only exception to the requirement to update is when changes occur because your marital status changes. In that case, you need not update.

Student Aid Index (SAI): The number that appears on your Student Aid Report (SAR), telling you about your Pell Grant eligibility. The SAI is the result of a series of calculations based on the information you reported when you applied for federal student aid.

At-a-Glance Financial Aid Calendar

When	What To Do
Junior Year of High School	
■ October	☞ Take PSAT
	☞ Send for college brochures and financial aid information
	☞ Begin campus tours; talk to financial aid advisers at colleges
Senior Year of High School	
■ September to December	☞ Narrow down your college choices
	☞ Ask schools for admission applications and financial aid forms
	☞ Send in applications for admission
■ January 1	☞ Send in financial aid applications
■ April 1	☞ Most college acceptances and rejections have been sent out
■ May 1	☞ Your financial aid application must be received by the processing agency listed on the form
■ June 30	☞ Your school's financial aid office must have received your application and student aid report

Answer Key and Scoring Sheet for Practice Exam I

English				Mathematics			
	Answer	Usage/ Mechanics	Rhetorical		Answer	Pre-Alg./ Elem. Alg.	Int. Alg./ Coord. Geom.	Geom./ Trig.
1.	C	___		1.	A	___		
2.	J		___	2.	G	___		
3.	D		___	3.	B			___
4.	G	___		4.	F			___
5.	A	___		5.	A	___		
6.	H	___		6.	H		___	
7.	C		___	7.	E	___		
8.	F	___		8.	K	___		
9.	B	___		9.	D	___		
10.	G	___		10.	G	___		
11.	D	___		11.	B			
12.	H	___		12.	H	___		
13.	C		___	13.	E	___		
14.	H		___	14.	J	___		
15.	D	___		15.	E	___		
16.	F	___		16.	G	___		
17.	B	___		17.	C			___
18.	J		___	18.	F		___	
19.	D	___		19.	B		___	
20.	H	___		20.	F			
21.	A	___		21.	E		___	
22.	J	___		22.	J		___	
23.	A		___	23.	E			___
24.	H		___	24.	F			___
25.	C	___		25.	E			___
26.	J		___	26.	F	___		
27.	A	___		27.	B	___		
28.	J		___	28.	K			
29.	C	___		29.	E			___
30.	F		___	30.	H			___
31.	A	___		31.	E		___	
32.	J	___		32.	G			
33.	B		___	33.	C			___
34.	G	___		34.	H			___
35.	D	___		35.	B	___		
36.	G		___	36.	F		___	
37.	A		___	37.	D			
38.	H		___	38.	G			
39.	B	___		39.	E		___	
40.	J		___	40.	F			___

Answer Key and Scoring Sheet for Practice Exam I (continued)

	English				**Mathematics**			
	Answer	Usage/ Mechanics	Rhetorical		Answer	Pre-Alg./ Elem. Alg.	Int. Alg./ Coord. Geom.	Geom./ Trig.
41.	A	____		41.	E			____
42.	H	____		42.	H		____	
43.	D		____	43.	B			____
44.	H	____		44.	G			____
45.	B		____	45.	A			____
46.	J		____	46.	H		____	
47.	B		____	47.	C	____		
48.	F	____		48.	H			____
49.	D		____	49.	E		____	
50.	H		____	50.	F	____		
51.	B	____		51.	B	____		
52.	F	____		52.	G		____	
53.	D	____		53.	E	____		
54.	G	____		54.	F		____	
55.	D		____	55.	A	____		
56.	J		____	56.	G		____	
57.	C	____		57.	D			____
58.	H	____		58.	H		____	
59.	A		____	59.	A			____
60.	G		____	60.	G		____	
61.	A	____						
62.	H		____					
63.	B		____					
64.	J	____						
65.	D		____					
66.	H	____						
67.	C	____						
68.	G		____					
69.	B		____					
70.	F	____						
71.	D	____						
72.	J	____						
73.	C		____					
74.	F		____					
75.	A		____					

Raw Score	Total Correct (by category) ____ ____	Total Correct (by category) ____ ____ ____	
	Grand Total Correct (English) ____	Grand Total Correct (Mathematics) ____	

Using the chart on page 325, convert the above raw score to an approximate standardized score.

Approx. Standardized Score		

Answer Key and Scoring Sheet for Practice Exam I (continued)

	Reading			Science Reasoning	
	Answer	Social St./Science	Arts/Lit.	Answer	Science Reasoning
1.	B		____	1. D	____
2.	H		____	2. F	____
3.	C		____	3. D	____
4.	J		____	4. G	____
5.	A		____	5. C	____
6.	G		____	6. G	____
7.	A		____	7. C	____
8.	H		____	8. H	____
9.	D		____	9. A	____
10.	F		____	10. H	____
11.	C		____	11. D	____
12.	F		____	12. G	____
13.	D		____	13. C	____
14.	F		____	14. J	____
15.	B		____	15. D	____
16.	H		____	16. G	____
17.	A		____	17. A	____
18.	H		____	18. J	____
19.	D		____	19. D	____
20.	G		____	20. H	____
21.	A	____		21. A	____
22.	J	____		22. G	____
23.	B	____		23. D	____
24.	J	____		24. F	____
25.	B	____		25. C	____
26.	F	____		26. H	____
27.	C	____		27. B	____
28.	H	____		28. G	____
29.	A	____		29. A	____
30.	H	____		30. H	____
31.	C	____		31. B	____
32.	G	____		32. H	____
33.	D	____		33. B	____
34.	J	____		34. H	____
35.	B	____		35. D	____
36.	H	____		36. J	____
37.	A	____		37. C	____
38.	J	____		38. H	____
39.	A	____		39. A	____
40.	H	____		40. G	____

Raw Score

Total Correct (by category) ____ ____

Grand Total Correct (Reading) ____

Total Correct ____

Grand Total Correct (Science Reasoning) ____

Answer Key and Scoring Sheet for Practice Exam I (continued)

Using the chart on page 325, convert the above raw score to an approximate standardized score.

Approx. Standardized Score		

CONVERSION TABLE

Number Answered Correctly				Approximate Standardized Score
English	Mathematics	Reading	Science Reasoning	
0–2	0–2	0–2	0–1	1
3–4	3	3	2	2
5–6	4–5	4	3–4	3
7–8	6	5	5	4
9–10	7	6	6	5
11–12	8–9	7	7–8	6
13–14	10	8	9	7
15–16	11	9–10	10	8
17–18	12–13	11	11	9
19–20	14	12	12	10
21–23	15	13	13–14	11
24–25	16–17	14–15	15	12
26–27	18–19	16	16	13
28–29	20	17	17	14
30–31	21–22	18	18	15
32–33	23–24	19	19	16
34–35	25–26	20	20	17
36–37	27	21	21	18
38–39	28–29	22	22	19
40–41	30–31	23	23	20
42–44	32–33	24	24–25	21
45–46	34–35	25	26	22
47–48	36–38	26	27	23
49–50	39–40	27	28	24
51–52	41–42	28	29	25
53–54	43	29	30	26
55–57	44–46	30–31	31	27
58–60	47–48	32	32	28
61–63	49–50	33	33	29
64–65	51–52	34	34	30
66–68	53–54	35	35	31
69–70	55–56	36	36	32
71	57	37	37	33
72–73	58	38	38	34
74	59	39	39	35
75	60	40	40	36

Explanatory Answers for Practice Exam I

1. English Test

1. **(C)** A semicolon is used between clauses joined by a coordinating conjunction when one or more of the clauses contains commas.

2. **(J)** This is redundant and not necessary to the sentence.

3. **(D)** The correct adjective is *characteristic*. *Characteristic* means distinctive.

4. **(G)** *When* is not used with *is*. The correct expression is *is that*.

5. **(A)** *Has become* is correct in both number and tense.

6. **(H)** Numbers are generally written out, especially at the beginning of a sentence.

7. **(C)** *As* is the standard usage for comparison.

8. **(F)** The dash is used for separation and emphasis.

9. **(B)** The apostrophe is used to show possession.

10. **(G)** The comma is needed for separation and clarity.

11. **(D)** *One's* is the correct possessive pronoun.

12. **(H)** Quotation marks indicate that *bowl* is used in an unusual way.

13. **(C)** The correct adjective is *distinguished*. *Distinguished* means separated from others by extraordinary qualities.

14. **(H)** The question gives the reader the main focus of the passage and piques his interest.

15. **(D)** The quoted material is the words of the imaginative Italian observer mentioned in the second sentence.

16. **(F)** *Easily* is the correct adverb modifying the verb *die*.

17. **(B)** *Likely* should be used to indicate probability. *Liable* implies something undesirable or unwanted.

18. **(J)** This is redundant and not necessary to the sentence since sociologists, by definition, study sociology.

19. **(D)** *Those kind* is a nonstandard expression. *Those* is plural and *kind* is singular.

20. **(H)** The correct adverb is *around*.

21. **(A)** The verb *compared* continues the past tense used throughout the sentence.

22. **(J)** Commas are used to separate items in a list or series.

23. **(A)** Criminology is a topic in the study of sociology, but the passage is not technical in nature, thus choice B is wrong. Choice C is too general, while choice D is too specific.

24. **(H)** Paragraph 1 refers to the nineteenth century, Paragraph 3 to the turn of the century, and Paragraph 2 to the twentieth century.

25. **(C)** *Shows* is necessary for agreement with the singular subject *history*.

26. **(J)** *In depth* is the correct prepositional phrase.

27. **(A)** *Effects* is the noun meaning *results*.

28. **(J)** This information has no relevance to the paragraph.

29. **(C)** A comma is used to separate words, phrases or clauses in a series.

30. **(F)** An example of the risks being discussed would make the discussion more concrete to the reader.

31. **(A)** *An* is used before a word beginning with a vowel.

32. **(J)** *Neither* agrees with *nor* in the sentence.

33. **(B)** *And years to come* is redundant and not necessary to the sentence.

34. **(G)** *Persistence* is the correct noun.

35. **(D)** *Compared* is the correct verb and *to* is the correct preposition.

36. **(G)** No punctuation is necessary.

37. **(A)** Paragraph (1) clearly introduces the topic of the entire essay: modern pollution problems. Therefore, only choices A and C need to be considered. Paragraph (3) starts with *These*

arguments which must refer to arguments previously mentioned. This happens only when paragraph (2) comes before paragraph (3) as in choice A.

38. **(H)** The passage discusses pollution problems, not a history of technology; thus F is wrong. Because the information presented is general, not technical, in nature, G is also wrong. J is too narrow; the passage covers radioactive substances and more.

39. **(B)** *Remaining* is the correct gerund. The addition of *around* or *up* is unnecessary.

40. **(J)** Use of the word *of* in place of *have* is nonstandard. *Maybe* is an adverb, not a verb.

41. **(A)** *Most* is used correctly to modify the adjective *able*.

42. **(H)** Commas are used to set off adverbs that compare or contrast some preceding idea.

43. **(D)** *Disrepute* is the correct noun. It means having a bad reputation.

44. **(H)** The singular pronoun *his* is needed for agreement with the singular noun *researcher*.

45. **(B)** The paragraph discusses a theory about the usefulness of the researcher after age 40. Thus discussing contributions of older researchers would now be appropriate. Choices A and D are irrelevant; choice C is too general. The correct answer is B.

46. **(J)** *Of long ago* is redundant and not necessary to the sentence.

47. **(B)** *Considered* is the correct verb.

48. **(F)** *In* is the correct preposition.

49. **(D)** The most logical order is to contrast views of creativity in the past (3) with those of the present (2) and (1), and then salary guideposts of the past (4) to those of today (5).

50. **(H)**

51. **(B)** *Who* is correct as the subject of the verb *have chosen*.

52. **(F)** Question marks are used after direct questions.

53. **(D)** *Greater* is the correct comparative adjective. *Greatest* is in the superlative and not required in this sentence.

54. **(G)** *Through* meaning by means of is the correct preposition. *Threw* is the past tense of the verb throw.

55. **(D)** *In the past* is redundant.

56. **(J)** The conjunction *that* is the only word needed to introduce the clause that follows.

57. **(C)** *But* establishes the contrast between the two clauses and parallels the construction of the previous sentence.

58. **(H)** *Rising*, which means moving upward, is correct. *Raising* means causing to move upward.

59. **(A)** *Quite the contrary* is the only phrase that makes sense in the sentence.

60. **(G)** The paragraph discusses the contributions that science and engineering have made. Therefore, specific examples are appropriate.

61. **(A)** No punctuation is required here.

62. **(H)** The passage is concerned with solving problems in the fields of science and engineering. It begins by addressing those who have chosen these fields.

63. **(B)** Paragraph 1 introduces the main concern of this section. Paragraphs 4, 2, and 3 begin with First, Second, and Third respectively. Paragraph 5 summarizes the author's point of view; hence, it is the conclusion.

64. **(J)** The singular subject *youth* requires the singular verb *is*.

65. **(D)** *This here* is nonstandard usage for the pronoun this.

66. **(H)** *Similarities* is not completed by *from*. It requires the preposition *to* (similarities *to* the American market).

67. **(C)** *Market's* is the correct possessive. The apostrophe followed by an *s* is used to show singular possession.

68. **(G)** The adverb *increasingly* correctly modifies the adjective *high*.

69. **(B)** The use of the comma creates a run-on sentence. The two sentences must be separated by a period.

70. **(F)** *Transatlantic* is one word. It is an adjective, not a proper noun. No capitalization is necessary.

328 / ACT

71. **(D)** *Adopted*, meaning to have taken up and practiced as one's own, is the correct verb. *Adapted* means to have adjusted.

72. **(J)** *Between* is used for two persons or things and *among* is used for more than two persons or things.

73. **(C)**

74. **(F)** The passage deals with the youth markets of Western Europe and America; therefore, its readers would probably be people interested in the consumer patterns of youth.

75. **(A)**

2. Mathematics Test

1. **(A)** If two numbers add to zero, they are additive inverses.

   $a + (-a) = 0$

   The additive inverse is the opposite of the original value.

   $+\frac{2}{3}$ is the additive inverse of $-\frac{2}{3}$

2. **(G)** $x^2 + 6x + 8 = 0$
   $(x + 4)(x + 2) = 0$
   $x + 4 = 0 \quad x + 2 = 0$
   $x = -4 \quad x = -2$

3. **(B)** Angle AOC is a central angle. Arc $AC = 70°$, a central angle is equal to its intercepted arc.

   $\angle ABC = 35°$

   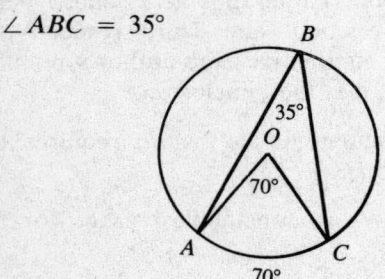

   An inscribed angle is equal to $\frac{1}{2}$ the measure of its intercepted arc.

   $m\angle ABC = \frac{1}{2}m\widehat{AC}$

4. **(F)**

   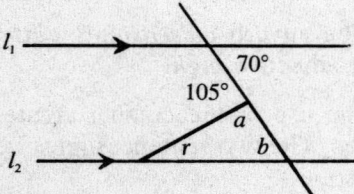

   The measure of $\angle b = 70°$. It is an alternate interior angle with angle x.

   The measure of $\angle a = 75°$. It is the supplement of angle y.

   $m\angle r + m\angle a + m\angle b = 180°$. They form a triangle.

   $m\angle r + 75° + 70° = 180°$
   $m\angle r = 35°$

5. **(A)** $A = \dfrac{2gr}{g + r}$

   $4 = \dfrac{2g(1)}{g + (1)} \rightarrow 4 = \dfrac{2g}{g + 1}$

   By cross-multiplication:

   $4(g + 1) = 2g$
   $4g + 4 = 2g$
   $2g = -4$
   $g = -2$

6. **(H)** A V-shaped graph is usually indicative of an absolute value function.

   By substituting the given coordinates (2, 2), (0, 0), and (−3, 3) into the answer choices, only $y = |x|$ satisfies all the ordered pairs.

7. **(E)** The distributive property:
   - of multiplication over addition $a(b + c) = ab + ac$
   - of multiplication over subtraction $a(b - c) = ab - ac$

   $x(x + 2) = x^2 + 2x$

8. **(K)** The sales tax is 7% of $600.

   $\left(\dfrac{7}{100}\right)(600) =$

   $\dfrac{7(600)}{100} = \$42$

   The total cost is $600 + $42 = $642

ACT Practice Exam I / 329

9. **(D)** $-x^2 - 2x^3$

   Substitute the value -1 for x
   $$-(-1)^2 - 2(-1)^3 =$$
   $$-(1) - 2(-1) =$$
   $$-1 + 2 = 1$$

10. **(G)** Average $= \dfrac{\text{Sum of the numbers}}{\text{Quantity of numbers}}$
    $$= \dfrac{(n+3) + (2n-1) + (3n+4)}{3}$$
    $$= \dfrac{6n+6}{3} = 2n+2$$

11. **(B)** Substitute $x = 9$
    $$9^0 + 9^{1/2} + 9^{-2}$$
    $$= 1 + \sqrt{9} + \dfrac{1}{9^2}$$
    $$= 1 + 3 + \dfrac{1}{81}$$
    $$= 4\dfrac{1}{81}$$

12. **(H)** $4\sqrt{3} + 3\sqrt{27}$

    To add radicals, the number in the square root must be the same.
    NOTE: $\sqrt{27} = \sqrt{9}\sqrt{3} = 3\sqrt{3}$
    $$4\sqrt{3} + 3\sqrt{27} =$$
    $$4\sqrt{3} + 3(3\sqrt{3}) =$$
    $$4\sqrt{3} + 9\sqrt{3} = 13\sqrt{3}$$

13. **(E)** Average $= \dfrac{\text{Sum of the test scores}}{\text{Quantity of tests}}$
    $$90 = \dfrac{87 + 93 + 86 + x}{4}$$
    By cross-multiplication:
    $$4(90) = 87 + 93 + 86 + x$$
    $$360 = 266 + x$$
    $$x = 94$$

14. **(J)** Each dime is 10 cents. Three dimes would be $3(10) = 30$ cents.

    $4x$ dimes would be $4x(10) = 40x$ cents.

15. **(E)** The ● indicates either $\geq$ or $\leq$. The ○ indicates either $>$ or $<$ without the equal. The arrow to the left indicates less than ($<$). The arrow to the right indicates greater than ($>$).

    The graph indicates $x \leq -5$
    $$x > 3$$
    The answers are connected by an "or."
    $$x \leq -5 \quad \text{or} \quad x > 3$$

16. **(G)** $2\dfrac{2}{5} - 1\dfrac{7}{8} = \dfrac{12}{5} - \dfrac{15}{8}$

    The lowest common denominator is 40.
    $$\dfrac{12}{5} - \dfrac{15}{8} = \dfrac{96}{40} - \dfrac{75}{40} = \dfrac{21}{40}$$

17. **(C)** Circumference $= 2\pi r = 2\pi(6) = 12\pi$ in length. 2π is $\dfrac{2\pi}{12\pi} = \dfrac{1}{6}$ of the circumference. In turn, the central angle is $\dfrac{1}{6}(360°) = 60°$

    or
    $$\dfrac{\text{arc length}}{\text{circumference}} = \dfrac{x°}{360°}$$
    $$\dfrac{2\pi}{12\pi} = \dfrac{x}{360}$$
    $$\dfrac{1}{6} = \dfrac{x}{360}$$
    $$6x = 360$$
    $$x = 60$$

18. **(F)** $\dfrac{2x}{3\sqrt{2}} = \dfrac{3\sqrt{2}}{x}$

    By cross-multiplication
    $$2x(x) = (3\sqrt{2})(3\sqrt{2})$$
    $$2x^2 = 9(2) = 18$$
    $$x^2 = 9$$
    $$x = \pm 3$$
    The positive value of x is 3.

19. **(B)** $f(x) = 2x - x^2$
    $$f(2) = 2(2) - (2)^2$$
    $$= 4 - 4 = 0$$
    $$g(x) = x - 4$$
    $$g(0) = 0 - 4$$
    $$= -4$$
    $$\therefore g(f(2)) = g(0) = -4$$

20. **(F)** $|5 - 2x| = 7$

    $$5 - 2x = -7 \qquad 5 - 2x = 7$$
    $$-2x = -12 \qquad -2x = 2$$
    $$x = 6 \qquad\qquad x = -1$$

    Check the solutions
    $$|5 - 2x| = 7 \qquad |5 - 2x| = 7$$
    $$|5 - 2(6)| = 7 \qquad |5 - 2(-1)| = 7$$
    $$|5 - 12| = 7 \qquad |5 + 2| = 7$$
    $$|-7| = 7 \qquad\qquad 7 = 7$$
    $$7 = 7$$

21. **(E)** $\dfrac{3 - \dfrac{3}{x}}{x - 1}$

Multiply the top and bottom of the complex fraction by the lowest common denominator, which is x.

$$\dfrac{x\left(3 - \dfrac{3}{x}\right)}{x(x-1)} = \dfrac{x(3) - x\left(\dfrac{3}{x}\right)}{x(x-1)} = \dfrac{3x - 3}{x(x-1)}$$

$$= \dfrac{3(x-1)}{x(x-1)} = \dfrac{3}{x}$$

22. **(J)** slope $= m = \dfrac{y_2 - y_1}{x_2 - x_1}$

$$m = \dfrac{7 - 5}{4 - (-3)} = \dfrac{2}{7}$$

23. **(E)**

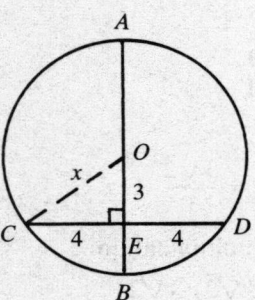

A radius or diameter drawn perpendicular to a chord, bisects the chord. Therefore $\overline{AB}$ bisects $\overline{CD}$.
Construct radius $\overline{OC}$.
This forms right triangle OEC with $\overline{OC}$ as the hypotenuse.

$$(\text{Leg 1})^2 + (\text{Leg 2})^2 = (\text{Hypotenuse})^2$$
$$(\overline{OE})^2 + (\overline{CE})^2 = (\overline{OC})^2$$
$$3^2 + 4^2 = x^2$$
$$25 = x^2$$
$$x = 5$$

24. **(F)**

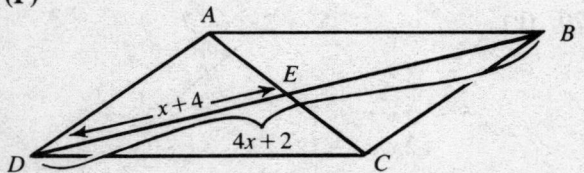

The diagonals of a parallelogram bisect each other.
$$\overline{DB} = 2(\overline{DE})$$
$$4x + 2 = 2(x + 4)$$
$$4x + 2 = 2x + 8$$
$$2x = 6$$
$$x = 3$$

25. **(E)**

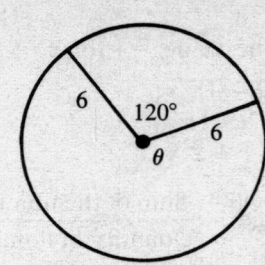

$$\dfrac{\text{area of sector}}{\text{area of circle}} = \dfrac{\text{central angle}}{360°}$$

$$\dfrac{x}{\pi r^2} = \dfrac{120°}{360°}$$

$$\dfrac{x}{36\pi} = \dfrac{1}{3}$$

By cross-multiplication
$$3x = 36\pi$$
$$x = 12\pi$$

26. **(F)** If a statement is true, its contrapositive must be true. The contrapositive is the converse of the inverse or the inverse of the converse of the original statement. If the original statement is $p \to q$, the contrapositive is $\sim q \to \sim p$.

27. **(B)** Compare all the answer choices to the original using cross-multiplication.

original: $\dfrac{a}{b} = \dfrac{r}{t} \to at = br$

choice A: $\dfrac{a}{r} = \dfrac{b}{t} \to at = br$ ✓

choice B: $\dfrac{a}{t} = \dfrac{b}{r} \to ar = bt$ No ←

choice C: $\dfrac{a+b}{b} = \dfrac{r+t}{t} \to t(a+b) = b(r+t)$
$$at + bt = br + bt$$
$$at = br \checkmark$$

choice D: $\dfrac{b}{a} = \dfrac{t}{r} \to at = br$ ✓

choice E: $at = br$ ✓

28. **(K)** $-2x + 5 = 2 - (5 - 2x)$
$$= 2 - 5 + 2x$$
$$= -3 + 2x$$

$$\begin{aligned}-2x + 5 &= -3 + 2x\\ +2x &= +2x\end{aligned}$$

$$5 = -3 + 4x$$
$$+3 = +3$$
$$8 = 4x$$
$$x = 2$$

29. **(E)** $\dfrac{(1+\sin x)(1-\sin x)}{(1+\cos x)(1-\cos x)}$
$= \dfrac{1 - \sin x + \sin x - \sin^2 x}{1 - \cos x + \cos x - \cos^2 x}$
$= \dfrac{1 - \sin^2 x}{1 - \cos^2 x}$

Using the identity $\sin^2 x + \cos^2 x = 1$
solve for $\sin^2 x$: $\sin^2 x = 1 - \cos^2 x$
solve for $\cos^2 x$: $\cos^2 x = 1 - \sin^2 x$
By substitution
$\dfrac{1 - \sin^2 x}{1 - \cos^2 x} = \dfrac{\cos^2 x}{\sin^2 x}$
$= \left(\dfrac{\cos x}{\sin x}\right)^2$
$= \cot^2 x$

30. **(H)** The median to the hypotenuse of a right triangle is equal in length to half the hypotenuse.

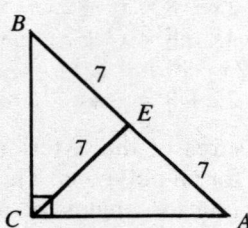

$\overline{BE} = \overline{AE} = \overline{CE}$

31. **(E)** y varies directly as $x \rightarrow \dfrac{y_1}{x_1} = \dfrac{y_2}{x_2}$

$\therefore \dfrac{10}{\frac{1}{5}} = \dfrac{y}{\frac{1}{2}}$

By cross-multiplication
$\dfrac{1}{2}(10) = \dfrac{1}{5}y$
$5 = \dfrac{y}{5}$
$y = 25$

32. **(G)** $\dfrac{(-1)(2)(-3)(4)(-5)}{(1)(-2)(3)(-4)(5)} = \dfrac{-120}{+120} = -1$

or

By rearranging the denominator
$\dfrac{(-1)(2)(-3)(4)(-5)}{(1)(-2)(3)(-4)(5)}$
$= (-1)(-1)(-1)(-1)(-1) = -1$

33. **(C)** The product of the segments of one chord is equal to the product of the segments of the other.
$(\overline{CE})(\overline{ED}) = (\overline{AE})(\overline{EB})$
$x(6x) = 6(4)$
$6x^2 = 24$
$x^2 = 4$
$x = \pm 2$
$\therefore x = 2$

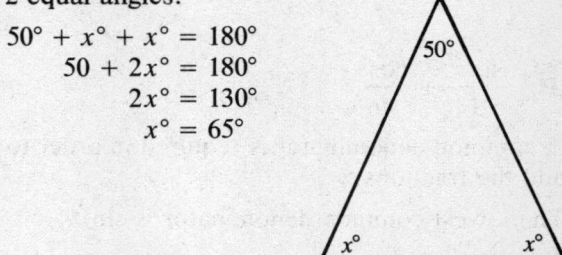

34. **(H)** An isosceles triangle has 2 equal sides and 2 equal angles.
$50° + x° + x° = 180°$
$50 + 2x° = 180°$
$2x° = 130°$
$x° = 65°$

35. **(B)** The median is the "middle" data element when the data is arranged in numerical order.
20,20,20,20,30,30,30,30,50,50,50,50,50,50,50
                      ↑
The "middle" data element is 30.

36. **(F)** $x^2 - 2x - 3 > 0$
$(x - 3)(x + 1) > 0$
$x = 3$ $x = -1$

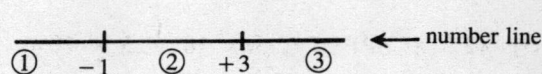

Use a numerical value to test each of the three circled intervals.
Test interval ①, x is less than -1. Use the test element $x = -2$.
$(x-3)(x+1) > 0 \rightarrow (-2-3)(-2+1) \overset{?}{>} 0$
$(-5)(-1) \overset{?}{>} 0$
$5 > 0$
True
$\therefore$ Interval ① is part of the solution set.
Test interval ②, $-1 < x < +3$. Use the test element $x = 0$.
$(x-3)(x+1) > 0 \rightarrow (0-3)(0+1) \overset{?}{>} 0$
$(-3)(1) \overset{?}{>} 0$
$-3 > 0$ False
$\therefore$ Interval ② is *not* part of the solution set.

332 / ACT

Test interval ③, $x > 3$. Use the test element $x = 4$.

$(x - 3)(x + 1) > 0 \rightarrow (4 - 3)(4 + 1) \overset{?}{>} 0$
$(1)(5) \overset{?}{>} 0$
$5 > 0$ True

∴ Interval ③ is part of the solution set.

Because $(x - 3)(x + 1) > 0$ has only a greater than sign (>) and not a greater than or equal sign (≥), the values $x = -1$ and $x = 3$ are hollow (○).

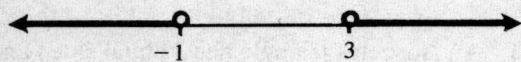

37. **(D)** $\dfrac{\sin x}{1} + \dfrac{\cos^2 x}{\sin x}$

A common denominator is required in order to add the fractions.

The lowest common denominator is $\sin x$.

$\dfrac{\sin x}{1} \cdot \dfrac{\sin x}{\sin x} + \dfrac{\cos^2 x}{\sin x} = \dfrac{\sin^2 x}{\sin x} + \dfrac{\cos^2 x}{\sin x}$

$= \dfrac{\sin^2 x + \cos^2 x}{\sin x}$

but $\sin^2 x + \cos^2 x = 1$.

∴ $= \dfrac{1}{\sin x}$

38. **(G)** $(2.5 \times 10^5)^2 = (2.5 \times 10^5)(2.5 \times 10^5)$
$= 6.25 \times 10^{10}$

39. **(E)** $A * B = \dfrac{AB - B}{-B}$

$-2 * 2 = \dfrac{(-2)(2) - 2}{-2} = \dfrac{-4 - 2}{-2} = \dfrac{-6}{-2} = 3$

40. **(F)** Substitute the root into the equation for the value of x.

$x^2 + kx - 12 = 0$
$(4)^2 + k(4) - 12 = 0$
$16 + 4k - 12 = 0$
$4k + 4 = 0$
$4k = -4$
$k = -1$

41. **(E)**

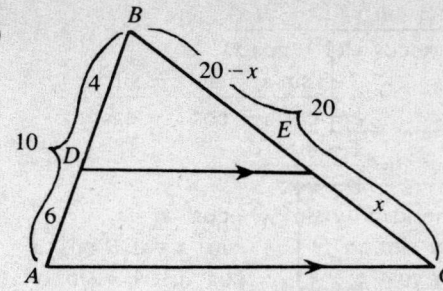

The triangles ($\triangle ABC$ and $\triangle DBE$) are similar. ∴ create a proportion.

NOTE: If $\overline{AB} = 10$ and $\overline{BD} = 4$, then $\overline{DA} = 6$, and if $\overline{BC} = 20$ and $\overline{EC} = x$, then $\overline{BE} = 20 - x$.

$\dfrac{4}{10} = \dfrac{20 - x}{20}$
$80 = 200 - 10x$
$-120 = -10x$
$x = 12$

42. **(H)**
$(x + 2)(x - 4) = x^2 - 4x + 2x - 8 = x^2 - 2x - 8$
$(x + 4)(x - 2) = x^2 - 2x + 4x - 8 = x^2 + 2x - 8$
$(x^2 - 2x - 8) - (x^2 + 2x - 8) =$
$x^2 - 2x - 8 - x^2 - 2x + 8 = -4x$

43. **(B)** The sum of the measures of the exterior angles of a polygon is 360° for all polygons. The sum of the measures of interior angles of a polygon can be expressed as $180°(n - 2)$, where n is the number of sides.

∴ $180(n - 2) = 360$

Divide by 180

$(n - 2) = 2$
$n = 4$

44. **(G)** If the perimeter = 12, then each side is $\dfrac{12}{3} = 4$. The area of an equilateral triangle can be expressed as:

$A = \dfrac{s^2}{4}\sqrt{3}$, when s is the length of the side of the equilateral triangle

$A = \dfrac{4^2}{4}\sqrt{3} = 4\sqrt{3}$

45. **(A)** Let $8x$ = the degree measure of one of the angles
$1x$ = the degree measure of the other angle

Complementary angles add to 90°

$8x + 1x = 90$
$9x = 90$
$x = 10$

46. **(H)** 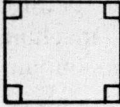 The square has 4 right angles.

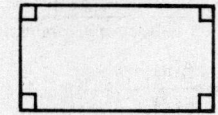 The rectangle has 4 right angles.

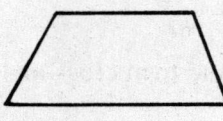 The trapezoid does not have 4 right angles.

 The circle does not have 4 right angles.

Probability of 4 right angles

$= \dfrac{\text{number of successes}}{\text{number of possibilities}} = \dfrac{2}{4} = \dfrac{1}{2}$

47. **(C)**

distance = rate × time → rate = $\dfrac{\text{distance}}{\text{time}}$

$\dfrac{320 \text{ miles}}{8 \text{ hrs}} = 40 \text{ mph} \quad 40 \text{ mph} \times 2 \text{ hrs} = 80 \text{ miles}$

48. **(H)** Use the common denominator $\sin x \cos x$.

$\dfrac{\sin x}{\cos x} \cdot \dfrac{\sin x}{\sin x} + \dfrac{\cos x}{\sin x} \cdot \dfrac{\cos x}{\cos x} =$

$\dfrac{\sin^2 x}{\sin x \cos x} + \dfrac{\cos^2 x}{\sin x \cos x} =$

$\dfrac{\sin^2 x + \cos^2 x}{\sin x \cos x} =$

$\dfrac{1}{\sin x \cos x}$

49. **(E)** The mode is the data element with the greatest frequency.

mode = 91

50. **(F)** $\dfrac{\text{part}}{\text{whole}} \times 100 = \dfrac{9}{30} \times 100 = 30\%$

51. **(B)** First rearrange the expression:

$6t^2 - 7t - 3$
$(3t + 1)(2t - 3)$

52. **(G)** If $2^{x^2+2x} = 2^{-1}$
then $x^2 + 2x = -1$
$x^2 + 2x + 1 = 0$
$(x + 1)(x + 1) = 0$

$x + 1 = 0 \quad\quad x + 1 = 0$
$x = -1 \quad\quad\quad x = -1$

53. **(E)** If Joshua is x years old now and Jessica is 3 years younger, then Jessica is now $x - 3$ years old. Four years ago she was $(x - 3) - 4 = x - 7$ years old.

54. **(F)** (the number of students)(amount each contributed) = amount collected

$(x)(y) = 18$
$(x + 3)(y - 1) = 18$

55. **(A)** $\dfrac{1}{2}\sqrt{112} = \dfrac{1}{2}\sqrt{16}\sqrt{7} = \dfrac{1}{2}(4)(\sqrt{7}) = 2\sqrt{7}$

$\sqrt{28} = \sqrt{4}\sqrt{7} = 2\sqrt{7}$

$2\sqrt{63} = 2\sqrt{9}\sqrt{7} = 2(3)\sqrt{7} = 6\sqrt{7}$

$2\sqrt{7} - 2\sqrt{7} + 6\sqrt{7} = 6\sqrt{7}$

56. **(G)** Add the two equations.

$\dfrac{1}{x} + \dfrac{1}{y} = \dfrac{1}{4}$

$\dfrac{1}{x} - \dfrac{1}{y} = \dfrac{3}{4}$

$\dfrac{2}{x} = 1$

By cross-multiplication

$x = 2$

57. **(D)** The sum of the lengths of any two sides of a triangle must exceed the length of the third side.

choice A: 1 + 3 is not greater than 6
choice B: 2 + 4 is not greater than 7
choice C: 2 + 10 is not greater than 12
choice D: 4 + 6 > 8
$\quad\quad\quad\;\;$ 4 + 8 > 6 ✓
$\quad\quad\quad\;\;$ 6 + 8 > 4
choice E: 4 + 4 is not greater than 10

58. **(H)** To eliminate the variable y, multiply the first equation by -1 and add the equations

$\begin{matrix}-1(ax + y = b)\\ 2ax + y = 2b\end{matrix} \rightarrow \begin{matrix}-ax - y = -b\\ \underline{2ax + y = 2b}\\ ax \quad\quad = b\\ x \quad\quad = \dfrac{b}{a}\end{matrix}$

Substitute the value of x into the first equation and solve for y.

$$ax + y = b$$
$$a\left(\frac{b}{a}\right) + y = b$$
$$b + y = b$$
$$y = 0$$

The solution set is: $\left\{\frac{b}{a}, 0\right\}$

59. **(A)**

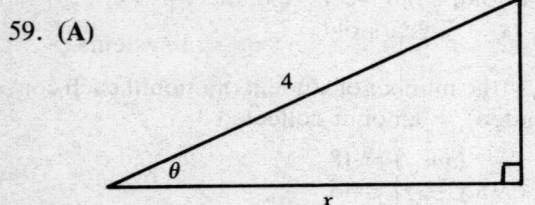

Find the third side of the triangle using the Pythagorean theorem. Label the third side x.

$$x^2 + r^2 = 4^2$$
$$x^2 + r^2 = 16$$
$$x^2 = 16 - r^2$$
$$x = \sqrt{16 - r^2}$$

$$\cos\theta = \frac{\sqrt{16 - r^2}}{4}$$

60. **(G)** The number of sheets is directly proportional to the number of machines and also directly proportional to the amount of time.

Mathematically this can be expressed as:

$$\frac{\text{sheets}}{(\text{number of machines})(\text{time})} = \frac{\text{sheets}}{(\text{number of machines})(\text{time})}$$

$$\frac{300}{3(3)} = \frac{600}{6(t)}$$

$$\frac{300}{9} = \frac{600}{6t}$$

Reduce the fractions and then cross-multiply

$$\frac{100}{3} = \frac{100}{t}$$
$$100t = 300$$
$$t = 3$$

3. Reading Test

1. **(B)** Burton's use of the nickname Larry tells us that he and Olivier are friends.

2. **(H)** In paragraph 4, Burton uses the analogy of Casanova, a lover, to describe Olivier's attitude toward his hand.

3. **(C)** In paragraph 3, Burton says the speech had "a freshness, a newness, an illusion of the first time . . ."

4. **(J)** The scene is described as "A beautiful dance of the hands!"

5. **(A)** The first sentence of paragraph 4 describes Olivier as ". . . the same old Larry—expert and crisp. . ."

6. **(G)** When he came to the end of the speech, Olivier chopped off his hand.

7. **(A)** Olivier ". . . let out one of his hair-raising shrieks. . ."

8. **(H)** Burton says that ". . . for one awful moment, I believed it!"

9. **(D)** Olivier needed all the pauses to give him time to remove the artificial hand.

10. **(F)** The story is punctuated by exclamation marks. Burton sounds amazed at the skill and cleverness of his friend, Olivier.

11. **(C)** The image of the world hanging in a certain position leads the reader to believe that the world is at a standstill.

12. **(F)** The word "shutter" evokes the sound of a shutter being closed.

13. **(D)** The visual image of black clouds on a white sky is one of severe contrast.

14. **(F)** Line 1 states: ". . . the lightning fluttered perpetually . . ." The repetition of the word *flutter* brings back the image of lightning.

15. **(B)** Both phrases refer to the shadows of the huge trees in the landscape.

16. **(H)** The man alternates hatred with tenderness in a short period of time. His mental state is one of confusion.

17. **(A)** Paragraph 1 mentions a long march and the character's hatred of his captain; thus, it probably took place after a battle in which he was hurt.

18. **(H)** The color blue and the adjectives cool and tender suggest calmness.

19. **(D)** The passage describes the landscape and the character's thoughts and feelings through a series of word pictures.

20. **(G)** All of the descriptions are bleak and revolve around sickness, thirst, and pain.

21. **(A)** The first sentence states that ". . . the last possible line of defense was established instinctively. . ."

22. **(J)** The garrison was insufficient and the soldiers were scattered sparsely.

23. **(B)** The passage states that ". . . the soldiers were scattered almost as sparsely as sentinels." Therefore II is correct. I cannot be correct. III is not discussed in the passage.

24. **(J)** The passage states that ". . . the assailants were unprovided with scaling ladders." These would be special equipment.

25. **(B)** Their supposed victory and yells of exultation imply an initial advantage.

26. **(F)** The last two sentences describe the unfortunate terrain.

27. **(C)** The last sentence tells the reader that the attackers refused to leave their refuge.

28. **(H)** The "human billow" was the attacking force of the assailants.

29. **(A)** The passage describes the soldiers in grey uniforms carrying muskets. This would have occurred during the Civil War.

30. **(H)** The passage tells a very dramatic story of war.

31. **(C)** The second paragraph states: "Hamiltonian theory describes with powerful generality the overall properties of optical systems. . ."

32. **(G)** The benefits of Hamiltonian theory are conceptual and indirect.

33. **(D)** The second paragraph says that Hamiltonian theory ". . . has made little direct contribution to techniques for optical instrument design."

34. **(J)** Answers F and G are wrong, as the author states that the reader of the book should be a master of the subject. Therefore those just beginning in the field or those who are merely interested would not have sufficient knowledge to grasp the book. Choice H is also wrong, as the book *would* be useful to such a person.

35. **(B)** The other choices have nothing to do with what is being discussed.

36. **(H)** Paragraph 3 states Buchdahl's knowledge of practical optics and his significant contributions to optical theory.

37. **(A)** Paragraph 2 states that the indirect effects of the Hamiltonian theory have been large.

38. **(J)** The last sentence of the selection supports choice J.

39. **(A)** The passage discusses Buchdahl's book from a reviewer's point of view.

40. **(H)** The last paragraph states that physicists and engineers would consider the book to be quite mathematical. To professional mathematicians, however, the book would seem non-mathematical.

4. Science Reasoning Test

1. **(D)** period of revolution for Mercury
   $= .25 \times$ (period of revolution for Earth)
   $= .25 \times (365.3 \text{ days})$
   $=$ approximately 90

   period of rotation for Mercury
   $= 60 \times$ (period of rotation for Earth)
   $= 60 \times (1 \text{ day})$
   $= 60$

   ratio of revolution to rotation
   $= \dfrac{90}{60} = \dfrac{3}{2}$

2. **(F)** Mercury has a relative density to Earth of 1.
   $\text{density} = \dfrac{\text{mass}}{\text{volume}}$

   $\text{density Mercury} = \dfrac{\text{mass Mercury}}{\text{volume Mercury}}$

   $= \dfrac{.58 \times (\text{mass Earth})}{.58 \times (\text{volume Earth})}$

   $= \dfrac{\text{mass Earth}}{\text{volume Earth}}$

   $=$ density Earth

3. **(D)** Rate equals distance divided by time. Divide the average distance to the sun by the period of revolution to get relative rate. The smallest relative rate is the slowest. In this specific case, the planet with the greatest relative period of revolution orbits the sun at the slowest rate.

4. **(G)** Gravity depends on both the distance between the centers of objects (and thereby the volume—assuming the planets are roughly spherical in shape) and on the mass of the objects. Compare Mars and Mercury to see the effect of volume (by considering their diameters). Mars is more massive, but the smaller size of Mercury gives it an equivalent surface gravity. Density, a ratio of mass and volume, is not enough, because gravity depends on the *amount* of mass and the *amount* of distance, not their ratio.

5. **(C)** $\dfrac{\text{volume Pluto}}{\text{volume Earth}} = .729$

   $\dfrac{\frac{4}{3}\pi r^3_{\text{Pluto}}}{\frac{4}{3}\pi r^3_{\text{Earth}}} = .729$

   $\dfrac{r^3_{\text{Pluto}}}{r^3_{\text{Earth}}} = .729$

   $\dfrac{r_{\text{Pluto}}}{r_{\text{Earth}}} = \sqrt[3]{.729} = .9$

   $r_{\text{Pluto}} = .9 \times r_{\text{Earth}}$
   diameter Pluto $= 2 \times (.9 \text{ radius Earth})$
   $= 1.8 \text{ radius Earth}$

6. **(G)** The neighbors furthest from each other are Uranus and Neptune.
   Relative distance to sun:

Mercury	Venus	Earth	Mars	Jupiter
0.4	0.7	1	1.5	5.3

Saturn	Uranus	Neptune	Pluto
10	19	30	40

   The largest difference $(30 - 19 = 11)$

7. **(C)** Choice **A** exhibits a drop from 120 to 118.
   $\dfrac{120 - 118}{120} = 1.6\%$

   Choice **B** exhibits a drop from 118 to 115.
   $\dfrac{118 - 115}{118} = 2.5\%$

   Choice **C** exhibits a drop from 100 to 70.
   $\dfrac{100 - 70}{100} = 30\%$

   Choice **D** exhibits an *increase* from 70 to 90.

8. **(H)** The samples *must* start with the same values to be sure we are comparing equivalent populations. Choice **F** *might* weaken the validity of the comparison depending on when and how many mice died. As long as the methods agree or can be correlated, choice **G** is no problem. Choice **J** refers to the end of the experiment; although it happens that this condition is true, validity of an experiment is not determined by the final results.

9. **(A)** The total amount of hormone X in the average mouse is equal to the product of the average body weight and the hormone concentration. The amount of hormone X at the 132-hour mark of experiment 2 is equal to the average body weight (80g) times the average hormone concentration (85μg/g). Amount = 80g × 85μg/g = 6800μg.

10. **(H)** Choices **F** and **G** imply a cause-and-effect relationship that has not been proved. We do not know whether the hormone causes the change in body weight; all we know from the data is that when the hormone concentration increases, a weight drop occurs approximately a day later. Choice **J** is not true throughout the entire range of the experiment.

11. **(D)** Experiment 1 suggests normal conditions because the mice exhibit no large change in their weight or hormone concentration. To find the normal concentration of hormone X, use the dashed line graph and read the hormone concentration on the right-hand scale. The mice maintain a level of approximately 20 throughout the experiment. Note that their initial and final concentration levels are 20.

12. **(G)** The sharpest sloping curve is for potassium nitrate (KNO_3).

13. **(C)** Look at the solubility of NaCl and $NaNO_3$. We observe that the two sodium salts have different solubilities, indicating that their solubility depends on more than the nature of sodium. Therefore, choices **A** and **B** must be incorrect. Choice **D** is incorrect because we do not know whether we have seen the solubility curves for *all* sodium compounds. Choice **C** is correct because it takes into account the differences in solubilities of different sodium salts.

14. **(J)** The table gives data only for *aqueous* solutions, not alcoholic.

15. **(D)** Since the solubility curves cross at 72° F, the temperature needs to be known.

16. **(G)** Soda goes flat as gas (carbon dioxide) leaves the liquid. The warmer the soda, the faster it goes flat. Choice **F** shows the effect of pressure, not temperature, on solubility. Choice **H** shows solubility of a solid (sugar), which has nothing to do with the solubility characteristics of a gas. Choice **J** deals with relative densities of gases, and not with solubilities.

17. **(A)** Per the chart, the dinosaur icon appears in the Triassic through Cretaceous periods.

18. **(J)** Three types of fossils are shown in layer F of outcrop II: flowering plants, dinosaurs, and insects. Based on the chart, the three species are only present concurrently during the Cretaceous Period. Also present during that period (per the chart) are ammonites. The only rock layer in outcrop I that contains only organisms existing during the Cretaceous Period is layer D. Layers A, B, and C contain fossils from older time periods; therefore, only layer D could be from the Cretaceous Period.

19. **(D)** The chart shows that flowering plants survived to the present (0 years).

20. **(H)** The spirifers died out approximately 136 million years ago; the appearance of flowering plants also occurred at that time period.

21. **(A)** Layer E contains two types of fossils: insects and flowering plants. The chart indicates that these two species of land organisms are found in rock layers of either the Cretaceous Period or the Tertiary Period. Rock layer E of outcrop II must have been formed during one of these periods. Of the two possible answers, Cretaceous or Tertiary, only Tertiary is among the answer choices available.

22. **(G)** A clear division between marine and land creatures is seen in the diagram.

23. **(D)** Compare Trials 2 and 3 to see what changing concentration of only one component has on rate. In this case we see no change in rate with change in concentration of *A*, so rate is independent of concentration.

24. **(F)** Compare Trials 2 and 4, or Trials 1 and 3.

25. **(C)** Compare Trials 1 and 4, or Trials 2 and 3.

26. **(H)** Averaging or intermediate mechanisms do not work because one mechanism has no dependence on *A* with regard to rate. Choice **G** is unlikely because a well-mixed solution should be homogeneous and have no pockets for mechanism 1 or 2.

27. **(B)** This is a subtle question. Choices **C** and **D** are incorrect because they overgeneralize from a single case. How can we say for certain that mechanisms can *always* be changed (choice **C**), or that in *every* case the mechanism depends on solvent effects (choice **D**)? Answer choice **A** is a special case of answer choice **D**, where we make a claim that *all* reactions are solvent dependent. Choice **B** alone

allows for the possibility that solvents need not have an effect (note the word *may*).

28. **(G)** acceleration $= \frac{\Delta v}{\Delta t} = \frac{\text{change in velocity}}{\text{change in time}}$

Experiment 1 (steel ball)

The acceleration is constant at 3.50 m/sec². This can be demonstrated by choosing a time interval and dividing the corresponding velocity change during the time interval by the length of the time interval. For example, between 1 and 2 seconds the velocity changes from 3.5 m/sec to 7 m/sec; therefore, acceleration $= \frac{\Delta v}{\Delta t} = \frac{7-3.5}{2-1} = \frac{3.5}{1} = 3.5$ m/sec². If we used the time interval from 0.5 seconds to 1 second, the corresponding velocity would change from 1.75 m/sec to 3.5 m/sec; therefore, the acceleration $= \frac{\Delta v}{\Delta t} = \frac{3.5 - 1.75}{1 - 0.5} = \frac{1.75}{0.5} = 3.5$ m/sec².

Experiment 2 (sled)

The acceleration is constant at 4.9 m/sec². For example, the change in velocity corresponding to the time interval from 0.5 seconds to 1 second is 4.90 m/sec − 2.45 m/sec = 2.45 m/sec; therefore, acceleration $= \frac{\Delta v}{\Delta t} = \frac{4.90 - 2.45}{1 - 0.5} = \frac{2.45}{0.5} = 4.9$ m/sec².

Experiment 3 (box)

The acceleration is constant at .66 m/sec².

29. **(A)** When friction is reduced in Experiment 4, the sled and ball still travel at about the same accelerations as in the previous experiments. This can be demonstrated by using the equation $d = \frac{1}{2} at^2$, which relates the distance an object travels starting from rest to the time (traveling at constant acceleration) it takes to travel the indicated distance. Since the board is 10 meters in length, the distance each travels is 10 meters.

For the sled: $d = \frac{1}{2} at^2$

$10 = \frac{1}{2} a(2.02)^2$

note: $(2.02)^2$ is approximately 4

$10 = \frac{1}{2} (a)(4)$

$a = 5$ m/sec²

For the ball: $d = \frac{1}{2} at^2$

$10 = \frac{1}{2} a(2.39)^2$

note: $(2.39)^2$ is approximately 5.7

$10 = \frac{1}{2} a(5.7)$

$a = 3.50$ m/sec²

Because the ball and sled still travel at about the same accelerations before and after oiling, the difference in their relative accelerations must be due to something other than friction. This difference is the rolling of the ball.

30. **(H)** Experiment 4 shows that friction affects the relative acceleration between the box and either the sled or ball. Calculating the acceleration for the box in Experiment 4 as we did for the sled and ball in problem 29, we get:

For the box: $d = \frac{1}{2} at^2$

$10 = \frac{1}{2} a(4.08)^2$

note: $(4.08)^2$ is approximately 16

$10 = \frac{1}{2} a(16)$

$a = 1.25$ m/sec²

Because the oiling in Experiment 4 caused a change in the box's acceleration, friction is a factor. Rolling must also be a factor as per the answer explanation to question 31.

31. **(B)** The acceleration for the ball is constant at 3.50 m/sec² (either Experiment 1 or 4). The acceleration of the sled is constant at 4.90 m/sec² (either Experiment 2 or 4). The ratio is:

ratio $= \frac{3.50}{4.90} = \frac{5}{7}$

32. **(H)** Although the acceleration of the ball is relatively insensitive to the amount of friction, the acceleration of the box is very sensitive to friction. Therefore, in a ratio, the effect of changing the amount of friction will change the numerator (ball acceleration) only slightly, whereas the denominator (box acceleration) will change significantly depending on fric-

tion. Choice **J** is not correct because within each experiment the acceleration remains constant.

33. **(B)** Two species genetically distant cannot breed successfully.

34. **(H)** For early modern humans to completely replace Neanderthals, there could not have been a region containing Neanderthals that did not contain early modern humans as well.

35. **(D)** Neither hypothesis necessarily rules out isolated communities. Both are concerned about areas where contact occurred.

36. **(J)** This information suggests that early modern humans killed Neanderthals, which supports Scientist 2.

37. **(C)** This fact shows that even if two species can breed, they may not do so voluntarily. Scientist 2 can therefore use this case as an example of the fact that two genetically compatible but dissimilar-looking animals choose not to interbreed. Choice **D** is not readily relevant because lions and tigers are brought together artificially. No one disputed the notion that animals can interbreed, so choice **A** does not enter the argument. Choice **B** is incorrect because lions and tigers do not share the same niche (tigers are solitary forest hunters while lions are group-hunting plains dwellers), and their ranges rarely overlap.

38. **(H)** The mixing of traits is part of Scientist 2's objections to Scientist 1's hypothesis.

39. **(A)** Both hypotheses attribute the disappearance of Neanderthals to early modern humans.

40. **(G)** Choice **F** is a perfectly logical argument but does not strengthen Scientist 1; it only offers a hypothesis that does not strengthen Scientist 2. Choice **J** does not strengthen Scientist 1 since there is no way to prove from the information given whether others also died violently (clubs may have been used, or spearpoints that were used may have been valuable and were taken by the victors). Even if you accept choice **J**, it does not strengthen Scientist 1. It only casts doubt on Scientist 2. Choice **H** is true in general. The only possible answer that *strengthens* a scientist's argument is Choice **G**.

Answer Sheet for Practice Exam II

1. English Test

1 A B C D	11 A B C D	21 A B C D	31 A B C D	41 A B C D	51 A B C D	61 A B C D	71 A B C D
2 F G H J	12 F G H J	22 F G H J	32 F G H J	42 F G H J	52 F G H J	62 F G H J	72 F G H J
3 A B C D	13 A B C D	23 A B C D	33 A B C D	43 A B C D	53 A B C D	63 A B C D	73 A B C D
4 F G H J	14 F G H J	24 F G H J	34 F G H J	44 F G H J	54 F G H J	64 F G H J	74 F G H J
5 A B C D	15 A B C D	25 A B C D	35 A B C D	45 A B C D	55 A B C D	65 A B C D	75 A B C D
6 F G H J	16 F G H J	26 F G H J	36 F G H J	46 F G H J	56 F G H J	66 F G H J	
7 A B C D	17 A B C D	27 A B C D	37 A B C D	47 A B C D	57 A B C D	67 A B C D	
8 F G H J	18 F G H J	28 F G H J	38 F G H J	48 F G H J	58 F G H J	68 F G H J	
9 A B C D	19 A B C D	29 A B C D	39 A B C D	49 A B C D	59 A B C D	69 A B C D	
10 F G H J	20 F G H J	30 F G H J	40 F G H J	50 F G H J	60 F G H J	70 F G H J	

2. Mathematics Test

1 A B C D E	9 A B C D E	17 A B C D E	25 A B C D E	33 A B C D E	41 A B C D E	49 A B C D E	57 A B C D E
2 F G H J K	10 F G H J K	18 F G H J K	26 F G H J K	34 F G H J K	42 F G H J K	50 F G H J K	58 F G H J K
3 A B C D E	11 A B C D E	19 A B C D E	27 A B C D E	35 A B C D E	43 A B C D E	51 A B C D E	59 A B C D E
4 F G H J K	12 F G H J K	20 F G H J K	28 F G H J K	36 F G H J K	44 F G H J K	52 F G H J K	60 F G H J K
5 A B C D E	13 A B C D E	21 A B C D E	29 A B C D E	37 A B C D E	45 A B C D E	53 A B C D E	
6 F G H J K	14 F G H J K	22 F G H J K	30 F G H J K	38 F G H J K	46 F G H J K	54 F G H J K	
7 A B C D E	15 A B C D E	23 A B C D E	31 A B C D E	39 A B C D E	47 A B C D E	55 A B C D E	
8 F G H J K	16 F G H J K	24 F G H J K	32 F G H J K	40 F G H J K	48 F G H J K	56 F G H J K	

3. Reading Test

1 A B C D	6 F G H J	11 A B C D	16 F G H J	21 A B C D	26 F G H J	31 A B C D	36 F G H J
2 F G H J	7 A B C D	12 F G H J	17 A B C D	22 F G H J	27 A B C D	32 F G H J	37 A B C D
3 A B C D	8 F G H J	13 A B C D	18 F G H J	23 A B C D	28 F G H J	33 A B C D	38 F G H J
4 F G H J	9 A B C D	14 F G H J	19 A B C D	24 F G H J	29 A B C D	34 F G H J	39 A B C D
5 A B C D	10 F G H J	15 A B C D	20 F G H J	25 A B C D	30 F G H J	35 A B C D	40 F G H J

4. Science Reasoning Test

1 A B C D	6 F G H J	11 A B C D	16 F G H J	21 A B C D	26 F G H J	31 A B C D	36 F G H J
2 F G H J	7 A B C D	12 F G H J	17 A B C D	22 F G H J	27 A B C D	32 F G H J	37 A B C D
3 A B C D	8 F G H J	13 A B C D	18 F G H J	23 A B C D	28 F G H J	33 A B C D	38 F G H J
4 F G H J	9 A B C D	14 F G H J	19 A B C D	24 F G H J	29 A B C D	34 F G H J	39 A B C D
5 A B C D	10 F G H J	15 A B C D	20 F G H J	25 A B C D	30 F G H J	35 A B C D	40 F G H J

1. ENGLISH TEST

45 Minutes—75 Questions

DIRECTIONS: In the passage(s) below, certain words and phrases are underlined and numbered. In the right-hand column, you will find choices for each underlined part. You are to select the one that best expresses the idea, makes the statement appropriate for standard written English, or is worded most consistently with the style and mood of the passage as a whole. If you think the original version is best, choose "NO CHANGE." You will also find questions about a section of the passage, or about the passage as a whole. These questions are indicated by a number or numbers in a box. For each question in the test, choose the choice you consider best and blacken the corresponding space on your answer sheet. Read each passage through once before you begin to answer the questions that accompany it. You cannot determine most answers without reading several sentences beyond the phrase in question.

Passage I

> The following paragraphs may or may not be in the most sensible order. Each paragraph is numbered in parentheses, and item 12 will ask you to choose the sequence of paragraph numbers that is most sensible.

(1)

Innovations have been variously introduced as ways to break out of the rigid system which

marches students, lock-step fashion, through a series of identical classrooms in which teachers do most of the talking and students have little opportunity to respond.

1. **A.** NO CHANGE
   B. Introducing various innovations
   C. Having been introduced various innovations
   D. Various innovations have been introduced

2. **F.** NO CHANGE
   G. marching
   H. march
   J. marched

(2)

Between these innovations are team teaching and teacher aides, nongraded elementary and secondary schools, independent study, curricula

3. **A.** NO CHANGE
   B. In between
   C. Of between
   D. Among

focused on helping students discover things for theirselves rather than on trying to tell them everything, and schools designed for maximum flexibility so that students can work alone, or in small groups, or take part in large-group instruction via diverse media.

4. F. NO CHANGE
G. oneself
H. themselves
J. himself

(3)

The aim of all these innovations—organizational, curricular, and technological—is to adapt instruction most precise to the needs of each

5. A. NO CHANGE
B. more precisely
C. more precise
D. precise

individual student. Many people whom have an aversion to organizing instruction scientifically

6. F. NO CHANGE
G. people, that
H. people, which
J. people who

and to having brought new technology into the schools and colleges fail to realize that the present system is in many respects mechanical and rigid.

7. A. NO CHANGE
B. bringing
C. being brought
D. brings

The vast differences in the ways students learn is disregarded when they are taught the same thing, in the same way, at the same time.

8. F. NO CHANGE
G. was
H. are
J. have

(4)

Theirs no escaping the evidence that many students themselves feel little enthusiasm and even outright hostility for the present way schools and colleges are organized. And instruction is handled. Many of them resent technology, but what they object to is usually technology patched on as an expedient for handling a large number of students.

9. A. NO CHANGE
B. There is no escaping
C. Their is no way to escape
D. They're escaping

10. F. NO CHANGE
G. organized. (And instruction is handled.)
H. organized, and instruction being handled.
J. organized and instruction is handled.

Or it is programming which merely reproduces conventional classroom teaching.

(5)

What instruction requires is an arrangement of resources whereby the student responds and learns, <u>reaching new plateaus from which to climb</u>₁₁ <u>to higher levels of understanding.</u> Implicit in such an arrangement, if it is to be effective, is the adaptability of the process to the individual students's differences—in pace, temperament, background, and style of learning. ☐12 ☐13

11. A. NO CHANGE
    B. (Place after *resources*)
    C. (Place after *student*)
    D. (Place after *responds*)

12. Choose the order of paragraph numbers that will make the essay's structure most logical.
    F. NO CHANGE
    G. 3, 2, 1, 4, 5
    H. 1, 3, 2, 5, 4
    J. 4, 2, 3, 1, 5

13. Is the use of the dash appropriate in this passage?
    A. No, because the dash is never used in formal writing.
    B. No, because commas would have been effective for emphasis.
    C. Yes, because the dash is used to set off interruptions, additions, and illustrations.
    D. Yes, because the dash adds excitement to the passage.

Passage II

Many individuals first learn of investment opportunities through <u>advertising in a newspaper or magazine, on</u>₁₄ radio or television, or by mail. Phone solicitations are also regarded as a form of advertising <u>unlike phone</u>₁₅ <u>surveys.</u>₁₅ In practically every area of investment activity, false or misleading advertising is illegal. <u>They are</u>₁₆ subject to civil, criminal, or regulatory penalties.

14. F. NO CHANGE
    G. advertising—in a newspaper or magazine,
    H. advertising, in a newspaper or magazine,
    J. advertising in a newspaper, or magazine,

15. A. NO CHANGE
    B. except phone surveys
    C. in addition to
    D. OMIT the underline section

16. F. NO CHANGE
    G. They will be
    H. It is
    J. It will be

Bear in mind that advertising is able to display only
limited information, and the most attractive features
are most likely to be highlighted. In accordance with
this, it is never wise to invest solely, on the basis of
an advertisement. The only *bona fide* purposes of investment advertising are calling your attention to an
offering and to encourage you to obtain additional information. In the securities industry, "suitability"
rules require that investment advice be appropriate for
the particular customer. [22]

If you make any investment, you have the right to
seek and obtain information about the investment. You
also have the right to call or write for information
about firms with whom you would be doing
business to find out whether it has a "track
record." [25] [26] [27]

17. A. NO CHANGE
    B. is capable of displaying
    C. is able to convey
    D. conveys
18. F. NO CHANGE
    G. to be highlighted
    H. to be most highlighted
    J. OMIT underlined section
19. A. NO CHANGE
    B. Accordingly,
    C. In accord with this,
    D. Accordantly,
20. F. NO CHANGE
    G. invest, solely on the basis of
    H. invest solely on the basis of
    J. invest on the basis of
21. A. NO CHANGE
    B. is calling
    C. are to call
    D. is to call
22. The writer's mention of the "suitability" rules is inappropriate because
    F. the average reader would not be familiar with this term.
    G. it departs from the focus of this paragraph.
    H. the passage is not directed toward particular customers.
    J. it provides redundant information.
23. A. NO CHANGE
    B. request
    C. make a phone call or write a letter for
    D. demand
24. F. NO CHANGE
    G. it will have
    H. they have
    J. they will have
25. In order to be helpful to the intended audience, this paragraph would need
    A. NO CHANGE
    B. actual phone numbers and addresses.
    C. an explanation of what is meant by a "track record."
    D. more specific information about the type of investment to which the writer refers.
26. The continuation of this passage would probably include
    F. additional rights of potential investors.
    G. specific advice about real estate deals.
    H. additional types of investments that are safe.
    J. guidelines for reinvestment plans during retirement years.

27. This passage would be most helpful to
   A. an investment banker.
   B. a veteran investor.
   C. someone contemplating a first investment.
   D. a newly formed investment firm.

Passage III

A rosebud holds the entire flower in miniature. The unfolding petals reveal nothing which they did not harbor in microcosmic existence. They merely exemplify more fully the nature of the beauty which is indigenous to it. When we
<u>28</u>
view the ages of man unfolding through the

centuries. We see, not a Utopian fulfillment of
<u>29</u>
idealistic beginnings, but the perennial problem of man's enduring fallibility in approaching and handling the enigmas that face him.

   We turn back several centuries of the corona of
   <u>30</u>
civilization, we may find the same dichotomy of values inherent in twentieth century mortals. English kings of the fourteenth century kept the people preoccupied with foreign wars in order to mollify them at home. The Magna Carta had been no panacea for the ills of the land, and seeds of rebellion came to fruition in the Peasants' Revolt of 1381. The Plague <u>had already ravaged</u> the
                                        31
country and subsequent disruption of labor practices left the land in utter chaos. Although Christianity had preserved civilization and

28. F. NO CHANGE
    G. them
    H. they
    J. theirs

29. A. NO CHANGE
    B. centuries; we
    C. centuries, we
    D. centuries we

30. F. NO CHANGE
    G. Until we turn back several centuries
    H. If we turn back several centuries
    J. OMIT the underlined portion.

31. A. NO CHANGE
    B. has already ravaged
    C. all ready ravaged
    D. already has ravaged

fostering education throughout the "Dark Ages," nevertheless, Wycliffe led the Lollards in protest against Church weaknesses, such as those which allowed pardoners preying upon the poor, and which permitted a Western Schism and an Avignon Papacy to occur.

    Several epidemics of the Black Death caused a mushroom-like cloud to hang over the populace. The tavern became the temple where the gods Bacchus and Venus were diligently worshipped. The liturgical theme was "Eat, drink, and be merry, for tomorrow we die"—and again ironically the horror of death was palliated by a *Danse Macabre*. There was no other paladin for the peasantry than their own timorously bold, superstitions impotent affront to personified Death.

    Folks in medieval times in the "Dark Ages" were well aware of the paradox of the mutability of time and the permanence of human nature. They looked to the heavens for both eternal salvation and for astrological guidance, but whereas religion could bring the former, science strove in vain to achieve the latter. Twentieth-century man has his wars, poverty, sickness, and disenchantment with efforts of his leaders, but while death constantly pursues him, he ignores

32. F. NO CHANGE
    G. foster
    H. fosters
    J. fostered

33. A. NO CHANGE
    B. to prey
    C. for preying
    D. had preyed

34. F. NO CHANGE
    G. are diligently
    H. were diligent
    J. with diligence

35. A. NO CHANGE
    B. ; ironically,
    C. : ironically,
    D. , ironically,

36. F. NO CHANGE
    G. superstition
    H. superstitiously
    J. superstitious

37. A. NO CHANGE
    B. of the "Dark Ages"
    C. at the "Dark Ages"
    D. OMIT the underlined portion.

38. F. NO CHANGE
    G. previous
    H. latter
    J. last

the Bomb and puts his sight on the moon and the stars. The rose opens continuously, revealing beauty alongside the thorns. [39]

39. This passage was probably intended for readers who
    A. are against nuclear research
    B. are experts in astrology
    C. have some familiarity with the events of the Middle Ages
    D. have read *Danse Macabre*

Passage IV

John Harold Drake is a man of deep compassion, and has wrote a book that pleads for the cause of children in need of love. *Children, Little Children* is an honest book, overflowing with concern and it shows anguish.

The difficult trick of living inside another person's mind, and being able to put your reader inside that same mind, is only a facility held by writers of exceptional skill and talent. Mr. Drake has compounded the problem by making a 10-year-old boy his central character, the boy does not for a moment come across as a real child. Irresponsible parents abandoned him, his grandfather despised him, he took everything literally, and begging everyone for love. Bret is being used to make a point. His musings are too poetic, his responses too pat, and the contrasts of good and evil too simplistic for real life. He was to be manipulated by someone behind the scenery trying to tell us something.

40. F. NO CHANGE
    G. have wrote
    H. has written
    J. written

41. A. NO CHANGE
    B. showing anguish
    C. anguish
    D. being full of anguish

42. F. NO CHANGE
    G. is a facility held only
    H. only is a facility held
    J. is held as a facility only

43. A. NO CHANGE
    B. character the
    C. character, this
    D. character. The

44. F. NO CHANGE
    G. is begging
    H. begged
    J. begs

45. A. NO CHANGE
    B. has been
    C. was being
    D. is being

For fifteen years the author has been director of psychodrama therapy at the V.I.T. Neuropsychiatric Institute. He has actively been involved in this field at other institutions for a quarter of a century. This book is a form of acting out, through the puppet that is Bret, the pain of a rejected child. If one understands the book in those terms, one may be willing to suspend disbelief.

If viewed in this light, the exaggerated movements and reactions become less obtrusive of the characters and therefore more meaningful. The excessively poetic passages of description and emotion, seen as stage flats made more colorful than nature in order to look real from afar, are acceptable in a drama moreover they are irritating in a novel. The one-sided characterizations—insane father, immature mother, mean old grandmother, selfish aunt, cruel neighbors, and totally misunderstood Bret—are figures moving across a lit stage to dramatize a message. The true-to-life ending, without resolution or growth or development, might work on a stage, it is contrary to everything a novel should do.

Calling the book a novel is the publisher's mistake; the work is more nearly a drama. Perhaps it is one of Mr. Drake's psychodramas in

46. F. NO CHANGE
    G. ; through the puppet that is Bret,
    H. through the puppet that is Bret
    J. OMIT the underlined portion.

47. A. NO CHANGE
    B. (Place after *movements*)
    C. (Place after *reactions*)
    D. (Place after *meaningful*)

48. F. NO CHANGE
    G. consequently
    H. therefore
    J. whereas

49. A. NO CHANGE
    B. stage it
    C. stage; it
    D. stage, however, it

print and should so be judged. ☐50

50. Is the use of the hyphen appropriate in this passage?
   F. No, because hyphens are only used to show division between syllables.
   G. No, because they are not used in formal writing.
   H. Yes, because a hyphen adds excitement to a passage.
   J. Yes, because the hyphen is used between single words to express the idea of a unit.

Passage V

As America has grown in size and <u>divergent of</u>⁵¹ population, political power is no longer <u>wielded</u>⁵² by one or two influential groups. Elected politicians appear to govern the land, but they are <u>influencing</u>⁵³ and manipulated by a multitude of special interest groups. Some of these groups are highly organized and well financed <u>and have large amounts of money.</u>⁵⁴ Since these groups tend to focus on one or two issues from the standpoint of their own <u>self-interest; the</u>⁵⁵ pressure they exert can sometimes work against the national interest.

One such pressure group is the National Rifle Association (NRA). <u>Spokesman</u>⁵⁶ for this influential lobby cite the Second Amendment to the <u>Constitution. That which guarantees</u>⁵⁷ the right of all citizens to own and bear arms, as justification for their position. They claim that every citizen

51. A. NO CHANGE
    B. diverse
    C. in diversity
    D. in diverse

52. F. NO CHANGE
    G. welded
    H. welding
    J. wielding

53. A. NO CHANGE
    B. influence
    C. influences
    D. influenced

54. F. NO CHANGE
    G. and have some money.
    H. by having money.
    J. OMIT the underlined portion.

55. A. NO CHANGE
    B. self-interest the
    C. self-interest, the
    D. self-interest. The

56. F. NO CHANGE
    G. Spokesmen
    H. Spokesperson
    J. The people who talk

57. A. NO CHANGE
    B. Constitution—guaranteeing
    C. Constitution. Which guarantees
    D. Constitution, that which guarantees

should be permitted to own a gun, provided that he or she can demonstrate proficiency in its care
                                            58
and use and familiarity with rules of safety. [59]

According to the NRA, a person has the *right* to own a gun even if he does not *need* to own a gun. These spokesmen claim that if many people owned guns, criminals might be deterred because they could expect retaliatory fire at any time. A slogan of the NRA is "If guns are outlawed, only outlaws will have guns".
                                          60

The danger in this position is that guns, being easy to procure, fall into the hands of careless people. Thus, there are many accidental deaths occurring from mishandling of
                                           61
guns. [62] [63]

58. F. NO CHANGE
    G. it is
    H. it's
    J. its'

59. Is the author's use of the pronouns "he or she" in the second paragraph appropriate?
    A. No, because it weakens the passage's focus on special interest groups.
    B. Yes, the use of the pronouns shows agreement and gives emphasis to the antecedent "every citizen."
    C. No, the pronouns "he or she" should not be used in formal writing.
    D. Yes, because the pronouns help the reader understand a difficult idea.

60. F. NO CHANGE
    G. guns!
    H. guns."
    J. guns"

61. A. NO CHANGE
    B. accidentally
    C. accident
    D. Omit the underlined portion.

62. The writer could most effectively strengthen the passage at this point by adding which of the following?
    F. the sentence "Guns are to blame for these deaths."
    G. a definition of accidental death
    H. a description of the proper methods of handling firearms
    J. specific examples of how carelessness and mishandling of firearms can lead to accidents

63. Is the use of parentheses appropriate in this passage?
    A. Yes, they add emphasis.
    B. No, because parentheses are only used to enclose figures within a sentence.
    C. Yes, because parentheses are used to enclose parenthetical material, specific details, and examples.
    D. No, they are not used in formal writing.

Passage VI

The following paragraphs may or may not be in the most sensible order. Each paragraph is numbered in parentheses, and item 75 will ask you to select the sequence of paragraph numbers that is most sensible.

(1)

The United States are the most energy hungry
                        ‾‾
                        64
country in the world. Our economy is based upon manufacturing processes which consume a great deal of fuel. Our lifestyle involves frequent travel, commitment to personnel comfort obtained by
                            ‾‾‾‾‾‾‾‾‾
                               65
maintaining constant indoor temperature all year around and extensive use of powered gadgets for pleasure and convenience.

(2)

While the governments of the Persian Gulf countries were stable and unambitious, all went well for us. However, with awakening national awareness and a sudden realization that the world was dependent upon it, the oil-rich nations have
                       ‾‾
                       66
begun to take advantage of their power. These countries have discovered that they can raise their prices to exorbitant heights; and that they can
                            ‾‾‾‾‾‾‾‾‾‾‾‾
                                 67
bend the policies of other nations to their will by withholding oil from the world market. The
‾‾‾‾‾‾‾‾‾‾‾‾‾‾‾‾‾‾‾‾‾‾‾‾‾‾‾‾‾‾‾‾‾‾‾‾‾‾‾
                     68
political situation around the world has become one of tyranny by the oil-rich nations.

64. F. NO CHANGE
    G. be
    H. is
    J. was

65. A. NO CHANGE
    B. personalize
    C. personify
    D. personal

66. F. NO CHANGE
    G. them
    H. themselves
    J. itself

67. A. NO CHANGE
    B. heights: and
    C. heights and
    D. heights, and

68. F. NO CHANGE
    G. for withholding oil from the world market
    H. to withholding oil from the world market
    J. OMIT the underlined portion.

(3)

To attempt to counter this situation, the President of the United States has urged austerity in the American behavior, rationing has been
                                          ——————————————
                                                69
proposed, and alternate means for obtaining the required energy are being explored. [70]

69. A. NO CHANGE
    B. behavior. Rationing has been
    C. behavior, rationing being
    D. behavior. By rationing being

70. The writer could most effectively strengthen the passage at this point by adding which of the following?
    F. the sentence "Conservation is extremely important."
    G. specific examples of political situations that have occurred as a result of oil-rich nations withholding oil
    H. a definition of austerity
    J. examples of actions that have been taken by the American people in order to conserve energy

(4)

At one time the United States, was able to
                    ————————————
                           71
satisfy its own energy needs with the help of its extensive coal resources and its own oil supply. However, the demand for energy has expanded so rapidly that our ability meeting our own needs has
                                 ———————
                                    72
been outstripped. In addition, recent realization of the health hazards inherent in the air pollution created by burning coal has resulted in greater demand for cleaner burning oil. And so, we have
                ———————————
                      73
turned to foreign sources to supply that oil. In the

71. A. NO CHANGE
    B. United States, were
    C. United States were
    D. United States was

72. F. NO CHANGE
    G. meets
    H. meet
    J. to meet

73. A. NO CHANGE
    B. cleaner-burning oil
    C. cleaner, burning oil
    D. oil that is more clean to burn

past few decades, the bulk of our imported oil has come from the Persian Gulf area. There oil is found in abundance and, with the assistance of American technology, production has been able to keep up with world demand. [74] [75]

74. Readers are likely to describe this passage by which of the following terms?
   F. inspirational
   G. critical
   H. informational
   J. satirical

75. Choose the sequence of paragraph numbers that will make the essay's structure most logical.
   A. NO CHANGE
   B. 1, 4, 2, 3
   C. 1, 3, 4, 2
   D. 4, 3, 2, 1

STOP!

This is the end of the English Test.
Do not proceed to the next section until the allotted
time expires.

2. MATHEMATICS TEST

60 Minutes—60 Questions

DIRECTIONS: Solve each problem. Then select the correct answer from among the five choices and darken the corresponding space on the answer sheet.

Solve as many problems as you can since they all have the same point value. Do not spend too much time on a single problem. Remember: you are not penalized for incorrect answers; only those answered correctly contribute to your final score.

NOTE: Unless otherwise stated, assume the following:

- All figures lie in a plane.
- Figures are not necessarily drawn to scale.
- All lines are straight.

---

1. In rhombus $ABCD$, if $\overline{AB} = 4x - 2$ and $\overline{BC} = 3x + 3$ then $x = ?$

    A. 5
    B. 4
    C. 3
    D. 2
    E. 1

2. Which of the following is an illustration of the commutative property for multiplication?

    F. $a(b + c) = ab + ac$
    G. $a(bc) = (ab)c$
    H. $a + b = b + a$
    J. $(ab)c = (ba)c$
    K. $0 \cdot a = 0$

3. What is the product of $3x^2$ and $2x^3$?

    A. $6x^5$
    B. $6x^6$
    C. $5x^5$
    D. $5x^6$
    E. $12x$

4. $|-6| - |2| - |-2| = ?$

    F. 10
    G. 8
    H. 6
    J. 4
    K. 2

DO YOUR FIGURING HERE.

GO ON TO THE NEXT PAGE.

5. Two adjacent sides of a rectangle measure 4 and 7. What is the perimeter of the rectangle?

   A. 11
   B. 18
   C. 22
   D. 28
   E. 44

6. In circle R, the coordinates of the endpoints of diameter $\overline{AB}$ are $A(2, 5)$ and $B(8, 1)$. What are the coordinates of the center of the circle?

   F. $(6, -4)$
   G. $(5, 3)$
   H. $(6, 4)$
   J. $(3, 5)$
   K. $(10, 6)$

7. If $F = \dfrac{9}{5}C + 32$, what is the value of C when $F = 77$?

   A. 25
   B. 30
   C. 35
   D. 40
   E. 45

8. If $f(x) = |2x + 3|$, then $f(-5) = ?$

   F. -7
   G. 7
   H. 10
   J. -13
   K. 13

9. In the figure below, $\triangle ABC$ is similar to $\triangle XYZ$, and the measure of angle A is equal to the measure of angle X. If $\overline{AB}:\overline{XY} = 4:5$ and $\overline{BC} = 20$, then what is the length of $\overline{YZ}$?

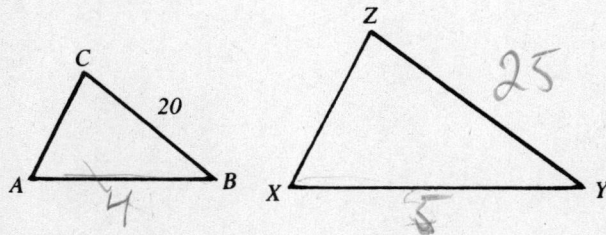

   A. 15
   B. 16
   C. 20
   D. 24
   E. 25

GO ON TO THE NEXT PAGE.

10. Which of the following is equivalent to $3\sqrt{18}$?

    F. $9\sqrt{2}$
    G. $3\sqrt{2}$
    H. $3\sqrt{6}$
    J. $9\sqrt{3}$
    K. $\sqrt{54}$

11. What is the difference when $x^2 - 7$ is subtracted from $3x^2 - 4$?

    A. $2x^2 + 3$
    B. $2x^2 - 3$
    C. $2x^2 - 11$
    D. $2x^2 + 11$
    E. $4x^2 - 11$

12. Which ordered pair is the solution set for the following system of equations?

    $$3x + y = 5$$
    $$2x - y = 5$$

    F. $(1, 2)$
    G. $(2, 1)$
    H. $(4, 3)$
    J. $(2, -1)$
    K. $(2, 3)$

13. What is the quotient when $12x^4 - 3x^3 + 6x^2$ is divided by $3x^2$?

    A. $9x^2 - 3$
    B. $5x^2$
    C. $4x^2 - 3x + 2$
    D. $4x^2 - x + 2$
    E. $4x^2 - x$

14. If 5% of a number is 30, what is the number?

    F. 1.5
    G. 6
    H. 15
    J. 60
    K. 600

GO ON TO THE NEXT PAGE.

ACT Practice Exam II / 359

15. If $x + ay = m$, then $y = ?$

    A. $\dfrac{m - x}{a}$
    B. $\dfrac{m + x}{a}$
    C. $\dfrac{m}{a} - x$
    D. $\dfrac{m}{a} + x$
    E. $\dfrac{m}{x + a}$

DO YOUR FIGURING HERE.

16. In the circle below, O is the center of the circle. If radius $\overline{OS} = 10$ and the perpendicular distance from O to chord $\overline{RTS}$ is 6, what is the length of $\overline{RS}$?

    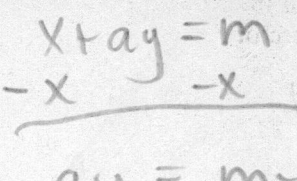

    F. 6
    G. 8
    H. 10
    J. 12
    K. 16

17. The length of two of the sides of an equilateral triangle are represented by $2a + 7$ and $3a - 4$. What is the perimeter of the triangle?

    A. 29
    B. 57
    C. 63
    D. 78
    E. 87

    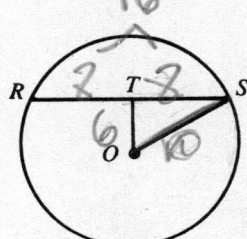

18. What are the factors of $3y^2 + 4y - 4$?

    F. $(3y - 2)(y + 2)$
    G. $(3y - 4)(y + 1)$
    H. $(3y + 2)(y - 2)$
    J. $(3y + 1)(y - 4)$
    K. $(3y + 4)(y - 1)$

19. What is the value of x if $3^{x-2} = 81$?

    A. 7
    B. 6
    C. 5
    D. 4
    E. 3

    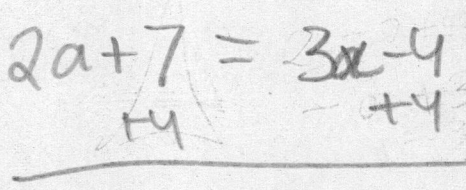

GO ON TO THE NEXT PAGE.

360 / ACT

20. In quadrilateral *ABCD* below, the measure of ∠*A* = 120°, the measure of ∠*B* = 82° and the measure of ∠*D* = 93°. What is the measure of ∠*C*?

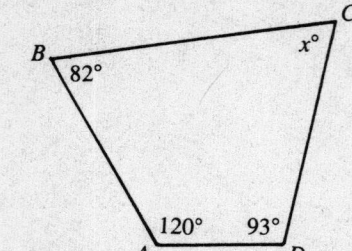

F. 60°
G. 65°
H. 78°
J. 103°
K. 295°

21. What is the value of $2b^0 + b^{-1/2}$ when $b = 16$?

A. -4
B. -2
C. -8
D. $\dfrac{9}{4}$
E. $\dfrac{7}{4}$

22. What is the average (arithmetic mean) of $x + 1$ and $3x - 3$?

F. $2x - 4$
G. $4x - 2$
H. $2x - 1$
J. $2x + 4$
K. $2x + 1$

23. What is the sum of $\dfrac{a + b}{3}$ and $\dfrac{a - b}{2}$?

A. $\dfrac{5a - b}{6}$
B. $\dfrac{2a}{5}$
C. $\dfrac{-a - b}{6}$
D. $\dfrac{5a - 5b}{6}$
E. $\dfrac{2a - 3b}{6}$

24. Jessica needs a total of $80 to buy a bicycle. She has already saved $35. If she saves $10 a week from her earnings, what is the least number of weeks she must work to have enough money to buy the bicycle?

F. 3
G. 4
H. 5
J. 6
K. 8

DO YOUR FIGURING HERE.

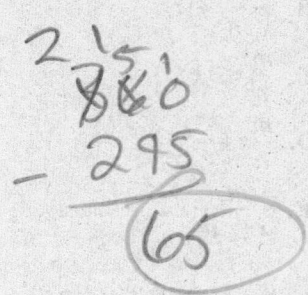

GO ON TO THE NEXT PAGE.

25. What is the solution set for the equation $|y - 5| = 2$?

   A. {7}
   B. {3}
   C. {7, −7}
   D. {7, 3}
   E. {3, 7, −7}

26. The measure of an angle is $(50 - n)$ degrees. In terms of n, what is the degree measure of the complement of the angle?

   F. $40 - n$
   G. $40 + n$
   H. $130 - n$
   J. $130 + n$
   K. $220 - n$

27. What is the slope of a line parallel to the line whose equation is $y = -\frac{2}{3}x + 4$?

   A. 4
   B. $\frac{3}{2}$
   C. $-\frac{3}{2}$
   D. $\frac{2}{3}$
   E. $-\frac{2}{3}$

28. What are the coordinates (x, y) at which $2x + y = 4$ intersects $x - 2y = 2$?

   F. (0, 0)
   G. (0, 2)
   H. (2, −1)
   J. (−2, 1)
   K. (2, 0)

29. If the diameter of a circle is 8, what is the length of the circumference?

   A. 64π
   B. 16π
   C. 8π
   D. 4π
   E. 2π

GO ON TO THE NEXT PAGE.

362 / ACT

30. Which of the following represents the prime factors of $2x^3 + x^2 - 6x$?

   F. $(2x^2 + 3x)(x - 2)$
   G. $x(2x - 3)(x + 2)$
   H. $x(2x + 3)(x - 2)$
   J. $x^2(2x + 1)(-6x)$
   K. $x(x + 3)(2x - 2)$

31. The expression $\dfrac{6 \times 10^8}{3 \times 10^2} = $?

   A. 2×10^6
   B. 2×10^4
   C. 2×10^{-6}
   D. 2×10^{-4}
   E. 120

32. The expression $\dfrac{6}{\frac{1}{2} + \frac{1}{3}} = $?

   F. 30
   G. $\dfrac{36}{5}$
   H. 5
   J. $\dfrac{6}{5}$
   K. $\dfrac{5}{6}$

33. In △NJL below, what is the value of $(\sin N)(\cos L)$?

   A. $\dfrac{6}{25}$
   B. $\dfrac{7}{25}$
   C. $\dfrac{16}{25}$
   D. $\dfrac{12}{25}$
   E. $\dfrac{9}{25}$

34. $\sqrt{27} + \sqrt{12} = $?

   F. $6\sqrt{5}$
   G. $\sqrt{39}$
   H. $13\sqrt{3}$
   J. $5\sqrt{6}$
   K. $5\sqrt{3}$

DO YOUR FIGURING HERE.

GO ON TO THE NEXT PAGE.

35. Which of the graphs below represents the solution set of $-1 \leq x < 4$?

A.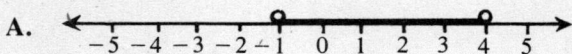

B.

C.

D.

E.

36. In the trapezoid ABCD below, $\overline{BC} \parallel \overline{AD}$. If $\overline{BC} = 7$, $\overline{BE} = 4$, and $\overline{AD} = 12$, what is the area of the trapezoid?

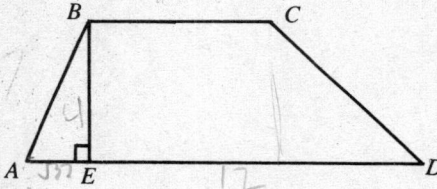

F. 23
G. 38
H. 48
J. 76
K. 336

37. In the figure below l_1 and l_2 are parallel. What is the value of x?

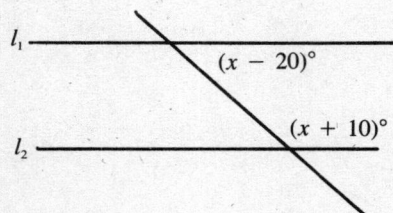

A. 50
B. 75
C. 85
D. 95
E. 185

GO ON TO THE NEXT PAGE.

364 / ACT

38. Which of the following is the equation of a line with a slope of 2 and passing through the point $(-1, -2)$?

   F. $y + 2 = 2(x + 1)$
   G. $y - 2 = 2(x - 1)$
   H. $x + 1 = 2(y + 2)$
   J. $x - 1 = 2(y - 2)$
   K. $y + 2 = \frac{1}{2}(x + 1)$

39. Based on the table below, what is the median for the set of data?

Measure	Frequency
70	4
85	3
90	2
95	1

   A. 70
   B. 81
   C. 85
   D. 87.5
   E. 90

40. In the triangle below, if the value of $\tan \theta = \frac{4}{3}$, then $\overline{RS} = ?$

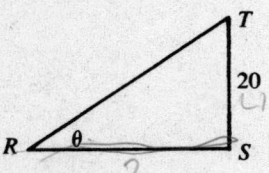

   F. 15
   G. 16
   H. 20
   J. 25
   K. $26\frac{2}{3}$

41. $\dfrac{5}{2 - \sqrt{3}} = ?$

   A. $10 + 5\sqrt{3}$
   B. $-2 - \sqrt{3}$
   C. $-10 - 5\sqrt{3}$
   D. $2 + \sqrt{3}$
   E. $\dfrac{5(2 + \sqrt{3})}{7}$

GO ON TO THE NEXT PAGE.

42. $(1 - \cos \theta)(1 + \cos \theta) = ?$

   F. $\sin \theta$
   G. $\cos \theta$
   H. $\tan^2 \theta$
   J. $\cos^2 \theta$
   K. $\sin^2 \theta$

43. If $f(x) = x + 4$ and $g(x) = x^2 - 3$, what is the value of $f(f(2))$?

   A. -2
   B. 5
   C. 7
   D. 10
   E. 33

44. Which is the converse of the statement, "If it is a goldfish, then it is a tropical fish"?

   F. If it is not a goldfish, then it is not a tropical fish.
   G. If it is not a tropical fish, then it is not a goldfish.
   H. If it is not a goldfish, then it is a tropical fish.
   J. If it is a tropical fish, then it is a goldfish.
   K. If it is a tropical fish, then it is not a goldfish.

45. The length of one leg of a right triangle is 5 and the length of the hypotenuse is $\sqrt{29}$, what is the length of the other leg?

   A. 2
   B. 4
   C. $\sqrt{24}$
   D. $\sqrt{54}$
   E. 24

46. If the ratio of the corresponding diagonals of two similar figures is $4:9$, then what is the ratio of their perimeters?

   F. $2:3$
   G. $4:9$
   H. $6:12$
   J. $8:27$
   K. $16:81$

47. What is the distance between the points whose coordinates are $(2, 7)$ and $(8, -1)$?

   A. $\sqrt{12}$
   B. $\sqrt{14}$
   C. $\sqrt{28}$
   D. $\sqrt{72}$
   E. 10

DO YOUR FIGURING HERE.

GO ON TO THE NEXT PAGE.

48. Which of the following is true about the nature of the roots of the equation
$x - 1 = x^2 - 2x + 1$?

F. Rational and unequal
G. Rational and equal
H. Irrational and unequal
J. Imaginary
K. Real and equal

49. What is the slope of a line perpendicular to the line $(y - 1) = 3(x - 6)$?

A. $\frac{1}{3}$
B. $\frac{1}{6}$
C. $-\frac{1}{3}$
D. -3
E. 6

50. The figure below represents a circle with a diameter of length 6 inscribed in a square. What is the area of the shaded region?

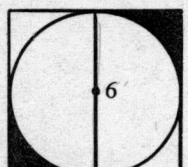

F. $18 - \frac{9}{2}\pi$
G. $18 - 9\pi$
H. $36 - 6\pi$
J. $36 - 9\pi$
K. $36 + 9\pi$

51. If the perimeter of a square is $3x$, then in terms of x, what is its area?

A. $6x$
B. $9x$
C. $\frac{9x^2}{16}$
D. $\frac{9x^2}{4}$
E. $9x^2$

52. If $i = \sqrt{-1}$, simplify $i^{10} + i^8 + i^6 + i^2$

F. -2
G. 0
H. 2
J. 4
K. $1 + i$

DO YOUR FIGURING HERE.

GO ON TO THE NEXT PAGE.

53. A jar contains 2 red marbles, 3 green marbles, and 4 orange marbles. If a marble is picked at random, what is the probability that the marble is not orange?

   A. $\frac{1}{4}$
   B. $\frac{1}{3}$
   C. $\frac{4}{9}$
   D. $\frac{5}{9}$
   E. 5

54. In the figure below, what is the value of sin L?

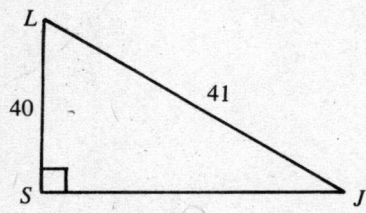

   F. $\frac{1}{41}$
   G. $\frac{7}{41}$
   H. $\frac{9}{41}$
   J. $\frac{27}{41}$
   K. $\frac{40}{41}$

55. What is the value of $x + y^2 + z$, if $x = y = z = -1$?

   A. -1
   B. 0
   C. 1
   D. 2
   E. 3

56. If $\sqrt{x+1} + 2 = 0$, what is the solution set for all real values of x?

   F. $\{-1\}$
   G. $\{2\}$
   H. $\{3\}$
   J. $\{5\}$
   K. $\{\ \}$

GO ON TO THE NEXT PAGE.

57. The area of a sphere varies directly as the square of the radius. If the area is 36π square centimeters when the radius is 3 centimeters long, what is the area, in centimeters, when the radius is 6 centimeters long?

   A. 9π
   B. 18π
   C. 72π
   D. 108π
   E. 144π

58. Jessica can paint a room in 6 hours. What percent of the room can she paint in x hours?

   F. $\dfrac{x}{6}\%$
   G. $\dfrac{100x}{6}\%$
   H. $\dfrac{6}{x}\%$
   J. $\dfrac{600}{x}\%$
   K. $\dfrac{x}{600}\%$

59. Which of the following is true of the graph of the equation $y = 2x^2 - 5x + 3$?

   A. It is tangent to the x-axis.
   B. It intersects the x-axis at only two distinct points.
   C. It intersects the x-axis at more than two distinct points.
   D. It lies completely below the x-axis.
   E. It lies completely above the x-axis.

60. Which of the following represents the multiplicative inverse of $1 - \sqrt{2}$?

   F. $1 + \sqrt{2}$
   G. $\dfrac{1 + \sqrt{2}}{2}$
   H. $-1 - \sqrt{2}$
   J. $\sqrt{2} - 1$
   K. $\dfrac{\sqrt{2} - 1}{2}$

DO YOUR FIGURING HERE.

STOP!

This is the end of the Mathematics Test.
Do not proceed to the next section until the allotted time expires.

3. READING TEST

35 Minutes—40 Questions

DIRECTIONS: There are four passages in this test. Each passage is followed by ten questions. After reading a passage, select the most appropriate answer to each question and blacken the corresponding space on your answer sheet. You may refer to the passages as often as you feel necessary.

Passage I

Bulgaria's Communist Party leader makes a speech lasting six hours. In Washington, they're shorter . . . but maybe only because nobody will listen that long.

The Bulgarian Communist Party is having its annual party congress in Sofia. It's a time when the party leaders come in from the provinces . . . get a look at such bright lights as Sofia has . . . get a few free meals . . . and get treated for a few days as if they were important . . . vote as they're told to vote . . . and go home. It's a standard ritual in the Communist world . . . a week or so of public sweetness and agreement . . . and private bickering. You never see their party leaders having a public argument, as ours always do. They settle differences in private and then announce the result in public . . . everyone says yes, that's fine . . . and it's all over.

When the leader of the Bulgarian Communist Party made his speech to the congress he started talking . . . and didn't stop for six hours. Six hours. And his audience sat through it because it had to. The Communist states have made remarkable progress in some areas, but obviously not in this one. The Bulgarian leader still holds . . . as do some of Russia's leaders . . . that a speech isn't truly important unless it runs for hours and hours. And so they drone away for hours to an audience that must listen, or at least sit there and stay awake, or appear to.

The U.S. Senate has in the past had a few members afflicted with this disease—voxophilia, or something like that—whose symptom is a love of hearing one's own voice. But here nobody has to listen. Senators can walk out, and do. Often, speeches on the Senate floor are delivered before an audience of one or two, out of a membership of 100. And the speaker does not complain . . . because next week somebody will make a speech he doesn't want to sit through . . . and he will walk out on that. It's a pretty amiable arrangement. Everybody gets to talk . . . but nobody has to listen. It has to be that way in a town like Washington . . . where we have a vast oversupply of talkers . . . and a critical shortage of listeners.

In Washington . . . brief remarks generally run 10 to 20 minutes. A speech runs an hour or more . . . but seldom much more. In the House of Representatives, there are so many members . . . 435 . . . they have a one-minute rule for speakers. One-minute speeches usually run from two minutes up to five, or ten. Except for filibusters, nobody here to my knowledge has ever equaled or even approached the Bulgarian chairman's six hours. Because we lack one essential ingredient found only in the police state . . . the power to force anybody to listen. We have talkers, all right, including some who might be willing to go six hours. But, fortunately, we don't have the listeners.

1. Bulgarian leaders gather in Sofia primarily in order to

   A. enjoy the bright lights.
   B. secretly meet other politicians.
   C. vote as they are told to vote.
   D. receive treatment due such important people.

2. According to this passage, what is one experience common to politicians in both Sofia and Washington?

   F. Listening to speeches
   G. Free meals
   H. Flattering treatment
   J. Bright lights and parties

369

3. What does the author suggest about Bulgarian politicians?

   A. They are more polite than American politicians.
   B. They make more important speeches than American politicians.
   C. They have great confidence in their party leaders.
   D. They are afraid to walk out on their leaders' speeches.

4. According to this passage, the activities of the Bulgarian Party Congress are typical of those found in

   F. both Bulgaria and the United States.
   G. all Communist countries.
   H. Bulgaria only.
   J. many European countries.

5. From the passage, the reader can most safely conclude that the arguments among American political leaders

   A. take place in public.
   B. are settled in private.
   C. occur infrequently.
   D. are settled in a friendly manner.

6. In the United States Congress, Senators may talk longer than Representatives do because

   F. Senators are elected for their speaking ability.
   G. The Senators have to pass more bills.
   H. The Senate deals with more important topics which need longer speeches.
   J. A time limit is imposed on speeches by Representatives but not on those by Senators.

7. According to this passage, which idea(s) is(are) suggested about the United States Senate?

   I. There are few Senators who like to speak.
   II. There is a shortage of Senators willing to listen to long speeches.
   III. Few take advantage of the opportunities to listen and learn before voting.

   A. I only
   B. II and III
   C. I and II
   D. I, II, and III

8. The House of Representatives has a rule that members can speak for

   F. one minute.
   G. two minutes to four minutes.
   H. five minutes to ten minutes.
   J. one hour.

9. The author most likely believes that Congressional rules concerning speeches should

   A. force more members of Congress to listen.
   B. allow only party leaders to speak.
   C. forbid filibusters.
   D. be kept as they are now.

10. The author feels that the major difference between customs in Sofia and Washington regarding politicians is that

    F. Washington is more efficient than Sofia.
    G. Bulgarian political leaders never disagree.
    H. a free country has politicians who do not listen to speeches.
    J. the Sofia Congress meets for a longer time than the Washington Congress.

Passage II

When I arrived at a few minutes before seven, I found the platoon assembled and ready to go. It was cold, and in the ranks the men were shivering and dancing up and down to keep warm. I was only the second-in-command of the platoon at that time, under instruction from a senior lieutenant, who was the platoon commander. Punctually at seven I said to Broadhurst, "March off, Sergeant. To the aerodrome, at the double."

Broadhurst asked doubtfully whether we shouldn't wait for the platoon commander, who had not turned up. Unversed in the ways of the army, I said, "No, march off. The men are cold." We doubled off.

Three or four minutes later the platoon commander, who had about fourteen years of service, appeared. He was in a towering rage. He rushed straight up to Broadhurst and asked him furiously what he meant by marching off without permission.

Broadhurst said, "I'm sorry, sir."

My feet wouldn't move. My mouth wouldn't open. I made a gigantic effort and said, "Sir--" But the lieutenant had given Broadhurst a final blast and taken command. I looked at Broadhurst, but he was busy. After parade I apologized to him, but I never explained to the lieutenant. Broadhurst told me the incident wasn't worth worrying about.

Does this seem a small crime to remember all one's life? I don't think so. It was the worst thing that I ever did in the army, because in it I showed cowardice and disloyalty. The only excuses I could find for myself were that it happened quickly and that I was very young. It had a result, though. I had been frightened of the lieutenant, frightened of being reprimanded, frightened of failure even in the smallest endeavor. I discovered now that being ashamed of yourself is worse than any fear. Duty, orders, loyalty, obedience—all things boiled down to one simple idea: whatever the consequences, a man must act so that he can live with himself.

11. The narrator probably gave the order to march off because he

   A. wanted a chance to show his authority.
   B. was considerate of the troops.
   C. secretly wanted Broadhurst to receive a reprimand.
   D. wanted to be in good favor with the troops.

12. Which factor contributed most to the narrator's mistake?

   F. His desire to impress Broadhurst
   G. His inexperience with army routine
   H. His unfamiliarity with the army post
   J. His liking for the troops

13. From the passage the reader can most safely conclude that the narrator never explained the truth to the platoon commander because

   A. army custom forbade his doing so.
   B. he felt that the incident was unimportant.
   C. he hoped that Broadhurst would do it for him.
   D. he feared the reaction of the platoon commander.

14. Which statement can most safely be made about the platoon commander?

   F. He refused to give the narrator any instructions.
   G. He gave command of the troops to Broadhurst.
   H. He expected his subordinates to execute orders on their own.
   J. He observed army customs to the letter.

15. In the passage, Broadhurst seems to be a man who

   A. has the courage to stand up for his rights.
   B. is willing to overlook an error.
   C. greatly resents authority.
   D. cannot understand other people's mistakes.

16. From the passage the reader can most safely conclude that Broadhurst was

   F. familiar with army routine.
   G. proud of the platoon.
   H. friendly with the platoon commander.
   J. higher in rank than the platoon commander.

17. In looking back on the episode which he describes, the narrator concludes that the episode

   A. proved that he had been improperly trained in army discipline.
   B. caused him to "lose face" with the troops.
   C. helped him to gain self-understanding.
   D. encouraged him to obey orders without question.

18. It is most probable that before this episode took place

   F. plans had been made for the troops to march.
   G. the narrator had not been told the time of departure.
   H. the narrator had given several other incorrect orders.
   J. the platoon commander had relied greatly upon the narrator.

19. This passage was probably excerpted from

   A. an army manual.
   B. a personal narrative.
   C. a spy novel.
   D. an apology.

20. The title that best expresses the main idea of this passage is

   F. "Living in the Army."
   G. "A Friend in Need."
   H. "A Lesson Learned."
   J. "Youth and Duty."

Passage III

Discoveries in science and technology are thought by "untaught minds" to come in blinding flashes or as the result of dramatic accidents. Sir Alexander Fleming did not, as legend would have it, look at the mold on a piece
[5] of cheese and get the idea for penicillin there and then. He experimented with antibacterial substances for nine years before he made his discovery. Inventions and innovations almost always come out of laborious trial and error. Innovation is like hockey: Even the best players
[10] miss the net and have their shots blocked much more frequently than they score.

The point is that the players who score most are the ones who take the most shots on the net—and so it goes with innovation in any field of activity. The prime difference
[15] between innovators and others is one of approach. Everybody gets ideas, but innovators work consciously on theirs, and they follow them through until they prove practicable or otherwise. They never reject any thought that comes into their heads as outlandish. What ordinary
[20] people see as fanciful abstractions, professional innovators see as solid possibilities.

"Creative thinking may mean simply the realization that there's no particular virtue in doing things the way they have always been done," wrote Rudolph Flesch, the lan-
[25] guage guru. This accounts for our reaction to deceptively simple innovations like plastic garbage bags and suitcases on wheels that make life more convenient: "How come nobody thought of that before?"

Creativity does not demand absolute originality. It often
[30] takes the form of shooting an old puck with a new twist.

The creative approach begins with the proposition that nothing is as it appears. Innovators will not accept that there is only one way to do anything. Faced with getting
[35] from A to B, the average person will automatically set out on the best-known and apparently simplest routing. The innovator will search for alternate courses, which may prove easier in the long run and are bound to be more interesting and challenging even if they lead to dead
[40] ends.

Highly creative individuals really do march to a different drummer.

21. Which person would the author probably consider to have an "untaught mind" (lines 1–2)?

A. A high school dropout
B. A citizen of a society that restricts personal freedoms
C. A superstitious person
D. A person ignorant of the method of laboratory experimentation

22. According to the author, what separates innovators from noninnovators?

F. The variety of ideas they have
G. The number of successes they achieve
H. The way they approach problems
J. The manner in which they present their findings

23. According to the author, what is the common response to a new invention?

A. Surprise at its simplicity
B. Acceptance of its utility
C. Questioning of its necessity
D. Dependent on its convenience

24. In lines 30 and 31, the author uses the imagery of shooting the puck to explain the

F. significance of form.
G. importance of a fresh perspective.
H. importance of perspective.
J. relationship between science and athletics.

25. In keeping with the context of the passage, what would the innovator probably state about going from point A to point B?

A. A straight line is the most direct and proven approach.
B. The shortest route is the most advantageous.
C. The most challenging route will eventually prove to be the easiest.
D. The advantages of various routes must be carefully considered.

26. The phrase "march to a different drummer" (lines 33–34) suggests that highly creative individuals are

F. diligent in pursuing their goals.
G. committed to perfection.
H. motivated by their own perceptions of life.
J. unconcerned about society's needs.

27. The tone of this passage is

A. jovial.
B. arrogant.
C. instructive.
D. argumentative.

28. The main idea of this passage can best be summarized in line(s)

    F. 1–2.
    G. 33–34.
    H. 8–9.
    J. 26.

29. The quote by Rudolph Flesch (lines 22–24) is appropriate because

    A. it strengthens the assertion of the author that creative individuals look for new ways of doing things.
    B. Rudolph Flesch is the best expert in the field of creativity.
    C. the reader will believe a quotation more than he will believe the author's point of view.
    D. the quotation adds a new twist to the information previously presented.

30. The author would most likely go on to discuss

    F. some examples of creative individuals in different fields of endeavor.
    G. a universal definition of creativity.
    H. a different view of creativity.
    J. an explanation of the author's view of creativity.

Passage IV

During the past four decades the fishery scientists of the West have studied the dynamics of fish populations with the objective of determining the relation between the amount of fishing and the sustainable catch. They have developed a substantial body of theory that has been applied successfully to a large number of animal populations and has led to a major improvement in the management of some of the major marine fisheries.

The theory has been developed for single-species populations with man as a predator. Much of it is based on the Darwinian concept of a constant overpopulation of young that is reduced by density-dependent mortality resulting from intraspecific competition. The unfished population tends toward a maximum equilibrium size with a relatively high proportion of large, old individuals. As fishing increases, both population size and proportions of large, old individuals are reduced, but growth is increased and natural mortality is reduced. Fishing mortality eventually takes the place of most natural mortality. If the amount of fishing is increased too much, the individuals will tend to be taken before realizing their potential growth, and total yield will be reduced. The maximum sustainable yields can be taken at an intermediate population size that in some populations is about one-third to one-half the unfished population size.

G. V. Nikolskii, of Moscow State University, develops his theory from a different approach. He is a non-Darwinian and is (he says) a nonmathematician; rather he considers himself an ecologist and a morphologist. He argues that Darwin's concept of constant overpopulation has led to the neglect of the problem of protecting spawners and young fish. He argues also that Darwin's concept of a variety as an incipient species has led to extensive mathematical analysis of racial characteristics without understanding of the adaptive significance of the characters. Nikolskii considers the main laws of population dynamics to be concerned with the succession of generations; their birth, growth, and death. The details are governed by the relative rates of adaptation and environmental change. The mass and age structure of a population are the result of adaptation to the food supply. The rate of growth of individuals, the time of sexual maturity, and the accumulation of reserves vary according to the food supply. These factors in turn influence the success of reproduction in ways that tend to bring the size of the population into balance with its food supply.

31. Nikolskii disagrees with Darwin on the concept of

    A. ecology.
    B. constant overpopulation.
    C. morphology.
    D. racial characteristics.

32. The researchers discussed in this passage were mainly concerned with

    F. species of fish faced with extinction.
    G. the ecology of fishing.
    H. the effects of pollution on fishing.
    J. commercial fishing.

33. The theories based on the concepts of Darwin assume that fish population is controlled mainly by the

    A. size of the fish caught within a species.
    B. amount of fishing pressure on the species.
    C. racial characteristics of the species.
    D. life expectancy within the species.

34. Nikolskii theorizes that fish population is controlled mainly by the

    F. size of the fish caught within a species.
    G. racial characteristics of the species.
    H. amount of food available to the species.
    J. death rate within a species.

35. The purpose of the passage is to

    A. compare two different approaches to the dynamics of fish populations.
    B. develop a new theory of fish populations.
    C. refute a long-held theory of fish populations.
    D. review all theories of fish populations.

36. The author indicates the main difference between the theories of Darwin and Nikolskii is the

    F. effect of food supply on the size of the fish.
    G. amount of fish that can be harvested.
    H. methods used to catch fish.
    J. cause of population variation in fish.

37. All of the following are mentioned as affecting fish population EXCEPT

    A. quality of environment.
    B. fishing methods.
    C. fishing pressure.
    D. management techniques.

38. Darwinian theory applied to sustainable catch and the amount of fishing is based on

    F. species of fish caught.
    G. areas that are fished.
    H. population size and proportions of large fish in the population.
    J. number of species in a given fished area.

39. In considering the maximum sustainable yields

    A. more fish taken will better the species because of natural selection and survival of the fittest.
    B. more fish taken will tend to decrease the size of the population and proportion of large fish.
    C. an intermediate population size can be no more than one-third the unfished population size.
    D. there is no need to consider size and proportion of a population of fish.

40. Increasing fishing according to Darwinian theory is an implied benefit because

    F. it reduces population size.
    G. it reduces proportion of older fish.
    H. it reduces natural mortality and increases growth.
    J. it produces a species better fit to survive in a heavily fished environment.

STOP!

This is the end of the Reading Test.
Do not proceed to the next section until the allotted
time expires.

4. SCIENCE REASONING TEST

35 Minutes—40 Questions

DIRECTIONS: Each passage in this test is followed by several questions. After reading a passage, select the most appropriate answer to each question and blacken the corresponding space on your answer sheet. You may refer to the passages as often as you feel necessary.

Passage I

Two strains of bacteria were grown on identical nutritive agar culture dishes. In Experiment 1, a few individuals of each type of bacteria were introduced onto separate culture media; the bacteria populations increased according to the graph in Figure 1. In Experiments 2–4, a few individuals of both species were introduced onto the same culture dish; the populations grew according to the information in Figures 2–4. All conditions of temperature, light, and pH were identical for all culture dishes. The results of the experiments are pictured in the diagrams that appear below.

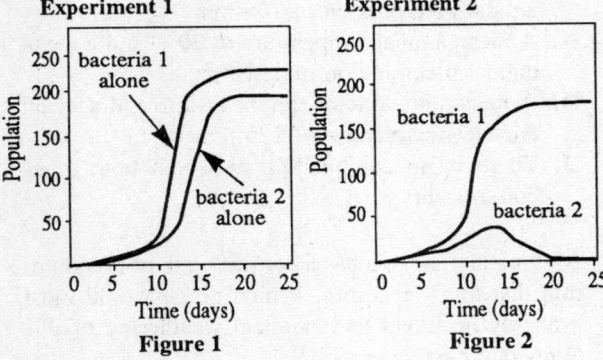

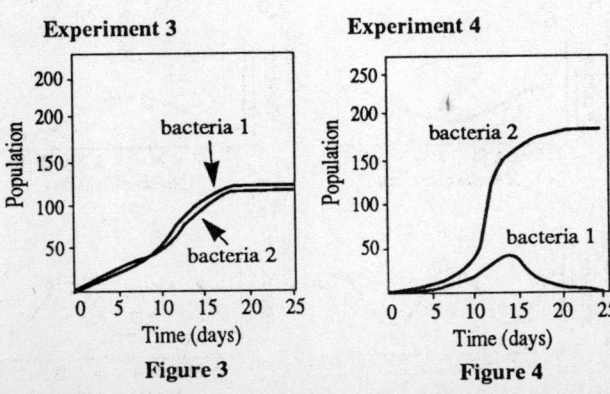

1. For bacteria 1, which portion of the graph in the first experiment represents a constant rate of growth?

   A. 5–10 days
   B. 10–12 days
   C. 12–15 days
   D. 15–20 days

2. A researcher hypothesized that bacteria 1 was a more efficient competitor for limited resources than bacteria 2. Which of the experiments *least* supports her theory?

   F. Experiment 1
   G. Experiment 2
   H. Experiment 3
   J. Experiment 4

3. Bacteriologists have discovered that similar strains of bacteria in close proximity usually separate from each other and restrict themselves to a fraction of their available environment. Which of the four experiments here most likely represents such behavior?

   A. Experiment 1
   B. Experiment 2
   C. Experiment 3
   D. Experiment 4

4. On the basis of the information compiled from Experiments 2 and 4, which of the following conclusions can one draw about bacteria strains 1 and 2?

   F. The life spans of bacteria 1 and 2 are both approximately 20 days.
   G. Bacteria 2 requires a daily per capita intake of nutrients greater than that of bacteria 1.
   H. The natural reproductive rates of bacteria 1 and bacteria 2 are equal.

375

J. Bacteria 1 and bacteria 2 exhibit interspecific competition that results in extinction of one strain.

5. According to the results of Experiment 2, which of the following is true?

   A. The life span of bacteria 1 is longer than bacteria 2.
   B. The life span of bacteria 2 is longer than bacteria 1.
   C. The life span of bacteria 1 is equal to that of bacteria 2.
   D. Cannot be determined on the basis of the results given

Passage II

The graph below represents various types of weathering for different climatic conditions.

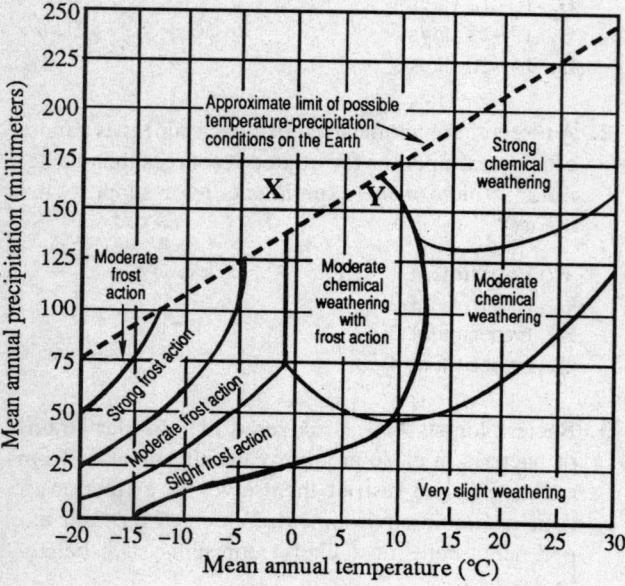

6. Which climatic conditions would produce moderate frost action, but no chemical weathering?

   F. A mean annual temperature of $-10°C$ and a mean annual precipitation of 100 mm
   G. A mean annual temperature of 10°C and a mean annual precipitation of 75 mm
   H. A mean annual temperature of $-5°C$ and a mean annual precipitation of 75 mm
   J. A mean annual temperature of $-15°C$ and a mean annual precipitation of 50 mm

7. Why is no frost action shown for locations with a mean annual temperature greater than 13°C?

   A. Very little freezing takes place at these locations.
   B. Chemical weathering eliminates frost action.
   C. Very little precipitation falls at these locations.
   D. Too much precipitation falls at these locations.

8. At location Y, moderate chemical weathering and frost action dominate, yet at location X, with a mean annual temperature just slightly lower, no particular type of weathering occurs. Why?

   F. Only chemical weathering would occur under these conditions.
   G. Conditions at X probably do not occur on Earth.
   H. Any weathering at Y is an anomaly.
   J. There is too much precipitation at X.

9. The relationship between absolute mean annual precipitation and absolute mean annual temperature is best described as

   A. logarithmic.
   B. inverse.
   C. direct.
   D. There is no relationship.

10. At what combination of precipitation and temperature would strong frost action and strong chemical action occur simultaneously?

    F. A mean annual temperature of $-5°C$ and a mean annual precipitation of 100 mm
    G. A mean annual temperature of 20°C and a mean annual precipitation of 150 mm
    H. A mean annual temperature of 5°C and a mean annual precipitation of 125 mm
    J. There is no combination at which both types could occur.

11. Assume that an area has a constant rate of precipitation that totals 160 mm. Which graph would most probably represent the chemical weathering of this temperate area's bedrock?

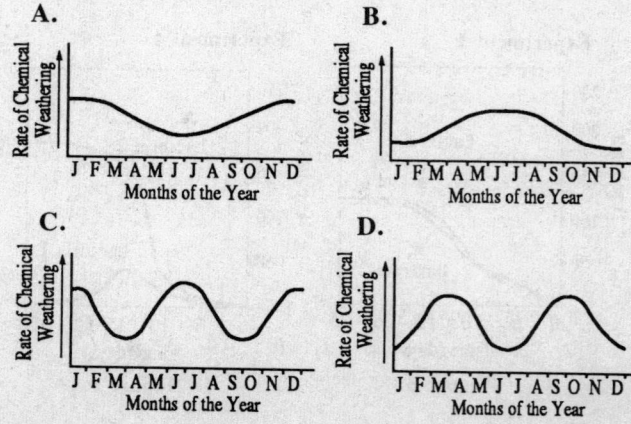

Passage III

Two scientists are debating the nature of the evolutionary process.

Scientist 1

Clearly species have evolved gradually over time. Slight mutations accumulating over thousands of generations compose the evolutionary history of speciation. Random mutations and inheritable competitive advantages spread slowly through a population until, after several million years, they dominate and characterize the species. Deoxyribonucleic acid (DNA) molecules, the building blocks of life that are carried on chromosomes, code for these minute changes. For example, consider the case of the giraffe. At one point, all giraffes had short necks; however, some members of the population who had slightly longer necks enjoyed a competitive advantage in being able to reach food higher off the ground. These members ate more, were healthier, and were more likely to pass their "long-necked" genes on to offspring. Over time, this competitive selection favored giraffes with longer and longer necks, until the species arrived at the form we recognize today. In many cases, some environmental condition creates a reproductive barrier, which geographically isolates a segment of the population; after several million years, that segment can evolve so that reproduction between the two original populations is impossible. Thus, in these respects the process of speciation is marked by gradualism.

Scientist 2

Such a conventional interpretation of the evolutionary process is elegant, but fundamentally flawed. The fossil record does not support gradualism, but rather a crisis-initiated speciation process—punctuated equilibrium. On an evolutionary time scale, the creation of new species is extremely rapid—almost immediate. Actually, there is very little change in a species over vast periods of time, and then some ecological crisis gives rise by chance to a population quite different from its ancestral species. It is quite probable that some crises wiped out the food source for all but the longer-necked giraffes, and these were the only remaining members of the species left to reproduce at all. Their "long-necked" DNA codes were the only ones to be passed on to the next generation, so it is logical to assume that the species quickly evolved into the one we recognize today through a series of such critical episodes. Gradual changes certainly serve their function; they fine-tune the adaptations of the species in equilibrium.

12. One of the principal disagreements between the two scientists concerns

   F. whether there is ample evidence to prove that speciation occurs.
   G. whether fossils are adequate evidence with which to analyze speciation.
   H. the rate of speciation.
   J. the presence or absence of ecological disturbances during speciation.

13. Which of the following diagrams best represents the process of gradualism espoused by Scientist 1?

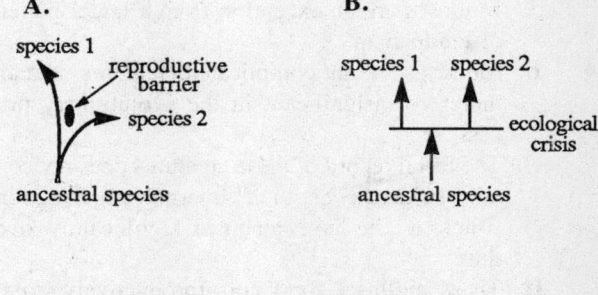

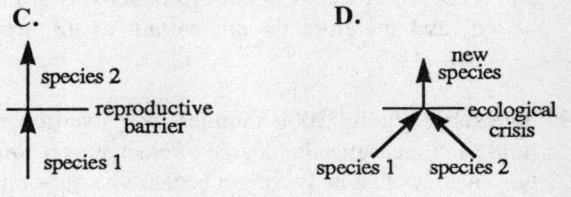

14. Which of the following would most weaken the argument of Scientist 2?

   F. The sudden discovery of a complete fossil record that exhibited no sudden discontinuities
   G. A finding that reproductive barriers are NOT effective in creating new species
   H. A new theory that asserts that giraffes have not changed significantly in one million years
   J. None of the above

15. Scientist 1 would be most likely to assert which of the following?

   A. Fossils are unimportant in the contemplation of the evolutionary process.
   B. Ecological crisis is the most significant factor in the creation of new species.
   C. The question of speciation is less important than that of identifying reproductive barriers.
   D. One may define two species as distinct if they are unable to reproduce with each other.

16. Which theory seems to support the idea of selective pressures on the evolutionary process that weed out unfit members of a population?

   F. Scientist 1's theory
   G. Scientist 2's theory
   H. Neither scientist's theory
   J. Both scientist's theories

17. It has been determined that a complete fossil record of molluscs—shelled creatures with no internal skeleton—exhibits very little change over vast periods of time. How might Scientist 1 analyze this evidence in light of his beliefs?

   A. Molluscs are an exception from a larger pattern of gradualism.
   B. Molluscs are not complicated creatures, and are therefore insignificant in the evolutionary process.
   C. The fossil record of these creatures does not contain evidence of their internal organization, which might have changed significantly over time.
   D. These molluscs were not reproductively isolated, and therefore do not pertain to the argument.

18. Scientist 2 studies 2000 families over five generations, and measures the degree of change over time; he concludes that he is correct because he finds minimal evolutionary change. Humans, he concludes, are in a period of equilibrium. How might Scientist 1 react?

   F. He would support the conclusion.
   G. He would deny the relevance of the results, since humans are too genetically complicated to use in the experiment.
   H. He would deny the relevance of the results, since Scientist 2 did not examine human fossils.
   J. He would deny the relevance of the results, asserting that even rapid evolutionary change covers thousands of years.

Passage IV

The resistance (R) of a material is directly proportional to the resistivity (r) of the material. Resistivity is measured in ohm-meters. The voltage (V, measured in volts) in a circuit is directly proportional to both the resistance (R, measured in ohms) and the current (I, measured in amperes). Resistors in series act as one resistor according to the formula:

$$R_s = R_1 + R_2 + R_3 + \ldots;$$

and resistors in parallel act as one resistor according to the formula:

$$\frac{1}{R_p} = \frac{1}{R_1} + \frac{1}{R_2} + \frac{1}{R_3} + \ldots$$

The resistivities of several materials are listed below.

Substance	Resistivity (r) (ohm-meters)
Aluminum	2.63×10^{-8}
Copper	1.72×10^{-8}
Germanium	6.00×10^{-1}
Silicon	2.30×10^{3}
Silver	1.47×10^{-8}
Sulfur	1.00×10^{15}

19. According to the information above, the best formula for the voltage in a circuit, where voltage is V, current is I, and resistance is R is

   A. $V = \dfrac{I}{R}$.
   B. $V = I + R$.
   C. $V = IR$.
   D. $V = I - R$.

20. According to the information above, how would the voltage in a circuit with a silver resistor compare to the voltage in a circuit with a germanium resistor of the same size? (Current is the same in both circuits.)

   F. The voltage in the silver circuit would be greater.
   G. The voltage in the germanium circuit would be greater.
   H. The voltage would be the same in both circuits.
   J. Cannot be determine from the information given.

21. Two resistors with R=2 are placed in series. How does the voltage in the circuit compare with the voltage in a circuit with only one resistor, R=2? (Assume current remains constant.)

   A. The voltage is doubled.
   B. the voltage is halved.
   C. The voltage is the same.
   D. The voltage is zero.

22. A resistor with R=4 is put in parallel with an identical resistor, R=4. What is Rp?

   F. 0
   G. $\frac{1}{2}$
   H. 1
   J. 2

23. Power is defined as $P = I^2R$. If R is constant, then power would increase _____ with an increase in the current. (Fill in the blank space with the best answer choice.)

   A. Logarithmically
   B. Directly
   C. Exponentially
   D. Inversely

24. In order to keep the current in a circuit constant, if one increases the voltage, one must

   F. lengthen the circuit.
   G. shorten the circuit.
   H. Decrease the resistance.
   J. increase the resistance.

Passage V

Diagram I below represents the path of a stream with locations A–F. Diagram II represents a geologic cross-section of the area over which the stream flows. (Assume that the width and volume of the stream are constant.)

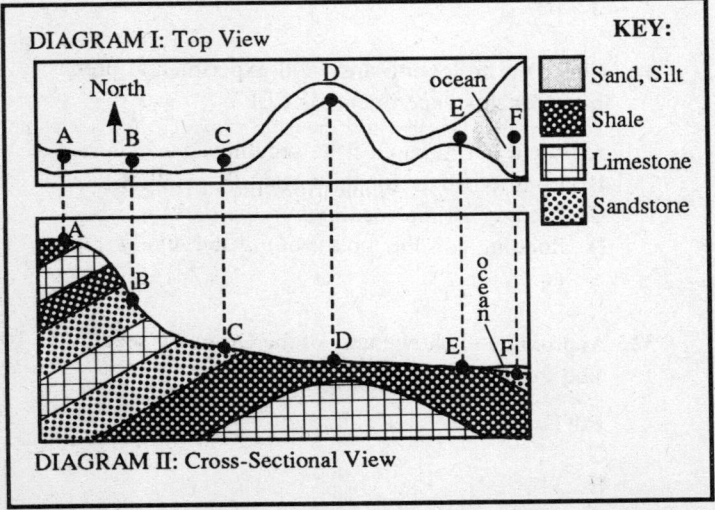

25. At which point would the stream's velocity be greatest?

   A. A
   B. B
   C. D
   D. F

26. The stream's potential energy is greatest at

   F. A
   G. B
   H. C
   J. F

27. Deposition of sediment in the ocean between points E and F is most likely caused by a(n)

   A. loss of potential energy by the current between E and F.
   B. increase in potential energy of the current between E and F.
   C. loss of kinetic energy by the current between E and F.
   D. increase in kinetic energy of the current between E and F.

28. An observer looks downstream from a location just above point D and draws a cross section of the streambed at point D. Which diagram would probably best represent this cross section?

   F.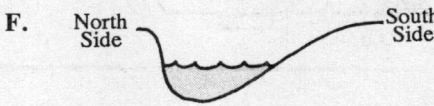

   G.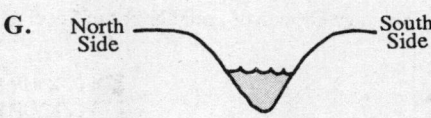

   H.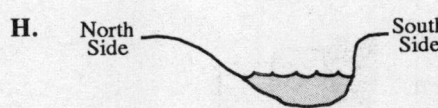

   J.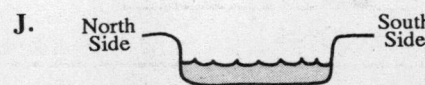

29. Assuming that there have been no upheavals in the bedrock, at which point is the stream flowing over the oldest bedrock?

   A. A
   B. C
   C. D
   D. F

Passage VI

Seedlings of the variety *Osmuda cinnamomea* were planted in 2" × 2" seedling pots. There were four groups of seedlings, and four pots were planted for each group. Group I consisted of 1 seedling per pot; Group II consisted of 5 seedlings per pot; Group III consisted of 10 seedlings per pot; Group IV consisted of 20 seedlings per pot. The average shoot height of the seedlings in each group was measured after one and two weeks. The diagrams below summarize the results of the experiment.

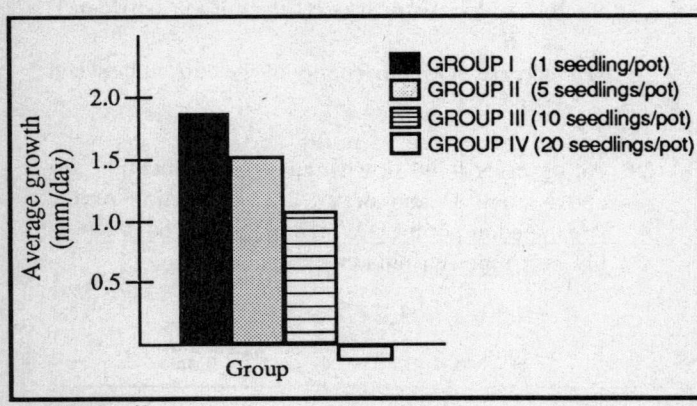
Figure 1

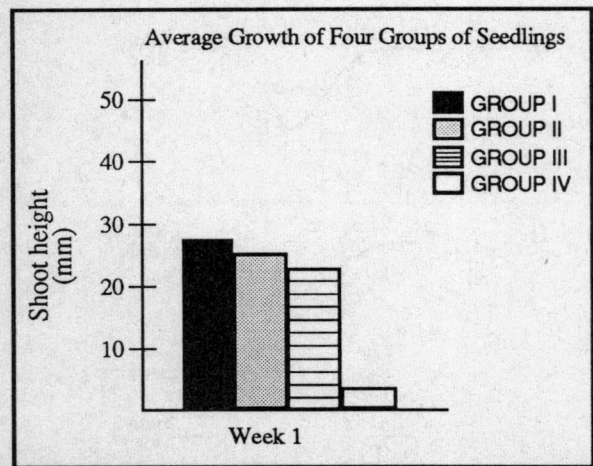
Figure 2

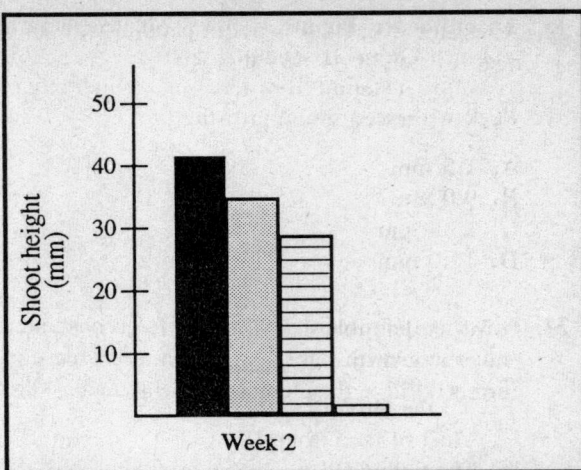
Figure 3

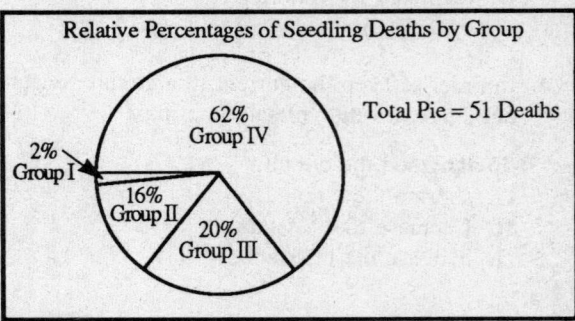
Figure 4

30. How many seedlings were planted in total?

    F. 36
    G. 121
    H. 144
    J. 180

31. All of the following are valid experimental procedures for this experiment EXCEPT

    A. not watering any of the seedlings.
    B. using fertilizer for the Group IV seedlings.
    C. keeping all the seedlings in the dark.
    D. flooding all the pots with water every other day.

32. Approximately how many of the Group IV seedlings died during the experiment?

    F. 11
    G. 32
    H. 51
    J. 62

33. According to Figure 1, approximately how high would a Group II seedling shoot be after 1 week, assuming it started from zero and the first day of the week witnessed initial growth?

   A. 1.5 mm
   B. 9.0 mm
   C. 10.5 mm
   D. 12.0 mm

34. How is it possible that Group IV seedlings exhibit a negative growth rate?

   F. All the Group IV seedlings died.
   G. Most of the Group IV seedlings died.
   H. The Group IV seedlings grew steadily, but were the slowest growers out of the four groups.
   J. Over the two weeks, the Group IV plants withered and had shorter shoots at the end of the experiment.

35. If the number of Group III deaths increases by 5, and the total deaths remain at 51, what is the new approximate relative percentage death rate for Group III plants?

   A. 23%
   B. 25%
   C. 30%
   D. 51%

Passage VII

Four groups of 1000 men each were placed on strict diets that contained different intakes of cholesterol. The men stayed on the diets for 40 years, and their history of illnesses over that time is recorded below.

| | Death rate, standardized/1000 ||||
| | | Men taking in a daily average of |||
Illness	No cholesterol	0–5 grams	6–20 grams	20+ grams
Cancer				
Colon	0.01	0.03	0.04	0.02
Prostate	2.02	0.06	1.03	4.01
Lung	0.03	0.06	0.40	0.20
Coronary				
Thrombosis	5.02	1.01	4.00	10.05
Arrest	6.00	0.98	5.09	11.00
Cardiovascular	5.96	0.65	4.97	9.08
Cerebral Clot	4.01	0.02	0.50	4.01
Depression	5.01	0.30	0.30	0.30

36. Which of the following statements is best supported by the data?

   F. A man ingesting no cholesterol is approximately twice as likely to die of prostate cancer than a man ingesting 10 grams per day.
   G. Any ingestion of cholesterol decreases the risk of dying from all three forms of cancer listed here.
   H. Ingestion of cholesterol seems unrelated to the probability of coronary disease.
   J. Cerebral clots are the most prevalent forms of death among the group consuming the most cholesterol.

37. What might one conclude about the relationship between cholesterol ingestion and depression on the basis of the information above?

    A. Cholesterol causes depression.
    B. Ingestion of cholesterol has no effect on the occurrence of depression.
    C. Small amounts of cholesterol are most effective in combating depression.
    D. Large and small amounts of cholesterol are equally effective in reducing the depression death rate.

38. For which of the following diseases does the highest cholesterol diet increase the probability of death most, compared *relatively* to the non-cholesterol diet (i.e., which increases by the highest percentage)?

    F. Cerebral clots
    G. Coronary arrest
    H. Cardiovascular disease
    J. Coronary thrombosis

39. For which of the following groups of diseases does a daily intake of 0–5 grams of cholesterol reduce the probability of death regardless of initial cholesterol intake?

    A. Cerebral clot, coronary thrombosis, lung cancer
    B. Cerebral clot, depression, colon cancer
    C. Depression, coronary arrest, prostate cancer
    D. Depression, coronary thrombosis, colon cancer

40. What might be involved in determining a standardized death rate for men?

    F. Ignoring deaths that do not conform to the average results
    G. Adjusting death rates according to discrepancies in age
    H. Assuming that the natural death rate is 0 deaths per 1000 men
    J. Comparing data with a similar experiment involving women

STOP!

This is the end of the Science Reasoning Test.
When the allotted time for this section expires,
the entire test is completed.

Answer Key and Scoring Sheet for Practice Exam II

	English				Mathematics		
	Answer	Usage/ Mechanics	Rhetorical		Answer	Pre-Alg./ Elem. Alg.	Int. Alg./ Coord. Geom.	Geom./ Trig.
1.	D			1.	A			____
2.	F	____		2.	J	____		
3.	D	____		3.	A	____		
4.	H	____		4.	K	____		
5.	B	____		5.	C			____
6.	J	____		6.	G		____	
7.	B	____		7.	A	____		
8.	H	____		8.	G		____	
9.	B	____		9.	E	____		
10.	J		____	10.	F	____		
11.	A		____	11.	A	____		
12.	F		____	12.	J		____	
13.	C		____	13.	D	____		
14.	G	____		14.	K	____		
15.	D		____	15.	A	____		
16.	H	____		16.	K			____
17.	C	____		17.	E			____
18.	F	____		18.	F	____		
19.	B	____		19.	B		____	
20.	H	____		20.	G			____
21.	C	____		21.	D		____	
22.	G		____	22.	H	____		
23.	B		____	23.	A	____		
24.	H	____		24.	H	____		
25.	C		____	25.	D		____	
26.	F		____	26.	G			____
27.	C		____	27.	E		____	
28.	G		____	28.	K	____		
29.	C		____	29.	C			____
30.	H		____	30.	G	____		
31.	A		____	31.	A	____		
32.	J	____		32.	G	____		
33.	B	____		33.	E			____
34.	F	____		34.	K	____		
35.	D	____		35.	D		____	
36.	H	____		36.	G			____
37.	D		____	37.	D			____
38.	A		____	38.	F		____	
39.	C		____	39.	C	____		
40.	H	____		40.	F			____

Answer Key and Scoring Sheet for Practice Exam II (continued)

	English				**Mathematics**			
	Answer	Usage/ Mechanics	Rhetorical		Answer	Pre-Alg./ Elem. Alg.	Int. Alg./ Coord. Geom.	Geom./ Trig.
41.	C	___		41.	A		___	
42.	G		___	42.	K			___
43.	D	___		43.	D		___	
44.	H	___		44.	J	___		
45.	D	___		45.	A			___
46.	F		___	46.	G			___
47.	C		___	47.	E		___	
48.	J		___	48.	F		___	
49.	C		___	49.	C	___		
50.	J		___	50.	F			___
51.	C		___	51.	C			___
52.	F	___		52.	F		___	
53.	D	___		53.	D		___	
54.	J		___	54.	H			___
55.	C	___		55.	C	___		
56.	G	___		56.	K		___	
57.	D		___	57.	E		___	
58.	F	___		58.	G	___		
59.	B		___	59.	B		___	
60.	H	___		60.	H		___	
61.	A		___					
62.	J		___					
63.	C		___					
64.	H	___						
65.	D	___						
66.	G	___						
67.	C	___						
68.	F		___					
69.	B		___					
70.	J		___					
71.	D	___						
72.	J	___						
73.	B	___						
74.	H		___					
75.	B		___					

Raw Score

Total Correct (by category) ___   ___   Total Correct (by category) ___ ___ ___

Grand Total Correct (English) ___   Grand Total Correct (Mathematics) ___

Using the chart on page 386, convert the above raw score to an approximate standardized score.

Approx. Standardized Score

Answer Key and Scoring Sheet for Practice Exam II (continued)

	Reading				Science Reasoning	
	Answer	Social St./Science	Arts/Lit.		Answer	Science Reasoning
1.	C	___		1.	B	___
2.	F	___		2.	J	___
3.	D	___		3.	C	___
4.	G	___		4.	J	___
5.	A	___		5.	D	___
6.	J	___		6.	H	___
7.	B	___		7.	A	___
8.	F	___		8.	G	___
9.	D	___		9.	C	___
10.	H	___		10.	J	___
11.	B		___	11.	B	___
12.	G		___	12.	H	___
13.	D		___	13.	A	___
14.	J		___	14.	F	___
15.	B		___	15.	D	___
16.	F		___	16.	J	___
17.	C		___	17.	C	___
18.	F		___	18.	J	___
19.	B		___	19.	C	___
20.	H		___	20.	G	___
21.	D		___	21.	A	___
22.	H		___	22.	J	___
23.	A		___	23.	C	___
24.	G		___	24.	J	___
25.	D		___	25.	B	___
26.	H		___	26.	F	___
27.	C		___	27.	C	___
28.	G		___	28.	F	___
29.	A		___	29.	C	___
30.	F		___	30.	H	___
31.	B	___		31.	B	___
32.	J	___		32.	G	___
33.	B	___		33.	C	___
34.	H	___		34.	J	___
35.	A	___		35.	C	___
36.	J	___		36.	F	___
37.	B	___		37.	D	___
38.	H	___		38.	J	___
39.	B	___		39.	C	___
40.	H	___		40.	G	___

Raw Score

Total Correct (by category) ___ ___

Grand Total Correct (Reading) ___

Total Correct ___

Grand Total Correct (Science Reasoning) ___

Answer Key and Scoring Sheet for Practice Exam II (continued)

Using the chart below, convert the above raw score to an approximate standardized score

Approx. Standardized Score

CONVERSION TABLE

Number Answered Correctly				Approximate Standardized Score
English	Mathematics	Reading	Science Reasoning	
0–2	0–2	0–2	0–1	1
3–4	3	3	2	2
5–6	4–5	4	3–4	3
7–8	6	5	5	4
9–10	7	6	6	5
11–12	8–9	7	7–8	6
13–14	10	8	9	7
15–16	11	9–10	10	8
17–18	12–13	11	11	9
19–20	14	12	12	10
21–23	15	13	13–14	11
24–25	16–17	14–15	15	12
26–27	18–19	16	16	13
28–29	20	17	17	14
30–31	21–22	18	18	15
32–33	23–24	19	19	16
34–35	25–26	20	20	17
36–37	27	21	21	18
38–39	28–29	22	22	19
40–41	30–31	23	23	20
42–44	32–33	24	24–25	21
45–46	34–35	25	26	22
47–48	36–38	26	27	23
49–50	39–40	27	28	24
51–52	41–42	28	29	25
53–54	43	29	30	26
55–57	44–46	30–31	31	27
58–60	47–48	32	32	28
61–63	49–50	33	33	29
64–65	51–52	34	34	30
66–68	53–54	35	35	31
69–70	55–56	36	36	32
71	57	37	37	33
72–73	58	38	38	34
74	59	39	39	35
75	60	40	40	36

Explanatory Answers for Practice Exam II

1. English Test

1. **(D)** This is the only word order that makes sense in the sentence.

2. **(F)** *Marches* is the correct present plural verb.

3. **(D)** *Among* is used with more than two persons or things. *Between* is used with two persons or things.

4. **(H)** *Theirselves* is nonstandard usage for the reflexive pronoun *themselves*. *Oneself* and *himself* are singular and cannot refer to the plural antecedent *students*.

5. **(B)** The adverb *precisely* is needed to modify the verb *adapt*. *More* joins *precisely* to form the comparative.

6. **(J)** *Who* is required as the subject of the verb *have*. *That* is used to introduce essential clauses and, therefore, should not be preceded by a comma. *Which* refers to animals or things.

7. **(B)** *Bringing* is the correct verbal form and should be used to avoid a needless shift in tense.

8. **(H)** The plural subject *differences* requires the plural verb *are*.

9. **(B)** *There* is the correct adverb. *They're* is a contraction for *they are*; *their* and *theirs* are possessive pronouns.

10. **(J)** No punctuation is needed. *And* is an appropriate conjunction.

11. **(A)** The phrase is correctly placed.

12. **(F)** Paragraph 1 introduces the topic of the entire passage, innovations in teaching methods. Paragraph 2 names some of the innovations. Paragraph 3 presents the aims of these innovations and introduces the topic of students which is further discussed in paragraph 4. Paragraph 5 makes a recommendation about innovations and student differences based on the previous paragraphs.

13. **(C)** The dashes set off illustrations of previously mentioned items.

14. **(G)** Choice G is correct because the three prepositional phrases that follow the dash give specific examples of the preceding word, *advertising*. Choice F creates ambiguity since the last two prepositional phrases have no clear antecedent. Choice H is grammatically acceptable but stylistically confusing because of the series commas that follow in the same sentence. Choice J includes an unnecessary comma.

15. **(D)** Choice D is correct since the underlined section is irrelevant to the topic of this paragraph.

16. **(H)** Choice H is correct because the singular antecedent demands a singular pronoun and verb, and the passage is written in the present tense. Both choices G and J introduce a future tense and choice F features a plural pronoun and plural noun.

17. **(C)** Choice C is correct because it is the only wording that uses the better vocabulary choice, *convey*, and features the other verb, *is able to*, that renders the sentence most logical.

18. **(F)** Choice F is correct because the superlative *most* is properly placed before *likely*. Choice H misplaces the superlative, choice G omits it, and J would render the sentence meaningless.

19. **(B)** Choice B is the most economical way to express this transition. Choices F and H are awkward and non-idiomatic. Choice J features a nonexistent word.

20. **(H)** Choice H is correct. Choices F and G, by misplacing the comma, create illogical or unintended meanings, and choice J, by omitting "solely," creates an unintended meaning.

21. **(C)** Choice C is correct because it provides a plural verb to agree with the plural subject and maintains parallel structure with the second infinitive phrase.

22. **(G)** Choice G is correct. This paragraph has focused on warning the reader to consider investment advice very carefully. The final sentence shifts to a new, unrelated concern for the would-be investor.

23. **(B)** Choice B is the best choice since it is succinct and consistent with the tone of the rest of the passage. Choices A and C are wordier versions, and D introduces an inconsistently harsh tone.

24. **(H)** Choice H is correct because it provides the plural pronoun and verb required by the plural antecedent. Choices F and G feature singular pronouns; choice J shifts to future tense.

25. **(C)** Choice **C** is correct because the intended audience, those new to investment options, would be unlikely to know what the writer means by a firm's "track record."

26. **(F)** Choice **F** is correct because the purpose of the passage is clearly to provide investors with advice about what they are entitled to expect in the investment world. Choices **G** and **H** both suggest information too specific to be consistent with the intended purpose, and choice **H** assumes a different purpose altogether.

27. **(C)** Choice **C** is correct. The passage does not offer advice to those offering investments at all, so choices **A** and **D** are incorrect. Choice **B** is wrong because the advice offered in the passage would be too simple and somewhat obvious for a veteran investor.

28. **(G)** *Them* is the correct plural pronoun and agrees with the antecedent *they*.

29. **(C)** A comma is used to set off a long adverbial clause or phrase preceding the subject. Using a period creates a sentence fragment.

30. **(H)** Subordinating the first clause to the second one corrects the original comma splice. *If* is appropriate for a clause of supposition.

31. **(A)** The past perfect (*had ravaged*) is correct to indicate an action completed before another past action (*left*). *Already* means *previously*; *all ready* means *everybody or everything ready*.

32. **(J)** This clause has a compound predicate and the verbs must agree in tense. *Fostered* is correct verb tense.

33. **(B)** The infinitive *to prey* is the correct verbal form.

34. **(F)** The auxiliary verb *were* agrees with the past tense verb *worshipped*. The adverb *diligently* correctly modifies *worshipped*.

35. **(D)** Commas are used to set off parenthetical material.

36. **(H)** The adverb *superstitiously* correctly modifies the adjective *impotent*.

37. **(D)** *In the "Dark Ages"* is redundant. The Medieval period is also referred to as the "Dark Ages."

38. **(A)** *Former* meaning *the first of two* is used with *latter* meaning *the second of two*.

39. **(C)** The author mentions events in the Middle Ages (Magna Carta, Peasants' Revolt, etc.) which he expects the reader to know.

40. **(H)** *Has written* is the present perfect tense and this tense is used to express past time extending to the present.

41. **(C)** The noun *anguish* is best to parallel the noun *concern*.

42. **(G)** *Only* should be placed next to the word it modifies (*held*).

43. **(D)** The use of the comma creates a run-on sentence. The sentences must be separated by a period.

44. **(H)** The past tense *begged* is needed to agree with the other verbs in the sentence (*abandoned, despised*).

45. **(D)** The present progressive form (*is being manipulated*) is correct for an activity continuing from the past into the present.

46. **(F)** The comma is used to set off parenthetical material.

47. **(C)** The phrase *of the characters* describes *movements and reactions* and should be placed immediately after *reactions*.

48. **(J)** The adverb *whereas* indicates the contrast intended between what is acceptable in drama and in novels. *Moreover*, *consequently* and *therefore* all indicate a result.

49. **(C)** The semicolon is used between two clauses not joined by a conjunction.

50. **(J)** See *10-year-old* in paragraph 2 and *one-sided* in paragraph 4.

51. **(C)** The correct noun is *diversity* meaning variety. *Divergent* is an adjective meaning separating from each other.

52. **(F)** The past participle *wielded* is the correct verbal form. The verb *wield* means to have full control over.

53. **(D)** The past tense form *influenced* is required to balance *manipulated*.

54. **(J)** *And have large amounts of money* is redundant.

55. **(C)** Commas are used to set off a long adverbial clause or phrase preceding the subject.

56. **(G)** The plural noun *spokesmen* agrees with the verb *cite*.

57. **(D)** The clause *that which guarantees the right of all citizens to own and bear arms* further explains the Second Amendment and should be set off by commas.

58. **(F)** *Its* is the correct possessive pronoun. *It's* is a contraction for the words *it is*.

59. **(B)**

60. **(H)** The period is always placed within the quotation marks.

61. **(A)** The adjective *accidental* is correct to modify the noun *deaths*.

62. **(J)** Examples of the mishandling of guns would provide a stronger case for gun control.

63. **(C)** The abbreviation NRA is appropriately enclosed in parentheses following *National Rifle Association*.

64. **(H)** The verb *is* is correct because it agrees in number with the singular subject *United States*, and in tense with the rest of the paragraph.

65. **(D)** The adjective *personal* meaning relating to or affecting an individual person is correct. *Personnel* is a noun meaning persons usually employed by some type of organization.

66. **(G)** *Them* is the correct plural pronoun to agree with the plural subject *nations*.

67. **(C)** *And* is the correct conjunction. No punctuation is required.

68. **(F)** *By* is the correct preposition to express the means of accomplishing something. The phrases are essential to the meaning of the sentence.

69. **(B)** A period is needed to correct the original comma splice. D creates an ungrammatical second sentence.

70. **(J)** Examples would provide concrete material to illustrate his point.

71. **(D)** A comma should not be used to separate the subject from the verb. A singular verb is used to refer to the United States as a unit.

72. **(J)** The infinitive *to meet* is the correct verbal form.

73. **(B)** A hyphen is used to join two or more words that serve as a single adjective before a noun. D is wordy.

74. **(H)** The passage provides information on the energy situation in the United States.

75. **(B)** Paragraph 1 introduces the problem of energy in the U.S. Paragraph 4 provides a historical perspective. Paragraph 2 gives depth to the problem. Paragraph 3 offers a solution.

2. Mathematics Test

1. **(A)**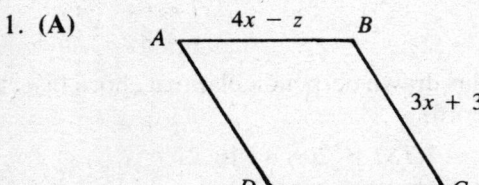

   The sides of a rhombus are equal.
   $4x - 2 = 3x + 3$
   $x = 5$

2. **(J)** The commutative property involves the change of position. The commutative property of addition $(a + b) + c = (b + a) + c$. The commutative property of multiplication $(ab)c = (ba)c$.

3. **(A)** $(3x^2)(2x^3) = 6x^5$

4. **(K)** $|-6| = 6$, $|2| = 2$, $|-2| = 2$
   $|-6| - |2| - |-2| = 6 - 2 - 2 = 2$

5. **(C)**

   Perimeter $= 4 + 7 + 4 + 7 = 22$

6. **(G)**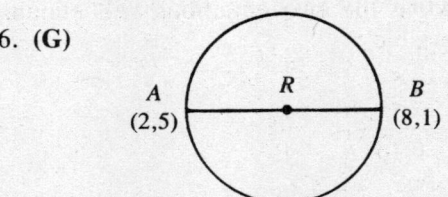

   Midpoint $x = \dfrac{x_1 + x_2}{2}$ Midpoint $y = \dfrac{y_1 + y_2}{2}$

   $= \dfrac{2 + 8}{2}$ $= \dfrac{5 + 1}{2}$

   $= 5$ $= 3$

   $(5, 3)$

7. **(A)** $F = \frac{9}{5}C + 32$

$77 = \frac{9}{5}C + 32$

Subtract 32 from each side of the equation.

$45 = \frac{9}{5}C \rightarrow \frac{9C}{5} = 45$

By cross-multiplication:

$9C = 5(45)$
$C = 25$

8. **(G)** $f(-5) = |2(-5) + 3| = |-10 + 3| = |-7| = 7$

9. **(E)** The sides of similar triangles are proportional.

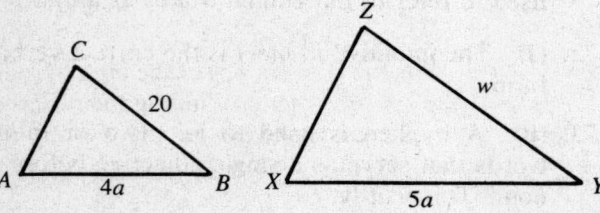

Let $\overline{AB} = 4a$
$\overline{XY} = 5a$

$\frac{4a}{5a} = \frac{20}{w}$

$\frac{4}{5} = \frac{20}{w}$

$4w = 100$
$w = 25$

10. **(F)** $3\sqrt{18} = 3\sqrt{9}\sqrt{2}$
$= 3(3)\sqrt{2}$
$= 9\sqrt{2}$

11. **(A)** $(3x^2 - 4) - (x^2 - 7)$
$3x^2 - 4 - x^2 + 7$
$2x^2 + 3$

12. **(J)** Adding the two equations will eliminate the y variable.

$3x + y = 5$
$2x - y = 5$
$\overline{5x \quad\quad = 10}$
$x \quad\quad = 2$

Substitute $x = 2$ into the first equation and solve for y.

$3x + y = 5$
$3(2) + y = 5$
$6 + y = 5$
$y = -1$

The solution is: $(2, -1)$

13. **(D)** $\frac{12x^4 - 3x^3 + 6x^2}{3x^2} = \frac{12x^4}{3x^2} - \frac{3x^3}{3x^2} + \frac{6x^2}{3x^2}$
$= 4x^2 - x + 2$

14. **(K)** $\frac{\text{is}}{\text{of}} = \frac{\text{percent}}{100}$

$\frac{30}{x} = \frac{5}{100}$

$x = 600$

15. **(A)** $x + ay = m$

First subtract x from each side of the equation.

$\begin{aligned} x + ay &= m \\ -x & \quad\quad -x \end{aligned}$
$\overline{ ay = m - x}$

Divide both sides by a.

$\frac{ay}{a} = \frac{m - x}{a}$

$y = \frac{m - x}{a}$

16. **(K)**
By the Pythagorean theorem,

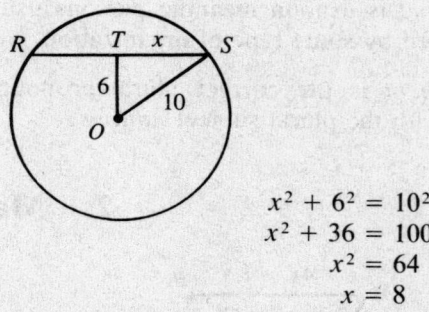

$x^2 + 6^2 = 10^2$
$x^2 + 36 = 100$
$x^2 = 64$
$x = 8$

A radius drawn perpendicular to a chord bisects the chord.

$\therefore \overline{RS} = 2(\overline{TS}) = 2(8) = 16$

17. **(E)**

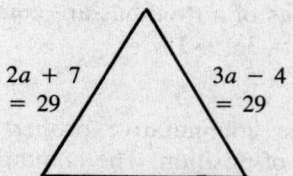

All three sides of an equilateral triangle are equal.

$\therefore 2a + 7 = 3a - 4$
$11 = a$

$\left. \begin{aligned} \therefore 2a + 7 &= 2(11) + 7 = 29 \\ 3a - 4 &= 3(11) - 4 = 29 \end{aligned} \right\}$, each side is 29

Perimeter $= 3s = 3(29) = 87$

18. **(F)** $3y^2 + 4y - 4$
    $(3y - 2)(y + 2)$

19. **(B)** $3^{x-2} = 81$
    $3^{x-2} = 3^4$
    $\therefore x - 2 = 4$
    $x = 6$

20. **(G)** The sum of the measures of the four angles of a quadrilateral is 360°.
    $m\angle A + m\angle B + m\angle C + m\angle D = 360°$
    $120 + 82 + x + 93 = 360$
    $295 + x = 360$
    $x = 65$

21. **(D)** $b^0 = 1 \quad b^{-1/2} = 16^{-1/2} = \dfrac{1}{4}$
    $2b^0 + b^{-1/2} = 2(1) + \dfrac{1}{4} = \dfrac{9}{4}$

22. **(H)** Average =
    $\dfrac{\text{Sum of the items}}{\text{Quantity of items}} = \dfrac{(x+1) + (3x-3)}{2}$
    $= \dfrac{4x - 2}{2}$
    $= 2x - 1$

23. **(A)** Addition of fractions requires a common denominator. In this case 6 is the lowest common denominator.
    $\dfrac{(a+b)(2)}{3 \quad (2)} + \dfrac{(a-b)(3)}{2 \quad (3)} = \dfrac{2a + 2b + 3a - 3b}{6}$
    $= \dfrac{5a - b}{6}$

24. **(H)** $\$80$
    -35 saved
    $\$45$ still required

    At $\$10$/wk it takes a minimum of 5 weeks to save the $\$45$

25. **(D)** $|y - 5| = 2$

    $y - 5 = -2 \quad | \quad y - 5 = 2$
    $y = 3 \quad\quad | \quad\quad y = 7$

    Check

    $|y - 5| = 2 \quad | \quad |y - 5| = 2$
    $|3 - 5| = 2 \quad | \quad |7 - 5| = 2$
    $|-2| = 2 \quad | \quad |2| = 2$
    $\sqrt{} \; 2 = 2 \quad\; | \quad\;\; 2 = 2 \; \sqrt{}$

26. **(G)**

    Two complementary angles sum to 90°.
    $x + (50 - n) = 90$
    $x = 40 + n$

27. **(E)** Parallel lines have the same slope. The equation of a line can be written as $y = mx + b$, where m is the slope. If $y = -\dfrac{2}{3}x + 4$, the slope $= -\dfrac{2}{3}$, and a line parallel to this line also has a slope of $-\dfrac{2}{3}$.

28. **(K)** Finding the coordinates of the intersection of two lines is equivalent to finding the ordered pair which is the solution to the system of equations.
    $2x + y = 4$
    $x - 2y = 2$

    To eliminate the y variable, multiply the first equation by 2 and add it to the second equation.

    $2(2x + y = 4) \rightarrow \quad 4x + 2y = 8$
    $x - 2y = 2 \quad\quad\quad\quad\;\; x - 2y = 2$
    $\quad\quad\quad\quad\quad\quad\quad\quad\; 5x \quad\quad = 10$
    $\quad\quad\quad\quad\quad\quad\quad\quad\;\; x \quad\quad = 2$

    Substitute $x = 2$ into the first equation and solve for y.
    $2x + y = 4$
    $2(2) + y = 4$
    $y = 0$

    The solution is: $(2, 0)$

29. **(C)** If the diameter $= 8$, $C = 2\pi r = \pi d = 8\pi$.

30. **(G)** $2x^3 + x^2 - 6x$
    $x(2x^2 + x - 6)$
    $x(2x - 3)(x + 2)$

31. **(A)** $\dfrac{6 \times 10^8}{3 \times 10^2} = \dfrac{6}{3} \times 10^{8-2}$
    $= 2 \times 10^6$

32. **(G)** $\dfrac{1}{2} + \dfrac{1}{3} = \dfrac{1}{2} \cdot \dfrac{3}{3} + \dfrac{1}{3} \cdot \dfrac{2}{2}$
    $= \dfrac{3}{6} + \dfrac{2}{6} = \dfrac{5}{6}$

    $\dfrac{6}{\dfrac{1}{2} + \dfrac{1}{3}} = \dfrac{6}{\dfrac{5}{6}} = \dfrac{6}{1} \cdot \dfrac{6}{5} = \dfrac{36}{5}$

33. (E)

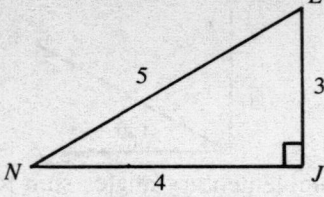

$\sin N = \dfrac{\text{side opposite angle } N}{\text{hypotenuse}} = \dfrac{3}{5}$

$\cos L = \dfrac{\text{side adjacent to angle } L}{\text{hypotenuse}} = \dfrac{3}{5}$

$(\sin N)(\cos L) = \left(\dfrac{3}{5}\right)\left(\dfrac{3}{5}\right) = \dfrac{9}{25}$

34. (K) $\sqrt{27} = \sqrt{9}\sqrt{3} = 3\sqrt{3}$
$\sqrt{12} = \sqrt{4}\sqrt{3} = 2\sqrt{3}$
$\sqrt{27} + \sqrt{12} = 3\sqrt{3} + 2\sqrt{3} = 5\sqrt{3}$

35. (D) The $-1 \le x$ indicates that the -1 is represented by a ● because of the "≤." x is greater than or equal to -1 is to the right of -1 on the number line.

The $x < 4$ indicates that the 4 is represented by a ○ because of the ">." x is less than 4 is to the left of 4 on the number line.

$-1 \le x < 4$ represents the intersection (overlap) of the two number line representations.

36. (G) Area $= \dfrac{1}{2}(\text{height})(\text{base}_1 + \text{base}_2)$

$= \dfrac{1}{2}(4)(7 + 12) = \dfrac{1}{2}(4)(19) = 38$

37. (D) The interior angles on the same side of the transversal are supplementary.
$(x - 20) + (x + 10) = 180$
$2x - 10 = 180$
$2x = 190$
$x = 95$

38. (F) Use the point-slope form of the equation of a line. $(y - y_1) = m(x - x_1)$ where $m =$ slope and (x_1, y_1) is a point on the line. If $m = 2$ and $(-1, -2)$ is on the line, then
$(y - (-2)) = 2(x - (-1))$
$y + 2 = 2(x + 1)$

39. (C) The median is the 'middle' score when the data is arrayed in increasing order.
70,70,70,70,85,85,85,90,90,95
85 is the median

40. (F)

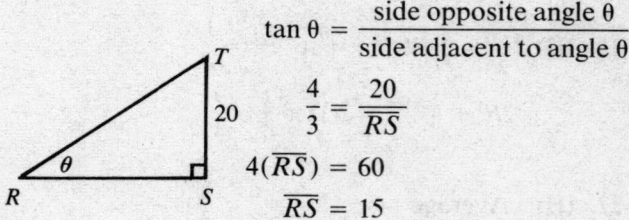

$\tan \theta = \dfrac{\text{side opposite angle } \theta}{\text{side adjacent to angle } \theta}$

$\dfrac{4}{3} = \dfrac{20}{\overline{RS}}$

$4(\overline{RS}) = 60$
$\overline{RS} = 15$

41. (A) Rationalize the denominator:
$\dfrac{5}{(2 - \sqrt{3})} \cdot \dfrac{(2 + \sqrt{3})}{(2 + \sqrt{3})} = \dfrac{5(2 + \sqrt{3})}{4 + 2\sqrt{3} - 2\sqrt{3} - \sqrt{9}}$
$= \dfrac{5(2 + \sqrt{3})}{4 - 3}$
$= 5(2 + \sqrt{3})$
$= 10 + 5\sqrt{3}$

42. (K)
$(1 - \cos\theta)(1 + \cos\theta) = 1 + \cos\theta - \cos\theta - \cos^2\theta$
$= 1 - \cos^2\theta$
but $\sin^2\theta + \cos^2\theta = 1 \rightarrow 1 - \cos^2\theta = \sin^2\theta$

43. (D) $f(x) = x + 4$
$f(2) = 2 + 4 = 6$
$f(6) = 6 + 4 = 10$
$f(f(2)) = f(6) = 10$

44. (J) The converse of a statement is the interchange of the hypothesis and conclusion. If the original statement is represented by $p \rightarrow q$, the converse is represented by $q \rightarrow p$.

45. (A)

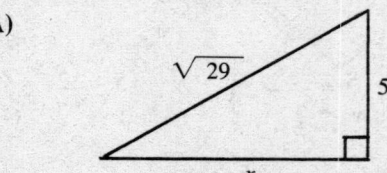

$x^2 + 5^2 = (\sqrt{29})^2$
$x^2 + 25 = 29$
$x^2 = 4$
$x = \pm 2$

The leg is 2.

ACT Practice Exam II / 393

46. (G) Line ratio = $\dfrac{\text{diagonal figure 1}}{\text{diagonal figure 2}}$

    $= \dfrac{\text{any line in figure 1}}{\text{corresponding line in figure 2}}$

    $= \dfrac{\text{perimeter of figure 1}}{\text{perimeter of figure 2}}$

    $\dfrac{4}{9}$ is also the perimeter ratio.

47. (E) $d = \sqrt{(x_2 - x_1)^2 + (y_2 - y_1)^2}$
    $= \sqrt{(8 - 2)^2 + (-1 - 7)^2}$
    $= \sqrt{6^2 + (-8)^2}$
    $= \sqrt{36 + 64}$
    $= \sqrt{100}$
    $= 10$

48. (F)

    Value of the discriminant ($b^2 - 4ac$)

	negative "−"	zero	positive perfect square	positive, not a perfect square
Nature of the roots	imaginary	real equal rational	real unequal rational	real unequal irrational
Graph	totally above or below the x-axis	tangent to the x-axis	intersects the x-axis at two distinct points	intersects the x-axis at two distinct points

    First arrange the quadratic equation into $ax^2 + bx + c = 0$ form.
    $x - 1 = x^2 - 2x + 1 \rightarrow x^2 - 3x + 2 = 0$
    $\therefore a = 1, b = -3, c = 2$
    The discriminant $= b^2 - 4ac$
    $= (-3)^2 - 4(1)(2)$
    $= 9 - 8$
    $= 1$

    With reference to the chart above if the discriminant $= 1$ the roots are real, unequal, rational and the graph intersects the x-axis at two distinct points.

49. (C) Written in point-slope form, the equation of a line is $(y - y_1) = m(x - x_1)$, where m is the slope of the line.

    For the equation $(y - 1) = 3(x - 6)$, the slope of the line $= 3$.

    Two lines are perpendicular if their slopes are negative reciprocals. The negative reciprocal of 3 is $-\dfrac{1}{3}$.

50. (F)

    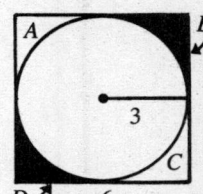

    The area of the 4 pieces (A, B, C, and D) can be found by subtracting the area of the circle (radius of 3) from the area of the square (side of 6).

    Area of $(A + B + C + D) =$ (area of the square) minus (area of the circle)
    $= (6)^2 - \pi(3)^2$
    $= 36 - 9\pi$

    The shaded area is regions B and D, which is
    $\dfrac{1}{2}(36 - 9\pi) = 18 - \dfrac{9}{2}\pi$

51. (C) Perimeter $= 4s = 4(\text{side}) = 3x$
    $\therefore \text{side} = \dfrac{3x}{4}$
    Area $= (\text{side})^2 = \left(\dfrac{3x}{4}\right)^2 = \dfrac{9x^2}{16}$

52. (F) recall: $i^1 = i$
    $i^2 = -1$
    $i^3 = -i$
    $i^4 = 1$
    $i^{10} = i^4 \cdot i^4 \cdot i^2 = (1)(1)(-1) = -1$
    $i^8 = i^4 \cdot i^4 = (1)(1) = 1$
    $i^6 = i^4 \cdot i^2 = (1)(-1) = -1$
    $i^2 = -1$

    $i^{10} + i^8 + i^6 + i^2 = (-1) + (1) + (-1) + (-1)$
    $= -1 + 1 - 1 - 1$
    $= -2$

53. (D) Probability of not orange =
    $\dfrac{\text{Number of ways not to pick an orange}}{\text{Number of ways to pick a marble}} =$
    $\dfrac{2 \text{ red} + 3 \text{ green}}{9 \text{ marbles}} = \dfrac{5}{9}$

394 / ACT

54. (H)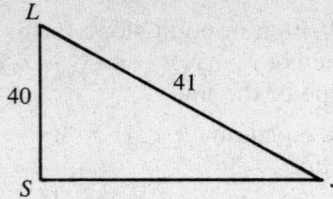

$$\sin L = \frac{\text{side opposite angle } L}{\text{hypotenuse}}$$

Find the side opposite angle L, $(\overline{SJ})$, using the Pythagorean theorem.

$$(\overline{SJ})^2 + (40)^2 = (41)^2$$
$$(\overline{SJ})^2 + 1600 = 1681$$
$$(\overline{SJ})^2 = 81$$
$$\overline{SJ} = 9$$

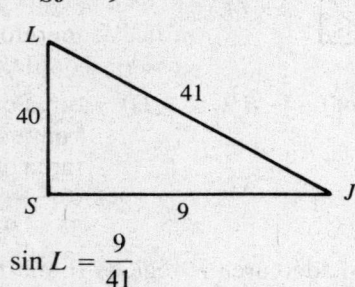

$$\sin L = \frac{9}{41}$$

55. (C) $x + y^2 - z = (-1) + (-1)^2 - (-1)$
$= (-1) + (1) - (-1)$
$= -1 + 1 + 1$
$= 1$

56. (K) $\sqrt{x+1} + 2 = 0$
$\sqrt{x+1} = -2$

Square both sides of the equation.
$(\sqrt{x+1})^2 = (-2)^2$
$x + 1 = 4$
$x = 3$

Check:
$\sqrt{x+1} + 2 = 0$
$\sqrt{3+1} + 2 \stackrel{?}{=} 0$
$\sqrt{4} + 2 \stackrel{?}{=} 0$
$2 + 2 \stackrel{?}{=} 0$
$4 = 0$ No

There are no solutions. The solution set is the null or empty set $\{\ \}$.

57. (E) The area A of a sphere varies directly as the square of the radius r.

This can be expressed mathematically as:

$$\frac{A}{r} = \text{constant} \quad \text{or} \quad \frac{A_1}{r_1} = \frac{A_2}{r_2}$$

If $A_1 = 36\pi$ when $r_1 = 3$, then what is A_2 when $r_2 = 6$?

$$\frac{A_1}{(r_1)^2} = \frac{A_2}{(r_2)^2} \rightarrow \frac{36\pi}{(3)^2} = \frac{A_2}{(6)^2} \rightarrow \frac{36\pi}{9} = \frac{A}{36}$$

$$4\pi = \frac{A}{36}$$

Use cross-multiplication

$$A = 4\pi(36)$$
$$= 144\pi$$

58. (G) $\left(\dfrac{\text{piece}}{\text{whole}}\right) 100 = \%$

$\left(\dfrac{x}{6}\right) 100 = \dfrac{100x}{6}\%$

59. (B)

Values of the discriminant ($b^2 - 4ac$)

	negative "−"	zero	positive perfect square	positive, not a perfect square
About the graph	Totally above or below the x-axis. Does not intersect the x-axis	Tangent to the x-axis	Intersects the x-axis at two distinct points	Intersects the x-axis at two distinct points

The discriminant ($b^2 - 4ac$) of the equation $2x^2 - 5x + 3 = 0$ is
$b^2 - 4ac = (-5)^2 - 4(2)(3)$
$= 25 - 24 = 1$

∴ The graph intersects the x-axis at only two distinct points.

ACT Practice Exam II / 395

60. **(H)** The multiplicative inverse of a number is that number which when multiplied by the original number gives a product of 1. The reciprocal of a number, times the original number yields a product of 1.

$$a \cdot \frac{1}{a} = 1$$

The reciprocal of $1 - \sqrt{2}$ is $\frac{1}{1 - \sqrt{2}}$.

Rationalize:

$$\frac{1}{(1 - \sqrt{2})} \cdot \frac{(1 + \sqrt{2})}{(1 + \sqrt{2})} = \frac{1 + \sqrt{2}}{1 + \sqrt{2} - \sqrt{2} - \sqrt{4}}$$

$$= \frac{1 + \sqrt{2}}{1 - \sqrt{4}} = \frac{1 + \sqrt{2}}{1 - 2}$$

$$= \frac{1 + \sqrt{2}}{-1} = -1 - \sqrt{2}$$

3. Reading Test

1. **(C)** The second paragraph states that party leaders "... vote as they're told to vote ..."

2. **(F)** Both Bulgarian and American politicians listen to speeches. American politicians, however, have the option to leave.

3. **(D)** The third paragraph states that the Bulgarian "... audience sat through it (the speech) because it had to."

4. **(G)** The third paragraph indicates that the Bulgarian Party Congress is typical of Party Congresses in all Communist states.

5. **(A)** Since everyone in Congress is allowed to speak, one can conclude that political arguments occur in public.

6. **(J)** The passage states the length of time given for members of the House of Representatives. No length of time is mandated for Senators.

7. **(B)** The next-to-last paragraph states that "Senators can walk out, and do."

8. **(F)** The last paragraph mentions the one-minute rule.

9. **(D)** The last sentence of the passage states: "But, fortunately, we don't have the listeners."

10. **(H)** The author stresses the fact that American politicians are free to leave when their colleagues make speeches.

11. **(B)** The narrator states in the second paragraph that the men are cold; therefore, he wants Broadhurst to march off.

12. **(G)** The second paragraph mentions that the narrator was unversed in the ways of the army.

13. **(D)** The narrator apologized to Broadhurst but did not approach the lieutenant. He says the act showed "cowardice"; therefore, it can be assumed that the narrator feared the lieutenant.

14. **(J)** The lieutenant was furious at Broadhurst for marching off without permission and did not give Broadhurst a chance to explain.

15. **(B)** Broadhurst was not terribly concerned or upset at being reprimanded through no fault of his own. He told the narrator to forget the incident.

16. **(F)** In the second paragraph Broadhurst expresses doubt about the wisdom of marching off before the platoon commander's arrival.

17. **(C)** The last paragraph summarizes what insights the narrator gained from this incident.

18. **(F)** The first sentence states that the narrator found "... the platoon assembled and ready to go."

19. **(B)** The passage recounts the author's experience and describes his feelings about the incident.

20. **(H)** The point of the passage is that the author learned that he must act in a way consistent with his image of himself.

21. **(D)** The author uses the phrase "untaught minds" to mean persons who lack specific education in distinct areas. The other choices refer to general categories of persons; therefore, they are incorrect.

22. **(H)** Paragraph 2 discusses the main difference between innovators and noninnovators as one of approach.

23. **(A)** Lines 25–28 describe "... our reaction of

deceptively simple innovations . . ." as "How come nobody thought of that before?"

24. **(G)** The key phrase is ". . . with a new twist." This tells the reader that the author is looking for a fresh perspective.

25. **(D)** The answer lies at the end of the fifth paragraph. It states that the innovator will consider alternate courses in his search for the best route.

26. **(H)** The phrase is preceded by a paragraph that tells us that the innovator will *not* automatically set out for the best-known and apparently simplest routing; instead, he will search for alternate courses. Thus he is motivated by his own thoughts and feelings about life.

27. **(C)** This passage is meant to teach us something about creativity; hence, it is instructive.

28. **(G)** The main idea of the passage is best and most simply stated at its conclusion. Creativity is following one's own perceptions, not being part of a crowd.

29. **(A)** The author uses the expertise of Rudolph Flesch to strengthen his assertion that creativity requires a new look at old things.

30. **(F)** The author has developed his thesis about creativity sufficiently at this point. He would most likely give some examples of creative individuals and their specific fields of endeavor. This would best strengthen and complement the passage.

31. **(B)** The third paragraph states that Nikolskii ". . . argues that Darwin's concept of constant overpopulation has led to the neglect of the problem of protecting spawners and young fish."

32. **(J)** The main focus of the research is concerned with commercial fishing.

33. **(B)** The amount of fishing pressure on a species is the basic concept behind the Darwinian theory.

34. **(H)** This choice is supported by the statement that the "mass and age structure of a population are the result of adaptation to the food supply."

35. **(A)** The passage compares the Darwinian concept of overpopulation of young fish with Nikolskii's alternative theories.

36. **(J)** Darwin claims fish population depends upon fishing pressure on the species, while Nikolskii's view is that population is a result of the food supply. This illustrates a major difference of opinion regarding population of a species.

37. **(B)** Of the answer choices listed only response B is not mentioned as affecting fish population.

38. **(H)** The second paragraph states: "The unfished population tends toward a maximum equilibrium size with a relatively high proportion of large, old individuals."

39. **(B)** The second paragraph states that as fishing increases, population size and proportions of old fish are reduced.

40. **(H)** The authors state in paragraph 2 that fishing mortality eventually takes the place of most natural mortality.

4. Science Reasoning Test

1. **(B)** This question asks for a constant rate of growth, or for the part of the curve that exhibits a constant slope. The slope of a curve is defined as the rate of change, and a constant rate of change represents a straight line. Choice **A** describes a part of the curve that rises exponentially; choices **C** and **D** describe logarithmic portions of the curve. This type of S-shaped curve is called the logistic growth curve.

2. **(J)** In Experiment 4 the population of bacteria 1 decreased to zero by day 25. In Experiments 2 and 3, bacteria 1 grew faster than bacteria 2, and would therefore be considered a more efficient competitor. Experiment 1 does not directly support a hypothesis on competition.

3. **(C)** If the two strains of bacteria restricted themselves to only part of the available environment, both populations would grow, but both growth curves would be lower than the ideal curves of Experiment 1, in which the bacteria could utilize all the resources of the culture dish.

4. **(J)** In Experiments 2 and 4, one strain of bacteria outcompetes the other; the outcomes of these experiments are reversed. Choice **F** is incorrect because we are not given any information on the individual

lifespans of the bacteria; the 20 days represented on the *x*-axis represent the duration of the experiment. While we cannot conclusively analyze the nutrient requirements or individual reproductive rates of the bacteria (**G** and **H**), it is evident that some form of interspecific competition—competition between different species that often results in the extinction of one of the species—is involved.

5. **(D)** This question tests to see if you understand the limits of the experiment. The experimental procedure measures **population growth** but does not deal directly with the lifespans of the individual members of the populations. Actual population growth involves complicated calculations of birth rates and death rates, but this experiment does not address those issues.

6. **(H)** This question merely asks you to read from the graph. Choice **F** results in strong frost action; choice **G** in moderate chemical weathering with frost action; and choice **J** also results in strong frost action.

7. **(A)** Since the freezing point of water is 0°C, there is very little freezing at 13°C, which is equivalent to over 50°F. Choice **C** is wrong because there can be a great deal of precipitation at 13°C; choice **D** is incorrect because "too much" precipitation is imprecise and probably by itself would not eliminate frost action.

8. **(G)** The dotted line on the graph represents the limit of possible temperature–precipitation conditions on Earth. For the given temperature at location X, the precipitation conditions are beyond the possible limit of Earth. Choice **F** goes beyond the scope of the information given; location Y lies just within the possible limit of Earth conditions; and there cannot be too much precipitation at X, since those conditions could not exist.

9. **(C)** This question asks you to determine the nature of the absolute temperature–precipitation relationship. As the limit line suggests, as temperature rises, precipitation rises. This is the definition of a direct relationship.

10. **(J)** These two types of weathering are at opposite ends of the graph, and there is no point of intersection between them. Therefore, both cannot occur simultaneously according to the information given.

11. **(B)** In a temperate region, with constant precipitation that totals 160 mm, the summer months would cause the most chemical weathering, and the colder months would cause the least.

12. **(H)** The main difference between the scientists, as the names of their theories imply, is the rate at which the creation of new species occur. Both agree that new species do arise, so choice **F** is incorrect. Scientist 2 merely says that the fossil record does not support gradualism, but he does not argue that it is irrelevant to the question of speciation. Choice **J** mentions ecological disturbances, but neither scientist questions their presence during evolution.

13. **(A)** According to the gradualism theory, two species are created when part of the original population breaks from the ancestral species, and some reproductive barrier isolates the segments until one has evolved along a different line from the other. There are no sharp breaks as in choice **B**. Choice **C** neglects the gradual evolution from an ancestral species; instead, one species replaces the other.

14. **(F)** Scientist 2 dismisses gradualism because of lack of evidence, but choice **F** provides the data to support Scientist 1's argument. Choices **G** and **H** both would tend to support Scientist 2.

15. **(D)** The central tenet of Scientist 1's argument is that species gradually grow apart, until the two segmented populations can no longer reproduce. Choice **A** disregards the main body of evidence of evolutionary research; choice **B** supports Scientist 2.

16. **(J)** In his third sentence, Scientist 1 argues that random mutations and inheritable competitive advantages can "dominate" a species. This is the classic definition of natural selection. Scientist 2 also asserts in his discussion of giraffes that an ecological crisis might render an entire segment of the population (giraffes with short necks) unable to secure food. This inability to adapt to a new environmental condition that results in extinction is another example of natural selection.

17. **(C)** It would be very unlikely that the only complete fossil record was an exception to the gradualism theory, and molluscs are certainly evolutionarily significant creatures. The question does not mention the conditions under which the molluscs were found (i.e., whether they were reproductively isolated), so choices **A**, **B**, and **D** are incorrect. Choice **C** is the only reasonable assertion Scientist 1 can make, since the soft innards of a mollusc would not fossilize.

18. **(J)** Five generations of human life is an insignificant passage of time on the evolutionary time-scale, which has stretched back millions of years. Evolutionary change would be infinitesimal for most species over such a short period of time. Punctuated equilibrium implies rapid change, but rapid in the

specific sense of evolutionary time. (20,000 years is considered fairly rapid in this sense.)

19. **(C)** Since voltage is directly related to current, voltage increases by the same factor as current if other variables are held constant. The same applies for resistance; therefore, the only correct formula is choice **C**.

20. **(G)** According to the formula $V = IR$, the circuit with the greater resistance would have the greater voltage. Since resistance is directly proportional to resistivity, the germanium circuit would have the greater resistance and voltage.

21. **(A)** The total resistance R_s of the series resistors is $R_1 + R_2 = 2 + 2 = 4$. This resistance is double that of the circuit where $R = 2$. If R doubles, then the voltage doubles as long as the current remains the same.

22. **(J)** According to the formula for resistors in parallel,
$$\frac{1}{R_p} = \frac{1}{4} + \frac{1}{4} = \frac{2}{4} = \frac{1}{2}$$
$$\frac{1}{R_p} = \frac{1}{2}$$
$$R_p = 2$$

23. **(C)** If R is constant, then P increases with I^2; this is a straightforward definition of exponential growth.

24. **(J)** If $V = IR$, then $I = \frac{V}{R}$. In order to keep I constant, if V increases, then R must be increased.

25. **(B)** According to Diagram II, which represents a lateral cross section of the stream, the slope of the ground is steepest at point B. This would probably be the point at which water flows fastest.

26. **(F)** Potential energy is the energy stored in the stream that has not been translated into kinetic or heat energy. This would occur at the highest point of the stream, where the water has the most potential to flow downhill.

27. **(C)** As the water flows from the stream into the wider mouth of the ocean, the flow slackens and loses kinetic energy. Sediment that had been caught in the turbulence of the flow would settle out between E and F.

28. **(F)** The stream would acquire the most kinetic energy on the north side of the turn. The water velocity is greater on the outside of the bend (in this case, north) and slower on the inside (south). The greater north side water speed will cause the north bank to erode faster, leading to a steeper stream bank. The slower south side water speed would cause a slower, more gradual erosion on the south side. Choice **F** represents the faster erosion into the north bank and slower, more gradual erosion on the south side.

29. **(C)** Assuming no upheavals, the oldest rock would have been deposited first, and would occupy the lowest bedrock layer. The shale at point D is the "lowest" and oldest layer that the stream encounters. Note that the limestone under the shale is older, but that the stream does not come in contact with it.

30. **(H)** There are four pots for each group. The math is $20 \times 4 = 80$ for Group IV; $10 \times 4 = 40$ for Group III; $5 \times 4 = 20$ for Group II; and $1 \times 4 = 4$ for Group I. The total is $80 + 40 + 20 + 4 = 144$. Choice **F** accounts for only 1 pot for each group.

31. **(B)** The key to this question is that all procedures that are applied *equally* to all the pots are valid. Choices **A**, **C**, and **D** are not conducive to growth, but they are valid so long as the conditions are the same for all the seedlings. Only choice **B** violates that rule.

32. **(G)** The pie graph (Figure 4) depicts a *total* of 51 deaths, so immediately choices **H** and **J** are incorrect. The question boils down to: what is 62 percent of 51 total deaths; 62 percent of 51 is approximately 32.

33. **(C)** The average daily growth rate of Group II seedlings was approximately 1.5 mm/day. Over a period of seven days, the seedling would have grown $1.5 \times 7 = 10.5$ mm. This question was easy so long as you noted the label on the y-axis of Figure 1.

34. **(J)** A negative growth rate can only imply that the seedlings were shrinking; it is not connected to seedling deaths, and even slow growers would exhibit a small positive rate.

35. **(C)** This question involves several steps. First you must determine what the original number of Group III deaths was. Since 20 percent of 51 is 10.2, you may express the number of plant deaths simply as 10. If 5 more Group III seedlings die, and the total deaths remain at 51, then Group III deaths account for 15 of the 51 total deaths. All that remains is to approximate what percentage is 15 of 51. The equation boils down to $51 \times Y = 15$; or $Y = 15/51$. You may approximate the percentage as $Y = 15/50$, which reduces to $3/10$, or 0.3. Thus the answer is 30%. (The actual value will be slightly less than 30%, since the denominator of the equation is slightly larger than 50.)

36. **(F)** The death rate for the 6–20 gram/day choles-

terol eater from prostate cancer is 1.03, while that for a non-cholesterol eater is 2.02. Thus, choice **F** is correct. Choice **G** contradicts the data for colon cancer; choice **H** ignores the direct relationship between coronary deaths and cholesterol intake; and cardiac arrest is a more common form of death than cerebral clots for the 20+ eaters.

37. **(D)** The death rate for all three groups of cholesterol eaters from depression is 0.30. This number is lower than for non-cholesterol eaters, so choices **A** and **B** are both wrong. According to the data, large amounts of cholesterol are just as effective in combating depression as small amounts, so choice **C** is incorrect.

38. **(J)** Although the 20+ diet increases coronary arrest to the highest absolute death rate, the percentage increase is less than 100% (from 6.00 to 11.00). The percentage increase for coronary thrombosis is greater than 100% (from 5.02 to 10.05).

39. **(C)** This question merely requires you to read off the chart, and choice **C** is the only group in which low intake of cholesterol decreases the death rate from all three diseases. Intake of 0–5 grams raises the probability of death for lung and colon cancer only. This question is probably best answered by recognizing that fact and eliminating those choices that include either lung or colon cancer.

40. **(G)** Standardizing the death rate involves correcting for variables inherent in the subject groups but not involved in the experiment. Age, weight, genetic histories, and accidental deaths are just some of the variables that the scientist must consider when working with human subjects. However, choice **F** does not correct for intrinsic variables; rather it ignores results that might not conform to a "neat" result. This does not standardize the death rate so much as "fudge" it. Choice **H** involves an arbitrary assumption that is in fact incorrect. Assuming a zero death rate in the male population distorts the result of this experiment and does not correct for variations within the subject groups. Choice **J** is incorrect because this experiment does not consider women at all. It might be valid to compare results with a different experiment involving men, but the actual death rates for men and women for different diseases are not necessarily similar. Consider, for example, the gender-related differences for breast cancer.

Answer Sheet for Practice Exam III

1. English Test

2. Mathematics Test

3. Reading Test

4. Science Reasoning Test

1. ENGLISH TEST

45 Minutes—75 Questions

DIRECTIONS: In the passage(s) below, certain words and phrases are underlined and numbered. In the right-hand column, you will find choices for each underlined part. You are to select the one that best expresses the idea, makes the statement appropriate for standard written English, or is worded most consistently with the style and mood of the passage as a whole. If you think the original version is best, choose "NO CHANGE." You will also find questions about a section of the passage, or about the passage as a whole. These questions are indicated by a number or numbers in a box. For each question in the test, choose the choice you consider best and blacken the corresponding space on your answer sheet. Read each passage through once before you begin to answer the questions that accompany it. You cannot determine most answers without reading several sentences beyond the phrase in question.

Passage I

The following paragraphs may or may not be in the most sensible order. Each paragraph is numbered in parentheses, and item 12 will ask you to choose the sequence of paragraph numbers that is most sensible.

(1)

No contemporary American has thought more about peace, fought longer for it, or written clearer about it than William R. Marshall.
        1

(2)

He began to get started in the late nineteenth
             2

century when he met Anton Gates, who established the "International Peace Foundation".
                     3

Gates is long since gone but his foundation survives, and Marshall still expounds inter-

1. **A.** NO CHANGE
   B. writes clearer
   C. written more clearly
   D. more clearly writes

2. **F.** NO CHANGE
   G. starting
   H. to start
   J. OMIT the underlined portion.

3. **A.** NO CHANGE
   B. International Peace Foundation
   C. (International Peace Foundation)
   D. international peace foundation

nationalism with the undiminished conviction that

man can govern themselves.
            ―――――――――――――
                  4

(3)

Despite Marshall's papers span the whole of
―――――
   5

our twentieth century, they are not dated. They
              ―――――――――――
                    6
prove conclusively that intergovernmental organizations will not be able to maintain peace unless governments give up to them enough of their own sovereignty. Marshall, however, does not advocate world government in a form that would irritate anyone but a card-carrying Internationalist.

(4)

The final section of the volume deals with Mr. Gates' ideals and Mr. Marshall's attempts, through international organization, to eliminate
                                            ――――――――――
                                                 7
armed struggle. The author is frank about his disillusionment and honest in his criticism. He makes the point that we will not lose our democracy through stronger international government, but that this here represents the only way to maintain
     ―――――――
        8

it in a increasingly militaristic world.
       ―――――――――――――――――――――
                  9

4. F. NO CHANGE
   G. self-govern
   H. govern himself
   J. be governed by itself

5. A. NO CHANGE
   B. However
   C. Though
   D. OMIT the underlined portion.

6. F. NO CHANGE
   G. century; they
   H. century they
   J. century: they

7. A. NO CHANGE
   B. eliminated
   C. eliminates
   D. eliminating

8. F. NO CHANGE
   G. them there
   H. this
   J. these

9. A. NO CHANGE
   B. an increasing militaristic
   C. a militaristic increasing
   D. an increasingly militaristic

404 / ACT

(5)

The first part of this volume, discusses the
great increase in the power of the Presidency to determine foreign policy, and how the growing impact of international affairs on our internal affairs adds to this power.

10. F. NO CHANGE
G. volume;
H. volume:
J. volume

(6)

Part two outlines the differences in the development of the federal system in the United States and that of the South American Republics. Federalism is now sufficiently understood so that it can operate in any manner needed to meet man's demands, whether on a national or international basis. Federalism, as Lincoln proved is never static but grows as necessity demands. [12]

11. A. NO CHANGE
B. —as Lincoln proved,
C. as Lincoln proved
D. , as Lincoln proved,

12. Select the order of paragraph numbers that will make the essay's structure most logical.
F. NO CHANGE
G. 1, 2, 6, 5, 3, 4
H. 1, 2, 3, 4, 6, 5
J. 1, 2, 3, 5, 6, 4

Passage II

Of all the areas of learning the most important are the development of attitudes. Emotional reactions as well as logical thought processes effect the behavior of most people.

"The burnt child fears the fire" is one instance; another is the rise of despots like Hitler. Both these examples also point up the fact that atti-

13. A. NO CHANGE
B. was
C. is
D. were

14. F. NO CHANGE
G. affect
H. effecting
J. affecting

15. A. NO CHANGE
B. Each
C. Each of
D. All

tudes stem from experience. In the one case the experience was direct and impressive, in the other case it was indirect and cumulative. The Nazis were indoctrinated largely by the speeches they heard and the books they read. [16]

The classroom teacher in the elementary school is in a strategic position to influence attitudes. This is true partly being that children acquire atti-
                              ——17——
tudes from those adults whose word they respect.

Another reason it is true is because pupils often
                                  ——18——
delve somewhat deeply into a subject in school that has only been touched upon at home or has possibly never occurred to them before. To a child who had previously acquired little knowledge of Mexico, his teacher's method of handling such a unit would greatly affect his attitude toward Mexicans the people of Mexico.
                                   ——19——

The medium through which the teacher can
      ——20——
develop wholesome attitudes are innumerable. Social studies (with special reference to races, creeds, and nationalities), science matters of health and safety, the very atmosphere of the classroom—these are a few of the fertile fields for the inculcation of proper emotional reactions.
                                    ——21——
However, when children come to school with undesirable attitudes, it is unwise for the

16. Is the use of examples in this paragraph appropriate?

F. No, because they detract from the main thesis.
G. No, because the examples are irrelevant to the topic being discussed.
H. Yes, because the examples give substance to the assertion that attitudes come from experience.
J. Yes, because the examples are an integral part of the main point being made.

17. A. NO CHANGE
    B. being as
    C. being
    D. because

18. F. NO CHANGE
    G. that
    H. since
    J. until

19. A. NO CHANGE
    B. Mexico's people
    C. people in Mexico
    D. OMIT the underlined portion.

20. F. NO CHANGE
    G. media
    H. medium of exchange
    J. channel

21. A. NO CHANGE
    B. emotionally
    C. emotionalism
    D. emotions

teacher to attempt to change his feelings by
cajoling or scolding them. She can achieve the
proper effect by helping them obtain constructive
experiences. [23]

Finally, a teacher who constantly evaluates her
own attitudes, because her influence can be
deleterious if she has personal prejudices. This is
especially true in respect to controversial issues
and questions on which children should be
encouraged to reach their own decisions as a
result of objective analysis of all the facts. [25]

22. F. NO CHANGE
    G. its
    H. her
    J. their

23. The author could most effectively strengthen the passage here by adding which of the following?
    A. The sentence "Teachers are important."
    B. A paragraph containing illustrations of constructive experiences at school which can help change undesirable attitudes
    C. A definition of undesirable attitudes
    D. An example of a teacher scolding her students for the undesirable attitudes they hold

24. F. NO CHANGE
    G. who is constantly evaluating
    H. must constantly evaluate
    J. constantly evaluating

25. Is the use of parentheses appropriate in this passage?
    A. No, because formal writing requires no extra punctuation mark.
    B. No, because parentheses are only used to enclose figures or letters within a sentence.
    C. Yes, because parentheses are used to enclose parenthetical material, specific details, and examples.
    D. Yes, they add emphasis.

Passage III

> The following paragraphs may or may not be in the most sensible order. Each paragraph is numbered in parentheses, and item 37 will ask you to choose the sequence of paragraph numbers that is most sensible.

(1)

Like the United States today, Athens had courts where a wrong might be righted.
                                                       26

Any citizen might accuse another of a crime,
       27
the Athenian courts of law were very busy. In fact, unless a citizen is unusual peaceful or very
                                             28
unimportant, he would be sure to find himself in the courts at least once every few years.

(2)

At a trial both the accuser plus the person
                                 29
accused were allowed a certain time to speak.

The length of time to be marked by a water
                        30
clock. Free men testified under oath as they do today, while the oath of a slave was counted as
             31
worthless.

(3)

Judging a trial, a jury was chosen from the
  32
members of the assembly who had reached 30 years of age. The Athenian juries were very

26. F. NO CHANGE
    G. right
    H. fixed
    J. changed

27. A. NO CHANGE
    B. Anyone who was a citizen
    C. Although any citizen
    D. Since any citizen

28. F. NO CHANGE
    G. was unusual peaceful
    H. is unusually peaceful
    J. was unusually peaceful

29. A. NO CHANGE
    B. and
    C. or
    D. also

30. F. NO CHANGE
    G. was marked
    H. being marked
    J. marked

31. A. NO CHANGE
    B. since
    C. but
    D. until

32. F. NO CHANGE
    G. To judge
    H. Judge
    J. Judged

large, often consisting of 201; 401; 501; 1,001 or more men, depending upon the importance of the case being tried. The juryman swore by the gods to listen careful to both sides of the question and to give his honest opinion of the case. Each juryman gave his decision by depositing a white or black stone in a box. To keep citizens from being too careless in accusing each other, there was a rule that if the person accused did not receive a certain number of negative votes, the accuser was condemned instead. [36] [37]

33. A. NO CHANGE
    B. 201: 401: 501: 1,001
    C. 201. 401. 501. 1,001
    D. 201, 401, 501, 1001

34. F. NO CHANGE
    G. to be careful in listening
    H. to carefully listen
    J. to listen carefully

35. A. NO CHANGE
    B. to be careless
    C. being too careless
    D. careless

36. This passage was probably excerpted from
    F. a political science text.
    G. a newspaper article.
    H. a grammar textbook.
    J. a monograph on jurisprudence in Greece and America.

37. Choose the sequence of paragraphs that will make the essay's structure most orderly.
    A. NO CHANGE
    B. 3, 2, 1
    C. 2, 1, 3
    D. 1, 3, 2

Passage IV

Back in 1892, when Baron Pierre deCoubertin re-created the Olympics, the purpose of the games was to foster friendly competition between athletes and nations. The Olympic arena was to be the showcase for the strongest, the fleetest, the athletes who were most graceful of every nation.

Unfortunately, deCoubertins dream has been subverted by increasing politicization of the games. Adolph Hitler began this trend in 1936.

38. F. NO CHANGE
    G. betwixt
    H. about
    J. among

39. A. NO CHANGE
    B. the athletes of most grace
    C. the most graceful
    D. the more graceful

40. F. NO CHANGE
    G. deCoubertins'
    H. deCoubertin's
    J. deCoubertin

The 1936 games were held in Berlin, Germany, and the American black athlete, Jesse Owens, won four gold medals. Departing from the tradition by which the leader of the host nation congratulates gold medalists, Hitler refusing to shake hands with a black man.

In 1968, the medal ceremony was again used as a political vehicle. This time three black Americans whom had won medals in a track and field event displayed the black power sign as they stood on the stand to receive there medals.

The Olympic Committee it has perpetuated the politicization of the games with its ongoing debate over which Chinese delegation—the People's Republic of China (Red China) or the Nationalist Republic of China (Taiwan)—should represent the Chinese people.

The bleaker of all years in modern Olympic history was 1972. First, committees of predominantly Communist judges handed down blatant biased rulings in boxing matches, gymnastic competitions, and basketball games. Then, far worse, a group of Palestinian terrorists attacked the Israeli quarters, took hostages, and held siege. Eleven innocent Israeli athletes were killed.

41. A. NO CHANGE
    B. was held
    C. were to be held
    D. being held

42. F. NO CHANGE
    G. refused
    H. refuses
    J. refuse

43. A. NO CHANGE
    B. who
    C. which
    D. what

44. F. NO CHANGE
    G. they're
    H. some
    J. their

45. A. NO CHANGE
    B. oneself
    C. themselves
    D. itself

46. F. NO CHANGE
    G. bleakest
    H. more bleak
    J. most bleakest

47. A. NO CHANGE
    B. blatantly biased rulings
    C. blatant rulings that were biased
    D. blatant, biased rulings

In light of this history, it is difficult to understand the public outcry against politicization by boycott of the 1980 games. The purpose of the 1980 boycott is to protest the invasion in late December 1979 of Afghanistan by the U.S.S.R. The locale of the 1980 Olympics in Moscow, and the presents there of international press, dignitaries, and athletes is a powerful propaganda opportunity for the Russians. Russia can show its own people how popular and important it is; the world can be shown the brightest aspects of life in the U.S.S.R. Boycott of the Olympics by a large portion of the free world would seriously damage the propaganda value of the games.

A show of solidarity by the governments and the athletes of the "free world" might demonstrate to the Russians that conquest and domination of weaker countries will no longer be tolerated. The Olympics might, in an oblique way, turn out to be the instrument of peace and freedom for small nations. [49] [50]

48. F. NO CHANGE
    G. present
    H. presence
    J. arrival

49. The style of this passage can best be described as
    A. didactic
    B. prose fiction.
    C. narrative.
    D. historical.

50. The author's primary purpose in writing this passage was most probably to
    F. discourage politicization of the Olympic games.
    G. provide a purely historical account of the Olympic games.
    H. protest the killing of Olympic athletes in 1972.
    J. encourage support of the 1980 boycott of the Olympic games.

Passage V

Had I lived in ancient Rome I might of sipped a
                                        ―――
                                         51
broth made by soaking Allium cepa—an onion—in
warm water to relieve the symptoms of the common cold. In Colonial America you might have relied on pennyroyal tea or an herbal concoction made from such unmedicinal sounding plants as (sage, hyssop, yarrow, black cohash, buckthorn, coltsfoot, goldenseal, cube berries or bloodroot.)
In grandmas time, the combination of lemon and
   ―――――――――
       52

honey were a favorite recipe, or in extreme cases,
      ――――
       53
a hot toddy laced with rum—the amount of same determined by the age of the drinker.

Today, if you don't have an old reliable remedy to fall back on, you might take one of literally thousands of drug preparations available without prescription. Some contain ingredients reminiscence of the folk medicine of the
        ――――――――――――
              54

past, others are formulated with sophisticated
    ―――――――
       55
chemical creations. Old or new, simple or sophisticated, many of these remedies will relieve some of the familiar cold symptoms, such as a stopped-up nose or hacking cough. But not a

51. A. NO CHANGE
    B. have
    C. had
    D. OMIT the underlined portion.

52. F. NO CHANGE
    G. grandmas' time
    H. old folks' time
    J. grandma's time

53. A. NO CHANGE
    B. is
    C. has
    D. was

54. F. NO CHANGE
    G. reminding
    H. reminiscent
    J. remiss

55. A. NO CHANGE
    B. past others
    C. past; others
    D. past. Others which

single one of these products—on which Americans spend an estimated $700 million a year—will prevent, cure, or even shorten the course of the common cold.

So says a panel of non-government experts called on by the Food and Drug Administration to study the safety, the effectiveness, and the accuracy of claims of some 50,000 cold, cough, allergy, bronchodilator, and antiasthmatic drug products made on the labels. [58]

56. F. NO CHANGE
    G. where Americans spend an estimated $700 million a year
    H. a lot of money gets spent on them
    J. OMIT the underlined portion.

57. A. NO CHANGE
    B. (Place after *accuracy*)
    C. (Place after *claims*)
    D. OMIT the underlined portion.

58. Suppose at this point in the passage the writer wanted to add more information about this study. Which of the following additions would be most relevant to this paragraph?
    F. the sentence "The panel is only an advisory panel."
    G. a description of the selection process used in choosing panel members
    H. a definition of nonprescription drugs
    J. a sentence explaining the role of the panel and the desired goals of the project

---

Questions 59 to 62 refer to the passage as a whole.

---

59. This passage was probably written for readers who
    A. have careers in the medical field
    B. have suffered or who are currently suffering from the common cold
    C. represent large pharmaceutical firms
    D. are engaged in scientific research regarding the common cold

60. Is the writer's use of the pronoun "I" appropriate in the essay?
    F. Yes, because this passage is more interesting in the first person.
    G. No, because the writer alternately uses first and second person in the passage and only the second person should be used.
    H. Yes, because it gives emphasis to a common problem—the cold.
    J. No, because the use of the pronoun "I" is never used in formal writing.

61. Is the use of the dash appropriate in this passage?
    A. Yes, because the dash is used to set off interruptions, additions, and illustrations.
    B. No, because a colon would be more effective.
    C. No, because the dash is never used in formal writing.
    D. Yes, because commas are too distracting to the reader.

62. Is the use of parentheses appropriate in this passage?
    F. Yes, because formal writing requires extra punctuation marks.
    G. Yes, because parentheses are used to enclose parenthetical material.
    H. No, because parentheses are only used to enclose figures or letters used for enumeration within a sentence.
    J. No, because essential information should be enclosed in parentheses.

Passage VI

> The following paragraphs may or may not be in the most sensible order. Each paragraph is numbered in parentheses, and item 75 will ask you to choose the order of paragraph numbers that is most sensible.

(1)

Mention the word caffeine, says George E. Boecklin, president, of the National Coffee Association, and most people will think you are talking about coffee. "When a story breaks about caffeine, it's immediately translated in the consumer's mind to coffee," he declared. "He doesn't think about Coca-Cola, just coffee."

63. A. NO CHANGE
    B. president of the National Coffee Association—
    C. president of the National Coffee Association,
    D. president of the National Coffee Association

(2)

But today the makers of soft drinks are the big user of caffeine, and in 1985, soft drinks surpassed coffee for the first time as the favorite beverage of Americans. (People all over the world enjoy soft drinks.)

64. F. NO CHANGE
    G. more bigger
    H. biggest
    J. most big

65. A. NO CHANGE
    B. (People in other countries enjoy soft drinks.)
    C. (Soft drinks are enjoyed by people all around the world.)
    D. OMIT the underlined portion.

(3)

It's not surprising that caffeine and coffee are

viewed like being almost synonymous. Coffee has
been around for centuries. For years it has been
America's most-popular beverage and the largest
single source of caffeine in the human diet.

(4)

Coffee consumption reached its peak in the United States in 1962, when nearly three out of four Americans were consuming the beverage. Today, slightly more than half the population drinks coffee. [68]

Today, according to the coffee industry survey, nearly six out of every ten persons (58 percent) include soft drinks in they're daily diet.

(5)

In addition to the steady drop in the percentage of the U.S. population that drinks coffee, consumption among coffee drinkers has also dropped—from more than four cups a day per person in 1962 to 3.38 cups daily in 1987, meanwhile, consumption of decaffeinated coffee rose from 4 percent of the

66. F. NO CHANGE
G. as like
H. for
J. as

67. A. NO CHANGE
B. 1962. When
C. 1962; when
D. 1962 and when

68. The writer could most effectively strengthen the passage at this point by adding which of the following?
F. a definition of the term soft drink
G. the sentence "Twenty-five years ago, only about one of three persons consumed soft drinks."
H. a list of the most popular brands of coffee sold in the United States
J. a description of the marketing techniques used to promote the sale of soft drinks

69. A. NO CHANGE
B. their
C. there
D. the

70. F. NO CHANGE
G. 1987; Meanwhile
H. 1987. Meanwhile
J. 1987 meanwhile

population in 1962 to the current 17.5 percent

now.
———
71

71. A. NO CHANGE
    B. at the present time
    C. presently
    D. OMIT the underlined portion.

Questions 72 to 75 refer to the passage as a whole.

---

72. Is the hyphen used appropriately throughout the passage?
    F. No, the hyphen has been used between single words to express the idea of a unit when it was unnecessary.
    G. Yes, because the hyphen adds clarity to the passage.
    H. No, because hyphens are only used to show division between syllables.
    J. Yes, because the hyphen is used between single words to express the idea of a unit.

73. Is the use of direct quotation in the passage appropriate?
    A. No, because the passage is not specific enough for quotation marks.
    B. No, because quotation marks indicate a conversation.
    C. Yes, because the passage is giving the reader information about coffee.
    D. Yes, because the passage is strengthened by the direct quotation from a leader in the coffee industry.

74. Is the writer's use of statistical information in this passage appropriate?
    F. Yes, because it is easier to read figures.
    G. Yes, because the statistics give the reader important additional information.
    H. No, because statistical information is never used in formal writing.
    J. No, because the reader is confused by the statistical information.

75. Choose the sequence of paragraph numbers that will make the essay's structure most sensible.
    A. NO CHANGE
    B. 1, 3, 2, 4, 5
    C. 1, 2, 4, 3, 5
    D. 5, 1, 2, 3, 4

STOP!

This is the end of the English Test.
Do not proceed to the next section until the allotted
time expires.

2. MATHEMATICS TEST

60 Minutes—60 Questions

DIRECTIONS: Solve each problem. Then select the correct answer from among the five choices and darken the corresponding space on the answer sheet.

Solve as many problems as you can since they all have the same point value. Do not spend too much time on a single problem. Remember: you are not penalized for incorrect answers; only those answered correctly contribute to your final score.

NOTE: Unless otherwise stated, assume the following:
- All figures lie in a plane.
- Figures are not necessarily drawn to scale.
- All lines are straight.

---

1. In the figure below, the spinner has five equal sections numbered 1 through 5. If the arrow is equally likely to land on any of the sections, what is the probability that it will land on an even number on the next spin?

   A. $\dfrac{1}{5}$
   B. $\dfrac{2}{5}$
   C. $\dfrac{3}{5}$
   D. $\dfrac{4}{5}$
   E. 1

2. Which of the following is the equation of a line parallel to the line $y - 1 = 3x$?

   F. $y = -\dfrac{1}{3}x + 1$
   G. $y = 2x + 1$
   H. $y = 3x - 1$
   J. $y = -3x + 1$
   K. $y = 2x - 1$

DO YOUR FIGURING HERE.

GO ON TO THE NEXT PAGE.

3. Circle O has center $(1, 2)$ and diameter $\overline{AB}$. If the coordinates of A are $(-3, -2)$, what are the coordinates of B?

   A. $(-1, 0)$
   B. $(-2, 0)$
   C. $(5, 6)$
   D. $(-5, -4)$
   E. $(5, 2)$

4. If $x = -2$, then $-x^2 - 2x - 3 = $?

   F. -11
   G. -7
   H. -6
   J. -5
   K. -3

5. What is the solution set, in terms of r, of the following system of equations?

   $3x + y = 2r$
   $x + y = r$

   A. $\{r, 0\}$
   B. $\left\{\dfrac{r}{2}, \dfrac{r}{2}\right\}$
   C. $\left\{2r, \dfrac{r}{2}\right\}$
   D. $\{r, -r\}$
   E. $\left\{\dfrac{r}{2}, 2r\right\}$

6. In the figure below, two tangent semicircles are drawn in a square. If the length of a side of the square is 4, what is the area of the shaded portion of the figure?

   F. $8 - 2\pi$
   G. $8 - 4\pi$
   H. $16 - 2\pi$
   J. $16 - 4\pi$
   K. $16 - 16\pi$

   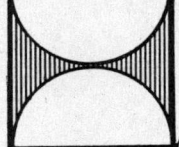

7. The area of an equilateral triangle is $\dfrac{25\sqrt{3}}{4}$. What is the perimeter of the triangle?

   A. 5
   B. 12
   C. 15
   D. $3\sqrt{3}$
   E. $\dfrac{3\sqrt{3}}{2}$

GO ON TO THE NEXT PAGE.

418 / ACT

8. The measures of the angles of a triangle are in the ratio of 3:5:7. What is the measure, in degrees, of the smallest angle?

   F. 12°
   G. 24°
   H. 36°
   J. 72°
   K. 84°

9. The expression $(x - y)(x^2 + xy + y^2)$ is equivalent to which of the following?

   A. $x^2 - y^2$
   B. $x^3 - xy^2$
   C. $x^3 - y^3$
   D. $x^3 + y^3$
   E. $x^3 - x^2y + y^2$

10. What is the value of $(2a^2 - a^3)^2$ when $a = -1$?

    F. 0
    G. 1
    H. 4
    J. 9
    K. 16

11. If $\sin x = \frac{1}{3}$, which of the following could be a value of $\tan x$?

    A. $\frac{1}{4}$
    B. $\frac{\sqrt{2}}{4}$
    C. $\frac{1}{2}$
    D. $\frac{\sqrt{3}}{4}$
    E. $\frac{3}{4}$

12. In the figure below, ABCD is a parallelogram. If $\overline{EC} = 31$, $\overline{EB} = 27$ and $\overline{AE} = 4x - 5$, then $x = ?$

    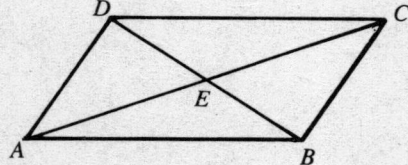

    F. 7
    G. 8
    H. 9
    J. 10
    K. 11

DO YOUR FIGURING HERE.

GO ON TO THE NEXT PAGE.

13. In the diagram below, △ABC is similar to △DBF. If $\overline{DF} = 3$, $\overline{BD} = \overline{BF} = 6$ and $\overline{AC} = 4$, what is the perimeter of △ABC?

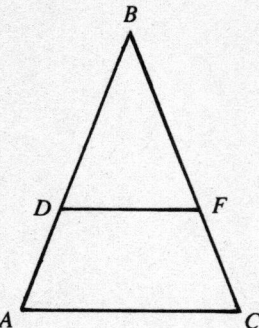

A. 8
B. 18
C. 20
D. 24
E. 32

14. Two roads intersect at right angles. A pole is 30 meters from one road and also 40 meters from the other road. How far (in meters) is the pole from the point where the roads intersect?

F. 30
G. 40
H. 50
J. 60
K. 70

15. From the town of Williston Park to Albertson there are 3 different roads. From the town of Albertson to Mineola there are 5 routes. How many different paths are there to go from Williston Park to Mineola through Albertson?

A. 2
B. 8
C. 12
D. 14
E. 15

16. What is the y-intercept of the line whose equation is $(y - 5) = \frac{1}{2}(x + 2)$?

F. 2
G. 4
H. 6
J. 8
K. 10

DO YOUR FIGURING HERE.

GO ON TO THE NEXT PAGE.

420 / ACT

DO YOUR FIGURING HERE.

17. For which value of c will the roots of the equation $x^2 + 4x + c = 0$ be real and equal?

    A. 1
    B. 2
    C. 3
    D. 4
    E. 5

18. Given the true statement, "If it is raining, then the sky is green." Which of the following is also a true statement?

    F. If the sky is green, then it is raining.
    G. If it is not raining, the sky is not green.
    H. If the sky is not green, then it is not raining.
    J. If the sky is not green, then it is raining.
    K. If it is not raining, then the sky is blue.

19. If $f(x) = 2x - 5$ and $g(x) = \dfrac{x + 5}{2}$ what is the value, in terms of m, of $f(g(2m))$?

    A. m
    B. $2m$
    C. m^2
    D. $4m^2$
    E. $m + 2$

20. Which graph represents the solution set of the inequality $(x - 1)(x + 3) < 0$?

    F.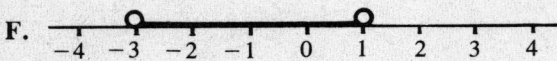
    G.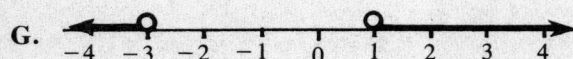
    H.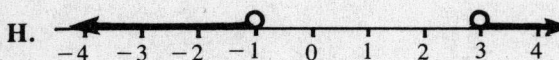
    J.
    K.

21. The area of a square is represented by K. What is the perimeter of this square in terms of K?

    A. $4K$
    B. $\sqrt{K}$
    C. $4\sqrt{K}$
    D. $\dfrac{K}{4}$
    E. $2K$

GO ON TO THE NEXT PAGE.

22. $\dfrac{1 + \dfrac{1}{x}}{1 + \dfrac{1}{y}} = ?$

   F. 1
   G. $\dfrac{y}{x}$
   H. $\dfrac{xy + 1}{xy}$
   J. $\dfrac{xy + y}{xy + x}$
   K. $\dfrac{x + 1}{y + 1}$

23. If y varies inversely as the square root of x, then when x is multiplied by 4, which of the following is true for the value of y?

   A. It is halved.
   B. It is doubled.
   C. It is quartered.
   D. It is multiplied by 4.
   E. It is unchanged.

24. What is the slope of a line perpendicular to the line whose equation is $y = 3x + 2$?

   F. $-\dfrac{1}{3}$
   G. -2
   H. 2
   J. 3
   K. $\dfrac{1}{3}$

25. Joshua can buy 12 candy bars for 17¢. At this rate, how many can he buy for $1.02?

   A. 2
   B. 43
   C. 60
   D. 72
   E. 78

26. $\dfrac{-|3 - (-2)|}{|-3 + 2|} = ?$

   F. -5
   G. -4
   H. -1
   J. 1
   K. 5

GO ON TO THE NEXT PAGE.

422 / ACT

27. If the length of an edge of a cube is represented by $5x$, which of the following expressions represents the volume of the cube?

   A. 15^3
   B. 25^2
   C. 25^3
   D. 125^2
   E. $125x^3$

28. Which point does not lie on the graph of the equation $2x + y = 3$?

   F. $(-1, -1)$
   G. $(-1, 5)$
   H. $(0, 3)$
   J. $\left(\dfrac{1}{2}, 2\right)$
   K. $(-2, 7)$

29. $\dfrac{2^2 + 3^2}{5^2} + \dfrac{1}{10} = ?$

   A. $\dfrac{31}{50}$
   B. $\dfrac{14}{35}$
   C. $\dfrac{14}{10}$
   D. $\dfrac{11}{10}$
   E. $\dfrac{1}{2}$

30. Joshua received test scores of 89, 86, 81, 94, and 75. What is his average (arithmetic mean) score?

   F. 19
   G. 75
   H. 81
   J. 84
   K. 85

31. In the figure below, diameters $\overline{AB}$ and $\overline{CD}$ intersect at O. If the measure of arc AC is 40°, what is the degree measure of $\angle COB$?

   A. 140°
   B. 80°
   C. 70°
   D. 35°
   E. 20°

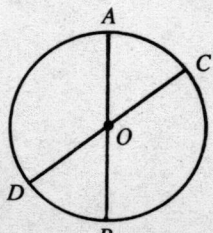

DO YOUR FIGURING HERE.

GO ON TO THE NEXT PAGE.

32. If the average (arithmetic mean) of 6 test scores is 84, what is the sum of the 6 test scores?

   F. 14
   G. 90
   H. 360
   J. 480
   K. 504

33. What is the length of the line segment whose end points are $(3, -2)$ and $(-4, 5)$?

   A. $5\sqrt{2}$
   B. $6\sqrt{2}$
   C. $7\sqrt{2}$
   D. $\sqrt{10}$
   E. 14

34. The distance from the center of a circle to a chord is 5. If the length of the chord is 24, what is the length of the radius of the circle?

   F. 13
   G. 7
   H. 5
   J. 10
   K. 17

35. The lengths of the sides of a triangle are 3, 4, and 5. What is the value of the sine of the larger acute angle of the triangle?

   A. $\frac{3}{4}$
   B. $\frac{5}{4}$
   C. $\frac{3}{5}$
   D. $\frac{4}{5}$
   E. $\frac{4}{3}$

36. $\dfrac{2}{3 - \sqrt{3}} = ?$

   F. $3 + \sqrt{3}$
   G. $\dfrac{3 + \sqrt{3}}{2}$
   H. $\dfrac{3 + \sqrt{3}}{3}$
   J. $\dfrac{2(3 + \sqrt{3})}{3}$
   K. $\dfrac{1}{3}$

GO ON TO THE NEXT PAGE.

424 / ACT

37. In △FGH below, sin F = $\frac{5}{7}$. What is the value of $\frac{\sec F}{\csc H}$?

A. $\frac{2\sqrt{6}}{7}$
B. $\frac{7}{2\sqrt{6}}$
C. 1
D. $2\sqrt{6}$
E. $\frac{5}{7}$

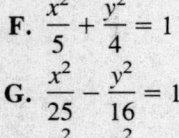

38. In an isosceles right triangle, the measure of an acute angle is represented by $(2x + 5)°$. What is the value of x?

F. 20
G. 22
H. 25
J. 27
K. 30

39. The length of a side of a square is $\sqrt{2}$. What is the length of a diagonal of the square?

A. $\sqrt{2}$
B. $2\sqrt{2}$
C. 2
D. $4\sqrt{2}$
E. 4

40. Which equation represents the graph of the ellipse shown below?

F. $\frac{x^2}{5} + \frac{y^2}{4} = 1$
G. $\frac{x^2}{25} - \frac{y^2}{16} = 1$
H. $\frac{x^2}{16} + \frac{y^2}{25} = 1$
J. $\frac{x^2}{25} + \frac{y^2}{16} = 1$
K. $xy = 20$

41. The set of rational numbers is a subset of which of the following?

A. Integers
B. Irrational numbers
C. Real numbers
D. Whole numbers
E. Natural numbers

DO YOUR FIGURING HERE.

GO ON TO THE NEXT PAGE.

42. The equation $3(2x + 1) = 6x + 3$ is an illustration of which of the following?

   F. Associative property of addition
   G. Distributive property of multiplication over addition
   H. Commutative property of multiplication
   J. Commutative property of addition
   K. Associative property of multiplication

43. What is the remainder when $4x^2 - 5x + 7$ is divided by $x - 1$?

   A. 16
   B. 8
   C. 6
   D. -2
   E. -4

44. Which ordered pair is the solution of the following system of equations?

$$3x + 2y = 4$$
$$-2x + 2y = 24$$

   F. $(2, -1)$
   G. $(-4, 8)$
   H. $(-4, -8)$
   J. $(2, -5)$
   K. $\left(1, \dfrac{1}{2}\right)$

45. Which fraction has the greatest value:

$$\frac{5}{8}, \frac{7}{11}, \frac{2}{3}, \frac{3}{5}, \frac{4}{7}$$

   A. $\dfrac{5}{8}$
   B. $\dfrac{7}{11}$
   C. $\dfrac{2}{3}$
   D. $\dfrac{3}{5}$
   E. $\dfrac{4}{7}$

46. How many inches are there in $(3x - 2)$ feet?

   F. $12x$
   G. $\dfrac{3x - 2}{12}$
   H. $36x - 2$
   J. $36x - 24$
   K. $9x - 6$

DO YOUR FIGURING HERE.

GO ON TO THE NEXT PAGE.

47. If $n + 1$ represents an even integer, which expression also represents an even integer?

   A. n
   B. $n + 2$
   C. $n + 3$
   D. $n - 2$
   E. n^2

48. If $2x - 3y = 7$, what is the value of $6y - 4x$?

   F. -14
   G. -7
   H. 7
   J. 14
   K. It cannot be determined from the given information.

49. What is the difference when $2x - 3y$ is subtracted from $7x + 8y$?

   A. $5x + 11y$
   B. $9x + 5y$
   C. $5x + 5y$
   D. $-5x - 11y$
   E. $5x - 11y$

50. If the yearly income from a $1,000 investment is $50, what is the annual interest rate?

   F. 0.5%
   G. 2%
   H. 5%
   J. 20%
   K. 50%

51. $\dfrac{\left(\dfrac{6}{x} \div \dfrac{3}{x}\right) \div \dfrac{x}{3}}{6} = ?$

   A. x
   B. $\dfrac{1}{x}$
   C. 1
   D. x^2
   E. $\dfrac{1}{x^2}$

52. In the figure below, $\tan \theta = \dfrac{m}{n}$. What is the value of $\sin \theta$?

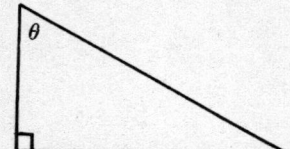

F. $\dfrac{n}{\sqrt{m^2 + n^2}}$

G. $\dfrac{n}{m}$

H. $\dfrac{m}{\sqrt{m^2 + n^2}}$

J. $\dfrac{1}{\sqrt{m^2 - n^2}}$

K. $\dfrac{1}{\sqrt{m^2 + n^2}}$

53. In the figure below, what is the ratio of the measure of $\angle ACB$ to the measure of $\angle AOB$?

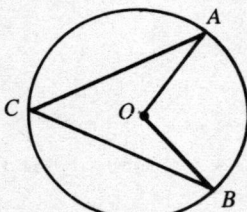

A. 1:1
B. 2:1
C. 1:2
D. 3:1
E. 3:2

54. In the figure below two circles are tangent to each other and each is tangent to three sides of the rectangle. If the radius of each circle is 3, what is the area of the shaded portion?

F. $72 - 18\pi$
G. $72 - 36\pi$
H. $36 - 18\pi$
J. $36 - 9\pi$
K. $18 - 9\pi$

GO ON TO THE NEXT PAGE.

55. What is the converse of the statement, "If it has green horns, then it is a fizzgig"?

    A. No fizzgig has green horns.
    B. If it is a fizzgig, then it has green horns.
    C. If it is not a fizzgig, then it does not have green horns.
    D. If it does not have green horns, then it is a fizzgig.
    E. If it does not have green horns, then it is not a fizzgig.

56. Two trains leave from the East Williston station at the same time and travel in opposite directions. The train headed north is traveling at an average speed of 60 m.p.h. After 3 hours the trains are 255 miles apart. What is the average speed in miles per hour of the train headed south?

    F. 25
    G. 20
    H. 15
    J. 10
    K. 5

57. $\dfrac{x}{x-1} - \dfrac{x}{1-x} =$

    A. 1
    B. 2
    C. $\dfrac{x}{x-1}$
    D. $\dfrac{2x}{x-1}$
    E. 0

58. Which is true for the set of numbers {4, 7, 12}?

    F. A range of 3 and a median of 7
    G. A range of 8 and a median of 7
    H. A range of 12 and a median of $7\dfrac{2}{3}$
    J. A range of 8 and a median of $7\dfrac{2}{3}$
    K. An average of $7\dfrac{2}{3}$ and a median of 8

DO YOUR FIGURING HERE.

GO ON TO THE NEXT PAGE.

59. Using the data in the table below, which statement is true?

Measure	Frequency
8	1
10	3
14	2

A. Mean = median
B. Mean > median
C. Mean < median
D. Median > mode
E. Mean = mode

60. If $n! = n(n-1)(n-2) \ldots (1)$, what is the value of $\frac{6!}{3!}$?

F. 2!
G. 6
H. 30
J. 60
K. 120

STOP!
This is the end of the Mathematics Test.
Do not proceed to the next section until the allotted time expires.

3. READING TEST

35 Minutes—40 Questions

DIRECTIONS: There are four passages in this test. Each passage is followed by ten questions. After reading a passage, select the most appropriate answer to each question and blacken the corresponding space on your answer sheet. You may refer to the passages as often as you feel necessary.

Passage I

The energy crunch, which is being felt around the world, has dramatized how the reckless despoiling of the earth's resources has brought the whole world to the brink of disaster. The overdevelopment of motor transport, with its spiral of more cars, more highways, more pollution, more suburbs, more commuting, has contributed to the near-destruction of our cities, the disintegration of the family, and the pollution not only of local air, but also of the earth's atmosphere. The catastrophe has arrived in the form of the energy crunch.

Our present situation is unlike war, revolution, or depression. It is also unlike the great natural catastrophes of the past. Worldwide resource exploitation and energy use have brought us to a state where long-range planning is crucial. What we need is not a continuation of our present perilous state, which endangers the future of our country, our children, and our earth, but a movement forward to a new norm in order to work rapidly and effectively on planetary problems.

This country has been reeling under the continuing exposures of loss of moral integrity and the revelation that lawbreaking has reached into the highest places in the land. There is a strong demand for moral reinvigoration and for some commitment that is vast enough and yet personal enough to enlist the loyalty of all. In the past it has been only in a war in defense of their own country and their own ideals that any people have been able to invoke a total commitment.

This is the first time that we have been asked to defend ourselves and what we hold dear in cooperation with all the other inhabitants of this planet, who share with us the same endangered air and the same endangered oceans. There is a common need to reassess our present course, to change that course, and to devise new methods through which the world can survive. This is a priceless opportunity.

To grasp it, we need a widespread understanding of the nature of the crisis confronting us—and the world—a crisis that is no passing inconvenience, no by-product of the ambitions of the oil-producing countries, no figment of environmentalists' fears, no by-product of any present system of government. What we face is the outcome of the inventions of the last four hundred years. What we need is a transformed lifestyle. This new lifestyle can flow directly from science and technology, but its acceptance depends on an overriding commitment to a higher quality of life for the world's children and future generations.

1. The speaker feels that the energy crisis has brought the entire world close to

   A. cooperation.
   B. revolution.
   C. destruction.
   D. transformation.

2. What device does the speaker use in the first paragraph to emphasize overdevelopment?

   F. Repetition of a key word
   G. Comparison of destruction in cities and suburbs
   H. Examples of the effects of pollution
   J. Alliteration

3. Which condition does the speaker feel has nearly destroyed our cities?

   A. Lack of financial planning
   B. The breakup of the family
   C. Natural disasters in many regions
   D. The excessive growth of motor transportation

430

4. According to the speaker, what is one example of our loss of moral integrity?

F. Disregard for law
G. Lack of loyalty
H. Lack of cooperation
J. Exploitation of resources

5. This type of writing could best be classified as

A. literary.
B. argumentative.
C. prosaic.
D. epic.

6. Why is the speaker's repetition of the word "no" effective in the conclusion of the speech?

F. It reinforces the audience reaction.
G. It parallels her introduction.
H. It emphasizes that there are no easy answers.
J. It emphasizes her discouraged attitude.

7. By comparing past problems with present ones, the speaker draws attention to the

A. significance of this crisis.
B. inadequacy of governments.
C. similarity of the past to the present.
D. hopelessness of the situation.

8. What commitment does the speaker feel people must now make?

F. Search for new energy sources
G. Outlaw motor transportation
H. Accept a new lifestyle
J. Adopt a new form of government

9. The author of this passage is probably a (an)

A. businessman.
B. developer.
C. student.
D. environmentalist.

10. Which order does the speaker follow in this speech?

F. Comparison and contrast of past and present
G. Statement of problem, history and development, appeal for solution
H. Chronological order of the events leading to the problem
J. Appeal to all nations, history, statement of problem, solution

Passage II

One potential hideaway that until now has been completely ignored is De Witt Isle, off the coast of Tasmania. Its assets are 4,000 acres of jagged rocks, tangled undergrowth, and trees twisted and bent by battering winds. Settlers have avoided it like the plague, but the bandicoots (ratlike marsupials native to Australia), wallabies, eagles, and penguins think De Witt is just fine.

So does Jane Cooper, 18, a pert Melbourne high school graduate, who emigrated there with three goats, several chickens, and a number of cats brought along to stand guard against the bandicoots. Why De Witt? "I was frightened at the way life is lived today in our cities," says Jane. "I wanted to be alone, to have some time to think and find out about myself."

She has been left alone to write poems and start work on a book, play the flute, and dive for crayfish and abalone to supplement her diet of cereal, canned goods, and home-grown vegetables.

Her solitary life isn't easy. "Dear God," she wrote in her diary on her first day ashore, "how I love this island . . . but I don't know if I'm strong enough to stay. I found myself walking along the rocks crying." Then her mood began to change: "I'm going to conquer this island. I won't let it beat me . . . I had been feeling so sorry for myself that I was unaware of the beauty that surrounded me." Recently she sent a letter home via the local fishermen. She wrote: "I feel very old and very young. I'm more determined than ever to stay here." She has made a friend—a penguin named Mickey Mouse—and she is beginning to feel that "this is my world and my life . . . it is so beautiful here I can't imagine Melbourne any longer." To millions of city-bound Australians, Jane has become something of a heroine.

11. Which phrase best expresses the main idea of this passage?

A. "Life in Melbourne"
B. "Planning a Wildlife"
C. "The Pesky Bandicoots"
D. "True Grit"

12. The author's description of De Witt Isle suggests that it contains

F. many secret coves.
G. many primitive settlements.
H. inhospitable areas.
J. elaborate wildlife refuges.

13. At one point in her experience on the isle, Jane coped with

    A. a raid by bandicoots.
    B. the loss of her livestock.
    C. an attack of self-pity.
    D. a feeling of resentment at her plight.

14. Of the following, which word best describes Jane?

    F. Versatile
    G. Self-important
    H. Shy
    J. Sly

15. Which inference can best be made on the basis of the passage?

    A. Jane never doubted her ability to survive.
    B. The Isle's weather proved quite an obstacle.
    C. Jane is basically rather unemotional.
    D. Jane's days on the Isle are very full ones.

16. From this passage we can most safely conclude that Jane is

    I. a religious fanatic.
    II. a fancy cook.
    III. a strong swimmer.

    F. I only
    G. I and III only
    H. III only
    J. I, II, and III

17. Jane's words "I feel very old and very young" suggest that she

    A. wants to grow up too soon.
    B. has grown with experience.
    C. craves human companionship.
    D. wants some form of support from home.

18. By the end of the passage we realize that Jane

    F. is still rather lonesome.
    G. has apparently won the battle.
    H. will probably go home.
    J. greatly needs encouragement.

19. In the first paragraph, which word is used in an ironic sense?

    A. "Hideaway"
    B. "Coast"
    C. "Assets"
    D. "Winds"

20. Jane's purpose in going to De Witt Isle was to

    F. escape reality.
    G. live the good life as she saw it.
    H. think and engage in self-discovery.
    J. participate in an adventure.

Passage III

He never could pinpoint, with his dazzled and watery eyes, Armande's silhouette among the skiers. Once, however, he was sure he had caught her, floating and flashing, bare-headed, agonizingly graceful, there, there, and now there, jumping a bump, shooting down nearer and nearer, going into a tuck— and abruptly changing into a goggled stranger.

Presently she appeared from another side of the terrace, in glossy green nylon, carrying her skis, but with her impressive boots still on. He had spent enough time studying skiwear in Swiss shops to know that shoe leather had been replaced by plastic, and laces by rigid clips. "You look like the first girl on the moon," he said, indicating her boots, and if they had not been especially close fitting, she would have wiggled her toes inside as a woman does when her footwear happens to be discussed in flattering terms (smiling toes taking over the making of mouths).

"Listen," she said as she considered her Mondstein Sexy (their incredible trade name), "I'll leave my skis here, and change into walking shoes and return to Witt with you *a deux* . . . I've quarreled with Jacques, and he has left with his dear friends. All is finished."

21. The passage can best be described as

    A. descriptive.
    B. didactic.
    C. technical.
    D. convincing.

22. Which phrase best expresses the focus of this passage?

    F. "The ski slopes"
    G. "An attractive girl"
    H. "The walking shoes"
    J. "Jacques' friends"

23. In the first paragraph, where is "He" positioned?

    A. Alongside a group of skiers
    B. In a group of skiers
    C. Immediately behind a group of skiers
    D. At the base of a ski slope

24. In the first paragraph, the expression "agonizingly graceful" is written from the point of view of

   F. the "He" of the passage.
   G. Armande.
   H. the skiers.
   J. Jacques.

25. In the third paragraph, the term "Mondstein Sexy" refers to

   A. Armande.
   B. ski boots.
   C. nylon laces.
   D. walking shoes.

26. The reader can infer from the passage that Armande's clothing is

   F. inexpensive.
   G. thin.
   H. shapeless.
   J. stylish.

27. In this passage, the "He" most probably is trying to see Armande because he

   A. would like to meet her.
   B. could learn to ski better by watching her.
   C. is fond of her.
   D. is a dear friend of Jacques.

28. In the second paragraph, the expression "You look like the first girl on the moon" is most probably meant to be

   F. a protest.
   G. a statement of fact.
   H. an insult.
   J. a compliment.

29. The passage would probably next go on to

   A. the conversation between the author and Armande.
   B. Armande's discussion with Jacques.
   C. a description of the ski slopes.
   D. a comparison of Armande and the author.

30. It can be inferred that the author is

   F. dispassionate in his presentation of Armande.
   G. a friend of Jacques.
   H. enamored of Armande.
   J. undecided about Armande.

Passage IV

Scientific interest in caves began in seventeenth- and eighteenth-century Europe with the development of elaborate (but erroneous) theories of the hydrologic cycle in which cave systems were essential elements. The beginnings of a correct understanding of the geology of caves date from about 1850 in Europe and 1900 in North America. In Europe, emphasis was on karst hydrology, particularly on subterranean streams. Early biological studies emphasized faunal surveys and descriptions of the degenerate eyes of cavernicolous animals (cavernicoles); only after 1900 were a few experimental studies made.

In the early twentieth century Racovitza and Jeannel sparked the spectacular rise of modern biospeleology in Europe. This period was, in general, an interlude for cave science in the United States, during which the only additions to knowledge about North American caves and their life were made by Europeans on field trips in North America.

Biospeleology advanced slowly in the United States from 1930 to 1950, even though this was the time of a lively debate over the origin of caves. The central point was whether caves form above or below the local water table. Davis proposed cave development deep below the water table, by random circulation of slowly percolating groundwater ("phreatic" origin). This view became textbook doctrine for many years. Other theories placed the zone of cave development at or above the local water table ("vadose" origin). This debate and Davis's reputation as an authority had two stifling effects on cave studies: (1) the implied random pattern of cave development discouraged search for specific hydrological mechanisms causative of cave system patterns, and (2) the argument over the location of the water table tended to reduce the research that was done to a sterile classification of some particular cave as having a vadose or phreatic origin.

Factors influencing reactivation of geological cave research and continued progress in biospeleology in the past decade include amassment of a large body of descriptive data collected mainly by non-professional explorers and surveyors within the National Speleological Society; growing acquaintance with the large body of European literature that had been largely ignored by American theoreticians of the 1930s; near-completion of a systematic description of many groups of cave organisms and their distribution, which permitted biologists to turn to ecological and physiological problems; and finally, involvement of younger researchers whose interest arose from exploration and field experience.

31. The main purpose of this passage is to
    A. settle some of the long-standing disputes over cave developments.
    B. present a short history of the study of caves.
    C. outline the author's point of view before presenting a detailed discussion.
    D. briefly explain many theories about caves.

32. Biospeleology is understood to be the study of cave
    F. life.
    G. hydrology.
    H. development.
    J. research.

33. Between 1900 and 1920, most of the research carried out on U.S. caves was done by
    A. amateurs.
    B. the National Speleological Society.
    C. Davis.
    D. Europeans.

34. The work of W. M. Davis on American speleological research had the effect of
    F. lessening the amount and value of the research.
    G. permitting biologists to turn to ecological and physiological problems.
    H. making cave research a reputable science.
    J. interesting young researchers in cave science.

35. If a cave were of phreatic origin, it would have developed
    A. at the top point of the water table.
    B. as the result of unusual flooding.
    C. completely underwater.
    D. as a result of water seepage.

36. Prior to 1900 research in biospeleology was principally
    F. better in Europe than in North America.
    G. surveys and descriptions of plant and animal life.
    H. characterized by few experimental models of cave life.
    J. done by Racovitza and Jeannel.

37. Recent interest in geological cave research was sparked by all of the following EXCEPT
    A. information provided by nonprofessionals/nonscientists.
    B. reading previous research done in Europe.
    C. recent understanding of the physiology of cave organisms.
    D. younger scientists who have explored caves and done field work in biospeleology in their training.

38. An erroneous theory of caves was the
    F. biospeleological.
    G. phreatic.
    H. geologic.
    J. hydrologic.

39. This passage could have been excerpted from a
    A. news magazine.
    B. scientific journal.
    C. general magazine.
    D. biology textbook.

40. The National Speleological Society was an organization of
    F. nonprofessional people interested in caves.
    G. professional surveyors.
    H. scientists and engineers.
    J. laymen.

STOP!

This is the end of the Reading Test.
Do not proceed to the next section until the allotted time expires.

4. SCIENCE REASONING TEST

35 Minutes—40 Questions

DIRECTIONS: Each passage in this test is followed by several questions. After reading a passage, select the most appropriate answer to each question and blacken the corresponding space on your answer sheet. You may refer to the passages as often as you feel necessary.

Passage I

The physical form that matter takes—its phase—depends on the temperature and pressure to which the material is subjected. The most common phases are solid, liquid, and gas (plasmas, less common by far, are found primarily in the interiors of stars). The solid phase is normally the densest phase, with the particles as close together as possible. The particles in the solid phase always have the least mobility relative to each other. Particles in the liquid phase are generally less closely packed than in solids. The particles in the liquid phase can move past one another. We observe this as fluidity—liquids can be poured. The resistance to pouring, called viscosity, is due in part to the jostling of particles as they move. Just as you would find it more difficult to move through a crowd that is milling about than one that is stationary or has everyone moving in your direction, so, too, molecules in a fluid experience less resistance to movement if the kinetic energy of surrounding molecules is decreased. The less compressed the fluid, the less likely molecules are to get in the way, which will also cause a decrease in the viscosity. In a gas the particles are spread very far apart compared to their density in liquids or solids. In the chart below, the phase diagram for compound X is presented. Pressure is in units of atmospheres; temperature, which is the average kinetic energy of the particles of X, is measured on the Kelvin scale.

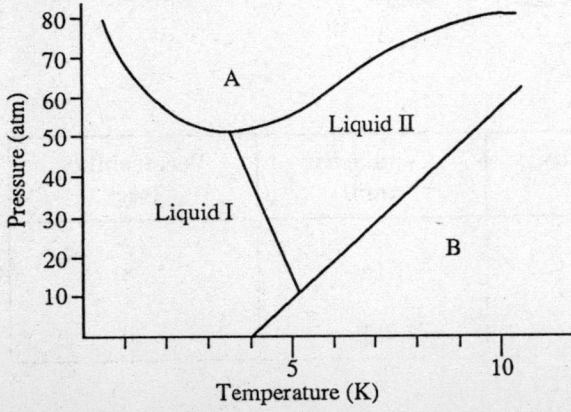

1. Which of the following most likely designates the solid region of the phase diagram?

   A. A
   B. B
   C. A and B together
   D. Cannot be determined

2. Which of the following most likely designates the gas region of the phase diagram?

   F. A
   G. B
   H. A and B together
   J. Neither A nor B

3. What would happen if you cooled a sample of X at 32.5 atm pressure from 10K to 8.5K?

   A. The gas would condense into liquid I.
   B. The gas would condense into liquid II.
   C. The solid would melt into liquid I and liquid II.
   D. No change in phase would occur.

4. What is the boiling point of X at 57.5 atm, assuming region B were the gas phase and region A were the solid phase?

   F. 2K
   G. 5.37K
   H. 5.87K
   J. 10.125K

5. At what temperature will gaseous X begin to condense into a liquid at 57.5 atm, assuming that region B were the gas phase?

   A. 2K
   B. 5.37K
   C. 5.87K
   D. 10.125K

6. Which of the following most accurately describes the situation obtained at 4.0K and 40.0 atm pressure?

   F. Liquid I is turning into liquid II.
   G. Liquid II is turning into liquid I.
   H. Both F and G
   J. Neither F nor G

   B. A is the superfluid because it exists at pressures higher than any of the other phases.
   C. Liquid II is the superfluid; its particles are forced to flow more evenly because the pressure exerted is greater than in the other liquid.
   D. B is the superfluid because it exists at temperatures higher than any of the other phases.

7. A superfluid is a liquid that has no viscosity. Select the choice that best explains which liquid is the superfluid.

   A. Liquid I is the superfluid because the particles are at lower temperatures and/or pressures than any of the other phases.

Passage II

Experiments were performed using the design given below:

Three similar tubes, each containing a specific soil of uniform particle size and shape, were used to study the effect that different particle size has on porosity (the amount of open space between particles, usually expressed as a percentage comparing volume of open space to volume of material), capillarity (the ability of water to rise within a column of soil, usually expressed in terms of height) and permeability (the ease with which water flows through a material, usually expressed in terms of time).

A fourth tube containing soil that was a mixture of the various sizes found in the other tubes was also studied, and its data are recorded in the table. (Assume that the soils were perfectly dry between the parts of the investigation.)

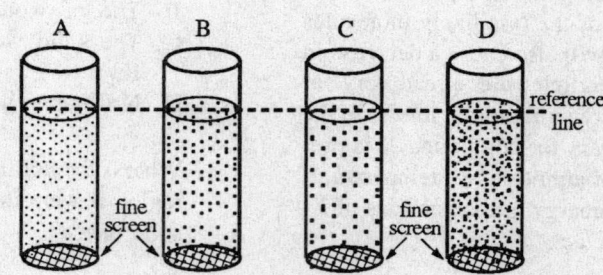

Tube	Particle Size (diameter in cm)	Porosity (%)	Capillarity (mm)	Permeability (sec)
A	Fine (0.025 cm)	40	20	14
B	Medium (0.1 cm)	40	15	8
C	Coarse (0.3 cm)	40	7	6
D	Mixed (0.025 to 0.3 cm)	20	12	20

The graph below indicates the relationship of transported particle size to water velocity. This generalized graph shows the water velocity needed to maintain—but not start—movement. Variations occur due to differences in particle density and shape.

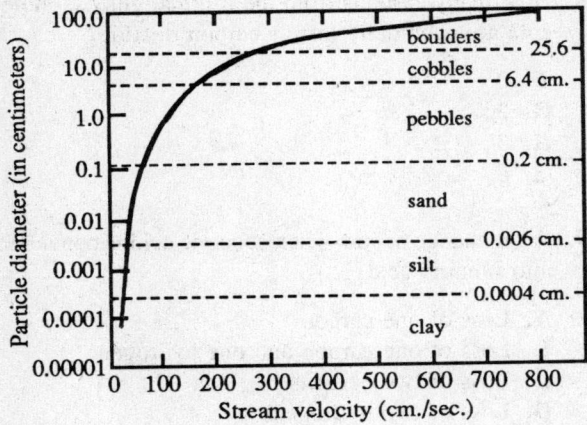

8. When water was poured into the top of each tube at the same time, which tube allowed the water to pass through most quickly?

   F. A
   G. B
   H. C
   J. D

9. What is the relation between particle size and porosity?

   A. As particle size increases, porosity increases.
   B. As particle size increases, porosity decreases.
   C. Porosity is a constant.
   D. There is no direct relation between porosity and particle size.

10. Each tube was placed in a shallow pan of water. In which tube did the water rise the highest?

    F. A
    G. B
    H. C
    J. D

11. The bottom of each tube was closed and the water was slowly poured into each tube until the reference line was reached. Which statement best describes the water held in the tubes?

    A. Tube D held the most water.
    B. Tube C held the most water.
    C. Tube C held the least water.
    D. Tube D held the least water.

12. What is the apparent relation between capillarity and permeability?

    F. Capillarity increases as the permeability time decreases.
    G. Capillarity increases as the permeability time increases.
    H. Capillarity is not related to permeability time.
    J. Capillarity is inversely proportional to permeability time.

13. A handful of material from tube D was dropped into a fifth tube filled with water only. In which order would the particle sizes of this soil settle in the tube from top to bottom, assuming that all particles were made from the same material?

    A. Fine, Coarse, Medium
    B. Coarse, Medium, Fine
    C. Fine, Medium, Coarse
    D. Coarse, Fine, Medium

14. Into which category would the soil sample in tube C be classified?

    F. Pebbles
    G. Silt
    H. Cobbles
    J. Sand

GO ON TO THE NEXT PAGE.

Passage III

The Krebs cycle is the completion of the aerobic breakdown of glucose, $C_6H_{12}O_6$, a compound which is ultimately obtained from plants. Glucose is first broken down in a process called glycolysis. Glycolysis yields two molecules of pyruvic acid. In the Krebs cycle each molecule of pyruvic acid is broken down into carbon dioxide and water, while the energy from the molecule is stored in other molecules (notably ATP). Each step of the reaction is controlled by enzymes. A simplified scheme is presented below:

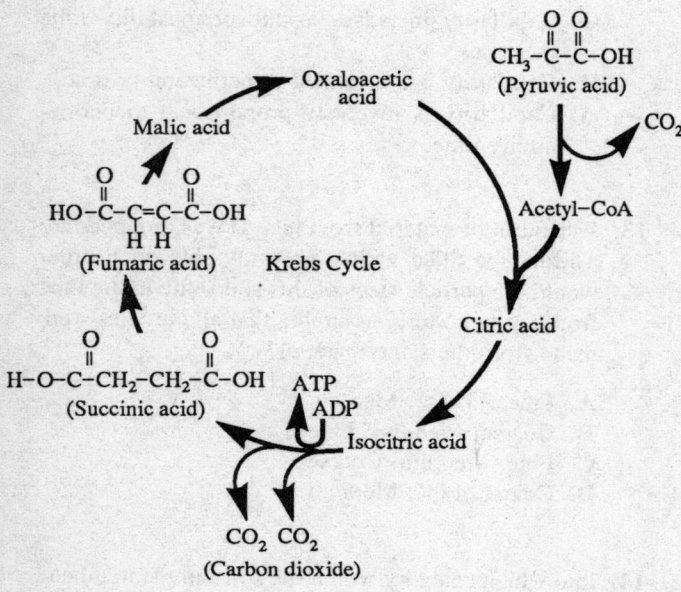

15. Two molecules of glucose give rise to how many molecules of pyruvic acid?

    A. 1
    B. 2
    C. 4
    D. 6

16. Assuming that each step of the Krebs cycle requires only one enzyme and that each enzyme is specific for each step, how many different enzymes are required for the Krebs cycle itself?

    F. 4
    G. 5
    H. 6
    J. 8

17. How many adenosine triphosphate (ATP) molecules are produced per turn of the cycle?

    A. 1
    B. 6
    C. 2
    D. 0

18. How many carbons from the original glucose molecule are eventually lost as carbon dioxide?

    F. 0
    G. 2
    H. 3
    J. 6

19. What change occurs when succinic acid is converted into fumaric acid?

    A. Loss of one carbon
    B. Loss of one carbon and one hydrogen
    C. Loss of two carbons
    D. Loss of two hydrogens

20. What is the source of the energy found in glucose?

    F. A Krebs cycle in plants
    G. Heat
    H. Minerals
    J. Light

Passage IV

Metals are characterized by the ease with which at least some of their electrons are removed. This is why metals are so valuable as conductors of electricity. While it is relatively easy to remove electrons from metals, it does require some energy. In the following sets of experiments, the number and speeds of electrons released by the surface of a polished one-square-centimeter piece of Mu metal is studied as a function of the intensity (the number of light particles called *photons* striking the surface per second) and frequency (an intrinsic property related to the wavelength of the light) of light shined on the surface.

Experiment 1

Light of frequency 1 and intensity 1 was shined on a polished one-centimeter piece of Mu metal. The speed and number of electrons released were recorded using photomultiplier tubes. No electrons were observed. The experiment was repeated at the same frequency and twice the intensity of light used the first time (intensity 2). No electrons were observed. The experiment was repeated a third time at the same frequency using an intensity three times greater than the first trial (intensity 3). No electrons were observed.

Experiment 2

Light of frequency 2 (greater than frequency 1) and intensity 1 (identical to intensity 1 in the first experiment) was shined on the Mu metal. Using the same experimental set-up as Experiment 1, researchers obtained the curve in Figure 1 labelled I1.

Subsequent trials using double and triple the initial intensity at the same frequency were plotted in the same diagram and are labelled "I2" and "I3" respectively.

Experiment 3

Experiment 3 used the exact same procedure as in Experiments 1 and 2 except that the frequency of light used in Experiment 3, frequency 3, was greater than the frequency used in Experiment 2. The results are presented in Figure 2.

Experiment 4

Experiment 4 used the exact same procedure as in all the preceding experiments except that the frequency of light used in Experiment 4, frequency 4, was greater than the frequency used in Experiment 3. The results are presented in Figure 3.

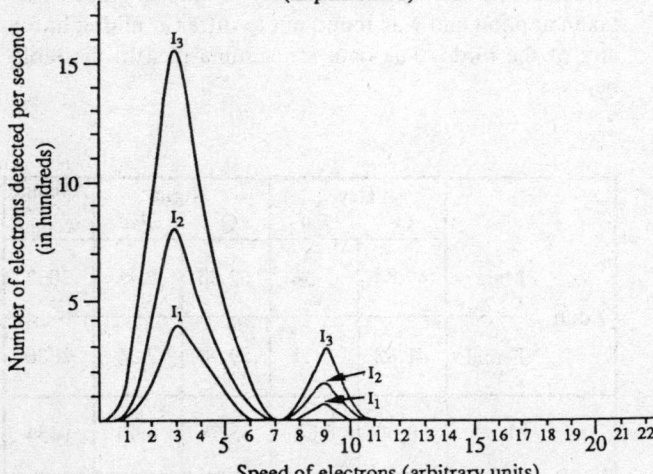

Figure 1

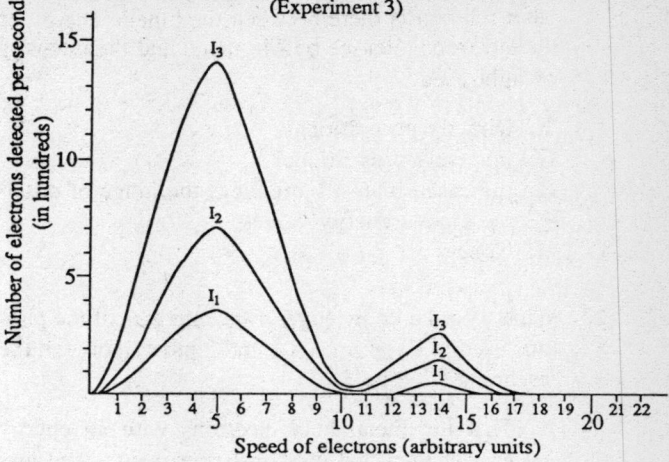

Figure 2

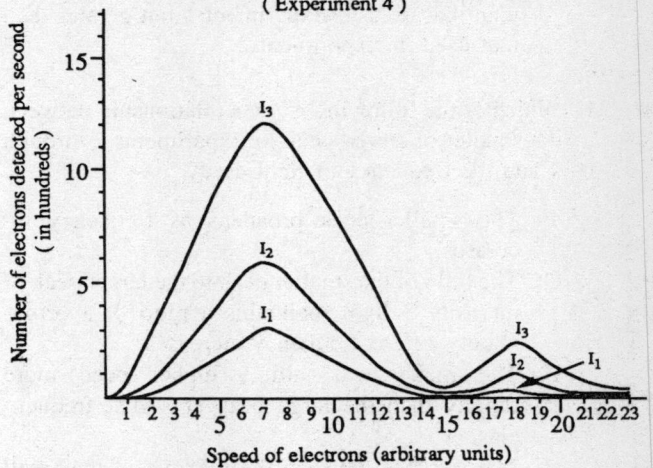

Figure 3

21. Based on the information presented, which frequency has the greatest energy?

A. Frequency 1
B. Frequency 2
C. Frequency 3
D. Frequency 4

22. Based on the information presented in Experiment 3, what relation is there between the kinetic energy of the electrons released by Mu metal and the intensity of light used?

    F. Directly proportional
    G. Inversely proportional
    H. Increased intensity broadens the range of possible kinetic energy values.
    J. None

23. What would a knowledge of the energies of the photons used in Experiments 1 and 2 most likely tell the researcher?

    A. That the metal held electrons with an energy greater than that used in Experiment 1 and less than that used in Experiment 2.
    B. That the metal held photons with an energy greater than that used in Experiment 1 and less than that used in Experiment 2.
    C. That the metal held electrons with an energy less than that used in Experiment 1 but greater than that used in Experiment 2.
    D. That the metal held photons with an energy less than that used in Experiment 1 but greater than that used in Experiment 2.

24. Which of the following is *not* a relationship between the smaller observed peak in Experiments 2 through 4 and the frequency of light used?

    F. The smaller peak broadens as frequency increases.
    G. The ratio of the smaller peak to the larger peak of intensity 3 light maintains a ratio of approximately 1:5 as frequency increases.
    H. The smaller peak shifts to higher speeds more rapidly than the large peak at higher frequencies.
    J. The distance between the maxima of the small and large peaks in speed units decreases as frequency increases.

25. Which of the following is the likeliest cause of the smaller peak in Experiments 2 through 4?

    A. The electrons in the smaller peak absorbed only one photon of light.
    B. The electrons in the smaller peak absorbed exactly two photons of light.
    C. The electrons in the smaller peak absorbed two or more photons of light.
    D. The electrons in the smaller peak received more energy by collisions with other electrons.

26. If it were true that energy and frequency were directly proportional, and that frequency and wavelength were inversely proportional, what would the shapes of the curves in Experiments 2 through 4 imply?

    F. That the range of speeds available increases as wavelength increases
    G. That the range of speeds available decreases as wavelength decreases
    H. That the range of speeds available decreases as energy increases
    J. That the range of speeds available increases as energy decreases

Passage V

Homeostasis refers to the ability of a living organism to organize its biochemical and physico-biochemical processes in such a way as to promote a stable internal environment. To accomplish this, thousands of specific catalysts called *enzymes* regulate the many steps of the complex chemical reactions. In a recent study of Barnum's pigeon, the relationship between the amount of body fat and a substance Q, believed to regulate the amount of fat in the body, was studied. This study was done by averaging the concentration (in micrograms per milliliter) of Q found in the blood of twenty birds per sample group drawn at noon for the day reading, and the concentration of Q in the blood of the same birds drawn at midnight for the night reading. The fat content (in grams) of the birds was determined by buoyancy readings done immediately before blood was drawn. The body weight (in grams) was taken at noon and was found not to differ at midnight for any of the birds. The data are summarized in the table below.

		Day Q	Day Fat	Night Q	Night Fat	Average body weight
Adult	Male	42.84	7.34	62.00	7.45	3033
Adult	Female	41.82	7.22	59.98	7.34	2880
Baby	Male	30.00	6.84	35.58	6.90	1454
Baby	Female	28.42	6.59	34.92	6.85	1530

(Note: 1 microgram is equal to one millionth of one gram.)

27. Which of the following best describes the relation between the body weight of males and females in Barnum's pigeon?

   A. Males are about 5% heavier than females.
   B. Males are about 10% heavier than females.
   C. Females are 5% heavier than males when newborn, but are 5% lighter at maturity.
   D. Females are 10% heavier than males when newborn, but are 10% lighter at maturity.

28. Which of the following has the greatest percentage of fat per gram of body weight?

   F. Baby male
   G. Baby female
   H. Adult male
   J. Adult female

29. If 10% of a baby female's mass is blood, and the blood has a density of 1 g/ml, approximately how many micrograms of Q are there in an average female baby?

   A. 61 μg
   B. 43 μg
   C. 18 μg
   D. 7 μg

30. Why does the amount of fat in the bird increase at night?

   F. To keep it warm
   G. Because the bird uses its fat reserves during the day
   H. Because of the increased amount of Q in the blood
   J. Insufficient data are provided.

31. An unmarked sample of pigeon blood was found to have a Q level of 60.5 micrograms per milliliter. Which of the following is the most reasonable conclusion that can be drawn about the source of the blood?

   A. It was drawn from an adult male at night.
   B. It was drawn from an adult female at night.
   C. It was drawn from an adult at night.
   D. It was drawn from two baby males at night.

32. If males and females mature at the same time, which sex gains body weight at the faster rate?

   F. Females
   G. Males
   H. Both gain at the same rate.
   J. Insufficient data are provided.

Passage VI

Did dinosaurs have four-chambered hearts? Two different views are presented below.

Scientist 1

Dinosaurs almost certainly had four-chambered hearts. A four-chambered heart allows for the creation of two circuits for the circulatory system. One circuit takes deoxygenated blood and sends it to the lungs. The lungs then allow for an exchange of gases—carbon dioxide from the blood is traded for oxygen. This blood is then returned to the heart for the second circuit. The oxygenated blood is sent from the heart to the entire body. This division of the circulatory system is very efficient because only oxygenated blood is sent from the heart to the body. On the other hand, the three-chambered heart of the reptiles is not as efficient. The oxygenated blood that the lungs return to the heart is mixed with some deoxygenated blood before being sent out to the body. Less oxygen means less energy available for the animal, because energy is generated by the "burning" of food with oxygen. If dinosaurs had three-chambered hearts, they would have been incapable of moving quickly. Predators could have eaten herbivorous dinosaurs before the dinosaur could have run more than a few yards. Also, if current theories are correct, dinosaurs were warm-blooded and, therefore, would have required greater energy. Finally, since it is acknowledged that birds, with their four-chambered hearts, are the closest descendants of the dinosaurs, it follows that the dinosaurs also possessed four-chambered hearts.

Scientist 2

Dinosaurs were the most successful organisms of their time. They dominated their landscape until the great dying-out period during the Cretaceous, 65 million years ago. But their success does not imply that they were as sophisticated biologically as creatures are today, only that they were the most sophisticated of their own time. At that time their only real competition for the land came from the amphibians. Granted that the amphibians had three-chambered hearts, but they were also tied to the water, both to keep their skin moist and to breed. It was on this second difference that the dinosaurs capitalized. Their tougher skin and shelled eggs allowed the dinosaurs and other reptiles to take possession of the inland regions that were inaccessible to their amphibian ancestors and competitors. There is no need to assume that dinosaurs needed a second advantage to dominate over the amphibians. There is, in fact, no reason to assume that dinosaurs differed in any fundamental way from reptiles that are found today. Also, it does not follow that a three-chambered heart doomed the dinosaurs to a life of sluggish movement. Komodo dragons, which reach lengths of ten feet, are reptiles that regularly hunt and catch *deer*!

33. What assumption does Scientist 1 make about dinosaurs?

    A. Dinosaurs were slow.
    B. Dinosaurs had four-chambered hearts.
    C. Related animals have similar biologies.
    D. All of the above

34. How does Scientist 2 counter the argument that three-chambered hearts make animals slow?

    F. He does not address that issue.
    G. He presents an analogy.
    H. He presents a counterexample.
    J. He shows that the dinosaurs are closely related to the amphibians.

35. Which of the following, if true, would most weaken Scientist 2's argument?

    A. Alligators are large, slow-moving reptiles.
    B. Dinosaurs were much larger than Komodo dragons.
    C. Bone studies show that dinosaurs were warm-blooded.
    D. Dinosaurs are not related to birds.

36. Which of the following would Scientist 2 predict to be the fastest animal?

    F. A small mammal
    G. A dinosaur
    H. An amphibian
    J. He would say that relative speeds cannot be predicted.

37. Which of the following would Scientist 1 predict to be the fastest animal?

    A. A large mammal
    B. A large reptile
    C. A large amphibian
    D. He would say that relative speeds cannot be predicted.

38. Which of the following would most weaken Scientist 1's argument based on the descent of birds from dinosaurs?

    F. Not all dinosaurs were two-legged.
    G. Amphibians gave rise to reptiles which also had three-chambered hearts.
    H. Fish with two-chambered hearts gave rise to amphibians with three-chambered hearts.
    J. Birds are warm-blooded.

39. Which of the following would be the most effective argument Scientist 2 could use to counter Scientist 1's claim based on dinosaur running speeds?

    A. There was no need to run fast if the predator's running speed was also slow because it had the same type of heart.
    B. The dinosaurs could not have had four-chambered hearts because they were reptiles.
    C. Birds do not, in general, run fast.
    D. Four-chambered hearts do not guarantee fast speeds.

40. Which of the following, if true, most strengthens Scientist 1's argument based on the descent of birds?

    F. Some dinosaurs were two-legged.
    G. Amphibians gave rise to dinosaurs, which also had three-chambered hearts.
    H. Fish with two-chambered hearts gave rise to amphibians that had three-chambered hearts.
    J. Birds are warm-blooded.

STOP!

This is the end of the Science Reasoning Test.
When the allotted time for this section expires,
the entire test is completed.

Answer Key and Scoring Sheet for Practice Exam III

	English				Mathematics			
	Answer	Usage/Mechanics	Rhetorical		Answer	Pre-Alg./Elem. Alg.	Int. Alg./Coord. Geom.	Geom./Trig.
1.	C	___		1.	B		___	
2.	J		___	2.	H	___		
3.	B	___		3.	C		___	
4.	H		___	4.	K	___		
5.	C		___	5.	B		___	
6.	F	___		6.	J			___
7.	A	___		7.	C			___
8.	H	___		8.	H			___
9.	D	___		9.	C		___	
10.	J	___		10.	J	___		
11.	D	___		11.	B			___
12.	J		___	12.	H			___
13.	C	___		13.	C			___
14.	G	___		14.	H			___
15.	A	___		15.	E		___	
16.	H		___	16.	H	___		
17.	D	___		17.	D		___	
18.	G	___		18.	H	___		
19.	D		___	19.	B		___	
20.	G		___	20.	F		___	
21.	A	___		21.	C			___
22.	J	___		22.	J		___	
23.	B		___	23.	A		___	
24.	H		___	24.	F	___		
25.	C		___	25.	D	___		
26.	F		___	26.	F	___		
27.	D	___		27.	E			___
28.	J	___		28.	F		___	
29.	B	___		29.	A	___		
30.	G	___		30.	K	___		
31.	C	___		31.	A			___
32.	G	___		32.	K			___
33.	D	___		33.	C		___	
34.	J	___		34.	F			___
35.	A		___	35.	D			___
36.	F		___	36.	H			___
37.	A		___	37.	C			___
38.	J	___		38.	F			___
39.	C		___	39.	C			___
40.	H	___		40.	J			___

Answer Key and Scoring Sheet for Practice Exam III (continued)

	English				**Mathematics**			
	Answer	Usage/ Mechanics	Rhetorical		Answer	Pre-Alg./ Elem. Alg.	Int. Alg./ Coord. Geom.	Geom./ Trig.
41.	A	———		41.	C		———	
42.	G	———		42.	G	———		
43.	B	———		43.	C	———		
44.	J	———		44.	G	———		
45.	D	———		45.	C	———		
46.	G	———		46.	J	———		
47.	B		———	47.	C	———		
48.	H	———		48.	F	———		
49.	A		———	49.	A	———		
50.	J		———	50.	H	———		
51.	B		———	51.	B	———		
52.	J	———		52.	H			———
53.	D			53.	C			———
54.	H		———	54.	F			———
55.	C	———		55.	B	———		
56.	F		———	56.	F	———		
57.	C		———	57.	D		———	
58.	J		———	58.	G	———		
59.	B		———	59.	B	———		
60.	G		———	60.	K	———		
61.	A		———					
62.	J		———					
63.	C		———					
64.	H	———						
65.	D		———					
66.	J	———						
67.	A	———						
68.	G		———					
69.	B	———						
70.	H	———						
71.	D		———					
72.	F		———					
73.	D		———					
74.	G		———					
75.	B		———					

Raw Score

Total Correct (by category) ——— ———

Grand Total Correct (English) ———

Total Correct (by category) ——— ——— ———

Grand Total Correct (Mathematics) ———

Using the chart on page **446**, convert the above raw score to an approximate standardized score.

Approx. Standardized Score

Answer Key and Scoring Sheet for Practice Exam III (continued)

	Reading			Science Reasoning	
	Answer	Social St./Science	Arts/Lit.	Answer	Science Reasoning
1.	C	___		1. A	___
2.	F	___		2. G	___
3.	D	___		3. D	___
4.	F	___		4. J	___
5.	B	___		5. D	___
6.	H	___		6. H	___
7.	A	___		7. A	___
8.	H	___		8. H	___
9.	D	___		9. D	___
10.	G	___		10. F	___
11.	D		___	11. D	___
12.	H		___	12. G	___
13.	C		___	13. C	___
14.	F		___	14. F	___
15.	D		___	15. C	___
16.	H		___	16. H	___
17.	B		___	17. A	___
18.	G		___	18. J	___
19.	C		___	19. D	___
20.	H		___	20. J	___
21.	A		___	21. D	___
22.	G		___	22. J	___
23.	D		___	23. A	___
24.	F		___	24. J	___
25.	B		___	25. B	___
26.	J		___	26. G	___
27.	C		___	27. C	___
28.	J		___	28. F	___
29.	A		___	29. B	___
30.	H		___	30. J	___
31.	B	___		31. C	___
32.	F	___		32. G	___
33.	D	___		33. C	___
34.	F	___		34. H	___
35.	C	___		35. C	___
36.	G	___		36. J	___
37.	C	___		37. A	___
38.	J	___		38. H	___
39.	B	___		39. A	___
40.	F	___		40. G	___

Raw Score

Total Correct (by Category) ___ ___   Total Correct ___

Grand Total Correct (Reading) ___   Grand Total Correct (Science Reasoning) ___

Answer Key and Scoring Sheet for Practice Exam III (continued)

Using the chart below, convert the above raw score to an approximate standardized score

Approx. Standardized Score

CONVERSION TABLE

Number Answered Correctly				Approximate Standardized Score
English	Mathematics	Reading	Science Reasoning	
0–2	0–2	0–2	0–1	1
3–4	3	3	2	2
5–6	4–5	4	3–4	3
7–8	6	5	5	4
9–10	7	6	6	5
11–12	8–9	7	7–8	6
13–14	10	8	9	7
15–16	11	9–10	10	8
17–18	12–13	11	11	9
19–20	14	12	12	10
21–23	15	13	13–14	11
24–25	16–17	14–15	15	12
26–27	18–19	16	16	13
28–29	20	17	17	14
30–31	21–22	18	18	15
32–33	23–24	19	19	16
34–35	25–26	20	20	17
36–37	27	21	21	18
38–39	28–29	22	22	19
40–41	30–31	23	23	20
42–44	32–33	24	24–25	21
45–46	34–35	25	26	22
47–48	36–38	26	27	23
49–50	39–40	27	28	24
51–52	41–42	28	29	25
53–54	43	29	30	26
55–57	44–46	30–31	31	27
58–60	47–48	32	32	28
61–63	49–50	33	33	29
64–65	51–52	34	34	30
66–68	53–54	35	35	31
69–70	55–56	36	36	32
71	57	37	37	33
72–73	58	38	38	34
74	59	39	39	35
75	60	40	40	36

Explanatory Answers for Practice Exam III

1. English Test

1. **(C)** To parallel the other items in the series (*thought more* and *fought longer*), the past participle (*written*) followed by a comparative (*more clearly*) is best.

2. **(J)** *Began* means *to get started*; thus, the phrase is unnecessary.

3. **(B)** Capitalization is necessary for proper nouns. Quotation marks are not used for the title of an organization.

4. **(H)** *Man* is singular and takes the singular reflexive *himself*.

5. **(C)** *Though* is the subordinate conjunction needed to connect the dependent clause to the clause on which it depends.

6. **(F)** Commas are used to set off a long adverbial clause or phrase preceding the subject.

7. **(A)** The infinitive *to eliminate* is the correct verbal form.

8. **(H)** *This here* is nonstandard usage for the pronoun *this*.

9. **(D)** *An* is used before a vowel sound and *a* is used before a consonant sound. The adverb *increasingly* is needed to modify the adjective *militaristic*.

10. **(J)** The comma is superfluous. A comma should not be used to separate the subject from the verb.

11. **(D)** *As Lincoln proved* is a parenthetical element. Use a comma both before and after a parenthetical element within a sentence.

12. **(J)** Paragraphs 1 and 2 introduce William Marshall. Paragraph 3 introduces his papers. Paragraph 5 discusses the beginning of the volume, paragraph 6, the middle and paragraph 4, the end.

13. **(C)** The singular subject *development* requires a singular verb *is* in the present tense.

14. **(G)** *Affect*, meaning *to influence*, is used correctly only as a verb. *Effect* functions as a noun meaning *the result* or a verb meaning *to bring about*.

15. **(A)** *Both* is the correct conjunction meaning *two considered together*. *Each* means *one of two or more*.

16. **(H)** Both examples support the primary assertion of the paragraph. One illustrates the idea that attitudes can change due to immediate experience; the other shows that less direct experience may lead to change as well.

17. **(D)** *Being that* is nonstandard usage for the conjunction *because*.

18. **(G)** *Because* is redundant. In formal writing the conjunction *that* should follow the noun *reason*. *Reason* means *cause*.

19. **(D)** *The people of Mexico* is redundant. *Mexican* means *a person from Mexico*.

20. **(G)** *Media* is the plural of *medium*. The plural is necessary for agreement with the plural verb *are*.

21. **(A)** The adjective *emotional* meaning *of or relating to emotion* is used correctly to modify the noun *reactions*.

22. **(J)** *Their* is the correct plural pronoun and it agrees with the antecedent *children*.

23. **(B)** The paragraph deals with the undesirable attitudes of children and how to change them. Giving concrete examples would strengthen the passage.

24. **(H)** This is the only choice that creates a main clause on which the subordinate clause can depend.

25. **(C)**

26. **(F)** *Righted* is used correctly as the past tense form of the verb *right* meaning *to relieve from wrong*.

27. **(D)** *Since* establishes the cause and effect relationship between the two clauses and corrects the comma splice by making one clause subordinate to the other.

28. **(J)** *Was*, the past tense form, is required to avoid a needless shift in tense. The adverb *unusually* is needed to modify the adjective *peaceful*.

29. **(B)** Do not use *plus* to mean *and*.

30. **(G)** Without the addition of *was* the statement is a fragment, not a sentence.

31. **(C)** *But* is the correct conjunction. The conjunction *while* usually refers to time and should not be used in place of *and* or *but*.

32. **(G)** The infinitive *to judge* is the correct verbal form.

33. **(D)** The comma is used to separate items in a series.

34. **(J)** The adverb *carefully* correctly modifies *to listen*. H creates a split infinitive, which is to be avoided in formal writing.

35. **(A)** The correct idiom is *to keep someone from being*.

36. **(F)** The passage describes the Athenian system of justice. Therefore, it would most likely appear in a political science textbook.

37. **(A)** Paragraph 1 introduces the subject, the courts of Athens. Paragraph 2 describes the trial. Paragraph 3 describes the decision process.

38. **(J)** *Among* is used for more than two persons or things, and *between* is used for two persons and things.

39. **(C)** The superlative *most graceful* is best to parallel the other two superlatives (*strongest* and *fleetest*).

40. **(H)** *deCoubertin's* is the correct possessive. The apostrophe followed by an *s* is used to show singular possession.

41. **(A)** The past tense is required.

42. **(G)** The past tense form *refused* is required.

43. **(B)** *Who* is correct as the subject of the verb *had won*.

44. **(J)** *Their* is the correct possessive pronoun. The adverb *there* means *in that place*.

45. **(D)** The committee as a unit takes the singular intensive pronoun *itself*.

46. **(G)** *Bleakest* is the correct superlative adjective.

47. **(B)** The adverb *blatantly* correctly modifies *biased*.

48. **(H)** *Presence* meaning *the fact or condition of being present* is the correct noun. The noun *presents* means *gifts*.

49. **(A)** The passage has a definite point of view about the Olympic games and the boycotts of the games. The author wants to persuade the reader toward his point of view. Therefore, the passage is didactic (intending to instruct).

50. **(J)** The last paragraph indicates the writer's support of the 1980 boycott to show that "conquest . . . of weaker countries will no longer be tolerated."

51. **(B)** *Of* is nonstandard usage for *have*.

52. **(J)** The apostrophe followed by an *s* is used to show singular possession.

53. **(D)** The singular verb *was* is required for the singular subject *combination*.

54. **(H)** *Reminiscent* is the correct adjective meaning serving to remind. *Reminiscence* is a noun meaning a remembered experience.

55. **(C)** The semicolon is used between two main clauses not joined by a coordinating conjunction. D creates a fragment.

56. **(F)** The original version is best, providing relevant additional information to the passage. G represents an incorrect use of *where* and H an incorrect use of *gets*.

57. **(C)** The phrase *made on the label* modifies *claims* and should be placed next to that word.

58. **(J)** The paragraph is discussing the findings of the panel. An explanation of the role of the panel and its desired goals would be informative.

59. **(B)** The entire passage deals with the cold and its remedies, past and present. It is written in laymen's terms; therefore, A, C, and D are incorrect. B is the only correct choice.

60. **(G)** The passage should be second person throughout.

61. **(A)** A dash is used to give special emphasis to the word or phrase set off. It is particularly appropriate in an informal passage such as this one.

62. **(J)** Parentheses are used to enclose nonessential information. The information enclosed in parentheses in paragraph 1 is essential to the sentence.

63. **(C)** The phrase *president of the National Coffee Association* is an appositive that describes George E. Boecklin. It should be set off by two

ACT Practice Exam III / 449

commas.

64. **(H)** *Biggest* is the correct superlative adjective.

65. **(D)** This sentence is not relevant to the paragraph.

66. **(J)** *As* is the correct conjunction. *Like* is never used as a conjunction.

67. **(A)** The dependent clause starting with *when* should not be separated from the clause on which it depends by either a period or a semicolon.

68. **(G)** The paragraph compares coffee drinkers in 1962 to coffee drinkers today. It is logical to follow with a parallel comparison of soft drink consumers in 1962 to soft drink consumers today.

69. **(B)** *Their* is the correct possessive pronoun. *They're* is a contraction for the words they are. *There* is an adverb.

70. **(H)** The use of the comma creates a run-on sentence. The sentences must be separated by a period.

71. **(D)** *Current* means belonging to the present time. The addition of the word *now* is unnecessary.

72. **(F)** In paragraph 2 *soft-drink* does not require a hyphen. In paragraph 3 *most-popular* does not require a hyphen.

73. **(D)**

74. **(G)** Paragraphs 4 and 5 use statistical information to strengthen the passage and its effect.

75. **(B)** Paragraph 1 introduces the topic with a quote. Paragraph 3 explains why the quote is true. Paragraph 2 offers a contrast to information presented in paragraph 3. Paragraph 4 provides statistics to verify facts in paragraph 3. Paragraph 5 presents additional information related to paragraph 4.

2. Mathematics Test

1. **(B)** Probability of an even number =
$$\frac{\text{possibility of success}}{\text{number of possibilities}} = \frac{2}{5}$$

2. **(H)** Two lines are parallel if they have the same slopes. If the equation of a line is represented as $y = mx + b$, the value of m is the slope.

$y - 1 = 3x$
$y = 3x + 1$

The slope is 3.

choice F: slope $= -\frac{1}{3}$
choice G: slope $= 2$
choice H: slope $= 3$ ←
choice J: slope $= -3$
choice K: slope $= 2$

3. **(C)**

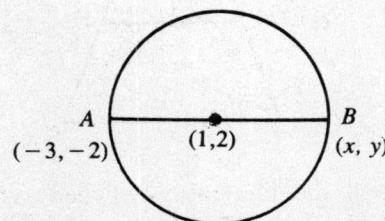

The center (1, 2) represents the midpoint of diameter $\overline{AB}$.

x-midpoint $= \frac{x_1 + x_2}{2}$ y-midpoint $= \frac{y_1 + y_2}{2}$

$1 = \frac{-3 + x}{2}$ $2 = \frac{-2 + y}{2}$

$-3 + x = 2$ $-2 + y = 4$
$x = 5$ $y = 6$

(5, 6)

4. **(K)** $-x^2 - 2x - 3 = -(-2)^2 - 2(-2) - 3$
$= -(4) + 4 - 3$
$= -4 + 4 - 3$
$= -3$

5. **(B)** To eliminate the variable y, multiply the first equation by -1 and then add the two equations.

$-1(3x + y = 2r) = -3x - y = -2r$
$x + y = r \qquad\qquad\quad x + y = r$
$\qquad\qquad\qquad\qquad\overline{-2x \quad\quad = -r}$

$x = \frac{-r}{-2} = \frac{r}{2}$

Substitute $x = \frac{r}{2}$ into the second equation and solve for y.

$x + y = r$
$\frac{r}{2} + y = r$
$y = r - \frac{r}{2} = \frac{r}{2}$

The solution set is: $\left\{\frac{r}{2}, \frac{r}{2}\right\}$

6. (J) 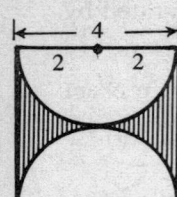 Area of the square = $s^2 = (4)^2 = 16$.

Area of the 2 semicircles = $2\left[\dfrac{1}{2}\pi r^2\right]$

$= 2\left(\dfrac{1}{2}\right)\pi(2)^2$

$= 4\pi$

The shaded area is the area of the square minus the area of the two semicircles.

Shaded area = $16 - 4\pi$

7. (C) The area of an equilateral triangle can be expressed as:

$A = \dfrac{s^2}{4}\sqrt{3}$, when s = side of the equilateral triangle

$\dfrac{s^2}{4}\sqrt{3} = \dfrac{25\sqrt{3}}{4}$

$s^2 = 25$
$s = 5$

Perimeter = $3s = 3(5) = 15$

8. (H)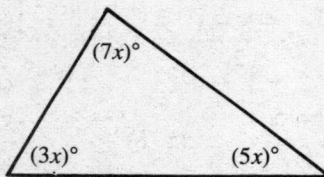

Let $3x$ = the measure of one of the angles
$5x$ = the measure of the 2nd angle
$7x$ = the measure of the 3rd angle

$3x + 5x + 7x = 180$
$15x = 180$
$x = 12$

The smallest angle = $3x = 36°$

9. (C) $(x - y)(x^2 + xy + y^2)$

$= x(x^2) + x(xy) + x(y^2) - y(x^2)$
$\quad - y(xy) - y(y^2)$

$= x^3 + x^2y + xy^2 - yx^2 - xy^2 - y^3$

$= x^3 - y^3$

10. (J) $(2a^2 - a^3)^2$ when $a = -1$

$(2(-1)^2 - (-1)^3)^2 = (2(1) - (-1))^2$
$= (2 + 1)^2$
$= 3^2$
$= 9$

11. (B) Draw a right triangle and represent

$\sin x = \dfrac{1}{3} = \dfrac{\text{side opposite angle } x}{\text{hypotenuse}}$

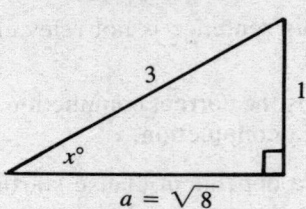

Calculate the third side of the triangle using the Pythagorean theorem.

$a^2 + 1^2 = 3^2$
$a^2 + 1 = 9$
$a^2 = 8$
$a = \sqrt{8}$

$\tan x = \dfrac{\text{side opposite angle } x}{\text{side adjacent to angle } x}$

$= \dfrac{1}{\sqrt{8}} = \dfrac{1}{2\sqrt{2}} \cdot \dfrac{\sqrt{2}}{\sqrt{2}} = \dfrac{\sqrt{2}}{4}$

12. (H)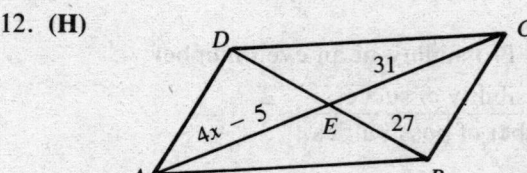

The diagonals of a parallelogram bisect each other.

$\therefore \overline{AE} = \overline{EC}$
$4x - 5 = 31$
$4x = 36$
$x = 9$

13. (C)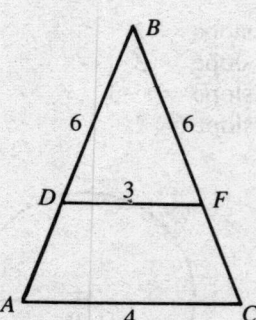

Establish the line ratio between $\triangle DBF$ and $\triangle ABC$.

$\dfrac{\text{side of } \triangle DBF}{\text{corresponding side of } \triangle ABC} = \dfrac{\text{perimeter of } DBF}{\text{perimeter of } \triangle ABC}$

$$\frac{3}{4} = \frac{(3+6+6)}{x}$$
$$\frac{3}{4} = \frac{15}{x}$$
$$3x = 60$$
$$x = 20$$

14. **(H)**

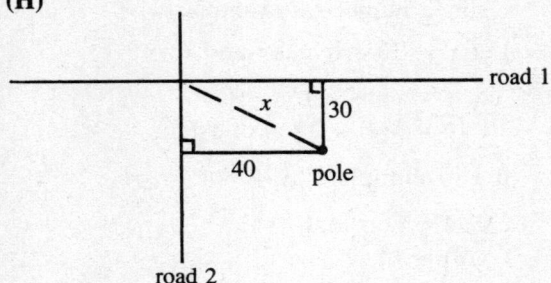

Using the Pythagorean theorem:
$$(30)^2 + (40)^2 = x^2$$
$$900 + 1600 = x^2$$
$$2500 = x^2$$
$$x = 50$$

15. **(E)**

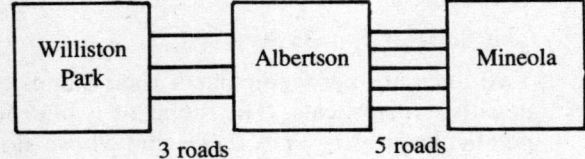

There are $3 \times 5 = 15$ different paths from Williston Park to Mineola through Albertson.

16. **(H)** If the equation of a line is written in the form $y = mx + b$, m represents the slope and b represents the y-intercept.

$$y - 5 = \frac{1}{2}(x + 2)$$

Multiply each side of the equation by 2.

$$2(y - 5) = (x + 2)$$
$$2y - 10 = x + 2$$
$$2y = x + 12$$
$$y = \frac{1}{2}x + 6$$

The slope $= \frac{1}{2}$, the y-intercept $= 6$.

17. **(D)** For the roots of a quadratic equation to be real and equal, the discriminant $(b^2 - 4ac)$ must equal zero.

Value of the discriminant $(b^2 - 4ac)$

	negative "−"	zero	positive perfect square	positive, not a perfect square
Nature of the roots	imaginary	real	real	real
		equal	unequal	unequal
		rational	rational	irrational
	graph is totally above or below the x-axis	graph is tangent to the x-axis	graph intersects the x-axis at two distinct points	graph intersects the x-axis at two distinct points

Given: $x^2 + 4x + c$ $\quad a = 1$
$\quad b = 4$
$\quad c = c$

$$b^2 - 4ac = (4)^2 - 4(1)(c) = 0$$
$$16 - 4c = 0$$
$$4c = 16$$
$$c = 4$$

18. **(H)** The contrapositive of a true statement is always true. If $p \to q$ represents the original statement, then $\sim q \to \sim p$ represents the contrapositive.

19. **(B)**
$$g(x) = \frac{x+5}{2}$$
$$g(2m) = \frac{2m+5}{2}$$
$$f(x) = 2x - 5$$
$$f\left(\frac{2m+5}{2}\right) = 2\left(\frac{2m+5}{2}\right) - 5$$
$$= 2m + 5 - 5$$
$$= 2m$$
$$\therefore f(g(2m)) = f\left(\frac{2m+5}{2}\right) = 2m$$

20. **(F)** $(x - 1)(x + 3) < 0$
$\quad x = 1 \mid x = -3$

 ← number line

Use a numerical value to test each of the three circled intervals.

Test interval ①, $x < -3$. Use the test element $x = -4$.

$(x - 1)(x + 3) < 0 \rightarrow (-4 - 1)(-4 + 3) \stackrel{?}{<} 0$
$(-5)(-1) \stackrel{?}{<} 0$
$5 < 0$
False

∴ Interval ① is *not* part of the solution set.

Test interval ②, $-3 < x < 1$. Use the test element $x = 0$.

$(x - 1)(x + 3) < 0 \rightarrow (0 - 1)(0 + 3) \stackrel{?}{<} 0$
$(-1)(3) \stackrel{?}{<} 0$
$-3 < 0$ True

∴ Interval ② is part of the solution set.

Test interval ③, $x > 1$. Use the test element $x = 2$.

$(x - 1)(x + 3) < 0 \rightarrow (2 - 1)(2 + 3) \stackrel{?}{<} 0$
$(1)(5) \stackrel{?}{<} 0$
$5 < 0$ False

∴ Interval ③ is *not* part of the solution set.

Because $(x - 1)(x + 3) < 0$ has only a less than sign ($<$) and not a less than or equal ($\leq$), the values of $x = 1$ and $x = -3$ are hollow (○).

$$\overset{\circ\circ}{\underset{-31}{\rule{4cm}{0.4pt}}}$$

21. **(C)** $A = s^2 = K$
∴ $s = \sqrt{K}$
$P = 4s = 4\sqrt{K}$

22. **(J)** $\dfrac{1 + \dfrac{1}{x}}{1 + \dfrac{1}{y}}$

Multiply the top and bottom of the complex fraction by the lowest common denominator, which is xy.

$$\dfrac{xy\left(1 + \dfrac{1}{x}\right)}{xy\left(1 + \dfrac{1}{y}\right)} = \dfrac{xy(1) + xy\left(\dfrac{1}{x}\right)}{xy(1) + xy\left(\dfrac{1}{y}\right)} = \dfrac{xy + y}{xy + x}$$

23. **(A)** y varies inversely as the $\sqrt{x}$ can be expressed as:

$y_1\sqrt{x_1} = y_2\sqrt{x_2}$ or $y\sqrt{x} =$ constant

If $y\sqrt{x} =$ constant, multiplying the x by four increases the left side of the equation two-fold (by the $\sqrt{4}$). The value of y would have to be cut in half to cancel the effect.

Using a numerical example:

Let $x = 16$ originally and $y = 3$

$y\sqrt{x} =$ constant
$3\sqrt{16} = 3(4) = 12 =$ constant

If x is multiplied by 4 ∴ $x = 64$

$y\sqrt{64} =$ constant $= 12$
$y(8) = 12$
$y = \dfrac{3}{2}$

NOTE: The value of y went from $y = 3$ to $y = \dfrac{3}{2}$. It was halved.

24. **(F)** In the form $y = mx + b$, m is the slope of the line and b is the y-intercept.

The slope of $y = 3x + 2$ is 3.

Two lines are perpendicular if their slopes are negative reciprocals. The slope of a line perpendicular to $y = 3x + 2$ is a line whose slope is the negative reciprocal of 3.

The negative reciprocal of 3 is $-\dfrac{1}{3}$.

25. **(D)** Establish a ratio of candy bars to cents. NOTE: $1.02 is 102¢.

$\dfrac{\text{candy bars}}{\text{cents}}: \dfrac{12}{17} = \dfrac{x}{102}$

$17x = 12(102)$
$x = 72$

26. **(F)** $-|3 - (-2)| = -|3 + 2| = -(5) = -5$
$|-3 + 2| = |-1| = 1$

$\dfrac{-|3 - (-2)|}{|-3 + 2|} = \dfrac{-5}{1} = -5$

27. **(E)** Volume $=$ (edge)³
$= (5x)^3 = 125x^3$

28. **(F)** If a point does *not* lie on the graph of an equation, then it does *not* satisfy the equation.
choice F: $(-1, -1)$ $\quad 2x + y = 2(-1) + (-1)$
$\qquad\qquad\qquad\qquad\quad = -3 \neq 3$
choice G: $(-1, 5)$ $\quad 2x + y = 2(-1) + (5) = 3$
choice H: $(0, 3)$ $\qquad 2x + y = 2(0) + 3 = 3$
choice J: $\left(\dfrac{1}{2}, 2\right)$ $\quad 2x + y = 2\left(\dfrac{1}{2}\right) + 2 = 3$
choice K: $(-2, 7)$ $\quad 2x + y = 2(-2) + 7 = 3$

29. **(A)** $\dfrac{2^2 + 3^2}{5^2} + \dfrac{1}{10} = \dfrac{4 + 9}{25} + \dfrac{1}{10}$
$\qquad\qquad\quad = \dfrac{13}{25} + \dfrac{1}{10}$

The lowest common denominator is 50.

$\qquad\qquad\quad = \dfrac{26}{50} + \dfrac{5}{50} = \dfrac{31}{50}$

30. **(K)** Average = $\dfrac{\text{Sum of the scores}}{\text{Number of scores}}$
$\qquad\qquad = \dfrac{89 + 86 + 81 + 94 + 75}{5}$
$\qquad\qquad = \dfrac{425}{5} = 85$

31. **(A)**

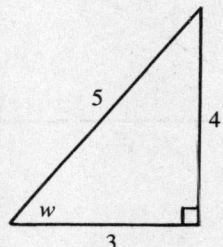

Since $\overline{AB}$ is a diameter, arc AC + arc CB = 180° ∴ arc CB = 140°. $\angle COB$ is a central angle and a central angle is equal in measure to its intercepted arc ∴ $\angle COB$ = 140°.

32. **(K)** Average = $\dfrac{\text{Sum of items}}{\text{Quantity of items}}$
$\qquad 84 = \dfrac{\text{Sum}}{6}$
$\qquad \text{Sum} = 504$

33. **(C)** $d = \sqrt{(x_2 - x_1)^2 + (y_2 - y_1)^2}$
$\qquad = \sqrt{(3 - (-4))^2 + (-2 - 5)^2}$
$\qquad = \sqrt{7^2 + (-7)^2}$
$\qquad = \sqrt{49 + 49} = \sqrt{98} = \sqrt{49}\sqrt{2}$
$\qquad = 7\sqrt{2}$

34. **(F)**

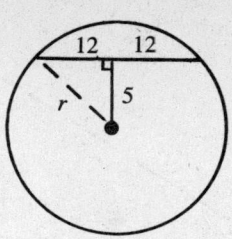

A radius drawn perpendicular to a chord bisects the chord. Construct the radius as shown above.
$\qquad 5^2 + 12^2 = r^2$
$\qquad 25 + 144 = r^2$
$\qquad\qquad r^2 = 169$
$\qquad\qquad r = 13$

35. **(D)**

NOTE: A triangle with sides 3-4-5 is a right triangle.

The larger acute angle is opposite the larger (non-hypotenuse) side. We will denote the larger acute angle by the letter w.

$\sin w = \dfrac{\text{side opposite angle } w}{\text{hypotenuse}} = \dfrac{4}{5}$

36. **(H)** Rationalize the denominator
$\dfrac{2}{(3 - \sqrt{3})} \cdot \dfrac{(3 + \sqrt{3})}{(3 + \sqrt{3})} = \dfrac{2(3 + \sqrt{3})}{9 + 3\sqrt{3} - 3\sqrt{3} - \sqrt{9}} =$
$\dfrac{2(3 + \sqrt{3})}{9 - \sqrt{9}} = \dfrac{2(3 + \sqrt{3})}{9 - 3}$
$= \dfrac{2(3 + \sqrt{3})}{6}$
$= \dfrac{3 + \sqrt{3}}{3}$

454 / ACT

37. **(C)**

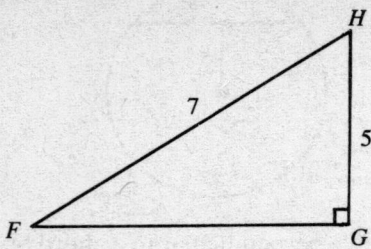

$(\overline{FG})^2 + 5^2 = 7^2$
$(\overline{FG})^2 + 25 = 49$
$(\overline{FG})^2 = 24$
$\overline{FG} = \sqrt{24} = 2\sqrt{6}$

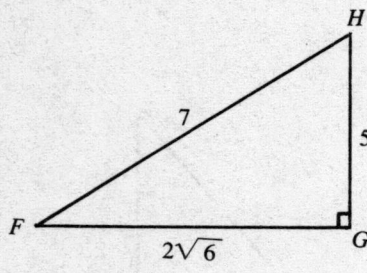

$\dfrac{\sec F}{\csc H} = \dfrac{\dfrac{1}{\cos F}}{\dfrac{1}{\sin H}} =$

$\dfrac{\sin H}{\cos F} = \dfrac{\dfrac{2\sqrt{6}}{7}}{\dfrac{2\sqrt{6}}{7}} = \left(\dfrac{2\sqrt{6}}{7}\right)\left(\dfrac{7}{2\sqrt{6}}\right) = 1$

38. **(F)** The angles of an isosceles right triangle are 45°-45°-90°. Each acute angle is 45°

$\therefore\ 2x + 5 = 45$
$2x = 40$
$x = 20$

39. **(C)**

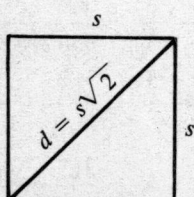

Diagonal of a square = (side)($\sqrt{2}$)
$d = (\sqrt{2})(\sqrt{2}) = 2$

40. **(J)** The ellipse is of the form $\dfrac{x^2}{a^2} + \dfrac{y^2}{b^2} = 1$ where $a = 5$ and $b = 4$.

$\dfrac{x^2}{5^2} + \dfrac{y^2}{4^2} = 1 \rightarrow \dfrac{x^2}{25} + \dfrac{y^2}{16} = 1$

41. **(C)**

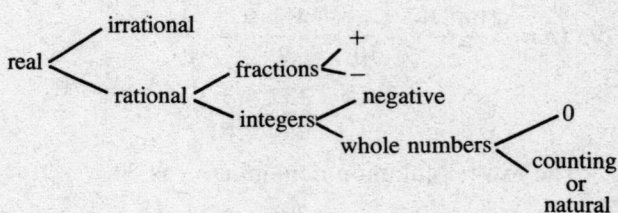

Rational numbers are a subset of real numbers.

42. **(G)** $3(2x + 1) = 6x + 3$ is an example of the distributive property of multiplication over addition.

43. **(C)** By long division:

$$\begin{array}{r} 4x - 1 \\ x - 1 \overline{\smash{)}4x^2 - 5x + 7} \\ -\underline{4x^2 - 4x} \\ -x + 7 \\ -\underline{-x + 1} \\ 6 \leftarrow \text{remainder} \end{array}$$

By synthetic division:

$$\underline{1]}\ \ \begin{array}{rrr} 4 & -5 & 7 \\ & 4 & -1 \\ \hline 4 & -1 & \underline{|6} \leftarrow \text{remainder} \end{array}$$

44. **(G)** To eliminate the y, multiply the first equation by -1 and add the equations.

$\begin{array}{l} -1\,(3x + 2y = 4) \\ -2x + 2y = 24 \end{array} \rightarrow \begin{array}{l} -3x - 2y = -4 \\ \underline{-2x + 2y = 24} \\ -5x = 20 \\ x = -4 \end{array}$

Substitute $x = -4$ into the first equation and solve for y.

$3x + 2y = 4$
$3(-4) + 2y = 4$
$-12 + 2y = 4$
$2y = 16$
$y = 8$

The solution is $(-4, 8)$.

45. **(C)** $\frac{5}{8} = .625,\ \frac{7}{11} = .636\ldots,\ \frac{2}{3} = .666\ldots,$
$\frac{3}{5} = .6,\ \frac{4}{7} = .571\ldots$

$\frac{2}{3}$ is the largest.

46. **(J)** To convert feet to inches multiply by 12. For example:

3 feet are $3(12) = 36$ inches

$(3x - 2)$ feet are $(3x - 2)(12) = 36x - 24$ inches

47. **(C)** The sum of two even integers is always even. If $n + 1$ is an even number, then $(n + 1) + 2$ is also even.

$(n + 1) + 2 = n + 3$

48. **(F)** Multiply the given equation by -2.

$-2[2x - 3y = 7] = -4x + 6y = -14$

Rearrange the equation as follows:

$6y - 4x = -14$

49. **(A)**
$(7x + 8y) - (2x - 3y) = 7x + 8y - 2x + 3y$
$= 5x + 11y$

50. **(H)** $\dfrac{\text{interest received}}{\text{amount invested}} \times 100$

$\dfrac{50}{1000} \times 100 = 5\%$

51. **(B)** $\dfrac{6}{x} \div \dfrac{3}{x} \to \dfrac{6}{x} \cdot \dfrac{x}{3} = \dfrac{6x}{3x} = 2$

$2 \div \dfrac{x}{3} \to \dfrac{2}{1} \cdot \dfrac{3}{x} = \dfrac{6}{x}$

$\dfrac{\left(\dfrac{6}{x} \div \dfrac{3}{x}\right) \div \dfrac{x}{3}}{6} = \dfrac{2 \div \dfrac{x}{3}}{6} = \dfrac{\dfrac{6}{x}}{6} = \dfrac{6}{x} \cdot \dfrac{1}{6} = \dfrac{1}{x}$

52. **(H)**

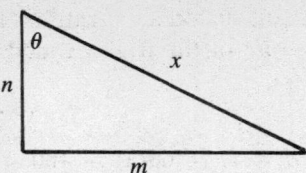

Find the third side of the triangle using the Pythagorean theorem. Label the third side x.

$m^2 + n^2 = x^2$

$x = \sqrt{m^2 + n^2}$

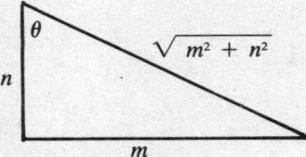

$\sin \theta = \dfrac{m}{\sqrt{m^2 + n^2}}$

53. **(C)**

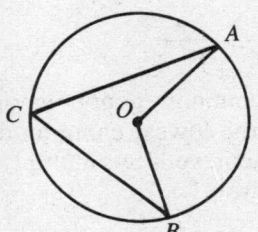

$\angle ACB$ is an inscribed angle. Its measure is $\dfrac{1}{2}$ the measure of arc AB. $\angle AOB$ is a central angle. Its measure is equal to arc AB.

$\dfrac{\text{measure of } \angle ACB}{\text{measure of } \angle AOB} = \dfrac{\dfrac{1}{2} \text{ measure of arc } AB}{\text{measure of arc } AB} = \dfrac{1}{2}$

54. **(F)** The shaded area is the area of the rectangle minus the area of the two circles.

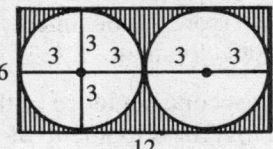

Area of the rectangle $= 6(12) = 72$
Area of circle $= \pi r^2 = 9\pi$
Shaded area $= 72 - 2(9\pi) = 72 - 18\pi$

55. **(B)** The converse of a statement involves reversing the position of the hypothesis and conclusion.

If the original statement is $p \to q$, the converse is $q \to p$.

"If it is a fizzgig, then it has green horns."

56. (F) Recall: distance = rate × time ($d = rt$).
Let r = rate of the train headed south.

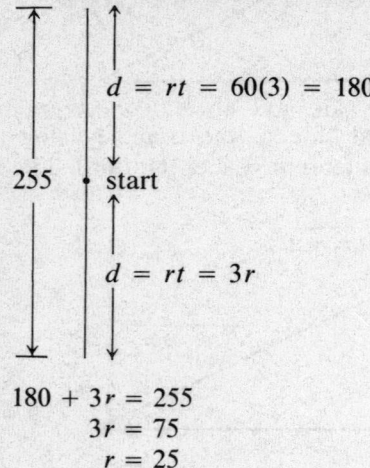

$180 + 3r = 255$
$3r = 75$
$r = 25$

57. (D) $\dfrac{x}{x-1} - \dfrac{x}{1-x}$

Find a common denominator. In this case $x - 1$ is the lowest common denominator and can be achieved by multiplying the second fraction by -1.

$\dfrac{x}{x-1} - \dfrac{x(-1)}{(1-x)(-1)} = \dfrac{x}{x-1} + \dfrac{x}{x-1} = \dfrac{2x}{x-1}$

58. (G) Range: The difference between the maximum and minimum values. The range of $\{4, 7, 12\}$ is $12 - 4 = 8$.

Median: The middle number when the elements are arranged in numerical sequence. The median of $\{4, 7, 12\}$ is 7.

Average (Mean) = $\dfrac{\text{The sum of the numbers}}{\text{The quantity of numbers}}$

$= \dfrac{4+7+12}{3} = \dfrac{23}{3} = 7\dfrac{2}{3}$.

Choice G is correct.

59. (B) 8, 10, 10, 10, 14, 14

Average (Mean) = $\dfrac{\text{Sum of the numbers}}{\text{Quantity of numbers}}$

$= \dfrac{8+10+10+10+14+14}{6}$

$= 11$.

Median: The "middle" number when arranged in numerical sequence. The median is 10.

Mode: The number with the greatest frequency. The mode is 10.

Choice B is correct.

60. (K) $\dfrac{6!}{3!} = \dfrac{6 \cdot 5 \cdot 4 \cdot 3 \cdot 2 \cdot 1}{3 \cdot 2 \cdot 1} = 6 \cdot 5 \cdot 4 = 120$

3. Reading Test

1. (C) The first sentence of the passage states that "The energy crunch . . . has brought the whole world to the brink of disaster."

2. (F) The second sentence of the passage uses the word "more" four times, thus emphasizing the overdevelopment.

3. (D) The second sentence of the passage states that the overdevelopment of motor transport ". . . has contributed to the near-destruction of our cities . . ."

4. (F) The first sentence in the third paragraph discusses the widespread lawbreaking.

5. (B) The passage argues a definite point of view. Therefore, it is considered argumentative.

6. (H) The use of the word "no" in the last paragraph boldly emphasizes the magnitude of the problem.

7. (A) The comparison to past problems in paragraph 2 dramatizes the urgency of the problem.

8. (H) The last paragraph discusses the need for a change in lifestyle.

9. (D) The author expresses concern throughout the passage about the use of energy resources. Choices A and B would be concerned about the making of money, choice C is irrelevant. Therefore, the answer is D.

10. (G) Paragraph 1 states the problem. Paragraphs 2 and 3 provide a history and development. Paragraphs 4 and 5 appeal for a solution.

11. (D) The passage describes the experiences of Jane Cooper on an isolated and difficult island in Australia.

12. (H) Paragraph 1 describes its ". . . jagged rocks, tangled undergrowth, and trees twisted and bent by battering winds."

13. **(C)** In the last paragraph Jane describes feeling sorry for herself and crying.

14. **(F)** The third paragraph describes Jane's many talents.

15. **(D)** Paragraph 3 describes how Jane spends her time on the island.

16. **(H)** Jane dives for crayfish and abalone to supplement her diet; therefore, she must be a strong swimmer.

17. **(B)** The experiences of De Witt Isle have helped Jane to mature.

18. **(G)** Jane seems optimistic by the end of the passage.

19. **(C)** The rocks and undergrowth are hardly assets for De Witt Isle.

20. **(H)** In the second paragraph Jane states: "I wanted to be alone, to have some time to think and find out about myself."

21. **(A)** The passage uses numerous adjectives to describe the ski slopes, Armande, and her clothing.

22. **(G)** The main focus of this passage is Armande.

23. **(D)** He is looking at the silhouette of Armande from a distance; therefore, he is at a point beneath the skiers.

24. **(F)** The entire first paragraph is written from his point of view.

25. **(B)** "Mondstein Sexy" is the trade name of the ski boots.

26. **(J)** The second paragraph describes Armande's fashionable clothing.

27. **(C)** His close observation of Armande shows his fondness for her.

28. **(J)** The sentence ends with the comment that the footwear was being discussed ". . . in flattering terms."

29. **(A)** Armande offers to return to Witt with the author. The passage might then describe their conversation.

30. **(H)** The author watches Armande painstakingly as she skis and describes her in only flattering terms.

31. **(B)** This selection presents a history of the study of caves. The article does not do any of the things suggested by the other answers.

32. **(F)** Biospeleology is first mentioned in paragraph two in relation to caves and their life. "Bio" also means "life."

33. **(D)** Paragraph 2 also clearly explains that most research of North American caves during the early twentieth century was done by Europeans.

34. **(F)** Mr. Davis' research had two stifling effects on cave studies, which hampered the research. Choice F reflects the negative products of Davis' findings.

35. **(C)** Paragraph 3 points out that Davis proposed cave development deep below the water table (phreatic origin).

36. **(G)** The author states in the first paragraph: "Early biological studies emphasized faunal surveys and descriptions of the . . . eyes of . . . animals . . ."

37. **(C)** Cave organisms and their physiology are not discussed in the passage.

38. **(J)** The first sentence of the passage states that elaborate, but erroneous, theories of the hydrological cycle were propounded in the seventeenth and eighteenth centuries in Europe.

39. **(B)** The passage deals with cave history in depth; therefore, it would have come from some scientific journal or magazine.

40. **(F)** The last paragraph states that the National Speleological Society consists of ". . . nonprofessional explorers and surveyors."

4. Science Reasoning Test

1. **(A)** The solid phase is the one that has the particles most tightly bound. High pressure will tend to force the particles together. In addition, low temperatures will ensure that the particles have little kinetic energy available for them to move relative to each other. In addition, things tend to solidify at low temperatures. The region that has both high pressure (top of graph) and low temperature (left of graph) is region A. It is extremely unlikely that both A and B are solid phases because that would mean that as you reduced the pressure from 80 to 10 atm at 6K you would cause a solid to melt (at 62.5 atm) and then freeze again (at 18.7 atm). Because the particles of region B are not forced together as much as are the particles of region A (because they are at lower pressures), and because the particles have more kinetic energy available to use to separate from each other, region B is unlikely to be a solid.

2. **(G)** To use an argument similar to the one in the first question, the gas phase will be the one in which the particles have the *least* incentive to stay together. Lower pressure means less force pushing the particles together. Higher temperatures mean that the molecules will be able to escape from each other because of their high kinetic energy. The region that has the lowest pressure and highest temperature will be in the lower right corner of the diagram, region B.

3. **(D)** First find the point marking 32.5 atm and 10K. Move on the horizontal to the left. This corresponds to lowering the temperature while maintaining the same pressure. At 8.5K we note that we have not crossed any boundaries. Because we have not crossed any boundaries, we have not changed the phase.

4. **(J)** Boiling occurs when there is a transition between the liquid and gas phases such that the vapor pressure of the gas equals the applied pressure. On the diagram this point is the boundary between the liquid and gas phases. If you draw a horizontal line at 57.5 atm, it intersects the liquid-gas (region B) border at 10.125K.

5. **(D)** The condensation point occurs when there is a transition between gas and liquid phases such that the vapor pressure of the gas equals the applied pressure. On the diagram this point is the boundary between the gas and liquid phases. If you draw a horizontal line at 57.5 atm, it intersects the gas (region B)-liquid border at 10.125K. Questions 4 and 5 illustrate the fact that the boiling and condensation points are identical. This is because the boiling and condensation points describe the same equilibrium situation between two phases. This same line of reasoning also applies to melting and freezing points (water freezes and ice melts at 0°C).

6. **(H)** The border between two phases marks a transition between the two phases. At the transition there is a shuttling back and forth between one phase and the other. For example, at 0°C ice melts *and* water freezes. To apply this to the current case, liquid I turns into liquid II *and* liquid II turns into liquid I. Thus, both choices **F** and **G** are correct. If only **F** or **G** were correct, that would mean that at that combination of pressure and temperature, one would find only liquid I or liquid II after some time had elapsed. This would mean that the point ought to be *within* either liquid I's or liquid II's region of the phase diagram, which is not the case.

7. **(A)** The introduction to the passage points out that the greater the jostling, the more difficult it is for the molecules to flow past each other. Since temperature is, as was noted in the introduction, the average kinetic energy of the particles, the higher the temperature, the more the particles jump around. We would therefore expect the superfluid, which has *no* viscosity, to exist at the lower temperature range. We would also expect the viscosity to decrease as the pressure decreased because the particles would find themselves less pressed together at lower pressures. The region with the lowest pressure and the lowest temperature is liquid I.

8. **(H)** Permeability is a measure of the time required for water to pass through. The table indicates that the least amount of time for water to pass through occurred in tube C. Since the permeability for tube C was 6 seconds, the least of the four tubes, the coarse particles in tube C are the most permeable.

9. **(D)** Samples A, B, and C all have different particle sizes but the same porosity. Therefore, there is no direct relation between particle size and porosity. This rules out choices **A** and **B**. Choice **C** is ruled out because the porosity has a different value in tube D from its value in the others, and it is therefore not a constant.

10. **(F)** Capillarity is a measure of the ability of water

to rise in small openings. In loose material, the smaller the particle size, the greater the capillarity. The table indicates that tube A has the greatest capillarity of the four tubes.

11. **(D)** Porosity is a measure of the amount of space between the particles within a mass. Tubes A, B, and C each have a porosity of 40%. This means that each contains the same percentage of space between particles to hold water. By comparison, the porosity of the soil in tube D is only 20%. This means that the soil in tube D can hold only half as much water as the other three tubes.

12. **(G)** In order to compare capillarity to permeability, we need to exclude the experiment done in tube D, because the soil in this tube has a different porosity than the other tubes, which would introduce another variable. Considering the other three experiments, we see that as the time required for the water to pass through the soil increases, the height that the water can climb relative to a reservoir also increases. This makes sense because in both cases we are measuring the ability of water to "stick" to the soil. As the ability of water to stick to the soil increases, the height it is able to crawl up the soil should increase. As the stickiness increases, we would also expect the water to have more difficulty working its way out of a sample, and thus to have a longer permeability time.

13. **(C)** All things being equal (for example, density), the largest particles will settle out of a solution first and the smallest will settle out last. Therefore, the smallest particles will be on top, and will be listed first.

14. **(F)** The graph, which indicates the relationship of particle size to water velocity, also shows the relationship of particle size to category, ranging from clay to boulders. Tube C has a particle size of 0.3 cm, which falls into the category of pebbles (0.2 cm to 6.4 cm).

15. **(C)** The text indicates that the process of glycolysis yields two molecules of pyruvic acid from each molecule of glucose. Therefore, two glucose molecules can generate four pyruvic acid molecules.

16. **(H)** Each step of the reaction would take us to a brand new product. The steps of the reactions in the Krebs cycle are shown by the arrows. Counting the arrowheads in the reaction, we see that there are six steps. The question asks us to assume that there is one unique enzyme for each step, so we conclude that there were six enzymes used within the cycle.

17. **(A)** This question requires you to keep careful track of all reactions in the diagram. We see that one ATP is made before succinic acid.

18. **(J)** Note that the question asks for the number of carbons that *eventually* are lost as carbon dioxide. As we see as we look through the cycle, there is a loss of three carbon dioxides from the initial pyruvic acid. But each glucose produces two molecules of pyruvic acid, so the six carbons in glucose are all ultimately lost as carbon dioxide.

19. **(D)** By counting the number of carbons, hydrogens and oxygens in each compound, we obtain:

	Succinic acid	Fumaric acid	Change
C:	4	4	none
H:	6	4	lost 2
O:	4	4	none

20. **(J)** We are told in the introduction that the glucose is ultimately obtained from plants. Where do plants get their food? They make their own food by the process of photosynthesis. As the "photo" in the word implies, the plants use light, which is a form of energy, to make their food. Therefore, the energy found in glucose was originally the energy the plant received from the sun.

21. **(D)** The introduction states that the electrons are removed from the metal using energy. This energy comes from the light that impinges on the surface. The energy that the electrons have once they leave the surface of the metal must also come from the light because there is no other source for that energy. The energy these electrons exhibit is the energy of motion, which is called kinetic energy. The faster the motion of the particle, the more energy it has. It follows that the frequency that gave rise to the fastest electrons must have had the most energy to give. Looking at the diagrams, we see that the maxima for the largest peaks for frequencies 2, 3, and 4 are 3 units, 5 units, and 7 units respectively. This would suggest that frequency 4 had the most energy to give. Analysis of the smaller peaks gives the same results—9 units, 14 units, and 18 units for frequencies 2, 3, and 4 respectively.

22. **(J)** We see that the average speed of the electron in Experiment 3, which is roughly near the maximum of the big peak (not exactly because of the smaller peak at 14 units) does not shift as we go from inten-

sity 1 to intensity 2 to intensity 3. We get the same curve, but higher—meaning that there are more electrons released. This means that the intensity does not affect how fast the electrons go, it affects only the number of electrons that take off from the surface of the Mu metal. As we observed before, the faster an object goes, the greater is its kinetic energy. All of the other answers claim that there is a change in the kinetic energy, and therefore on the speed of the electrons, depending on the intensity of light. If choice **F** were correct, the peaks would shift to the right so that the speeds got higher as the intensity increased. If choice **G** were right, the peak would shift to the left, so that the speed would decrease as the intensity increased. If choice **H** were correct, the points on the curve where no electrons were found (at 0, 10, and 17 units) would shift for each intensity.

23. **(A)** The experiment is designed to tell us about the behavior of the *electrons* bound to the metal. This should make us suspicious of answers **B** and **D**, which talk about the photons of light directed at the metal. In the first experiment no electrons were observed. Either there was a problem with the apparatus (somebody forgot to turn it on?) or the electrons did not leave the metal. Assuming for the moment that everybody was doing his or her job, the fact that the electrons did not leave means that the light did not have enough energy to take away the electron from the metal. Therefore, the metal must hold the electrons with an energy greater than the energy associated with frequency 1. Also, the smallest energy that we know about that could overwhelm the metal is the energy associated with the slowest moving electrons. Thus, the metal could not have a hold on the electrons stronger than the energy associated with frequency 2. If you were confused by the answer choices, it might be helpful to attempt to answer the question in your own words first.

24. **(J)** Choice **F** is true.

    Frequency 2: base $7\frac{1}{2}$ to $10\frac{1}{3} = 3$

    Frequency 3: base 11 to 17 = 6
    Frequency 4: base 15 to 23 = 8

    Choice **G** is true.

    $$\text{Ratio} = \frac{\text{Intensity (I}_3\text{) small peak}}{\text{Intensity (I}_3\text{) large peak}}$$

Frequency 2	Frequency 3	Frequency 4
$\frac{3}{15.5} = .19$	$\frac{2.75}{14} = .2$	$\frac{2.5}{12} = .21$

    A ratio of 1:5 is $\frac{1}{5} = .2$, this approximate ratio is maintained.

    Choice **H** is true.

	Frequency 2		Frequency 3		Frequency 4
large peak:	3	→	5	→	7
small peak:	9	→	14	→	18

    The small peak is shifting faster than the larger peak as frequency increases.

    Choice **J** is False.

    distance between large and small peaks:

Frequency 2	Frequency 3	Frequency 4
9 − 3 = 6	14 − 5 = 9	18 − 7 = 11

    The distance between peaks increases with frequency.

25. **(B)** The likeliest cause for any electron's moving would be its being struck by a photon. Therefore, the largest peak should be due to electrons being struck by one photon. This rules out choice **A**. If choice **C** were correct, we would expect the peak to have at least some "ridges"—each ridge would be from electrons absorbing a different number of photons. We would expect a separation by speed because electrons struck by two photons receive twice as much energy as those struck only once, while those struck three times receive three times as much energy, and so on. The more energy the electrons receive, the faster they should go. Choice **D** is probably not correct because the transferral of energy to these faster electrons would require that some electrons *lose* their energy. Therefore, we should see yet another peak for slower electrons that gave up their energy. Choice **B**, therefore, is the best, because the energy of the electrons is consistent with a common amount of energy among them, and an absorption of two photons is the second likeliest event.

26. **(G)** If energy is directly proportional to frequency, and frequency is inversely proportional to wavelength, then energy is inversely proportional to wavelength. We observe in the diagrams that the base of the signals increases in width as the frequency, and hence the energy, increases. Therefore, the range of speeds must increase as the wavelength *decreases* because wavelength and energy are inversely proportional.

27. **(C)** Ten percent of the adult's body weight would be about 300 grams. The difference in body weight between male and female adults is only around 150 grams. Therefore, any answer that claims a ten percent difference between adults can be eliminated—

choices **B** and **D**. The difference in weight between adults is half of ten percent (5%), with the males being heavier. However, note that baby males are *lighter* than baby females (1454 to 1530 grams). Therefore, **A** is inaccurate because it does not qualify its assertion about males.

28. **(F)** If we look down both Fat columns, we notice that there is not a lot of variation from day to night or from male to female or even from adult to baby. The lowest fat reading is 6.59 grams, and the highest is less than a gram more than that. Therefore, the lightest bird is the one with the highest percentage of fat. The newborn male, who is a full 76 grams lighter than the newborn female, has the greatest percentage of fat per gram of body weight.

29. **(B)** If 10% of the baby female's mass is blood, she has about 150 grams (10% of 1530 = 153) of blood. If the blood has a density of 1 gram for every milliliter, then the volume of 150 grams of blood is 150 ml. The chart indicates volume of a little under 28.5 micrograms of Q per 100 ml of blood in the baby female. Using a proportion of micrograms of Q to milliliters of blood:

$$\frac{28.5}{100} = \frac{x}{150}$$

$$x = 42.75$$

There are approximately 43 micrograms of Q in the female baby.

30. **(J)** The question asks for an explanation of what has been observed. There is absolutely no cause-and-effect relationship that can be inferred from the material presented. Choices **F** and **G** are *possibly* correct, but there is no support in the data for either viewpoint. For example, if the bird lived only at sea level at the equator then **F** would not be a factor. We do not know what the behavior of the bird is, and knowing whether the bird is diurnal or nocturnal matters when considering when it would use its fat reserves. Finally, **H** is not a good choice because the introduction points out that scientists believe only that Q regulates fat reserves.

31. **(C)** The blood sample has a concentration that is close to that of adult males (59.98) and adult females (62.00) at night. Considering that the quoted values are *averages*, and that we are *not* told what the accepted ranges in values are, it is impossible to say that the reading is too low for a female, or too high for a male. Neither **A** nor **B** is therefore justified; they are too specific. Choice **D** is incorrect because it shows a misunderstanding of intrinsic properties. (An intrinsic property is a property that does not depend on the amount of material present. Blue ink is blue whether you have a gallon of it or only a drop. Concentration is also an intrinsic property. You cannot make a weak cup of coffee strong by pouring more of it. The *concentration* of Q should be the same for one baby male as for two.)

32. **(G)** If males and females mature over the same time, the one who picks up the most weight over that time must gain weight at a faster rate. This follows from the definition of rate, which is the change in a quantity over time. Since in this case the denominator, time, remains the same, it follows that the sex with the larger numerator, weight gained, has the bigger rate of gain. Males go from 1454 to 3033 grams, about 1600 grams (actually 1579 grams). Females go from 1530 to 2880 grams, only 1350 grams. Therefore, males gain weight at a faster rate.

33. **(C)** Remember that the question asks about *assumptions*. Scientist 1 states that dinosaurs have four-chambered hearts. An assumption is always unstated. This therefore rules out both choices **B** and **D**. Scientist 1 assumes that dinosaurs were *not* slow, and because he assumes that they were not slow, he makes the claim that they must have had four-chambered hearts. He assumes that animals that are related have similar biologies; otherwise there was no reason for pointing out that birds were both descendents of the dinosaurs and had four-chambered hearts. The correct choice is therefore **C**.

34. **(H)** Scientist 2 refutes the idea that reptiles with three-chambered hearts are doomed to slowness by mentioning that the Komodo dragon can catch a swift mammal that (because it is a mammal) has a four-chambered heart. This is an example that runs counter to what Scientist 1 claims. Choice **J**, while true, does not in itself deal with the problem of speed. Choice **F** is incorrect, because Scientist 2 brings up the fact about the dragon to contradict Scientist 1. Choice **G** is incorrect because he does not compare two unlike situations, which is the heart of an analogy.

35. **(C)** The point of a counterexample is that a rule is not necessarily true in every case. To show a case that follows a rule does not defeat a counterexample. Therefore **A** does not weaken the argument. Choice **B**, though better, is still weak. If it could be shown that increasing size above a certain level makes the

three-chambered heart hopelessly inefficient, Scientist 2's argument would be in trouble. But as it is, **B** is not a strong choice. Choice **D** is poor because the close relation of dinosaurs to birds is an important point in Scientist 1's arguments. Choice **C** is the best choice because it points out at least one crucial difference between the circulatory system of the dinosaurs and that of modern reptiles. This would refute Scientist 2's argument that there is no reason to believe that dinosaurs were biologically different from other reptiles.

36. **(J)** The whole point Scientist 2 made with the example of the Komodo dragon was that one could not predict speed of movement based solely on the circulatory system of the animal. Therefore **J** is the only appropriate response.

37. **(A)** Scientist 1 makes the key point in his argument that speed is related to the efficiency of the heart. Therefore the mammal, the only choice that has a four-chambered heart, would be the fastest according to Scientist 1.

38. **(H)** Scientist 1 argues that the ancestor must have a four-chambered heart because the descendant has the same. Choice **G** follows this line of reasoning. Choice **F** focuses on an extraneous fact. Choice **J** is not a problem for Scientist 1, because he accepts that dinosaurs were probably warm-blooded too. Choice **H** points out that even though birds may be descended from dinosaurs, and even though birds have four-chambered hearts, it does *not* follow that the dinosaur passed that trait to them, since the fish did not pass its two-chambered heart to its descendant, the amphibian.

39. **(A)** Choice **B** is poor because it merely restates the contention. Choice **C** fails because birds may not run quickly for a number of reasons having nothing to do with their type of heart (because they fly, for example). Choice **D** is better because it points out that the heart might not be the solution to the mobility problem. However, Scientist 1 could easily counter that a four-chambered heart allows at least for the *possibility* of increased speed. Choice **A** is the best choice because it reduces to irrelevance the whole problem of the absolute rate of speed. If the predator does not run quickly, the prey need not be Speedy Gonzalez either!

40. **(G)** As was pointed out in the explanation of question 38, **G** allows for the extrapolation of the traits of the descendant back to the traits of the ancestor.

Answer Sheet for Practice Exam IV

1. English Test

1 Ⓐ Ⓑ Ⓒ Ⓓ	11 Ⓐ Ⓑ Ⓒ Ⓓ	21 Ⓐ Ⓑ Ⓒ Ⓓ	31 Ⓐ Ⓑ Ⓒ Ⓓ	41 Ⓐ Ⓑ Ⓒ Ⓓ	51 Ⓐ Ⓑ Ⓒ Ⓓ	61 Ⓐ Ⓑ Ⓒ Ⓓ	71 Ⓐ Ⓑ Ⓒ Ⓓ
2 Ⓕ Ⓖ Ⓗ Ⓙ	12 Ⓕ Ⓖ Ⓗ Ⓙ	22 Ⓕ Ⓖ Ⓗ Ⓙ	32 Ⓕ Ⓖ Ⓗ Ⓙ	42 Ⓕ Ⓖ Ⓗ Ⓙ	52 Ⓕ Ⓖ Ⓗ Ⓙ	62 Ⓕ Ⓖ Ⓗ Ⓙ	72 Ⓕ Ⓖ Ⓗ Ⓙ
3 Ⓐ Ⓑ Ⓒ Ⓓ	13 Ⓐ Ⓑ Ⓒ Ⓓ	23 Ⓐ Ⓑ Ⓒ Ⓓ	33 Ⓐ Ⓑ Ⓒ Ⓓ	43 Ⓐ Ⓑ Ⓒ Ⓓ	53 Ⓐ Ⓑ Ⓒ Ⓓ	63 Ⓐ Ⓑ Ⓒ Ⓓ	73 Ⓐ Ⓑ Ⓒ Ⓓ
4 Ⓕ Ⓖ Ⓗ Ⓙ	14 Ⓕ Ⓖ Ⓗ Ⓙ	24 Ⓕ Ⓖ Ⓗ Ⓙ	34 Ⓕ Ⓖ Ⓗ Ⓙ	44 Ⓕ Ⓖ Ⓗ Ⓙ	54 Ⓕ Ⓖ Ⓗ Ⓙ	64 Ⓕ Ⓖ Ⓗ Ⓙ	74 Ⓕ Ⓖ Ⓗ Ⓙ
5 Ⓐ Ⓑ Ⓒ Ⓓ	15 Ⓐ Ⓑ Ⓒ Ⓓ	25 Ⓐ Ⓑ Ⓒ Ⓓ	35 Ⓐ Ⓑ Ⓒ Ⓓ	45 Ⓐ Ⓑ Ⓒ Ⓓ	55 Ⓐ Ⓑ Ⓒ Ⓓ	65 Ⓐ Ⓑ Ⓒ Ⓓ	75 Ⓐ Ⓑ Ⓒ Ⓓ
6 Ⓕ Ⓖ Ⓗ Ⓙ	16 Ⓕ Ⓖ Ⓗ Ⓙ	26 Ⓕ Ⓖ Ⓗ Ⓙ	36 Ⓕ Ⓖ Ⓗ Ⓙ	46 Ⓕ Ⓖ Ⓗ Ⓙ	56 Ⓕ Ⓖ Ⓗ Ⓙ	66 Ⓕ Ⓖ Ⓗ Ⓙ	
7 Ⓐ Ⓑ Ⓒ Ⓓ	17 Ⓐ Ⓑ Ⓒ Ⓓ	27 Ⓐ Ⓑ Ⓒ Ⓓ	37 Ⓐ Ⓑ Ⓒ Ⓓ	47 Ⓐ Ⓑ Ⓒ Ⓓ	57 Ⓐ Ⓑ Ⓒ Ⓓ	67 Ⓐ Ⓑ Ⓒ Ⓓ	
8 Ⓕ Ⓖ Ⓗ Ⓙ	18 Ⓕ Ⓖ Ⓗ Ⓙ	28 Ⓕ Ⓖ Ⓗ Ⓙ	38 Ⓕ Ⓖ Ⓗ Ⓙ	48 Ⓕ Ⓖ Ⓗ Ⓙ	58 Ⓕ Ⓖ Ⓗ Ⓙ	68 Ⓕ Ⓖ Ⓗ Ⓙ	
9 Ⓐ Ⓑ Ⓒ Ⓓ	19 Ⓐ Ⓑ Ⓒ Ⓓ	29 Ⓐ Ⓑ Ⓒ Ⓓ	39 Ⓐ Ⓑ Ⓒ Ⓓ	49 Ⓐ Ⓑ Ⓒ Ⓓ	59 Ⓐ Ⓑ Ⓒ Ⓓ	69 Ⓐ Ⓑ Ⓒ Ⓓ	
10 Ⓕ Ⓖ Ⓗ Ⓙ	20 Ⓕ Ⓖ Ⓗ Ⓙ	30 Ⓕ Ⓖ Ⓗ Ⓙ	40 Ⓕ Ⓖ Ⓗ Ⓙ	50 Ⓕ Ⓖ Ⓗ Ⓙ	60 Ⓕ Ⓖ Ⓗ Ⓙ	70 Ⓕ Ⓖ Ⓗ Ⓙ	

2. Mathematics Test

1 Ⓐ Ⓑ Ⓒ Ⓓ Ⓔ	9 Ⓐ Ⓑ Ⓒ Ⓓ Ⓔ	17 Ⓐ Ⓑ Ⓒ Ⓓ Ⓔ	25 Ⓐ Ⓑ Ⓒ Ⓓ Ⓔ	33 Ⓐ Ⓑ Ⓒ Ⓓ Ⓔ	41 Ⓐ Ⓑ Ⓒ Ⓓ Ⓔ	49 Ⓐ Ⓑ Ⓒ Ⓓ Ⓔ	57 Ⓐ Ⓑ Ⓒ Ⓓ Ⓔ
2 Ⓕ Ⓖ Ⓗ Ⓙ Ⓚ	10 Ⓕ Ⓖ Ⓗ Ⓙ Ⓚ	18 Ⓕ Ⓖ Ⓗ Ⓙ Ⓚ	26 Ⓕ Ⓖ Ⓗ Ⓙ Ⓚ	34 Ⓕ Ⓖ Ⓗ Ⓙ Ⓚ	42 Ⓕ Ⓖ Ⓗ Ⓙ Ⓚ	50 Ⓕ Ⓖ Ⓗ Ⓙ Ⓚ	58 Ⓕ Ⓖ Ⓗ Ⓙ Ⓚ
3 Ⓐ Ⓑ Ⓒ Ⓓ Ⓔ	11 Ⓐ Ⓑ Ⓒ Ⓓ Ⓔ	19 Ⓐ Ⓑ Ⓒ Ⓓ Ⓔ	27 Ⓐ Ⓑ Ⓒ Ⓓ Ⓔ	35 Ⓐ Ⓑ Ⓒ Ⓓ Ⓔ	43 Ⓐ Ⓑ Ⓒ Ⓓ Ⓔ	51 Ⓐ Ⓑ Ⓒ Ⓓ Ⓔ	59 Ⓐ Ⓑ Ⓒ Ⓓ Ⓔ
4 Ⓕ Ⓖ Ⓗ Ⓙ Ⓚ	12 Ⓕ Ⓖ Ⓗ Ⓙ Ⓚ	20 Ⓕ Ⓖ Ⓗ Ⓙ Ⓚ	28 Ⓕ Ⓖ Ⓗ Ⓙ Ⓚ	36 Ⓕ Ⓖ Ⓗ Ⓙ Ⓚ	44 Ⓕ Ⓖ Ⓗ Ⓙ Ⓚ	52 Ⓕ Ⓖ Ⓗ Ⓙ Ⓚ	60 Ⓕ Ⓖ Ⓗ Ⓙ Ⓚ
5 Ⓐ Ⓑ Ⓒ Ⓓ Ⓔ	13 Ⓐ Ⓑ Ⓒ Ⓓ Ⓔ	21 Ⓐ Ⓑ Ⓒ Ⓓ Ⓔ	29 Ⓐ Ⓑ Ⓒ Ⓓ Ⓔ	37 Ⓐ Ⓑ Ⓒ Ⓓ Ⓔ	45 Ⓐ Ⓑ Ⓒ Ⓓ Ⓔ	53 Ⓐ Ⓑ Ⓒ Ⓓ Ⓔ	
6 Ⓕ Ⓖ Ⓗ Ⓙ Ⓚ	14 Ⓕ Ⓖ Ⓗ Ⓙ Ⓚ	22 Ⓕ Ⓖ Ⓗ Ⓙ Ⓚ	30 Ⓕ Ⓖ Ⓗ Ⓙ Ⓚ	38 Ⓕ Ⓖ Ⓗ Ⓙ Ⓚ	46 Ⓕ Ⓖ Ⓗ Ⓙ Ⓚ	54 Ⓕ Ⓖ Ⓗ Ⓙ Ⓚ	
7 Ⓐ Ⓑ Ⓒ Ⓓ Ⓔ	15 Ⓐ Ⓑ Ⓒ Ⓓ Ⓔ	23 Ⓐ Ⓑ Ⓒ Ⓓ Ⓔ	31 Ⓐ Ⓑ Ⓒ Ⓓ Ⓔ	39 Ⓐ Ⓑ Ⓒ Ⓓ Ⓔ	47 Ⓐ Ⓑ Ⓒ Ⓓ Ⓔ	55 Ⓐ Ⓑ Ⓒ Ⓓ Ⓔ	
8 Ⓕ Ⓖ Ⓗ Ⓙ Ⓚ	16 Ⓕ Ⓖ Ⓗ Ⓙ Ⓚ	24 Ⓕ Ⓖ Ⓗ Ⓙ Ⓚ	32 Ⓕ Ⓖ Ⓗ Ⓙ Ⓚ	40 Ⓕ Ⓖ Ⓗ Ⓙ Ⓚ	48 Ⓕ Ⓖ Ⓗ Ⓙ Ⓚ	56 Ⓕ Ⓖ Ⓗ Ⓙ Ⓚ	

3. Reading Test

1 Ⓐ Ⓑ Ⓒ Ⓓ	6 Ⓕ Ⓖ Ⓗ Ⓙ	11 Ⓐ Ⓑ Ⓒ Ⓓ	16 Ⓕ Ⓖ Ⓗ Ⓙ	21 Ⓐ Ⓑ Ⓒ Ⓓ	26 Ⓕ Ⓖ Ⓗ Ⓙ	31 Ⓐ Ⓑ Ⓒ Ⓓ	36 Ⓕ Ⓖ Ⓗ Ⓙ
2 Ⓕ Ⓖ Ⓗ Ⓙ	7 Ⓐ Ⓑ Ⓒ Ⓓ	12 Ⓕ Ⓖ Ⓗ Ⓙ	17 Ⓐ Ⓑ Ⓒ Ⓓ	22 Ⓕ Ⓖ Ⓗ Ⓙ	27 Ⓐ Ⓑ Ⓒ Ⓓ	32 Ⓕ Ⓖ Ⓗ Ⓙ	37 Ⓐ Ⓑ Ⓒ Ⓓ
3 Ⓐ Ⓑ Ⓒ Ⓓ	8 Ⓕ Ⓖ Ⓗ Ⓙ	13 Ⓐ Ⓑ Ⓒ Ⓓ	18 Ⓕ Ⓖ Ⓗ Ⓙ	23 Ⓐ Ⓑ Ⓒ Ⓓ	28 Ⓕ Ⓖ Ⓗ Ⓙ	33 Ⓐ Ⓑ Ⓒ Ⓓ	38 Ⓕ Ⓖ Ⓗ Ⓙ
4 Ⓕ Ⓖ Ⓗ Ⓙ	9 Ⓐ Ⓑ Ⓒ Ⓓ	14 Ⓕ Ⓖ Ⓗ Ⓙ	19 Ⓐ Ⓑ Ⓒ Ⓓ	24 Ⓕ Ⓖ Ⓗ Ⓙ	29 Ⓐ Ⓑ Ⓒ Ⓓ	34 Ⓕ Ⓖ Ⓗ Ⓙ	39 Ⓐ Ⓑ Ⓒ Ⓓ
5 Ⓐ Ⓑ Ⓒ Ⓓ	10 Ⓕ Ⓖ Ⓗ Ⓙ	15 Ⓐ Ⓑ Ⓒ Ⓓ	20 Ⓕ Ⓖ Ⓗ Ⓙ	25 Ⓐ Ⓑ Ⓒ Ⓓ	30 Ⓕ Ⓖ Ⓗ Ⓙ	35 Ⓐ Ⓑ Ⓒ Ⓓ	40 Ⓕ Ⓖ Ⓗ Ⓙ

4. Science Reasoning Test

1 Ⓐ Ⓑ Ⓒ Ⓓ	6 Ⓕ Ⓖ Ⓗ Ⓙ	11 Ⓐ Ⓑ Ⓒ Ⓓ	16 Ⓕ Ⓖ Ⓗ Ⓙ	21 Ⓐ Ⓑ Ⓒ Ⓓ	26 Ⓕ Ⓖ Ⓗ Ⓙ	31 Ⓐ Ⓑ Ⓒ Ⓓ	36 Ⓕ Ⓖ Ⓗ Ⓙ
2 Ⓕ Ⓖ Ⓗ Ⓙ	7 Ⓐ Ⓑ Ⓒ Ⓓ	12 Ⓕ Ⓖ Ⓗ Ⓙ	17 Ⓐ Ⓑ Ⓒ Ⓓ	22 Ⓕ Ⓖ Ⓗ Ⓙ	27 Ⓐ Ⓑ Ⓒ Ⓓ	32 Ⓕ Ⓖ Ⓗ Ⓙ	37 Ⓐ Ⓑ Ⓒ Ⓓ
3 Ⓐ Ⓑ Ⓒ Ⓓ	8 Ⓕ Ⓖ Ⓗ Ⓙ	13 Ⓐ Ⓑ Ⓒ Ⓓ	18 Ⓕ Ⓖ Ⓗ Ⓙ	23 Ⓐ Ⓑ Ⓒ Ⓓ	28 Ⓕ Ⓖ Ⓗ Ⓙ	33 Ⓐ Ⓑ Ⓒ Ⓓ	38 Ⓕ Ⓖ Ⓗ Ⓙ
4 Ⓕ Ⓖ Ⓗ Ⓙ	9 Ⓐ Ⓑ Ⓒ Ⓓ	14 Ⓕ Ⓖ Ⓗ Ⓙ	19 Ⓐ Ⓑ Ⓒ Ⓓ	24 Ⓕ Ⓖ Ⓗ Ⓙ	29 Ⓐ Ⓑ Ⓒ Ⓓ	34 Ⓕ Ⓖ Ⓗ Ⓙ	39 Ⓐ Ⓑ Ⓒ Ⓓ
5 Ⓐ Ⓑ Ⓒ Ⓓ	10 Ⓕ Ⓖ Ⓗ Ⓙ	15 Ⓐ Ⓑ Ⓒ Ⓓ	20 Ⓕ Ⓖ Ⓗ Ⓙ	25 Ⓐ Ⓑ Ⓒ Ⓓ	30 Ⓕ Ⓖ Ⓗ Ⓙ	35 Ⓐ Ⓑ Ⓒ Ⓓ	40 Ⓕ Ⓖ Ⓗ Ⓙ

1. ENGLISH TEST

45 Minutes—75 Questions

DIRECTIONS: In the passage(s) below, certain words and phrases are underlined and numbered. In the right-hand column, you will find choices for each underlined part. You are to select the one that best expresses the idea, makes the statement appropriate for standard written English, or is worded most consistently with the style and mood of the passage as a whole. If you think the original version is best, choose "NO CHANGE." You will also find questions about a section of the passage, or about the passage as a whole. These questions are indicated by a number or numbers in a box. For each question in the test, select the choice you consider best and blacken the corresponding space on your answer sheet. Read each passage through once before you begin to answer the questions that accompany it. You cannot determine most answers without reading several sentences beyond the phrase in question.

Passage I

Why is there a difference in the calorie needs between women and men? The answer lies in differences in body size and body composition. The amount of energy (calories) expended through physical activity also plays a major role.

1. **A.** NO CHANGE
   B. of women and men
   C. among men and women
   D. had by women and men

2. **F.** NO CHANGE
   G. expended by
   H. used by
   J. people expend by

Calorie need is related to size as well as to gender and activity. This means that a 6-foot man can consume several hundred more calories without gaining weight than a woman seven inches shorter. Because he weighs more he will probably use a few more calories than a woman who has engaged in the same activity.

3. **A.** NO CHANGE
   B. more—he will
   C. more. He will
   D. more, he will

4. **F.** NO CHANGE
   G. who engage
   H. engaging
   J. often engaged

Adding to nature's unfairness, even when the woman is the same height as the man, the recommended weight

465

for her is about 10 pounds lighter than him.
                                    5

This introduces another factor. There is a difference in the composition of the poundage gained by boys and girls beginning at puberty. The weight girls put on contains proportionately more fat; that for boys
                                    6
contains more lean body tissue. Fat tissue is

less denser than leaner, so that if a girl and boy
       7

add to the same weight, the girl may appear to have
        8

gained more. ⬚9 ⬚10

Passage II

Americans have believed always that a good
              11

education is one of the most sure of ways to success.
                  12

That belief is as true today for blacks, Hispanics, and
                                13

5. A. NO CHANGE
   B. lighter than for him
   C. more light than his
   D. lighter than for them

6. F. NO CHANGE
   G. more fat, that
   H. more fat, even though that
   J. more fat: that

7. A. NO CHANGE
   B. less dense or lean
   C. less dense than lean
   D. less dense then lean

8. F. NO CHANGE
   G. grow to the same weight, the
   H. add the same number of weight, the
   J. add the same weight, the

9. Is it appropriate to start the passage with a question?
   A. No, because it implies the author does not know his or her subject.
   B. Yes, because it tells the reader what problem the passage will address.
   C. No, because the reader should be asking the questions, not the author.
   D. Yes, because it gives the author a chance to organize his or her thoughts.

10. This passage implies that
    F. all men should weigh more than all women.
    G. all women look fatter than all men.
    H. men's and women's diets should be different.
    J. only women should try to lose weight.

11. A. NO CHANGE
    B. always believe
    C. have always believed
    D. always believed

12. F. NO CHANGE
    G. one of the surest means of being a success
    H. one way sure to be successful
    J. one of the surest ways to success

13. A. NO CHANGE
    B. for blacks, Hispanics and the Asians,
    C. for blacks Hispanics and Asians
    D. for blacks and Hispanics and Asians,

Asians as it was for European immigrants in the early
segment of this century. For example, since 1940 as
much as two-thirds of the income gain for young blacks
has been attributed increases in years of schooling and
improvement in the quality of the schools they attend.

The benefits of education are colorblind. [17]

For whites, blacks, and Hispanics who are
completing the last two years of high school reduces by
about 60 percent the odds of being in poverty as an
adult. Today the typical high school graduate
will earn $441,000, more over a lifetime than a high
school dropout, and a college graduate will earn
$1,082,000 more.

A good elementary and secondary education is also
more critical for a chance of going to college for
students from low-income families than it is for other
students. Among students from low-income
backgrounds—those who perform well in school are
nearly three times as likely to attend college as those
who do not perform well.

14. F. NO CHANGE
G. in the early part of this century
H. earlier than this in the century
J. a portion of years earlier in this century

15. A. NO CHANGE
B. is attributable with
C. attributes itself to
D. is attributable to

16. F. NO CHANGE
G. have been attended
H. have been attending
J. would attend

17. In the first paragraph, the relationship between the last sentence and the rest of the paragraph is

A. question and answer.
B. summary and examples.
C. point and counterpoint.
D. argument and digression.

18. F. NO CHANGE
G. Hispanics who have completed
H. Hispanics, completing
J. Hispanics completing

19. A. NO CHANGE
B. earns $441,000, more
C. will earn $441,000 more
D. earns $441,000—more

20. F. NO CHANGE
G. more critical to the chances
H. more than critical for the chance
J. more critical than the chance

21. A. NO CHANGE
B. backgrounds: Those who perform
C. backgrounds, those, who perform
D. backgrounds, those who perform

Passage III

This year, we Americans will have been spending
                          ——————————————
                                22
billions of dollars on products that do nothing for us—

or may even harm us. And we'll do it for the

same reason people have done it since ancient

times: we want to believe in miracles. We want to find
——————
   23

simple solutions and shortcuts to better healthiness.
                                  ——————————————
                                         24
It's hard to resist. All of us, at one time or another,

have seen or hear about a product—a new and exotic
——————————
      25

pill, device, or potion—that can most easily solve our
                              ——————————————————
                                      26
most vexing problem. With this product, we're told,

we can eat all we want and still lose weight. We can
                                 ————
                                  27

grow taller, or, build a bigger bustline. Or we can
     ————————
        28

overcome baldness, age, arthritis, or maybe even
                        ————————————————
                                 29

cancer. [30]
——————

It sounds too good to be true—and it is. But

we're tempted to try the product in spite of all we
——————————————
       31
know about modern medical science—or perhaps

because of it. After all, many treatments we take for

22. **A.** NO CHANGE
    B. spend
    C. have been spending
    D. will spend

23. **F.** NO CHANGE
    G. times, we want
    H. times due to we want
    J. times because we want

24. **A.** NO CHANGE
    B. more healthiness
    C. better health
    D. having more healthiness

25. **F.** NO CHANGE
    G. seen or have heard
    H. saw or have heard
    J. have seen or heard

26. **A.** NO CHANGE
    B. can easily solve
    C. can be easily solved by
    D. can solve with great ease

27. **F.** NO CHANGE
    G. we can lose
    H. they lose
    J. they lost

28. **A.** NO CHANGE
    B. taller—or, build
    C. taller or build
    D. taller; or, build

29. **F.** NO CHANGE
    G. arthritis and even cancer
    H. arthritis or possible cancer
    J. arthritis, even cancer

30. In the first sentence of the second paragraph, to what does the word "It's" refer?

    A. The promise of health-restoring products.
    B. The pull of historical trends.
    C. Spending billions of dollars.
    D. Being healthy.

31. **F.** NO CHANGE
    G. we've been tempted by trying
    H. we're tempted by trying
    J. we've tempted to try

granted today were once to be considered miracles.
                    —————————————————————
                              32

How can we tell the difference? ☐33

Passage IV

Of the three artificial sweeteners that has whetted the
                                       ——————————
                                           34
palates of millions of Americans over the years, the
                                  ——————————————
                                        35
one souring ingredient common to them all has been controversy.

Saccharin which has no calories yet is 300 times
——————————————
      36
sweeter than sugar, and aspartame, which has the same amount of calories as sugar yet is 180 to 200 times as sweet, are currently available to help satisfy Americans twin cravings for sweets and slimness.
——————————————————
         37
Cyclamate, calorie-free yet 30 times sweeter than sugar, was banned by the Food and Drug Administration in 1970 because of concerns over its
                              ————————————————————
                                       38
safety.
——

Some 69 million Americans, 18 and over, are now
                          ——————————————————————
                                     39
consuming products containing saccharin, aspartame, or eat a combination of the two. Howard Roberts, vice
   ————————————————————
           40
president of science and technology for the National Soft Drink Association, has reported that the share of

32. A. NO CHANGE
    B. we once were considered
    C. once we consider
    D. were once considered

33. The next paragraph might logically talk about
    F. how to identify a miracle.
    G. how to identify false advertising.
    H. the miracles of modern science.
    J. examples of ancient treatments.

34. A. NO CHANGE
    B. have wet
    C. have whet
    D. has whet

35. F. NO CHANGE
    G. during the years
    H. for years
    J. over all those years

36. A. NO CHANGE
    B. Saccharin that has
    C. Saccharin has
    D. Saccharin, which has

37. F. NO CHANGE
    G. Americans' twins' cravings
    H. American's twin cravings
    J. Americans' twin cravings

38. A. NO CHANGE
    B. due to concerns of safety
    C. because of worries of safety
    D. OMIT the underlined portion.

39. F. NO CHANGE
    G. Americans 18 and over are
    H. Americans—18 and over—are
    J. Americans 18 and over, are

40. A. NO CHANGE
    B. a combination of
    C. some of both of
    D. combining

the soft drink market held by diet beverages rose from
15 percent in 1982 to more than 20 percent in 1984.

A regular 12-ounce soft drink has about 150 calories which is compared to none in most diet beverages. However, there is little documented evidence that consumption of artificially sweetened foods has contributed to weight loss among Americans. [43]

Besides dieters, diabetics are regular users of artificial sweeteners. The American Diabetes Association says that although aspartame had not been tested extensively in diabetic patients, those could use the sweetener as long as consumption is not excessive.

Over the years, all of the three artificial sweeteners has undergone long periods of review and debate. Controversy surrounding the sweeteners has tended to cloud public understanding of the complex issues involved. [46]

41. F. NO CHANGE
G. has risen
H. has rised
J. risen

42. A. NO CHANGE
B. which compares to none
C. compared to none
D. while there is none

43. Which best describes the relationship between the first and second sentences in the fourth paragraph?
F. Statement and supporting evidence.
G. Argument and clarification.
H. Point and counterpoint.
J. Statement and explanation.

44. A. NO CHANGE
B. it could use the sweetener
C. they could be used
D. they could use the sweetener

45. F. NO CHANGE
G. each of the three artificial sweeteners have undergone
H. all three artificial sweeteners has undergone
J. each of the three artificial sweeteners has undergone

46. What could follow this passage to best strengthen its point?
A. A short history of each sweetener.
B. A description of the chemical makeup of each sweetener.
C. A paragraph focusing on saccharin.
D. A list of popular foods containing artificial sweeteners.

Passage V

The following paragraphs may or may not be in the most logical order. Each paragraph is numbered in parentheses, and item 60 will ask you to choose the sequence of paragraph numbers that is most logical.

(1)

Money has taken many forms throughout history, some have been very unusual. Cowrie shells, for example, were once used as money in Africa.

The inhabitants of the Pacific island of Yap used stone money. Even dead rats have been used to mean money! But for more than 2,500 years, coins have been among the most popular forms of money in existence.

(2)

Because of its extrinsic value, however, gold has historically been the most highly valued metal for the minting of coins. It is estimated that more than 20,000 different gold coin designs have been issued by various countries during the least 2,500 years.

(3)

It is believed that the first coins was minted between 685 and 652 B.C. by King Gyges of Lydia (modern-day Turkey). Lydia's first gold coin was

47. A. NO CHANGE
B. history; some has been
C. history. Some have been
D. history. Some has been

48. F. NO CHANGE
G. The inhabitators of
H. Inhabitants on
J. Habitators of

49. A. NO CHANGE
B. were taken for
C. have been taken to mean
D. have been used as

50. F. NO CHANGE
G. intimate
H. intrinsic
J. extinct

51. A. NO CHANGE
B. We estimate
C. They estimate
D. They estimated

52. F. NO CHANGE
G. during last
H. among the last
J. during the past

53. A. NO CHANGE
B. were minted
C. minted
D. had been minted

54. F. NO CHANGE
G. Lydia; modern-day Turkey
H. Lydia that is modern-day Turkey
J. Lydia, which had been modern-day Turkey

oblong and stamps with the king's heraldic emblem.
                   ―――――
                     55
Other early coins were struck in silver and "base"

metals like bronze and copper.

(4)

Each ancient empire had its own monetary systems
                                  ――――――――――――――――
                                         56
and its own coinage. The Babylonians, the Greeks, and

the Romans had complex monetary systems with

banks, credit, and they had distinctive coinage. The
          ―――――――――――――――――――――――――――――――
                        57

world's first coin dealers were these countries' rulers,
                               ―――――――――――――――――
                                       58

who authorized the creation of coinage and put them
                                          ――――――――
                                             59
into circulation. Later, as economies grew more

complex, bankers became prominent coin

dealers. [60] [61]

55. A. NO CHANGE
    B. used to be stamped
    C. was stamped
    D. has been stamped

56. F. NO CHANGE
    G. monetary system
    H. system of monies
    J. money's system

57. A. NO CHANGE
    B. and also they had distinctive coinage
    C. and distinctive coinage
    D. OMIT the underlined portion.

58. F. NO CHANGE
    G. this country's
    H. these country's
    J. these countrys'

59. A. NO CHANGE
    B. then put them
    C. put it
    D. then they put it

60. What is the best order for the above paragraphs?

    F. 1, 2, 3, 4
    G. 1, 3, 4, 2
    H. 1, 3, 2, 4
    J. 1, 2, 4, 3

61. This passage is most likely

    A. an introduction to an economics textbook.
    B. an introduction to a bank teller's handbook.
    C. an introduction to a coin-collector's handbook.
    D. a conclusion to an accounting textbook.

Passage VI

Smokeless tobacco appears in different forms. You
                                    ——
                                    62
may know it as chewing tobacco or snuff. Some kids

use it because they think it looks cool. Others may
——————
      63

because their friends, coach, or relatives does. But
                                              ——
                                               64

your doctor or dentist can tell you that to be using
                                        ——————
                                            65
tobacco in any form—dipping, chewing or smoking—

is very bad for your health and can turn off friends.
                                ——
                                66

Using smokeless tobacco can cause cancer especially
                                  ————————
                                       67
in your cheeks, gums, and throat. But even before

cancer develops, changes can occur into your mouth—
                               —————
                                 68
sometimes after only a few weeks of dipping. Your

gums and lips can sting, crack, bleed, wrinkle, and get

sores and white patches may become cancerous.
                         ——
                         69

Stopping to use smokeless tobacco can make the white
——————
   70
patches go away.

Kids who dip, or chew often can use a can of snuff
         ——————
            71
or a pouch of chew every day or two. The cost adds up

62. A. NO CHANGE
    B. comes in
    C. shows itself in
    D. can be made to be

63. F. NO CHANGE
    G. use it—because
    H. use it, because
    J. use it; because

64. A. NO CHANGE
    B. both do
    C. both does
    D. do

65. F. NO CHANGE
    G. doing
    H. using
    J. to be doing

66. A. NO CHANGE
    B. it can
    C. also it can
    D. OMIT the underlined word.

67. F. NO CHANGE
    G. cancer—especially
    H. cancer. Especially
    J. cancer; especially

68. A. NO CHANGE
    B. happen on the inside
    C. occur in
    D. appear and within

69. F. NO CHANGE
    G. that may
    H. which may
    J. that they may

70. A. NO CHANGE
    B. To stop using
    C. Stopping use of
    D. Stop using

71. F. NO CHANGE
    G. dip, or chew,
    H. dip; or chew
    J. dip or chew

by the week, month, and year. Why would anyone
want to pay to hurt his or her looks and

health?

72. A. NO CHANGE
    B. months, and year
    C. month, and years
    D. months and a year

73. The question at the end of the passage can best be described as

    F. argumentative.
    G. rhetorical.
    H. explanatory.
    J. contradictory.

74. To best support the passage's argument, the next paragraph should be which of the following?

    A. A description of someone with cancer.
    B. A quote from someone with cancer.
    C. Elaboration on tobacco's physical effects on the body.
    D. The passage is complete as it is.

75. This passage was most likely designed to

    F. keep youngsters from starting to smoke.
    G. encourage youngsters to stop chewing tobacco.
    H. promote the sale of chewing tobacco.
    J. educate adults about the dangers of chewing tobacco.

STOP!

This is the end of the English Test.
Do not proceed to the next section until the allotted
time expires.

2. MATHEMATICS TEST

60 Minutes—60 Questions

DIRECTIONS: Solve each problem. Then select the correct answer from among the five choices and darken the corresponding space on the answer sheet.

Solve as many problems as you can since they all have the same point value. Do not spend too much time on a single problem. Remember: you are not penalized for incorrect answers; only those answered correctly contribute to your final score.

NOTE: Unless otherwise stated, assume the following:

- All figures lie in a plane.
- Figures are not necessarily drawn to scale.
- All lines are straight.

---

1. Joshua bought two dozen apples for 3 dollars. At this rate, how much will 18 apples cost?

    A. $27.00
    B. $ 4.00
    C. $ 2.50
    D. $ 2.25
    E. $ 1.50

2. What is the y-intercept of the line with equation $\frac{x}{3} - \frac{y}{2} = 1$?

    F. 3
    G. 2
    H. $\frac{3}{2}$
    J. $\frac{2}{3}$
    K. -2

DO YOUR FIGURING HERE.

GO ON TO THE NEXT PAGE.

3. In the figure below, △NJL is a right triangle. The length of $\overline{JL}$ is $\sqrt{3}$ and the length of $\overline{NL}$ is 4. What is the length of $\overline{NJ}$?

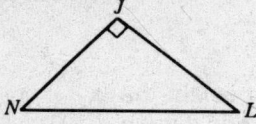

A. $4\sqrt{3}$
B. $4 - \sqrt{3}$
C. $\sqrt{13}$
D. $\sqrt{19}$
E. $4 + \sqrt{3}$

4. In the figure below, square WXYZ is formed by connecting the midpoints of the sides of square ABCD. If the length of $\overline{AB} = 6$, what is the area of the shaded region?

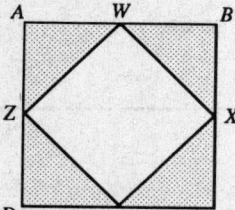

F. 36
G. 24
H. 18
J. 12
K. 6

5. Seth bought $4\frac{5}{6}$ pounds of peanuts. He gave $\frac{1}{4}$ of his purchase to his sister. How many pounds of peanuts did Seth keep for himself?

A. 3
B. $3\frac{5}{8}$
C. $3\frac{3}{4}$
D. $3\frac{5}{6}$
E. $3\frac{7}{8}$

6. $3a - (3b - (3c - 3d) - 2e)$ is equivalent to which of the following?

F. $3a - 3b - 3c + 3d - 2e$
G. $3a - 3b + 3c - 3d - 2e$
H. $3a - 3b - 3c - 3d - 2e$
J. $3a - 3b + 3c + 3d - 2e$
K. $3a - 3b + 3c - 3d + 2e$

GO ON TO THE NEXT PAGE.

7. The slopes of two non-vertical parallel lines are represented by m_1 and m_2 respectively. Which one of the following statements must be true?

A. $m_1 = \dfrac{1}{m_2}$

B. $m_1 = -\dfrac{1}{m_2}$

C. $m_1 m_2 = -1$
D. $m_1 - m_2 = 0$
E. $m_1 + m_2 = 0$

8. $\dfrac{2^2 \cdot 2^3}{2^{-2} \cdot 2^{-3}} = ?$

F. 2^{-1}
G. -1
H. 1
J. 2^{10}
K. 2^{12}

9. In the standard (x,y) coordinate plane, the points $(1,1)$ and $(-1,-1)$ are how many units apart?

A. 1
B. $\sqrt{3}$
C. 2
D. $2\sqrt{2}$
E. 4

10. What is the value of $-x^2 - 2x - 1$, when $x = -2$?

F. -9
G. -7
H. -1
J. 1
K. 2

11. In the polygon below, the vertices are hinged to open and close. What integer value is the maximum possible length of the side $\overline{CD}$?

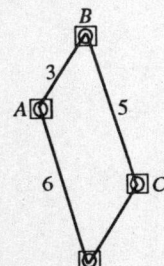

A. 11
B. 12
C. 13
D. 14
E. 15

DO YOUR FIGURING HERE.

GO ON TO THE NEXT PAGE.

12. For $0 < \theta < \frac{\pi}{2}$, if $\sin \theta = \frac{4}{7}$, then $\frac{1}{\tan \theta} = ?$

   F. $\frac{\sqrt{33}}{4}$

   G. $\frac{\sqrt{33}}{7}$

   H. $\frac{7}{4}$

   J. $\frac{\sqrt{65}}{4}$

   K. $\frac{\sqrt{65}}{7}$

13. $\dfrac{-\frac{1}{3}}{3} - \dfrac{3}{-\frac{1}{3}} = ?$

   A. $8\frac{8}{9}$

   B. 6

   C. $-\frac{2}{9}$

   D. -9

   E. $-9\frac{1}{9}$

14. Which one of the following sets contains ONLY prime numbers?

   F. {2, 3, 5, 29}
   G. {3, 5, 17, 27}
   H. {2, 3, 6, 12}
   J. {3, 5, 7, 9}
   K. {2, 4, 6, 8}

15. If the ratio of $4a$ to $3b$ is 8 to 9, what is the ratio of $3a$ to $4b$?

   A. $\frac{4}{3}$

   B. $\frac{9}{8}$

   C. 1

   D. $\frac{3}{4}$

   E. $\frac{1}{2}$

GO ON TO THE NEXT PAGE.

16. In the figure below, secant $\overline{AP}$ is 6 units long and secant $\overline{DP}$ is 8 units long. If $\overline{AB} = 4$, what is the length of $\overline{CP}$?

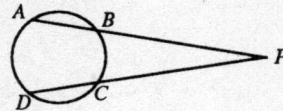

F. $\frac{1}{2}$
G. 1
H. $1\frac{1}{2}$
J. 2
K. $2\frac{1}{2}$

17. What is the average (arithmetic mean) of $x^2 - 9$, $x^2 + 9$ and $x^2 + 3x + 6$?

A. $x + 2$
B. $2x + 3$
C. $x^2 + 2x + 3$
D. $x^2 + x + 2$
E. $3x^2 + 3x + 6$

18. The temperature in degrees Celsius (C) can be formulated from the temperature in degrees Fahrenheit (F) as follows: Subtract 32 from the Fahrenheit temperature and multiply the resulting difference by $\frac{5}{9}$. Which of the following expresses this relationship?

F. $C = \frac{5}{9}(32 - F)$
G. $F = \frac{5}{9}(C - 32)$
H. $C = \frac{5}{9}(F - 32)$
J. $C = \frac{5}{9}F - 32$
K. $C = F - \frac{5}{9}(32)$

19. Dawn's average for four math tests is 80. What score must she receive on her next exam to increase her average by three points?

A. 83
B. 86
C. 89
D. 92
E. 95

20. Which of the following choices represents 20 + 200 + 2,000 expressed in scientific notation?

   F. 8×10^3
   G. 4.2×10^3
   H. 2.22×10^3
   J. 2.22×10^2
   K. 2.22×10^1

21. Jessica caught five fish with an average weight of 10 pounds. If three of the fish weigh 9, 9 and 10 pounds respectively, what is the average (arithmetic mean) weight of the other two fish?

   A. 11
   B. 22
   C. 28
   D. 32
   E. 33

22. In the figure below, the circle has center O. The measure of $\angle BAC$ is 100°. If chords $\overline{AB}$ and $\overline{AC}$ are congruent, what is the measure of arc $\stackrel{\frown}{AB}$?

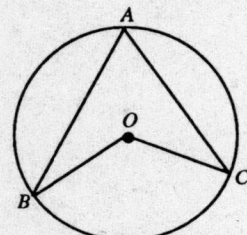

   F. 60°
   G. 80°
   H. 100°
   J. 160°
   K. 200°

23. What is the value of
$$\left(\cos \frac{\pi}{6}\right)\left(\cos \frac{\pi}{6}\right) + \left(\sin \frac{\pi}{6}\right)\left(\sin \frac{\pi}{6}\right)?$$

   A. $\frac{1}{2}$
   B. $\frac{\sqrt{2}}{2}$
   C. $\frac{\sqrt{3}}{2}$
   D. $\frac{\sqrt{3}}{3}$
   E. 1

24. In the standard (x, y) coordinate plane, what is the equation of a circle with center at $(0, -1)$ and a radius of 4?

   F. $x^2 + (y - 1)^2 = 16$
   G. $x^2 + (y + 1)^2 = 16$
   H. $x^2 + (y - 1)^2 = 4$
   J. $x^2 + (y + 1)^2 = 2$
   K. $x^2 + (y - 1)^2 = 2$

25. $-|-3 - 4| - |3| - |-4| = ?$

   A. -14
   B. -8
   C. 0
   D. 8
   E. 14

26. What is the equation of the line perpendicular to $y = -\frac{1}{3}x + 2$ and passing through the point $(1, 1)$?

   F. $y = \frac{1}{3}x + \frac{2}{3}$
   G. $y = -3x + 2$
   H. $y = -3x + 4$
   J. $y = 3x - 2$
   K. $y = 3x - 4$

27. In the right triangle shown below, what is the length of $\overline{BC}$, if the measure of $\angle A$ is 42° and the length of $\overline{AC}$ is 6?

   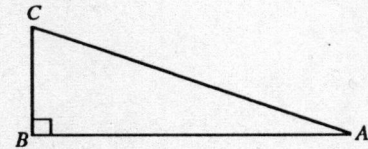

   A. $6 \sin 42°$
   B. $6 \cos 42°$
   C. $6 \tan 42°$
   D. $\dfrac{6}{\sin 42°}$
   E. $\dfrac{6}{\cos 42°}$

28. $\left(\sqrt{3}\right)^5 - \left(\sqrt{3}\right)^3 = ?$

   F. $6\sqrt{6}$
   G. $6\sqrt{3}$
   H. $3\sqrt{3}$
   J. 9
   K. 3

29. The expression $\frac{a^2}{a} - 1 \ (a \neq 0)$ is equivalent to which of the following?

   A. $a - 1$
   B. $1 - a$
   C. $\frac{a - 1}{a}$
   D. $\frac{1 - a}{a}$
   E. 0

30. Which graph below represents the solution set for the inequality

$$3x - 4(x + 2) \leq 7$$

   F.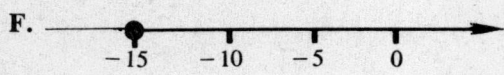
   G.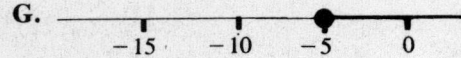
   H.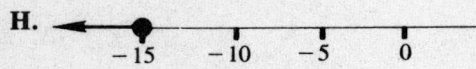
   J.
   K.

31. A number is divisible by 3 if the sum of its digits is divisible by 3. Which one of the following is divisible by 15?

   A. 55,155
   B. 11,511
   C. 52,225
   D. 53,335
   E. 56,665

32. $3.714 \div \frac{1}{5} = ?$

   F. 1857.0
   G. 185.7
   H. 18.57
   J. 1.857
   K. .1857

GO ON TO THE NEXT PAGE.

33. If the cost of a party is to be split equally among 11 friends, each would pay $15.00. If 20 persons equally split the same cost, how much would each person pay?

   A. $8.05
   B. $8.15
   C. $8.25
   D. $8.35
   E. $8.45

34. $\sqrt{4 + 4^2} = ?$

   F. 2
   G. 4
   H. $2\sqrt{3}$
   J. $2\sqrt{5}$
   K. 20

35. Thirty thousand two hundred and forty minutes is equivalent to how many weeks?

   A. 1
   B. 2
   C. 3
   D. 4
   E. 5

36. What is the sum of the solutions to the equation $|3x - 4| = 5$?

   F. 3
   G. $2\frac{2}{3}$
   H. $2\frac{1}{3}$
   J. $1\frac{2}{3}$
   K. $1\frac{1}{3}$

37. In the figure below, line l_1 is parallel to line l_2. Transversals t_1 and t_2 are drawn. What is the value of $a + b + c + d$?

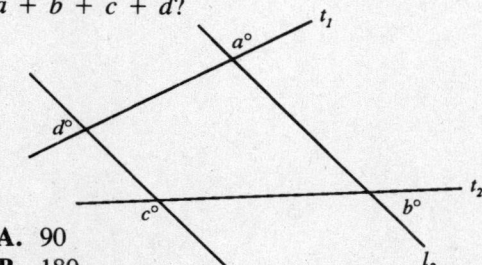

   A. 90
   B. 180
   C. 270
   D. 360
   E. Cannot be determined.

DO YOUR FIGURING HERE.

GO ON TO THE NEXT PAGE.

38. In the figure below, rectangle ABCD has sides of length 6 and 8 as shown. If X (not shown) is the midpoint of $\overline{CD}$ and Y (not shown) is the midpoint of $\overline{AD}$, what is the perimeter of △ XDY?

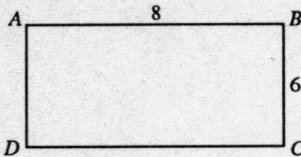

F. 5
G. 6
H. $7 + 3\sqrt{3}$
J. $7 + 4\sqrt{3}$
K. 12

39. What is the absolute value of the product of the two solutions for x in the equation $2x^2 - 3x - 2 = 0$?

A. $-\frac{1}{2}$
B. 1
C. $\frac{3}{2}$
D. 2
E. 6

40. In the figure below, $\overline{KJ}$ bisects $\angle J$. The measure of $\angle K$ is 40° and the measure of $\angle L$ is 20°. What is the measure of $\angle N$?

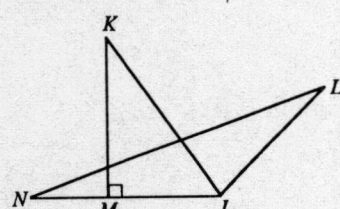

F. 40°
G. 45°
H. 50°
J. 60°
K. 70°

41. A car travels from town A to town B, a distance of 360 miles in 9 hours. How many hours would the same trip have taken had the car travelled 5 mph faster?

A. 6
B. 6.5
C. 7
D. 7.5
E. 8

42. In the figure below, what is the area of △NKL?

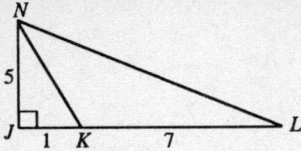

F. 2.5
G. $\sqrt{26}$
H. $\sqrt{89}$
J. 17.5
K. 20

43. A line passes through the points (0, 4) and (3, 0). Which of the following does NOT represent the equation of this line?

A. $y - 4 = -\frac{4}{3}(x - 0)$
B. $y = -\frac{4}{3}x + 3$
C. $y - 0 = -\frac{4}{3}(x - 3)$
D. $\frac{x}{3} + \frac{y}{4} = 1$
E. $4x + 3y - 12 = 0$

44. In the figure below, chords $\overline{AB}$ and $\overline{CD}$ intersect at E. If the length of $\overline{AB} = 6$, $\overline{AE} = 2$ and $\overline{CE} = 1$, what is the length of $\overline{ED}$?

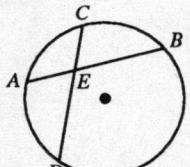

F. 4
G. 5
H. 6
J. 7
K. 8

45. In the figure below $m\angle N = (9x - 40)°$, $m\angle J = (4x + 30)°$ and $m\angle JLR = (8x + 40)°$. What is the measure of $\angle J$?

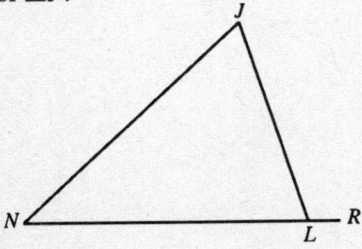

A. 50°
B. 60°
C. 70°
D. 80°
E. 120°

GO ON TO THE NEXT PAGE.

46. $(\sqrt{18} - \sqrt{8})^2 = ?$

    F. 10
    G. 7
    H. 4
    J. 3
    K. 2

47. Line l is graphed in the figure below in the standard (x, y) coordinate plane. What is the y-intercept of the line?

    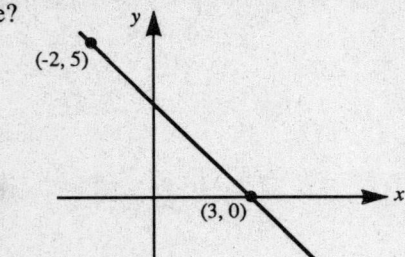

    A. 1
    B. 2
    C. 3
    D. 3.5
    E. 4

48. $16^{\frac{3}{4}} + 16^{\frac{1}{4}} = ?$

    F. 3
    G. 8
    H. 10
    J. 12
    K. 16

49. Which of the following is equivalent to $\dfrac{1 - \sin^2 \theta}{\cos \theta}$?

    A. $\dfrac{1}{\sin \theta}$
    B. $\dfrac{1}{\cos \theta}$
    C. $\sin \theta$
    D. $\cos \theta$
    E. $\tan \theta$

50. The expression $xy + 2x + 3y + 6$ is equivalent to all of the following EXCEPT?

    F. $(x + 3)(y + 2)$
    G. $x(y + 2) + 3(y + 2)$
    H. $y(x + 3) + 2(x + 3)$
    J. $(x + 2)(y + 3)$
    K. $y(3 + x) + 2x + 6$

GO ON TO THE NEXT PAGE.

51. What is the sum of the solutions, x and y, to the following system of equations? $2x - y = 7$
$x + 2y = 11$

A. 4
B. 5
C. 6
D. 7
E. 8

52. For all x, $x \neq -y$, $\dfrac{x^2 + x + xy + y}{x + y} = ?$

F. $x + 1$
G. $x^2 + xy$
H. $3x + y$
J. $2x + xy$
K. $x + y$

53. In the figure below, if $\dfrac{1}{\tan \theta} = \dfrac{4}{7}$, what is the value of $\dfrac{1}{\sin \phi}$?

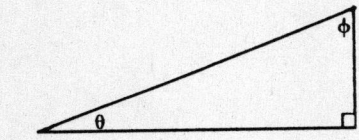

A. $\dfrac{\sqrt{65}}{7}$
B. $\dfrac{\sqrt{65}}{4}$
C. $\dfrac{\sqrt{33}}{7}$
D. $\dfrac{\sqrt{33}}{4}$
E. $\dfrac{4\sqrt{65}}{65}$

54. What is the area of a circle that is inscribed in a square with a diagonal of 8?

F. 2π
G. 4π
H. 6π
J. 8π
K. 10π

GO ON TO THE NEXT PAGE.

488 / ACT

55. In the figure below, line segment $\overline{AB}$ is divided into three pieces as shown in the diagram. If the ratio of $\overline{AC}:\overline{CD}$ is 2:3 and the ratio of $\overline{CD}:\overline{DB}$ is 2:5, what is the length of $\overline{AB}$ if $\overline{AC} = 4$?

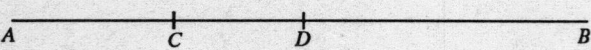

A. 15
B. 18
C. 20
D. 25
E. 40

56. For all θ, $\dfrac{\sin^2 3\theta + \cos^2 3\theta}{\sin^2 2\theta + \cos^2 2\theta} =$

F. $\dfrac{1}{3}$
G. $\dfrac{9}{4}$
H. $\dfrac{1}{2}$
J. $\dfrac{3}{2}$
K. 1

57. What is $\dfrac{1}{10}$% of $\dfrac{1}{10}$ of 10?

A. .1
B. .01
C. .001
D. .0001
E. .00001

58. $4^3 + 4^3 + 4^3 + 4^3 = ?$

F. 4^4
G. 16^3
H. 4^{12}
J. 16^{12}
K. 4^{81}

59. If an x-intercept of the parabola $y = -x^2 + 2x + k$ is -1, what is the value of k?

A. -3
B. -1
C. 1
D. 2
E. 3

DO YOUR FIGURING HERE.

GO ON TO THE NEXT PAGE.

60. If $y = \frac{x+1}{x-1}$ ($x \neq 1$ and $y \neq 1$), which of the following is the solution for x in terms of y?

F. $\frac{y+1}{y}$

G. $\frac{y-1}{y}$

H. $\frac{y+1}{y-1}$

J. $\frac{y-1}{y+1}$

K. $1 - \frac{1}{y^2}$

DO YOUR FIGURING HERE.

STOP!
This is the end of the Mathematics Test.
Do not proceed to the next section until the allotted time expires.

3. READING TEST

35 Minutes—40 Questions

DIRECTIONS: There are four passages in this test. Each passage is followed by a number of questions. After reading a passage, select the most appropriate answer to each question and blacken the corresponding space on your answer sheet. You may refer to the passages as often as necessary.

Passage I

Water is necessary to us, but a waterfall is not. It is something extra, a beautiful ornament. We need daylight and to that extent it is utilitarian, but moonlight we do not need. When it comes, it serves
5 no necessity. It transforms. It falls upon the banks and the grass, separating one long blade from another; turning a drift of brown, frosted leaves from a single heap to innumerable flashing fragments; or glimmering lengthways along wet twigs
10 as the trunks of trees, their clarity fading as they recede into the powdery, misty distance of beech woods at night. In moonlight, two acres of coarse bent grass, undulant and ankle deep tumbled and rough as a horse's mane, appear like a bay of waves,
15 all shadowy troughs and hollows. The growth is so thick and matted that even the wind does not move it, but it is the moonlight that seems to confer stillness upon it. We do not take moonlight for granted. It is like snow, or like the dew on a July
20 morning. It does not reveal but changes what it covers. And its low intensity—so much lower than that of daylight—makes us conscious that it is something added to the down, to give it, for only a little time, a singular and marvelous quality that we
25 should admire while we can, for soon it will be gone again.

1. The feeling established in the passage is one of
   A. suspense.
   B. liveliness.
   C. admiration.
   D. joy.

2. In lines 8–9, the use of the words "innumerable flashing fragments" provides a
   F. calm and tranquil description of the beams.
   G. lively vision of a pile of moonlit leaves.
   H. precise picture of meadow grass.
   J. detailed image of the wet twigs in moonlight.

3. Which statement best explains lines 10–12, "their clarity fading as they recede into the powdery, misty distance of beech woods . . ."?
   A. The moon is rising too high in the sky.
   B. The clouds are passing over and hiding the moon.
   C. The undergrowth causes the beams to disappear.
   D. The distance erases the sharpness of each beam.

4. As used in line 14, the words "like a bay of waves" describes the
   F. grass.
   G. horse's mane.
   H. water.
   J. moonbeams.

5. Which statement best expresses the main idea of this passage?
   A. Many things are useful and therefore beautiful.
   B. Water and light are necessary to life.
   C. One can discover a foreign world after dark.
   D. The beauty of moonlight should be appreciated.

6. Which statement best rephrases the author's description "a singular and marvelous quality that we should admire while we can" (lines 24–25)?

   F. Moonlight is beautiful and short-lived.
   G. Night provides the earth with a marvelous quality.
   H. Daylight reveals beauty better than moonlight does.
   J. Dew changes the appearance of whatever it covers.

7. Which idea appears first in the passage?

   A. Moonlight transforms.
   B. Moonlight confers stillness.
   C. Moonlight is unnecessary.
   D. Moonlight has a singular quality.

8. The style of the passage is

   F. didactic.
   G. informal.
   H. expository.
   J. circumlocutory.

9. The function of the first two sentences of the passage is to

   A. introduce the concept of beauty in natural phenomena.
   B. compare and contrast a waterfall to moonlight.
   C. compare beauty and necessity in reference to water.
   D. provide an interesting contrast to moonlight.

10. The author would probably appreciate all of the following EXCEPT

    F. an ocean wave.
    G. a starry night.
    H. a bare light bulb.
    J. a candlelit dinner.

Passage II

We might as well accept it as a fact that our present mode of living, with its intricate technical aspects, requires a correspondingly intricate organization. It would be foolish to talk of turning this clock back
5 or slowing its pendulum to the tempo of Walden Pond. Corporations and labor unions have conferred great benefits upon their employees and members as well as upon the general public. But if a power becomes too concentrated in a corporation or a
10 union and its members are coerced into submission, or if either assumes and selfishly exploits a monopolistic position regardless of the public interest, the public safeguards of individual freedom are weakened. Tyranny is tyranny, no matter who
15 practices it; corruption is corruption. If citizens get used to these things and condone them in their private affairs, they school themselves to accept and condone them in public affairs.
   But it is not so much these more flagrant (and less
20 frequent) transgressions as it is the everyday organizational way of life that threatens individual freedom. For the obvious transgressions there are obvious remedies at law. But what shall we say about the endless sterile conferences held in sub-
25 stitution for individual inventiveness; the public opinion polls whose vogue threatens even our moral and aesthetic values with the pernicious doctrine that the customer is always right; the unctuous public relations counsels that rob us of both our
30 courage and our convictions? This continuous, daily deferral of opinion and judgment to someone else becomes a habit. The undeveloped negative remains a negative. It conjures a nightmare picture of a whole nation of yes-men, of hitchhikers and eaves-
35 droppers, tiptoeing backwards offstage with their fingers to their lips—this, the nation whose prophets once cried "Trust thyself!"

11. As used in line 11, the word "either" refers to

    A. tyranny or corruption.
    B. a corporation or a union.
    C. the public interest or a power.
    D. turning the clock back or slowing the pendulum.

12. Which does the author regard as unchangeable?

    F. The complexity of modern life
    G. Public interest
    H. The integrity of our traditions
    J. The deterioration of public morality

13. As used in line 20, the word "transgressions" most nearly means

    A. institutions.
    B. criminals.
    C. crimes.
    D. freedoms.

14. The author suggests that in people's everyday lives, they should

    F. join worthwhile organizations.
    G. treat their rivals with contempt.

H. improve their knowledge of world affairs.
J. respect their own views.

15. The author would most likely believe in which of the following maxims?

    A. Self-love is the greatest of all flatterers.
    B. The spirit is willing, but the flesh is weak.
    C. To thine own self be true.
    D. History repeats itself.

16. The last two sentences of the passage suggest that people

    F. value their right to disagree.
    G. are becoming conformists.
    H. are overwhelmed by helpful opinions.
    J. resent the actions of those who disagree with them.

17. The author's main purpose in writing this passage seems to be to

    A. arouse the public to action.
    B. praise a previous way of life.
    C. show the function of law in modern society.
    D. explain the intricacies of modern life.

18. The type of writing exemplified by this passage is

    F. narrative.
    G. poetic.
    H. literary.
    J. purposeful.

19. The author mentions Walden Pond in order to

    A. compare and contrast to modern times.
    B. look yearningly to former times.
    C. hold up a standard to be emulated.
    D. confuse the reader with obfuscations.

20. The passage implies that the author believes in

    F. the value of public opinion.
    G. the lessons of the past.
    H. the necessity of thinking for oneself.
    J. the status quo.

Passage III

Iona sees a hall porter with some sacking, and decides to talk to him.
"Friend, what sort of time is it?" he asks.
"Past nine. What are you standing here for? Move on."
Iona moves on a few steps, doubles up, and abandons himself to his grief. In less than five minutes he straightens himself, holds his head up as if he felt some sharp pain, and gives a tug at the reins; he can bear it no longer. "The stables," he thinks, and the little horse, as if it understood, starts off at a trot.
About an hour and a half later Iona is seated by a large dirty stove. Around the stove, on the floor, on the benches, people are snoring; the air is thick and suffocatingly hot. Iona looks at the sleepers, scratches himself, and regrets having returned so early.
One of the cabdrivers half gets up, grunts sleepily, and stretches toward a bucket of water.
"Do you want a drink?" Iona asks him.
"Don't I want a drink!"
"That's so? Your good health! But listen, mate—you know, my son is dead . . . Did you hear? This week, in the hospital . . . It's a long story."
Iona looks to see what effect his words have, but sees none—the young man has hidden his face and is fast asleep again. The old man sighs, and scratches his head. Just as much as the young one wants to drink, the old man wants to talk. Is it nothing to tell?
"I'll go and look after my horse," thinks Iona; "there's always time to sleep. No fear of that!"
He puts on his coat, and goes to the stables to his horse; he thinks of the corn, the hay, the weather. When he is alone, he dares not think of his son; he can speak about him to anyone, but to think of him, and picture him to himself, is unbearably painful.
"Are you tucking in?" Iona asks his horse, looking at its bright eyes, "Go on, tuck in. Though we've not earned our corn, we can eat hay."
Iona is silent for a moment, then continues:
"That's how it is, my old horse. There's no more Kuzma Ionitch. Now let's say, you had a foal, you were the foal's mother, and suddenly, let's say, that foal went and left you to live after him. It would be sad, wouldn't it?"
The little horse munches, listens, and breathes over its master's hand . . .
Iona's feelings are too much for him, and he tells the little horse the whole story.

21. Iona most probably regrets going to the room with the stove because

    A. his horse has not been fed.
    B. there is no room for him.

C. the sleepers are unfriendly to him.
D. there is no one who will listen to him.

22. In his encounter with the cabdriver, Iona shows

    F. patriotism.
    G. resignation.
    H. suspicion.
    J. ill will.

23. In this story it is ironic that

    A. the cabdriver wants a drink.
    B. the hall porter tells Iona to move on.
    C. Iona tells his story to his horse.
    D. Iona has run out of food for his horse.

24. Iona's grief is strongest when he

    F. is seated by the stove.
    G. realizes that he is dying.
    H. speaks with the cabdriver.
    J. is alone.

25. The setting for this story is probably a nineteenth-century

    A. American city.
    B. Eastern European city.
    C. Northern European farm.
    D. American small town.

26. The author's purpose in using the present tense is most probably to

    F. make the story seem modern.
    G. increase the length of the story.
    H. heighten the reader's sense of immediacy.
    J. reinforce the first person point of view.

27. This passage is characterized by

    A. few extra words.
    B. over-writing, in the form of too many ornate adjectives.
    C. too-long paragraphs.
    D. frequent use of figures of speech.

28. The title that best expresses the main idea of the passage is

    F. "A Father's Grief."
    G. "A Horse and Its Master."
    H. "A Day in the Life of a Groom."
    J. "A Senile Old Man."

29. Iona goes to take care of his horse. He does so most probably to

    I. have something to do.
    II. show his great love for his horse.
    III. remove his feelings of guilt.
    IV. prove that he does not resent the cabdriver's action.

    A. I only
    B. I and II
    C. I, II, and III
    D. II and IV

30. The tone of the passage is one of

    F. sadness.
    G. gaiety.
    H. impartiality.
    J. destruction.

Passage IV

The ear is indeed a remarkable mechanism; it is so complicated that its operation is not well-understood. Certainly it is extremely sensitive. At the threshold of audibility, the power requirement is inconceivably tiny. If
5 all the people in the United States were listening simultaneously to a whisper (20 decibels), the power received by all their collective eardrums would total only a few millionths of a watt—far less than the power generated by a single flying mosquito.
10 This aural organ is also remarkable for its ability to distinguish various pitches and other qualities of sound. In the range of frequencies where the ear is most sensitive (between 500 and 4,000 vibrations per second), changes in pitch of only .3 percent can be detected. Thus, if a
15 singer trying to reach the octave above middle C (512 vibrations per second) is off-key by only 1.5 vibrations per second, the fault can be detected.
 The normal ear can respond to frequencies ranging from 20 to 20,000 vibrations per second. In this range, it is
20 estimated that the ear can distinguish more than half a million separate pure tones; that is, 500,000 differences in frequency or loudness. The range varies somewhat from ear to ear and becomes somewhat shorter for low-intensity sounds. Above the audible range, air vibrations
25 similar to sound are called supersonic vibrations. These may be generated and detected by electrical devices and are useful particularly for depth sounding at sea. The time for the waves to travel from the generator to the bottom of the ocean and back again is a measure of the depth of
30 that particular spot. Supersonic vibrations apparently can be heard by some animals—notably bats. It is believed that bats are guided during flight by supersonic sounds

(supersonic only to humans) which they emit and which are reflected back to their ears in a kind of natural radar.

35 Humans can tell approximately where a sound comes from because we have two ears, not one. The sound arriving at one ear a split second before its arrival at the second ear gives the brain information, which the latter organ interprets to note the direction from which the
40 sound originally came.

The ear is divided into three parts: the outer ear, the middle ear, and the inner ear. The outer ear consists of a canal closed at the inner end by a membrane, the eardrum. The middle ear contains a system of three bone
45 levers, known as the hammer, the anvil, and the stirrup. These bones serve to transmit the sound vibrations from the eardrum to the membrane-window covering the inner ear. The principal feature of the inner ear is the cochlea, a peculiar spiral bony enclosure that looks much like a
50 snail shell. Contained in the cochlea is the vital organ of hearing, the basilar membrane of the organ of corti.

Surrounding the basilar membrane is a liquid. The sound vibrations are transmitted to this liquid, and then, apparently, through the liquid for a distance that is
55 dependent on the frequency of the sound vibration. Lower frequencies are transmitted to the farther end of the basilar membrane; higher frequencies are able to penetrate only a short distance through the liquid. Along the basilar membrane are located the auditory nerve endings.
60 When a particular portion of the basilar membrane is stimulated by the sound vibrations, the brain records the disturbance as a certain pitch. More vigorous oscillation is interpreted as a louder sound.

31. Which of the following statements about normal human hearing is true?

    A. All ear vibrations occur at frequencies between 2,000 and 20,000 vibrations per second.
    B. Vibrations below 20 or above 20,000 per second cannot be detected.
    C. All human beings can hear sounds if the vibrations are within a range of between 2 and 200,000 vibrations per second.
    D. Many women can detect vibrations below 4 per second.

32. The amount of wattage received by the normal eardrum

    F. indicates high electrical energy.
    G. is extremely sensitive to heat.
    H. is extraordinarily small.
    J. can be harnessed to do useful work.

33. A sound coming from a person's left side would

    A. irritate the cortex.
    B. hit both ears at the same time.
    C. not be perceived by a brain-damaged child.
    D. hit the left ear first.

34. Which of the following would cause the most vigorous vibration in the human ear?

    F. Supersonic vibration.
    G. Police whistle.
    H. Loud bass drum.
    J. Shot from a cannon.

35. Sound is transmitted immediately past the eardrum by

    A. a series of bone levers.
    B. nerve endings.
    C. cochlea.
    D. membranes.

36. The tone of the passage is

    F. argumentative.
    G. didactic.
    H. disdaining.
    J. approving.

37. The passage would most likely go on to discuss

    A. other parts of the body.
    B. pitch and frequency in the ear.
    C. how oscillation affects the ear.
    D. more details about the workings of the ear.

38. This passage is probably excerpted from a

    F. news magazine.
    G. textbook on human anatomy.
    H. popular magazine dealing with scientific topics.
    J. medical textbook.

39. The best title for the passage is

    A. The Ear—An Amazing Part of the Body.
    B. How Sounds Affect the Ear.
    C. The Three Parts of the Ear.
    D. The Range of the Ear.

40. The direction of sound can be detected

   F. by combining kinesthetic and tactile data.
   G. by the inner ear alone.
   H. by the frequency and duration of the sound.
   J. because sound arrives in each ear at different time intervals.

STOP!

This is the end of the Reading Test.
Do not proceed to the next section until the allotted
time expires.

4. SCIENCE REASONING TEST

35 Minutes—40 Questions

DIRECTIONS: Each passage in this test is followed by several questions. After reading a passage, select the most appropriate answer to each question and blacken the corresponding space on your answer sheet. You may refer to the passages as often as you feel necessary.

Passage I

The lower the energy of a system, be it a box on an incline or sub-atomic particles in a nucleus, the more stable the system. The graph below relates the energy level of the negatively charged electrons in a bond between two atoms, X and Y, to the distance between the centers of the positively charged nuclei of X and Y. This internuclear distance is called the bond length. The electrons possess discrete energies corresponding to the horizontal "levels" labelled in the diagram below.

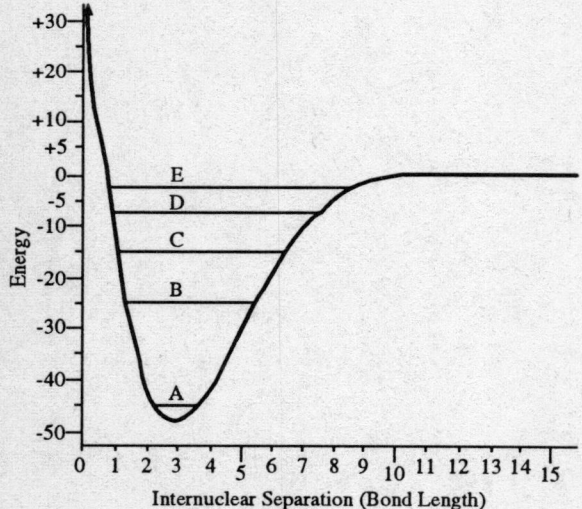

1. According to the diagram, which of the following is the most stable bond length?

   A. 0 units
   B. 1 unit
   C. 3 units
   D. 13 units

2. What is the most likely explanation for the change in energy as the bond length decreases from 3 units?

   F. The bond is getting stronger.
   G. The energy is increasing.
   H. The nuclei are repelling each other.
   J. The nuclei are attracting each other.

3. What is the significance of the zero energy level?

   A. It corresponds to a state where X and Y do not interact at all.
   B. It corresponds to a state where there is no net interaction.
   C. It corresponds to a maximum repulsion between the two atoms.
   D. It corresponds to a minimum repulsion between the two atoms.

4. What energy level is not available when X and Y are 5 units apart?

   F. A
   G. B
   H. C
   J. All are available.

5. If an electron has the lowest possible energy in an X–Y bond that is 3.1 units long, what is the smallest amount of energy it can absorb?

   A. − 45 units
   B. − 40 units
   C. + 20 units
   D. + 45 units

6. The fact that the energy of the system decreases to a stable minimum as large internuclear separations decrease explains why molecules

F. are stable.
G. react rapidly.
H. can rotate in free space.
J. have characteristic compositions.

Passage II

A clinical study was initiated to determine the effect of a new drug on the levels of five hormones (A, B, C, D, and E) found in the bloodstream. For the study, 20 genetically and physically similar rats were divided into four groups—one control group and three groups receiving different doses of the new drug. The experimental groups were injected with a predetermined dose of the drug every day. The control group was injected with a volume of water equal to the injection volume of the other groups. Blood samples were analyzed on the fifth and tenth days of the experiment. The figures presented below are the average values obtained for the rats in each group. The dose is reported in mg/kg-body weight; hormone concentrations in micrograms per ml of blood.

Time on Drug (Days)	Dosage	Hormone: A	B	C	D	E
0	0	12.4	18.6	25.0	66.0	142
5	0	12.3	18.7	25.0	66.0	142
5	1	10.0	19.2	21.4	34.0	146
5	2	9.6	18.6	6.0	19.6	160
5	4	9.2	4.8	9.6	17.8	124
10	0	12.4	18.6	24.9	66.1	142
10	1	22.0	25.8	25.0	19.6	98
10	2	18.2	16.6	8.8	15.8	104
10	4	33.4	11.8	13.6	14.4	86

7. Which hormone returned to its initial concentration at some non-zero dosage during the course of the study?

A. A
B. B
C. C
D. B and C

8. What effect does the drug have on the concentration of hormone E during the course of the experiment?

F. It initially increases the concentration of E, but later lowers the concentration below normal for all dosages studied.
G. It initially decreases the concentration of E, but later raises the concentration above normal for all dosages studied.
H. It initially raises or lowers concentration depending on the dosage, but ultimately lowers the concentration of E for all dosages studied.
J. It initially raises or lowers the concentration depending on the dosage, but ultimately raises the concentration of E for all dosages studied.

9. If hormone B is the key growth hormone for the rat, what dosage in mg per GRAM body weight should be used to grow the smallest rat possible?

A. 0.004 mg/g-body weight
B. 0.4 mg/g-body weight
C. 2 mg/g-body weight
D. 4 mg/g-body weight

10. Which of the following hormones is the most active after 10 days' treatment at the highest dosage tested?

F. A
G. E
H. C
J. Cannot be determined.

11. Which of the following hormones had the greatest percentage loss in concentration after 10 days of treatment?

A. A
B. E
C. C
D. D

12. Which of the following statements most accurately describes the effect of the 4 mg/kg-body weight dosage?

F. It depresses the concentrations of all hormones.
G. It depresses the concentrations of all hormones after 10 days, though not after only 5 days.
H. It depresses all hormone concentrations after 5 days, but not after 10 days.
J. It increases the concentration of hormone A.

13. What happens to the ratio of the concentrations of E to A over the course of the 2 mg/kg-body weight treatment?

    A. The ratio increases then decreases.
    B. The ratio decreases then increases.
    C. The ratio remains constant.
    D. The ratio decreases.

14. Which hormone concentrations declined to lethal levels by day 5 of the 4 mg/kg-body weight treatment?

    F. All
    G. A, C, and E
    H. None
    J. Cannot be determined.

Passage III

The change in temperature of an object depends on three variables. First, the rise in temperature depends on the amount of heat energy supplied. Secondly, it depends on the amount of material to be heated. A greater amount of material requires more heat than a smaller amount of material for the same rise in temperature. Thirdly, the nature of the material plays a role in the temperature rise. This factor or property is called the heat capacity of the material. A formula that relates all these variables is:

$$Heat = mC\triangle T$$

Where m is the mass, C is the heat capacity measured in $J/g - °C$, and $\triangle T$ is the change in temperature in degrees Celcius. In the following experiments electrical work is used to generate heat in the sample fluids. The work generated is identical to the heat given, and is calculated by the following formula:

$$Work = IVt$$

Where I is the current in amperes, V is the voltage, and t is the length of time voltage was applied.

Experimental Procedure:
For each trial a liquid was placed in a Dewar flask that allowed heat to neither enter nor escape. At the base of the flask an electrical circuit was set up to produce electrical work when hooked up to a battery. Some liquids were used only once, others may have been used in several trials. The table summarizes the data collected:

Trial Number	Mass (g)	Current (amp)	Voltage (V)	Time (sec)	$\triangle T$ (°C)
1	5	10	2	3	4
2	2	2	16	5	x
3	10	y	2	10	6
4	10	5	4	5	10
5	1	5	4	3	20
6	z	4	8	5	10
7	10	5	2	5	1

15. The liquid used in trial 1 could be the same liquid used in which other trial?

    A. 7
    B. 4
    C. 5
    D. None of the above.

16. If the same liquid was used in trials 3 and 4, what must have been the current y used in trial 3?

    F. 3 amps
    G. 6 amps
    H. 1 amp
    J. Not enough data.

17. If 5 grams of liquid A experiences the same rise in temperature as 10 grams of liquid B under the same conditions, the ratio of the heat capacity of B to the heat capacity of A is

    A. 1/2
    B. 2
    C. 1
    D. 50

18. If the liquid used in trial 6 has a heat capacity of 2 $J/g - °C$, what mass z must have been used in the trial?

    F. 4 g
    G. 8 g
    H. 2 g
    J. 1 g

19. What would happen to the heat capacity of a substance if both the current used and the duration of heating were doubled?

    A. It would increase by a factor of 4.
    B. It would decrease to 1/4 of its value.
    C. It would cause a change in the voltage.
    D. It would be unaffected.

20. Is it possible for two entirely different substances to have identical heat capacities?

F. No, but they can have very similar ones.
G. No, because the heat capacity is a property of the substance.
H. Yes, because heat capacity depends on the applied heat.
J. Yes, because heat capacity is not related to a single unique feature of a substance.

Passage IV

Pest control is a serious problem for the agricultural community. Not only must the crops be protected from the ravages of various pests, but the method of control must be environmentally safe. Two compounds, X and Y, were recently tested as means of controlling the beetle *magister ineptus*.

Experiment 1

A fish tank kept under constant temperature, humidity and lighting conditions was stocked with 2 kilograms each of apricots, apples, and pears. Each type of fruit rested on a digital pan balance that was set at zero. Into this environment were placed 30 mature male beetles. At the end of every hour a researcher recorded the amount of each type of fruit eaten and reset the balance to zero. Diagram IV-1 depicts the consumption pattern of the beetles over the course of 10 hours. (The length of a fruit's bar at any time equals the amount of that fruit consumed over the course of the hour. For example, the bar for apricots at time = 5 hours indicates that 0.1g of apricots were consumed from the beginning to the end of the fifth hour of the experiment.

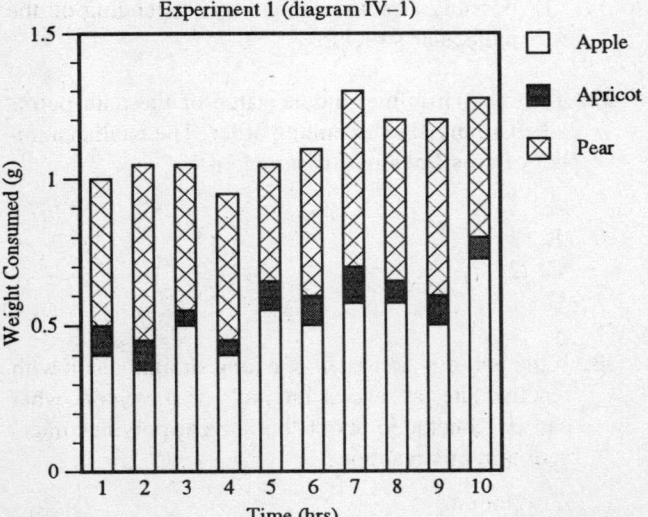

Experiment 2

Conditions identical to the conditions in Experiment 1 were set up, except that all fruit in the tank was equally sprayed with a total of 50 mg of compound X. The results are presented in Diagram IV-2.

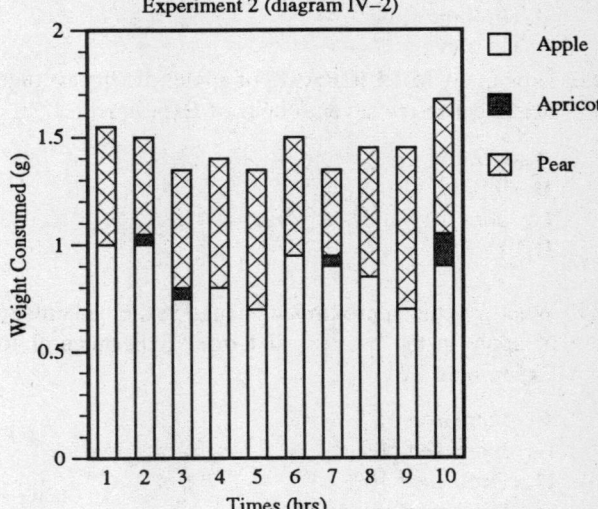

Experiment 3

Conditions identical to the conditions in Experiment 1 were set up, except that all fruit in the tank was equally sprayed with a total of 50 mg of compound Y. The results are presented in Diagram IV-3.

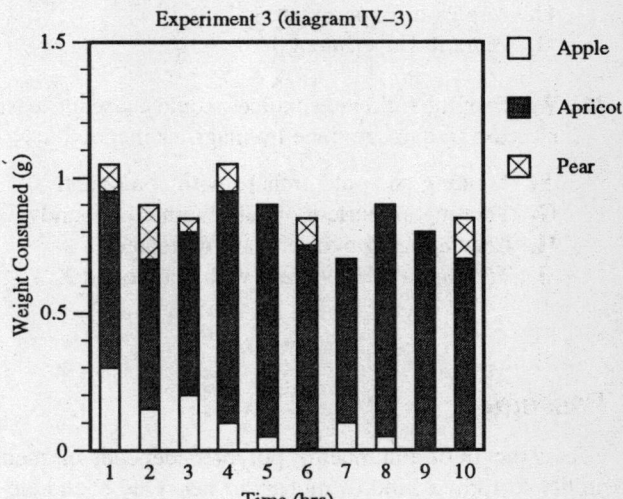

21. How many grams of pear were consumed during the course of Experiment 2?

A. 5.65 g
B. 0.565 g
C. 5.65/30 g
D. 5.65/300 g

22. What was the approximate average hourly fruit consumption of the beetles in Experiment 1?

    F. 11.2 g
    G. 1.12 g
    H. 0.04 g
    J. 0.40 g

23. How many MILLIGRAMS of apples did the average beetle eat in the seventh hour of Experiment 2?

    A. 0.9
    B. 0.03
    C. 30
    D. 15

24. What was the approximate change in the percentage of apple in the beetles' diet from Experiment 1 to Experiment 2?

    F. Increased 15%
    G. Increased 60%
    H. Decreased 10%
    J. Remained constant.

25. Which of the following was consumed in the lowest quantity?

    A. Apricots in Experiment 1.
    B. Apricots in Experiment 2.
    C. Apples in Experiment 3.
    D. Pears in Experiment 3.

26. Which of the following choices would cause the least increase in damage done by magister ineptus?

    F. Treating an apple orchard with compound X.
    G. Treating an apricot orchard with compound Y.
    H. Leaving an apricot orchard untreated.
    J. Treating a pear orchard with compound X.

Passage V

The strength of a number of polymers depends on their ability to form a kind of molecular net. One of the elements important to net making is a process called crosslinking. Crosslinking occurs when reactive sites on a polymer bond (link) to other reactive sites. This can happen intramolecularly (between reactive sites on the same molecule) or intermolecularly (between reactive sites on different molecules). Reaction conditions can often influence both the amount of crosslinking and whether the crosslinking will be intra- or intermolecular. In the results presented below, obtained from viscosity (resistance to flow) studies, only intramolecular crosslinking is assumed to occur.

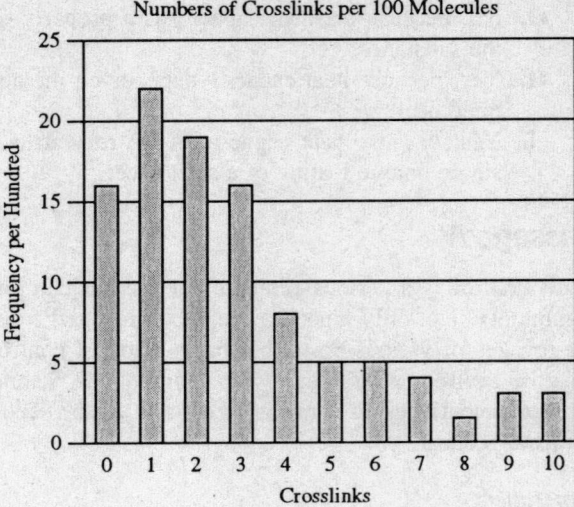

27. According to the graph, the proportion of molecules with six or more crosslinks is

    A. less than one tenth.
    B. less than one eighth but greater than one tenth.
    C. one eighth.
    D. greater than one eighth.

28. If the reaction took place in a highly concentrated solution, the assumption that the crosslinking was intramolecular would be

    F. strongly supported.
    G. less likely to be true.
    H. unaffected by this information.
    J. possibly affected either way, depending on the molecular structure.

29. The median is the middle value of the data points when arranged in ascending order. The median number of crosslinks in this sample is

    A. 5
    B. 3
    C. 2
    D. 1

30. If the polymer consisted of a long straight chain with reactive sites at regular intervals on the chain, what can be concluded about the solvent-polymer interaction in this reaction?

    F. Nothing.
    G. There is a strong attraction between polymer and solvent.

H. There is a strong repulsion between polymer and solvent.

J. There is a temperature dependent attraction between polymer and solvent.

31. What is the likelihood that if a molecule has one crosslink, it has at least four other crosslinks?

A. 8%
B. 19%
C. 27%
D. 81%

32. What is the likelihood of there being only one crosslink in a polymer?

F. 22%
G. 38%
H. 62%
J. 78%

Passage VI

How did Venus' cloud cover originate? Two differing views are presented below.

Scientist 1

Venus is a planet with a surface gravity similar to the surface gravity of the Earth. Venus is also much closer to the sun than the Earth is. Because of this, Venus receives solar winds that are much more concentrated than the wind that reaches our own planet. These winds are rich in gaseous matter from the surface of the sun. As Venus sweeps through its orbit its gravitational field pulls some of this gaseous material into its own atmosphere. Once the gas has entered the atmosphere it is difficult for it to escape again. First of all, the molecules that enter the atmosphere lose their kinetic energy through countless collisions with other molecules in the atmosphere. Thus it becomes very difficult to develop the "escape velocity" required to leave the gravitational field of the planet. Second, the second law of thermodynamics states that the universe moves to a more disordered (mixed) state. This would favor the molecules' staying "dissolved" in the atmosphere. Strong evidence for the solar origin of the Venusian clouds is provided by the observed change in cloud density on that planet during solar storms, when large plumes of gas, called flares, are released by the sun. The density of the clouds increases dramatically during these times. It is also true that the color of Venus' clouds changes during the storm. This indicates that the gases expelled by the sun during a flare differ in composition from gases expelled at other times.

Scientist 2

There is no need to assume that Venus has pilfered anyone but herself to bedeck herself in the luxuriant mantle of clouds over her surface. Many planets farther away from the solar winds have developed thick atmospheres. Jupiter, for example, has an atmosphere so thick that it crushes whatever probe we send towards the surface of the planet. It is possible that the moon Titan, a satellite of Jupiter, may also have an atmosphere. The Earth herself has a fairly extensive cover without taking much material from the solar wind. The thickness of Venus' clouds have a much simpler explanation than the capturing of material from the sun. Venus is near enough to the sun to make her surface several times hotter than the surface of the Earth. Because of that, a lot of the material that would be liquid, or even "frozen" solid on Earth would be vaporized in the heat of Venus' surface. The changes in Venus' atmosphere during solar flares might be explained by remembering that the surface temperature of that planet probably reaches even higher levels during solar storms. This increase in temperature would make the clouds thicker, and also could change the composition and the color of the clouds as the less volatile components of Venus' surface finally evaporate at the elevated temperatures.

33. According to the hypothesis of Scientist 1, the density of the Venusian cloud over time should

A. increase.
B. decrease.
C. remain constant.
D. fluctuate.

34. Scientist 2 would most likely argue that the increase in Venus' cloud density in the presence of solar flares is due to

F. trapping the solar gases by Venus' gravity.
G. only temporarily trapping the gases by Venus' gravitational field.
H. an increase in the volatility of the surface.
J. chemical reactions in the cloud cover.

35. Scientist 2 would most likely counter the argument based on the color change of the cloud cover during the solar flare by pointing out that

A. the color has nothing to do with the chemical properties of the clouds.
B. the color does not persist after the flare.
C. there is no color change independent of the flares.
D. the color change occurs at the same time as the change in density.

36. Which of the following, if true, would most weaken Scientist 1's argument?

   F. The molecules present in the Venusian atmosphere are different from the molecules found in the solar flares.
   G. The atoms found in the cloud cover are present in different amounts from those present in the solar flares.
   H. Venus has a weaker gravitational field than does Earth.
   J. The molecules of the Venusian atmosphere are composed of different elements from those present in the solar flares.

37. According to Scientist 1's hypothesis, which planet should have the greatest cloud cover?

   A. Mercury
   B. Venus
   C. Earth
   D. Pluto

38. What assumption does Scientist 1 make about the cloud cover on Venus?

   F. That it is chemically similar to the cloud cover on Earth.
   G. That it is different from the surface in chemical composition.
   H. That it is chemically inert.
   J. That it contains only elements found in solar winds.

39. If the sun had been extinguished soon after Venus was formed, how would the hypotheses compare on predictions about the nature of the Venusian atmosphere?

   A. Scientist 2 would predict a heavy cloud cover, while Scientist 1 would predict no cloud cover.
   B. Scientist 2 would predict no cloud cover, while Scientist 1 would predict a heavy cloud cover.
   C. Both would predict no cloud cover.
   D. Both would predict a heavy cloud cover.

40. If Scientist 1 were correct, what should the surface of Venus look like over time?

   F. Many mesas.
   G. Flat and smooth.
   H. Mountainous.
   J. Jagged cliffs overlooking valleys.

STOP!

This is the end of the Science Reasoning Test.
When the allotted time for this section expires,
the entire test is completed.

Answer Key and Scoring Sheet for Practice Exam IV

English				Mathematics			
	Answer	Usage/ Mechanics	Rhetorical		Answer	Pre-Alg./ Elem. Alg.	Int. Alg./ Coord. Geom.	Geom./ Trig.
1.	B			1.	D	___		
2.	F			2.	K		___	
3.	D	___		3.	C			___
4.	H	___		4.	H			___
5.	B		___	5.	B	___		
6.	F		___	6.	K	___		
7.	C	___		7.	D	___		
8.	J		___	8.	J		___	
9.	B		___	9.	D		___	
10.	H		___	10.	H	___		
11.	C		___	11.	C			___
12.	J		___	12.	F			
13.	A	___		13.	A	___		
14.	G		___	14.	F			
15.	D	___		15.	E		___	
16.	F	___		16.	H	___		
17.	B		___	17.	D	___		
18.	H	___		18.	H	___		
19.	C		___	19.	E	___		
20.	G		___	20.	H	___		
21.	D		___	21.	A			
22.	D	___		22.	G			___
23.	F	___		23.	E			___
24.	C	___		24.	G		___	
25.	J	___		25.	A	___		
26.	B		___	26.	J		___	
27.	F	___		27.	A			___
28.	C	___		28.	G		___	
29.	J	___		29.	A	___		
30.	A		___	30.	F	___		
31.	F	___		31.	A			
32.	D		___	32.	H			
33.	G		___	33.	C			
34.	C	___		34.	J	___		
35.	F		___	35.	C	___		
36.	D	___		36.	G			
37.	J	___		37.	D			___
38.	A	___		38.	K			___
39.	G	___		39.	B		___	
40.	B		___	40.	J			___

Answer Key and Scoring Sheet for Practice Exam IV (continued)

		English					Mathematics		
		Answer	Usage/ Mechanics	Rhetorical			Answer	Pre-Alg./ Elem. Alg.	Int. Alg./ Coord. Geom.	Geom./ Trig.
	41.	F	___			41.	E	___		
	42.	C	___			42.	J			___
	43.	H		___		43.	B		___	
	44.	D	___			44.	K			___
	45.	J		___		45.	C			___
	46.	A		___		46.	K		___	
	47.	C	___			47.	C		___	
	48.	F	___			48.	H		___	
	49.	D	___			49.	D			___
	50.	H		___		50.	J		___	
	51.	A	___			51.	E		___	
	52.	J	___			52.	F		___	
	53.	B	___			53.	B			___
	54.	F	___			54.	J			___
	55.	C	___			55.	D	___		
	56.	G		___		56.	K			___
	57.	C		___		57.	C	___		
	58.	F		___		58.	F	___		
	59.	C		___		59.	E		___	
	60.	H		___		60.	H		___	
	61.	C		___						
	62.	B	___							
	63.	F	___							
	64.	D	___							
	65.	H	___							
	66.	A		___						
	67.	G	___							
	68.	C		___						
	69.	G	___							
	70.	C	___							
	71.	J	___							
	72.	A	___							
	73.	G		___						
	74.	C		___						
	75.	G		___						

Raw Score	Total Correct (by category) ___	Total Correct (by category) ___ ___ ___	
	Grand Total Correct (English) ___	Grand Total Correct (Mathematics) ___	

Using the chart on page 507, convert the above raw score to an approximate standardized score.

Approx. Standardized Score

Answer Key and Scoring Sheet for Practice Exam IV (continued)

	Reading				Science Reasoning	
	Answer	Social St./Science	Arts/Lit.		Answer	Science Reasoning
1.	C			1.	C	
2.	G			2.	H	
3.	D			3.	B	
4.	F			4.	F	
5.	D			5.	C	
6.	F			6.	F	
7.	C			7.	C	
8.	H			8.	H	
9.	A			9.	A	
10.	H			10.	J	
11.	B	___		11.	D	___
12.	F	___		12.	H	___
13.	C	___		13.	A	___
14.	J	___		14.	H	___
15.	C	___		15.	C	___
16.	G	___		16.	F	___
17.	A	___		17.	A	___
18.	J	___		18.	G	___
19.	A	___		19.	D	___
20.	H	___		20.	J	___
21.	D		___	21.	A	___
22.	G		___	22.	G	___
23.	C		___	23.	C	___
24.	J		___	24.	F	___
25.	B		___	25.	B	___
26.	H		___	26.	H	___
27.	A		___	27.	D	___
28.	F		___	28.	G	___
29.	A		___	29.	C	___
30.	F		___	30.	G	___
31.	B	___		31.	B	___
32.	H	___		32.	F	___
33.	D	___		33.	A	___
34.	J	___		34.	H	___
35.	A	___		35.	B	___
36.	G	___		36.	J	___
37.	D	___		37.	A	___
38.	H	___		38.	J	___
39.	A	___		39.	C	___
40.	J	___		40.	G	___

Raw Score

Total Correct (by category) ___ ___

Grand Total Correct (Reading) ___

Total Correct ___

Grand Total Correct (Science Reasoning) ___

Answer Key and Scoring Sheet for Practice Exam IV (continued)

Using the chart on page 507, convert the above raw score to an approximate standardized score.

Approx. Standardized Score

CONVERSION TABLE

Number Answered Correctly				Approximate Standardized Score
English	Mathematics	Reading	Science Reasoning	
0–2	0–2	0–2	0–1	1
3–4	3	3	2	2
5–6	4–5	4	3–4	3
7–8	6	5	5	4
9–10	7	6	6	5
11–12	8–9	7	7–8	6
13–14	10	8	9	7
15–16	11	9–10	10	8
17–18	12–13	11	11	9
19–20	14	12	12	10
21–23	15	13	13–14	11
24–25	16–17	14–15	15	12
26–27	18–19	16	16	13
28–29	20	17	17	14
30–31	21–22	18	18	15
32–33	23–24	19	19	16
34–35	25–26	20	20	17
36–37	27	21	21	18
38–39	28–29	22	22	19
40–41	30–31	23	23	20
42–44	32–33	24	24–25	21
45–46	34–35	25	26	22
47–48	36–38	26	27	23
49–50	39–40	27	28	24
51–52	41–42	28	29	25
53–54	43	29	30	26
55–57	44–46	30–31	31	27
58–60	47–48	32	32	28
61–63	49–50	33	33	29
64–65	51–52	34	34	30
66–68	53–54	35	35	31
69–70	55–56	36	36	32
71	57	37	37	33
72–73	58	38	38	34
74	59	39	39	35
75	60	40	40	36

Explanatory Answers for Practice Exam IV

1. English

1. **(B)** Answer B is correct because *of* expresses the correct relationship between *the calorie needs* and *women and men*. The other three choices are used incorrectly.

2. **(F)** Answer F is correct because choices G and H make *physical activity* the subject of the verb *expend*. Choice J is redundant.

3. **(D)** Answer D is correct because a comma is necessary to separate the dependent clause from the independent clause. Choice A provides no punctuation. Choice B is incorrect because a dash indicates an abrupt change. Choice C creates a sentence fragment.

4. **(H)** Answer H is correct because using the gerund, *engaging*, affixes no time limit to the activity. Choice F puts the action in the past; choice G uses a plural verb with a singular subject; choice J does not make sense.

5. **(B)** Answer B is correct because the phrase *lighter than for him* is parallel to the previous phrase *for her*.

6. **(F)** Answer F is correct because the two independent clauses need separating punctuation, and a semicolon is used to separate two independent but related clauses. Choices G and H do not separate the clauses; choice J, using the colon, is incorrect. A colon is used when the second part of a sentence describes the first part before the colon.

7. **(C)** Answer C is correct because it expresses the proper relationship between the two adjectives, *dense* and *lean*. The adjective after *less* must always be followed by *than* to express the relationship.

8. **(J)** Answer J is correct because it properly explains that boys and girls can gain the same amount of weight and still look different. Choices F and H are wordy and unidiomatic; in choice G, *grow to the same weight* is awkward.

9. **(B)** Answer B is correct because starting the passage with a question is a good way to pinpoint the subject of the passage and to capture the reader's attention.

10. **(H)** Answer H is correct because the passage discusses different nutritional needs of men and women, thereby implying that different diets might work. The other three choices are not addressed by the passage.

11. **(C)** Answer C is correct because choice A is phrased awkwardly; choice B puts the verb in the present tense, and the word *today* in the second sentence implies that the first sentence must be in the past by contrast. Choice D makes the verb *believed* a definitive past action, and it is not over—we still believe in education.

12. **(J)** Answer J is correct because choices F and G are wordy, and choice H is awkward—*sure to be successful* is incorrectly used.

13. **(A)** Answer A is correct because commas are necessary to separate the list of nouns. In choice B, the word *the* before *Asians* is unnecessary; choice C is lacking the punctuation to separate the series of nouns and choice D uses too many *and*'s.

14. **(G)** Answer G is correct because *part* is a more appropriate word choice than *segment*. Choices H and J are wordy.

15. **(D)** Answer D is correct because the verb *attribute* needs *to* after it, excluding choices A and B. Choice C is wrong because the verb *attribute* must be in the passive voice to make sense in the sentence.

16. **(F)** Answer F is correct because the simple present tense is needed to complement the pronoun *they*.

17. **(B)** Answer B is correct because the last sentence sums up the thoughts of the rest of the paragraph. The other choices are incorrect because those relationships are not shown.

18. **(H)** Answer H is correct because the first phrase, ending with the word *Hispanics*, tells to whom the second phrase refers. Choices F and G result in sentences without a subject for the verb *reduces*; choice J omits the comma necessary to separate the phrases.

19. **(C)** Answer C is correct because it is the only choice that is correctly punctuated.

20. **(G)** Answer G is correct because *chances* must be plural to agree with *students*.

21. **(D)** Answer D is correct because though there is a comma needed after *backgrounds* to separate the first dependent clause from the following independent clause, there is no need for a full stop (choices A and B), nor for a comma after *those* (choice C).

22. **(D)** Answer D is correct because the rest of the passage talks about events to come—so the future tense is necessary.

23. **(F)** Answer F is correct because a colon is necessary to separate the two independent clauses, since the second explains the first. Choices H and J introduce unnecessary words.

24. **(C)** Answer C is correct because *health* is the proper form of the noun.

25. **(J)** Answer J is correct because it is the only choice in which the two verbs agree in tense.

26. **(B)** Answer B is correct because the other choices are excessively wordy.

27. **(F)** Answer F is correct because there is no need to insert a pronoun before *lose*.

28. **(C)** Answer C is correct because the pronoun *we* applies to the entire sentence, so there is no need to separate the two phrases.

29. **(J)** Answer J is correct because the other choices are excessively wordy.

30. **(A)** Answer A is correct because the entire passage deals with the lure of health-restoring products. Choices B, C and D are secondary themes and do not refer to *It*.

31. **(F)** Answer F is correct because the verb *tempted* must be passive, eliminating choice J. Choices G and H are incorrect because *tempt* takes the word *to* after it when it is followed by a verb. We are *tempted by* things.

32. **(D)** Answer D is correct because the verb should be in the past tense, eliminating choices A and C. Choice B is incorrect because it incorrectly makes *we* the object of the verb *considered*.

33. **(G)** Answer G is correct because the passage's tone implies that these *cures* are not all they promise. Choices F and J are irrelevant, and choice H is too general to be a follow-up to this passage.

34. **(C)** Answer C is correct because the verb *have* must be plural to agree with *sweeteners*, and *whet* is the correct verb form.

35. **(F)** Answer F is correct because choice G makes the time period too specific; choice H makes it too general, and choice J is excessively wordy.

36. **(D)** Answer D is correct because a comma is needed to set off the modifying clause.

37. **(J)** Answer J is correct because *Americans* needs to be plural and possessive, and *twin* is being used as an adjective.

38. **(A)** Answer A is correct because choices B and C are awkward, and choice D eliminates a meaningful phrase from the sentence.

39. **(G)** Answer G is correct because no punctuation is needed to separate *Americans* from *18 and over*.

40. **(B)** Answer B is correct because in the parallel construction of the sentence, adding the verb *eat* is redundant, eliminating choice A. Choice C is overly wordy, and choice D offers a verb, *combining*, for which there is no subject.

41. **(F)** Answer F is correct because the simple past tense is appropriate here.

42. **(C)** Answer C is correct because choice A is excessively wordy; choice B is awkward, and in choice D the verb *is* does not agree with the implied subject, *calories*, in number.

43. **(H)** Answer H is correct because the word *however* signifies two opposing intents. The other relationships in choices F, G and J do not apply here.

44. **(D)** Answer D is correct. Choices A and B are incorrect because the pronoun *they* refers correctly to *patients*. Choice C makes *they* the object, rather than the subject, of the verb.

45. **(J)** Answer J is correct because in choices F, G and H, the subjects and verbs do not agree in number. In choice G, *each* does not agree with the plural *have*. In choices F and H, *all* does not agree with the singular *has*.

46. **(A)** Answer A is correct because choice B would add little to the meaning of the passage. Choice C would be unnecessary—there is no need to focus on just one of the sweeteners. Choice D would not add to the passage's discussion of the controversy over these sweeteners.

47. **(C)** Answer C is correct because two sentences are necessary here. Choice D is incorrect because the verb *has* does not agree with the subject *some*.

48. **(F)** Answer F is correct because *inhabitants* is the correct form of the noun. Choice H is incorrect because *inhabitants* must be followed by the preposition *of*, not *on*.

49. **(D)** Answer D is correct because choices A and C are excessively wordy. In choice B, the verb has the wrong tense.

50. **(H)** Answer H is correct because the other choices do not make sense. *Intrinsic* means basic or inherent.

51. **(A)** Answer A is correct because the impersonal pronoun, *it*, is appropriate here—it is a general statement.

52. **(J)** Answer J is correct because the other choices show incorrect usage.

53. **(B)** Answer B is correct because it is the only choice in which the verb *were* agrees with the subject *coins* and is in the right tense.

54. **(F)** Answer F is correct because the parenthetical statement is an aside, and should not be taken out of the parentheses. Choices H and J are awkward and wordy.

55. **(C)** Answer C is correct because the two characteristics of the coin must be described in parallel fashion—*was oblong* and *was stamped*.

56. **(G)** Answer G is correct because *system* should be singular to agree with *empire*. Choices H and J show awkward usage.

57. **(C)** Answer C is correct because it maintains the sentence's parallel structure. Choices A and B insert the unnecessary pronoun *they*; choice D leaves the sentence incomplete.

58. **(F)** Answer F is correct because it is the only choice in which the pronoun *these* is plural and the noun *countries* agrees. In choice J, *countrys'* is misspelled.

59. **(C)** Answer C is correct because in choice A, the plural object pronoun *them* does not agree with the singular subject *coinage*; choice B is excessively wordy; choice D unnecessarily repeats the pronoun *they*.

60. **(H)** Answer H is correct because in any other order, the paragraphs do not make sense. Paragraph 1 introduces money throughout history. Paragraph 3 discusses the first coins minted. Paragraph 2 is a general discussion, and paragraph 4 discusses ancient empires and their coinage.

61. **(C)** Answer C is correct because the focus of the piece is on the coins themselves, not on their financial significance.

62. **(B)** Answer B is correct because choice A is awkward, and choices C and D are excessively wordy.

63. **(F)** Answer F is correct because no pause is necessary; therefore, no punctuation is needed.

64. **(D)** Answer D is correct because the plural verb *do* is necessary to agree with *friends, coach, or relatives*. The word *both* in choices B and C is unnecessary.

65. **(H)** Answer H is correct because the gerund *using* is the proper form here.

66. **(A)** Answer A is correct because the word *can* is necessary, but repeating the subject *it* is not.

67. **(G)** Answer G is correct because though a pause is necessary to separate the clause, a full stop—as in choices H and J—is not.

68. **(C)** Answer C is correct because in choice A, the word *into* is incorrectly used with the verb *occur*. Choices B and D are awkward.

69. **(G)** Answer G is correct because *that* is used to introduce a restrictive clause. The word *which* is used for a non-restrictive clause.

70. **(C)** Choice C is correct. In choice A, the gerund *stopping* cannot be followed by the infinitive *to use*. Choice B is awkward, and choice D, the imperative, has no subject in the sentence.

71. **(J)** Answer J is correct because no separating punctuation is necessary between the two verbs, *dip* and *chew*.

72. **(A)** Answer A is correct because nouns listed in a parallel series must agree in number. *Week, month* and *year* are all singular nouns.

73. **(G)** Answer G is correct because the question is not expected to be answered. That is the definition of a rhetorical question.

74. **(C)** Answer C is correct because it would best strengthen the passage's position.

75. **(G)** Answer G is correct because the passage deals with the harmful effects of chewing tobacco on young people.

2. Mathematics

1. **(D)** Use a ratio of apples to dollars.

   $\dfrac{\text{apples}}{\text{dollars}} \rightarrow \dfrac{24}{3} = \dfrac{18}{x}$

   $8 = \dfrac{18}{x}$

   $8x = 18$

   $x = 2.25$

2. **(K)** $\dfrac{x}{a} + \dfrac{y}{b} = 1$

   is the intercept form of a line equation
   where $a = x$-intercept
   $b = y$-intercept

   $\therefore$ the y-intercept is -2

   or

   $\dfrac{x}{3} - \dfrac{y}{2} = 1$

   multiply the equation by 6 and format into $y = mx + b$ form

   $6\left(\dfrac{x}{3} - \dfrac{y}{2} = 1\right) \rightarrow 2x - 3y = 6$

   $-3y = -2x + 6$

   $y = \dfrac{2}{3}x - 2$

   the y-intercept is -2.

3. **(C)** $(\text{Leg 1})^2 + (\text{Leg 2})^2 = (\text{Hypotenuse})^2$

   $(\overline{NJ})^2 + (\overline{JL})^2 = (\overline{NL})^2$

   $x^2 + (\sqrt{3})^2 = (4)^2$

   $x^2 + 3 = 16$

   $x^2 = 13$

   $x = \sqrt{13}$

4. **(H)**

   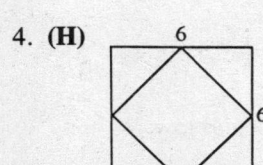

   the area of a square $= (\text{side})^2$

   or

   $= \dfrac{(\text{diagonal})^2}{2}$

   Area of $\square ABCD = (\text{side})^2 = 6^2 = 36$

   Area of $\square WXYZ = \dfrac{(\text{diagonal})^2}{2} = \dfrac{6^2}{2} = 18$

   Shaded area $= 36 - 18 = 18$.

5. **(B)** He kept $\dfrac{3}{4}$ of his peanuts

   $\dfrac{3}{4}\left(4\dfrac{5}{6}\right) = \dfrac{3}{4}\left(\dfrac{29}{6}\right) = \dfrac{29}{8} = 3\dfrac{5}{8}$

6. **(K)** $3a - (3b - (3c - 3d) - 2e)$
   $= 3a - (3b - 3c + 3d - 2e)$
   $= 3a - 3b + 3c - 3d + 2e$

7. **(D)** Parallel lines have equal slopes.

   $\therefore m_1 = m_2$
   $m_1 - m_2 = 0$

8. **(J)** $\dfrac{2^2 \cdot 2^3}{2^{-2} \cdot 2^{-3}} = \dfrac{2^5}{2^{-5}} = 2^{5-(-5)} = 2^{10}$

9. **(D)** $d = \sqrt{(x_2 - x_1)^2 + (y_2 - y_1)^2}$
   $= \sqrt{(1 - (-1))^2 + (( ) - (-1))^2}$
   $= \sqrt{2^2 + 2^2}$
   $= \sqrt{8}$
   $= 2\sqrt{2}$

10. **(H)** $-x^2 - 2x - 1$
    $= -(-2)^2 - 2(-2) - 1$
    $= -4 + 4 - 1$
    $= -1$

11. **(C)** The maximum length of $\overline{CD}$ occurs when the polygon is opened just shy of a straight line. The maximum length of $\overline{CD}$ is less than $5 + 3 + 6$ $\therefore 13$.

    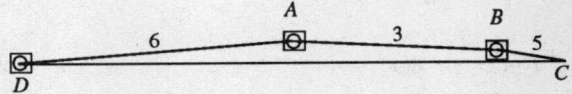

12. **(F)**

    $x^2 + 4^2 = 7^2$

    $x^2 = 33$

    $x = \sqrt{33}$

    $\tan \theta = \dfrac{\text{opposite}}{\text{adjacent}} = \dfrac{4}{\sqrt{33}}$

    $\dfrac{1}{\tan \theta} = \dfrac{\sqrt{33}}{4}$

13. **(A)** $\dfrac{-\dfrac{1}{3}}{3} - \dfrac{3}{-\dfrac{1}{3}} = \dfrac{-\dfrac{1}{3}}{\dfrac{3}{1}} - \dfrac{\dfrac{3}{1}}{-\dfrac{1}{3}}$

$= -\dfrac{1}{3}\left(\dfrac{1}{3}\right) - \dfrac{3}{1}\left(-\dfrac{3}{1}\right)$

$= -\dfrac{1}{9} + 9$

$= 8\dfrac{8}{9}$

14. **(F)** A prime number is an integer greater than 1, that is divisible only by itself and one.

4, 6, 8, 9, 12 and 27 are *not* prime numbers.

15. **(E)** $\dfrac{4a}{3b} = \dfrac{8}{9}$

multiply each side of the equation by $\dfrac{9}{16}$

$\dfrac{\cancel{4}a}{\cancel{3}b} \cdot \dfrac{\cancel{9}^{3}}{\cancel{16}_{4}} = \dfrac{8}{\cancel{9}} \cdot \dfrac{\cancel{9}}{16}$

$\dfrac{3a}{4b} = \dfrac{1}{2}$

16. **(H)** $\overline{(AP)}\overline{(BP)} = \overline{(DP)}\overline{(CP)}$

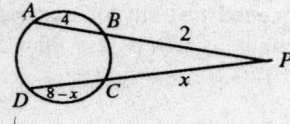

$(6)(2) = 8(x)$
$8x = 12$
$x = 1\dfrac{1}{2}$

17. **(D)** $\dfrac{(x^2 - 9) + (x^2 + 9) + (x^2 + 3x + 6)}{3}$

$= \dfrac{3x^2 + 3x + 6}{3} = \dfrac{3(x^2 + x + 2)}{3}$

$= x^2 + x + 2$

18. **(H)** $C = \dfrac{5}{9}(F - 32)$

19. **(E)** The sum of Dawn's scores for the first four tests is $80(4) = 320$.

$\dfrac{320 + x}{5} = 83$

$320 + x = 415$

$x = 95$

20. **(H)** $\begin{array}{r}20\\200\\2000\\\hline 2220\end{array} = 2.22 \times 10^3$

21. **(A)** $\dfrac{9 + 9 + 10 + x + y}{5} = 10$

$28 + x + y = 50$

$x + y = 22$

the average of x and y is

$\dfrac{x + y}{2} = \dfrac{22}{2} = 11$

22. **(G)**

$\widehat{mBC} = 2(m\angle BAC)$
$= 2(100)$
$= 200°$

$\widehat{AB} = \widehat{AC} = 80°$

23. **(E)** $\sin^2\theta + \cos^2\theta = 1$ for all θ

$\left(\cos\dfrac{\pi}{6}\right)\left(\cos\dfrac{\pi}{6}\right) + \left(\sin\dfrac{\pi}{6}\right)\left(\sin\dfrac{\pi}{6}\right)$

$= \cos^2\dfrac{\pi}{6} + \sin^2\dfrac{\pi}{6} = 1$

24. **(G)** A circle with center: (h, k) and radius r has the equation

$(x - h)^2 + (y - k)^2 = r^2$

c: $(0, -1)$ and radius $= 4$
$(x - 0)^2 + (y + 1)^2 = 4^2$
$x^2 + (y + 1)^2 = 16$

25. **(A)** $-|-3 - 4| - |3| - |-4|$
$= -|-7| - |3| - |-4|$
$= -(7) - (3) - (4)$
$= -14$

26. **(J)** The slope of $y = -\dfrac{1}{3}x + 2$ is $-\dfrac{1}{3}$

The slope of a line perpendicular to $y = -\dfrac{1}{3}x + 2$ is $+3$

$\left(+3 \text{ is the negative reciprocal of } -\dfrac{1}{3}\right)$

$m = 3 \quad pt = (1, 1)$

$y = mx + b$
$y = 3x + b$
$1 = 3(1) + b$
$b = -2$
$\therefore y = 3x - 2$

27. (A)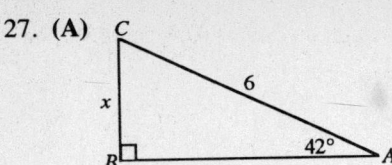

$\sin 42° = \dfrac{x}{6}$

$x = 6 \sin 42°$

28. (G) $(\sqrt{3})^5 - (\sqrt{3})^3$

$= \underbrace{(\sqrt{3})(\sqrt{3})}_{3} \underbrace{(\sqrt{3})(\sqrt{3})}_{3} (\sqrt{3}) - \underbrace{(\sqrt{3})(\sqrt{3})}_{3} (\sqrt{3})$

$= 9\sqrt{3} - 3\sqrt{3}$

$= 6\sqrt{3}$

29. (A) $\dfrac{a^2}{a} - 1 = \dfrac{a^2}{a} - \dfrac{a}{a} = \dfrac{a^2 - a}{a} =$

$\dfrac{a(a-1)}{a} = a - 1$

30. (F) $3x - 4(x + 2) \leq 7$
$3x - 4x - 8 \leq 7$
$-x - 8 \leq 7$
$-x \leq 15$
$x \geq -15$

31. (A) To be divisible by 15, a number must be divisible by 3 and 5.

	divisible by 3	divisible by 5	divisible by 15
55,155	✓	✓	✓
11,511	✓	x	x
52,225	x	✓	x
53,335	x	✓	x
56,665	x	✓	x

32. (H) $\dfrac{3.714}{\frac{1}{5}} = (3.714)(5) = 18.57$

33. (C) $\dfrac{x}{11} = 15$

$\therefore x = 165$

$\dfrac{165}{20} = 8.25$

34. (J) $\sqrt{4 + 4^2}$
$= \sqrt{4 + 16}$
$= \sqrt{20}$
$= 2\sqrt{5}$

35. (C) 1 week = 7 days
1 day = 24 hours
1 hour = 60 minutes

$\dfrac{30{,}240}{7(24)(60)} = 3$

36. (G) $|3x - 4| = 5$

$3x - 4 = 5 \quad | \quad 3x - 4 = -5$
$3x = 9 \quad\quad | \quad\quad 3x = -1$
$x = 3 \quad\quad\; | \quad\quad\; x = -\dfrac{1}{3}$

$3 + \left(-\dfrac{1}{3}\right) = 2\dfrac{2}{3}$

37. (D)

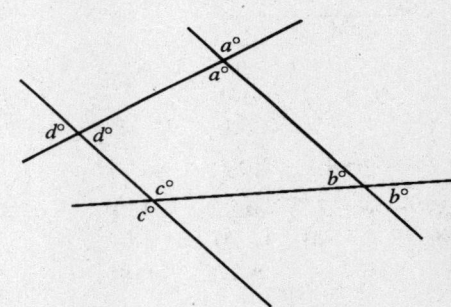

The sum of the interior angles of a quadrilateral is 360°
$\therefore a + b + c + d = 360$

38. (K)

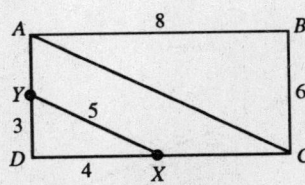

$\overline{DX} = \tfrac{1}{2}(\overline{DC}) = \tfrac{1}{2}(\overline{AB}) = \tfrac{1}{2}(8) = 4$

$\overline{DY} = \tfrac{1}{2}(\overline{AD}) = \tfrac{1}{2}(\overline{BC}) = \tfrac{1}{2}(6) = 3$

$\overline{XY} = 5$ (Pythagorean triple)

perimeter of $\triangle XDY = 3 + 4 + 5 = 12$

39. **(B)** $2x^2 - 3x - 2 = 0$
$(2x + 1)(x - 2) = 0$

or Product $= \dfrac{c}{a}$

$= \dfrac{-2}{2} = -1$

$|-1| = 1$

$2x + 1 = 0 \;|\; x - 2 = 0$
$x = -\dfrac{1}{2} \;|\; x = 2$

$\left| \left(-\dfrac{1}{2}\right)(2) \right| = |-1| = 1$

40. **(J)**

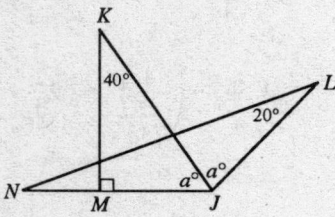

$40 + 90 + a = 180$
$a = 50$
$m\angle J = 2(50) = 100°$
$m\angle N + m\angle J + m\angle L = 180°$
$m\angle N + 100° + 20° = 180°$
$m\angle N = 60°$

41. **(E)** Distance = rate × time
$360 = r(9)$
$r = 40$

If r were $40 + 5 = 45$
$d = rt$
$360 = 45t$
$t = 8$

42. **(J)**

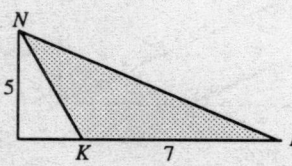

Area $\triangle NKL = \dfrac{1}{2}(b)(h)$

$= \dfrac{1}{2}(7)(5) = 17.5$

43. **(B)** The line through the points (0,4) and (3,0) has:
an x-intercept = 3
a y-intercept = 4
a slope = $-\dfrac{4}{3}$

Choice B shows the incorrect equation.

It should read $y = -\dfrac{4}{3}x + 4$.

44. **(K)**

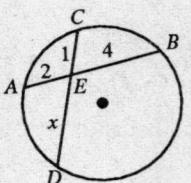

$(\overline{AE})(\overline{EB}) = (\overline{CE})(\overline{ED})$
$(2)(4) = (1)(x)$
$x = 8$

45. **(C)**

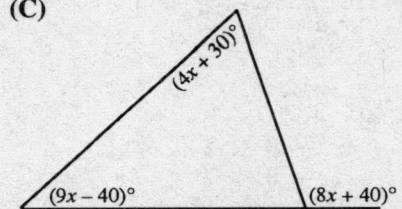

An exterior angle of a triangle is equal to the sum of the two remote interior angles.

$8x + 40 = (9x - 40) + (4x + 30)$
$8x + 40 = 13x - 10$
$5x = 50$
$x = 10$
$m\angle J = (4x + 30)° = (40 + 30)° = 70°$

46. **(K)** $(\sqrt{18} - \sqrt{8})^2$
$= (3\sqrt{2} - 2\sqrt{2})^2$
$= (\sqrt{2})^2 = 2$

47. **(C)** $(-2, 5)$ and $(3, 0)$

slope $= m = \dfrac{\triangle y}{\triangle x} = \dfrac{5}{-5} = -1$

equation of line: $(y - 0) = -1(x - 3)$

To find y-intercept, let $x = 0$
$(y - 0) = -1(x - 3)$
$y = -1(0 - 3) = 3$

y-intercept is 3

48. **(H)** $16^{\frac{3}{4}} + 16^{\frac{1}{4}}$

$= 2^3 + 2^1$
$= 8 + 2$
$= 10$

49. **(D)** $\sin^2 \theta + \cos^2 \theta = 1$

$\therefore 1 - \sin^2 \theta = \cos^2 \theta$

$\dfrac{1 - \sin^2 \theta}{\cos \theta} = \dfrac{\cos^2 \theta}{\cos \theta} = \cos \theta$

50. **(J)** Choice J is equivalent to:

$xy + 3x + 2y + 6$

51. **(E)** Multiply the second equation by -2 and add it to the first.

$\begin{array}{r} 2x - y = 7 \\ -2(x + 2y = 11) \end{array} \rightarrow \begin{array}{r} 2x - y = 7 \\ -2x - 4y = -22 \\ \hline -5y = -15 \\ y = 3 \end{array}$

Substitute $y = 3$ into the first equation.
$2x - y = 7$
$2x - 3 = 7$
$2x = 10$
$x = 5$

The sum $x + y = 5 + 3 = 8$.

52. **(F)** $\dfrac{x^2 + x + xy + y}{x + y}$

factor by grouping

$= \dfrac{x(x + 1) + y(x + 1)}{x + y}$

$= \dfrac{(x + 1)(x + y)}{(x + y)} = x + 1$

53. **(B)**

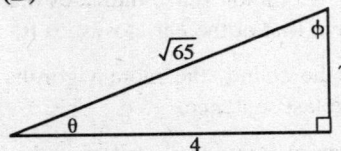

$7^2 + 4^2 = x^2$
$x^2 = 49 + 16$
$x = \sqrt{65}$

$\sin \phi = \dfrac{4}{\sqrt{65}}$

$\dfrac{1}{\sin \phi} = \dfrac{\sqrt{65}}{4}$

54. **(J)**

$x^2 + x^2 = 8^2$
$2x^2 = 64$
$x = 4\sqrt{2}$

The side of the square $= 4\sqrt{2}$.

The radius of the circle $= \dfrac{1}{2}(4\sqrt{2}) = 2\sqrt{2}$.

$A = \pi r^2$
$= \pi(2\sqrt{2})^2 = 8\pi$

55. **(D)** $\dfrac{\overline{AC}}{\overline{CD}} = \dfrac{2}{3}$ if $\overline{AC} = 4$, then $\overline{CD} = 6$

$\dfrac{\overline{CD}}{\overline{DB}} = \dfrac{2}{5}$ if $\overline{CD} = 6$, then $\overline{DB} = 15$

$\overline{AB} = 4 + 6 + 15 = 25$

56. **(K)** $\sin^2 x + \cos^2 x = 1$

$\therefore \dfrac{\sin^2 3\theta + \cos^2 3\theta}{\sin^2 2\theta + \cos^2 2\theta} = \dfrac{1}{1} = 1$

57. **(C)** $\dfrac{1}{10}\% = \dfrac{1}{1000}$

$\dfrac{1}{1000} \cdot \dfrac{1}{10} \cdot \dfrac{10}{1} = \dfrac{1}{1000} = .001$

58. **(F)** $4^3 + 4^3 + 4^3 + 4^3 = 4(4^3) = 4^4$

59. **(E)** The x-intercept has coordinates $(-1, 0)$.

$y = -x^2 + 2x + k$
$0 = -(-1)^2 + 2(-1) + k$
$0 = -1 - 2 + k$
$k = 3$

60. **(H)** $\dfrac{y}{1} = \dfrac{x + 1}{x - 1}$

$y(x - 1) = 1(x + 1)$
$xy - y = x + 1$
$xy - x = y + 1$
$x(y - 1) = y + 1$

$x = \dfrac{y + 1}{y - 1}$

3. Reading Test

1. **(C)** The author speaks of natural beauty in positive, admiring tones.

2. **(G)** The "flashing fragments" are rays of moonlight on leaves.

3. **(D)** The beams of moonlight become less clear in the wooded distance.

4. **(F)** The "bay of waves" refers to lines 12–13 "two acres of coarse bent grass."

5. **(D)** The passage specifically describes the beauty of moonlight with numerous examples.

6. **(F)** The passage ends with "for soon it will be gone again."

7. **(C)** Line 4 states "moonlight we do not need."

8. **(H)** The passage serves to explain and provide examples of the beauty of moonlight; therefore, it is expository.

9. **(A)** The use of water and the waterfall serve as an introduction to utilitarian and nonutilitarian aspects of nature. The passage goes on to discuss the "beautiful ornament" that is moonlight.

10. **(H)** An ocean wave, a starry night and a candlelit dinner all have aspects of beauty; thus the author would appreciate each of them. A bare light bulb is harsh; therefore, it is the best response.

11. **(B)** The sentence talks about power becoming too concentrated in a corporation or union.

12. **(F)** The first sentence states that our present mode of living, ". . . with its intricate technical aspects . . ." is unchangeable.

13. **(C)** Transgressions threaten individual freedom and have ". . . obvious remedies at law." Therefore, they are crimes.

14. **(J)** The last sentence in the passage warns of ". . . a nightmare picture of a whole nation of yes-men . . ."

15. **(C)** The author is critical of the organizational way of life because it threatens individual freedom and robs us of our courage and our convictions.

16. **(G)** ". . . a whole nation of yes-men . . ." are conformists.

17. **(A)** The author is appalled by this development. He wishes the readers to put a halt to the tendency.

18. **(J)** The author wants to alert the public to the dangers of conformity.

19. **(A)** He says "It would be foolish to talk of turning the clock back . . . to the tempo of Walden Pond." Thus it is meant to contrast with modern living.

20. **(H)** The second paragraph warns of the dangers to individual freedom and the negative effects conformity can bring.

21. **(D)** Iona looks at the sleeping men and regrets having no one with whom to talk.

22. **(G)** Iona ". . . sighs, and scratches his head." He accepts the situation.

23. **(C)** It is ironic that Iona has no one to talk to except his horse.

24. **(J)** When he is alone, the subject of his son "is unbearably painful."

25. **(B)** The son's name, Kuzma Ionitch, is a Russian or Eastern European name.

26. **(H)** The use of the present tense makes the reader feel as though he were living in the story.

27. **(A)** The story uses few descriptive words.

28. **(F)** The story tells of Iona's grief for his dead son.

29. **(A)** The horse does not seem to want for anything. Taking care of the horse gives Iona something to do.

30. **(F)** The passage is pervaded by a sense of Iona's loss and his loneliness.

31. **(B)** See lines 19–20.

32. **(H)** See the last sentence of Paragraph 1.

33. **(D)** The fourth paragraph (lines 35–40) tells us that sound arrives at one ear a split second before it arrives at the other. Common sense indicates that the sound would arrive first at the ear closest to it.

34. **(J)** The louder the sound, the more vigorous the vibration. See the last sentence.

35. **(A)** Transmission of sound is described in the fifth paragraph.

36. **(G)** The passage is an explanation of the workings of the ear. It is neither positive nor negative; therefore, Choices H and J are wrong. It does not argue; thus, Choice F is incorrect. The correct answer is G, didactic (instructive).

37. **(D)** The passage ends with a discussion of the inner ear. Choices B and C have already been discussed. A is far too general. Therefore, the best answer is D.

38. **(H)** The passage deals with the ear, explaining to laymen how it works. It is too simplistic for advanced science students; thus G and J are wrong. Choice F is not relevant. Choice H is the best response.

39. **(A)** The passage begins by describing the ear as a remarkable mechanism. It explains what the ear can do and how it operates. Choices B, C and D are too specific. Choice A is the best answer.

40. **(J)** Paragraph 4 states that human beings have two ears. Sound arrives ". . . at one ear a split second before its arrival at the second ear . . ."

4. Science Reasoning Test

1. **(C)** The most stable bond length corresponds to the lowest energy level, as pointed out in the introduction to the passage. The lowest energy level on the energy curve is −45 which corresponds to the horizontal line marked "A". The only bond length, from the choices provided, which can achieve energy level "A" is at an internuclear separation of 3 units. Answer choice A points to where the molecule is most unstable. Choice D is a bond length at which no interaction occurs, and choice B occurs at energies higher than those corresponding to a bond length of 3 units.

2. **(H)** The nuclei are both positive, and as the distance between them decreases they begin to repel. At bond lengths greater than 3, the attraction the nuclei have for the electrons in the bond is greater than the repulsion. Below 3 units, the attraction is no longer sufficient to compensate for the nuclear repulsions. Choice J is incorrect because the nuclei are not attracting. Choice F is wrong because the energy is increasing, which means the bond is less stable (getting weaker). Choice G merely records the fact that the energy is increasing; it does not explain a probable cause.

3. **(B)** There are two places on the graph where the energy is at zero. The region on the far right side of the graph is where the atoms are too far apart to notice each other and, therefore, neither attract nor repel each other. There is a second place, at an internuclear separation of about 0.75 units. At slightly greater separations the energy is lowered; at slightly smaller separations the energy increases tremendously. These changes in energy must be due to forces, so that at 0.75 units the forces must exactly cancel out. Only choice B takes into account both places that have zero energy. Choice A ignores the point at 0.75 units. C is wrong because one would not expect atoms to repel each other when they are very far apart. D is wrong because there are negative energy levels in the diagram.

4. **(F)** Draw a vertical line at the internuclear separation of 5 units. You will see that the only energy level not touched is the "A" level.

5. **(C)** At 3.1 units of energy the lowest level available is "A" at −45 units. The next available level is above "A" at −25 units. The difference is 20 units in the positive direction.

6. **(F)** As was pointed out in the introduction to the passage, the lower the energy the more stable the system. The fact that the energy decreases as the atoms approach each other points out that the atoms can "stick" together as a molecule. J is incorrect because there is no information given about compositions. While the fact that the bond formed is only stable over a very small range of internuclear separations argues that molecules should be able to react, it doesn't give any information as to how rapidly a reaction will occur. H is incorrect because the formation of a bond gives no information on the movement of the molecule in space.

7. **(C)** At a dosage of 1 mg/kg-body weight, hormone C returned to its original concentration level of 25 micrograms/ml after 10 days. Hormone C had an initial level of 25 micrograms per ml, changed to 21.4 at day 5 and went back to 25 at day 10. We are looking for evidence of change (either increase or decrease) in hormone level prior to returning to the initial hormone level. The change is necessary to affirm a fluctuation and a return, rather than having remained constant. Choice B exhibits an 18.6 concentration for hormone B at a dosage level of 2 mg/kg-body weight after 5 days; this is the same as the initial value of 18.6. However, we do not know if the hormone remained constant during the 5 day interval or returned from a fluctuation. Hormone A did not return to a concentration of 12.4 at some nonzero dosage during the course of the experiment.

8. **(H)** For dosages of 1 and 2 mg/kg-body weight the concentration of E rises from 142 to 146 and 160

respectively after 5 days. However, there is a DECREASE after 5 days for the 4 mg dose, to 124. By day 10 the concentrations for all groups receiving the drug are below 142.

9. **(A)** The table indicates that the 4 mg/kg-body weight dosage most effectively lowers the hormone B concentration. The question asks for mg per GRAM body weight. One gram is $\frac{1}{1000}$ of a kilogram, therefore we require $\frac{1}{1000}$ of the number of mgs in order to maintain the ratio constant. Four mg/kg-body weight is equivalent to .004 mg/g-body weight.

10. **(J)** We do not know what, if any, relation there is between concentration and activity of the hormones in the study. Therefore, we cannot determine the increase or decrease in activity.

---

11. **(D)** We need only consider the lowest concentration of each hormone at day 10 of the study. For hormone A, all concentrations increased, eliminating Choice **A**.

hormone E	hormone C	hormone D
lowest concentration after 10 days is 86	lowest concentration after 10 days is 8.8	lowest concentration after 10 days is 14.4
% change = $\frac{142-86}{142} \times 100$	% change = $\frac{25-8.8}{25} \times 100$	% change = $\frac{66-14.4}{66} \times 100$
= $\frac{56}{142} \times 100$	= $\frac{16.2}{25} \times 100$	= $\frac{51.6}{66} \times 100$
= 40% (approx)	= 60% (approx)	= 80% (approx)

---

12. **(H)** It is important to look at the correct rows in the table. You want only the 4 mg/kg-body weight rows. We see that while all concentrations in the 5 days at dose 4 are lower than at the start of the experiment, the concentration of A at the end of 10 days is higher than its initial concentration. Only choice **H** takes both facts into account.

13. **(A)** The initial ratio was 142/12.4, which is about 12. Then the ratio after 5 days is 160/9.6. Because the numerator is larger than the initial numerator AND the denominator is less than the initial denominator, we can conclude that this ratio is larger than the initial one. The ratio then becomes 104/18.2 which, because its numerator is less than the original numerator AND its denominator greater, we can conclude is smaller than the initial one.

14. **(H)** This question is NOT similar to question 11. Consider, if any hormone concentration at 5 days was at a lethally low level, the animal would have DIED. If that happened, how could we have gotten its hormone concentrations on day 10?

15. **(C)** If two samples are of the same material, they must have the same physical properties under similar conditions. In the current instance the physical property that we can calculate is the heat capacity. We know from the introduction to the passage that the electrical work is equal to the heat so:

(1) $IVt = \text{work} = \text{heat} = mC\Delta T$
(2) $IVt = mC\Delta T$
(3) $C = \frac{IVt}{m\Delta T}$

Use equation 3 to calculate the heat capacity of the liquid used in trial 1:

$$C = \frac{(10)(2)(3)}{(5)(4)} = 3$$

Using the same equation with the information for the liquid in trial 5 we find:

$$C = \frac{(5)(4)(3)}{(1)(20)} = 3$$

The liquid in trial 4 has a heat capacity of 1; the liquid in trial 7 has a heat capacity of 5. Only the liquid in trial 5 could be the same as the liquid in trial 1.

16. **(F)** If the liquids are the same they must have the same heat capacity. Using equation 3 from answer 15, we find that the heat capacity of trial 4 is 1. Using this value in equation 3 with the values given in trial 3:

$$C = \frac{IVt}{m\triangle T}$$

$$1 = \frac{(y)(2)(10)}{(10)(6)}$$

$$y = 3$$

17. **(A)** Let C_A represent the heat capacity of A
Let C_B represent the heat capacity of B

$$\triangle T = \frac{IVt}{mC}$$

$$\triangle T = \frac{IVt}{5C_A} = \frac{IVt}{10C_B}$$

Since I, V, t and $\triangle T$ are the same for A and B

$$\frac{1}{5C_A} = \frac{1}{10C_B}$$

By cross-multiplication:

$$10C_B = 5C_A$$

$$\frac{C_B}{C_A} = \frac{5}{10} = \frac{1}{2}$$

18. **(G)** $C = \frac{IVt}{m\triangle T}$

$$2 = \frac{(4)(8)(5)}{(z)(10)}$$

$$z = 8$$

19. **(D)** It was stated in the introduction that the heat capacity was a property of the material. If it is a property of the material it is not dependent on external conditions.

20. **(J)** While a material has a particular heat capacity there is no reason to suppose that the heat capacity of one substance can't be the same as the heat capacity of another substance. A similar line of reasoning would indicate that two totally different foods can have the same calorie content. This rules out Choices **F** and **G**. Choice **H** is ruled out because the heat capacity is a property of the material and therefore does not depend on the applied heat.

21. **(A)** Each mark along the left side of the graph indicates 0.1 gram of fruit consumed. To find total grams of pear consumed, figure out how many grams of pear were eaten in each hour and then add all 10 weights together: 0.55g (hour 1) + 0.45g (hour 2) + 0.55g (hour 3), etc. The total is 5.65 grams. If you were asked for the average HOURLY consumption, **B** would have been correct. If asked for the average consumption per beetle, choice **C** would have been right. Choice **D** gives the average beetle's hourly consumption. Only **A** gives the grand total.

22. **(G)** To find the total consumption of fruit add the hourly TOTALS together. For example, the total for hour 5 is 1.05 grams. The grand total is 11.2 grams. Therefore, the average number of grams consumed per hour is 11.2 grams/10 hours = 1.12 g/hr. However, had we examined the entire graph for Experiment 1 we would have observed that fruit consumption for each hour was between 1 and 1.3 grams. The only answer choice which approximates the average is 1.12 grams.

23. **(C)** The beetles ate 0.9 grams during hour 7. There were 30 beetles in the tank, so each beetle ate 0.9/30 = 0.03 grams. The question, however, asks for MILLIGRAMS. There are 1000 mg per gram, so the beetles ate 0.03 × 1000 = 30 mg.

24. **(F)** In experiment 1, 5 g of the 11.2 g consumed were apple. This is a bit less than 50% of the total. In Experiment 2, 8.6 g of the 14.55 g consumed were apple. This is about 60% of the total. There was a definite change in the percentage, so **J** is ruled out. **H** is ruled out because there was an increase. **G** is eliminated because we want the CHANGE in the percentages, which is certainly not 60%, but approximately 60% minus 50% or about 10%. The correct answer is therefore **F**.

or $\frac{5}{11.2} = .446 = 45\%$ (approx)

$\frac{8.6}{14.55} = .591 = 60\%$ (approx)

the change is: 60% − 45% = 15%

25. **(B)** 0.95 grams of apricots were consumed in Experiment 1. In Experiment 2 only 0.30 g were consumed. In Experiment 3, 0.95 g of apples and 0.70 g of pears were consumed. The lowest figure was choice **B**.

26. **(H)** Choice **H** indicates no treatment; there is therefore no change (zero increase) as compared to itself. A visual comparison of the apple consumption between the control (Experiment 1) and treatment with compound X (Experiment 2) indicates a marked increase in apple consumption. This eliminates Choice **F** as compared to Choice **H**.

An examination of the control against compound Y treatment (Experiment 1 vs 3) visually indicates a marked increase in apricot consumption, eliminating Choice **G** as compared to **H**.

Choice **J** requires a more careful comparison. The control indicates 5.25 g consumed against 5.65 g in Experiment 2. This increase, even though slight, is still greater than a zero increase as in answer Choice **H**.

27. **(D)** There are 14 molecules out of every hundred that have 6, 7, 8, 9, or 10 crosslinks (add the frequencies for all these numbers of crosslinks). Fourteen out of 100 is 14%. One eighth is 12.5% (this can be remembered as half of one quarter). Therefore, slightly more than one eighth of the molecules have six or more crosslinks.

28. **(G)** If the solution were concentrated, the odds of the reactive site of one molecule coming across the reactive site of another molecule are greatly enhanced. This would increase the likelihood of intermolecular crosslinking, because contact is required for a reaction to occur, and thereby reduce the likelihood of the assumption that only intramolecular crosslinking occurred.

29. **(C)** If the values were arranged in ascending order:
    the first 16 would have a value of zero.
    the next 22 would have a value of one.
    the 39th through 57th value would be two.

    The median value is the middle value when the elements are arranged in ascending order. The median of 100 items falls between the 50th and 51st item. In this case, since the value of both the 50th and 51st item is 2, the median value is 2. [If they had different values, the median would be the average (arithmetic mean) of the two values.]

30. **(G)** Notice that the graph is skewed towards fewer crosslinks. This signifies that there are few contacts between crosslinking sites. This implies that the molecule must be stretched out so that the sites can't get together. Therefore, the molecule has extended its contact with solvent. If it weren't attracted to the solvent it would curl up to minimize contact with it.

31. **(B)** The question is really asking how likely it is that there are five (four plus the original crosslink) or more crosslinks. Add up the molecules in the 5, 6, 7, 8, 9, and 10 crosslink categories. The total is 19 out of the hundred, or 19%.

32. **(F)** In this case you need look only at the 1 crosslink column and note that there are 22 of the hundred molecules in that category.

33. **(A)** If Venus is always picking up new material from the solar wind, and has no mechanism (at least as presented) to get rid of the material, the material will accumulate. The result would be an increase in the density of the atmosphere.

34. **(H)** Since he discounts the solar flare theory entirely, both Choices **F** and **G** are incorrect. Scientist 2 relates the changes to an increase in the surface temperature of the planet with the subsequent evaporation of some of the higher boiling components of the surface. Choice **J** does not necessarily explain an increase in density because if the chemical reaction is a synthesis, that could result in a decrease in cloud density.

35. **(B)** If the color change is due to newly absorbed solar material, what happens to this material when the color fades after the flare? Scientist 1 never offers an explanation for this point.

36. **(J)** It is possible that the molecules that enter the atmosphere from the solar flare undergo chemical reaction. So it is not fatal that the molecules in the clouds do not match those in the flare. But, unless there are nuclear reactions, the types of atoms in the flares should match those in the clouds if Scientist 1 is correct.

37. **(A)** Mercury is the closest planet to the sun and should therefore receive the most concentrated solar wind.

38. **(J)** Scientist 1 has no comment about the surface of the planet, so Choice **G** is unnecessarily strong. Choices **F** and **H** are unnecessary in light of the explanation given concerning Choice **F** for question 36. Scientist 1's only concern is to establish the solar parentage of the atoms found in the Venusian atmosphere.

39. **(C)** Scientist 1 requires solar winds to supply Venus' atmosphere with material. Scientist 2 requires the heat of the sun to volatize material at the surface of the planet. So both mechanisms would be interrupted by the extinguishing of the sun.

40. **(G)** As the atmosphere gets thicker we would expect wind erosion of the surface to increase. Erosion would smooth out the surface of the planet, and all raised features such as mesas, mountains, and cliffs would be wiped off the surface of Venus.

ALSO FROM THE PUBLISHERS OF ARCO BOOKS—

MONARCH NOTES–Selected Titles
Available at Fine Bookstores Everywhere

ACHEBE - Things Fall Apart
AESCHYLUS - The Plays
ARISTOTLE - The Philosophy
AUSTEN - Emma/Mansfield Park
AUSTEN - Pride and Prejudice
BECKETT - Waiting for Godot
Beowulf
BRADBURY- The Martian Chronicles
BRONTE - Jane Eyre
BRONTE - Wuthering Heights
BUCK - The Good Earth
CAMUS - The Stranger
CERVANTES - Don Quixote
CHAUCER - Canterbury Tales
CHEKHOV - The Plays
CHOPIN - The Awakening
CONRAD - Heart of Darkness/Secret Sharer
CONRAD - Lord Jim
CRANE - Red Badge of Courage
DANTE - The Divine Comedy
DE BEAUVOIR- The Second Sex
DESCARTES - The Philosophy
DICKENS - David Copperfield
DICKENS - Great Expectations
DICKENS - Hard Times
DICKENS - Oliver Twist
DICKENS - A Tale of Two Cities
DINESEN - Out of Africa
DOCTOROW- Ragtime
DONNE - The Poetry & The Metaphysical Poets
DOSTOYEVSKY - Brothers Karamazov
ELIOT - Silas Marner
ELIOT - Murder in the Cathedral & Poems
ELLISON - Invisible Man
EURIPIDES - The Plays
FAULKNER - As I Lay Dying
FAULKNER - Light in August
FAULKNER - The Sound and the Fury
FIELDING - Joseph Andrews
FIELDING - Tom Jones
FITZGERALD - The Great Gatsby
FITZGERALD - Tender is the Night
FLAUBERT - Madame Bovary/Three Tales
FROST - The Poetry
GARCIA-MARQUEZ - One Hundred Years of Solitude
GOETHE - Faust
GOLDING - Lord of the Flies
Greek and Roman Classics
GREENE - Major Works
HAMMETT - The Maltese Falcon/Thin Man
HARDY - The Mayor of Casterbridge
HARDY - The Return of the Native
HARDY - Tess of the D'Urbervilles
HAWTHORNE - House of the Seven Gables/ Marble Faun
HAWTHORNE - The Scarlet Letter
HELLER - Catch-22
HEMINGWAY- A Farewell to Arms
HEMINGWAY - For Whom the Bell Tolls
HEMINGWAY - Major Works
HEMINGWAY - The Old Man and the Sea
HEMINGWAY - The Sun Also Rises
HOMER - The Iliad
HOMER - The Odyssey
HUXLEY - Major Works
IBSEN - The Plays
JAMES - The Turn of the Screw
JOYCE - A Portrait of the Artist as a Young Man
KAFKA - Major Works
KEATS - The Poetry
KNOWLES - A Separate Peace

LAWRENCE - Sons and Lovers
LEE - To Kill A Mockingbird
LEGUIN - The Left Hand of Darkness
LEWIS - Babbitt
LOCKE & HOBBES - The Philosophies
MACHIAVELLI - The Prince
MARLOWE - Dr. Faustus
MELVILLE - Billy Budd
MELVILLE - Moby Dick
MILLER - The Crucible/A View from the Bridge
MILLER - Death of a Salesman
MILTON - Paradise Lost
MORRISON - Beloved
Mythology
NIETZSCHE - The Philosophy
O'NEILL - The Plays
ORWELL - Animal Farm
ORWELL - 1984
PATON - Cry the Beloved Country
PLATO - The Republic and Selected Dialogues
POE - Tales and Poems
REMARQUE - All Quiet on the Western Front
SALINGER - Catcher in the Rye
SARTRE - No Exit/The Flies
SCOTT - Ivanhoe

SHAKESPEARE - Antony and Cleopatra
SHAKESPEARE - As You Like It
SHAKESPEARE - Hamlet
SHAKESPEARE - Henry IV, Part 1
SHAKESPEARE - Henry IV, Part 2
SHAKESPEARE - Julius Caesar
SHAKESPEARE - King Lear
SHAKESPEARE - Macbeth
SHAKESPEARE - The Merchant of Venice
SHAKESPEARE - A Midsummer Night's Dream
SHAKESPEARE - Othello
SHAKESPEARE - Richard II
SHAKESPEARE - Richard III
SHAKESPEARE - Romeo and Juliet
SHAKESPEARE - Selected Comedies
SHAKESPEARE - The Taming of the Shrew
SHAKESPEARE - The Tempest
SHAKESPEARE - A Winter's Tale
SHAKESPEARE - Twelfth Night

SOPHOCLES - The Plays
SPENSER - The Faerie Queene
STEINBECK - The Grapes of Wrath
STEINBECK - Major Works
STEINBECK - Of Mice and Men
STEINBECK - The Pearl/Red Pony
SWIFT - Gulliver's Travels
THACKERAY - Vanity Fair/Henry Esmond
THOREAU - Walden
TOLSTOY - War and Peace
TWAIN - Huckleberry Finn
TWAIN - Tom Sawyer
VIRGIL - The Aeneid
VOLTAIRE - Candide/The Philosophies
WALKER - The Color Purple
WHARTON - Ethan Frome
WILDE - The Plays
WILDER - Our Town/Bridge of San Luis Rey
WILLIAMS - The Glass Menagerie

Call 1-(800)-223-2336 for a complete list of Monarch Note Titles

Try these fine references from America's best-selling family of dictionaries.

**Webster's New World Dictionary®
Third College Edition**

**Webster's New World™
Compact Dictionary
of American English**

**Webster's New World™
Pocket Dictionary**

**Webster's New World™
Vest Pocket Dictionary**

**Webster's New World™
Large-Print Dictionary**

**Webster's New World™
Children's Dictionary**

**Webster's New World Dictionary®
for Young Adults**

**Webster's New World™ Thesaurus
New Revised Edition**

**Webster's New World™
Speller/Divider**

AVAILABLE AT FINE BOOKSTORES EVERYWHERE

"HOW TO" GUIDES FOR STUDENTS

How to Develop and Write a Research Paper
How to Read and Write About Drama
How to Read and Write About Fiction
How to Read and Interpret Poetry
How to Write Book Reports
How to Write Poetry
How To Write Short Stories
How to Write Themes and Essays
How to Write a Thesis

AVAILABLE AT BOOKSTORES EVERYWHERE

weeded 1/12